SECOND EDITION

Foundations of American Education

Purpose and Promise

Peter S. Hlebowitsh
University of Iowa

WADSWORTH
™
THOMSON LEARNING

AUSTRALIA · CANADA · MEXICO · SINGAPORE · SPAIN · UNITED KINGDOM · UNITED STATES

For Margaret, Paul, Nadia, Nikolai, and Erica

WADSWORTH

THOMSON LEARNING

Education Editor: Dan Alpert
Associate Development Editor: Tangelique Williams
Editorial Assistant: Alex Orr
Marketing Manager: Becky Tollerson
Marketing Assistant: Ingrid Hernandez
Project Editor: Trudy Brown
Print Buyer: Tandra Jorgensen
Permissions Editor: Stephanie Keough-Hedges
Production Service: Strawberry Field Publishing

Text Designer: Sandy Drooker
Photo Researcher: Meyers Photo-Art
Copy Editor: Tom Briggs
Illustrator: Lotus Art
Cover Designer: Liz Harasymczuk
Cover Image: Stone/Darrell Gulin
Compositor: TBH Typecast, Inc.
Cover and Text Printer: Maple Vail

Printed in Canada
3   4   5   6   7   04   03   02

For permission to use material from this text, contact us
by **Web:** http://www.thomsonrights.com
Fax: 1-800-730-2215 **Phone:** 1-800-730-2214

Library of Congress Cataloging-in-Publication Data
Hlebowitsh, Peter S.
    Foundations of American education : purpose and promise /
    Peter S. Hlebowitsh.—2nd ed.
        p. cm.
    Rev. ed. of: American education, purpose and promise, 1997.
    Includes bibliographical references and index.
    ISBN 0-534-57043-7
    1. Education—United States—Philosophy—History.
2. Education—Social aspects—United States.   3. Education—
Aims and objectives—United States.   I. Hlebowitsh, Peter S.
American education, purpose and promise.   II. Title.
LA205.H544 2000
370'.973—dc21   00-049790

Wadsworth/Thomson Learning
10 Davis Drive
Belmont, CA 94002-3098
USA

For more information about our products, contact us:
Thomson Learning Academic Resource Center
1-800-423-0563
http://www.wadsworth.com

International Headquarters
Thomson Learning
International Division
290 Harbor Drive, 2nd Floor
Stamford, CT 06902-7477
USA

UK/Europe/Middle East/South Africa
Thomson Learning
Berkshire House
168-173 High Holborn
London WC1V 7AA
United Kingdom

Asia
Thomson Learning
60 Albert Street, #15-01
Albert Complex
Singapore 189969

Canada
Nelson Thomson Learning
1120 Birchmount Road
Toronto, Ontario M1K 5G4
Canada

CONTENTS

PREFACE   *xi*

PART I   *The Teacher and the School*

CHAPTER I   *Teaching in the American School Tradition*   *3*

Goals for the American Schools   *5*

The Teacher and the Comprehensive School   *17*

Teaching for Individual-Personal Growth   *22*

Teaching for Socio-Civic Growth   *26*

Teaching for Academic Growth   *30*

Teaching for Vocational Growth   *34*

Summary   *37*

Questions and Activities   *38*

References   *40*

CHAPTER 2   *The Teacher and the Classroom*   *43*

Who Educates the Masses?   *45*

The Status of the Teaching Profession   *50*

Job Satisfaction Issues   *58*

Professional Decision Making   *59*

LEVELS OF PROFESSIONALISM   *61*

FACTORS IN PROFESSIONAL DECISION MAKING   *66*

Classroom Issues   *73*

PROBLEMATIZING TEACHER EFFECTIVENESS   *73*

TEACHING TO THE TEST   *76*

CLASSROOM CONTROL   *79*

Summary   *87*

Questions and Activities   *88*

References   *89*

CHAPTER 3 *Philosophies of Teaching* 93

    Education in the Conservative Tradition 95

        PERENNIALISM *95*

        ESSENTIALISM *100*

    Education in the Progressive Tradition *105*

        EXPERIMENTALISM *107*

        ROMANTIC NATURALISM *110*

    Education in the Radical Tradition *115*

        SOCIAL RECONSTRUCTIONISM *115*

        POSTMODERNISM *118*

    Summary *122*

    Questions and Activities *123*

    References *126*

CHAPTER 4 *The Laws and Ethics of Teaching* 129

    Professional Ethics *133*

        LEGAL ETHICS AND THE IDEA OF "CONDUCT UNBECOMING" *133*

    Teacher Liability *142*

    Freedom of Expression *146*

        TEACHERS' ACADEMIC FREEDOM *147*

        TEACHERS' PERSONAL VIEWS *151*

        STUDENTS' VIEWS *152*

    Teacher Tenure and Teacher Dismissal *157*

    Student Searches and Seizures *165*

    Summary *170*

    Questions and Activities *172*

    References *173*

PART II *The History of the American School Experience*

CHAPTER 5 *The Emerging Public School in Early America* *177*

    New England School Life *178*

        THE DAME SCHOOL AND THE LATIN GRAMMAR SCHOOL *181*

        CURRICULUM MATERIALS *185*

Virginia and the Middle Colonies *187*

The Early Education of Blacks *191*

EDUCATIONAL OPPORTUNITIES PRIOR TO THE
INDUSTRIAL REVOLUTION *194*

INCREASED OPPRESSION FOLLOWING THE INDUSTRIAL
REVOLUTION *199*

Summary *201*

Questions and Activities *202*

References *203*

CHAPTER 6 *Public Schooling and the Secular Mandate* *207*

Changes in School Orientation *208*

THE AMERICAN-STYLE ACADEMY *208*

SCHOOL GOVERNANCE *211*

Education in the New Nation *212*

The Struggle for the American Public School *215*

INSTRUCTIONAL METHODS *216*

INDUSTRIAL DEVELOPMENT AND THE NEW NATIONAL
CONSCIOUSNESS *217*

EARLY FUNDING AND GOVERNANCE *220*

Horace Mann and the Rise of State Authority *221*

**The Upward and Outward Extension
of Schooling** *224*

The Birth of Teacher Education *226*

**The Evolution of Teacher Associations and Teacher
Unions** *231*

THE NATIONAL EDUCATION ASSOCIATION *232*

THE AMERICAN FEDERATION OF TEACHERS *238*

Summary *241*

Questions and Activities *243*

References *244*

CHAPTER 7 *The School Experience at the Turn of the Twentieth
Century* *247*

The Ascendancy of the Traditional Liberal Arts *248*

THE DOCTRINE OF MENTAL DISCIPLINE *248*

THE COMMITTEE REPORTS AND THE IDENTIFICATION OF
THE CURRICULUM *251*

The Child-Centered Counterreaction *256*

THE DOCTRINE OF ORIGINAL GOODNESS *256*

EUROPEAN PIONEERS IN PEDAGOGIC PRACTICES *257*

American Child-Centeredness *267*

THE AMERICANIZATION OF JOHANN PESTALOZZI *267*

G. STANLEY HALL AND THE CHILD STUDY MOVEMENT *273*

THE AMERICAN KINDERGARTEN AND THE RISE—AND
FALL—OF FROEBEL *276*

THE PROGRESSIVE CRITICISM
OF CHILD-CENTEREDNESS *283*

Summary *285*

Questions and Activities *286*

References *287*

CHAPTER 8 *The School Experience into the
Twentieth Century* *291*

Progressivism and the Cause of Social Reform *292*

JOHN DEWEY AND THE DEMOCRATIC COMMUNITY *293*

LESTER WARD AND THE PROGRESSIVE PRINCIPLE OF
ENVIRONMENTALISM *298*

Progressive Ideas in Action *299*

BOOKER T. WASHINGTON, W. E. B. DU BOIS, AND THE
BLACK STRUGGLE FOR SCHOOLING *300*

FRANCIS PARKER AND THE QUINCY METHODS *306*

JANE ADDAMS AND THE SETTLEMENT HOUSE
MOVEMENT *309*

THE CARDINAL PRINCIPLES REPORT OF 1918 AND A TIDAL
CHANGE FOR SECONDARY EDUCATION *312*

GEORGE COUNTS AND A MORE RADICAL
PROGRESSIVISM *316*

Education and the Rise of Social Efficiency *319*

FREDERICK TAYLOR AND THE IDEAL OF EFFICIENCY *320*

FRANKLIN BOBBITT, CURRICULUM DESIGN, AND SOCIAL
EFFICIENCY *322*

SPECIFICITY IN THE CURRICULUM AND IQ TESTING *325*

Summary *328*

Questions and Activities *329*

References *330*

PART III *The School and Society*

CHAPTER 9 *The Structure of American Education* *335*

Grade- and School-Level Orientations *336*

School Governance *341*

THE ROLE OF THE STATE *341*

THE ROLE OF LOCAL SCHOOL DISTRICTS *343*

THE ROLE OF THE FEDERAL GOVERNMENT *347*

Funding Public Education *348*

Church, State, and Public Education *360*

THE ESTABLISHMENT AND FREE EXERCISE CLAUSES *360*

SCHOOL PRAYER *373*

RELIGIOUS HOLIDAYS AND RELIGIOUS SYMBOLS *377*

THE TEACHING OF CREATIONISM *380*

STATE AID TO RELIGIOUS SCHOOLS *383*

Summary *387*

Questions and Activities *388*

References *389*

CHAPTER 10 *School Equity Issues* *395*

Curriculum Tracking *397*

DEFINING TRACKING *397*

REASONS FOR USING TRACKING *400*

INEQUITIES IN TRACKING *401*

RESPONSES TO CRITICISMS OF TRACKING *406*

ALTERNATIVES TO TRACKING *407*

School Desegregation *407*

LEGAL AND LEGISLATIVE INFLUENCES *408*

THE EFFECTS OF DESEGREGATION *419*

Gender and School Education *423*

GENDER BIAS *424*

SEXUAL HARASSMENT *435*

Summary   *438*

Questions and Activities   *440*

References   *441*

CHAPTER 11   *The Condition of American Education*   *445*

The Issue of School Achievement   *447*

The National Assessment of Educational Progress   *450*

THE READING REPORT CARD   *451*

THE MATHEMATICS REPORT CARD   *460*

School Dropouts   *466*

Poverty, Home Environments, and School Achievement   *473*

School Safety   *479*

Summary   *485*

Questions and Activities   *486*

References   *487*

CHAPTER 12   *The Culture and Language of Schooling*   *491*

Cultural Diversity and Commonality   *492*

The Culture of Schooling   *495*

SOURCES OF A COMMON CULTURE   *495*

MULTICULTURAL EDUCATION   *502*

CULTURE AND CRITICAL THEORY   *507*

The Language of Schooling   *511*

BILINGUAL EDUCATION   *512*

Summary   *522*

Questions and Activities   *523*

References   *525*

CHAPTER 13   *School Reform and the Sociopolitical Context Since the 1950s*   *529*

Getting "Back to Basics" in the 1950s   *530*

THE COLD WAR AND THE SPACE RACE   *531*

THE SUBJECT-CENTERED FOCUS ON MATH AND SCIENCE   *532*

Humanizing the Schools in the 1960s *535*

A NEW RADICAL/ROMANTIC RHETORIC *536*

OPEN EDUCATION *537*

Getting "Back to Basics"—Again—in the 1970s *539*

Promoting Academic Excellence in the 1980s *541*

Extending Academic Excellence into the 1990s *543*

NATIONAL STANDARDS AND SCHOOL CHOICE
OPTIONS *543*

CRITICISMS OF NATIONAL STANDARDS *548*

Summary *551*

Questions and Activities *555*

References *556*

CHAPTER 14 *The Idea of School Choice* *559*

Public School Choice Programs *560*

INTRADISTRICT AND INTERDISTRICT OPTIONS *561*

CHARTER SCHOOLS *561*

FOR-PROFIT EDUCATION CORPORATIONS *563*

MAGNET SCHOOLS *565*

**Privatization, Vouchers, and the Debate over School
Choice** *568*

ARGUMENTS FOR AND AGAINST VOUCHERS *570*

THE MILWAUKEE PARENTAL CHOICE PROGRAM
(MPCP) *574*

Home Schooling *576*

Summary *580*

Questions and Activities *581*

References *582*

INDEX *585*

PREFACE

This book is the second embodiment of an earlier text published by Wadsworth in 1997. It is not a second edition as much as it is a reconstruction built in the image of a course I teach at the University of Iowa. The new text is more encyclopedic than the earlier one and better attuned to the issues classroom teachers face, a feature making it unique for a foundations text. However, it still casts its main analytical gaze at the institution of public schooling, focusing on the core historical purposes of the public school.

ORGANIZATION OF THE TEXT

Part 1 gives an overview of school practices and purposes. Chapter 1 frames the purposes of the school at the national and state levels. It sets down the comprehensive agenda of public schooling and suggests ways for teachers to take this agenda seriously in their own professional lives. Chapter 2 brings the idea of teacher professionalism to the forefront of discussion by focusing on professional development concerns. The demographics of the teaching profession are detailed, and a considerable effort is made to portray the problems in the profession, including issues related to salary and work conditions. The chapter also explores what it means to conduct a professional classroom, a point of analysis that leads inevitably to a discussion of the main sources for professional judgment and ultimately to some consideration of classroom-based issues, such as teaching to the test, classroom management, and the teacher effectiveness literature. Chapter 3 deals with the profound issue of educational philosophy and the driving theoretical forces that help to shape our educational purposes. The philosophical underpinnings of teacher judgment are examined in relation to three overarching positions: (1) a cultural transmission perspective advanced by philosophical conservatives, (2) a progressive perspective, ranging from child-centered to more experimentalist views, and (3) a radical perspective. These are portrayed in historical contexts and are analyzed according to the sources of professional judgment described in Chapter 2. Part 1 concludes with a detailed analysis of teacher ethics and school law issues. Specifically, Chapter 4 examines the legal dimensions of teacher ethics and the legalistic foundation for teacher liability, teacher expression, teacher tenure, and various student freedoms.

Part 2 offers a historical survey of how the public school came into existence in America, explaining the uniquenesses of the American school system while also underscoring the importance of its most progressive features. The historical story starts in colonial America. Chapter 5 describes the formative stages in the development of the public school as emerging from the Puritan desire to support a religious education with general taxes and the compulsion of the law. The idea of locally controlled, tax-supported education for all youths has its foundation in these efforts. The secularization of public schooling is described in Chapter 6. The need to build a new nation led to more regulation from secular authorities with secular agendas. The chapter examines the historical evolution of state-level governance over the operation of the school, including its involvement in the licensing and educating of professional educators. The major theoretical arguments emerging in the struggle to shape the character of the school experience are explored in Chapters 7 and 8. These chapters deal with the important events and persons influencing curriculum formulations, with the focus on questions about what, how, and why we should teach. Various theoretical streams run through the channels of school practices and offer fundamental historical lessons on the way we conduct public schooling today. As Dewey reminds us, the history of the past is always the history of the present; what we derive from the past only makes sense and has relevance as it touches upon current conditions and problems. In writing this section, I tried to take this wisdom to heart.

Finally, Part 3 examines the relation of the school to society and highlights issues of school structure, school equity, school achievement, and school reform. Chapter 9 discusses the governance and structure of American schooling, explaining its uniquely decentralized makeup, its complicated funding design, and its vastly misunderstood relation with religion. Chapter 10 examines school equity concerns from the standpoint of three broad policy themes: desegregation, curriculum tracking, and gender bias. The chapter looks at how the school has had some hand in perpetuating inequities but also shows its constructive role in acting as an agent for the improvement of society. In discussing the issue of school achievement in Chapter 11, I tried to offer a balanced appraisal, scrutinizing achievement in relation to family issues and societal causes, and taking care to detail the national composite on school achievement. Although the problems of American education are considerable, there is quite a bit of good news to report that gets lost in the clamor over its failings. Chapter 12 focuses on issues of cultural and linguistic diversity. Much of the analysis attempts to resolve the tension between the need to build a common culture and the need to honor the diversity in society. Multicultural education and bilingual education are described in terms that serve the development of a common culture but also in terms that can be viewed as threatening to our sense of commonality. Chapter 13 examines the nature of school reform from a historical perspective and shows the linkage between school change and sociopolitical conditions. The current regard for national standards in discussed in some detail. Finally, Chapter 14 analyzes the main rationales for and against the most important educational policy issue of our time—school choice. The school choice movement represents an important phenomenon for anyone interested in public education. The increasing popularity of the privatization argument threatens to turn the school agenda in the direction of a familial mandate (what parents want for their children) instead of a societal mandate (what society wants for its children).

FEATURES OF THE TEXT

A course in the foundations of American education is typically offered as part of the course sequence required for teacher certification. It is, in other words, a teacher training course and must speak to the prospective schoolteacher. I tried to keep this charge in mind throughout the book. The book offers six feature boxes per chapter (Thinking About the Data, Web Points, Scholarly Voices, Debating the Issues, Research Inquiry, and The Historical Context) that extend the ideas in the narrative and provide readers with the opportunities to pursue new ideas on their own. In addition, each chapter opens with an outline listing the key chapter concepts and concludes with a summary and a list of questions and activities to aid in the review process. Tables and figures present key data in an easy-to-reference format, and photos illustrate important ideas. Finally, the instructor's manual accompanying the text provides some instructional ideas, forged in the heat of practice by the teaching assistants in my own foundations of education course.

In the end, my hope is that the book will fund the knowledge bank of the new teacher and will provoke productive conversations about what it means to be a good teacher working in a good school for the benefit of a good society.

ACKNOWLEDGMENTS

The manuscript for this textbook has gone through so many iterations and so many different review stages that I cannot possibly reconstruct the list of people who have been kind enough to offer helpful suggestions. The many blind reviews commissioned by my editor helped to transform the piece into its comprehensive new form. I've also been lucky to have a few good friends and colleagues who not only supported my work but also offered opportunities for professional conversations that always seem to leave me better off. No one has been more important to this end than Gregory Hamot and William Wraga. They didn't always know it, but they were the first ones to be tested with freshly written ideas. I have also been especially fortunate to have worked with two first-rate graduate students, Ted Caron and Randy Lange. Their work on the instructor's manual and, more importantly, their work as teaching assistants have helped to develop the manuscript more than either of them can probably appreciate.

I would also like to thank the following reviewers: Patty Adeeb, Nova Southeastern University; John Caruso Jr., Western Connecticut State University; Kate Friesner, College of Santa Fe; James E. Green, California State University, San Bernadino; C. Bobbi Hansen, University of San Diego; Olivet I.W. Jagusah, Eastern Illinois University; Harvey R. Jahn, Radford University; James M. Jennings, Hendrix College; Kenneth D. McCracken, University of Tennessee at Martin; Mark A. McJunkin, Arkansas State University; Lucy L. Payne, University of St. Thomas; Domingo A. Rodriguez, Rio Hondo College; Rita Seedorf, Eastern Washington University; Charles R. Teeter, University of North Texas; and Connie Titone, The College of New Jersey.

My main source of inspiration and strength, of course, has come from my family—my wife and my children. This book is dedicated to them.

PART I

The Teacher and the School

And you, America
Cast you the real reckoning for your present?
The lights and shadows of your future, good or evil?
To girlhood, boyhood look, the teacher and the school.

—WALT WHITMAN

CHAPTER 1

Teaching in the American School Tradition

Goals for American Schools

The Teacher and the Comprehensive School

Teaching for Individual-Personal Growth

Teaching for Socio-Civic Growth

Teaching for Academic Growth

Teaching for Vocational Growth

Summary

Questions and Activities

References

T HE AMERICAN PUBLIC SCHOOL has always carried a heavy burden of responsibility. Its mandate historically has underscored the importance of offering learning experiences that contribute not only to the academic and intellectual growth of students but also to their personal, social, and vocational growth. The American public expects nothing less from the school and, if anything, expects quite a bit more. Today, for instance, publicly financed schools are expected to socialize each generation of youths in the principles of democracy; to instill in them the skills needed to advance the interests of business and industry; to play a direct role in the psychological, social, intellectual, and physical betterment of each child; to have a hand in curbing virtually every social ill that prevails in society; and to provide the intellectual capital needed for the defense of the nation. As a public agency, the school is counted on to work in the interests of social progress and widespread social enlightenment.

The notion that popular education exists to serve society, of course, has been made over the centuries by many prominent thinkers. In Plato's *Republic,* for instance, the very essence of a good society implied a set of educational policies and practice that would give life to the highest ideals of the society. To Plato, societies were created not by whim or accident, but by a deliberate and conscious socialization process at the community level. In the early history of the United States, the core of Plato's idea was applied, at least at the rhetorical level, to the popularization of the common public school (Cremin, 1965). American intellectuals like Thomas Jefferson promoted the universalization of public schooling as essential to an enlightened, vital citizenry. To his mind, there could be no democracy unless the upcoming generations had the skills, knowledge, and ethical convictions needed to operate and preserve such a complex social arrangement. He believed that such a mission could be carried out only through the agency of mass public schooling. This line of thought continued into the nineteenth century with the work of Horace Mann, who used his position of superintendent of schools in Massachusetts to make common schooling mandatory through the elementary grades (Butts, 1988). Similarly, Lester Ward (1883) and John Dewey (1916) both held that schools were essential to developing the dispositions, skills, and general insights needed to maintain a democratic society. Dewey (1916), in fact, observed that the role of the school was to provide an enlarging experience that went beyond the less encompassing nature of education in the home, church, and community. Under these circumstances, the school is framed in the broad role that we find it occupying today.

GOALS FOR AMERICAN SCHOOLS

The basic governance structure of the American school system is decentralized, with most power wielded at the state level. As a result, the so-called American school system is actually fifty school systems (one for each state), all of which regulate themselves in significantly different ways. How, then, can there be an American school tradition under such an arrangement?

Any effort to represent a set of educational goals for the American schools is likely to run into disagreement and debate. Still, over the years, some nationalizing influences have affected the schools in rather uniform ways. Recent urges to formulate national standards for public education, to pass federal legislation encouraging certain school reforms, and to use various media outlets and government-sponsored commissions to sway public perceptions of schooling testify to these influences. The national popularity of certain exams and textbooks in the school curriculum also points to some national identity in the school curriculum. There is, in fact, no escaping some national sense of schooling if we believe that public education is an agency of democracy or, to paraphrase Dewey, the chief engine for social improvement in our democracy.

In a decentralized system of school governance, the challenge in establishing a set of national educational goals for the schools is designing it in a way that provides direction and guidance without offering curricular or instructional prescriptions. In other words, the goals themselves should be general enough to mean different things to different people, leaving room for interpretation and adaptation according to state and local circumstances. But they should also be solid enough to give us a common sense of national purpose and identification.

The federal Department of Education monitors the nation's progress on a set of national education goals adopted in 1990. The purpose of the goals is to give the states some collective identity and to hold each state accountable to common benchmarks of performance and progress. Originally fashioned in a report known as *America 2000* (U.S. Department of Education, 1990), which referred to the national goals that the public schools needed to attain by the year 2000, the goals now are well established and are used to judge both the national performance of the schools and the constituent performances of the fifty state school systems.

Note that the goals are constructed in highly general terms and do very little to detail a sense of the school experience. In fact, some of the goals are not specific to schooling at all, although each either affects or is affected by schooling. The goals are as follows:

1. All children in America will start school ready to learn.

2. The high school graduation rate will increase to at least 90 percent.

3. Students will leave grades 4, 8, and 12 having demonstrated competency over challenging subject matter, including English, mathematics, science, foreign languages, civics and government, economics, arts, history, and geography. Also, every school in America will ensure that all students learn to use their minds well, so they may be prepared for responsible citizenship, further learning, and productive employment in the nation's modern economy.

4. The nation's teaching force will have access to programs for the continued improvement of their professional skills and the opportunity to acquire the knowledge and skill needed to instruct and prepare all American students for the next century.

5. American students will be first in the world in mathematics and science achievement.

6. Every adult American will be literate and will possess the knowledge and skills necessary to compete in a global economy and to exercise the rights and responsibilities of citizenship.

7. Every American school will be free of drugs, violence, and the unauthorized presence of firearms and alcohol, and will offer a disciplined environment conducive to learning.

8. Every school in America will promote partnerships that increase parental involvement in the social, emotional, and academic growth of children (U.S. Department of Education, 1990).

Where there are goals, there must also be ways of determining whether they have been effectively met. To this end, the National Center for Education Statistics (NCES) has formulated a set of performance benchmarks to make these determinations. For instance, in assessing the extent to which goal 1 has been met, NCES collected data on the following measures: (1) the proportion of infants with one or more of four health risks, (2) the percentage of 2-year-olds who have been fully immunized against preventable childhood diseases, (3) the percentage of 3- to 5-year-olds whose parents read to them or tell them stories, and (4) the gap, expressed in percentages, in preschool participation by 3- to 5-year-olds from high- and low-income families. Collecting these data on an ongoing basis allows certain conclusions to be drawn about the state of progress relative to goal 1. Each year, different data are compared to the baseline performance figures established in 1990, when the goals were first created. In 1990, 37 percent of

One of the national educational goals is that students leave grades 4, 8, and 12 having demonstrated competency in challenging subject matter, so they are prepared for responsible citizenship, further learning, and productive employment in our nation's modern economy.

infants in America were born with one or more health risks; by 1996 the rate was down to 34 percent. In 1990, 75 percent of 2-year-olds were fully immunized; by 1996, it was up to 78 percent. In each case, of course, we could reasonably conclude that progress was being made on this essential national goal. Feature 1-1 documents some of the other efforts made to evaluate progress on the national goals; Feature 1-2 provides an opportunity to access updated information on the national goals. There are some problems with the way the national goals scorecard of progress is kept, which we will deal with in later chapters. The key point here is that awareness of these national goals exists at a general level, and data are being collected to enable assessments of the performance of state systems in terms of these national goals.

However, if we look a little more closely at the school experience, and at the school curriculum in particular, we find that four major goals historically have captured the essence of a public school education. These goals have no official sanction in government, but they do represent a historical, if not traditional, sense of what public schools are committed to doing. They include broadly defined goals related to (1) individual-personal growth, (2) socio-civic growth, (3) academic-intellectual growth, and

I-I THINKING ABOUT THE DATA
National Education Goals at the State Level

The national education goals supported by the Department of Education have resulted in an annual appraisal of each state's progress in relation to the national goals. Here is a selective sample of results from five highly populated states, representing different regions of the country. Can you draw any conclusions from these data? Check the progress of your state or get updated numbers on the states listed here from the National Education Goals Panel, *Data Volume for the National Education Goals Report* (Washington, DC: U.S. Government Printing Office) or on the National Education Goals Panel website: www.negp.gov.

	U.S. Baseline	CA	FL	IL	NY	TX
Goal 1: Readiness to Learn						
Children's Health Index						
The percentage of infants born in the state with one or more of four health risks (1997)*	37	—	29	32	—	29
Immunizations						
The percentage of fully immunized 2-year-olds (1997)	75	76	79	76	79	75
Low Birthweight						
The percentage of infants born at low birthweight (1997)	7	6	8	8	8	7
Early Prenatal Care						
The percentage of mothers receiving prenatal care (1997)	76	82	84	82	81	79
Preschool Programs for Children with Disabilities						
The increase in the number of children with disabilities in preschool (per 1,000 3- to 5-year-olds) (1998)	—	35	47	49	61	36
Goal 2: School Completion						
High School Completion Rate						
The percentage of 18- to 24-year-olds who have a high school credential (1997)	86	81	84	87	85	80

* Risks are late (in third trimester) or no prenatal care, low maternal weight gain (less than 21 pounds), mother smoked during pregnancy, or mother drank during pregnancy.

	U.S. Baseline	CA	FL	IL	NY	TX
Goal 3: Student Achievement and Citizenship						
Reading Achievement						
The percentage of students who meet the National Goal Panel's performance standard in reading (based on National Assessment of Educational Progress testing) (1998)						
Grade 4	29	20	23	—	29	29
Grade 8	—	22	23	—	34	28
Writing Achievement						
The percentage of students who meet the National Goal Panel's performance standard in writing (based on National Assessment of Educational Progress testing) (1998)						
Grade 8	—	20	19	—	21	31
Mathematics Achievement						
The percentage of students who meet the National Goal Panel's performance standard in writing (based on National Assessment of Educational Progress testing) (1996)						
Grade 4	18	11	15	—	20	25
Grade 8	15	17	17	—	22	21
Science Achievement						
The percentage of students who meet the National Goal Panel's performance standard in science (based on National Assessment of Educational Progress testing) (1996)						
Grade 8	29	20	21	—	27	23
Advanced Placement						
The number of advanced placement examinations (per 1,000 eleventh- and twelfth-graders) receiving a grade of 3 or higher	55	137	112	96	155	82

(continued)

I-I THINKING ABOUT THE DATA *(continued)*

National Education Goals at the State Level

	U.S. Baseline	CA	FL	IL	NY	TX
Goal 4: Teacher Preparation and Professional Development						
Teacher Preparation						
The percentage of secondary school teachers who hold an undergraduate or graduate degree in their main teaching assignment (1994)	66	51	62	72	75	51
Teacher Professional Development						
The percentage of teachers reporting that they participated in professional development programs on one or more topics since the end of the previous school year (1994)	—	94	88	81	76	93
Teacher Induction Programs						
The percentage of public school teachers participating in formal induction programs during their first year (1994)	22	35	48	20	31	30
Goal 5: Mathematics and Science Achievement						
International Mathematics Achievement The state's international ranking on international assessments of mathematics (out of forty-one countries, 1996)						
Grade 8	20	25	22	25	19	19
International Science Achievement The state's international ranking on international assessments of science (1996)						
Grade 8	9	20	13	16	10	10
Mathematics and Science Degrees The percentage of math and science degrees awarded (as a percentage of all degrees awarded, 1996)						
All students	39	47	37	40	44	38
Minorities	39	45	38	35	43	36
Females	35	44	35	36	43	35

	U.S. Baseline	CA	FL	IL	NY	TX
Goal 6: Adult Literacy and Lifelong Learning						
Adult Literacy						
The percentage of adults who score at above level 3 in prose literacy	—	66	50	61	71	54
Civic Participation						
The percentage of adults who reported that they:						
Registered to vote	70	71	69	72	70	69
Voted	61	61	56	59	59	52
Goal 7: Safe, Disciplined, and Alcohol- and Drug-free Schools						
Teacher Victimization						
The percentage of public school teachers reporting that they were threatened or injured at school (1994)	—	9	21	12	19	14
Disruptions in Class by Students						
The percentage of public school teachers reporting that student disruptions interfere with teaching and learning	—	43	58	49	55	46
Lack of Parental Involvement						
The percentage of teachers reporting a lack of parental involvement in their schools as a serious problem	—	32	33	25	29	36

I-2 WEB POINTS
The National Education Goals Panel

The National Education Goals Panel (NEGP) keeps its own website (www. negp.gov), which offers updated data on how all of the school systems in all the states and territories of the United States are faring against the panel's expressed national goals. State-by-state comparisons can be made for up to three states at a time. One also has access to the NEGP's publications, which are free and easily downloaded. Finally, links to important state and federal education agencies are also provided.

The National Education Goals Panel
Building a Nation of Learners

● *Home*
○ Search
○ Feedback
○ Site Overview

About NEGP   Goals   What's New   Data   Publications   News and Events   Links

Click here to view webcasts of the National Education Goals Panel's most recent Field Hearings in Vermont and Los Angeles focusing on bringing all students to high academic standards, as well as the *Creating a Framework for High Achieving Schools* teleconference. To view these webcasts you will need the free Realplayer 7 downloaded to your computer. You can download Realplayer 7 here for free!

The National Education Goals Panel (NEGP) is a unique bipartisan and intergovernmental body of federal and state officials created in July 1990 to assess and report state and national progress toward achieving the National Education Goals.

Below you will find our highly acclaimed newsletters that will keep you up to date with the latest news and information in the field of education.

The NEGP Weekly
The *NEGP Weekly* is a weekly news update on America's Education Goals and school improvement effort.

The NEGP Monthly
The *NEGP Monthly* reports state and local practices identified by policy makers in states making the most improvement or achieving at the highest levels on one or more indicators related to the National Education Goals.

E-Mail List
Have the Weekly and Monthly Highlights e-mailed to you as they become available!

(4) career-based or vocational growth. In combination, the four goals represent a comprehensive framework for the design of the school experience. What is important to remember is that a good public education is not strictly an academic education. Obviously, the development of vital academic skills is valued in a public school education, but it is only one facet of the public schooling experience.

We must return to the broad conception of schooling that Dewey supported to begin to understand the American school tradition. Individual-personal goals in the school encompass a range of concerns pertaining to the emotional and physical well-being of students, to the pursuit of their

Some socio-civic goals in public schooling aim at finding ways to encourage cooperation.

interests and aptitudes, to their sense of aesthetic or existential understanding, and, ultimately, to their constructions of self-identity. Socio-civic goals speak directly to interpersonal relations, which include dealing with different cultures and opposing viewpoints, developing the skills of compromise and negotiation, and cultivating the values of compassion and concern for others. Socio-civic goals also involve issues of citizenship, such as democratic participation and the workings of government, while also seeking to raise consciousness for global understanding, universal human rights, and the appreciation of cultural differences. The socio-civic side of public education also serves the interests of moral and character education by stressing moral integrity, an understanding of truth, and critical interpretations of good and evil. The initial academic-intellectual goals in the school involve establishing the basics for literacy and numeracy. In the early grades, this means mastery of the fundamental processes, or what we might view as the basics skills of reading, writing, and arithmetical operations. Thinking skills, problem-solving skills, inquiry skills, and the accumulation and application of general as well as specialized knowledge also have their place among academic-intellectual goals. Finally, the school promotes vocational goals that affect career outlooks and choices, that inculcate habits and attitudes of craftsmanship, and that encourage a positive attitude toward work. The full and complete range of goals, taken from Goodlad's work (1984), is expressed in the following outline.

GOALS FOR AMERICAN SCHOOLING

I. Individual-Personal
- A. Emotional and physical well-being
  1. Develop the willingness to receive emotional impressions and to expand one's affective sensitivity
  2. Develop the competence and skills for continuous adjustment and emotional stability, including coping with social change
  3. Acquire a knowledge of one's own body and adopt health practices that support and sustain it, including avoiding the consumption of harmful or addictive substances
  4. Learn to use leisure time effectively
  5. Develop physical fitness and recreational skills
  6. Cultivate the ability to engage in constructive self-criticism
- B. Creativity and aesthetic expression
  1. Learn to deal with problems in original ways
  2. Learn to be tolerant of new ideas
  3. Learn to be flexible and to consider different points of view
  4. Learn to experience and enjoy different forms of creative expression
  5. Learn to evaluate various forms of aesthetic expression
  6. Develop the willingness and ability to communicate through creative work in an active way
  7. Seek to contribute to cultural and social life through one's artistic, vocational, and avocational interests
- C. Self-realization
  1. Learn to search for meaning in one's activities, and develop a philosophy of life
  2. Develop the self-confidence necessary for knowing and confronting one's self
  3. Learn to assess realistically and to live with one's limitations and strengths
  4. Recognize that one's self-concept is developed in interaction with other people
  5. Develop skill in making decisions with purposes
  6. Learn to plan and organize the environment in order to realize one's goals
  7. Develop a willingness to accept responsibility for one's own decisions and their consequences

8. Develop skill in selecting some personal lifelong learning goals and the means to attain them

II. Socio-Civic
  A. Interpersonal understandings
    1. Acquire knowledge of opposing value systems and their influence on the individual and society
    2. Cultivate an understanding of how members of a family function under different family patterns, as well as within one's own family
    3. Develop skill in communicating effectively in groups
    4. Learn to identify with and advance the goals and concerns of others
    5. Learn to form productive and satisfying relations with others based on respect, trust, cooperation, consideration, and caring
    6. Develop a concern for humanity and an understanding of international relations
    7. Cultivate an understanding and appreciation of cultures different from one's own
  B. Citizenship participation
    1. Develop historical perspective
    2. Acquire knowledge of the basic workings of the government
    3. Develop a willingness to participate in the political life of the nation and the community
    4. Develop a commitment to the values of liberty, government by consent of the governed, representational government, and one's responsibility for the welfare of all
    5. Cultivate an understanding of the interrelationships among complex organizations and agencies in a modern society and learn to act in accordance with it
    6. Exercise the democratic right to dissent in accordance with one's conscience
    7. Develop economic and consumer skills necessary for making informed choices that enhance one's quality of life
    8. Cultivate an understanding of the basic interdependence of the biological and physical resources of the environment
    9. Develop the ability to act in light of this understanding of interdependence

C. Enculturation
1. Acquire insight into the values and characteristics, including the language, of the civilization of which one is a member
2. Develop an awareness and understanding of one's cultural heritage, and become familiar with the achievements of the past that have inspired and influenced humanity
3. Cultivate an understanding of the manner in which traditions from the past are operative today and influence the direction and values of society
4. Understand and adopt the norms, values, and traditions of the groups of which one is a member
5. Learn how to apply the basic principles and concepts of the fine arts and humanities to the appreciation of the aesthetic contributions of other cultures

D. Moral and ethical character
1. Learn to evaluate events and phenomena as good or evil
2. Develop a commitment to truth and values
3. Learn to utilize values in making choices
4. Develop moral integrity
5. Cultivate an understanding of the necessity for moral conduct

III. Academic-Intellectual
A. Mastery of basic skills and fundamental processes
1. Learn to read, write, and handle basic arithmetical operations
2. Learn to acquire ideas through reading and listening
3. Learn to communicate ideas through writing and speaking
4. Learn to utilize mathematical concepts
5. Learn to utilize available sources of information

B. Intellectual development
1. Learn to think rationally, including problem-solving skills, application of principles of logic, and skill in using different modes of inquiry
2. Learn to use and evaluate knowledge, to think critically and independently, so as to make judgments and decisions in a wide variety of life roles—citizen, consumer, worker—as well as in intellectual activities
3. Accumulate a general fund of knowledge, including information and concepts in mathematics, literature, natural science, and social science

    4. Develop positive attitudes toward intellectual activities, including intellectual curiosity and a desire for further learning

    5. Cultivate an understanding of change in society

IV. Vocational

  A. Career-vocational education

    1. Learn how to select an occupation that will be personally satisfying and suitable to one's skills and interests

    2. Learn to make decisions based on an awareness and knowledge of career options

    3. Develop salable skills and specialized knowledge that will prepare one to become economically independent

    4. Develop habits and attitudes, such as pride in good workmanship, that will make one a productive participant in economic life

    5. Develop positive attitudes toward work, including acceptance of the necessity of making a living and an appreciation of the social values and dignity of work

SOURCE: From J. I. Goodlad, "A Place Called School." Copyright © 1984 McGraw-Hill. Reprinted with permission.

These goals, in general terms, outline the comprehensive mandate for public education in America. They set the conditions and the context for the American belief in publicly educating youths in one unified school setting.

THE TEACHER AND THE COMPREHENSIVE SCHOOL

The notion that all youths in a democratic society should be educated in one unified setting, as opposed to separate academic and vocational schools, goes hand in hand with the commitment to a comprehensive school design. Feature 1-3 brings us the words of two important American educators who echo these sentiments. This commitment is moved by a democratic spirit, by a belief in using the school as an instrument of democracy where all youths can be taught together under one roof, without regard to their class status. Because of its inclusive nature, a unified school setting has to be sure that something educationally worthwhile is being offered to everyone enrolled. This means showing sensitivity to individual differences and to different career outlooks, but it also means being sure that all youths are equipped with the skills they will need to conduct intelligent lives in a democratic society. This is especially important in a pluralistic society such as ours,

I-3 SCHOLARLY VOICES
The Unified System, the Comprehensive School, and Democracy

In 1926, George Counts (1926, p. 1) discussed the difference between the dual system of schooling and the single system. The unified or single system, he stated, expresses the genius of the American people:

> America transformed the dual educational system of the Old World into a single system. This achievement constitutes a major contribution to the evolution of educational institutions and to the growth of civilization. In no other social institution has the genius of the American people been more fully expressed.

Several decades later, James B. Conant (1959, p. 8), one-time president of Harvard University and champion of the American comprehensive high school, observed a linkage between the unified comprehensive school and the democratic ideals of our society:

> I think it is safe to say that the comprehensive high school is characteristic of our society and further that it has come into being because of our economic history and our devotion to the ideals of equality of opportunity and equality of status.

What do you think about these observations? Is the unified school arrangement vital to our democracy?

George Counts

AP/Wide World Photos

James B. Conant

© Bettmann/Corbis

where the commonality of the school experience encourages social understanding and the forging of common values and outlooks.

The standard organizational arrangement for most secondary schools in a unified system of schooling is known as the comprehensive high school.

The curriculum of the comprehensive high school endeavors to provide an education in citizenship (common learnings), to offer elective and exploratory courses for individual improvement, and to support strong specialized programs for both academic and vocational learning (Tanner and Tanner, 1995). Its purpose is to educate all youths in one setting, making use of common learning experiences to develop common insights and supporting differentiated learning experiences for the development of individual talents, needs, and interests. Feature 1-4 presents some criticisms of the comprehensive school and suggests some resources for extending one's knowledge of the concept.

Note that this kind of school arrangement is not likely to be found in other advanced nations. In fact, the school tradition outside of the United States, especially at the secondary level, is typically a dual or bipartite system in which schoolchildren are enrolled in separate schools according to separate career purposes. Children entering into preadolescence in such societies, for instance, will often be identified and divided into "curriculum tracks" or "curriculum streams" and then sent off to separate schools designated by academic and terminal-vocational categories. Thus, a small percentage of the student population attends a college-preparatory high school, but the majority are funneled into vocational schools, technical schools, and assorted job-training schools. Although many American schools practice some version of curriculum tracking, the idea of separate schools linked to different life destinies and different career-based skills has not been part of the American school tradition.

The notion of constructing the school experience comprehensively has long been supported not only by educators but by parents as well. Goodlad's study of the American school system in the early 1980s found that parents and teachers, although believing that academic-intellectual goals were most important in the education of youths, held that the school also had an obligation to provide comprehensive educational experiences dealing with various personal, socio-civic, and vocational concerns. As Goodlad (1984, p. 39) stated, "When it comes to education, it appears that most parents want their children to have it all." This, of course, is understandable. Parents, ever more preoccupied with workplace concerns, sensibly find comfort when the school takes an active role in giving their children a well-rounded education, one that educates not only for academic prowess but also for social and moral development, individual well-being, and eventual performance in the workplace.

But if schoolchildren are going to "have it all" in public education, teachers have to find a way to support the many facets of the comprehensive learning agenda. For elementary school teachers, this is a natural agenda. The teaching expectations placed on these teachers are removed from the

1-4 DEBATING THE ISSUES
Criticism of the Comprehensive High School

Many school reformers believe that the best hope for school improvement involves reducing the school curriculum to its most academic and intellectual tradition. This belief often is inspired by a desire to immerse youths in a rigorous, discipline-centered liberal arts education. Any education that falls short of this mark is viewed as potentially anti-intellectual, especially if it includes opportunities for vocational study, physical education, performance arts, and even, in some cases, elective studies.

Among contemporary thinkers, Theodore Sizer is well known for his efforts to return the school to academic traditionalism. Regarding high schools, Sizer (1984) has been forthright in acknowledging his bias against the design of the comprehensive school. "High schools cannot be comprehensive and should not try to be comprehensive," he declared. "Helping students to use their minds is a large enough assignment" (p. 216). Sizer developed this theme in his widely read work *Horace's Compromise*. Among the teachers portrayed in this book is a high school English teacher named Horace Smith, whose life as a professional represents, at least to Sizer, the fundamental problem with schooling today. Though Smith is an educator with considerable talent and enthusiasm for his chosen profession, he simply cannot fulfill his educational charge. He is overcome by excessive demands on his time and energy, and he eventually has to resort to a professional life of compromises. Sizer's point is that the problem that Smith faces is systemic to a schooling structure that, by virtue of its comprehensiveness, attempts to do too much and, as a consequence, labors with a highly fragmented and wasteful curriculum. In short, Sizer tries to show how the comprehensive high school is an ineffective arrangement for learning, one that runs counter to the central task of developing a student's mind. He captures the logic of this idea by advancing the proposal that "less is more" when applied to the curriculum of a school. This essentially means that more can be gained by committing the school to the all-inclusive but less encompassing task of cultivating the intellect through the omniscient academic disciplines.

Disparaging the significance of a wide and extensive educational offering has been the message from several conservative scholars for many years. Mortimer Adler, the well-known philosopher and long-time critic of progressive education, is a case in point. He denigrates progressive thinkers for attempting to bring about a comprehensive school system that attempts to "be all things to all people." To Adler, the school's function should be limited to academic concerns believed to have generalizable effects in the development of one's intellect and character. Critics of Adler say that such a view places the academic at odds with the nonacademic and reinforces a mind-versus-body dualism. In the latter case, matters of the mind are separated from matters of the body, with one becoming worthy of the school and the other not. Thus, the academic curriculum (e.g., acquisition of discipline-centered knowledge, mastery of basic skills) takes precedence while other so-called nonacademic phases of the curriculum (e.g., vocational education, interdisciplinary citizenship education, elective study) take on a secondary status in the school.

If you're interested in looking further into this debate or merely in exploring the topic of the comprehensive high school, here's a selective bibliography:

- Bureau of Education, Department of Interior. (1918). *Cardinal Principles of Secondary Education: A Report of the Commission on the Reorganization of Secondary Education,* appointed by the National Education Association. Bulletin 35. (Washington, DC: U.S. Government Printing Office). The original blueprint for the comprehensive high school.

- Educational Policies Commission. (1994). *Education for ALL-American Youth.* (Washington, DC: National Education Association). An idealized example of a comprehensive school in operation during the post–World War II period.

- Conant, J. B. (1959). *The American High School Today: A First Report to Interested Citizens.* (New York: McGraw-Hill). A defense of the comprehensive high school against conservative critics asking for a dual system of schooling during the early years of the Cold War.

- Powell, A. G., Ferrar, E., and Cohen, D. K. (1985). *The Shopping Mall High School: Winners and Losers in the Educational Marketplace.* (Boston: Houghton Mifflin); and Sizer, T. (1984). *Horace's Compromise: The Dilemma of the American High School.* (Boston: Houghton Mifflin). Criticisms, direct and indirect, against the comprehensive school.

- Wraga, W. G. (1994). *Democracy's High School: The Comprehensive High School and Educational Reform in the United States.* (Lanham, NY: University Press of America). A history of the comprehensive high school.

For access to ongoing discussion and debate on the comprehensive high school, visit the NYU Seminar on the Future of the Comprehensive School, a website maintained by Floyd Hammack, at the New York University School of Education (www.nyu.edu/education/faculty).

pressures of college preparation and its inherent association with specialized knowledge. Although some elementary school teachers might feel pressure to teach the basic skills—and nothing but the basic skills—in most cases, lessons taught in elementary school are not strictly academic. Because elementary education teachers usually work with the same group of students all day, they teach a wide range of subject areas that can be integrated in many creative and engaging ways. Linking ideas to social concerns, setting up experiences that account for individual differences, allowing individual talents and interests to find some expression in the classroom, encouraging the development of a core or common experience in democracy—all are part of the elementary school teacher's day. High school teachers, by contrast, whose training and experience often are linked to a specific discipline (mathematics, English, history, etc.) inherit certain limitations in this regard. Their contribution to the comprehensive school agenda is sometimes compromised by the specific obligations they have to teach their specialized subject area. This problem can be alleviated to some extent by the way in which the school curriculum is organized. Depending on how the curriculum is arranged, some high school teachers are expected to seek interdisciplinary linkages, to connect their classroom to community outreach efforts, and to find ways to encourage individual talents and interests. But because of the specializing influences on the high school teacher, the school has to be vigilant about arranging the curriculum in a way that serves the comprehensive schooling mandate.

As mentioned, four major objectives frame the comprehensive school experience. But these are not formulated as exclusive objectives. In fact, they are complementary and often overlap in the school experience. The four objectives, however, do set out a rather explicit charge to teachers, reminding them of their wide-ranging teaching duties. But how can teachers actually organize and apply the curriculum to achieve the four major objectives in the classroom and to help advance a comprehensive education?

TEACHING FOR INDIVIDUAL-PERSONAL GROWTH

The individual-personal aspects of the school experience should emphasize the development of a sense of individual responsibility; cultivate individual talents and skills; assist youths in their emotional, cognitive, and physical development; and generally serve the objectives of self-understanding and self-expression.

One feature of the individual-personal aspect of the curriculum goes directly to the question of individual interests and aptitudes. To put it simply, schools are expected to help develop the aptitudes and interests of individual students. Students showing a high aptitude in, say, mathematics, art, music, writing, or athletics should have access to some outlet in the school that affords them the opportunity to continue to develop that skill. Conversely, those with limited aptitudes or with particular disabilities should receive remedial assistance. The school, besides considering options within the classroom, might also point to provisions in the curriculum (e.g., advanced placement courses, various enrichment opportunities, remedial assistance, or experiences external to the school) that support individual talents and address individual weaknesses. The same rules apply to student interests. Most schools make some effort to represent individual interests in the design of their curriculum. In most elementary schools, individualization is the responsibility of the teacher, who tries to find some way to deal with individual concerns within a self-contained classroom. But it is not unusual to find pullout programs for remedial education or for the education of the so-called gifted and talented. At the middle and high school levels, however, individualization usually takes shape through systematically designed course work that might get promoted as elective study, advanced placement, or remedial/foundations education. Classroom teachers, of course, continue to do their part as well.

Instructional concerns related to individual-personal growth also have a lot to do with issues of individual well-being, such as maintaining emotional stability, coping with change, taking care of one's health, engaging in fulfilling leisure time activities, and maintaining an honest and constructive self-image. This means that teachers might direct some attention to introspective issues, to habits of individual responsibility, to constructive uses of leisure time, and ultimately to finding balance and perspective in life.

The guiding principle here is that attending to the unique needs of children is what the individual-personal phase of the curriculum is generally about. This could include making adjustments in instruction, which might include pacing differences and differences in the structure of the teaching strategy (as influenced by, say, developmental processes). But, as indicated, the individual-personal phase of the curriculum is directly tied into the exploration of personal abilities and individual interests, and into the development of the emotional and physical well-being of each child.

In the classroom, individualization can be accomplished through individual and group projects and through various extraclassroom activities. All this means is that certain students will have the opportunity to participate in certain projects on their own (or in small groups) for the purpose of pursuing a question or an interest that they personally find worthwhile. The teacher, of course, has to spark this initiative by providing options for extended exploratory education. Students might spontaneously suggest ideas for a project, but most projects should be deliberately designed in the classroom as opportunities to pursue issues raised in the classroom and to develop new interests.

A teacher could, for example, list ways to extend and further develop interests related to the classroom. To the mathematics educator, this might mean getting students involved in a math club or in other extraclassroom initiatives focusing on numeracy. In high school, extraclassroom activities or even classroom-based activities—such as a schoolwide group dedicated to polling student views on various social issues, or a consumer advocacy group interested in discerning the best local buys for various items typically purchased by students, or a computer group interested in exploring fractals —could all be possibilities for cultivating student interest in mathematics. For students showing a particular aptitude and keen interest in advanced mathematics, the teacher's role usually is limited, but curriculum options for elective study or study outside the school should be available.

The teacher can also reserve some time each day for the pursuit of individualized programs of studies related to students' own interests. During this period, small groups might meet to work on their projects, some students might go to the library to conduct research, other students might have a quiet reading session with their favorite books, and still others might pursue an interest in an area like computers.

It should be stressed, however, that a classroom period devoted to individual interests does not translate into a laissez-faire, "do-your-own-thing" classroom climate. The teacher must be an active participant in each student's work and should have a fundamental sense of what each student intends to do during these sessions. To accomplish this, the teacher might require that all projects be approved before being pursued in class and establish a list of generic activities that all students could do during the so-called individual period. In an elementary school, for example, each individual period might allow for a reasonable number of children to read or research in the library (or another quiet area), to read the local newspaper or magazines for children, to work in the computer lab or on classroom computers, or to work on approved ongoing projects.

It is important for all teachers to realize that the role of individualizing the curriculum is not simply for students to pursue preexisting interests, which is undoubtedly important, but also to widen and explore new interests. Thus, educators should try to keep an inventory of what each student in doing in the individualized phase of the curriculum. It is probably not in the student's interest to devote all of his or her time to one area of interest during the course of an academic year. For example, a student who only works on the computer or who only reads to himself all of the time needs to be encouraged, if not required, to widen his areas or bases of participation.

In the elementary school, this could also be a time when students with particular talents and aptitudes might receive special instruction outside the classroom. For instance, a child with particular gifts in the visual arts might arrange to work with the art teacher during this period; a child with an aptitude for writing, when not using her time to work on her short stories or other writing projects, could arrange for opportunities to read her work to other classrooms. At the high school level, advanced placement courses are a valuable method for providing special instruction.

Individualization can be accomplished in other ways as well. Students typically will have time in school when their work in the other phases of the curriculum is completed. Individualization can also be accomplished through optional homework assignments. Often, teachers do not have the luxury of isolating a period devoted to individual interests, which means that such projects must be pursued in the time between other classroom-based experiences or during times outside the classroom.

Finally, teachers must consider the mental, emotional, and physical well-being of each student in terms of self-realization, spiritual growth, and aesthetic understanding. Although there are clear prohibitions on any actions a teacher might take to establish a religious point of view in the classroom, religion, per se, is not banned from school. Thus, on an individual basis, there is room to explore religious or spiritual convictions and to examine, in more general terms, the aesthetics of what stirs students and gives their lives purpose and meaning. Specifically, students might pursue interests in music, art, poetry, dance, sports, and other forms of recreation. Activities that encourage varied modes of expression, that spark the imagination and a sense of wonder, that give life purpose or place it in perspective, or that help us define or see how we understand virtues such as love, trust, honesty, and courage—all have a place here. To high school English teachers, and perhaps to elementary school teachers, these instructional concerns are more customary than in other, more specialized classrooms, but they should not be limited to such places. Figure 1-1 lists some activities that might play a central role in the individual-personal phase of the curriculum.

FIGURE I-I
**Curricular and Instructional Possibilities
for Individual-Personal Growth**

FIGURE I-I

**Curricular and Instructional Possibilities
for Individual-Personal Growth**

1. Classroom activities might include library research related to any topic, interest, or pending school assignment; recreational reading, which might include the daily newspaper, various magazines, or any book of interest; ongoing individual or small-group projects based on interest; and remedial assistance within the classroom in a particular area or with a particular skill.

2. Extraclassroom activities might include a hobby or club activity reflecting student interests; advanced study, by arrangement with outside experts, for students with high aptitudes; and various experiences in sports and the fine arts.

3. Curricular arrangements, usually at the high school level, could highlight advanced placement courses and a menu of elective courses. Also, remedial assistance based on pullout programs could be provided.

TEACHING FOR SOCIO-CIVIC GROWTH

Public schools have long been viewed as fundamental agencies in the social development of children. Most public schools, after all, try to stress the highest ideals of the society in their policies and practices. In recent years, however, this aspect of the school curriculum has been dealt with rather dismally in the practice of teaching. Often, the mission of socio-civic learning has been relegated to extraclassroom experiences and to the belief that socio-civic issues are served naturally in the ebb and flow of school life (e.g., in team sports, classroom interactions, and cafeteria conversations).

In a democratic society, the public schools need to provide experiences that embody civic virtues like social responsibility, cooperation, tolerance, and equity, preferably in a social context that is characteristic of the society's population. The schools should support experiences that promote the development of interpersonal relations, that speak directly to the roles and responsibilities of democratic citizenship, that enculturate the student population into a common heritage, and that teach students to develop a critical moral perspective on their own conduct.

It is probably fair to say that in recent years most schools have undervalued these ideals and practices. In high school, socio-civic education often is linked to the disciplines of social studies and history or to extraclassroom activities like student government. In lower schools, it is believed to be served by social interactions and by some components of the social studies curriculum. Few schools, however, devote an actual block of time to citizenship education. Still, in most cases, the public school continues to represent the best hope for providing an experience in democratic living that cannot be captured in the home or the church, or any other societal institution, for that matter. Public schools sometimes do this so well that parents may perceive them as threatening institutions with a public mandate that violates certain principles or values in the home.

How does one operationalize socio-civic learning throughout the grades? What might the curriculum look like in either an elementary, middle, or secondary school, and how might it be operationalized in a school long accustomed to departmentalized subject area requirements?

Depending on the organizational structure of the school, elementary teachers can operationalize socio-civic traditions of learning in many ways. The first step is to specify a time in the classroom schedule to deal specifically with socio-civic issues in the school and community. During these common learning sessions, for instance, children in first grade could be taught a unit on the people who provide important services in their homes, neighborhood, or town. In third grade, students could prepare a formal newscast that deals with vital social concerns in the school and community. In higher grades, students might develop a monthly classroom newsletter, invite guests from the community to discuss local issues, prepare interview questions for authorities in the community or survey questions for fellow students, engage in letter-writing campaigns to public officials, or prepare a series of occasional reports on important social issues (e.g., HIV/AIDS, propaganda in advertising, gun control, or gangs).

Each of these initiatives is difficult to realize in traditional subject areas, although, depending on the project, vital skills in reading, language arts, social studies, and science are developed. Thus, teaching events can also be organized lines of inquiry that raise socio-civic questions in separate subject areas. The science line of inquiry in elementary school, for instance, might include a series of units dealing with environmental concerns, with health and nutrition issues, or with issues of technology. The social studies line might deal systematically with current events, with upcoming election-year voter decisions, or with the Constitution and the Bill of Rights. The mathematics line might lead to the creation of a classroom or school store, a treatment of consumer issues, or an economic analysis of the sports industry. The language arts line might focus on maintaining an ongoing correspondence with a wide range of pen pals across the country or the world, or on an analysis of the language used in advertising, political campaigning, or newspaper writing. In short, we can see how common learning, at least in the elementary school, could replace the more traditional arrangement of subject matter in the curriculum.

Socio-civic learning, of course, does not always call for large-group meetings. Some of its mandate can be fulfilled using smaller groups that devote themselves to the analysis of various issues. For example, a four- to seven-member team could do mathematical analyses of how much water is wasted in a typical household in the community (showing, through extrapolation, cumulative effects). Another team could work on an artistic depiction of the cultures represented in the school. Still another team could study a social problem, such as the care of the aged in society, that might move the members to engage in actions that assist the local senior citizen community.

The community-based facet of common leaning is also important. Local problems should, of course, be studied in the classroom through reading, library work, and discussions with peers, but where possible, they should also be viewed through the lens of a volunteer service organization. Middle and high school students might get involved in a study of the quality of life for young children in their community. The students might then report their findings and views to local politicians and media sources, as well as offer their services to local recreational agencies or to organizations that care for children in need (e.g., battered children, homeless children). Students in elementary schools, with the guidance and assistance of parents and teachers, might participate in local recycling projects, local food drives, local civic events, and other activities that assist people in need and improve the civic life of the community. In addition to fulfilling the service duties associated with these projects, the students will be studying the social problems that underscore the projects.

Clearly, this facet of the curriculum is unlike any other. It is expressly civic in orientation and interdisciplinary in its subject matter or content area. The habits of mind and the skills and attitudes fundamental to informed participation in a democracy take center stage. Feature 1-5 describes one way to conduct a survey that tests students for anti-democratic attitudes.

There is some room for socio-civic learning in virtually all classrooms. Many schools, especially middle schools, are now designing the curriculum in a way that encourages cross-disciplinary teaching, including team teaching arrangements and block-time allocations expressly dedicated to the study of socio-personal issues and problems. Figure 1-2 summarizes some of the possibilities.

Measuring or otherwise understanding the civic skills of American youths has not been a very popular line of inquiry for education researchers. The National Assessment of Educational Progress periodically publishes a civic report card, detailing national finding on the civic knowledge of students. The last one was published was in 1998, and you can get it for free from the National Center for Education Statistics. Generally, however, very few studies are available on topics related to the socio-civic function of schooling. Research on the democratic attitudes of children, their knowledge of politics and government, their skills as citizens, and their levels of civic consciousness has not been at the top of the research agenda. Public schools have exhibited the same lack of interest. An enormous amount of time and energy is devoted to testing for academic achievement, usually in the traditional academic areas; but in the public schools, little effort is made to test for socio-civic competencies and attitudes.

In the 1950s, during the early phase of the Cold War, the Purdue Opinion Panel, directed by H. H. Remmers, conducted some interesting research on the antidemocratic attitudes of high school students. One part of this research asked students to answer questions that testified to or against a fascist, antidemocratic ideology. Here are the results of this part of the survey, given to high school seniors in 1952 and again in 1984. Conduct your own study using these questions. Compare your results to what you see below. Disaggregate the data by sex, race, ethnicity, income, and other variables, and see if anything interesting emerges.

RESPONSES TO FASCIST IDEOLOGY

	Agree 1952	Agree 1984	Disagree 1952	Disagree 1984	Uncertain 1952	Uncertain 1984
Obedience and respect for authority are the most important virtues that children should learn.	73%	62%	18%	23%	9%	14%
Whatever serves the interests of government best is generally right.	20	10	56	73	24	17
Most criminals and moral misfits should be prevented from having children.	44	12	36	69	21	16
What this country needs most is a few strong, courageous, tireless leaders in whom people can put their trust.	59	64	29	22	12	13
A large mass of the people is not capable of determining what is and what is not good for them.	51	33	33	46	16	20
There will always be strong groups and weak groups, and it is best that the strong continue to dominate the weak.	19	14	66	64	15	21
The right of some working groups to call a strike should be abolished, as it is a threat to democracy and not in the general interest of society.	37	25	47	53	16	21

SOURCE: From S. M. Elam, "Anti-Democratic Attitudes of High School Seniors in the Orwell Year." From *Phi Delta Kappan*, 64:331. Reprinted with permission.

> **FIGURE I-2**
> **Curricular and Instructional Possibilities for Socio-Civic Growth**
>
> **1.** General classroom initiatives could be dedicated to examining socio-civic issues. Examples might include classwide letter-writing campaigns to public officials, a classroom store, a monthly preparation of a classroom newsletter, a semester-long preparation of a show dramatizing the problems of the community or society, a collective art mural representing the dynamic dimensions of the community, or a classwide examination and discussion of emerging issues like censorship in the local library and gun control.
>
> **2.** Small-group initiatives could be dedicated to developing an occasional report on an emerging issue. At elementary school levels, topics might include bicycle safety, environmental conservation, the hazards of smoking, and illegal drugs. In middle or high school, topics might include sex, the censorship of various materials in the community, the sexist and violent lyrics in some popular music, abortion, and upcoming election-year decisions.
>
> **3.** Community-based initiatives could be dedicated to studying local problems through the lens of voluntary service organizations. Youths can get involved in service opportunities that aid children (homes for battered/homeless children), the aged, and the poor, as well as in projects devoted to civic and cultural enhancement. The idea is not only to participate in the agency but also to become well versed with the issues and problems that the agency is committed to addressing. On another front, youths can conduct neighborhood studies on the recreational problems and needs of the community or on its health conditions and needs.

TEACHING FOR ACADEMIC GROWTH

Academic growth concerns in the curriculum are most often associated with college entrance demands in middle school and high school, and with basic intellectual competencies in elementary school. Academic priorities are also usually related to the development of thinking skills (e.g., inquiry, logic, and evaluation), skills of literacy and numeracy, and knowledge in the traditional disciplines. Historically, the academic function of the curriculum has valued specialized knowledge and has been organized along rather strict subject-centered lines. In the high school, this has led to a traditional menu of course work covering a discipline-centered knowledge base. In the elementary school, the same type of content has been in place, as students jump from mathematics lessons to science lessons to reading lessons and so on. At all levels, academic concerns have dominated the curriculum. Academic learning in the elementary school has usually meant education in the so-called basic skills. This has often resulted in teaching that emphasized skill-drill routines and various rote and recitation exercises. Believing that inculcation of the basic skills is necessary preparation for later academic work in the disciplines, many elementary school teachers have been keen to develop these skills in focused isolation. Thus, this emphasis on the basic skills has been a mainstay in the elementary classroom.

But the idea of teaching the basic skills in relation to larger instructional ends, as means toward ends instead of as ends in and of themselves, is attracting more proponents in the classroom. The reality is that the basic skills (or fundamental processes, as they are also known) have no full and complete residency in any one particular subject area; rather, the skills of reading, writing, and numeracy are needed in all academic subject areas. Thus, the academic tradition in the elementary school is nonspecialized or non-subject-specific and is naturally multidisciplinary, if not interdisciplinary. A teacher can think of teaching reading not only in terms of a discrete skill (during reading instruction) but also in terms of a skill that finds application in the teaching of science, mathematics, and social studies. Similarly, the teaching of mathematical skills and skills related to effective communication (writing, speaking, debating, and artistic communication) has wide-ranging possibilities in virtually all subject areas. As a result, in the elementary school, there is a blending of academic goals with individual-personal and socio-civic ones.

This is not to say that there are no subject-specific knowledge requirements for elementary school teachers. Such requirements exist in science and social studies, and, as basic skills, in reading, language arts, and mathematics. But there is no pressure to convey a seriously specialized body of knowledge to the learner yet. Consequently, the teacher has a certain latitude to think about securing connections between academic goals and socio-civic ones: to build bridges across certain content areas, to design special supplemental units, to resequence certain materials in the text, or even to consider offering a set of independent materials as supplements to the textbook.

At the high school level, the instructional equation is a little different. The academic tradition in the secondary school essentially reflects two roles: (1) one that deals expressly with specialized knowledge in the pre-college curriculum, and (2) one that might have a place in interdisciplinary settings dedicated to socio-civic objectives. In the high school, for instance, youths need to be given the opportunity to enroll in specialized academic courses, especially as these courses serve the interests of students intent on pursuing a college education. Also, high schools often exert a specializing pressure by stipulating the need for a certain number of semesters of study within certain subject areas to graduate.

This tradition dates back to the turn of the twentieth century, when established learning doctrine upheld the view that certain subjects had the intrinsic qualities to strengthen the intellect. This doctrine of mental discipline was wedded to a concept of curriculum that equated learning with knowledge acquisition in an essential body of prescribed subject matter (Kliebard, 1986). The idea was that learning proceeded through an interaction with certain studies believed to be uniquely endowed with the power to exercise the mind. The biases inherent in the doctrine of mental discipline prejudiced certain studies over others, with the effect of giving low priority to the modern social sciences, interdisciplinary subject areas, vocational education, physical education, aesthetics, and other "nonacademic" pursuits. The elevation of certain subjects to the status of "intellective" placed all other studies in an anti-intellectual position, which itself perpetuated a rather narrow view of what was worthy in the school curriculum. Feature 1-6 places the doctrine of mental discipline in historical context.

Over the years, the doctrine of mental discipline has been defrocked in the literature, but its subject-centered legacy has lingered in the schools. Because postsecondary schools set their admissions criteria according to traditional subject areas, high schools have had trouble breaking away from them. Moreover, the preparation of high school teachers continues to be aligned with specialized training in one particular discipline, which also reinforces the subject-centered lines. As mentioned, some of this makes good sense; after all, the academic curriculum in the high school does need to provide highly specialized courses. This typically means that science will be broached through the standard specializations of biology, chemistry, and physics; mathematics through algebra, geometry, and trigonometry; social studies through civics and history; and English through grammar, composition, and classical literature. College entrance requirements and state-mandated objectives typically influence the character of these specialized offerings.

But the academic curriculum in the high school could allow for linkages to interdisciplinary and socio-civic concerns as well. Obviously, a broad field such as social studies has multiple claims on subject disciplines and multiple connections to socio-civic goals. But educators from science, math, and English also could direct their efforts toward the goal of making interdisciplinary connections in the socio-civic arena. In science education, for instance, the last decade witnessed the growth of a movement, known as Science-Technology and Society (STS), that used issue-centered themes that touch on critical social topics. Sanctioned by the National Science

1-6 THE HISTORICAL CONTEXT
The Doctrine of Mental Discipline

The high regard given to discipline-centered subjects and academic knowledge in the high school curriculum is partly a vestige of an Old World learning doctrine known as mental discipline. According to its advocates, the doctrine of mental discipline upheld a learning process that sought to expose students to a prescribed set of academic subjects believed to be uniquely endowed with the power to exercise the mind. Traditionally, Latin, classical literature, mathematics, and other classical liberal studies were the anointed subjects. The focus on the all-inclusive task of cultivating the mind created a tilt in the curriculum that put greater emphasis on subject-centered, academic, and mentalistic learning.

The spirit of this approach often was captured in the work of Robert Hutchins, one-time president of the University of Chicago and a scholar whose philosophical leanings favored the doctrine of mental discipline. "The ideal education," he once stated, "is . . . an education calculated to develop the mind" (Hutchins, 1936, p. 66). Elsewhere, he noted that "grammar disciplines the mind and develops the logical faculty" and that "correctness in thinking may be more directly and impressively taught through mathematics than in any other way" (Hutchins, 1936, pp. 62, 82).

Interestingly, early attempts to test the contention that certain subjects had an inherent power to train the mind failed to produce results that supported the doctrine of mental discipline. Studies conducted by Edmund Thorndike, the preeminent psychologist of his time, as well as verifying studies conducted throughout the century, made it clear that no particular subjects have a unique hold on intellectual development (Tanner and Tanner, 1995). Thorndike (1924) was fairly straightforward about his findings. He observed:

The expectation of any large difference in general improvement of the mind from one study rather than another seems doomed to disappointment. The chief reason why good thinkers seem superficially to have been made such by having taken certain school studies is that good thinkers have taken such studies. . . .When good thinkers studied Greek and Latin, these studies seemed to make good thinking. . . .If the abler students should all study Physical Education and Dramatic Art, these subjects seem to make good thinkers. (p. 98)

Today, the doctrine of mental discipline may not be with us in word as much as by effect. High schools continue to be locked into a subject-centered curriculum that puts a higher premium on academic learning. Vocational studies still suffer from accusations of anti-intellectualism, and subjects like Latin still are promoted for their mind-training endowments.

Examine the historical record. How did Thorndike set up an experiment to test the idea of mental discipline? What have other scholars done to verify Thorndike's work? Of particular interest might be the evaluation work of Tyler (1942) on the famous eight-year study. Why haven't these studies dissuaded certain scholars from continuing to advance the doctrine of mental discipline?

Teachers Association and sponsored by the National Science Foundation, STS has sought to transcend the discipline-centered lines of traditional science and to deal with points of argument that cut across a broad range of environmental, industrial, technological, social, and political problems (National Science Teachers Association, 1982; Yager, 1986). It unabashedly claims to prepare youths for constructive citizenship roles. English educators have gotten in on the action, mobilizing their energies to deal with the relation of their discipline to democratizing practices in the school. The teaching standards supported by the National Council of Teachers of English (1996), for example, include references to the teaching of language in the context of cultural diversity, to the teaching of literature as it relates to improving understanding of society, and to the encouragement of problem-focused research inquiries on various socio-personal issues and interests. Mathematics educators have acknowledged a similar position, arguing that an educated, informed electorate must have solid math literacy skills. Understanding issues such as environmental protection, nuclear energy, defense spending, space exploration, and taxation require high achievement in mathematics, according to the National Council of Teachers of Mathematics (1989). Thus, the academic merges, in some sectors of the curriculum, with the socio-civic.

Along these lines, we can begin to see certain formations in the curriculum encouraging the commingling of academic and socio-civic goals. "Academic" goals in social studies might result in a course on the problems of democracy. In science, a course dedicated to exploring environmental or health problems might be offered. In mathematics, a series of courses that deal with understanding sociological phenomena via quantitative means could be planned, and in English, the possibilities of linking the examination of literature to the social conditions of humankind are virtually endless. Figure 1-3 details the general landscape of instructional possibilities for the academic curriculum.

TEACHING FOR VOCATIONAL GROWTH

Part of the conventional wisdom about public schooling speaks to its importance in equipping youths with the skills, competencies, and attitudes needed to perform successfully in the labor markets. At the university level, "vocational" programs exist for the preparation of accountants, educators, engineers, economists, social workers, musicians, and physicists. In secondary schools, vocational programs exist in relation to employment in

---

FIGURE 1-3
Curricular and Instructional Possibilities for Academic Growth

1. Interdisciplinary initiatives associated with common learnings might draw out academic skills and knowledge in relation to socio-civic themes. These would predominate in elementary and middle schools, but would be reserved within a facet of the common learning component of the curriculum in high school. The math stream might include courses such as understanding and designing surveys, the economics of banking and the stock market, the role of taxation in a democracy, consumer math, and statistics in sports. The science stream might include courses on the history of innovation and technology, the science of environmental protection, medicine and the microscopic world, global disease, and the science of war. English courses could provide a literature-based treatment of any social problem. English teachers could offer biographies of key people in the history of the society's development and correlate the class reading schedule with any number of other interdisciplinary courses. The role of poetry and musical lyrics as social protest and the art of editorial writing also could come into play.

2. Specialized courses in each of the attendant academic traditions are designed for students planning to attend college. They include the typical menu of specialized courses affiliated with the broad fields of math (algebra, geometry, calculus, and trigonometry), science (biology, chemistry, and physics), social studies (history and government), and English. Such courses should not be widely used in elementary or middle school settings because specialized academic training, which is the province of higher education, has little compelling justification in the life of the elementary school student.

---

the agricultural, health, trade, and industrial sectors. Such programs have long been situated in comprehensive school settings, though one can find them in separate technical schools as well.

Vocational education is a phenomenon that applies mostly to middle and high school settings. Over the years, middle schools have offered courses in the prevocational arts in an attempt to offer youths an opportunity to explore vocational life-skills. These are viewed as exploratory courses that give preadoloscents an early exposure to consumer education courses or to general labor preparation courses. In the secondary school, however, vocational education courses become more specialized and more closely associated with the education of youths not destined for higher education. Still, aspects of vocational education in the high school retain their general orientation and are sometimes connected to socio-civic objectives (e.g., courses on the literature of work, ethics in business, or the history of technology and society). Moreover, vocational education courses in the high school are also offered as electives, especially for college-bound students. As it turns out, 98 percent of all high school graduates complete at least one course in vocational education (National Center for Education Statistics, 1992, p. 8).

Critics across the ideological spectrum have questioned the placement of vocational education in the comprehensive school design. Conservatives generally argue that vocational programs are anti-intellectual, cost too much, and lack value in the actual job market. They also claim that opportunities to enjoy a rigorous academic education are lost on students who participate heavily in vocational education programs. More liberal critics generally argue that vocational education is too specialized and too slow to respond to changes in the technological and occupational conditions of the marketplace. As a result, they criticize vocational education for restricting student career opportunities. Vocational education students, they claim, may become trained solely as, say, welders and nothing else, which gives them little flexibility in the job market and consequently more restricted options for social and economic advancement. In this manner, vocational education, which is largely populated by students from the lower socioeconomic sectors of society, serves as a mechanism that perpetuates the status quo.

The major criticism facing vocational education is one that raises doubts about its worth as a bridge between the school and the workplace. Data from the National Center for Education Statistics (NCES), however, are inconclusive. Of all the high school graduates from 1992 who chose not to opt for postsecondary schooling (two- or four-year college), 43 percent were employed full-time, 18 percent were working part-time, 10 percent were unemployed, and 29 percent were not in the labor force (NCES, 1992, p. 42). Among high school graduates with the most vocational education credits, the full-time employment rate was at 50 percent. The data, in fact, show a positive correlation between degree of participation in vocational education and full-time employment. At the same time, there was no difference between the rate of unemployment among high school graduates with no postsecondary schooling and the rate of unemployment among students with intensive exposure to vocational education. Furthermore, the amount of vocational preparation gained by a student in high school made no difference in terms of the wages earned by graduates (NCES, 1992, pp. 42, 46). Some of this might be explained by the fact that close to 40 percent of the students with a high degree of participation in vocational education opted to continue their educations, often in training schools and two-year community colleges, where their vocational education skills presumably were further cultivated. In other words, the true market worth of vocational education cannot be fully evaluated until the postsecondary education has been completed.

The organizational structure of vocational education targets both non-occupationally specific and occupationally specific education. To avoid a narrowness in training, the curriculum is organized in three parts: (1) consumer and homemaking education, which provides courses in child development, clothing, basic food preparation, and home management; (2) general labor market preparation, which offers courses in beginning word processing, industrial arts, work experience and career exploration, business math, and business English; and (3) specific labor market preparation, which includes introductory, advanced, and elective courses in agriculture, business, marketing and distribution, health, occupational home economics, trade and industry, and technical (NCES, 1992, p. xix).

The occupational focus notwithstanding, vocational studies is increasingly looking for stronger academic ties. A health-services cluster, for instance, could be seen as preparatory to several occupations, including nurse, medical technician, physical therapist, dental assistant, orderly, and dietitian. Such a program of courses would be vocational in terms of particular skills but would also have a strong academic base, especially as it relates to mathematics and the sciences. Another cluster might be business education, which, besides having a strong skill base in word processing, shorthand, and computer facility, would offer academic course work in mathematics, business principles, and English. Figure 1-4 outlines some curricular and instructional possibilities for vocational growth.

SUMMARY

Public schooling bears the profound responsibility of educating youths for informed participation in democratic society. This means that it must provide an education that equips youths with the general skills, competencies, knowledge, attitudes, values, and outlooks that they will need to conduct intelligent, fulfilling, and empowering lives—as individuals, workers, and citizens. Education for academic and intellectual growth has an undeniably significant place in such an agenda, but objectives more intimately attached to personal, social, and vocational learning also have their place. Thus, the school, operating in a unified setting, endeavors to produce a comprehensive and enlarging learning experience, where the full expression of the public mandate can be realized.

FIGURE 1-4
Curricular and Instructional Possibilities for Vocational Growth

1. Several prevocational courses might be offered as exploratory initiatives for middle school youths. They could be organized in broad categorical groups through the common curriculum or as elective options. The categories might include home economics education, which would include issues related to food and nutrition, clothing and textiles, child development, family and social relationships and, home management and family economics; or beginning courses in trade and industrial education, which might include an introduction to basic motor mechanics, carpentry skills, and drafting.

2. Courses in vocational and socio-civic education could link occupational concerns with socio-civic problems. These courses might deal with the problems of capitalism in a free society, the history of unionism in the nation, the role of technology as it relates to the freedoms of a democracy, basic consumer issues, and actual vocational life-skills (e.g., motor mechanics, computer literacy, and the skills related to most do-it-yourself home projects). These courses would apply to both middle and secondary schools.

3. Courses in vocational and occupational education could be designed for non-college-bound students. A program of courses might cover a comprehensive range of occupational skills related to a broad family of vocational competencies.

QUESTIONS AND ACTIVITIES

1. In what ways has the public school carried a heavy burden of responsibility?

2. Dewey (1916) once stated that "it is the office of the school environment to balance the various elements in the social environment, and to see to it that each individual gets an opportunity to escape from the limitations of the social groups in which he was born, and to come into living contact with a broader environment" (p. 20). How do you interpret this? Do you agree with it? Why or why not?

3. How can the public schools be regulated at the state level and still abide by some sense of national goals?

4. What are the four main objectives in a school committed to offering youths a comprehensive education? Explain their purposes.

5. What is the American unified system of schooling, and how does it differ from a dual or bipartite system?

6. In 1959, Rickover criticized the comprehensive high school for promoting a soft and anti-intellectual education: "In the American comprehensive high school, the pupils find a display of courses resembling the variegated dishes in a cafeteria. No wonder he often gorges himself on sweets instead of taking solid meat that must be chewed" (p. 143). What do you think of Rickover's metaphor? Is this a criticism that bears any resemblance to the experience you might have had in a comprehensive high school?

7. In 1996, Census Bureau data showed that only 45.6 percent of all citizens between the ages of 18 and 20 were registered to vote, and that only 31 percent actually voted (U.S. Bureau of Census, 1997). Should this be viewed, at least in part, as a failure in the school's mission to educate youths for socio-civic growth?

8. In his national study, Goodlad (1984) found that the emotional tone of the classroom in public school was flat, that the discourse of the classroom was dominated by teacher talk, and that the widespread use of worksheets resulted in frequent low-level and repetitive exercises. What does such a finding say about the comprehensive educational agenda in the school?

9. What are the main differences between the way the elementary school and the high school might deal with individual needs in the curriculum?

10. What are some classroom possibilities for an elementary school teacher wanting to address the individual needs and interests of his or her students?

11. How might community issues factor into the socio-civic education of children?

12. From your own experience as a student or as a student teacher, can you identify how socio-civic skills were taught in your school? Was there a common core of studies dedicated to the socio-civic curriculum?

13. If you were asked to redesign the high school or elementary school you attended, what might you do to better fulfill the comprehensive school agenda?

14. Develop a conceptual outline for an elementary school unit or a secondary school course dedicated to using mathematical skills for promoting socio-civic understanding.

15. What role has the doctrine of mental discipline played in the debate over the place of academics in the curriculum?

16. How might academic instruction factor into socio-civic education at the high school level?

17. Why are specialized courses much less necessary in elementary and middle schools than in high school?

18. Participation in vocational education programs at the high school level decreases as students' socioeconomic status, academic ability, and grades increase (NCES, p. xxii). Do you see this as a problem? Why or why not?

19. What have been the main criticisms of vocational education in a comprehensive high school?

20. Some reformers believe that vocational education is better placed at the postsecondary level, leaving the high school to focus on the other three major objectives in the curriculum. What do you think of such a reform? Are there general limitations or general strengths to the idea?

REFERENCES

Adler, M. (1997). *Reforming education: The schooling of a people and their education beyond schooling.* (Boulder, CO: Westview Press).

Butts, R. F. (1989). *The civic mission of educational reform.* (Stanford, CA: Hoover Institute Press).

Conant, J. B. (1959). *The American high school today.* (New York: McGraw-Hill).

Counts, G. S. (1926). The senior high school curriculum. *Supplementary Educational Monographs No. 29.* (Chicago: University of Chicago Press).

Cremin, L. A. (1965). *The genius of American education.* (New York: Vintage Books).

Dewey, J. (1916). *Democracy and education.* (New York: Macmillan).

Goodlad, J. I. (1984). *A place called school.* (New York: McGraw-Hill).

Hutchins, R. M. (1936). *The higher learning in America.* (New Haven, CT: Yale University Press).

Kliebard, H. M. (1986). *The struggle for the American curriculum.* (New York: Routledge & Kegan Paul).

National Center for Education Statistics. (1998). *Civics report card.* (Washington, DC: U.S. Department of Education).

National Center for Education Statistics. (1992). *Vocational education in the United States: 1969–1990.* (Washington, DC: U.S. Department of Education).

National Council of Teachers of English and the International Reading Association. (1996). *Standards for the English language art.* (Washington, DC: NCTE).

National Council of Teachers of Mathematics. (1989). *Curriculum and evaluation standards for school mathematics.* (Washington, DC: NCTM).

National Education Goals Panel. (1998). *Data volume for the National Education Goals Report.* (Washington, DC: U.S. Government Printing Office).

National Science Teachers Association. (1982). *Science-technology and society.* (Washington, DC: U.S. Government Printing Office).

Rickover, H. G. (1959). *Education and freedom.* (New York: Dutton).

Sizer, T. R. (1984). *Horace's compromise.* (Boston: Houghton Mifflin).

Tanner, D., and Tanner, L. N. (1995). *Curriculum development,* 3rd ed. (New York: Macmillan).

Thorndike, E. L. (1924). Mental discipline in high school studies. *Journal of Educational Psychology,* 15 (Feb.).

Tyler, R. W. (1949). *Basic principles of curriculum and instruction.* (Chicago: University of Chicago Press).

U.S. Bureau of Census. (1997). *Fertility and family statistics.* (Washington, DC: U.S. Government Printing Office).

U.S. Department of Education. (1990). *America 2000.* (Washington, DC: U.S. Government Printing Office).

Ward, L. (1883). *Dynamic sociology.* (New York: Appleton).

Yager, R. (1986). What's wrong with school science? *The Science Teacher,* 53(1):145–47.

CHAPTER 2

The Teacher and the Classroom

Who Educates the Masses?

The Status of the Teaching Profession

Job Satisfaction Issues

Professional Decision Making
LEVELS OF PROFESSIONALISM
FACTORS IN PROFESSIONAL DECISION MAKING

Classroom Issues
PROBLEMATIZING TEACHER EFFECTIVENESS
TEACHING TO THE TEST
CLASSROOM CONTROL

Summary

Questions and Activities

References

J OHN DEWEY ONCE OBSERVED that we are all born to be teachers as we are not born to be engineers or sculptors. His point was that teaching is preeminently a social act, one that attaches itself to real-life situations and people. To be human is, in many ways, to be a teacher. The very sustenance of society depends on the capacity of humanity to learn from itself and to encourage a sense of mutuality of interests and of social understanding. Today much of this process has been formalized in the school. We sometimes use dramatic language to portray the high purpose of the school, referring to it as the main building block of democracy, the place where children can learn what it means to be an American, the chief agency for the socialization of democratic skills and democratic values, and the one public experience deliberately designed to give youths a cosmopolitan understanding of the world. Teachers, of course, are the main workers in the fulfillment of the public schooling task, as close to 50 million public schoolchildren in America can attest. But education is not always a matter of schooling. Families, churches, and various special interest groups also have educating agendas. And in all cases, teachers, albeit of a different sort, are needed to get the job done. Thus, we find the skills of an educator manifesting obviously in the role of parent, spouse, sibling, citizen, worker, friend, and colleague. The native capacity to teach exists, to varying degrees, in all of us. It is part of our humanity.

Professional school teaching, however, especially in the context of public schools, involves a unique and profound responsibility. It is, without exaggeration, allied with arguably one of the most important tasks facing our society—the enlightenment of generations of immature youths for informed participation in society. Although various people have some role to play in this task, professional teachers are intentionally placed in the key role of actualizing a democratic social mandate in the school. They are, in effect, our appointed directors of social and democratic learning. We expect them to be role models for ethical and moral behavior, wise counselors, fair-minded authorities and disciplinarians, important gatekeepers of knowledge, and ultimately professionals whose judgments in the school are always made in the best interests of the learner.

The nobility of the teaching profession, in fact, resides in these many roles. Other professions, of course, have their own claims on nobility. Doctors save lives and attend to our health and physical well-being; judges preserve justice and the rule of law; and engineers help build our infrastructure and our base of technological know-how. But all of these professionals have necessarily had teachers in their lives, often public school teachers, who helped them develop their professional skills, as well as their life-skills as citizens and family members. The dignity inherent in the teach-

Academic, vocational, social, and individualistic learning needs should be served by the school.

ing profession is reflected in its commitment to social service, in its dedication to the long-term task of educating each generation in a way that will ensure a better life for those who are yet to be born.

WHO EDUCATES THE MASSES?

In preliterate societies, learning took place without the formal institution of schooling. Virtually every action of the society was imbued with life purpose. Food-gathering and hunting skills were taught by elders, who conveyed their wisdom to the younger generation through life applications. Teaching was not an academic exercise, but a life exercise, tied directly to the sustenance of the group. Motivation was not a concern; because education was so closely linked to survival, there was little need to generate learning interest. Learning was of interest because it was so completely associated with the act of living. No separation existed between the needs of living and the act of education.

Today, of course, the role of the educator has been formalized, and the educational agenda is not always tied directly to life. Academic, vocational, social, and individualistic needs are served by trained educators who employ formal techniques to capture the hearts and minds of youngsters.

Lessons are used, objectives are formulated, motivational techniques are considered, and various organizational frameworks (using different time allotments and group configurations) are weighed. Formal schooling, unlike an informal communal or societal arrangement, has a purpose that extends beyond the interests of the family or the parochial community. In America, it has to bring a multitude of cultures and languages together, and it has to embrace an ideal that transcends all community traditions. The professional educator has to carry out this cosmopolitan purpose in accordance with the definitive ideals of the profession.

Who are the people that our society has entrusted with the formal education of youngsters? What are their lives like in school, and what do we expect from them in the classroom? Are there problems in the demographics of the teaching profession or in the characteristics of the profession that speak to a failure in the public school classroom?

One of the interesting characteristics of the teaching profession is its gender distribution. Over 73 percent of the nation's 2.5 million public school teachers are women (National Center for Education Statistics, 1997a, p. 9). The percentage of women teachers working in elementary schools is even greater—over 90 percent. The dominance of women in the teaching profession probably has something to do with the early development of "normal schools," teacher training schools that focused on the teaching of methodology over subject matter. In the early nineteenth century, getting an education in subject matter, which was embodied in course work at the university or college level, was viewed as worthy for only men. It was a man's intellect, not a woman's, that was considered to be equal to the task of learning the subject matter. Long denied access to higher education, women could, by and large, only look to the normal school as a realistic source of postsecondary education. The normal school's commitment to the "lightweight" task of teaching methodologies posed no threat to and evinced little interest from males. The old maxim of "those who can't, teach" had a real-life application in the minds of many males. This prejudice, combined with an emerging popular cultural perspective that viewed teaching as an extension of mothering, as a gentle art for the gentle sex, helped to make teaching women's work. Today, of course, many female teachers recognize that the role they play as teacher often mirrors that of a mother, and most view this as an important aspect of their job, but the job obviously calls for more than mothering. Interestingly, at the secondary school level, where the children are obviously older, the gender distribution is much more balanced than at the elementary school level.

With respect to ethnicity, the nation's teaching force remains the domain of white, middle-class women. During the 1993–94 academic year, black

TABLE 2-1

Percentage Distribution of Public School Teachers According to Minority Enrollment in Their Schools, by Teacher Race-Ethnicity, 1993–94

Teacher Race-Ethnicity	Minority Enrollment in School				
	No Minority Students	1–10 percent	11–30 percent	31–50 percent	More Than 50 Percent
Total	4.9%	33.5%	22.8%	14.2%	24.6%
Black, non-Hispanic	0.4	3.4	11.8	16.1	68.3
White, non-Hispanic	5.6	37.7	24.3	14.2	18.2
Other*	0.8	8.6	13.0	12.7	64.8

NOTE: Percentage distributions may not sum to 100 due to rounding.

* Other includes Asian/Pacific Islanders, Hispanics of any race, American Indian/Alaskan Natives, and other racial-ethnic categories.

SOURCE: U.S. Department of Education, National Center for Education Statistics, Schools and Staffing Survey, 1993–94 (School Teacher Questionnaires).

(non-Hispanic) children represented about 16 percent of the public school enrollment, while the Hispanic enrollment stood at about 12 percent; combined, these students account for close to one-third of the overall enrollment. At the same time, only about 12 percent of all public school teachers were drawn from these two minority groups (National Center for Education Statistics, 1997a, p. 10). Indeed, even as the public schools' student population is becoming increasingly diverse, the race-ethnicity of teachers is not following suit. This situation does not show many signs of changing. Although 16 percent of beginning teachers (three years of experience or less) are now being drawn from minority groups, which is clearly an improvement, the growth is mostly in the Hispanic teaching population. The proportion of black, non-Hispanic teachers has shown no growth, standing at 6 percent among beginning teachers, and is arguably down when one considers the fact that 8 percent of teachers with twenty or more years of experience are black. (See Table 2-1.)

Clearly, it is important for all children to be exposed to the vast racial and ethnic diversity of our nation. Some have argued that it is especially important for minority children to be exposed to minority teachers, largely because of a belief that such teachers are more influential role models and are better prepared than nonminority teachers to deal with the motivational and performance-related concerns of minority children (Ladson-Billings, 1994). To this end, we find that minority teachers are indeed heavily represented in schools where more than half of the student

The nation's teaching force still lacks
sufficient minority representation.

population belongs to a minority group. (See Table 2-2.) Sixty-eight percent of all black non-Hispanic teachers work in largely minority schools.
This is both good and bad news. Although minority teachers seem to be
teaching where they might be most needed, their presence in all the schools
of America is still a benefit waiting to be reaped. Moreover, where there are
high minority student enrollments, there are often high poverty levels
among the children, as well as high numbers of limited-English-proficiency
(LEP) students. Thus, the lack of representative diversity cuts across the
student population not only by race and ethnicity but also by income level
and English language ability. If the public schools are schools of democracy,
then it seems axiomatic that the ethnic and racial composition of America's
schoolteachers must reflect America's student population. It currently does
not, and for many the remediation of this problem is at the core of any
future school reform.

Public school teachers are also a highly educated group of professionals.
About 47 percent of all public school teachers have an education beyond a
bachelor's degree; only about 1 percent do not hold a bachelor's degree
(National Center for Education Statistics, 1997a, p. 29). Teachers are often
encouraged to pursue graduate education by school districts that design
their salary schedules in a way that rewards teachers who continue to
advance their education. In several states, a master's degree is considered
the professional diploma for a public school educator. In New York, for

TABLE 2-2
**Percentage Distribution of Teachers According to Race-Ethnicity,
by Sector and Minority Enrollment in Their Schools, 1993–94**

	American Indian/ Alaskan Native	Asian/ Pacific Islander	Black, Non-Hispanic	Hispanic	White, Non-Hispanic
Total	0.4%	1.1%	7.9%	3.6%	87.0%
Public	0.4	1.1	8.6	3.7	86.2
Minority enrollment					
No minority students	0.5	0.1	0.8	0.1	98.5
1–10 percent	0.2	0.3	1.0	0.4	98.1
11–30 percent	0.4	0.7	4.3	1.5	93.2
31–50 percent	0.5	0.9	9.4	2.9	86.3
More than 50 percent	0.7	2.7	23.1	10.8	62.8
Private	0.3	1.2	3.4	2.8	92.3
Minority enrollment					
No minority students	0.1	—*	0.3	0.4	99.2
1–10 percent	0.1	0.3	0.6	0.8	98.2
11–30 percent	0.4	1.2	1.8	2.6	94.0
31–50 percent	0.2	2.1	2.8	5.1	89.7
More than 50 percent	0.7	4.6	18.7	11.0	65.1

NOTE: Percentage distributions may not sum to 100 due to rounding.
* —Too few cases for a reliable estimate.
SOURCE: U.S. Department of Education, National Center for Education Statistics, Schools and Staffing Survey, 1993–94 (School Teacher Questionnaires).

instance, a master's degree is required for permanent certification as a teacher. Unfortunately, across the nation, the distribution of teachers with more than a bachelor's degree is significantly lower in high-poverty schools, standing at around 42 percent, than in low-poverty schools, where it is about 58 percent (National Center for Education Statistics, 1997a, p. 20). Still, by international standards, American teachers are among the most highly educated in the world (Carson, Huelskamp, and Woodall, 1993).

The political and religious character of the teaching profession is balanced, if not slightly tilted to the political right. According to a study conducted by the Carnegie Foundation for the Advancement of Teaching (1990), 29 percent of public school teachers characterize themselves as liberal or moderately liberal, while 42 percent characterize themselves as conservative or moderately conservative. The remainder identify themselves as "middle of the road." This contradicts the popular image of a politically liberal profession that marches to the orders of the Democratic party. One-fourth of all teachers see themselves as deeply religious, and another 62 percent see themselves as moderately religious. Altogether, 88 percent of the public teaching force considers itself deeply or moderately religious. This is an important finding because many conservative religious critics of public schools like to describe them as soulless institutions operated by people who have no religious depth. The irony is that the secular nature of schooling is protected and served by highly religious individuals. Only 12 percent of teachers stated that they were indifferent to religion, and only 1 percent were opposed to it.

THE STATUS OF THE TEACHING PROFESSION

Participation in a profession typically requires credentials gained through some officially sanctioned method of certification whereby individuals are judged able to perform a particular set of specialized professional skills. This process of certification is usually associated with a training program that is, more often than not, consummated through an official licensing examination. Physicians, lawyers, dentists, and architects are not accorded full professional status until they pass a licensing exam at the conclusion of their educational training. This has not been the tradition in teaching, although increasingly states are requiring teacher-licensing examinations. Other characteristics of a profession include (1) the presence of an induction program that helps new professionals enter the field, (2) ongoing in-service training programs that keep professionals informed of any changes in their field, (3) an expectation of authority to exercise decision making in the workplace, and (4) good compensation, largely through salary and benefits, throughout the span of a career (National Center for Education Statistics, 1997b). These criteria, and several others, are outlined in an inquiry-based assignment highlighted in Feature 2-1. Not surprisingly, statistical analyses done by the National Center for Education Statistics (1997c) found that professional indices, such as teacher autonomy and teacher influence, higher end-of-career salaries, and assistance for teacher induction, were all positively associated with higher levels of reported teacher commitment, as well as the related traits of engagement, enthusiasm, and satisfaction. How does teaching generally fare when judged as a profession against these criteria?

2-1 RESEARCH INQUIRY
Grading the Profession

According to a report filed by the National Center for Education Statistics (1997b), a profession can be evaluated against six main levels of performance. These include the following:

1. *Credentials*—the extent to which hiring practices are based on credentials earned in professional training programs
   Ex.—all math teachers educated in Math?

2. *Induction*—the extent to which mentoring programs are in place to serve as effective inductions for newcomers into the profession

3. *Professional development*—the extent to which provisions and experiences are provided that allow for the continuing growth and development of the professional

4. *Specialization*—the extent to which there is a match between the specialized knowledge of the professional and specialized knowledge required in the job (e.g., Are high school math teachers knowledgeable in mathematics?)

5. *Authority*—the extent to which the professional is able to influence decisions in the workplace

6. *Compensation*—the extent of compensation offered through salary and benefits

How would you begin to use these criteria to grade the profession of teaching? Some evidence is provided in the text, but what other kinds of evidence would you look for to make a judgment on each criterion? How might you apply these criteria to other professions, and how might they score?

In terms of salaries, public school teachers across the country report an average salary of about $37,000 (American Federation of Teachers, 1995). Public school teachers at the start of their careers can expect to earn an average annual salary of about $22,000; after teaching for twenty years and earning a master's degree, they can expect to reach the $37,000 level. Because teachers are typically given a ten-month contract, they have an opportunity to augment their annual salary, which on the average results in about $2,500 in supplemental earnings (National Center for Education Statistics, 1997a, p. 73).

Teachers' salaries are often determined by negotiated salary schedules that take into account education and experience, but not, in most cases, grade level or subject taught. Teachers can usually expect pay raises based on the accumulation of experience and additional education, not on any judgment of classroom performance, although some school districts have experimented with performance pay for teachers. Over the past decade, the median salaries of teachers have remained, in constant dollars, more or less the same. Adjusting for inflation, the median salary for a schoolteacher in America in 1971 was $34,113; in 1998, the median salary was $35,099 (National Center for Education Statistics, 1999, p. 78). Feature 2-2 traces some historical trends, spanning three decades, on the annual median salaries of teachers.

Teachers continue to earn less than many other college graduates despite possessing similar literacy skills. The median salary for a college graduate (employed full-time) in 1998 was $37,399, while for a full-time professional public school teacher, as indicated, it was $35,099 (National Center for Education Statistics, 1999a, p. 78). The negative stereotype of a teacher, often inspired by media commentary, is built on the image of a low-achieving and poorly educated college graduate. But the evidence points to a fundamentally different conclusion. The Educational Testing Service released a study in 1999 (Bruschi and Coley, 1999) that documented the capabilities of teachers in dealing with prose, document, and quantitative problems, showing that their scores in prose and document literacy were higher than those of many other professionals and were no worse than those of most other professionals, including physicians. Figure 2-1 summarizes the document literacy data. Their quantitative skills were significantly lower than those of professionals in highly quantitative fields, such as engineering, accounting, and computer science, but were no worse than those of physicians and financial managers. In the words of the researchers, "What we can take away from this analysis is the assurance that our teachers measure up well with those in other professions and those with similar levels of education. This is contrary to the national view that has developed, proving that we need to abandon the currently negative stereotype" (Bruschi and Coley, 1999, p. 25).

Contrary to popular opinion, teachers do not work a shortened workweek. Teachers spend about 33 required hours per week at school, where their time is dedicated largely to teaching class, preparing lessons, attending staff meetings, and fulfilling any number of school-related responsibilities. However, this amounts to only about three-quarters of the teacher's workweek, because in addition to the required time in school, teachers devote approximately 12 more hours per week to activities involving students or

2-2 **THE HISTORICAL CONTEXT**

Teacher Salaries

Here are three different ways of viewing the distribution of the annual median salaries of teachers over three decades. Examine the trends. What conclusions can you draw from the three different representations? These data, and other, related information on teachers' salaries, can be found in the National Center for Education Statistics report, *Condition of Education, 1999.* You can access it from the NCES's website (www.nces.ed.gov), where all of the public reports on education can be ordered free of charge.

Percentage Distribution and Annual Median Salaries of Full-Time Elementary and Secondary Teachers, by Age, 1971–98

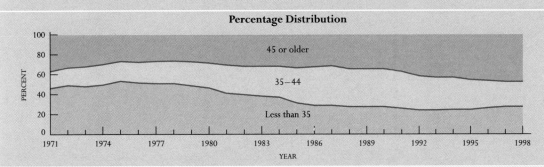

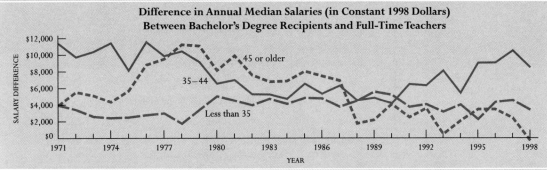

NOTE: Median salaries refer to the previous calendar year; for example, salaries reported in 1971 refer to salaries earned in 1970. The Consumer Price Index (CPI) was used to calculate constant dollars. Data include full-time public and private school teachers who taught grades 1–12.

SOURCE: National Center for Education Statistics (1999), *The condition of education* (Washington, DC: U.S. Department of Education), p. 79.

53

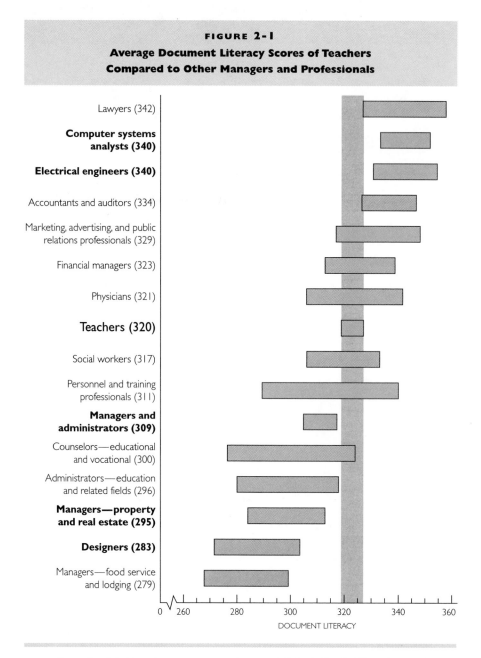

FIGURE 2-1

**Average Document Literacy Scores of Teachers
Compared to Other Managers and Professionals**

NOTE: Occupations in bold type have average scores that are statistically significantly different from teachers. While other score differences may appear large, they are not statistically significant. Bars represent the confidence intervals around the average scores. The vertical shaded area represents the confidence band for teachers' average score and is intended to facilitate comparisons.

SOURCE: National Center for Education Statistics (1992), *National adult literacy survey* (Washington, DC: U.S. Department of Education).

Contrary to popular opinion, teachers
do not work a shortened work week.

school-related work, such as grading and lesson preparation. These numbers
are more or less consistent between elementary and secondary schoolteachers. Thus, teachers, on the average, spend about 45 hours per week performing all of their teaching duties (National Center for Education
Statistics, 1997a, p. 47). This contrasts with the image of a reduced workweek. Other professions do not have a significantly longer workweek; for
example, physicians and lawyers report an average workweek of 49 hours.

The act of mentoring a beginning teacher, which is a fundamental principle in the concept of professionalism, occurs on a formal basis in only about
67 percent of public schools (National Center for Education Statistics,
1997b, p. 14). The increasing presence of formally designed induction programs is a positive development for the teaching profession. But the effectiveness of such programs is still highly uneven, largely because the
meetings between new and veteran teachers in these programs vary in frequency and quality. New teachers report that induction programs that
include frequent planning sessions and regularly scheduled collaborations
with veteran teachers, inside and outside of school, improve their teaching
(National Center for Education Statistics, 1999b, p. 34). Currently, about
45 percent of new teachers, defined as those who have been teaching for
three or fewer years, who reported to be mentored, claimed to benefit
"a lot" from the experience. Only 5 percent claimed not to benefit at all
(National Center for Education Statistics, 1999b, p. 33).

© Bob Rowan, Progressive Image/Corbis

Over 90 percent of public school teachers participate in school-sponsored workshops or in-service training.

In-service training for educators has a much longer and better-established tradition in the school than induction programs. Over 90 percent of public school teachers reported that they participated in school-sponsored workshops or in-service training. During the 1998 school year, many of these programs were dedicated to methods of teaching, student assessment, cooperative learning, the uses of educational technology for instruction, and the integration of state and district curriculum and performance standards in the classroom (National Center for Education Statistics, 1999b, p. 23). These programs have had, at least in the past, some impact. In 1993, a majority of teachers (about 60 percent) reported that such in-service programs caused them to change their teaching practices and to seek further information and training (National Center for Education Statistics, 1997a, p. 41). Efforts by school districts to support the ongoing or continuing education of teachers in postbaccalaureate settings could also be viewed as in-service. As of 1997, about one-third of public schools reimbursed teachers for the costs (tuition and course fees) associated with furthering their education (National Center for Education Statistics, 1997b, p. 18). This figure, however, has to be understood in relation to a teacher's salary schedule, which typically provides some financial rewards for the number of post-baccalaureate credits (or degrees) earned.

Teacher authority in the workplace, as demonstrated by teacher involvement in the critical affairs of the school, does not show the hallmarks of a profession. Data from the National Center for Education Statistics (1997a, p. 53) show that only 38 percent of teachers reported having a good deal of influence in setting discipline policy and establishing curriculum (which might include choosing textbooks and instructional materials, shaping curriculum standards and objectives, and determining schoolwide evaluation mechanisms). Only 31 percent of public school teachers claimed to have a good deal of influence over determining in-service content, and only 8 percent claimed to have a lot of influence in hiring new teachers (National Center for Education Statistics, 1997a, p. 53). From other accounts, we find that an overwhelming majority of teachers claim not to be at all involved in selecting new teachers, in evaluating teacher performance, or in selecting new administrators (Carnegie Foundation, 1990). These are not positive signs for the professionalization of teaching.

At the same time, teachers did report having extensive control over any number of classroom practices, including evaluating and grading students, determining the amount of homework, selecting teaching techniques, and actually disciplining students. However, only a small majority of teachers viewed some classroom practices, such as selecting the content, topics, and skills to be taught in school and selecting materials, as matters largely under their control (National Center for Education Statistics, 1997a, p. 52). The fact that many teachers believe that they either are not allowed or are not expected to make critical judgments about what is taught in the schools most likely speaks to the influence of state-mandated content requirements in the curriculum. Given the rise of the standards movement in education, and its accompanying proclivity to offer details on the content, topics, and skills of the school curriculum, this will remain problematic for teachers for some time.

In general, the teaching profession is not yet receiving passing grades on the central characteristics that we associate with professions. Salaries are improving, but they still seriously lag behind those in other professions. Induction and in-service programs are probably better designed and better funded today than in the past, but they are still idiosyncratic in nature; formal induction programs, in particular, are still not widely embraced in schools. Teacher authority seems to have a solid standing in the classroom, despite the presence of forces external to the school, such as state standards and statewide examinations, that affect what a teacher will teach. But at the schoolwide policy level, teacher authority is weak, having largely a subordinate status to the authority of the school administration. It is important to emphasize however, that teachers, despite the negative stereotype about their competency, clearly represent a highly educated group with literacy and quantitative skills equal to those of most other professionals, including physicians. New forms of state (and even national) licensing examinations seem to be the next step for the profession. Forms of compensation that reward performance, rather than raw experience, might also prove to be within range.

JOB SATISFACTION ISSUES

The record is mixed on self-reported indices of job satisfaction among teachers. The vast majority of teachers (82 percent) report overall satisfaction with their jobs, with 88 percent reporting satisfaction with job security, 87 percent reporting satisfaction with the intellectual challenge posed by the position, and 89 percent reporting satisfaction with the level of autonomy in their work (National Center for Education Statistics, 1997a, p. 90). However, this positive portrayal exists side by side with less-than-positive reports of teacher satisfaction. For instance, only 58 percent of public school teachers report satisfaction with the level of prestige accorded to their profession, only 56 percent are satisfied with their influence over policy and only 58 percent view their salaries as satisfactory. When teachers were asked if they would teach again, if given the opportunity to do things differently (a measure that tests teacher satisfaction against idealized career paths), about 65 percent answered that they would (National Center for Education Statistics, 1997a, p. 92). Among those who left the profession, the most prominent reason given was dissatisfaction with salary and with benefits, not professional workplace concerns (National Center for Education Statistics, 1997a, p. 91).

Teacher relations with principals and other school administrators are generally positive. According to national data, 86 percent of teachers reported that their principal communicated effectively with staff, and 80 percent said they worked with an administration that was supportive and encouraging. These numbers are always somewhat higher among elementary school teachers than secondary school teachers. Among colleagues, relations seem similarly positive. Eighty-four percent of teachers claimed to have colleagues who share beliefs and mission, and 77 percent agreed that a great deal of cooperative effort exists among staff. Again, these numbers are slightly higher among elementary faculty (National Center for Education Statistics, 1997a, pp. 82–84).

Teachers continue to identify parental problems and student misbehavior as problematic for their schools. For instance, 23 percent of all public school teachers reported that student apathy was a serious problem in their school, while 14 percent pointed toward absenteeism as a serious problem. Twenty-seven percent identified lack of parental involvement, and 13 percent cited parent alcohol or drug abuse as serious problems (National Center for Education Statistics, 1997a, pp. 18–21). All of these percentages were significantly higher in secondary schools than in elementary schools, and they were always highest in high-poverty secondary schools.

Teachers are now also reporting violence against themselves as a serious problem. Twenty-three percent reported that a student from their school had threatened to injure them, and 10 percent reported an actual physical attack, with the attacks being more likely in the high-poverty schools (National Center for Education Statistics, 1997a, p. 17). Almost half of all teachers reported physical conflict among students as a moderate or serious problem. Although one out of every ten public schools reported experiencing at least one serious violent crime (defined as murder, rape, suicide, physical attack with a weapon, or robbery) during the 1996–97 academic year (National Center for Education Statistics, 1998), most public schools actually are relatively safe places that employ only modest, low-level security measures. The most stringent forms of school security, which include metal detectors and full-time security guards, exist in only 2 percent of public schools (National Center for Education Statistics, 1998). Nevertheless, a new awareness of school security, influenced by national media coverage of school violence, has led schools to embrace various security precautions, including formal school violence prevention programs, and to implement controversial zero-tolerance policies regarding various student offenses, an issue we will revisit in another chapter.

PROFESSIONAL DECISION MAKING

The teacher is always the final arbiter of what occurs in the classroom. As a result, teachers face considerable pressure from forces external to the classroom seeking to influence their judgment. Pressures to raise test scores, to respond to emerging state or local standards, to follow the latest pedagogic fad, and to honor parental and community wishes—all push up against the classroom door. Whether these pressures find their way into the classroom and actually affect the school experience depends on the teacher.

In the final analysis, it is the teacher who decides what gets taught, how it gets taught, what gets greater or lesser attention, which readings are assigned, what assignments are used, and how it all gets assessed. Naturally, teachers cannot do whatever they please. They are required to attend to district and state policy, to execute professionally defensible judgments and to follow a curriculum that provides an equal opportunity to learn.

But teachers are not mere functionaries whose job is to follow an instructional script or someone else's instructional orders. We expect intelligence and creativity in the operation of a classroom, as well as a professional rationale supporting the actions and experiences undertaken there. As Dewey (1904) once observed, teachers "should be given to understand that they are not only permitted to act on their own initiative, but that they are expected to do so, and that their ability to take on a situation for themselves would be more important in judging them than their following any particular set method or scheme." Obviously, the freedom to act according to professional methods is fundamental to the development of positive educative environments.

Over the years, schoolteachers have been criticized, often appropriately, for failing to bring varied, innovative instructional methods to the classroom. Teachers have been faulted for using a stale and uniform methodology that tended to feature repetitive low-level exercises. This, however, is not a completely fair appraisal. Some evidence suggests considerable variance, both within and between public schools, in teaching styles and approaches, something that most of us have probably witnessed in our own experiences as students (National Center for Education Statistics, 1997a; Pauley, 1991; Stodolsky, 1988). Teachers seem to understand the complexity of the situation in which they find themselves, and they tend to apply different educational strategies in the classroom depending on the context of the school, community, and student population. Feature 2-3 on pages 62–63 graphically conveys some of the variation that a classroom teacher inherits from prevailing socioeconomic conditions.

We know that the act of teaching varies according to situational conditions. A high school teacher of mathematics engages in teaching approaches that vary, often considerably, from those of a teacher of, say, social studies or science. Math teachers, for instance, tend to spend more time working with individual students than do social studies teachers (Henke, Chen, and Goldman, 1999), while science teachers are more apt to integrate projects, experiments, and exploratory investigations in their classrooms (National Center for Education Statistics, 1997a, p. 64). Similarly, a teacher in elementary school typically engages in classroom actions that differ from those of the secondary school teacher. Children in elementary school classrooms, much more so than their secondary school counterparts, work individually on projects, spend time in small-group instruction, and discuss as a class work that has been done in small groups (Henke, Chen, and Goldman, 1999). But the situational context goes even deeper. Because each school is marked by a unique set of conditions, teachers always find themselves working within the context of different school missions and calling upon sets of behaviors particular to each local context. They have to deal with different levels of support and resources, different levels of parental involvement, and different styles of administrative leadership. Depending on local conditions, teachers, including high school teachers from varied disciplinary backgrounds, might find their teaching efforts entangled with community outreach programs, parent education efforts, and various extraclassroom experiences. But the issue is even more complex because each classroom within a school brings unique variation to the act of teaching. The student population within the classroom likely represents a broad range of variables related to family, income, ethnicity, and individual aptitude and maturation, to name just a few. Finding a way to teach all the children in the classroom requires some understanding of the diversity of the classroom population.

All of this underscores the complex dynamics of the classroom situation and the difficulties we encounter in trying to capture its essence with generalities. But, even while acknowledging the complexity of the classroom, we must develop some general sense of what we might call professional knowledge. All teacher decision making has to be enlivened by knowledge about learners, by the perception of the role of the school in society, and by the capacity to organize knowledge and experience in a manner that serves all youngsters. There is no one "right" way of teaching, but there is a principled sense of what it means to be an educator and what it means to make professionally justifiable decisions.

Levels of Professionalism

Teaching can be categorized according to three main levels of performance (Tanner and Tanner, 1995). Level I, known as imitative-maintenance, is the most simplistic. It is marked by routine and adoptive practices, with activities essentially scripted by teacher manuals, closed instructional systems, or a "teaching to the test" mentality. The notion that learning is based on emergent conditions is not part of the instructional calculation. Level II, known as mediative, registers at a higher professional scale because it represents a

2-3 THINKING ABOUT THE DATA
Teachers, Teaching, and the Socioeconomic Context

Here are some of the data demonstrating the differences across low- and high-poverty schools. All numbers were rounded. What might these data say about the teaching situation?

	PERCENTAGE OF TEACHERS WHO REPORTED	
	Low-Poverty Schools*	High-Poverty Schools†
School Safety		
That They Had Been Threatened or Attacked by a Student as a Serious Problem in School	20%	29%
Physical Conflicts Among Students as a Serious Problem in School	3	13
Robbery or Theft as a Serious Problem in School	2	6
Vandalism of School Property as a Serious Problem in School	3	9
Student Possession of Weapons as a Serious Problem in School	1	3
Student Misbehavior		
Tardiness as a Serious Problem in School	7	14
Absenteeism as a Serious Problem in School	10	17
Cutting Class as a Serious Problem in School	4	6
Verbal Abuse of Teachers as a Serious Problem in School	6	15
Student Problems		
Students Coming to School Unprepared to Learn as a Serious Problem in School	16	39
Student Apathy as a Serious Problem in School	18	25

movement away from simple maintenance and adoption and toward refinements or adjustments in practice based on some awareness of the unique condition of the classroom. Level II, in essence, is an acknowledgment that teaching is not solely a prefashioned affair in which the teacher does little more than follow someone else's instructional plan. Finally level III, generative-creative, stands as the highest ideal of professionalism, because teaching becomes a problem-solving process that requires the teacher to make judgments based on both the broadest school purposes and the evaluation of individual learning needs. It is important to note that these levels

	PERCENTAGE OF TEACHERS WHO REPORTED	
	Low-Poverty Schools*	High-Poverty Schools†
Student Problems *(continued)*		
Student Poor Nutrition as a Serious Problem in School	2	15
Student Poor Health as a Serious Problem in School	1	9
Student Pregnancy as a Serious Problem in School	2	6
Student Alcohol Use as a Serious Problem in School	13	5
Student Drug Abuse as a Serious Problem in School	7	4
Parental Problems		
Lack of Parental Involvement as a Serious Problem in School	13	40
Parent Alcohol or Drug Abuse as a Serious Problem in School	5	22
Poverty as a Serious Problem in School	4	39
Teacher Qualifications		
Bachelor's Degree as the Highest Degree	41	57
Master's Degree as the Highest Degree	52	38
Teacher Satisfaction		
Highest Willingness to Become a Teacher Again	41	38
Lowest Willingness to Become a Teacher Again	5	6

* (less than 5 percent of students on free or reduced lunch)
† (more than 40 percent of students on free or reduced lunch)

are not designed as developmental stages for teachers. No professional growth theory suggests that teachers must start at level I and, with experience, move to level III. All teaching professionals, novices and veterans alike, should be working at level III, but clearly factors related to school policy and to experience will have some hand in determining how successful a teacher might be in working at this level.

Level I: Imitative-Maintenance. Teachers who work at this level usually see the classroom in pure management terms. Reliant on routine activities that keep schoolchildren busy, level-I teachers readily use premade commercial materials in the interests of maintaining classroom order. The curriculum, even in the elementary school, is usually organized in a highly segmented manner, with no allowance for interconnections between subject areas, and managed according to disciplinary subject matter lines. Because of the concern for smooth operations, the classroom experience is largely reduced to low-level exercises and basic skills development. The idea of problem-focused inquiry or idea-centered learning poses a methodological concern for this teacher because it requires some assessment of classroom conditions and some imaginative planning beyond the scope of the textbook or workbook.

Teachers operating at level I are quasi-technicians whose main function in the classroom is to carry out the instructional directions of a prescribed system of learning. The popularity of competency-based instruction, mastery learning, teacher-proof materials, and programmed instruction all, in their own ways, testify to a level-I condition. Such instructional systems tend to reduce the teacher's role in the classroom to its most rudimentary and routine elements. The main duties of this teacher usually revolve around clerical acts, such as handing out worksheets and exams in proper sequence, documenting the results, and keeping students on task. Competency-based instruction, for instance, usually preidentifies all of the objectives in a particular instructional area and sets out an array of worksheets designed to help students learn the skills embodied in the objectives. When students are ready, they take an exam to demonstrate "mastery" of the particular skills learned. Once this mastery is achieved, they move on to to the next set of objectives (and the next set of worksheets and tests). Under these conditions, the teacher clearly has a limited instructional role.

Level-I teachers are also more prone to "teach to the test" than teachers working at a higher level of professional development. Teaching to the test, as we will discuss later, is controversial and takes on different forms in the classroom. But any teacher inclined to engage in the most blatant form of teaching to the test, such as taking past exam items and teaching directly to the items, is operating at level I. The use of reflective intelligence in the classroom to make adjustments in teaching based on interactions in the curriculum and on the emerging knowledge of the learner is lost at level I. Classroom assessment for the purpose of diagnosing learner weaknesses (with the presumption of making instructional corrections) essentially does not exist.

Level II: Mediative. Level II represents some professional awareness of the situational context of the classroom. As a result, it is a considerable jump up from level I. But teachers at the mediative level make only partial use of their classroom awareness, limiting their decisions to certain refinements and adaptations. Thus, we might find among level-II teachers some of the very instructional strategies supported by level-I teachers. But the strategies of the level-II teachers likely would be offered with some adaptations, reflecting an awareness of the unique context of the classroom. A competency-based method of learning, for instance, could still be used, but not without some refinements. Teachers at level II might note its effects in the classroom and make adjustments, such as skipping certain sections of the curriculum, adding supplementary materials here and there, or using another instructional approach along with the competency-based approach. Thus, we cannot expect any grand innovations in the curriculum from the teacher at level II, but certain modest changes, justified by some consideration of learners, will likely prevail.

Many teachers working at the mediative level are simply not able to work at a higher level. This is especially the case if a school district and/or certain superordinates require the use of a closed and instructionally prescriptive curriculum. Thus burdened by a curriculum that constricts judgment, teachers could at best make some curriculum alterations or perhaps offer some alternative instructional approaches. Pressures to teach to the test, to use certain textbooks, and to engage in instructional techniques favored by in-service training programs could have the same effect.

Level III: Generative-Creative. As indicated, level III represents the highest standard of professionalism. At level III, teaching is motivated by the broadest educational purposes of the school, not simply those that have priority on standardized tests or that are conveniently encapsulated in competency-based learning systems. Hence, classroom activity is wide ranging, concerned not only with academic and intellectual skills but also with socio-civic attitudes, individual interests and talents, an array of critical thinking and communication skills, constructive attitudes toward learning, and so forth. Activities in the classroom are problem-focused and idea-centered, and are planned and operated through the creative judgment of the teacher. In turn, the teacher's thinking is grounded in the nature of the learner, the values of society, and the knowledge embodied in the subject matter. The curriculum may be organized in any number of ways, but it often reflects interconnections between ideas and between disciplines, and shows good articulation between grades or age levels.

The level-III teacher is fundamentally a diagnostician, who reflects on the classroom in ways that draw from a wealth of instructional and assessment strategies. The idea of assessment is especially important because it demonstrates that the teacher is paying attention to whether instructional strategies have the desired effects. If they are not, the teacher (using experience, theory, and research) makes changes that will ultimately be retested in the experience of the classroom. Thus, the teacher at level III must be a consumer of research and must have the authority to exercise independent judgment in selecting materials and methods. Teaching-to-the test does not register here because no test could possibly cover everything that the teacher seeks in the education of the learner. Competency-based systems also go against the grain of level III because of their narrow skills base and their prescriptive instructional nature.

Factors in Professional Decision Making

What are essential factors in professional decision making? What do we expect professional educators to think about when they make instructional judgments? The progressive educational literature highlights the importance of three fundamental factors in the educational situation: (1) the nature of the learner, (2) the values and aims of society, and (3) the world of knowledge represented in organized subject matter (Tanner and Tanner, 1995). These three factors together represent a working framework for teacher judgment. Combined, the factors force educators to weight their decisions in light of learners' interests and developmental needs, in the spirit of democratic values and skills, and with ultimate regard for what is worthy knowledge.

The Nature of the Learner. Accounting for the nature of the learner essentially means holding the teacher responsible for responding to the interests and living conditions of students, as well as to the literature on how students learn. It also requires that the fundamental learning theory influencing classroom instruction be responsive to the values and aims of society. The net effect should be a classroom that has some meaningful role in students' lives, that deals with age-appropriate issues and problems, that identifies individual strengths and weaknesses, and that empowers the comprehensive objectives of the school experience.

Often, this requires practical action. Teachers, for instance, might take an inventory of their students' interests and explore their students' community life to identify group problems, needs, and traditions. This involves not only determining what children like to do but also trying to incorporate the dimensions of students' lives (interests, problems, issues) in the curriculum. These kinds of judgments help the teacher decide what should be taught and also provide important information on how certain skills, knowledge, and values should be taught.

Where group problems arise, the teacher might employ an investigative strategy. If middle school students, for instance, are found to be experimenting with cigarettes at an alarming rate, the teacher might look to the learner to get some insight into the problem. The teacher might find that advertisers are preying on impressionable preadolescents, that peer pressures are exerting a strong pull, that the children who are smoking have parents who smoke, and that the students are unaware of the facts of lung cancer. These locally derived insights could then inform the pedagogic strategy in teaching about the dangers of smoking or in the more general area of health care. A curriculum plan might focus on learning about the facts of lung cancer and the tactics of Madison Avenue advertisers. Pedagogic strategies might stress peer pressure scenarios that give students practical courses of action and group projects that involve the participation of parents—smokers and non-smokers alike. In this way, an investigation of the students' school and neighborhood life becomes a fundamental part of being responsive to the nature of the learner. Any number of tactics can be employed, including student interviews, student questionnaires, various testing efforts, social data on the community, newspaper reports, and customized surveys (Tyler, 1949).

Sometimes the investigative effort might be driven by certain professional priorities regarding the teaching of particular skills. For example, the teacher of reading might want to know what children are reading, if anything, at home, how often they are reading outside of school, and where they are reading. Answers to these questions could shape pedagogic tactics that aim to instill in children a love of reading. It might also offer the teacher some insight into what students should be reading in class. Here, examining circulation rates at the school library, taking reading interest inventories from children, asking parents to provide information on home reading behaviors, and noting the genre of reading interest among certain children all become potential sources for better responsiveness to the learner in reading instruction.

Responsiveness to the learner also means that teachers might scan the psychological literature to find insight into the developmental processes involved in teaching schoolchildren. Different-aged learners operate at qualitatively different levels of thinking and are under different social and biological pressures. The psychological literature in these areas might have useful implications for the construction of motivation in the classroom and for the development of lesson plans and learning objectives. Where a particular learning problem might arise in an individual, the effort to account for the nature of the learner might reveal a disability or a remediable deficiency.

The effort to respond to the nature of the learner brings the teacher face to face with the literature on developmental processes, the nature of human intelligence, and the cognitive and affective processes in learning. In recent years, for instance, researchers have offered new conceptions about intelligence and learning to assist the teacher in educating the whole child. Howard Gardner's work on multiple intelligence (1983) has allowed teachers and administrators to expand their notions of intelligence to include actions and processes not typically recognized in traditional views of intelligence. These include a range of intelligences that account for linguistic, musical, logical-mathematical, spatial, bodily kinesthetic, interpersonal and intrapersonal competence. Gardner's work points to the need for schools to attend to all of the abilities implied by these multiple intelligences, as opposed to only the linguistic and mathematical traditions that are typically stressed in the schools. Intelligence viewed in this way can be considered part of what we associate with the nature of the learner. Similarly, Benjamin Bloom's work on cognitive and affective processes (Bloom, 1956; Krathwohl, Bloom, and Masia, 1964), which provides teachers with working taxonomies that can be used to bring out more cognitive and affective variation in the classroom, and Jean Piaget's (1970) work on developmental processes, provide teachers with the ability to adapt certain teaching strategies to certain learners.

Accounting for the learner also means being conscious of meeting a hierarchy of basic needs. Abraham Maslow (1962) described the hierarchy, arguing that the most fundamental needs were physiological ones (e.g., sleep, shelter, clothing, food), followed by a succession of needs that included safety, love and acceptance, self-esteem, and self-actualization. This was Maslow's way of saying that children who come to school tired or hungry likely will not be able to learn. Maslow's work underscored the rationale for passage of the National School Lunch Act, which provides free or reduced-price lunches, and the Child Nutrition Act, which provides free or reduced-price breakfasts to needy children. The linkage between the need for proper nutrition and the cognitive and social development of young children has, of course, been established for many years. The implications of Maslow's work, however, go deeper, given the value he placed on needs related to safety, love and affection, and self-esteem. Children who attend schools where safety is an issue, or who have to deal with some form of dislocation in the home (e.g., an impending divorce or family illness), or who live in homes where love and acceptance might be in short supply, will have their school education compromised. Similarly, children who are routinely rejected or ridiculed by their peers, for whatever reasons, will not be poised to succeed in school. Thus, the teacher has a role to play in regulating these factors.

Finally, accounting for the nature of the learner means embracing a theory of learning that resonates with the values and aims of democracy. Such a learning theory must promote reflective thinking, problem solving, idea-oriented learning, and the teaching of a wide range of social values and attitudes. The learning theory of mental discipline, for instance, which suggested that certain subjects train the mind in a way that results in a learned and capable person, might have some problems justifying itself as a theory responsive to democracy. Because mental discipline implies a mentalistic view of learning that is deeply embedded in the subject matter, it might not be able to carry the weight of experiences that we might expect in a curriculum informed by the values and aims of democracy. Behavioristic traditions of learning, historically wedded to reinforcement strategies and to stimulus-response conditioning principles, face a similar problem. Inspired by the research on lower animals and motivated by a desire to put the learner under control, behaviorism tends to focus on lower cognitive processes, using motivational schemes that are largely reducible to reward and punishment strategies. It, too, is limited in its instructional reach. Gestalt- or field-based theories of learning, by contrast, put more emphasis on experience and on the active role of students in responding to and giving meaning to their own learning. Hence, the learner is in a position to emerge as an autonomously thinking and socially conscious individual. In emphasizing social processes and reflective thinking, cognitive field theory might also make more allowances for group work and social interactions. The point is that a learning theory must be able to actualize learning experiences appropriate for education in a democratic society. Such a judgment is, of course, ultimately left up to the teacher to make. Figure 2-2 lists some points to consider in responding to the nature of the learner.

The Values and Aims of Society. The factor of society provides a foundation for the kinds of knowledge, skills, and values that students should learn. It also influences the process of teaching by reminding the teacher that schooling is fundamentally moved by a social democratic theory and by some expression of hope for the kind of society we desire.

The factor of society points to the need to teach certain values and certain kinds of skills in the classroom—values and skills that transcend the subject matter. For example, all teachers, regardless of what they are teaching, need to embody various democratic processes and values in their teaching. With this concern in mind, the teacher might try to get children

> ### FIGURE 2-2
> ### Points to Consider in Responding to the Nature of the Learner
>
> **1.** Determining various aptitudes based on a broad construction of intelligence
>
> **2.** Determining student interests from an inventory of activities inside and outside of the school
>
> **3.** Determining the developmental or maturational stage of learning in the student population
>
> **4.** Determining the specifics of students' lives in the family, school, and community
>
> **5.** Constructing a vision of teaching rooted in a defined learning theory responsive to the values and aims of democracy
>
> **6.** Forming ideas about motivation, learning interests, and instruction from the perspective of students' aptitudes, interests, life issues and concerns, and developmental processes, as well as a democratically aligned learning theory

to learn how to consider the consequences of their actions in the lives of others, to guard the safety and health of each other, to believe in the worth of each individual, and to offer help where possible to those who are most needy. Or the teacher might cultivate in students an awareness of and willingness to do something about the problems that affect the quality of life, and a recognition of constitutional rights and civic responsibilities in the school environment. In accounting for the values of society, the teacher might embrace objectives that teach children to defend the rights and liberties of all people, to think critically about the world, and to believe that each person's participation and opinion are important. Or the teacher might take certain cognitive actions, such as teaching children to seek relevant information and alternative viewpoints, to communicate openly and honestly, to obtain information from credible and varied sources, to distinguish fact from opinion and reliable information from unreliable, and to detect logical errors, unstated assumptions, and unsupported statements. These actions all are laden with democratic values and aims. They are important for the education of all children in all places and thus represent an important source for teacher decision making.

But the factor of society also leads us to questions about what is taught. As indicated, teachers do not have free rein over what they are supposed to teach, but they do have a certain pedagogic leeway that allows them to make certain linkages with ideas, problems, and issues that might be rele-

FIGURE 2-3
Points to Consider in Responding to the Values and Aims of Society

1. Determining the types of skills, values, attitudes, and competencies required for informed participation in society

2. Recognizing the place of social issues and social problems in the school experience

3. Accounting for local conditions in terms of community, neighborhood, and school life

4. Reinforcing specific civic responsibilities and constitutional values

5. Applying instructional methods that encourage the development of democratic skills

vant to promoting a better understanding of society. So, the standard lineup of discipline-centered skills and knowledge in, say, a math, science, or history course can be transformed when they are taught in a context responsive to community or societal concerns. Quantitative reasoning, for instance, could become, at least partly, a method of social analysis; scientific knowledge, depending on its nature, could be presented in terms that show its application in the life experience.

Not all teachers can be active instructors of civics or social studies, or even of democracy, for that matter. But all teachers should conduct their classrooms in a manner attuned to the values and aims of democratic society. This means that all teachers, whether in kindergarten or in an advanced trigonometry course, should promote development of a wide range of skills and values. These might include a positive sense of self, social skills that encourage social responsibility and cooperation, thinking skills that engage the intelligence and produce analytical and discerning minds, inquiry skills that promote decision making based on the evaluation of evidence, and communication skills that recognize the importance of clear, persuasive writing and speaking. Just how these things will be taught, and how extensively, depends on the nature of the learner and certain subject matter requirements, which again underscores the complementary nature of the three factors. Figure 2-3 lists some points to consider in responding to the values and aims of society.

Subject Matter. There is no escaping the issue of subject matter. Students have to be taught something, and the question of what content or what knowledge is most worthwhile has been an enduring one for educators. We are essentially drawn to the question of what should be taught and how the knowledge will be encapsulated in organized subject matter.

The question of the content of the classroom is posed in relation to the learner and society. The school curriculum might carry some preidentified sense of what content is worthwhile. For teaching purposes, we expect the content to be age-appropriate—that is, within the developmental and experiential realm of the student—and justified as useful and empowering knowledge.

This aspect of teacher decision making is itself influenced by many factors. Statewide or locally derived content standards often play a role, not because of a need to script teachers' actions but because of a need to ensure some basis of equal opportunity for students to learn common knowledge and common skills.

For example, in mathematics, a teacher at the third-, fourth-, or fifth-grade level likely will be teaching the basic properties of number concepts. We might expect the teacher to exercise considerable creativity and instructional judgment in teaching the appropriate math skills, but the skills themselves likely will be part of some systemic (local or state) curriculum strategy or plan. They might include objectives related to learning about the relationships among fractions, decimals, mixed numbers, and whole numbers; about equivalent forms of basic percentages, fractions, and decimals; about the basic difference between odd and even numbers, and the meaning of place value; and so forth (National Council of Teachers of Mathematics, 1989). The skills are, of course, screened as age-appropriate and are certainly socially useful, but not until they are brought to students in an instructional experience that accounts for the learner and the society. The teacher, as a result, likely will try to find a way to apply the teaching of such mathematical skills in the life and social contexts of the student and in other ways implied by the two other sources for decision making. This is essentially what it means to be a generative-creative teacher.

Similarly, a high school history teacher charged with the responsibility of teaching, say, the characteristics of societies in the Americas, Western Europe, and Northern Africa in the fifteenth century might look to examine, among many other things, the economic changes affecting Western Europe at the time, the similarities and differences among Native American societies, the rise of centralized states and the development of urban centers, the economic importance of trans-Saharan slave trade in Africa, and European perceptions of Native American societies. The content in its most informational form gives the teacher ample opportunity to select learning experiences that reflect all three sources of decision making.

Can there be learning experiences without a sense of context? Such a condition would likely result in a free-form activity that offered only idiosyncratic connections to some basis of content and skill. And the other two

FIGURE 2-4
Points to Consider in Responding to the Subject Matter

1. Integrating age-appropriate knowledge and skills into instruction

2. Integrating socially useful and empowering knowledge into instruction

3. Accounting for any systemic plan or arrangement of content in the curriculum (content standards and scope and sequence traditions)

sources would be ignored because a free or open form of education is not accountable to a working learning theory appropriate for teaching the skills, competencies, values, and attitudes of democratic society. Figure 2-4 lists some points to consider in responding to the subject matter.

CLASSROOM ISSUES

The classroom, as suggested, is a dynamic environment. Still, some general problems and issues seem to prevail, in one form or another, in virtually all classrooms. Most of these issues are curricular in nature and are deeply embedded in the structure of the school experience—in the design of educational purposes and objectives, the adoption of materials and tests, the formation of local school policy, and the exercise of school leadership.

Problematizing Teacher Effectiveness

The manner in which teacher effectiveness is viewed in the context of teacher supervision, in-service training, and even teacher preparation affects what it means to be judged as an effective teacher. Historically, the determination of effectiveness has been closely tied to pure instructional behaviors, to the "how" of teaching and the management of established techniques or methodologies. With these kinds of instructional actions, the teacher's main concern is the mechanics of the lesson and its implementation. This might include concerns about, say, gaining the class's attention, or informing the class of the lesson's objective, or eliciting the so called "desired behavior" of the lesson. Questions pertaining to the appropriateness of the objective or to the fundamental educative character of the experience are of secondary importance.

A recent insight from the teacher effectiveness literature illustrates this point. For many years, researchers have been touting the importance of the principle of time on task in the classroom. It is, at its most superficial level, an unremarkable idea that espouses the need for teachers to keep learners engaged in classroom activities. Obviously, engagement is a requisite condition for learning. But when such a principle stands at the forefront of how we view good teaching, potential problems can occur. To put it simply, not all forms of engagement are necessarily educative. Because the time-on-task dictum does nothing to highlight or underscore the qualitative character of the task, it is of limited value. Thus, a teacher might achieve high grades from supervisors in keeping children on task, but if the task itself is not educationally worthwhile, the level of student engagement is not relevant. Time on task is clearly an idea that is rooted in instructional and managerial concerns.

Another manifestation of the same problem emerges from the teacher effectiveness research, which has identified and promoted the value of certain universally applicable instructional practices as effective. Research findings indicate, among other things, that effective teachers have high expectations for performance, that they convey enthusiasm in their teaching, and that they are vigilant about monitoring student work. But when the term "effective" is used in this context, we need to be able to show the criteria by which the term is being defined and operationalized. The term "effective" is theoretically neutral; after all, one could be an "effective" thief or an "effective" ax murderer. In the context of the teaching literature, the use of the term "effective" is tied into how well certain practices raise standardized test scores. The problem is that what a teacher might do to raise test scores may not always lead to enlightened pedagogy. For instance, one prominent teacher effectiveness researcher stated that "effective" teachers of basic skills "ask questions at a low cognitive level so that students can produce many correct responses" (Rosenshine, 1978). The practice of asking low-level questions might raise test scores in the basic skills, and therefore be judged to be effective teaching, but it comes at the expense of a vital and dynamic cognitive experience, which should be idea oriented and directed toward challenging students.

As Schulman (1987) has argued, the empirical research on effective teaching has oversimplified the teaching situation. "Critical features of teaching, such as the subject matter being taught, the classroom context, the physical and psychological characteristics of students, or the accomplishment of purpose not readily assessed on standardized tests, are typically ignored in the quest for general principles of effective teaching" (p. 6). A review of the effective teaching literature substantiates Schulman's point about its generally instructional/methodological orientation. Thus, "effective" teachers are expected to, among other things, focus clearly on academic goals, present information clearly, cover subject matter extensively, monitor student progress, and provide quick and well-targeted feedback. However, an educator might abide by all of these generalizations and still not offer educative experiences in the classroom. It might be important for a teacher to be clear, focused, on task, and organized, but it is equally important to identify the nature of what a teacher is organizing and being clear about; after all, one can be clear, organized, and vigilant about nonsense.

In-service training programs have sometimes shown the same preoccupation with methodological concerns. The popular Hunter (1980) approach is perhaps best known. Hunter's program, often referred to as the "Seven-Step Lesson" or the "Elements of Effective Instruction," was one of the most enduring features on the educational landscape during the 1980s and 1990s. It dominated teacher in-service programs throughout American schools, affecting the thinking and behavior of thousands of teachers. Some school districts even went so far as to adopt the Hunter model as their choice for assessing teacher performance and used it for promotion and salary decisions.

The Hunter approach lists various structural elements of a lesson as the foundation for effective pedagogy:

1. *Anticipatory set.* This phase is designed primarily to get students' attention. One of the problems Hunter noticed as she developed her lesson design was that some teachers began to teach before they had students' attention. The anticipatory set helps to focus learners on what is going to be taught. It is designed to "grab" the students' attention.

2. *Objective and purpose.* Once the students are attentive, the teacher, in clear and concise language, states what the students will be expected to learn and why.

3. *Input.* In this phase, the teacher provides the information that students need to meet the lesson's objective. For instance, she might help her students understand how to add fractions by performing examples on the board, asking for strategies that students might have in performing certain manipulations with fractions, or providing visual or hands-on demonstrations.

4. *Modeling.* Next, the teacher shows students the process, skill, or knowledge that is being taught. He might, for example, anticipate the errors students may make and model how students can correct their own errors. Here, the teacher should keep in mind that modeling can be enhanced when he "thinks out loud."

5. *Checking for understanding.* During the modeling phase, the teacher attempts to discover how many students understand the lesson's objective, and to what degree. Hunter included this phase because she noticed that many teachers would call only on students who knew the answer, or worse, simply ask if there were any questions, and move on.

6. *Guided practice.* In this phase, the students practice the lesson objective under the guidance of the teacher. For example, the teacher may put a practice problem on the board and help the class solve it together. Or she might put the problem on the board and ask students to work on it independently while she circulates around the room, checking students' work.

7. *Independent practice.* This is the phase of the lesson in which students work on exercises associated with the lesson's objective or objectives independently. In high school classes, independent practice is often used as homework. In elementary school, the teacher is more likely to allow students to complete their independent practice in school.

As one instructional method, the Hunter model is certainly worthy. But if used as an exclusive method that focuses only on the "how" of teaching (on the actual mechanics of the seven-step plan), the implication is that a good teacher is someone who follows the lesson design, irrespective of the nature of the activity justified by or operating through the design. The instructional elements of the lesson become the ends of a teacher's performance rather than the vital means toward an educative learning environment.

Teaching to the Test

Since the early 1980s, standardized testing in public education has gained popularity and authority in the school curriculum. In fact, the penchant for measurement has shaped virtually all facets of the classroom. In many schools, decisions affecting grade promotion, admission into gifted and talented programs, assignment into special education programs and various curriculum tracks, and even, in some cases, graduation from high school are based primarily, if not entirely, on the results obtained on some standardized test. In some schools, such tests also represent the key criterion for assessing teacher performance in the classroom and for judging the overall educational value of the school.

In all of these situations, the standardized test is granted a "high-stakes" status in the curriculum (Madaus, 1999). A test earns high-stakes status when it is used in a way that has a pronounced effect on the school destinies of children and on the professional destinies of teachers and administrators.

In a high-stakes testing environment, educators are persuaded or otherwise compelled to think that the best way to improve education (or at least to demonstrate improvement) is to raise standardized scores. And this inevitably leads to a form of teaching that tries to conform to the test.

The mandate to teach to the test emerges in the life of a classroom in various ways. School principals and district-level administrators are often key personnel in promoting the influence of high-stakes testing. School administrators are usually keen to show visible signs of improvement in their schools, and nothing meets this demand better than favorable school-wide results on norm-referenced standardized tests. With the public image of the school at stake, administrators will sometimes exert pressure to ensure favorable examination outcomes. If we consider the fact that realtors have not hesitated to tout local test scores as a "selling point" for homes in a particular neighborhood, we get an idea of how serious the public stakes can be. Under these conditions, the very evaluation of a teacher often is reduced to student performance outcomes on high-stakes tests. In other words, a good teacher is viewed as someone who can demonstrate high student performance outcomes on standardized exams. But support for teaching to the test can also emerge from the teachers themselves, who reasonably observe that, if student destinies are being dictated by examination results, then educators, like it or not, must do their utmost to boost these all-important scores. Other factors include school policies that have the effect of elevating the importance of a particular standardized test. For instance, the increasing popularity of grade retention policies, whereby students are promoted to the next grade only if they perform at or above some minimal score on a standardized exam, has given the standardized exam a prominent place in the curriculum. Grade retention obviously has a dramatic effect on a youngster's life, and aggregate grade promotion rates have considerable public relations currency. The stakes are indeed high when such policies are in place, compelling teachers to think first and foremost about how to teach in ways that raise standardized exam scores.

Naturally, a serious problem emerges under these circumstances. The test, which is supposed to be designed in a way that is responsive to the broader purposes of the school curriculum, instead takes on a life of its own. Schoolteachers, concerned about test scores, become fixated on the exam. As a consequence, depending on the intensity of high-stakes pressure, the exam becomes, quite literally, the whole of the school curriculum experience.

Some commentators have no problem with the act of teaching to the test, stating that whatever works to raise scores should be embraced as a viable instructional strategy. But critics counter that teaching to the test not only invalidates the test but creates a training atmosphere that concentrates mostly on teaching the skills most amenable to quantification. Such critics also contend that, when too great a faith is placed in the fallible mechanism of standardized testing, anything not systematically tested becomes marginalized in the school experience. The teacher, for instance, who aims to cultivate certain healthy values and attitudes toward learning, or who is dedicated to teaching children the values of respect, integrity, and honesty, or who wants to highlight the importance of higher-order thinking skills will find that such concerns typically have little or no place on the standardized school examination. Knowing this, the teacher in a high-stakes testing climate will have little incentive to teach such things; such initiatives will represent time lost to the all-consuming need to raise test scores. What we emphasize on the test is often the clearest sign of what we value instructionally in the classroom. This is increasingly the case as the test takes on a high-stakes status.

But the problem is not simply *what* gets taught; it is also a matter of *how* it gets taught. In one study, the self-reported commitment of elementary school teachers to various instructional strategies was compared against their commitment to openly teaching to a state-mandated test. Among elementary reading teachers, those most openly committed to teaching to the test were also those most overtly reliant on the teacher's manual. Among elementary math teachers, those reporting a high commitment to teaching to the test also reported a high commitment to skill-drill exercises, student memorization tactics, and the teacher's manual (Hlebowitsh, 1992). The correlations in the study pointed to the possibility that the teachers who were most inclined to teach directly to the exam were also those most broadly committed to instructional strategies that were low level and mechanical in orientation. This is another way of saying that where teaching to the test occurs, we are likely to find less instructional innovation and certainly less of the independence of thought that we expect from a generative-creative teacher.

Teaching to the test also raises ethical questions. In some forms, it amounts to little more than cheating, especially if teachers teach directly to actual test items. For example, one teacher was fired and ten others disciplined after officials in the Los Angeles Unified School District accused them of copying the actual items from an achievement exam and tailoring their instruction to the items (Hoff, 2000b). This has become a problem of growing proportions, an issue we will consider in detail in Chapter 4. Other ethical concerns have to do with the fact that, when students' school fortunes are so visibly linked to test scores, as they are with test-linked grade promotion and curriculum placement policies, the students most likely to fail will be disproportionately represented by low-income, limited-English, and minority group populations.

Classroom Control

When experienced teachers and principals are asked to identify the greatest problem facing a young teacher in the classroom, they will almost always point to classroom discipline and classroom control. The failure of a classroom teacher to maintain classroom discipline is very serious business. It can be, and sometimes is, viewed as grounds for dismissal of the teacher. In fact, the most commonly cited problem among teachers facing dismissal proceedings on the charge of incompetence is related to their inability to secure an orderly and well-functioning classroom (Fischer, Schimmel, and Kelly, 1999). Teachers have a professional obligation to engage students in purposeful and meaningful activities that aim to fulfill the educational agenda of the school, something that cannot be accomplished in a classroom troubled by disruption or disorder.

Most parents express positive views about the level of discipline found in the public schools. A national study found that 93 percent of parents with children in elementary school agreed or strongly agreed that their child's teacher maintained good discipline in the classroom. At the middle school level, the number drops to 87 percent, and it rises again at the high school level to 91 percent (National Center for Education Statistics, 1993). At the schoolwide level, student tardiness and absenteeism are the two main discipline issues cites by principals as serious or moderate problems in their schools (National Center for Education Statistics, 1998). Teacher seems to have control, as they must, of their classrooms; little leaning could take place if they did not.

To many people, the term "control" has negative connotations, being associated with acts of coercion and authoritarianism. The truth, however, is that elements of control are essential to every social arrangement and that, one way or another, they will prevail in every context of learning. Even the idea of freedom requires controls, lest anarchy or chaos result. Because the school is a deliberately designed and consciously conceived environment that aims to fulfill certain goals, it necessarily supports certain objectives, expectations, and controls. The question, then, is not whether there will be control, but what its nature will be.

Most teachers recognize the need for imposing external controls in the classroom. They set rules, enforce them, consider reward and punishment strategies, establish expectations and routines, and make independent authoritative decisions about what gets included into and excluded from the purview of the classroom experience. There is simply no getting away from some of these decisions. Professional advice on these matters can be found in various outlets, including the website outlined in Feature 2-4.

But professional educators also understand the importance of vesting control in the learning engagement and seek to teach their students responsibility and behavior management by placing them in a classroom where they can learn to be *in* control of their environment rather than *under* control of it. They concede, as Dewey (1916) observed, that "internal control through identity of interest and understanding is the business of education" (pp. 39–40). In this sense, classroom discipline relies primarily, though not exclusively, on learning activities and social engagements for control, and not on the exercise of threats, coercion, punishment, and other forms of authoritarianism (Dewey, 1938). The teacher does not so much keep order as create order through engagement in the learning experiences of the school. Thus, where there are failings in classroom discipline, there will usually be shortcomings in the quality of the learning activities in the classroom. Teacher problems with discipline often amount to teacher problems with teaching.

The role that motivation plays in contributing to classroom control is a case in point. Some teachers believe that schooling needs to be intrinsically arduous to be educative. They subscribe to the view that "good things do not come easy" and that part of being an educated person means learning to accept the pain of education—the hard work, industry, and perseverance required to be a successful student. Here, motivation might be secured by the looming threat of punishment. Other teachers might view motivation as a simple inducement strategy designed to make learning as palatable as possible. These teachers might, as a result, frequently resort to various reward mechanisms and to instructional methods designed to make learning as much fun as possible. In each of the two orientations, motivation is moved mostly by external conditions.

But another view of motivation distances itself from the idea that educators should always be looking to create or compel interest and instead proposes that motivation is inherent in the nature of the classroom experiences. The difference is fundamental. In one case, the interest is appended to the experience and is, to paraphrase Dewey (1902, p. 29), held in contrast to an alternate experience, such as receiving a scolding, being held up to ridicule, staying after school, or receiving low marks. In the other case, interest is umbilically tied, again to paraphrase Dewey (1902), to the consciousness of the child, to his or her own doings, thinkings and struggles

2-4 WEB POINTS
The Behavior Home Page

The Behavior Home Page (www.state.ky.us/agencies/behave/homepage.html) was designed by the Kentucky Department of Education and the University of Kentucky as a source for teachers interested in gaining more information and insight on disciplinary techniques. It showcases detailed advice on behavioral interventions, and offers opportunities for discussions and consultations.

The Behavior Home Page
Working to Make a Difference for Children Who Display Challenging Behavior

Navigational Menu

- Home

Sponsors

- KDE
- SERC at UK

Interactivity

- BHP Discussion Forum
- WebQuest Exercise
- CEC Discussion Forum
- (CECP) Author Online
- TEC Author Online Discussion
- Needs Assessment Results
- Guest book
- Guest Book Data

Behavioral Interventions

- Behavioral Interventions
- Effective Behavioral Support (EBS)
- Time-Out Procedures
- The Teacher's Encyclopedia of Behavior Management
- Sample IEP
- CEC Research Connections
- CECP-Addressing Problem Student Behavior
- CECP-Preventing School Failure and Antisocial Behavior

The **Kentucky Department of Education** (KDE) and the **Department of Special Education and Rehabilitation Counseling at UK** (SERC) are collaborating on this Web page on student behavior. The purpose is to provide a format that allows school personnel, parents, and other professionals to gain access to information, to share effective practices, and to receive ongoing consultation and technical assistance concerning the full range of behavior problems and challenges displayed by children and youth in school and community settings, as well as other behavioral issues that may affect their success in school.

Job Opportunities

- Behavior Consultant
  The Training Resource Center at Eastern Kentucky University has 3 Bridges Behavior Consultant positions available to be located in London, Hazard and Prestonsburg. **Position Description:** The Bridges Behavior Consultant is responsible for assisting Bridges schools within one Area Development region with the implementation of a school-wide system of effective behavior intervention and support.

Academic/Behavioral Connection

There is no question that students who exhibit challenging behavior also experience academic failure. If interventions are designed and implemented to directly address academic (e.g., reading) and behavioral deficiencies, schools can improve students' academic performance and reduce problem behavior. Follow the links below to explore the academic/behavioral connection:

- National Reading Panel, Teaching Children to Read: An Evidence-

Used with permission.

2-5 SCHOLARLY VOICES
Dewey on Motivation

John Dewey believed that the key to motivation resided in the design and application of attractive and meaningful learning experiences. Here, he describes what happens when this principle is lost and when a teacher becomes wedded to generating motivation through external controls:

The substitute for living motivation in subject matter is that of contrast-effects; the material of the lesson is rendered interesting, if not in itself, at least in contrast with some alternative experience. To learn the lesson is more interesting than to take a scolding, be held up to ridicule, stay after school, receive degradingly low marks, or fail to be promoted. And very much of what goes by the name of discipline and prides itself upon opposing the doctrines of soft pedagogy and upon upholding the banner of effort and duty, is nothing more or less than just this appeal to interest in its obverse aspect—to fear, to dislike of various kinds of physical, social and personal pain. The subject matter does not appeal; it cannot appeal; it lacks origin and bearing in a growing experience. So the appeal is to the thousand and one outside and irrelevant agencies which may serve to throw, by sheer rebuff and rebound, the mind back upon the materials from which it is constantly wandering. (Dewey, 1902, p. 29)

(Dewey, 1902, p. 29). From this perspective, motivation involves making an effort to construct learning experiences intrinsically appealing to youths. Interest is central to the experience, not external to it. Feature 2-5 directly quotes Dewey on the issue of motivation.

This is sometimes known as intrinsic motivation. When students are moved by an intrinsic motivation, they engage in a learning activity for its own sake, motivated not by a dangling carrot but by a genuine self-interest. Csikszentmihalyi (1990) has described the idea of intrinsic motivation as "flow," as a condition of being immersed in the enjoyment of the activity. Finding flow in the classroom is no easy task. But teachers who are responsive to the nature of learners, who give their students opportunities to make choices and to set some of their own goals, and who offer more idea-oriented and problem-focused activities have a better chance of achieving it.

Much of classroom control, especially as it manifests in classroom management practices, has been under the influence of a behavioristic psychology that touts the power of external controls. Behaviorism established itself as a distinct school of human psychology in the early twentieth century. Early spokespersons for behaviorism, such as John Watson, believed that they had developed the key to analyzing, interpreting, predicting, and controlling behavior. At the turn of the century, Watson urged psychologists to discard their preoccupation with mentalistic concepts, which often was justified by the doctrine of mental discipline, and to focus instead on objective human behaviors and acts. He was convinced that animal behavior held the key to understanding human behavior and so stressed the need for experimentation in the area of animal learning.

Given the focus on animal behavior, it was not long before the behaviorists hit upon the idea of the conditioned response. A response, they observed, is conditioned when it attaches itself or is associated with a stimulus. The Russian psychologist, Ivan Pavlov proved that hungry dogs could be conditioned to salivate at the sound of a bell instead of the sight of food. To early behaviorists, such as Watson, this work with animal learning pointed to the centrality of the stimulus-response bond in human learning. The vast complexity of human behavior could now be studied along its most rudimentary lines, its stimulus-response bonds, and learning could now be viewed, more powerfully, in relation to the influence of the environment. Children could be taught to learn through reinforcement and punishment strategies.

Behaviorism remains the driving psychology behind many classroom management strategies. This is because it can provide a ready handle on the management of behaviors (or misbehaviors) through the technique known as behavior modification. The process of behavior modification focuses on the consequences of student behavior for the purpose of modifying or correcting poor behavior and maintaining good behavior. Generally, all behavior is believed to be influenced by external controls, often manifesting as either rewards or punishments. To behave properly, children need to be under the control of their environment, understanding the consequences of desirable and undesirable behavior.

B. F. Skinner (1968), behaviorism's most celebrated advocate, observed that the act of teaching "is simply the arrangement of contingencies of reinforcement" (p. 33). That is, virtually every aspect of the classroom, from cognitive learning to behavioral conduct, can be reduced to a grid of operational objectives that can be met through conditioned responses. The equation for success is straightforward: Behavior that is positively reinforced will continue to be vital, while behavior that is negatively reinforced, or punished, will eventually be vanquished. There is, of course, much truth to such a view, but there is also quite a bit of truth to the view that behavior is shaped not only by external inducements but also by inner forces of industry, cooperation, ethics, and interest.

One does not have to be a behaviorist to understand the centrality of rewards and punishments in the classroom. Inevitably, they will be part of the ebb and flow of classroom life. But the manner and frequency with which they are managed will vary according to how deeply committed a teacher is to the use of external control structures.

Punishment is, of course, an oft-used action when a teacher seeks to control behavior. Behaviorism teaches us that the introduction of an aversive event will make it less likely that the behavior will reoccur. Most teachers see this as a helpful principle while also acknowledging that teaching is not always well served by punishment tactics. In fact, to argue for the role of punishment in the classroom immediately raises questions about its form and about its potential effects on students. Teachers who use educational activities as punishments (e.g., homework, writing assignments) must consider the kinds of latent messages they might send. For instance, the teacher contemplating a punishment that requires a child to write an essay on why his behavior was not acceptable might have a working rationale for the punishment that includes a desire for the child to think through his behavior, to acknowledge his wrong, and presumably to suffer the strain of writing. But because this punishment is associated with the act of writing, it could easily be seen as counterproductive, and even miseducative, in terms of teaching children to appreciate the communicative powers of good writing.

Teachers must also consider the effects of punishment as they might apply to specific students, accounting for factors related to a disability, family home life, and individual characteristics. Determining an appropriate punishment will have everything to do with previous problems the child might have had in class, with a detailed understanding of the incident, with a sense of her background, and with any other mitigating factors related to her. Depending on its nature, punishment could arouse resentment and even fear among some children. And if used frequently, it testifies to a basic lack of trust in the classroom, and perhaps even to an adversarial relationship between teacher and students. It could also reduce or undermine opportunities to develop a sense of responsibility and cooperation. All of this is not enough to dismiss the idea of punishment out of hand, but it certainly complicates the issue. Many of these considerations have been raised in the national debate over the practice of corporal punishment in schools; this debate is summarized in Feature 2-6.

Professional educators use punishment judiciously, issuing a fair warning before punishing and conveying it with a tone that communicates concern and disappointment, and perhaps even surprise, rather than anger or hostility. Professional teachers think about whether the punishment "fits the crime" and understand the importance of explaining the punishment to the student. They keep a watchful eye on student responses to the punishment,

2-6 DEBATING THE ISSUES
Corporal Punishment

The use of corporal punishment in American schools is controversial. Although corporal punishment in the schools is banned in twenty-seven states, there are no federal sanctions against it. And the twenty-three remaining states still practice it in some form.* One out of every eight schoolchildren in Mississippi is struck with a paddle by a teacher, making its corporal punishment rate the highest in the nation (Hoff, 2000a). Some states require a written parental approval for the practice before a student can be struck, and many local school districts have drafted their own policies, often ensuring that the punishment is reasonable and that it is witnessed by several authorities.

The infliction of physical pain as punishment is a troubling phenomenon to many educators and parents. In thinking about the issue, consider the latent effects that might accompany the use of corporal punishment. Does corporal punishment, for instance, teach children that hitting is an acceptable form of managing conflict? Does it create resentment, and even anger, toward school officials and schooling in general? Or is it, as many of its supporters believe, simply the best way to send a strong message to children about their behaviors, showing them, in classic behaviorist fashion, that there are painful (even humiliating) consequences for misbehavior?

Many groups are interested in this topic, including the National Coalition to Abolish Corporal Punishment in Schools. In 2000, the U.S. Department of Education released a report on corporal punishment in public schools, and various Internet sites, such as familyeducation.com, have taken an interest in the issue, too. Examine these sources as you begin to formulate your own view on the practice.

*The states where corporal punishment is legal are Alabama, Arizona, Arkansas, Colorado, Delaware, Florida, Georgia, Idaho, Indiana, Kansas, Kentucky, Louisiana, Mississippi, New Mexico, North Carolina, Ohio, Oklahoma, Pennsylvania, South Carolina, Tennessee, and Texas.

noting any hostile or otherwise unhealthy tendencies, and try to anticipate any latent negative effects.

Another response in a teacher's management repertoire is the tactic of omission training. In classrooms and schools, this usually manifests as something known as time-out. The rationale behind omission training is that the removal of the student from a pleasant or meaningful social environment will be motivation to change future behaviors. This strategy also has some overtones of punishment to it, especially if the act of removal has associated effects of humiliation or embarrassment.

But the removal of the opportunity to be positively rewarded is different from punishment. In most cases, it is less likely to generate many of the unwanted side effects associated with punishment. But most importantly, its success hinges on the proposition that the student is being removed from an attractive, meaningful, and engaging learning experiences. It is a negative experience only if the student is being removed from something worthwhile. Thus, the cornerstone to classroom control and classroom discipline, under these conditions, is the development of attractive and relevant learning experiences. This is, in fact, the basic premise of many school discipline techniques. Even the traditional idea of school suspension is based on the belief that the student is being suspended from a worthy and important experience, although in practice many school leaders probably hope that the family sees it as a punishing experience as well. If being suspended from school turns out to be a holiday from a repressive and stultifying experience, it can hardly be seen as an effective disciplining strategy.

Teachers, of course, also use positive reinforcement to manage behavior. In the classroom environment, the uses of verbal praise and verbal encouragement are among the more obvious forms. All children, of course, need to be recognized and praised for their accomplishments. Some teachers believe this so strongly that they routinely employ praising reinforcements in the classroom in large doses. But a teacher who praises students too often and who does so uncritically can do a disservice to them. If teachers, for instance, offer effusive praise for the smallest accomplishments, even with so-called low-achieving children, they might humiliate the children, especially if these are accomplishments that other students have already mastered with some ease. Similarly, rewarding or praising students for what they are already doing without external reinforcement could be viewed as unwise because it might tend to attenuate intrinsic motivational drives. In other words, if students have internalized certain constructive routines and behaviors, they need not be continuously praised for these actions.

All classrooms will likely have a handful of students whose behavioral problems are severe enough to warrant special attention. In fact, youths who exhibit persistent behavioral problems in school will usually, in due time, find their way to the school psychologist. Their problems, if severe enough, might result in special curricular attention, though federal legislation in recent decades has promoted the mainstreaming of special populations of students in the interest of keeping them in "regular" education. These students, who typically make up approximately 10 percent of a class, might simply be confused and frustrated in their personal lives; they might be from families whose lives have little consistency and even less love; or they might suffer from any number of emotional or neurological disorders. These will frequently be the students who challenge authority and undermine the educational process of others students. What works for others does not seem to work for them, and a teacher's own anger and frustration with their behavior could result in a spiraling negative relationship. Such students usually will force teachers to make concessions to external reinforcement strategies, because the thing that makes these particular students so frustrating is their inability to develop internal self-control and self-responsibility.

Teachers work in emergent situations, with students who have distinctively different personalities, varied home and family backgrounds, and different levels of ability, interest, and maturity. It is difficult, if not impossible, to find a universally accepted procedure for classroom management or classroom control. There is simply no substitute for the exercise of teacher intelligence as it supports the design and implementation of activities that are intrinsically engaging and controlling, and as it calculates appropriate reinforcement strategies.

SUMMARY

Teaching is still largely a profession conducted by white, middle-class women. Changes in this demographic pattern have been slow in coming, partly due to the limited postsecondary educational options historically available to women. Still, the signs of general professionalization among American schoolteachers are on the rise. The criteria for professionalization indicate improvements, but issues related to salary, public prestige, and decision-making authority still must be addressed. The ideal of the professional in the classroom is of someone who is actively engaged with the best research on teaching and learning, who diagnoses classroom problems and tests working solutions, and who is ultimately responsive to a vision of teaching that accounts for the nature of the learner, the values of the society, and the integration of worthy subject matter or knowledge. In the classroom, this professional perspective is sometime compromised by factors external to the school. The tradition of high-stakes testing, for instance, has put unhealthy pressure on teachers to teach to the test. Efforts to define effective teaching in mechanistic and instructionally generic ways, and to see classroom management as primarily a matter of managing external controls, have had a similar compromising effect.

QUESTIONS AND ACTIVITIES

1. Dewey (1973) once wrote the following about the role of the teacher in society: "Every teacher should realize the dignity of his calling; that he is a social servant set apart for the maintenance of proper social order and the securing of the right social growth. In this way the teacher always is the prophet of the true God and the usherer in of the true kingdom of God" (p. 454). What do you think he meant by this? How do you feel about such a statement?

2. Why is the teaching profession still comprised of mostly women?

3. What are some of the issues that might lead one to conclude that teaching still has a long way to go before it is recognized fully as a profession?

4. Do you agree that the teaching force needs to reflect the demographic composition of society? Do we hold other professions to the same standard?

5. Investigate the portrayal of teachers in the major national media outlets, including national news journals and newspapers, over the past several decades. What conclusions can you draw?

6. Observe professional teachers at work, and judge their classroom performance in relation to one of the three levels of professional development: level I—imitative-maintenance, level II—mediative, and level III—generative-creative. Detail the things that the teachers do (or do not do) to support your conclusions.

7. Examine a curriculum program, curriculum unit, or textbook adopted in a school, and determine the extent to which it allows a teacher to operate at the highest level of professional awareness (level III—generative-creative). What factors in the curriculum open up or restrict the opportunities?

8. Examine a school initiative or school reform idea by subjecting it to an analysis using the three sources for professional decision making: the learner, the society, and the subject matter. Using the three factors, how might you evaluate, for example, whole-language reading instruction, competency-based instruction, STS for science education, the Great Books Curriculum in English education, or a general reform concept, such as middle school education?

9. Visit a classroom and evaluate the nature of the school experience using the same three factors.

10. George Madaus (1999), a well-known specialist in testing, concluded that "the more any quantitative social indicator is used for social decision-making, the more likely it will be to distort and corrupt the social processes it is intended to monitor" (p. 79). What do you think he means by this? How does this apply to education and schooling?

11. Define high-stakes testing. Provide examples from your own experience of high-stakes testing experiences.

12. What factors inside and outside of school can contribute to the formation of high-stakes testing in a school? How do politicians, parents, principals, college officials, and even real estate agents factor into the problem?

13. How is control a fundamental attribute of freedom?

14. What is the distinction between external and internal control? What are the pedagogic implications of such a distinction?

15. What are the pedagogic implications to the proposition that children should be taught to be *in control* of their environments rather than *under control* of their environments?

16. What precautions should be taken before using punishment strategies in the classroom?

17. Is praise always a good thing? What factors should be considered when using praise in the classroom?

18. What makes the notion of time on task problematic in the curriculum?

19. Explain how problems with classroom discipline and classroom management could be linked to problems with teaching in general.

20. What are some of the theoretical problems associated with the effective teaching literature?

REFERENCES

American Federal of Teachers. (1995). *Survey and analysis of salary trends.* (Washington, DC: AFT).

Bloom, B. S. (1956). *Taxonomy of educational objectives: Cognitive domain.* (New York: David McKay).

Bruschi, B. A., and Coley, R. J. (1999). *How teachers compare: The prose, document and quantitative skills of America's teachers.* (Princeton, NJ: Educational Testing Service).

Carnegie Foundation for the Advancement of Teaching. (1990). *The condition of teaching.* (Princeton, NJ: Carnegie Foundation for the Advancement of Teaching).

Carson, C. C., Huelskamp, R. M., and Woodall, T. D. (1993). Perspectives on education in America. *Journal of Educational Research,* 86(5):259–310.

Csikszentmihalyi, M. (1990). *Flow: The psychology of optimal experience.* (New York: Harper & Row).

Dewey, J. (1973). My pedagogic creed. In J. J. McDermott (ed.), *The philosophy of John Dewey.* (Chicago: University of Chicago Press [1897]).

Dewey, J. (1938). *Experience and education.* (New York: Macmillan).

Dewey, J (1916). *Democracy and education.* (New York: Free Press).

Dewey, J. (1904). The relation of theory to practice in education. In the *National Society for the Study of Education, 3rd Yearbook, Part 1.* (Bloomington, IN: Public School Publishing).

Dewey, J. (1902). *The child and the curriculum.* (Chicago: University of Chicago Press).

Fischer, L., Schimmel, D., and Kelly, C. (1999). *Teachers and the law,* 5th ed. (White Plains, NY: Longman).

Gardner, H. (1983). *Frames of mind: The theory of multiple intelligences.* (New York: Basic Books).

Henke, R. R., Chen, X. and Goldman, G. (1999). What happens in classrooms? Instructional practices in elementary and secondary schools: 1994–1995. *Education Quarterly,* 1(2):7–13.

Hlebowitsh, P. S. (1992). Time on TAAS. *Texas Researcher,* 3:81–89.

Hoff, D. J. (2000a). Mississippi first in paddling. *Education Week* (9 Jan.).

Hoff, D. J. (2000b). LA teachers caught cheating. *Education Week* (9 Jan.).

Hunter, M. (1980). *Teach more—faster.* (El Segundo, CA: TIP Publications).

Krathwohl, D. L., Bloom, B. S., and Masia, B. B. (1964). *Taxonomy of educational objectives: Affective domain.* (New York: David McKay).

Ladson-Billings, G. (1994). *The dreamkeepers: Successful teachers of African-American children.* (San Francisco: Jossey-Bass).

Madaus, G. F. (1999). The influence of testing on the curriculum. In *Issues in curriculum: 98th yearbook of the National Society for the Study of Education.* (Chicago: University of Chicago Press).

Maslow, A. H. (1962). *Toward a psychology of being.* (New York: Van Nostrand Reinhold).

National Center for Education Statistics. (1999a). *The condition of education.* (Washington, DC: Department of Education).

National Center for Education Statistics. (1999b). *Quality counts: A report on the preparation and qualifications of public school teachers.* (Washington, DC: Department of Education).

National Center for Education Statistics. (1998). *Violence and discipline in U.S. public schools: 1996–97.* (Washington, DC: Department of Education).

National Center for Education Statistics. (1997a). *America's teachers: Profile of a profession, 1993–94.* (Washington, DC: Department of Education).

National Center for Education Statistics. (1997b). *The status of teaching as a profession.* (Washington, DC: Department of Education).

National Center for Education Statistics. (1997c). *Teacher professionalization and teacher commitment.* (Washington, DC: Department of Education).

National Center for Education Statistics. (1993). *Violence and discipline problems in the United States public schools, 1996–1997.* (Washington, DC: Department of Education).

National Council of Teachers of Mathematics. (1989). *Curriculum and evaluation standards for school mathematics.* (Washington, DC: National Council of Teachers of Mathematics).

Pauley, E. (1991). *The classroom crucible.* (New York: Basic Books).

Piaget, J. (1970). *Science of education and the psychology of the child.* (New York: Orion Press).

Rosenshine, B. (1978). Time, content and direct instruction. In P. L. Peterson and H. L. Walberg, (eds.), *Research on teaching: Concept, findings and implications.* (Berkeley, CA: McCutchen).

Shulman, L. (1987). Knowledge and teaching: Foundations of the new reform. *Harvard Educational Review,* 57(1):1–17.

Skinner, B. F. (1968). *The technology of teaching.* (New York: Appleton, Century, Crofts).

Stodolsky, S. S. (1988). *The subject matters: Classroom activity in math and social studies.* (Chicago: University of Chicago Press).

Tanner, D., and Tanner, L. N. (1995). *Curriculum development: Theory into practice,* 3rd ed. (New York: Macmillan).

Tyler, R. W. (1949). *Basic principles of curriculum and instruction.* (Chicago: University of Chicago Press).

CHAPTER 3

Philosophies of Teaching

Education in the Conservative Tradition
PERENNIALISM
ESSENTIALISM

Education in the Progressive Tradition
EXPERIMENTALISM
ROMANTIC NATURALISM

Education in the Radical Tradition
SOCIAL RECONSTRUCTIONISM
POSTMODERNISM

Summary

Questions and Activities

References

T HE ACT OF TEACHING is not a mechanical or objectively neutral process. It is an endeavor deeply embedded in a set of values that help dictate the nature of the experience and knowledge found in the classroom. And although teachers often inherit state- or district-mandated standards on what should be taught and, as described earlier, often feel the influence of various external interests, no philosophy toward schooling or learning is more important or more influential in the lives of schoolchildren than the teacher's.

Tyler (1949) likened the role of philosophy in the classroom and the school to a screen through which ideas are filtered in order to crystallize teacher's purposes and objectives, making them consistent with one another and sharpening teachers' sense of why they are doing what they are doing. Because a philosophy of teaching has answers to questions related to what it means to lead a good life in a good society, it will have a defined perspective on what is worth knowing and doing. This leads headlong into the framing of purpose in the school, the articulation of objectives, and the eventual design and implementation of allied experiences.

But there are limitations to the possibilities here. A philosophy of teaching has to be responsive to the three factors in decision making discussed in the previous chapter (learner, society, subject matter). A teacher does not have the right to exercise a fascist philosophy in an institution expressly dedicated to educating youths for participation in a democracy. Naturally, there are different philosophical ways of justifying actions and experiences that might be viewed as good for democracy, but an overtly antidemocratic philosophy cannot stand. Similarly, a teacher does not have the right to apply a philosophy that might result in experiences that have no legitimacy in the secular purposes of the school. For example, an overtly Christian (or other religion-based) philosophy has no legitimate place in the school unless it can be used subtly in ways that secure overtly secular purposes. A philosophy also has to have some linkage to the learner. There can be no philosophical justification for experiences that are not age-appropriate or that are in any way harmful to the mental, emotional, and physical well-being of the child. A teacher, for example, who has an earnest philosophical commitment to bringing the hard realities of life to the classroom has to be careful about overstepping certain boundaries in practice. Obviously, one does not teach children that fire burns by forcing their hands into the flames.

Any philosophy of teaching resonates at the center of the three sources for professional decision making. Articulating a given philosophy involves answers to questions like these: What is the conception of the learner supported by a particular philosophical point of view? What is the ideal of an educated citizen? What knowledge (subject matter) is most worth knowing, and how should it be organized and taught? Each of these points of departure leaves room for the expression of a different philosophical position and the formation of different school purposes and practices.

Formulating a school (or classroom) philosophy is not just a ritualistic exercise to reassure the public that the school is moved by high-minded purposes, but a serious commitment to some standard of conduct. The overall statement of philosophy for a school, which is typically required for accreditation procedures, often makes reference to objectives in the public mandate, such as fostering democratic values, assuring equal opportunities to learn, and nurturing an attitude for lifelong learning. Such statements of philosophy are profitable only if they are simultaneously viewed as commitments to practice. A philosophy, in this sense, represents a kind of resolution on the part of the school not only to reflect its expressed ideals in the classroom but also to be judged against them. It is easier to have ideals than to actually live by them. A philosophy of teaching is a matter of living by an ideal; it is a compass that orients the instructional or pedagogic methods in the school. Feature 3-1 addresses the issue of weighing community views in the formulation of a school philosophy.

EDUCATION IN THE CONSERVATIVE TRADITION

The conservative philosophy of teaching is essentially a subject-centered position. It holds that teaching is largely a matter of maneuvering through the accumulated wisdom embodied in elements of organized knowledge. The purpose of the school is primarily to transmit and preserve common cultural knowledge. Students are believed to be well served as citizens by this purpose because the school will have exposed them to and socialized them in the essential dimensions of society. Among young children, the focus of education is acquisition of the basic skills that will later be needed for mastery of the subject matter. This general orientation is viewed as conservative because it is committed to the preservation of humanity's wisdom as it is found in particular academic studies. Conservative educational philosophies are typically understood as two distinct schools of thought, known as perennialism and essentialism.

Perennialism

In the perennialist perspective, learning is unalterably rooted in the subject matter. Learning thus is primarily a matter of immersion in a set of subjects endowed with the verities and virtues of Western civilization. Grammar, reading, rhetoric, logic, mathematics, and the great literary books of

3-1 THINKING ABOUT THE DATA

Public Opinion on Good Schooling

Here are some results from a national poll taken by Public Agenda in 1998. It shows some consensus among parents, and among the public, teachers, and students, on what is important and valuable in the school experience. If the same kinds of views prevailed in the school where you were employed as a professional educator, how might your own philosophy toward schooling be affected?

The Views of the General Public, Teachers, and Students on Basic Skills, Mainstream Values, and Computers as Curriculum Priorities

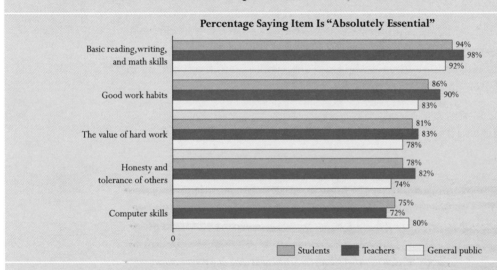

Percentage Saying Item Is "Absolutely Essential"

Item	Students	Teachers	General public
Basic reading, writing, and math skills	94%	98%	92%
Good work habits	86%	90%	83%
The value of hard work	81%	83%	78%
Honesty and tolerance of others	78%	82%	74%
Computer skills	75%	72%	80%

SOURCE: © Data copyrighted by Source. © Graphics copyrighted by Public Agenda 2000. No reproduction/distribution without permission.

humanity (the historic core of the liberal arts) have long stood as the main sources of content for perennialists—what Hutchins (1936) called the "permanent studies." The phrase "permanent studies" is revealing because it reflects the assumption that the educating powers of these studies persist over time; that is, they are perennial. In this sense, the subject matter itself, and the powers that accrue from it, represents the main ends of education. Learning arises from the activity generated in the learner's mind by the subject matter. Teachers might seek ways to guide, stimulate, and assist it, but the subject matter is the true teacher. And where teachers might focus on basic skills instruction (rather than content), especially with younger children, the rationale for their actions is that such skills are required to access the subject matter in a way that will allow students to eventually benefit from its mind-training possibilities. Believing that these subjects represent a

The Views of African American and White Parents on What Constitutes Good Schooling

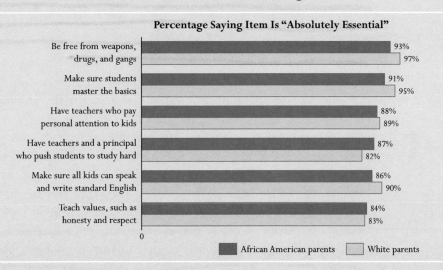

Percentage Saying Item Is "Absolutely Essential"

	African American parents	White parents
Be free from weapons, drugs, and gangs	93%	97%
Make sure students master the basics	91%	95%
Have teachers who pay personal attention to kids	88%	89%
Have teachers and a principal who push students to study hard	87%	82%
Make sure all kids can speak and write standard English	86%	90%
Teach values, such as honesty and respect	84%	83%

SOURCE: © Data copyrighted by Source. © Graphics copyrighted by Public Agenda 2000. No reproduction/distribution without permission.

kind of repository for the knowledge and wisdom of Western civilization, perennialists are confident that a well-managed and carefully supervised exposure to the permanent studies will produce the kind of rational, enlightened, and intellectually activated citizen that democracy demands.

The perennialist maintains that students must have an exclusive experience in the permanent studies to learn. Thus, the perennialist has a kind of one-size-fits-all mentality, a belief in one uniform curriculum for all students in virtually all places and all times. This insistence is rooted in the desire to expose all youths, not just the elite, to a form of education believed to be essential to democracy. Not only do students get smarter from experiences that discipline the mind, but they are granted their cultural inheritance and profit from a common foundation of knowledge. Through the eternal truths and virtues of perennial studies, the new generation can share a bond with previous generations and carry with it the shared outlook it will need to advance itself. As Hutchins (1972) put it, "The primary aim of the educational system in a democratic country is to draw out the common humanity of those committed to its charge" (p. 209). To Hutchins and other perennialists, this "common humanity" is reflected in the permanent studies.

This commitment to the mind is justified by the doctrine of mental discipline and is so intense that other areas of study, such as vocational studies, elective studies, physical education, and the performing arts, are viewed as anti-intellectual frivolities. This is especially true for vocational education, which, in the eyes of the perennialist, has no place in school because it drains time and resources from the central task of developing youths' minds and characters. During the 1980s, Mortimer Adler, who has long been a proponent of the perennialist position, argued for the elimination of all electives in the upper six years of schooling, with the exception of a choice of a second language, and the elimination of all specialized job training throughout. "The kind of vocational training that now goes on in schools is worse than useless," observed Adler (1988), "it is undemocratic in the extreme" (p. 281). Adler could see no value in job training in the schools given the key task of training minds. Vocational education took time away from the intimate tutoring that Adler believed each student needed in order to be brought through the canons of Western thought. This emphasis on matters pertaining to the mind over matters pertaining to the body leaves a mentalistic mark on the schooling experience; it stresses a rational, contemplative, abstract, and subject-centered approach to learning. To Adler, even physical education was justified for its contribution to mindful learning. In 1984, he described the two purposes of physical education in the school as "to develop the knowledge and habits requisite for the care of the body throughout life, and to provide some physical relief from the taxing brain work of schooling" (p. 161).

In the perennialist view, the elementary school teacher must give serious attention to the management of basic skills education, especially reading instruction. At this level, the development of the basic skills tends to take on a life of its own. These skills are the key needed to unlock the doors to civilization, the very tools that will enable students eventually to read and think their way through the subject matter. Thus, the instructional repertoire of the perennialist is unabashedly supportive of skill-drill strategies. As Adler (1984) observed, "Often painful, usually boring, drill is necessary. . . . Students have to develop error free habits. Repeating the act—i.e. experience—is indispensable" (p. 42).

But the elementary school is also the place where students get their first instructional experiences in reading and understanding the literary classics. This is where the "Great Books" curriculum, the centerpiece to perennialist

For the elementary school teacher, perennialism means that serious attention will be given to the management of basic skills education, especially reading instruction.

thinking, first takes hold. As one perennialist put it, "There should be no school in which the young mind fails to receive, like seeds destined to germinate in later years, a full sowing of sentences great men have spoken" (Van Doren, 1943, p. 95). The responsibility of the teacher, from elementary school to college, is to use the Great Books to bring the metanarrative of civilization to students. This calls for a varied set of instructional actions. One role is that of the seminar leader (Adler, 1984), the provocative facilitator who illuminates the power of the literature through questioning techniques that "catch the mind" and promote virtue. Another is that of the coach, the vigilant tutor who pays close attention to the work of students, offering immediate feedback, "shrewd" criticism, and relentless skill-drill repetitions.

The duty to coach or attend to the intellectual skills of individuals is often used by perennialists as the main justification not to embrace a more comprehensive school design. The argument is that, when the school tries to do too much, teachers cannot offer a close hand in the intellectual education of students. Why view education as an endeavor that is miles wide and inches deep, the perennialist might ask, when one can focus on mindful learning with precision and depth?

And what of the fact that until the nineteenth century the Great Books were all written by white European males? Adler (1977) responded that "the educational purpose of the great books is not to study Western civilization. Its aim is not to acquire knowledge of historical facts. It is rather to understand the great ideas" (p. xxxii). The fact that only great ideas could be had from the Great Books is nonproblematic to Adler because of his philosophical prejudices. The issue of diversity is irrelevant because learning is not about diversity; it is about training the mind, the will, and the character through the permanent studies.

During the 1980s, former U.S. Secretary of Education William Bennett often displayed his perennialist colors. In 1986, for instance, he helped to author a report on elementary education in the United States, entitled *First Lessons,* that outlined general curricular conditions for reform (Bennett, 1986). The report bore an unmistakable, if not proud, resemblance to the 1895 National Education Association's *Committee of Fifteen* report, authored by William Torrey Harris, a well-known mental disciplinarian. In framing the curriculum, Bennett cited the 1895 report, stating that "grammar, literature, arithmetic, geography and history are the five branches upon which the disciplinary work of the elementary work is concentrated" (p. 20). In 1987, Bennett authored a similar report, but this time focusing on the American high school. The report, entitled *James Madison High School,* represented another retrogradation to the nineteenth century. Stating that "schooling in the full set of core academic disciplines should be central to the true purposes of American secondary education," Bennett (1987, p. 2) proposed a set of courses that looked very much like the general course requirements found in the 1893 *Committee of Ten* report, which itself featured a classic mental disciplinarian approach to high school education. Feature 3-2 on pages 102–103 places the high school curriculum in historical context.

After his tenure as secretary concluded, Bennett remained an indefatigable critic of the public school, repeatedly alleging that it has neglected basic education and failed to give due deference to the literary works of Western civilization. He also helped to popularize perennialist causes by editing the *Book of Virtues* (Bennett, 1993), a compendium of "great" essays, poems, and stories, chosen for their enduring relevance as stories of virtue. Figure 3-1 on page 104 summarizes the conceptual features of perennialism.

Essentialism

Essentialists and perennialists are close cousins who share a basic commitment to training the intellect through subject-centered knowledge. The dividing line between the two mainly concerns what is the most worthy form of knowledge. The perennialist prefers to showcase the timeless intel-

Essentialism aims to provide an education in the "essentials" of our civilization, the indispensable features of our core cultural knowledge as it is organized in the academic disciplines.

lectual virtues of our Western cultural heritage, as it exists in the Great Books and the liberal arts, while the essentialist favors a more fundamentally modern outlook on the academic disciplines. The essentialist thus promotes a more strictly academic and disciplinary experience than one might find in the humanities approach of the perennialist.

Essentialist thinking, as implied, is rooted in the learning doctrine of mental discipline. So, the focus of the school is very much subject-centered, academic, and mentalistic. Logically organized academic disciplines—the very kinds of traditional disciplinary lines that one typically sees in the organization of a high school or even college curriculum—form the core of the curriculum. The general educational plan is disciplined study in language and grammar, mathematics, the sciences, history, and foreign language. The primacy of the subject matter in learning is justified as a perennialist might justify it. The subject matter not only trains the mind but also provides the basis needed to secure a common universe of discourse and understanding in society. Essentialism, in this way, is linked to the values of democracy.

The connection to democracy is important. At the turn of the century, William Bagley (1907) took an essentialist position by arguing that the

3-2 THE HISTORICAL CONTEXT

The High School Curriculum in 1987 and 1893

William Bennett suggested one set of courses for high school education in his 1987 report, *James Madison High School,* while the *Committee of Ten* suggested another set for high school education in its 1893 report. What are the similarities and differences? Will Bennett have a view of electives that might differ from that of a progressive? What do you think of the two proposed curriculum plans?

Bennett's 1987 Curriculum

Subject	1st Year	2nd Year	3rd Year	4th Year
English	Introduction to Literature	American Literature	British Literature	Introduction to World Literature
Social Studies	Western Civilzation	American History	Principles of American Democracy (*1 sem.*) and American Democracy and the World (*1 sem.*)	
Mathematics	Three Years Required From Among the Following Courses: Algebra 1, Plane and Solid Geometry, Algebra 11 and Trigonometry, Statistics and Probability (*1 sem.*), Pre-Calculus (*1 sem.*), and Calculus AB or BC			
Science	Three Years Required From Among the Following Courses: Astronomy/Geology, Biology, Chemistry, and Physics or Principles of Technology			
Foreign Language	Two Years Required in a Single Language From Among Offerings Determined by Local Jurisdictions		ELECTIVES	
Physical Education/ Health	Physical Education/ Health 9	Physical Education/ Health 10		
Fine Arts	Art History (*1 sem.*) Music History (*1 sem.*)			

school curriculum should be "a storehouse of organized race experience, conserved against the time when knowledge shall be needed in the constructive solution of new and untried problems" (p. 2). This statement touches on some of the main principles of the social theory behind the

The *Committee of Ten*'s 1893 Curriculum

1st Secondary School Year	2nd Secondary School Year

Latin.................................5p.
English Literature, 2p.⎤
English Composition, 2p.⎦........4p.
German [or French] ....5p.
Algebra.............................4p.
History of Italy, Spain,
   and France.......................3p.
Applied Geography (European
   political-continental and
   oceanic flora and fauna).........4p.
                25p.
	Latin...................................4p.
	Greek..................................5p.
	English Literature, 2p.⎤
	English Composition, 2p.⎦....4p.
	German, continued ....4p.
	French, begun.......................5p.
	Algebra,* 2p.⎤
	Geometry, 2p.⎦.................4p.
	Botany or Zoology..................4p.
	English History to 1688............3p.
	                33p.
	
	*Option of bookkeeping and
	  commercial arithmetic.

3rd Secondary School Year	**4th Secondary School Year**

Latin...................................4p.
Greek..................................4p.
English Literature, 2p.⎤
English Composition, 1p.⎬........4p.
Rhetoric, 1p.⎦
German ....4p.
French..................................4p.
Algebra,* 2p.⎤
Geometry, 2p.⎦.................4p.
Physics................................4p.
History, English and American....3p.
Astronomy, 3p. 1st 1/2 yr.⎤....3p.
Meterology, 3p. 2nd 1/2 yr.⎦
               34p.
 	
*Option of bookkeeping and
  commercial arithmetic.
	Latin...................................4p.
	Greek..................................4p.
	English Literature, 2p.⎤
	English Composition, 1p.⎬........4p.
	English Grammar, 1p.⎦
	German ....4p.
	French..................................4p.
	Trigonometry,⎤
	Higher Algebra,⎦.................2p.
	Chemistry............................4p.
	History (intensive) and
	   Civil Government...............3p.
	Geology or Physiography,⎤
	   4p. 1st 1/2 yr.⎬.....4p.
	Anatomy, Physiology, and⎦
	   Hygiene, 4p. 2nd 1/2 yr.
	               33p.

essentialist argument. Essentialism aims to provide an education in the "essentials" of our civilization, the indispensable features of our core cultural knowledge as it is organized in the academic disciplines. Bagley's reference to the race experience can be translated to mean the experience of

> **FIGURE 3-1**
> **Conceptual Features of Perennialism**
>
> **1.** *Ideal of the learner:* a disciplined mind immersed in the highest traditions, values, and wisdom of Western humanity
>
> **2.** *Ideal of society:* a democracy moved by its Western inheritance and the eternal truths and virtues that accompany it
>
> **3.** *Ideal of the subject matter:* a core of permanent studies, resembling the core of the liberal arts, that can discipline the mind and embody the wisdom of humanity

the human race (humanity), which he believed was warehoused in the academic disciplines. This body of core knowledge is transmitted to learners for the purposes of cultivating the faculties of thinking and reasoning and of promoting a common or shared culture. This is the essentialists' way of offering a general education to the population, an education in the knowledge one needs to lead an informed life in democratic society.

In their heyday, however, the essentialists were less influenced by democratic factors than by nationalistic ones. During the Cold War, the discipline-centered traditions of the essentialists looked to be the perfect foil to the perceived imperialistic designs of the Soviet state. The specialized academic education thought to be needed in the work force to dissuade the Soviets from their nefarious intentions fit hand and glove with the academic orientation of the essentialist curriculum. That is, the education of engineers, scientists, and mathematicians, the main workers in the technological (space-related) defense of the nation, required a highly academic, discipline-centered experience—as reflected in the federal sponsorship of discipline-centered curriculum projects in high schools during this era. The provision of intellectual training in the fundamental disciplines became the first duty of the school because it was viewed as crucial to the defense of the nation. Anything that could not be justified in this context was likely to be excluded from, or at least deemphasized in, the school curriculum.

But in the late 1980s the essentialists returned to the idea of general education, focusing not on nationalistic concerns but on the kind of public education students needed for participation in a democracy. The impetus for the refocus was a controversial book by E. D. Hirsch (1987), entitled *Cultural Literacy.* The gist of Hirsch's argument was that a spiraling decline in the shared knowledge of the citizenry was threatening the existence of American democracy. The book thus represented a kind of call to arms for the essentialist position. The term "cultural literacy" effectively echoed the main principle of essentialism, which is literacy in the core cultural traditions of Western civilization. Hisrch's book attempted to draw attention to the fact the much of the power of the content in the traditional academic disciplines had been lost in the schools. Students, Hirsch argued, did not know anything especially penetrating about their own cultural history and traditional literature; they did not benefit from scientific and mathematical knowledge; they were not culturally literate. This conclusion was buoyed by National Assessment of Educational Progress (NAEP) data documenting embarrassingly poor student performances on historical and literature-based knowledge tests (Finn and Ravitch, 1987). From the standpoint of the essentialist, two vital factors in the education of youths were being neglected. First, the students' minds were not being effectively trained or disciplined. Second, and more importantly, students were failing to gain the cultural background knowledge (the shared knowledge and vocabulary) they needed to forge a national identity and to participate in a common universe of understanding and insight. The antidote, of course, was to bring back the academic disciplines and place them front and center in a no-nonsense curriculum.

Hisrch has continued in his quest to revitalize the high academic tradition of the essentialist in the school and in the society. He has emerged as a leading critic of what he views as "contentless" teaching in the school and has sought to fill this perceived void by publishing a series of cultural literacy dictionaries, workbooks, and tests. He has also founded the tellingly titled Core Knowledge Foundation, which offers suggestions to schools on how to establish learnings in the core knowledge areas. Feature 3-3 gives a glimpse at the foundation's website.

In many ways, the American school, especially the high school, has continued to operate in the wake left by the essentialists during the Cold War, supporting discipline-centered graduation requirements, curriculum organization, and testing. And increasingly, advocates for the establishment of national standards and uniform content standards are offering a classic essentialist rationale: the need to give students a standard or uniform program of disciplined intellectual training in core academic areas. Figure 3-2 summarizes the conceptual features of essentialism.

EDUCATION IN THE PROGRESSIVE TRADITION

Whereas an advocate of a conservative perspective on schooling aims to preserve and transmit a core culture, a progressive aims to change it. The root word of *progressive* is "progress," which implies change by critical

3-3 WEB POINTS

Core Knowledge Foundation

E. D. Hirsch founded the Core Knowledge Foundation to help teachers establish the early foundations of knowledge in the education of children. This website (www.coreknowledge.org) has many lesson plans designed by teachers and general explanatory material about the nature of the foundation.

| About Core Knowledge | Schools | Bookstore | Lesson Plans | Conference |

Core Knowledge™

Welcome to the Core Knowledge Web Site.

Dedicated to excellence and fairness in early education, the Core Knowledge Foundation is an independent, non-profit, non-partisan organization founded in 1986 by **E. D. Hirsch, Jr.**, a professor at the University of Virginia and author of many acclaimed books including **Cultural Literacy: What Every American Needs to Know** and **The Schools We Need and Why We Don't Have Them.** The foundation conducts research on curricula, develops books and other materials for parents and teachers, offers workshops for teachers, and serves as the hub of a growing network of Core Knowledge schools.

New! Resources to Build On: An updated version of Books to Build On, a Core Knowledge Resource Guide for Parents and Teachers.

New Independent Study
In Oklahoma City a Rigorous Scientific Study Shows the Positive Equity Effects of Core Knowledge.
View a summary of the study conducted by Gracy Taylor and George Kimball of the Oklahoma Public Schools.

As you explore this site, you will find lesson plans, articles, and many other resources to help you use the Core Knowledge Sequence in your classroom and school. We invite you to learn more about the model curriculum guidelines developed by the Core Knowledge Foundation, and to discover why, as more schools "share the knowledge," they are discovering that

Core Knowledge is the common ground for uncommon success.

Reprinted with permission.

> **FIGURE 3-2**
> **Conceptual Features of Essentialism**
>
> **1.** *Ideal of the learner:* a rational mind immersed in the fundamental academic disciplines
>
> **2.** *Ideal of society:* a democracy dependent on a common or shared core of academic knowledge
>
> **3.** *Ideal of the subject matter:* a strictly academic and discipline-centered curriculum, attendant to the inner designs and intellective powers of the individual disciplines

evaluation for the sake of betterment or improvement. This shift in focus takes the progressive vision of schooling away from the subject-centered foundation of the conservatives and directly into some estimation of the actual skills, attitudes, knowledge, and competencies needed to respond to real-life challenges. Talk of mind training is replaced with discussion of the relevance of the life experience. Because progressives do not believe that subjects carry internal mind-training capacities, the subject matter loses it exalted status in the curriculum; it is no longer formulated as an end in itself but as a means toward the achievement or fulfillment of broader purposes and problems. The progressive tradition has two forms —the Deweyan form, known as experimentalism, and its more child-centered variant, known as romantic naturalism.

Experimentalism

Experimentalists conceive of the school as an agency for democracy, as the place where children are taught the values, skills, attitudes, knowledge, and general competencies they will need to lead a good life in a good society. The experimentalist variant to the progressive perspective is embodied in the work of John Dewey. Widely known as a philosopher of American democracy, Dewey had a strong interest in schooling. Philosophers historically have made their marks by writing their views on ethics, logic, religion, aesthetics, truth, and even reality, but very few have exercised their analytical acumen on the topic of schooling. Dewey, however, could not escape the connection that schooling had to his philosophical views, especially in relation to the concept of democracy; he even directed his own laboratory school at the University of Chicago, a rare activity for a philosopher indeed!

For the experimentalists, the center of the school experience is a problem-focused curriculum that highlights the importance of inquiry-based learning.

How does experimentalism begin to represent a philosophy that identifies with democracy? And why the term "experimentalism," which seems to connote some strange association with exotic laboratory techniques? To answer these questions, we must first identify what Dewey (1916) saw as the main basis of all education, which he described as that "reconstruction or reorganization of experience which adds to the meaning of experience and which increases ability to direct the course of subsequent experiences" (pp. 89–90). To understand experimentalism, we must understand this idea. To simplify matters, the "reconstruction or reorganization of experience" is really just another way of saying that one must learn from one's experience in a fashion that avoids repeating mistakes and that contributes to one's ability to make more informed decisions in the future. The implication is that learning is a process of experiential growth, that one is always in the state of becoming and, if properly managed, improving, but never achieving completeness or finality. This view of experience, however, does not emerge idiosyncratically. Some method of thinking, or some process of intelligence, has to be applied to help regulate it.

To Dewey, this intelligence could be cultivated using the scientific method. The scientific method applied to learning in school has several advantages from the standpoint of an experimentalist. First, it holds all truth up to ongoing inspection, a principle running counter to the conservative belief in the eternal value and truths of the Western canon. Given the tentative nature of truth, the process of inquiry and the use of evidence and reasoned argumentation in decision making assumes increased importance. Second, the scientific method is a problem resolution process that tests new ideas in the interests of producing improvements in existing conditions. This makes it an elegant method for living in a democracy because it poses problems as opportunities for new understanding and insight. Finally, the scientific method of thinking hones the important skill of reflective thinking, a required condition for informed participation in a democratic society. Thus, Dewey's insistence in seeing education as a "reconstruction of experience" was motivated by a desire to teach students a method of intelligent inquiry that gives them an effective handle on their personal and public lives. Inculcating in students the attitudes, habits of mind, and methods of scientific inquiry could give them not only, as Dewey (1938) put it, "freedom from control by routine, prejudice, dogma, unexamined tradition, [and] sheer self-interest" but also "the will to inquire, to examine, to discriminate, to draw conclusions only on the basis of evidence after taking pains to gather all available evidence" (p. 31).

The practical consequence of positioning the "reconstruction of experience" in the center of the school experience is a problem-focused curriculum that highlights the importance of inquiry-based learning. This obviously calls for a very different conception of subject matter than what might be expressed in a more conservative philosophy. But there is no single body of content that claims to have a warrant on intelligence among experimentalists. In fact, traditional subject matter lines are dissolved and then reconstituted topically, according to the problems and purposes of the educational situation. Because life problems are not easily located within disciplinary subjects, experimentalists place a premium on the interdisciplinary construction of subject matter. The cliche that "knowledge is power" has a very definite meaning for experimentalists. The power is not in the contribution that knowledge makes to one's mind, but in its contribution to one's behavior. To know that the act of smoking, for instance, carries certain side-effects that increase the odds of contracting serious illness, can be interpreted as mindful knowledge (one could know it but still smoke) or as applied knowledge (one knows it and acts accordingly). The experimentalists stake their claim with the latter.

The focus on behavior is especially important, because as a philosophy of democracy, experimentalism ultimately judges the effects of schooling against some standard of betterment or progress in the life experience. This is a principle associated with the roots that experimentalism has in a broader philosophical tradition known as pragmatism. The pragmatist's goal is to affect the here and now, to look at life as a matter of present significance, and not in terms of some ultimate judgment in some transcendental

---

FIGURE 3-3

Conceptual Features of Experimentalism

1. *Ideal of the learner:* a socially conscious, democratically inspired, and intellectually empowered problem solver

2. *Ideal of society:* a democracy whose citizenry is engaged in a common universe of social discourse and social understanding

3. *Ideal of the subject matter:* a problem-focused, idea-oriented curriculum directly responsive to the personal and socio-civic experience

---

realm. The key is to focus on experience and on the kind of intelligent conduct that will result in progress. As Dewey (1938) observed, "We always live at the time we live and not at some other time, and only by extracting at each present time the full meaning of each present experience are we prepared for doing the same thing in the future" (p. 51). Even the study of the past has relevance only as it grants understanding to the present. "The present," stated Dewey (1916), "generates the problems which lead us to search the past for suggestion, and which supplies meaning to what we find when we search" (p. 89).

Thus, we return to the primacy of experience in the school. Schooling, to paraphrase Dewey, is not a preparation for life, but is life itself and, in the case of American schooling, life in a democracy. This means that the whole child must be educated, and not just the mind. The curriculum, as a result, is comprehensive in its scope, is interdisciplinary in its overall organization and is activity-based in its sense of experience. And because the school is the engine of democracy, considerable emphasis is placed on shared experiences and the communion of values, outlooks, and problems that help to amalgamate democratic society. Figure 3-3 summarizes the conceptual features of experimentalism.

Romantic Naturalism

The first signs of a progressive movement in schools of the United States occurred at the turn of the twentieth century and were largely child-centered in orientation. Because the schools were so deeply ensconced in a conservative, subject-centered view of learning during the late nineteenth century, the conditions were conducive for a countermovement that would attempt to undo the extreme of subject centeredness. The child-centered movement in America was the counterreaction, offering a philosophy of learning unabashedly dedicated to providing children with a joyful, open-ended, activity-based education. Where the subject-centered view was mentalistic, the child-centered view was active; where the subject-centered view staked its claim in a uniform, knowledge-based, and planned experience, the child-centered view promoted an individualistic, emotional, and spontaneous experience. Where teacher-directed instruction, teacher authority, and a structured curriculum ruled in the school, child-centered advocates sought reforms that would allow children to direct their own learning and to determine for themselves what they learned and how and when they learned it. Feature 3-4 offers a way to loosely gauge the philosophical dispositions of teachers on a child-centered versus subject-centered continuum.

These expressions of child-centeredness unfolded under the influence of a romantic naturalist philosophy. Inspired by the philosopher Jean-Jacques Rousseau, whose disdain for both institutions and adults was legendary, the romantic naturalists argued that children were best educated in a free and largely unhampered environment, with only minimal adult intervention. Professing a commitment to the innate goodness and innocence of children, the romantic naturalists put little stock in the value of uniform experiences in the school or even in the act of curriculum or instructional planning. Rather, the emphasis was on the natural self-educating powers of the child. The key notion was that learning is so much a matter of individual choice and individual direction that the preferences and pleasures of children should be allowed to guide the process. Nature provided the inner processes needed for producing virtuous, self-actualized human beings. The romantic naturalists believed that schools tended to ruin this natural process by imposing an "educational" agenda on children that undermined their self-educating inclinations. Thus, the teacher's proper role was to help create a classroom environment that facilitated the pursuit of individual interests. One author put it this way: "What we need to do, and all we need to do, is bring as much of the world as we can into the school and the classroom; give the children as much help and guidance as they need and ask for, listen respectfully when they feel like talking; and then get out of the way. We can trust them to do the rest" (McCraken, 1973, p. 16).

The romantic naturalists sometimes represented their position under the banner of "learning by doing," arguing that there is educational virtue in essentially any task that the child is committed to perform in the classroom. In short, having an experience moved by student desire or student decision is ipso facto educational. But the experimentalists countered that

3-4 RESEARCH INQUIRY
Child-Centered Versus Subject-Centered Preferences

Here is a short questionnaire that can help you gauge the extent to which a person's philosophical position is tilted in the direction of either child-centeredness or subject-centeredness. If you wish, fill out the questionnaire yourself. For research purposes, however, think about giving it to teachers or principals from different school settings. Interpret the results in relation to variables such as grade level; years of experience; ethnicity, race, and gender; and the income level or percentage of minority students. What might be the significance of finding different levels of commitment to child-centered or subject-centered views in different school settings?

Rate each of these statements according to this scale. Compare your answers to the key below to determine your orientation.

Strongly disagree	Somewhat disagree	No opinion	Somewhat agree	Strongly agree
1	2	3	4	5

_____ 1. The education of children would be better served if we abandoned objectives and simply allowed children to explore their own heartfelt needs and interests.

_____ 2. Students should always be permitted to determine their own rules in the educational process.

_____ 3. The most important kind of education is one that is expressly dedicated to the cultivation of the mind.

_____ 4. Exposure to the strict academic disciplines is the most essential aspect in the education of youth.

_____ 5. Self-improvement and self-actualization are the most important components to a good public education.

_____ 6. Schools are primarily designed to maintain and preserve certain established values and ideas.

_____ 7. Memorization is the most important key to learning.

_____ 8. The most effective learning is usually unstructured and spontaneous.

_____ 9. Academics are most important to the education of youth; everything else is, more or less, a frill.

_____ 10. Good teachers try not to impose any cultural values on the student.

Key: 1. child-centered (C-C); 2. C-C; 3. subject-centered (S-C); 4. S-C; 5. C-C; 6. S-C; 7. S-C; 8. C-C; 9. S-C; 10. C-C.
Tally your score for each category and average them (divide by 5) to see where you stand.

not all experiences (doings) are necessarily educational and that a great many are, in fact, miseducative. So, while we might learn by doing, all doing is not a form of learning (Hook, 1973). This distinction exemplifies the difference between experimentalist and romantic naturalist thinking.

In historical context, we can appreciate the initial appeal of romantic naturalism. Many early progressives were keen to repudiate the assumption that children are innately evil (or are ordained as originally sinful). They were attracted to any idea that opened up possibilities for children to gain due consideration in the curriculum and that provided a foothold for active learning experiences in an institution that had long equated formal education with a stale uniformity of mental exercises and repressed physical motion. Anointing children in educational theorizing could bring activity and life to the school, freeing students from the timeworn but abstract and lifeless forms of schooling. Moreover, the progressive impulse to personalize schooling held possibilities for the outward extension of schooling, aligning it not with some elitist conceptions of high Western thought but with a recognition of something residing naturally in all human beings. As Boyd Bode (1938) put it, "The emphasis of progressive education on the individual, on the sinfulness of imposition, and on the necessity of securing free play for intelligence, is a reflection of the growing demand, outside of the school, for recognition of the common man" (p. 11).

This, however, did not prevent romantic naturalism from suffering early attacks from both conservative and progressive quarters. Critics targeted several theoretical problems. First, child-centered progressives were accused of advancing a form of education that denied children the central source of all learning—the individual wisdom of adults and the extended wisdom of humanity. To the conservatives, this meant that the power of the subject matter was eviscerated from the experience, an inexcusable failing. To the experimentalists, this meant that the learning would somehow proceed in a free form without any engagement with the social agenda of democracy. And both groups argued that the romantic naturalists failed to offer any vision of subject matter and any vision of society. Their abhorrence for the authority of direction and planning in the school experience led the romantic naturalists to support no systematic commitment to educating youths in a social or socially principled point of view. This not only removed the school from its historical role as an agency for democracy but also set the potential conditions for a form of antidemocratic education. Because the school program supported no social agenda, instead promoting only individualistic endeavors, it ran the risk of failing to systematically teach students the kinds of skills they would need to avoid being victims of antidemocratic authoritarian forces. Bode (1938) put it another way: "If

3-5 SCHOLARLY VOICES
Boyd Bode on Child-Centeredness

Boyd Bode was a progressive educator whose work was marked by trenchant criticism of a wide ideological range of viewpoints. Here he describes his dissatisfaction with child-centered thinking. Concerned that the progressive movement in education was drawing much of its inspiration from Rousseau, Bode warns against relying on child-centered thinking. Bode refers to the hope that education can rely on "interest, needs, growth, and freedom" as "pathetic." What do you think he means by this?

The faith of progressive education in the individual, and in the power of intelligence to create new standards and ideals in terms of human values and in accordance with changing conditions, entitles it to consideration as expressive of the spirit of democracy. As against this, however, stands the fact that it has never completely emancipated itself from the individualism and absolutism of Rousseau. Instead of turning to the ideal of democracy for guidance, it has all too often turned to the individual. It has nurtured the pathetic hope that it could find out how to educate by relying on such notions as interest, needs, growth, and freedom. (Bode, 1938, p. 10)

democracy is to have a deep and inclusive human meaning, it must have also a distinctive educational system" (p. 26). In Feature 3-5, Bode states his views against child-centeredness in strong terms.

Romantic naturalism was the by-product of those progressives who were absorbed in the individual and threatened by the limitations implied in any social theory or social mission of schooling. Although romantic naturalism sounds like a philosophy with little application to or basis in the realities of schooling, it did have its day in the educational sun both during the early stages of its development and again in the 1960s. The 1960s witnessed school reforms touting the value of open-ended experiences, self-directed learning, and facilitative teaching. The idea of open education and the open classroom encouraged a free form of teaching and learning, often in an open physical environment that resulted, in some cases, in classrooms without walls or doors. Popular best-selling authors preached a gospel of school renewal that portrayed emergent acts of love and compassion as the main basis for school improvement. Free and alternative schools, as well as concepts such as deschooling society (which implied that one could receive an education simply from freely chosen experiences in the wider society), gained popular currency. Much of this writing featured images of moribund and repressive schools that did little more than bore the life out of children

> **FIGURE 3-4**
> **Conceptual Features of Romantic Naturalism**
>
> **1.** *Ideal of the learner:* a self-educating force of nature whose education is best served with only minimal adult intervention
>
> **2.** *Ideal of society:* social fragmentation through multitudinous egoistic and individualistic pursuits
>
> **3.** *Ideal of the subject matter:* a content-neutral curriculum emphasizing free activity

and create unhappiness all around. Figure 3-4 summarizes the conceptual features of romantic naturalism.

EDUCATION IN THE RADICAL TRADITION

The romantic naturalist approach to education certainly could have been characterized as radical in its own right. Any view that essentially relativizes all school traditions and makes no effort to apply controlling principles to the school experience clearly has a radical element to it. But the radical philosophies discussed in this section are rooted primarily in an overtly ideological or political way of thinking that is, more often than not, explicitly designed to revolutionize, overthrow, or otherwise subvert the existing system of schooling. The social reconstructionist perspective, born during hurly-burly days of the Great Depression, was little more than an attempt to inject American schooling with a particular ideological outlook. Current radical thinking, often loosely categorized as postmodern in orientation, operates on a similar basis, although within a wide range of attendant political viewpoints.

Social Reconstructionism

To understand social reconstructionism, we must understand the fundamental social class analysis that gave it its start. During the 1920s and into the 1930s, a number of scholars vented their frustration with what they perceived as rampant class-based bias in the leadership and operation of the public schools. George Counts, who would emerge as the main historical voice of social reconstructionism, had preached this message throughout the decade of the Depression. His early work helped to expose some of the problems, showing, for instance, that disproportionately high numbers of student dropouts were from low-income families. He also examined school board memberships and found them to be comprised mainly of men drawn from the middle and upper classes. These general conditions, according to Counts (1922), encouraged the school to see its interests in terms not of the widest public good, but of the education of the wealthy and the accompanying promotion of the values of competitive and individualistic capitalism. The school, he alleged, was systemically, even ideologically, designed to perpetuate the socioeconomic status quo. It was the handmaiden of the ruling economic class, sustaining, instead of combatting, the evils of extreme poverty and social inequity.

Progressive thinkers had not given the problem of social class much standing in their philosophies. The child-centered romantic naturalists had no social theory behind their thinking whatsoever, and the experimentalists, although concerned about socioeconomic disparities, were not interested in framing an educational experience specifically designed to remedy a social problem. The experimentalists always linked education with democracy and expected the schools to produce an enlightened citizenry that could address its social problems. But they did not view the school as an instrument for dislodging or reforming a specific social ill.

So, it did not take long for the social class analysis offered by Counts and others to yield an educational philosophy that saw itself as an antidote to the crisis of classism in the schools. The thinking of the scholars who were earnestly offended by this perceived failing of the school on the socioeconomic front took shape in sharply ideological ways. Because the educational institution was itself accused by being ideological (deeply situated in the back pockets of business interest and socially conservative groups), some scholars had no reservations about flipping the ideological switch in the schools and forcing them in a direction that favored radical social transformation. One had to fight ideological fire, they claimed, with ideological fire.

Thus, social reconstructionism was born as a philosophy openly and unapologetically dedicated to educating youths in Socialist doctrine and the new social order it demanded. The duty of the teacher was to teach in a way that made a contribution to the social reconstruction of society along the lines of a collectivist Socialist society. Teachers had to understand that they were now caught up in a revolutionary struggle to wrest control of the school away from the ruling upper classes. This would call for abrupt and confrontational educational tactics. Counts (1932) stated the matter rather

© Peter D. Byron/PhotoEdit

The social reconstructionist philosophy is rooted in concerns over the school education of the poor.

bluntly: Education must "emancipate itself from the influence of the [ruling upper classes], face squarely and courageously every social issue, come to grips with life in all of its stark reality, establish an organic relation with the community, develop a realistic and comprehensive theory of welfare . . . and become less frightened than it is today at the bogeys of imposition and indoctrination" (pp. 9–10).

The educational plan was simple. Educators were not to fear indoctrination but to embrace it as a way to drive a stake through the heart of capitalistic-oriented schooling. In this way, education could become an enterprise dedicated to influencing students to accept the collectivist ideals of socialism, a position completely at odds with the experimentalist thinking of John Dewey. The social reconstructionists believed that this form of education was most suitable for democracy because their ideal of society involved not enlightened masses making reflective decisions based on a democratic ethic and the best available knowledge, but an indoctrinated citizenry prepared to defend the worthiness of a utopian social arrangement. Thus, the teacher became a kind of ideological missionary who emphasized the importance of economic equity, workers' rights, class analysis, and other collectivist ideals.

The social reconstructionists never gained much currency in the schools, but their criticisms remain a source of commentary. Today, the line of argumentation started by Counts continues to be played out by scholars claiming to embrace a critical theory of education. Critical theory aims to disclose all forms of injustice and inequity in schooling by revealing the interests served by the knowledge and actions brought to bear in the school setting. Critical theorists claim that the corporate ideology (capitalism) is behind the acts of injustice and inequity in schooling, although they also offer accusations of cultural hegemony or cultural imperialism, male authority, and white racism. The thesis is that the main function of schools is wedded to the reproduction of the socioeconomic order and the associated dominant groups. The school is said to offer knowledge and skills that empower the most privileged in a way that keeps social class divisions intact. Thus, the mode of analysis in this philosophy is to look closely for signs of how, not of whether, the school carries out its repressive mandate. Because schools do not openly tout their repressive actions, one has to search them out and make a case for how they function in the curriculum.

Critical theory is largely a theory or philosophy of protest, although some educators claim that they are involved in something known as critical pedagogy (Wink, 2000). McLaren (1989) states that critical pedagogy is about "how and why knowledge gets constructed the way it does, and how and why some constructions of reality are legitimated and celebrated by the dominant culture while others are clearly not" (p. 169). We can certainly appreciate the legacy of social reconstructionism in McLaren's statement. Concerns about dominant groups inevitably lead to a highly politicized form of teaching that encourages students to be more conscious of class, race, ethnic, and even gender differences, and more able to see their own victimization at the hands of society (or in the case of children from dominant groups, their own role as victimizers). Ideology stills prevails as the main educating force in the school. Figure 3-5 summarizes the conceptual features of social reconstructionism.

Postmodernism

Influenced by both conservative and some progressive philosophies, the public school is widely viewed as necessary to create the kind of society we live in. Conservatives embrace the grand narrative of the Western canon to bring insight to this process, while experimentalists embrace a set of values, attitudes, and general competencies believed to be required for informed participation in a democracy. These philosophies are accompa-

---

FIGURE 3-5

Conceptual Features of Social Reconstructionism

1. *Ideal of the learner:* a guardian of the highest principles of a collectivist doctrine

2. *Ideal of society:* a utopian social arrangement stressing economic and social equality

3. *Ideal of the subject matter:* politicized knowledge designed to promote the utopian causes of society

---

nied, with varying degrees of involvement, by so-called modernist assumptions. Faith in the idea of scientific progress, in rationalist thinking, in the power of evidence, in the reliability of social labels, and in the power of a common culture—all could be viewed, at least in part, as modernist in orientation. The postmodern perspective explodes these assumptions and actively seeks to "decenter" our way of viewing the world. This effort is motivated by a decidedly anti-Western sentiment, by a desire to expose and undermine "the privileging of Western patriarchal culture with its representations of domination rooted in a Eurocentric conception of the world" (Aronowitz and Giroux, 1991, p. 64). Postmodernists stress the value of individual initiative, the recognition of human intention, the unmasking of political ideology in knowledge, the taming of social control mechanisms in the school, and the general idea that society is marked by conflicting interests of class, gender, and culture.

Postmodernists are deeply involved in providing what might be called oppositional thought in the school experience. That is, they deny the validity of any grand claims about what is worth knowing and seek to preserve the dynamism of the lived experience in school, keeping the heterogeneity of the school experience intact. Thus, postmodernists challenge conventions and try to provide a better view of the plurality of thought in our experience. The school, which is perceived to be historically involved in transmitting established norms, becomes a place where knowledge is challenged, where its linkage to political ideology and to sources of power and domination is revealed. Such efforts are viewed as empowering because they lead to eye-opening moments that allow students to see themselves in a more authentic context. Oppositional thought also demands that the schools take an active role in revealing all forms of injustice and inequality, as well as the interests and institutions served by the knowledge transmitted by the schools.

Postmodernists believe that individuals need to escape from the forces of rationality in school. As a result, they are wary of the methods of science, arguing that science is really just an ideological cloak draped over acts of oppression. This is especially evident, they claim, in the manner in which science is used to create social categories in school. For example, special education labels, which typically include designations such as behaviorally disordered, emotionally disturbed, or learning disabled, might be viewed as instructional categories designed to offer special-needs children remedial education or other educational services. To the postmodernist, however, such categories must be "deconstructed" and understood in terms of the role they might play in sorting and slotting children in ways that result in the oppression of a disproportionately large number of minority and low-income children. As an instructional endeavor, special education is legitimated by a science of test scores, research findings, and other so-called objective data. Science validates both its existence and its utility. But the postmodernist frames special education in terms of its less obvious effects, which might include acknowledging how children in such settings suffer psychological handicaps that ultimately lead to the further deterioration of their academic competencies and life skills.

Postmodernists also place a strong emphasis on what might be called the "hidden curriculum," whereby school actions are justified by certain articulated intentions that give rise to certain latent or covert effects. For example, when teachers of mathematics teach, say, a set of computational sets, they are also, whether they know it or not, teaching certain attitudes toward mathematics, toward schooling, and toward various character or personality traits (such a patience, perseverance, and industry). These attitudinal concerns are part of the hidden curriculum. Postmodernists are strongly attracted to the idea of the hidden curriculum because it allows them to make certain statements about the subtext of schooling, about unstated and latent effects. For instance, when a teacher reminds children in a low-income school that they are all "such good workers," a postmodern analysis might deconstruct such a phrase as a latent reminder to the children that they are fated to be workers in a class-based society. When students are assigned the "Great Books" to read, the latent message is that only the thoughts and words of white European males have a claim on greatness. When schoolwork involves drudgery and keeps children from their heartfelt desires, the school could be interpreted as practicing a kind of breaking down of the spirit for the purposes of preparing the children for life roles that they would otherwise not embrace.

Postmodernists also value the concept of difference, a position decidedly at odds with virtually all other philosophical views of the school other than romantic naturalism. Because there are different ways of knowing, experiencing, and even labeling the world, the focus of learning has to be on these differences, on what is sometimes referred to as "otherness." To postmodernists, the conservative embrace of the Great Books represents a fundamental failure inspired by ethnocentrism and class bias (Aronowitz and Giroux, 1991). If the task of postmodernism is to help students develop unique identities, then they must be subjected to the full variance of experience, using narratives that reflect varied views of race, class, and gender. Marginalized or subordinate groups, usually women and minority groups, are especially important to the postmodern position because they represent a force that could be used to counter the dominant ideology. Such groups become a potential source of subversion, opposition, and ultimately transformation. The postmodernists' sympathy toward so-called subordinate groups, coupled with an uncontested denial, if not hatred, of dominant thinking, has sometimes resulted in the accusation that they are engaging politically correct thinking.

Because schools (and society in general) are believed to be heavily layered with corporate ideology, often peddled to the masses through the popular media, teachers are expected to keep an eye out for such incursions into the purposes and materials of the curriculum. But according to postmodernists, the mass of students must not be subjected to the transmission of knowledge, but should be taught to question knowledge, to see the misrepresentations in it, and to search for the imperialism, patriarchy, racism, and vulgar capitalism that has shaped it and that continues to sustain it.

Postmodernism, in the end, offers an escape for students from the social repressions inherent in knowledge and in the experience of living. Part of this freedom resides in the active questioning of everything that presumes to pass as truth or reason. But the process also embraces the idea of asking learners to look introspectively for a more authentic sense of self through meditation, intuition, imagination, and active interpretation of everyday events. This is part of the existentialist nature of postmodernism.

The postmodern educational route is sometimes so personal that much of the school experience resembles the features of romantic naturalism. For instance, in attempting to describe how a postmodern high school might begin to conduct its own version of education, Aronowitz and Giroux (1991) observe that the question about what will be studied "is a matter for local decision making" (p. 20). In the postmodern school, teachers and students have the final authority; no authority is granted in this matter to even legislative and governmental agents. "Instead," Giroux and Aronowiz continue, "students and teachers negotiate which courses, if any, are to be required" (p. 21). Teachers "try to persuade" students to engage in a certain

---

FIGURE 3-6
Conceptual Features of Postmodernism

1. *Ideal of the learner:* an emancipated individual seeking authentic meaning and identity in an ideologically layered world

2. *Ideal of society:* emancipated individuals and subordinate groups finding identity and understanding in a repressive society

3. *Ideal of the subject matter:* deconstructed knowledge, understood in relation to its linkage with the dominant ideology

---

regimen of courses. "The normal classroom now resembles an open classroom where small groups of students are simultaneously studying different aspects of the course of subject matter, and others are engaged in individual tutorials with the teacher or other knowledgeable persons" (p. 21). But these tutorials are decidedly political, which is where the comparison to the romantic naturalists begins to fray. Figure 3-6 summarizes the conceptual features of postmodernism; Feature 3-6 presents a hypothetical debate among proponents of the various philosophies of education.

SUMMARY

Philosophies of teaching play a crucial role in the classroom and school. They are the defining sources behind the considerable variations in teaching styles in classrooms and schools. This is not to say, however, that all philosophies necessarily have equal standing in the school. Fascist or authoritarian views, for instance, are obviously not reconcilable with the values of a democratic society. And where a philosophy seeks to inform a classroom, it must offer some insight into the three fundamental factors in the educative process: the learner, society, and the subject matter. In this way, a philosophy acts as a kind of screen through which ideas are filtered.

Three traditions of philosophical insight encapsulate the main positions on the purpose and practices of schooling. Conservative views are deeply subject-centered, still anchored in the psychology of mental discipline and very much wedded to the idea of transmitting the culture through the knowledge embodied in the traditional academic subjects and the Great Books. Progressive-experimentalist views are less mentalistic than the conservative views and are more attached to teaching the very skills, competencies, and attitudes needed to lead an intelligent life in a democratic society. Essential to this process is the involvement of the scientific method applied to social thinking. The romantic variant of the progressive education movement, rooted in the naturalist views of Rousseau, is child-centered. Finally, the radical tradition offers a social reconstructionist view that results in a politicized curriculum justified as the best way to rid the nation of capitalist oppression and a postmodern position that seeks inner understandings through the dislocation and deconstruction of dominant views.

QUESTIONS AND ACTIVITIES

1. Observe a teacher and make some determinations about the philosophical prejudices that might underpin his teaching. Interview him about why he does what he does.

2. Of the six orientations discussed in this chapter, where might your own views begin to settle? Is there a way to shape an eclectic approach to a philosophy of teaching, taking the best of each tradition?

3. Examine one phase of the school curriculum (e.g., multicultural education, the reading program, or the math program), and analyze the philosophical tradition behind it.

4. Get a copy of a school's mission statement, and analyze it in terms of the six orientations described in the chapter.

5. How might perennialists defend themselves against accusations of ethnocentrism?

6. What do perennialists mean when they declare the need for youths to be engaged in the permanent studies?

7. Conservatives share a commitment to the development of a common culture with experimentalists. Explain both the connection and the vital difference within it.

8. Ralph Tyler referred to philosophy as a screen through which ideas are filtered. Try another metaphor to explain the role of philosophy in teaching. In what way is philosophy like an engine, a foundation, a compass, or a recipe? How adequate are these metaphors? Construct your own metaphor.

9. Essentialist thinking thrived in the schools during the Cold War period in America. Why?

10. E. D. Hirsch wrote a book called *Cultural Literacy: What Every American Needs to Know.* If John Dewey wrote a book called *Cultural Literacy,* what might its subtitle be? Explain your choice.

3-6 DEBATING THE ISSUES
A Meeting of the Minds

Four friends, conducting their lives in a different reality from ours, sit down for coffee and conversation.

J.D. *(sipping his coffee)*: Well, George, it seems to me that, given the demise of Marxist-inspired societies on earth and the triumph of the free world, complete with its commitment to free market economies, that your social reconstructionist views have probably gotten quite a jolt.

G.C.: Not really, John. You're telling me that extreme poverty and social inequality still aren't problems on planet earth? It seems to me that the gaps between the rich and the poor have only widened since our day, and that there are still plenty of horrors associated with capitalism. Sweatshops, rampant materialism, inequitable health care, the suppression of worker rights, the abuse of the environment, and so on. If I could, I'd still go down there and try to make my case for using the school to socialize a generation of youths in Socialist causes.

J.R. *(in a French accent)*: But what madness is it that you're still proposing, George? The "chains of man" that encumbered children since the dawn of so-called civilization on earth hasn't fallen from their bodies since we left the planet. Now the invasion of man has crept even into the most intimate details of life. With the advent of the Internet, children can now push buttons on a computer and remove themselves almost entirely from engaging the world as their nature demands. No, if I could go down there I'd try to redirect the focus back to the inner spirit of the child in its natural condition. If you want to save children from the mutilations of our society, your only hope is to move inward.

11. Explain the term *experimentalism* and its association with the work of John Dewey.

12. What is the reconstruction of experience, and how is it vital to the work of John Dewey?

13. Explain the early attraction among progressive educators to romantic naturalism.

14. Here's one of Rousseau's aphorisms offered as advice to a student: "God makes all things good; man meddles with them and they become

G.C.: Do you honestly think, Jacques, that if we stroke the inner feelings of children we're going to build a better society?

J.D.: Hold on. This strikes me as interesting because George wants to tell children how to think and act, according to his own revolutionary ideology, and Jacques doesn't want to tell children anything for fear of crippling the possibilities for inner development. Neither position seems reconcilable with democracy, as I understand it.

R.H.: I've got to agree with John. We have our differences, but he and I at least believe that some common culture dedicated to a common conversation needs to be forged in the school. Children need to know something, and in my view, there is no better base of knowledge than what humanity has captured in the Great Books.

(Professor Postmodern enters the room and asks if she can join the group.)

Professor: I overheard your conversation and couldn't resist the chance of jumping in.

All together: Sure, sit down.

Extend the conversation, taking on the voice of Professor Postmodern. Where is the discussion likely to go, and how will each of the four other participants respond?

evil." Explain how this statement plays into a romantic naturalist view of the world.

15. In 1933, George Counts helped to author a report entitled *A Call to the Teachers of the Nation*. The report maintained that "teachers will have to emancipate themselves from the dominance of the business interests of the nation, cease cultivating the manners and association of bankers and promotion agents, repudiate utterly the ideal of material success as the goal of education, abandon the smug middle-class tradition on which they have been nourished in the past, acquire a realistic understanding of the forces that actually rule the world, and formulate a fundamental program of thought and action that will deal honestly and intelligently with the problems of industrial civilization" (p. 20). Do you believe that such things should be part of a teacher's responsibility? Why or why not?

16. Observe a classroom with an eye for evidence that supports or contradicts the social reconstructionist's view that public education serves capitalist interests.

17. Peter McLaren (1989) believes that teachers are treated in a way that makes them "clerks of the empire, whose dreams, desires and voices are often silenced in order to remove any distractions to industry's call for more entrepreneurial savvy among its future workers and its desire for a more compliant, devoted and efficient work force" (pp. 1–2). Do you agree? What evidence might support such a contention?

18. In what ways does postmodernism lead to child-centeredness?

19. What are the basic similarities between postmodernism and social reconstructionism?

20. Examine the literature used to teach English in middle or secondary school (language arts in elementary school). Conduct a postmodern analysis, looking for the dominant ideology used to color the worldviews of children, especially children from minority or subordinate groups.

REFERENCES

Adler, M. (1988). *Reforming education: The opening of the American mind.* (New York: Macmillan).

Adler, M. (1984). *The paideia program: An educational syllabus.* (New York: Macmillan).

Aronowitz, S., and Giroux, H. (1991). *Postmodern education: Politics, culture and social criticism.* (Minneapolis: University of Minnesota Press).

Bagley, W. (1907). *Classroom management.* (New York: Macmillan).

Bennett, W. J. (1993). *Book of virtues: A treasury of great moral stories.* (New York: Simon & Schuster).

Bennett, W. J. (1987). *James Madison high school.* (Washington, DC: U.S. Department of Education).

Bennett, W. J. (1986). *First lessons: A report on elementary education in America.* (Washington, DC: U.S. Department of Education).

Bode, B. H. (1938). *Progressive education at the crossroads.* (New York: Newson).

Committee of Ten. (1893). *Report of the Committee of Ten on secondary school studies.* (Washington, DC: National Education Association).

Counts, G. S. (1932). *Dare the schools build a new social order?* (New York: John Day).

Counts, G. S. (1922). *The selective character of American secondary education.* (Chicago: University of Chicago Press).

Dewey, J. (1938). *Experience and education.* (New York: Macmillan).

Dewey, J. (1916). *Democracy and education.* (New York: Free Press).

Finn, C., and Ravitch, D. (1987). *What do our 17-year-olds know?* (New York: Harper & Row).

Hirsch, E. D. (1987). *Cultural literacy: What every American needs to know.* (Boston: Houghton Mifflin).

Hook, S. (1973). John Dewey and his betrayers. In C. Troost (ed.), *Radical school reform: Critique and alternatives.* (Boston: Little, Brown).

Hutchins, R. M. (1972). The great anti-school campaign. In R. Hutchins and M. Adler (eds.), *The great ideas today.* (Chicago: Encyclopedia Britannica).

Hutchins, R. M. (1936). *The higher learning in America.* (New Haven, CT: Yale University Press).

McLaren, P. (1989). *Life in schools: An introduction to critical pedagogy in the foundations of education.* (New York: Longman).

McCraken, S. (1973). Quackery in the classroom. In C. Troost (ed.), *Radical school reform: Critique and alternatives.* (Boston: Little, Brown).

Tyler, R. W. (1949). *Basic principles of curriculum and instruction.* (Chicago: University of Chicago Press).

Van Doren, M. (1943). *Liberal education.* (New York: Henry Holt).

Wink, J. (2000). *Critical pedagogy: Notes from the real world.* (New York: Longman).

CHAPTER 4

The Laws and Ethics of Teaching

Professional Ethics
  LEGAL ETHICS AND THE IDEA OF "CONDUCT UNBECOMING"

Teacher Liability

Freedom of Expression
  TEACHERS' ACADEMIC FREEDOM
  TEACHERS' PERSONAL VIEWS
  STUDENTS' VIEWS

Teacher Tenure and Teacher Dismissal

Student Searches and Seizures

Summary

Questions and Activities

References

T
EACHERS OBVIOUSLY SHOULDER certain legal and ethical obligations. They have a legal duty to care for their students, which includes the responsibility to secure the safety of the classroom, to attend to the individual needs of the students, and to ensure that everyone has an equal opportunity to learn. Teachers are also expected to represent themselves as role models to the children of the school community, to make professionally defensible instructional decisions, and to abide by a code of professional ethics in their school behaviors. The ethics of teaching is grounded in the need to gain the respect and confidence of colleagues, students, and parents, and to strive to realize the highest ideals of democracy and to make the strongest commitment to learners in the school experience. It is as much a matter of professional conduct as of knowledge of subject matter and of good pedagogical and classroom management techniques.

In 1975, the National Education Association formally amended and readopted its own code of ethics for the profession. (See Figure 4-1.) According to the code, teachers are obligated to safeguard the safety of schoolchildren and to protect them from any form of social harassment or disparagement. This is supported not only from the standpoint of good pedagogy, in that no learning can take place if the safety and security of the learning environment is compromised, but also from the standpoint of the law, which subjects teachers to potential disciplinary actions if they fail to secure a safe and nondisruptive learning environment. The code also obligates teachers to widen the horizons of learning for children, to provide access to undistorted knowledge, and to encourage individualistic learning pursuits.

These ethical principles have their anchor in the idea of a democratic public education, in the desire to educate youths for informed participation in a pluralistic, constitutional democracy. As John Dewey (1916) once noted, a public school education is designed to broaden the base of experience for children in a way that transcends the more local or parochial nature of education in the home, church, or community. Children are expected to learn, see, and do enlightened things in the public school environment that they might not otherwise learn, see, or do. Society counts on the school to socialize each new generation in the skills, knowledge, dispositions, and values needed to contribute to its continuing growth and improvement. Thus, the ethical challenge in a public education is, among other things, to furnish a cosmopolitan experience that encourages independent inquiry, nurtures democratic principles, compels interactions with varied points of view, and ensures access to unpoliticized forms of information or knowledge.

FIGURE 4-1
NEA Code of Ethics for the Education Profession

Preamble

The educator, believing in the worth and dignity of each human being, recognizes the supreme importance of the pursuit of truth, devotion to excellence, and the nurture of the democratic principles. Essential to these goals is the protection of freedom to learn and to teach and the guarantee of equal educational opportunity for all. The educator accepts the responsibility to adhere to the highest ethical standards.

The educator recognizes the magnitude of the responsibility inherent in the teaching process. The desire for the respect and confidence of one's colleagues, of students, of parents, and of the members of the community provides the incentive to attain and maintain the highest possible degree of ethical conduct. The Code of Ethics of the Education Profession indicates the aspiration of all educators and provides standards by which to judge conduct.

The remedies specified by the NEA and/or its affiliates for the violation of any provision of this Code shall be exclusive and no such provision shall be enforceable in any form other than the one specifically designated by the NEA or its affiliates.

Principle I: Commitment to the Student

The educator strives to help each student realize his or her potential as a worthy and effective member of society. The educator therefore works to stimulate the spirit of inquiry, the acquisition of knowledge and understanding, and the thoughtful formulation of worthy goals.

In fulfillment of the obligation to the student, the educator—

1. Shall not unreasonably restrain the student from independent action in the pursuit of learning.

2. Shall not unreasonably deny the student's access to varying points of view.

3. Shall not deliberately suppress or distort subject matter relevant to the student's progress.

4. Shall make reasonable effort to protect the student from conditions harmful to learning or to health and safety.

5. Shall not intentionally expose the student to embarrassment or disparagement.

6. Shall not on the basis of race, color, creed, sex, national origin, marital status, political or religious beliefs, family, social or cultural background, or sexual orientation, unfairly—
   a. Exclude any student from participation in any program
   b. Deny benefits to any student
   c. Grant any advantage to any student

(continued)

FIGURE 4-1 *(continued)*
NEA Code of Ethics for the Education Profession

7. Shall not use professional relationships with students for private advantage.

8. Shall not disclose information about students obtained in the course of professional service unless disclosure serves a compelling professional purpose or is required by law.

Principle II: Commitment to the Profession

The education profession is vested by the public with a trust and responsibility requiring the highest ideals of professional service.

In the belief that the quality of the services of the education profession directly influences the nation and its citizens, the educator shall exert every effort to raise professional standards, to promote a climate that encourages the exercise of professional judgment to achieve conditions which attract persons worthy of the trust to careers in education, and to assist in preventing the practice of the profession by unqualified persons.

In fulfillment of the obligation to the profession, the educator—

1. Shall not in an application for a professional position deliberately make a false statement or fail to disclose a material fact related to competency and qualifications.

2. Shall not misrepresent his/her professional qualifications.

3. Shall not assist any entry into the profession of a person known to be unqualified in respect to character, education, or other relevant attribute.

4. Shall not knowingly make a false statement concerning the qualifications of a candidate for a professional position.

5. Shall not assist a noneducator in the unauthorized practice of teaching.

6. Shall not disclose information about colleagues obtained in the course of professional service unless disclosure serves a compelling professional purpose or is required by law.

7. Shall not knowingly make false or malicious statements about a colleague.

8. Shall not accept any gratuity, gift, or favor that might impair or appear to influence professional decisions or action.

Teachers, however, also have to understand their own rights and responsibilities in the school setting, as well as those of schoolchildren, in relation to the law. Ethical demands are, in fact, usually compelled by legal sanctions. Being aware of some of the fundamental issues in this area gives educators a working sense of how they might proceed with their own actions and behaviors, and how they might react to the actions and behaviors of others. Knowledge of the law allows teachers to err on the side of caution, compels them to think twice before acting, and lets them know when to seek professional advice. The reality is that the threat of lawsuits often looms in the school setting. A recent survey showed that 20 percent of school principals spend 10 hours a week documenting events to avoid litigation, and that 25 percent of principals have been involved in lawsuits or out-of-court settlements over the past two years (Zehr, 1999).

PROFESSIONAL ETHICS

The general terms of professional ethics are deeply influenced by legal considerations. As a result, certain guidelines, sanctioned by the courts, give us important direction when it comes to professional ethics. For instance, we can point to certain legal limits to a teacher's freedom of expression in the classroom. These are, generally speaking, ethical limits because they are designed in the interest of the public trust and are held to public accountability and public consequence. Hence, public school teachers need to be careful not to project religious or political views in their classrooms and not to use language or display behaviors that might be viewed as immoral or as "conduct unbecoming." Similarly, a teacher's personal life can come under scrutiny by school officials if they can show it to be relevant to the teacher's performance in the classroom. In some circumstances, even the sexual orientation of a teacher can be viewed as a relevant professional concern. Because the school community expects the teacher to be a role model to children, the teacher's personal life can be evaluated against some community standard of ethics and morality. The issue of ethics in teaching is not limited to the classroom.

Legal Ethics and the Idea of "Conduct Unbecoming"

The idea of "conduct unbecoming of a teacher" is a legalistic one. It is used to make a case against a teacher who presumably has violated a professional code of ethics, usually in relation to a moral issue. Conduct unbecoming is one of the main legal grounds for dismissing a teacher.

Personal Issues. Historically, school communities expected chaste behaviors from their teachers, who were supposed to be paragons of morality and virtue. Teachers who violated the moral norms of a community often found themselves without a job. At the turn of the twentieth century, some of the moral restrictions placed on teachers, especially female teachers, bordered on the absurd, including prohibitions against dancing, immodest dressing, and dating. Today, two questions prevail: (1) What reasonable moral norms can a school hold teachers up against? and (2) How far into the personal aspects of teachers' lives can these norms reach?

Teachers, like most professionals, believe that their personal life is their own business and no one else's. But, unlike many other professionals, teachers must understand that certain aspects of their private lives can be viewed as relevant to their professional responsibilities. This is because of the role model expectation and the belief that certain personal behaviors, if they become publicly known, can negatively affect a teacher's professional work.

The working principle in dismissing a teacher for conduct unbecoming is showing a nexus or connection to the teacher's performance in the classroom (Fischer, Schimmel, and Kelly, 1999). If a particular moral or ethical violation can be judged to be adversely affecting a teacher's potential to fulfill the teaching mission of the school, dismissal proceedings can go forward. This criterion, however, leaves any number of behaviors open to judgment. Serious criminal convictions, such as for felonies, can quickly and easily result in a teacher's dismissal. Any violent crime, and especially any serious crime involving a child, is, by its very nature, viewed as immoral and as evidence of an unfitness to teach. Any serious criminal conviction involving sexual or physical assault or the use of a gun, or any crime specifically targeted toward children would obviously be solid grounds for dismissal. However, other behaviors that are much less obviously immoral are more problematic.

Judgment of the moral turpitude of a teacher in relation to lesser criminal offenses, such as shoplifting, the possession of small amounts of marijuana, or speeding, will depend on the circumstances and on the evidence pertaining to the effect of the crime on the classroom performance of the teacher. For instance, can a teacher be dismissed, on grounds of conduct unbecoming, if he or she is convicted of drunk driving. The question immediately goes to the issue of whether such a crime can be established to negatively affect the performance of the teacher in the school (Fischer, Schimmel, and Kelly, 1999). Thus, the extent to which the drunk driving charge is publicly known might be a factor. A drunk driving arrest in another state during summer months might not even become an issue, but one that occurs in front of the school in broad daylight after school hours, and hits the front page of the local newspaper, is another matter. In addition, the degree to which the offense represents an established pattern of behavior, speaking to a defect in the character of the teacher, is a factor; it makes a difference if this was the fifth drunk driving charge as opposed to the first. Other contextual factors could also come into play. Was this a high school mathematics teacher or a teacher with a specific charge, as some health and physical education teachers carry, to teach about the dangers of drunk driving? If the latter, the teacher's publicly known problem with drinking and driving could be viewed as directly undermining his or her chances of conducting an effective educational experience with the children. Is there evidence that the parents have lost trust in the educator? Has a cloud of fear, distrust, and disrespect settled over the relationship between the teacher and the parents? If so, the teacher is again very much at risk of being dismissed.

Can these rules about the moral conduct of teachers also be applied to the personal lifestyle of the teacher, such as to his or her sexual preferences? For instance, should homosexual or transsexual teachers actually have to fear for their jobs? The fact is that some school districts still find homosexuality to be a moral or ethical breach. But it is only a breach with consequences if the district can demonstrate that it might undermine the teacher's ability to effectively teach in the classroom (Fischer, Schimmel, and Kelly, 1999). Thus, there would have to be some public knowledge of the homosexuality and some evidence of particular patterns of "homosexual" behavior that might be construed as contributing to a disruptive climate for teaching or that might result in distressed relations with parents. Homosexual teachers who lead a discreet lifestyle will not likely face any accusation of moral unsuitability. The transgendered teacher, however, is in an entirely different legal situation. A male teacher who undergoes a sex change over the summer and returns to school in the fall as a female is open to the accusation of conduct unbecoming. Obviously, there is no way for this action not to gain public notice. In the few cases tested on this issue, the main argument made against the teacher was that students and parents were so confused, and in some cases so frightened, by the sex change that healthy and educative engagements between the teacher and the students (and parents) were unlikely, if not impossible.

The issue of a teacher's moral suitability, as it relates to sexual matters, manifests in other ways as well. For instance, several school districts have attempted to dismiss unwed mothers, arguing that the condition of pregnancy outside of the institution of marriage violates the community's moral values and represents a living contradiction to the school's sex education message (Fischer, Schimmel, and Kelly, 1999). From the legalistic point of view, the unwed status of the teacher would have to be publicly known, but other contextual factors would also be weighed. It would likely matter, for instance, if the teacher worked at the high school as opposed to elementary school level, or if the teacher actually taught sex education. It would also likely matter if parents and students came to the support of the teacher. The same kinds of issues would prevail if a school sought to dismiss a teacher, on moral grounds, for unwed cohabitation.

Generally, conduct unbecoming only bears consequences when it can be shown to adversely affect the ability to teach. Homosexual activity, drunk driving, and small-time shoplifting, do not stand alone as justifiable grounds for dismissal (Fischer, Schimmel, and Kelly, 1999). If the teacher's competence in the classroom cannot be connected to any of these actions, it will not likely emerge as a viable legal case. Most felonious crimes, of course, are automatically seen as affecting teacher competence. And any immoral conduct involving a student, including sexual advances toward and drug or alcohol use with students, is usually viewed in the same light.

Classroom Issues. Teachers have an ethical obligation to conduct themselves in the classroom in a way that reflects the school's educational mission and that abides by professional standards of behavior. This means that teachers need to be attentive to the nature of their learners, to the overall purposes and policies of the school, to relevant laws and regulations, and to other factors related to the values of our society and the nature of the subject matter taught. These are a few of the main sources that help to shape and define professional conduct in the classroom.

Professional educators, however, are also expected to respect parental views on schooling and to reflect, within certain limits, various community prerogatives. The exercise of local/community control is, after all, one of the unique traditions of America's decentralized system of public schooling. But this can get complicated if community-supported desires, as parents might shape them, are at odds with some professionally grounded argument for the education of children. A teacher could find herself in a position of advancing a professional cause without community support or of rejecting a community cause that fails to meet a professional standard of performance. If teacher judgment is found to be out of alignment with community wishes, the resolution of the problem rests on a determination of the professional worth of the teacher's position. This is an easy task if the community prerogatives are outrageously misguided—for instance, if it is racist in its orientation and demands racist kinds of behaviors from teachers. But the schisms between teacher judgment and community desires are usually more subtle than this.

For instance, teachers generally cannot conduct themselves in the classroom in a manner that might be construed as supporting a religious or

Professional educators are expected to respect parental views on schooling and to reflect, within certain limits, various community prerogatives.

denominational point of view, even if the community desires it. (We'll discuss this issue more thoroughly in Chapter 9.) Teachers must also be conscious about avoiding any entanglement with partisan political views. Teachers are, by professional obligation, not allowed to proselytize or indoctrinate students into supporting or disdaining particular political perspectives. A teacher, for instance, may not openly endorse political candidates in the classroom or support political positions on controversial public issues without running the risk of being punished for unprofessional conduct. The teacher has an obligation to remain as neutral as possible on political matters and to present multiple points of views in the interests of broadening student understanding. With regard to religion, the obligation is to maintain a secular line of inquiry when dealing with religious matters. It is important to note that these rules apply only to the classroom and school, and not to the teacher's personal life. Unlike lifestyle issues related to moral behavior, the religious and political views and actions of teachers, when exhibited outside of school, are basically protected rights. In the arena of politics, there are a few exceptions, which will be dealt with later.

The tension between community mores, ethical restrictions against proselytizing, and a teacher's view of an educationally sound experience was evident in a recent case in Idaho (Richardson, 1993). Three high school teachers were suspended by the school board for allowing lesbian parents to speak to a group of students. The suspension unleashed deep community divisions. Action groups mobilized to defend the teachers or the school board. The problem was that some parents were very much against any interaction between their children and avowed adult homosexuals. One parent stated that "the majority of the school is Christian and Mormon and they're opposed to homosexuality. [The lesbian speakers] just shouldn't have been brought in" (Richardson, 1993). Other parents viewed the teachers' decisions to invite homosexuals to the classroom, without their prior consent, as a failure to respect parental rights. But do parents actually have a right to tell teachers what their children can or cannot experience in the school? Can the religious or political values of a community actually filter into the public school classroom? Does a teacher have an ethical responsibility to get approvals from parents before proceeding with a pedagogic strategy? Of course, the school must be sensitive to parental views or demands. And schools, in fact, often draft policies that allow students to opt out of certain experiences in the interest of community responsiveness and are required, under most conditions, to allow excusals for religious reasons.

What is interesting in the Idaho case is that the teachers' decision to invite a group of lesbians to their classroom, which was viewed by some parents as unprofessional and unethical, could also be viewed as fundamentally ethical, inspired by a professional obligation to broaden the school experience of students in a way that could strengthen their understanding of differences in their society. A key component in judging the teachers' success in doing this was determining whether the experience had educational merit or whether it involved promotion of a homosexual lifestyle, which some parents alleged. The course taught by the teachers was called American Character, and the topic of homosexuality, as it turned out, had a valid place in the textbook that was used in the class and was covered in the social studies curriculum. Eventually, the teachers were reinstated, the topic of homosexuality was deemed to be within the educational purposes of the school curriculum, and no evidence was found to support the idea of promoting a homosexual lifestyle.

Ethical considerations always pervade the classroom. Teachers, for instance, cannot use vulgar language or hateful language, nor can they verbally abuse students. Teachers are expected to protect the moral sanctity of the classroom and to be vigilant about any student-to-student harassment or inappropriate language or behaviors by students in the classroom. Their teaching methods are also subject to ethical screenings. Controversial teaching methods that walk the line between the ethical and the unethical

The public school teacher has an obligation to maintain a secular line of inquiry when dealing with religious matters.

provide interesting insights in this area. For example, what if an English teacher wants to encourage youngsters to be honest with their language and to openly express themselves in their writing assignments, with no fear of punishment, and if this results in a series of essays full of vulgar and highly offensive language? This teacher ostensibly is working within professional lines, trying to respond to the learners' lives and voices, and trying to find a way to enhance good writing. Can the teacher be charged with an ethical or professional infraction?

This is essentially the question that was tested in a suburban St. Louis high school in the mid-1990s. An English teacher with a reputation for using creative and innovative methods of teaching assigned her eleventh-grade students, all African American, to write and later produce a script for a play. The teacher abided by a long-held "no censorship" policy in her classroom, believing that it is important to encourage students to write freely and creatively from the basis of their experience and imagination. As the playwriting assignment went forward, the students decided that they wanted to videotape their plays being performed. The plays dealt with themes such as sex, teenage pregnancy, gangs, drugs, killings, and imprisonment, and the tapes showed the students using words like "m----r-f----r," "b---h," and "n----r" with some regularity. When the principal discovered the tapes, the teacher was suspended and eventually fired (Dieg-mueller, 1995).

Where such controversy prevails, it is incumbent on the teacher to demonstrate the educational viability of the classroom-based experience, making a case for it from the standpoint of its educational purpose and the maturational age of the student. It is also probably wise, as a matter of ethics and good pedagogy, to try to anticipate any problems that might arise under such circumstances and to apprise parents and students beforehand of the educational nature and purpose of the experience. The educational intentions of the teacher in the St. Louis case were not in question. The teacher had gotten positive reviews for her teaching in the past and had been widely praised in professional circles for her student-centered tech-niques. Although the teacher's action violated the school's formal policy on student profanity, this case was really about ethical and professional judg-ment. That is, could this particular activity be viewed as educationally sound, from the position of encouraging good writing and communication skills, while allowing, if not privileging, the use of vile language among the students? Some of the parents who saw the tape felt that the teacher was miseducating the youths into believing that such language was acceptable. Others argued that the teacher, who was white, was reinforcing vicious stereotypes by allowing the students to behave in such a manner (Dieg-mueller, 1995). In a case like this one, the answer to the question of profes-sionalism is debatable; in any event, the teacher was not reinstated.

But teachers often find themselves caught in potentially controversial teaching situations. What if a teacher assigns an essay or book laced with profane language or shows an R-rated movie in class? In 1999, Chicago school officials recommended the dismissal of a teacher who showed a fourth-grade class the R-rated movie *Striptease* (Class sees *Striptease,* 1997). In the movie, Demi Moore, who plays a stripper, appears partially nude. In this case, the teacher's actions could not be determined to be motivated by any educational purpose, and the movie itself, with its bawdy title and its R-rating, was fundamentally inappropriate to the age level of the children. In the same year, a school district in Oklahoma settled a claim by students who alleged that a teacher put them in a shower stall smeared with feces as part of a history lesson on slave ships ("Slave ship" case settled, 1998). If the allegations were true, the teacher might have been motivated by some per-verse desire to offer a realistic historical experience to the children. But here, the educational purpose was overwhelmed by the harm done to the children in subjecting them to a callous and unnerving experience.

Teachers also have used techniques that offended the ethical sensibilities of some administrators and parents but that proved, in the end, to be edu-

Teachers must be certain that all classroom-based experiences have a clear educational purpose and are responsive to the maturational age of the student.

cationally worthy. One well-known case, *Keefe v. Geanakos* (1969), again involving a high school English teacher, concerned an assignment that required students to read an *Atlantic Monthly* essay containing repeated references to the word "m----rf----r." Some parents complained, and the teacher, after refusing to comply with restrictions placed on his teaching, was dismissed. But when the courts examined the assignment in relation to the educational purposes of the school and reviewed the actual usage of the word in the essay, which was characterized by the judge as "scholarly and thoughtful," the teacher's action was supported. Interestingly, the judge concluded that "the sensibilities of offended parents are not the full measure of what is proper in education" (Fischer, Schimmel, and Kelly, 1999, p. 166), a point that returns us to the original tension explored between community (parental) and professionally argued views of learning.

Among the newer ethical issues being raised in classrooms is the ethics of testing. Increasingly, efforts at accountability have resulted in equating good schooling with high-test scores and in using state-sanctioned test measures as the main, if not sole, variable in judging teacher effectiveness. This has, unfortunately, led to growing incidences of teacher involvement in test-related misconduct.

Some teachers, for instance, have copied test booklets for the purpose of using them to help prepare students for upcoming exams. For example, in Rhode Island, state officials temporarily canceled English and mathematics exams after discovering teachers had used previous tests to prepare their students (Archer, 1999). A few teachers apparently had gotten into the habit of photocopying the exam from the previous year and using it as a platform for test preparation. If this resulted in actual test items being given to the students in preparation for the exam, it would certainly qualify as unprofessional teacher behavior, because such a practice would invalidate the exam. But teaching to the test does not always result in accusations of misconduct. In fact, some schools openly embrace it as a way to promote high achievement. Some school leaders argue that teachers have an obligation to teach students what tests will ask of them. So, rather than following the exam exactly, some teachers might track it topically in order to ensure that what they are teaching will pay a dividend on the test. To some, this is a borderline ethical transgression; to others, it is an acceptable form of pedagogy.

Some teachers also have been less than vigilant in following proper testing protocols and in some cases have been accused of altering student exams by erasing wrong answers and replacing them with correct ones. In the Houston Independent School District, a nine-month inquiry uncovered irregularities at 6 of the system's 280 schools. Investigators found that students were given oral prompting during the state exam, that answer keys were used to correct student answers, and that general test security was lacking (Johnston, 1999). State officials in Texas also put eleven school districts on notice, asking for an explanation for the high number of erasures found on their state tests over the years. Erasure mark analysis often raises a flag of suspicion. The state apparently has data on the number of erasures that can be reasonably expected on its tests, and anything falling outside those expectations becomes potential grounds for investigation. Figure 4-2 summarizes what might constitute conduct unbecoming.

TEACHER LIABILITY

The dismissal of teachers on the grounds of conduct unbecoming is one matter, but what legal liability do teachers carry for their behavior if students are injured at school under their watch? For example, if a child breaks an arm in a physical education class, can the physical education teacher be

---

FIGURE 4-2
Generalizations About the Idea of Conduct Unbecoming

1. The private life and actions of a teacher may be viewed as a professional concern if they can be linked in any way to the classroom performance of the teacher.

2. Felonious criminal charges against a teacher typically are prima facie grounds for dismissal; misdemeanor charges against a teacher may result in dismissal if they show some nexus or connection to the teacher's performance in the classroom.

3. The sexual orientation and the lifestyle choices of a teacher, including the decision to cohabitate outside of marriage, are private matters unless they can be shown to negatively affect the teacher's performance in the classroom.

4. The use of vulgar, hateful, or obscene language in the classroom by the teacher may be grounds for dismissal; the use of vulgar, hateful, or obscene language in the context of a school assignment or activity may be grounds for dismissal unless it can be shown to have a linkage to an expressed educational purpose that is within the boundaries of the school's mission and appropriate to the maturational level of the student.

5. Proselytizing a religious, political, or lifestyle point of view in the classroom may be grounds for dismissal.

---

held liable? If a student is mugged on a class trip, might the teacher be legally accountable?

Generally, a four-step process is followed when teachers are implicated in liability cases in school: (1) Did the teacher have a duty of care for the student at the time of the injury? (2) Was this duty breached by negligence? (3) Was there a causal connection between the purported negligence and the resulting injury? and (4) Did an actual injury result?

The concept of duty of care involves determining who was responsible for the supervision of students at the time of a given incident. Because teachers and administrators are considered "in loco parentis" (in the place of the parents), they have a general duty of care for all students. Specifically, they are expected to act with the same level of discretion and authority that a "normal" parent would display in a similar situation.

With regard to negligence, there must be an individual or individuals specifically charged with the duty of care. If an injury occurs under the territorial watch of a teacher—whether in the classroom or study hall or on the playground—there is little question about where the duty of care resides. But children cannot be supervised at every moment and in every

© Royalty Free/Corbis

Teachers working in vocational education shops, gymnasiums, and science labs must supervise students closely and give clear instructions.

situation and circumstance of schooling. When children go to the bathroom, for example, teachers are not expected to accompany them, although this might be the case with a special-needs learner or very young child. If an incident occurs as a student is moving between classrooms or on the way to the bathroom, the issue of duty of care may not apply to a particular teacher. This was the case in an elementary school in Georgia, where a teacher was exonerated from liability when a 6-year-old girl went to the bathroom unescorted and was sexually assaulted by a male teacher. The teacher was not obligated to escort the child because there was no foreseeable danger in the act of going to the bathroom (McCarthy, Cambron-McCabe, and Thomas, 1998).

Where students are gathered together for any stretch of time in the school, school personnel have a general duty of care. School personnel typically supervise study halls, playgrounds, and even parking lots. This author knows of one middle school that fails to provide any teacher supervision in its girls' locker room because it has no female physical education teachers on staff. If a serious injury occurs in the locker room, the school will be in danger of being found liable, because the duty of care (of supervision) clearly is not being fulfilled. Some public high schools have been sued for breaching their duty of care by parents whose children were injured or killed in car crashes after being allowed to leave campus during the lunch hour (Richard, 1999). The implication is that only a closed, vigilantly supervised campus can fulfill the duty of care. The courts, however, have not been clear in determining how much responsibility is accorded to the school once students leave campus.

Once duty of care is established, how is negligence determined in liability cases? The basic question here is to what extent a teacher's lack of vigilance, action, or foresight was related to the occurrence of an injury. For example, could the teacher have reasonably foreseen the collapse of a bookshelf that broke a student's arm? Were there any warning signs that the bookshelf might collapse? Did the teacher do anything to remedy the problem or protect students from potential injury, such as roping off the area until the shelf could be dismantled or repaired? Similarly, if a student is injured during recess, was the injury a function of the normal events associated with playground activity, or was it due to foreseeable circumstances that the teacher ignored or to a lack of proper supervision or instruction?

Determining appropriate levels of supervision depends on the circumstances of the school and on factors related to age and maturity of and the school's experience with the student, as well as the specific nature of the activity. Obviously, teachers working in vocational education shops, gymnasiums, and science labs are expected to provide increased supervision and more safety instructions, because there are known dangers in these settings that the teacher must anticipate, specifically caution against, and vigilantly guard against. Given awareness of potential danger, teachers must provide direct supervision as opposed to general supervision (Valente and Valente, 1998). This extends to the playground and to other contexts involving students known to have violent tendencies. Stricter supervision is also expected from teachers working with very young children, special-needs students, and students who have a history of problematic or recalcitrant behavior. Children age 7 and under are considered incapable of determining the degree of care necessary to prevent injury and are therefore rarely considered liable for their own injuries (Jasper, 1998, p. 74).

In short, teachers are expected to prevent foreseeable problems, weighing factors related to the nature of the learner, the special circumstances of the classroom, and any other emergent conditions. In their classrooms, they are expected to be on the scene and to be watchful. If a group of students is left unattended in the classroom and something happens, the teacher is clearly at risk of being found liable. But if a student, in clear violation of specific safety instructions and repeated interventions by the teacher, inadvertently sets his shirt ablaze when fooling around with a Bunsen burner during a science experiment, the teacher would have a good defense against a charge of negligence. The law essentially demands reasonable and prudent supervision and preventative action; there is no expectation of telepathic powers or of superhuman ability.

The third factor in assessing liability involves the principle of proximate cause, whereby a given injury can be clearly established as resulting from negligence. Sometimes, events occur in a classroom that have less relation to teacher negligence than to other factors. For example, if a fight breaks out in a classroom and a student is injured, some determination will have to be made about whether the fight was spontaneous and not foreseeable or whether the teacher should have been able to foresee and prevent it. And even if the fight occurred in an unsupervised classroom, authorities would have to determine whether a lack of supervision was the proximate cause of the injury. Perhaps no amount of supervision could have prevented the event from occurring, or perhaps the injury that ostensibly resulted from the fight was a preexisting injury suffered under circumstances that had nothing to do with the fight. As Jasper (1998, p. 73) notes, the courts use a "but for" test: Would the injuries have occurred but for the negligence of the teacher?

Finally, without real injury there is no real negligence. Therefore, establishing the validity of an injury is crucial to the general analysis used to determine liability. A manifest injury, such as a broken arm, is not an issue, but complications arise when students claim to suffer from ambiguous medical ailments, such as a stomach ache or mental distress. Feature 4-1 gives a set of scenarios that provide an opportunity to apply the four-step process for determining liability.

School districts are aware of their potential liability. They often provide liability coverage for their teachers, as do local teacher unions. School districts also commonly ask parents to sign consent forms releasing them from potential liability when students are engaged in activities outside of the school, such as field trips and sporting events. However, there is still a legal expectation, irrespective of the waiver, that the school will protect and secure the safety and welfare of children. And if they are negligent, the school and the involved teachers still can be found liable. Figure 4-3 summarizes some key issues in teacher liability.

FREEDOM OF EXPRESSION

Once a professional educator walks into a school, his or her First Amendment rights are subject to some restriction. The teacher's rights are not completely voided in the school. But the protection of the teacher's expressed views will always be weighed against factors pertaining to the

4-1 RESEARCH INQUIRY
Applying Knowledge of Liability

Here are three scenarios that require you to apply your knowledge of teacher liability. Remember the four components in the determination of teacher liability: duty of care, breach of duty, proximate cause, and validity of injury. Assuming that any injuries described are valid, for each scenario design a set of questions that will help you better establish whether the teacher was negligent.

1. A fourth-grade student is badly hurt while walking unescorted, with the teacher's permission, to the bathroom. He trips over materials left on the floor in the hallway by students in his classroom after they worked on a hallway bulletin board.

2. A student in a high school English class submits an essay to her teacher describing suicidal thoughts. She has been exploring this theme in her writing for over a month with the support of the teacher, who finds her work thoughtful and who has given her literary works to read dealing with the same theme. The student shows no outward signs of being depressed or despondent. In fact, her demeanor could be described as cheery. The next week, she commits suicide.

3. In kindergarten class, the children are working on an art project that requires them to glue together toothpicks. One of the children takes a toothpick and, in an unprovoked act, sticks it into the ear of another child, causing serious damage.

maintenance of quality educational experiences in the school. In other words, teacher speech is not protected if it is viewed as counter to the promotion of the central educational services of the school. Academic freedom is curtailed in the same way as are certain freedoms of association, personal speech, and even choice in personal appearance.

Teachers' Academic Freedom

Let us start with the concept of academic freedom, which was born in the context of German higher education, where scholars were given the freedom, unconstrained by government interference, to search for and to teach "the truth" (Hudgins and Vacca, 1995). In America, academic freedom is a derivative of the First Amendment right to free speech. It allows educators

FIGURE 4-3
Generalizations About Teacher Liability

1. School personnel have a legal duty of care for all students to the fullest extent possible.

2. Duty of care means that teachers need to make reasonable and prudent decisions to ensure the safety and security of the school environment.

3. The standards of reasonableness change depending on the characteristics of students and the nature of the school activity. Very young children and special-needs learners require stricter supervision. School environments that contain special dangers, such as vocational education shops and science laboratories, also require stricter supervision.

4. To avoid charges of negligence, teachers need to demonstrate reasonable foresight regarding circumstances that might lead to the injury of a student.

5. There is no negligence and no liability unless a real injury occurs.

to make decisions about reading materials, teaching methodologies, and study topics that may not always be popular with the community, school district, or government. It encourages experimentation with ideas and supports an open climate of criticism and debate. Academic freedom is a cornerstone of higher education in America, and it has also been applied, in a highly qualified way, to the K–12 setting.

As discussed previously, teachers are expected to exercise some independence and control in their classrooms. They need to have the freedom to select different pedagogic strategies and to make adjustments in the operation of the classroom based on the diagnosis of emergent problems and needs. This, however, does not translate into freedom to assign any topic or reading material or to try any unconventional or radical form of pedagogy they want to. All teacher actions have to meet some standard of professionalism. Teachers are essentially free to choose topics, materials, and teaching strategies, as long as their decisions are professionally defensible. This means that teacher judgments on these matters must be within the boundaries of the school's expressed educational purposes, appropriate for the age and maturity of the students, and not disruptive to the teaching/learning process of the school. For instance, a teacher will not have much of a leg to stand on if he insists on using pornographic readings to motivate adolescent boys to become better readers or if he uses blatantly racist materials without having a clear and high-minded instructional purpose or objective. In the former case, there are obvious standards of morality that would be violated, as well as issues pertaining to the appropriateness of the material

4-2 THE HISTORICAL CONTEXT
The Scopes Monkey Trial

The Scopes monkey trial, held in Dayton, Tennessee, in the summer of 1925, is considered by many to be the county's greatest courtroom trial. It reflected an emerging conflict between science and religion, and between traditional views of the world and more modern scientific ones. It pitted two legal titans—Clarence Darrow and William Jennings Bryan—against each other and supplied the nation with grandiose and dramatic courtroom scenes documented by the great American commentator H. L. Mencken.

But in the end, the Scopes monkey trial was really all about academic freedom. A young science teacher, John Thomas Scopes, had chosen to teach about evolution in his high school class, in violation of a Tennessee statute that explicitly stated that public schools cannot be used to "teach any theory that denies the story of the divine Creation of man taught in the Bible, and to teach that man has descended from lower order of animals." Scopes refused to follow the directive, believing that to do so amounted to teaching less than respectable science, an academic freedom issue he fought with the help of Darrow. But the statute was clear, as was Scopes' violation of it. The jury found him guilty, resulting in a $100 fine, which was later overturned on a legal technicality. Tennessee's statute would be eventually struck down as unconstitutional on the grounds that it represented an establishment of a religious point of view in public schooling.

based on age and maturity levels. In the latter case, there would also be issues of morality, linkage to school purposes, and the potential for disruptive classroom interactions.

Similarly, teachers cannot use the concept of academic freedom to justify ignoring or omitting prescribed course content. The courts have ruled that the content of the curriculum (but not the teaching methodology) is largely a matter of local school board authority, typically granted by state legislatures. Some schools encourage teachers to take a more daring approach to the content base of the curriculum, advocating different ways of capturing and even supplementing the content. But the content itself cannot be ignored in the name of academic freedom. Controversial topics and ideas have a place in the classroom, as long as they are related to the subject matter that the teacher has been assigned to teach. The famous Scopes monkey trial, highlighted in Feature 4-2, speaks to the historical power of the state in academic freedom cases.

The authority of local school boards over the curriculum was strengthened in the 1988 Supreme Court ruling in *Hazelwood v. Kuhlmeier*. Although the case dealt with the free speech rights of students, the ruling gave public school authorities wide discretion in dealing with controversial content in the school. But a school board's decisions cannot be idiosyncratic. For example, any decision to exclude material from the curriculum must be rooted in educational concerns. That is, restrictions on what teachers teach and what materials they use must be solidly based in arguments over the educational viability of the topics or materials, and not on a particular religious or political platform.

In a manner of speaking, the courts have tried to define the difference between the idea of censorship and the idea of educational judgment. School boards that insist on the removal of certain materials because they are offensive to certain political or religious standards in the community are engaging in censorship if their argument does not extend to the educational value of the material. Teachers are held to the same standard. Thus, if a teacher refuses to teach a certain book or deal with a certain topic because it conflicts with her personal political, religious, or philosophical beliefs, she is engaging in ideologically inspired censorship and can be dismissed. But a school board can decide not to allow the use of certain materials if it can show that the students do not have the emotional maturity needed to deal with the materials, that the materials themselves advance no palpably significant educational objectives, that the materials might create a condition that undermines the entire educational process of learning in the school, or that the materials violate the basic standards of civility. When decisions are made for legitimate educational reasons, they are not acts of censorship as much as they are acts of educational judgment.

Most schools like to leave these decisions to their teachers, but differences in opinion can occur. In Alabama, an English teacher assigned her high school junior class the novel *Welcome to the Monkey House,* by Kurt Vonnegut. The controversial assignment led the principal to dismiss the teacher, who was told that the story was "literary garbage'" condoning "the killing off of elderly people and free sex" (Thomas, Sperry, and Wasden, 1998, p. 162). But the teacher fought the dismissal. In *Parducci v. Rutland,* (1970), the issue before the Supreme Court was whether the dismissal was an act of censorship that violated the teacher's academic freedom or a valid, educationally defensible judgment by the principal attesting to the unprofessional behavior of the teacher. Was the story inappropriate to the maturity level of the students? Was it outside the educational purposes of the school? Did it cause a disruptive environment for learning? The Court ruled in favor of the teacher. In the words of the Court, "Since the board has failed to show either that the assignment was inappropriate reading for high school juniors, or that it created a significant disruption to the educational processes of this school, the Court concludes that the teacher's dismissal constituted an unwarranted invasion of her First Amendment right to academic freedom" (Thomas, Sperry, and Wasden, 1991, p. 162).

Teachers' Personal Views

There are, of course, other forms of freedom that involve teachers. Among the more controversial ones is the teacher's right to express personal views in public and in the school. Fundamentally, a teacher's First Amendment right to free speech is protected in the context of the school. If a teacher is upset about a certain school reform strategy or a particular funding referendum, she has the right to express her views. But, even here, there are a few constraints imposed on this freedom.

First, teachers' right to express themselves can be curtailed if their views have a negative effect on their performance in the classroom or on the overall educational operation of the school. In the famous *Pickering v. Board of Education* (1968) case, a teacher wrote a highly critical letter to a local newspaper about the manner in which the school board and superintendent were handling some school financing issues. The strongly worded letter contained false statements that were damaging to the reputations of certain school board members and school administrators (McCarthy, Cambron-McCabe, and Thomas, 1998, p. 272). The teacher was fired because the school district maintained that his relationship with his superiors was so damaged by the letter that he could no longer effectively carry out his teaching responsibilities. The teacher responded by arguing that his First Amendment right to free speech had been violated. Eventually, the case made its way to the Supreme Court, which sought to reconcile the issue by balancing the teacher's interest in expressing his views against the school's interest in providing effective educational services. The Court recognized that, if the fallout from the teacher's letter made it impossible for him to work effectively with administrators and other key school leaders, with clear negative effects in classroom performance, his dismissal could be upheld. In the end, however, the Court sided with the teacher, stating that his letter did not hinder the performance of his classroom duties or otherwise obstruct the educational operation of the school. The Court's ruling spoke directly to the issue of whether the teacher's expression impeded his ability to teach and whether it had an overall damaging effect on the educational functioning of the school. Although the teacher prevailed, *Pickering* reminds us that teacher expression in the context of school operations can be curtailed.

There are other situations in which a teacher's freedom of expression is not absolutely protected. A teacher, for instance, who verbally abuses her students can be terminated not only because such conduct is unprofessional but also because such conduct detracts from her ability to teach. It is not protected speech. Moreover, a teacher who expresses strong political opinions in the classroom may run the risk of being fired if such views disrupt the educational process or are seen as doctrinaire. Such viewpoints, of course, also must have educational merit. Clearly, the teacher's right of expression is subordinate to the educational livelihood of the school.

Teachers are free to pursue political activities outside of school, although there are some restrictions, depending on the state, on holding public office. In most cases, for instance, teachers cannot run for the school board in their school districts. And if they run for other public office, they must demonstrate that their political activities do not adversely affect their teaching or the educational operation of the school.

Students' Views

Students also face clear limits on expression. Generally, students' right to freedom of expression is also moderated by whether their viewpoints disrupt the educational process of the school. This typically is the strongest and most frequently used justification for restricting student speech, but it is not the only one.

Verbal Expression. One well-known case, *Bethel School District v. Fraser* (1986), concerned a high school student who presented a campaign speech to his peers in a school assembly. He used clever sexual innuendo in his speech to encourage the student body to vote for his friend, touting the virtue of his friend (to paraphrase one small part of his speech) because he was not only firm in character but firm in his pants. The reaction from the student body was predictably boisterous. The student who gave the speech was suspended from school, but he claimed that his First Amendment right to free speech had been breached. The Supreme Court, however, disagreed, observing that the speech had the effect of creating a disruptive environment and that lewd and indecent speech is not protected in a school environment. According to the Court, the school was well within its right to punish the student and to protect a captive student audience from lewd or

4-3 SCHOLARLY VOICES
Justice Burger on *Bethel v. Fraser*

Chief Justice Warren Burger delivered the opinion of the Court on *Bethel School District v. Fraser* (Valente, 1998, pp. 194–95). In this ruling, the Court outlined the unique conditions that apply to student speech in school, targeting the need to protect the student population from lewd and vulgar speech. The offending speech, given by a student (Fraser) in a school assembly, used graphic sexual metaphors to support a student candidate running for school office. The reaction of the student body to the speech was boisterous, including hooting and yelling and some gestures graphically simulating the sexual activities mentioned in the speech.

It does not follow that because the use of an offensive form of expression may not be prohibited to adults . . . the same latitude must be permitted to children in a public school. . . . Surely it is a highly appropriate function of public school education to prohibit the use of vulgar and offensive terms in public discourse. . . . The process of educating our youth for citizenship in public schools is not confined to books. . . . The schools, as instruments of the state, may determine that the essential lessons of civil, mature conduct cannot be conveyed in a school that tolerates lewd, indecent or offensive speech and conduct such as that indulged in by this confused boy. The pervasive sexual innuendo in Fraser's speech was plainly offensive to both teachers and students—indeed to any mature person. By glorifying male sexuality, and in its verbal content, the speech was acutely insulting to teenage girl students. . . . The speech could well be seriously damaging to its less mature audience, many of whom were only 14 years old and on the threshold of awareness of human sexuality. Some students were reported as bewildered by the speech and the reaction of the mimicry it provoked.

vulgar speech, even if there was no evidence of a disruption. Feature 4-3 contains an excerpt from one justice's opinion.

In similar cases, the courts upheld the suspension of students whose speech posed disruptive threats to the school, including the suspension of a boy who persisted in wearing a confederate flag on his sleeve in a racially tense school environment, and students who have made threatening or menacing remarks to teachers (McCarthy, Cambron-McCabe, and Thomas, 1998, p. 117). The confederate flag patch was considered symbolic speech, which can be readily restricted if it is determined to be potentially disruptive or otherwise lewd or inflammatory. Similarly, any "fighting words"—words that by their very utterance inflict injury—can be restricted.

Threats offered in the context of a legitimate school assignment can be especially difficult to decipher. In 1998, a student at a high school in Washington State handed in a short story to his English teacher for extra credit. The piece depicted a lonely student who roams the school and eventually draws a gun and kills twenty-eight people. "As I approached the classroom door, I drew my gun and threw open the door. Bang, Bang, Bang-Bang. When it was over, 28 were dead, and all I remember was not feeling any remorse, for I felt, I was, cleansing my soul . . ." (Walsh, 2000a). The boy was expelled from school. The question was whether, in the context of a story written to an English teacher, this could be viewed as a credible threat or was simply fiction. In the absence of any evidence that the story actually constituted a threat, a lower court eventually ruled in favor of the boy. In another case in Wisconsin, an eighth-grade boy who was disrupting the class, was asked to go in the hallway to do his writing assignment. Upset at being asked to leave the room, he wrote an essay that described a student who beheads his teacher with a machete (Walsh, 2000b). The school suspended the student for a year. The circuit court in this case, however, saw credibility in the student's threat. There was a resemblance between the teacher depicted in the essay and the actual teacher, and the written essay itself was a by-product of an assignment given by the teacher.

However, a school cannot restrict a student's speech simply because it does not like what the student is saying. The famous *Tinker v. Des Moines Independent School District* (1969) case concerned students who wore arm bands in protest of the Vietnam War. The Supreme Court upheld their right to conduct this silent method of protest, largely because it was found that it did not disrupt classwork or otherwise impede the educational operation of the school. The Court stated that school officials must have "more than a mere desire to avoid discomfort and unpleasantness that always accompany an unpopular viewpoint" in justifying a curtailment of student expression (McCarthy, Cambron-McCabe, and Thomas, 1998, p. 123). This was a strong signal that students enjoy First Amendment rights in the schools as they pertain to the expression of opinions on controversial issues.

But do schools have to wait for a disruption to occur before acting on it? As it turns out, a school may try to "forecast substantial disruption" based on credible evidence pertaining to an event. In the wake of the 1999 Columbine High shooting, many schools were quick to prohibit students from wearing black trench coats, the very type worn by the students who committed the murders in Columbine. The schools were able to forecast substantial disruption by showing that the wearing of such coats was associated with the searing media images of the killings at Columbine. The thinking was that such coats could create a very real atmosphere of tension in the school, enough to disrupt its educational operations.

Written Expression. Student writings can also be curtailed in the school, especially if the writings emerge from school-sponsored programs and give the appearance of representing the school. In *Hazelwood v. Kuhlmeier* (1988), the Supreme Court found that written student expression can indeed be regulated if it impedes the educational process in any way and if it does not have educational value or merit. In this case, high school journalism students in Hazelwood East High School, in Missouri, contended that their First Amendment rights had been violated when the principal of their school did not allow two articles to be published in the school's newspaper. The articles dealt with the sensitive topics of teenage pregnancy and the effects of divorce on teenagers, and they included stories about actual students in the high school, whose names had been changed to protect their identities. The principal objected to the articles on educational grounds. He feared that the identities of the individuals featured in the stories could be revealed and that the stories themselves, which contained some critical comments about a parent, could put the school at risk of a libel suit, which would harm the students and the school. Moreover, he felt that the articles, which made references to sexual activity and to birth control, were inappropriate for the most of the students attending the high school. The Supreme Court ruled in favor of the principal's action, maintaining that school officials can regulate material when it involves a legitimate educational interest. In the words of the Court, the First Amendment is not violated if educators "exercise editorial control over the style and content of student speech in school-sponsored expressive activities so long as their actions are reasonably related to legitimate pedagogical concerns" (Fischer, Schimmel, and Kelly, 1999, p. 182).

An important distinction emerges here. The Court's ruling made specific reference to "school-sponsored expressive activities," thereby distinguishing between school authority over school-sponsored student expression and over personal student expression. Personal speech falls under *Tinker* (and sometimes *Bethel*) and only speech that is disruptive or manifestly vulgar can be restricted. Thus, an underground student newspaper, operating without school funds, constitutes personal speech and so enjoys more constitutional protection because of it. The school cannot prevent an underground paper from discussing controversial topics or from criticizing school officials and school policies. The school can regulate the distribution of the paper, but it cannot ban the publication itself from the school unless it is found or forecasted to cause substantial disruption in school or to endanger the health and safety of students. School-sponsored speech, by contrast, falls under *Hazelwood;* this means that speech that is tied to pedagogic concerns can be curtailed for pedagogic purposes, even if it is not disruptive to the school (Valente and Valente, 1998, p. 178).

Symbolic Expression. Another area of concern is symbolic expression—modes of expression embodied in the way one dresses and grooms. Among teachers, there are clear regulations against wearing certain palpably religious clothes and jewelry, as discussed in Chapter 9. The courts have also given school districts wide latitude in enforcing grooming and dress codes for teachers. Among students, however, the regulations are slightly more complicated. Religious dress, for instance, is protected by the Constitution when worn by students. Unless the dress shows some affiliation to a disruptive event in the school or is in open violation of a school policy, it cannot be regulated.

Schools are, of course, well within their right to regulate student attire, but the regulations cannot be arbitrarily designed. Generally, clothing that is unsanitary, unsafe, obscene, or vulgar, or that is associated with a disruptive element in the school can be regulated. Sanitation issues are fairly straightforward, as are obscenity standards, which typically apply to scantily clad students who (especially in the context of a high school), by their very lack of dress, might pose a disruptive threat to the school. Safety issues might lead to the regulation of certain clothes in certain settings (e.g., loose-fitting clothes might not be permitted in a laboratory or vocational education setting).

More interesting are the efforts to regulate T-shirts containing various written and symbolic messages. Because *Bethel* made it clear that schools can punish students for lewd or indecent speech, a T-shirt or sweatshirt containing a lewd or indecent massage can be regulated. This is an easy call if the shirt is manifestly vulgar, as in one case in which a student wore a shirt containing a caricature of three school administrators boozing it up (Fischer, Schimmel, and Kelly, 1999, p. 464). But what if the message is more subtle. For instance, can a shirt containing the message "Drugs Suck" be regulated? It carries an antidrug message and is not as obviously vulgar as the prior example. The answer has do to with how the word "sucks" is interpreted. Other proeducational messages conveyed in a less-than-civil light run up against the same problem.

The courts have upheld the right of students to convey personal political messages on their T-shirts if they are not disruptive and not vulgar. Ironically, a T-shirt containing a picture of a marijuana plant with the wording "Legalize It" could and likely would be permitted, while a T-shirt that read "Drugs Suck," because of its association with a vulgar word, likely would be banned. But any T-shirt that carries a religious message (e.g., "Jesus Saves"), assuming that it is free of any association with disruptive circumstances, clearly is protected.

Finally, schools can prohibit any clothes viewed as gang-affiliated or affiliated with any potential disruption in the school. Some schools have banned the wearing of certain sports apparel, saggy pants, and jewelry because of known associations with gang or criminal activity. In such cases, however, the school must show a clear and factually based linkage between the wearing of such clothes and gang activity. Interestingly, some public schools are now experimenting with school uniform policies, arguing that school uniforms can contribute to a more conducive learning environment. See Feature 4-4 for a discussion of how one school district handled the issue.

In 1996, President Clinton endorsed the idea of school uniforms in a public address to the nation. Soon thereafter, the U.S. Department of Education released a manual on school uniform policy, which was sent to every school district in the nation. Some urban schools are using school uniform policies as a preemptive strike against gang activity—as a way to protect against the use of gang colors and gang affiliations in the school. The case law on school uniform policies has yet to play itself out. Under *Hazelwood,* school uniform policies could be legitimated if they were justified as essential to the maintenance of a legitimate educational interest. This would be an easier argument to make in a school threatened by recurrent gang or criminal activity than in one that has no such problems. Civil libertarians, however, argue that required uniforms violate students' free expression rights. Figure 4-4 on page 162 summarizes the key aspects of freedom of expression in the schools.

TEACHER TENURE AND TEACHER DISMISSAL

The employment process for teachers is managed at the local school level. The building principal, sometimes working with a committee of teachers and parents, typically will make the final appointment decision, contingent on the approval or sanction of the local school board. Local districts can require that teachers become residents of the district as a condition of appointment. They can also ask for a medical examination, screening for

4-4 DEBATING THE ISSUES
School Uniforms

A few school districts in the United States have adopted mandatory school uniform policies. In Polk County, Florida, the school district cited "increasingly disruptive and violent behavior and an increase in gangs and student participation in gang activities" in instituting its policy. Similar policies have been adopted by schools in Wilson County, Tennessee; Bossier Parish, Louisiana; Walker County, Alabama; and Louisville, Kentucky. In each case, an antiuniform group, usually comprised of parents, has emerged. In Polk County, hundreds of parents filed a suit in a federal court against the district, citing infringement of the First Amendment right to free expression and the right to privacy. In Kentucky, parents opposed to the school uniform policy adopted by their local high school (Atherton High School) have documented some of the problems in implementing a school uniform policy. Within the several months of implementation, for instance, over a thousand students were serving detention because of dress code violations. You can access the website for the parent opposition group to school uniforms at Atherton High School (www.historybox.com). The federal Department of Education *Manual on School Uniforms* can be found at its site (www.ed.gov); a comprehensive research study on the effect of school uniforms on schooling can be found at ETS's site (www.ets.org); and the point of view of the ACLU on school uniforms can be found at its site (www.aclu.org). Below is the official school uniform policy of Atherton High School in Louisville, Kentucky.

Atherton High School
Dress Code

Refer to the following for permissible clothing. Items not listed will be considered inappropriate and not allowed. Clothing must be sized to fit.

SHIRTS—must be tucked inside pants or skirts with belt showing, no blousing

Long/Short Sleeved Polos

- Collar

- 2 to 5 button placket (top button open only)

- Solid white or black

- "Official" Atherton white, gold, or mulberry

- No logos other than "official" Atherton

Long/Short Sleeved Oxfords

- Button-down color (top button open only)

- Solid white

- No logos

T-shirts

- Solid white (no writing or colors)
- Worn under polo shirt or oxford only

Turtlenecks

- Solid white
- Worn under approved long sleeved shirts or sweatshirts

SWEATSHIRTS—must be worn over collared polo, oxford, or turtleneck

- Crew neck only
- Must be banded at the bottom
- Solid white or black
- "Official" Atherton white, gold, mulberry, or gray
- No logos other than "official" Atherton
- No hoods
- Collar of shirt or turtleneck must be showing

OTHER

- No coats or jackets
- No garments tied around body
- No fleece

PANTS—trouser-style pants; cotton twill, cotton/polyester blend, or wool

- Khaki or black only
- Belt loops
- Visible belt
- Fastened with standard brown or black belt with standard buckle
- No stretch polyester or spandex
- No sagging (pants must be worn at waist)
- No cargo or patch pockets (pockets sewn on outside of pants)
- No jean cut, rivets, or denim
- No shorts

SKIRTS—cotton twill, cotton/polyester blend, or wool

- Khaki or black only
- "A" line, straight or pleated

(continued)

4-4 DEBATING THE ISSUES *(continued)*
School Uniforms

SKIRTS *(continued)*

- Fastened with standard brown or black belt with standard buckle if looped

- Length—must pass Flamingo test (Stand with both feet flat on the floor. Lift one foot and bend the leg at a 90 degree angle; the other leg must remain straight. If the back of the skirt touches the calf of the bent leg, the skirt is long enough. If the skirt does not touch the calf, the skirt is too short.)

- No stretch polyester or spandex

- No culottes, skorts, denim, or patch pockets

SHOES

- Closed toe and heel

JEWELRY, MISC.

- No medallions or necklaces worn outside the uniform shirt

- No visible key chains

- No jewelry with drug-, alcohol-, or violence-related information

- No jewelry that can be used as a weapon

- No body piercing except ears, earrings in earlobes only

- No visible tattoos

- No sweatbands, bandanas, combs/picks, curlers in hair

- Hair must be natural color

- Nothing hanging out of pockets

physical fitness, minimal vision and hearing, psychiatric conditions, and even, although this is controversial, drug use.

Schools offer two types of employment contracts to teachers: term contracts and tenure contracts. Term contracts are offered to new teachers for a fixed period of time, usually one or two years. After the contract expires, the school board can choose not to renew it for any reason—except, of course, for reasons that represent an infringement of constitutional rights (e.g., a decision based on a teacher's race, religion, sex, or protected speech, or that involves a "liberty" concern). The only requirement in a decision not to renew a term contract is timely notification, usually by

No clothing or jewelry should be worn in any manner representative of gang affiliation.

DRESS CODE VIOLATIONS/CONSEQUENCES

Students not in compliance with dress code policies will be referred to the administration. Parents may be notified and asked to bring appropriate clothing to the student.

1st Offense   go to ISAP. If violation is corrected, student will be assigned one day detention and sent back to class. If not corrected, student will be assigned one day detention and remain in ISAP.

2nd Offense   same consequences as first offense except with three day detention.

3rd Offense   student will be sent home.

4th Offense   student will be suspended for parent conference, which cannot be held on the day of the suspension. (ISAP may not be substituted for the suspension.)

The administrators will make final decisions on what is acceptable.
The School Climate and Safety Task Force recommends that the administration authorize specified dress down days as incentives for attendance, punctuality, etc. (For example students might be allowed to wear jeans on a specified Friday for reaching the district goal for our school on high attendance day.)

April 1 of the terminal year of the contract. Note that this is not a dismissal proceeding against a teacher, but a decision to not renew a contract after it expires. If a nontenured teacher is dismissed during the term of a contract period, the school must provide a formal and timely notice of the termination, detail its justification for termination, and hold a formal hearing or other forum so the teacher can hear and respond to the grounds for dismissal. This is known as due process, a procedure that will be detailed a little later. No due process is accorded to a nonrenewal, however, unless stipulated by state law or by union agreement, or triggered by a constitutional violation. Because the school district is under no legal obligation to

FIGURE 4-4
Generalizations About Freedom of Expression

1. Teachers have limited academic freedom. They are generally accorded academic freedom to choose teaching methodologies, curriculum materials, and certain topics, as long as these choices can be justified as within the educational mission of the school and are appropriate to the age and maturity level of the students. Their professional judgments also must not result in any disruption in the school environment. Choices based solely on political, religious, or lifestyle beliefs are not allowed.

2. Teachers do not have the right to not teach a state- or district-mandated curriculum.

3. Local school boards have legal authority over what can be taught, as long as they do not contradict state directives and as long as their decisions have educational merit. Decisions should be responsive to the manifest purposes of the school and the age level of the students, and must not result in any disruption to the educational process.

4. A teacher's right to free speech outside of school can be curtailed if this speech can be connected to an inability to maintain an effective teaching/learning environment in school.

5. Teachers can run for political office, but not if it proves or is foreseen to be disruptive to the school or to the ability of the teacher to maintain an effective learning environment

6. Personal student speech can be curtailed or punished if it is manifestly vulgar, lewd, or inflammatory, or is associated with some form of disruption in the school

7. School-related student speech associated with school-sponsored programs, such as school newspapers, can be regulated if it cannot be justified as having educational merit.

8. A school does not need to wait for a disruption to occur in order to regulate the conditions causing it. It may foresee disruption in the speech of teachers and students, making an argument from the standpoint of the available evidence.

9. Symbolic student speech in the form of clothing may be regulated if it is unsanitary, unsafe, disruptive, and/or vulgar.

10. Any clothes associate with gang affiliation or any element potentially disruptive to the school may be regulated.

11. Religious clothes worn by students may not be regulated unless they prove to be disruptive, unsanitary, unsafe, or vulgar.

12. School uniforms in public schools have yet to be adjudicated as freedom of expression violations, but public schools have argued for such policies as a means toward maintaining an educational environment in school.

provide a reason for the nonrenewal of a teacher's contract, the burden of proof in arguing that a nonrenewal was based on constitutionally impermissible action is with the probationary teacher.

Tenure contracts have an entirely different legal status and provide teachers with a layer of job security. Virtually every state has drafted laws supporting tenure contracts. Note that tenure is not a constitutionally protected right; it is a statutory provision (a matter of state law). Tenure originally was designed to eliminate the role of political patronage in government hiring processes, to guarantee teachers some right to academic freedom, and to otherwise protect good teachers from arbitrary or capricious actions by school officials. In most cases, tenure contracts are offered to teachers only after they have successfully demonstrated their professional worth during a fixed probationary period, usually about three years. During this probationary time, teachers work under term contracts. Once a tenure contract is offered, however, the teacher is automatically granted a contract renewal each year and comes under a new set of regulations governing disciplinary or dismissal decisions. Tenure grants "property right" status to the teacher's employment, which means that due process must be followed in any disciplinary proceedings or any attempt to terminate the teacher's employment.

Every American citizen has a constitutional right to due process; according to the Fourteenth Amendment to the Constitution, no state "shall . . . deprive a person of life, liberty or property without due process of the law." Such a right protects the accused from irresponsible and unwarranted punitive actions. Due process essentially means that a set of rules and principles must be followed when an individual is accused of an act that might lead to his dismissal or that might otherwise affect his livelihood or reputation. In the context of the school, this usually means that a teacher facing serious charges (1) must be informed in a timely manner of any proceedings or accusations, (2) must be given a fair opportunity to answer the charges, (3) has the right to obtain legal counsel and to mount a defense against the charges, and (4) must have an outlet for appeal.

With due process to consider, school districts cannot act arbitrarily toward teachers. The school has to be sure to abide by due process if the issue involves a liberty, life, or property concern. The courts have defined a liberty concern broadly as something involving the reputation, honor, or integrity of a person. So, if a nontenured teacher were facing a disciplinary action or even a nonrenewal that might implicate her character or subject her to public scorn, due process would have to be followed. For nontenured teachers, accusations pertaining to drinking and drug problems, sexual misconduct, mental instability, or extensive professional incompetence would likely result in due process, considering the stigmas associated with them (McCarthy, Cambron-McCabe, and Thomas, 1998, p. 368). However, for nontenured teachers, less serious job-related criticisms, such as an inability to get along with others, poor work habits, tardiness, absenteeism, and aggressive behavior, would not warrant due process. For tenured teachers, any charge carrying the possibility of disciplinary action is granted due process. Moreover, any decision to terminate a tenured teacher requires evidence of "dismissal for cause"; in this case, the burden of the proof rests with the school district, which often must provide a long and exhaustive record of documentation. Grounds for cause include incompetence, immorality, insubordination, financial exigency, and the rather vague "other good and just cause."

The most common reason for dismissal is incompetence, which is a charge with multifaceted characteristics. As indicated previously, many cases of incompetence revolve around issues of classroom management and control. A teacher who cannot maintain order and discipline cannot move forward with an educational mission—hence, the charge of incompetence. The charge could be sustained in other ways as well. Teachers who manifestly lack certain skills or certain subject matter knowledge also may face charges of incompetence. For example, an elementary school teacher whose teaching of spelling is compromised by his own inability to spell or a high school mathematics teacher who is obviously deficient in math skills can be fired on the charge of incompetence. But the burden of proof is on the school district if the charge involves a tenured teacher. Other grounds for dismissal due to incompetence include a failure to work effectively with colleagues and parents, excessive absenteeism, and an inability or unwillingness to teach district- or state-mandated curricula (Essex, 1999, p. 182).

Some states require that the school district first give the teacher an opportunity to correct deficient behavior; only then can the district move forward with a charge of "irremediable incompetence" (Thomas, Sperry, and Wasden, 1991, p. 93). Thus, for a teacher with classroom management problems, or a deficiency in a particular skill, or a poor absentee record, the district may give her assistance to make improvements before initiating dismissal proceedings. This preliminary action, in fact, often becomes part of the documented record eventually used in a teacher's dismissal proceeding. Naturally, some behaviors are so wrong and so completely unprofessional, especially if they involve unambiguous moral indiscretions, that they are viewed, prima facie (at face value), as irremediable.

Because school administrators are responsible for supervising the staff of a school, the failure of a teacher to follow a valid (within the scope of the administrator's authority) and reasonable directive from an administrator can be viewed as insubordination and thus as grounds for dismissal. The key here is that the school district has to document that the administrator's directive was reasonable and valid, and was not moved by any purpose other than a professional one. But if a principal asks a teacher to do something that might compromise the educational integrity or safety of the classroom, the teacher can refuse the directive and not fear an insubordination charge.

Other grounds for dismissal include the common argument of financial exigency, which has nothing to do with a teacher's performance and everything to do with the financial realities of supporting school programs and the faculty who teach them. Thus, a school that is experiencing dramatic drops in enrollment is well within its right to reduce its teaching force, including tenured teachers. Here, again, the school must follow due process, demonstrating a bona fide financial crisis and explaining how the reduction in staff will alleviate the crisis (Essex, 1999, p. 193). Most state tenure laws give tenured teachers priority over nontenured ones in retaining their jobs if a reduction-in-force action is being undertaken. Sometimes, school districts keep a recall list in case jobs open up as a result of improved financial conditions, retirements, or leaves of absence. Feature 4-5 shows some survey results on teacher tenure, attesting to its controversial, if not misunderstood, status among many citizens. Figure 4-5 summarizes some key points about teacher tenure and dismissal issues.

STUDENT SEARCHES AND SEIZURES

All American citizens have a constitutional protection, guaranteed by the Fourth Amendment, against unreasonable search and seizure. The purpose of the amendment is to safeguard the privacy and security of individuals against arbitrary invasions by government officials. The problem is that the amendment does not indicate precisely what constitutes an unreasonable search. As a result, a large body of case law has helped to define the boundaries of reasonableness. In most cases, the Fourth Amendment applies to police actions, requiring the police to abide by a principle known as probable cause. This means that no search of an individual's property or possessions is allowed unless the police can document a probable suspicion that the individual was involved in some wrong-doing. To search someone's home, the police need to obtain a warrant from the court certifying that they are operating within the boundaries of probable cause.

4-5 THINKING ABOUT THE DATA
Poll Data on Teacher Tenure

Here are a few questions taken from two surveys on teacher tenure. Do you agree with the sentiments emerging from the polls? How might you analyze the results? If you offered these questions to a random sample of adults in your community, would the results be similar?

1. Without the tenure system, many of the more experienced teachers would feel threatened and would consider leaving their jobs for something better (California Poll, Field Institute, 1983).

   27.9 % agree strongly
   27.9 % agree somewhat
   22.5 % disagree somewhat
   21.7 % disagree strongly

2. Tenure should be as difficult for teachers to get as it is for them to lose (Harris Poll, 1986).

   46.0 % agree strongly
   34.3 % agree somewhat
   10.6 % disagree somewhat
    7.4 % disagree strongly

3. Granting tenure to teachers is needed because it gives them the personal and academic freedom that they need to teach without fear of losing their jobs (California Poll, Field Institute, 1983).

   23.4 % agree strongly
   30.4 % agree somewhat
   20.2 % disagree somewhat
   26.0 % disagree strongly

4. Granting tenure to teachers lowers the quality of teaching because it makes tenured teachers less motivated since it is difficult for them to be fired (California Poll, Field Institute, 1983).

   37.5 % agree strongly
   27.9 % agree somewhat
   19.7 % disagree somewhat
   15.0 % disagree strongly

NOTE: Due to rounding, numbers may not add up to 100.

> **FIGURE 4-5**
> **Generalizations About Teacher Tenure and Teacher Dismissal**
>
> **1.** Term contracts are offered to nontenured teachers. Once the term of the contract expires, the school district can choose not to renew the contract for any reason except one that violates a constitutional right. The burden of proof for a constitutional violation resides with the teacher.
>
> **2.** A tenure contract represents an expectation of automatic renewal each year and gives the teacher a legal property right to the job.
>
> **3.** All tenured teachers are granted due process if disciplinary or dismissal proceedings are undertaken against them. Nontenured teachers are granted due process if they are being dismissed from a job while still under contract, but they can expect no due process in a nonrenewal decision unless a constitutional principle is involved, including "liberty" concerns, as interpreted by the courts.
>
> **4.** Tenured teachers can only be dismissed for cause, which means that a district has to prove incompetence, insubordination, conduct unbecoming, financial exigency, or other good and just causes. The burden of proof resides with the school district.

In the context of school, however, probable cause generally does not apply. Students, of course, do not give up their constitutional rights in school, but the school is unique because of the balance needed between individuals' Fourth Amendment right and the school's duty to provide a safe and secure learning environment. As a result, the courts have eased the search-and-seizure requirement in the context of the school from probable cause (probable suspicion that a crime has been committed) to reasonable cause (reasonable suspicion that a crime has been committed). This easing of the requirement reflects the unique standing of school officials in the lives of schoolchildren. School officials are in loco parentis (in the place of parents) to students. They have a role to fulfill in the school and a certain freedom to fulfill it that differs significantly from the police. In fact, any police action in the school still falls under probable cause requirements, and any student coming under suspicion off school property is also protected by probable cause.

But what are the general parameters of reasonable cause? An answer began to emerge in the 1985 landmark case, *New Jersey v. TLO*. In 1980, a teacher at a New Jersey high school determined that two girls were smoking cigarettes in the school lavatory, which was a violation of school rules.

The teacher brought the girls to the vice principal of the school, who questioned the girls. One of the girls admitted to the transgression, but the other, a 14-year-old freshman known as TLO in the court documents, offered no admission of guilt. Suspecting that the girl was not telling the truth, the vice principal searched TLO's purse, where he found a pack of cigarettes and some rolling papers. This confirmed the teacher's claim about smoking in the bathroom, but the discovery of the rolling papers raised new suspicions about potential marijuana use by the girl. In the vice principal's mind, there was a strong association between rolling paper and marijuana use. Thus, continuing with his search of TLO's purse, he discovered a small amount of marijuana, a considerable sum of one-dollar bills, an index card appearing to detail the names of students owing TLO money, a pipe, and a few other incriminating items (Essex, 1999, p. 38). TLO's eventual defense was that the search was not warranted, because there was no probable cause and no court-certified warrant. The Supreme Court, however, interpreted the matter differently and offered a new standard of reasonable suspicion as the basis for school-related search and seizure.

Reasonableness means that the search must be justified at its inception and limited in its scope. The accusation of smoking by the teacher and the denial by TLO justified (at its inception) a search of the girl's purse. If the vice principal at that point found only a pack of cigarettes, the search would stop, which speaks to the issue of scope. But because new evidence was uncovered in the original search, the scope of the search legitimately widened. The school, the Court reasoned, cannot be expected to obtain a warrant every time it needs to deal with issues speaking to the safety or security of the learning environment. The school simply has to have reasonable grounds, with pertinent evidence, to believe that a student has violated a school rule or policy. It cannot be a hunch or some intuitive feeling. Moreover, the school cannot decide to search everyone because of one violation of school rules. The determination of reasonableness also involves factors related to the student's age and history, the seriousness of the potential problem, the reliability of the information drawn from informants, the degree of urgency to search without delay, and the type of search (McCarthy, Cambron-McCabe, and Thomas, 1998, p. 219). Ultimately, students have a reasonable expectation of privacy, but school personnel certainly can search their personal property if reasonable suspicion prevails. This means that their lockers, book bags, purses, and other property are subject to searches based on reasonable suspicion.

In the case of physical searches, however, including either a physical pat-down or, at its most extreme, a strip search, the rules change. The school not only has to document a reasonable suspicion but also has to conduct a reasonable search, accounting for the nature of the crime, the age of the student, and other factors. In other words, a strip search of a student accused of stealing five dollars from the teacher's lounge is not a reasonable search even if there were reasonable suspicion. Similarly, no one will strip search a kindergarten student unless there was truly imminent danger, knowing that a 5-year-old child has no criminal culpability. Generally, physically intrusive searches require a higher standard of suspicion, one approaching probable cause. As one court stated, "We are of the view that as intrusiveness intensifies, the standard of the Fourth Amendment reasonableness approaches probable cause even in the school context" (Essex, 1999, p. 42).

Given the requirements in making a case of reasonable cause against a student, is the school still allowed to conduct general searches of all students, using devices such as metal detectors, sniffing dogs, or urine tests for drug use, or mere visual inspections of lockers? The answer is yes, provided that the school can demonstrate a need for such searches to protect the general safety of the school environment. Thus, metal detectors are permitted in schools where gun violence can be documented to exist in the surrounding neighborhood or within the student population itself. In 1998, an elementary school in Indianapolis took the unusual step of installing metal detectors after three students from the school, between the ages of 7 and 8, were arrested for gun possession in three separate incidents (Portner, 1998). A similar rationale applies to other forms of general searches. For instance, drug-sniffing dogs may be brought in for a general sweep of student automobiles and lockers, but only in relation to a general plan to protect students from an established threat of drug abuse in the school or community. And because the dogs represent a much more intrusive search of one's person than, say, metal detectors (which are minimally intrusive), they cannot be used on individual students unless individualized reasonable suspicion exists. Finally, with all general searches, every effort must be made to make the search truly general, not simply directed at a particular segment of the school population.

Searches conducted against segments of the population are allowed, if there is a reasonable suspicion of rules violations within the group. For example, one school learned from reliable sources about serious drug use among its student athletes. The school enacted a policy requiring participating students to submit a urine sample that would be tested for drugs. One student, who was never under any suspicion of drug use, refused to take the test, arguing that it was an unreasonable invasion. When the school suspended him, he took the school to court. In *Vernonia District v. Acton* (1992), the Supreme Court ruled that the school could institute such a policy as a measure against known drug use because it was conceived as a strategy to

---

FIGURE 4-6

Generalizations About Search and Seizure

1. School officials need to have reasonable suspicion to perform a search and seizure of a student's property and possessions.

2. Reasonable suspicion is affected by a number of factors, including the age of the student, the school history of the student, the reliability of the informant's information, the seriousness of the problem, and the nature of the search.

3. A search itself must be reasonable, meaning individualized, justified by its original intent, and limited in scope.

4. More invasive searches, such as strip searches, require a higher standard of suspicion, approaching the police standard of probable cause.

5. Police actions in school require establishment of probable cause.

6. Blanket search policies, involving metal detectors or sniffing dogs, can be conducted if they are part of a general plan to protect the school from a known and documented harm.

---

protect the general welfare. In addition, in this particular instance, it represented a relatively nonintrusive search, akin to simply going to the bathroom in a public restroom, among students who, by virtue of their participation in athletic programs, had lower expectations of privacy. Figure 4-6 summarizes the key points about search and seizure in the schools.

SUMMARY

The extensive body of case law on the legal and ethical behaviors of teachers has helped to give the schools some general guidelines in dealing with teacher indiscretions. Feature 4-6, in fact, offers a way to gain access to the actual narrative of the landmark Supreme Court cases.

When attempting to derive a sense of how the law might deal with the various issues discussed in this chapter, several generalizations hold. Regarding the idea of "conduct unbecoming," apart from a felonious crime or a blatantly immoral act (bordering on verbal, physical, sexual, or mental abuse), any teacher activity that might otherwise offend the ethical or moral sensibilities of school board members or school leaders is actionable only if it negatively affects the performance of the teacher in the classroom.

4-6 WEB POINTS

The Legal Information Institute's Supreme Court Collection

This website (www.law.cornell.edu) allows you to access over 600 of the most important historical decisions handed down by the Supreme Court. The site has also begun to document all the cases coming out of the Supreme Court since 1990. This allows you to take a close look of the language and argumentation of the Court on various school-related decisions.

LII
legal information institute

Supreme Court Collection

| collection home | search | tell me more | lii home |

contents & context

ways to access material

Pending cases:

This year we added a much-requested feature: the ability to search order lists and irregular orders for particular cases and any orders related to them. Database coverage goes back to the beginning of the October 1998 term. Complete details (and the search form) are here.

Decisions from 1990 to the present:

The Legal Information Institute offers Supreme Court opinions under the auspices of Project Hermes, the court's electronic-dissemination project. This archive contains nearly all opinions of the court issued since May of 1990. In addition, our collection of over 600 of the most important historical decisions of the Court is available on CD-ROM and (with reduced functionality) over the Net.

During our first four years of operation, the LII simply built finding aids -- such as tables of party names and searching tools -- which in turn pointed to the Hermes archive at Case Western Reserve University. In 1997, we acquired our own Hermes subscription and began streamed conversion of the decisions into HTML at the time of release. We have also converted the entire CWRU backlist to HTML.

As the foregoing implies, there are still some omissions and errata in this collection, and a high likelihood that in the process of conversion we've missed a few links here and there. If you run into a problem which is not mentioned in our list of errata and items under construction, do let us know.

At the start of the October 1997 term, the Court changed the file formats used in its Hermes distribution. Previously, opinions, syllabi, and order lists were distributed in WordPerfect 5.1 and flat ASCII

- Quick search:
  [ ] [Go]

- This month's decisions
- This month's order lists
- For the 1999-2000 term:
  - Highlights
  - Decisions arrayed by date
  - Orders granting and denying cert. and ruling on procedural matters in pending cases
  - Searchable database of orders in pending cases
  - Court calendar
  - Oral argument schedule
  - Questions presented in cases to be heard
- Historic decisions
  - Online
  - Purchase CD
- For the 1998-99 term:
  - Decisions arrayed by date
- Arrayed by topic:
  - Decisions from 1990-present
  - Historic decisions
- Arrayed by party name:
  - 1999 -- 1st. party, 2nd.

Reprinted with permission.

Regarding teacher liability, a straightforward process, involving four critical analytical steps, is used to determine negligence and eventual liability. Although the process is straightforward, finding unambiguous answers in the determining duty of care, breach of care, and proximate cause is deeply contextual and argumentative. Regarding academic freedom, public school teachers must understand that it exists in a limited and qualified form in the K–12 setting. School authorities can curtail what teachers are teaching and even how they are teaching if their actions cannot be justified from a valid educational or teaching perspective, or if they are associated in any way with some disruption of the school environment. The school can discipline personal teacher speech if that speech demonstrably undermines the teacher's ability to conduct an effective classroom. Student expression in the school can also be restricted. Personal student speech can be censored if it is vulgar or if it results in a disruption; school-related student speech (sponsored by the school) can be regulated if it does not fulfill a valid educational purpose, even if it does not cause a disruption.

Regarding employment issues, teachers generally are hired under two types of contracts: term contracts and tenure contracts. Term contracts typically run for a year or two and require the school to offer no explanation for the nonrenewal of the contract at its expiration (unless the reasons represent a constitutional infringement, which the teacher would have to prove). By contrast, tenure contracts, which are granted to teachers after a trial or probationary period, provide automatic yearly renewals and mean that teachers can only be dismissed with "cause" (for incompetence, insubordination, immoral behavior, or financial exigency), with the burden of proof resting on the school's shoulders.

Finally, with regard to search-and-seizure regulations, school officials must have only a reasonable suspicion of a rule-breaking activity, not the police standard of probable suspicion, to conduct a search of a student's property or possessions. The standard of reasonableness shifts in the direction of probable cause as the nature of the search becomes more intrusive. General searches or sweeps of student possessions and property (lockers and book bags) are allowable if the school can demonstrate a need for such measures to protect the safety and security of the school environment.

QUESTIONS AND ACTIVITIES

1. Can a teacher be dismissed from a teaching position on the basis of sexual orientation?

2. Can a teacher who preaches his politics and religion in class be dismissed?

3. Can a teacher accused of drunk driving be dismissed?

4. Can a teacher be fired for using vulgar or profane language?

5. Can a teacher show an R-rated film in class without fearing repercussions?

6. What criteria do the courts use to determine liability? Explain each characteristic of the criteria.

7. Explain how student age and various dangers associated with various classroom or teaching environments factor into the determination of negligence and liability.

8. What limitations must a teacher be aware of in considering the use of unconventional or controversial teaching methods?

9. Explain the implications of the *Pickering* case on teacher speech.

10. Describe the idea of in loco parentis, and explain how it factors into search-and-seizure regulations in school.

11. What was the essential implication of the ruling in *Bethel v. Fraser*?

12. How is the *Hazelwood* ruling significantly different from the *Tinker* ruling?

13. What are the general grounds for regulating student dress in school?

14. What are the main differences between term and tenure contracts?

15. What is due process?

16. Under what conditions can a probationary teacher claim a liberty right in asking for due process?

17. What are the main grounds for dismissal of tenured teachers, and why is it relatively difficult to dismiss a teacher once she is granted tenure?

18. Can probationary teachers have their contracts nonrenewed for no reason once their contract expires?

19. What are the main characteristics of reasonable suspicion when conducting a search of a student's property or possessions?

20. Are general sweeps for drug use allowed in school? If so, what are the particular conditions allowing them?

21. Are strip searches legal in school? If so, what are the particular conditions allowing them?

REFERENCES

Archer, J. (1997). Rhode Island halts exams in wake of wide-scale security breaches. *Education Week* (17 March).

Class sees *Striptease.* (1997). *Education Week* (28 May).

Dewey, J. (1916). *Democracy and education.* (New York: Free Press).

Diegmueller, K. (1995). Expletives deleted. *Education Week* (21 June).

Essex, N. L. (1999). *School law and the public schools: A practical guide for educational leaders.* (Boston: Allyn & Bacon).

Fischer, L., Schimmel, D., and Kelly, C. (1999). *Teachers and the law,* 5th ed. (White Plains, NY: Longman).

Hudgins, H. C. and Vacca, R. S. (1995). *Law and education.* (Charlottesville, VA: Michie Law).

Jasper, M. C. (1998). *Education law.* (Dobbs Ferry, NY: Oceana Publications).

Johnston, R. C. (1997). News: Texas presses districts in alleged test-tampering cases. *Education Week* (17 March).

McCarthy, M. M., Cambron-McCabe, N. H., and Thomas, S. B. (1998). *Public school law: Teachers' and students' rights.* (Boston: Allyn & Bacon).

Portner, J. (1998). Indianapolis uses metal detectors on elementary pupils. *Education Week* (3 June).

Richard, A. (1999). Policies on lunchtime scrutinized after deadly crash. *Education Week* (8 Dec.).

Richardson, J. (1993). Lesbian parents' school visit sparks a clash of cultures in Boise suburb. *Education Week.* (10 Feb.).

"Slave ship" case settled. (1998). *Education Week* (8 July): 4.

Thomas, G. J., Sperry, D. J., and Wasden, F. D. (1991). *The law and teacher employment.* (St. Paul: West).

Valente, W. D., and Valente, C. M. (1998). *Law in the schools.* (Upper Saddle River, NJ: Merrill).

Walsh, M. (2000a). A fine line between dangerous and harmless student speech. *Education Week* (8 March).

Walsh, M. (2000b). Law update: Violent essay. *Education Week* (12 Jan.).

Zehr, M. A. (1999). Threat of lawsuits a burden on principals, poll says. *Education Week* (15 Sept.).

PART II

The History of the American School Experience

Knowledge of the past is the key to understanding the present. History deals with the past, but this past is the history of the present.

—JOHN DEWEY

The *New-England* PRIMER

IMPROVED;

For the more eafy attaining the true Reading of ENGLISH.

To which is added,

The ASSEMBLY of DIVINES, and Mr. COTTON's

CATECHISM

PROVIDENCE

Printed and Sold by JOHN CAR-
TER, at *Shakefpear's Head.* 1775.

CHAPTER 5

The Emerging Public School
in Early America

New England School Life
THE DAME SCHOOL AND THE LATIN GRAMMAR SCHOOL
CURRICULUM MATERIALS

Virginia and the Middle Colonies

The Early Education of Blacks
EDUCATIONAL OPPORTUNITIES PRIOR TO THE INDUSTRIAL
REVOLUTION
INCREASED OPPRESSION FOLLOWING THE INDUSTRIAL
REVOLUTION

Summary

Questions and Activities

References

P UBLIC EDUCATION IN AMERICA arose out of an early union
between church and state. Because the dominant factor in the
founding of colonial America, especially in New England, was religion, public education became part of the orchestration of institutions used
to secure a church-based society. Interest in mass public education was
based solely on the desire to inject religion into the life of the state. The
Puritans took the first direct steps in this direction during the seventeenth
century, when they passed laws promoting state-sponsored schooling. To
them, publicly funded schools were simply public extensions of the church,
messengers of the Word. The religious homogeneity of the Massachusetts
Bay Colony made such an arrangement between church and state interests
virtually compulsory. What was good for the Puritan faith was also good for
government; there was no real separation. Colonial New England, after all,
was a settlement that, in the words of Lawrence Cremin (1977), was
founded in the unsettlement of Europe, in a movement to find new expression for religious conviction, and in a general mood of adventure believed
to be guided by God's grand design.

But elsewhere in the colonies, the idea of commingling state and church
concerns, as well as the idea of using public monies for public schools, was
problematic. The hurdles were obvious. For example, which church, which
doctrine, and which ecclesiastical slant on learning would be best for all of
the children in a religiously diverse region? Given the difficulties in answer-
ing such questions, much of the education of children outside of New
England occurred in nonpublic places, including the church and the household. The Puritan belief in using the public school for denominational purposes was simply not transportable to other regions and would, in time,
become increasingly difficult to manage even in New England. In the
South, social castes (ranging from black slaves, to white indentured servants, to white masters) made the idea of publicly funded mass education
inconceivable.

NEW ENGLAND SCHOOL LIFE

As mentioned, the history of American education dates back to the early
seventeenth-century settlements in New England. The center of the action
was the Massachusetts Bay Colony, where the Puritans took an active hand
in promoting publicly funded education at virtually every level of school
organization. The Puritans were well known for their efforts to provide a
beginning education, up to age 7, to all the children in their communities,

as well as for providing continued education, up to age 15, for a select group of boys. They also founded a number of colonial colleges, the first and most famous being Harvard College, which was chartered in 1636. Ultimately, they built an educational structure that formed the basis for a town-controlled system of compulsory education and that, by the close of the seventeenth century, could boast of having produced higher literacy rates than those achieved in England (Cohen, 1974).

The Puritans' attraction to public education was motivated not by democratic or egalitarian principles, but by a desire to use the school as an agency for church doctrine. Despite escaping religious harassment in Europe, the Puritans had no intention of establishing a New World community open to all religious creeds. To the Puritans, such an arrangement would inevitability lead to anarchy and to a serious falling away from God (Cohen, 1974). They were strong-headed about these matters, denying suffrage to nonchurch members and tolerating no dissent against the church. The Puritans' embrace of the state in establishing schools was motivated by a transparent desire to create and sustain a government in the image of their church.

Because the Puritans believed that mass education was needed to bring the gospel of Christian faith to all of their children, they committed themselves, with the urging of the church, to publicly funded schools that openly aimed to socialize youths in doctrinal faith. For the Puritans, the road to personal salvation was always traveled through the Bible, and unlike other colonial Americans, they were willing to collectively fund schools to serve as one of the main vehicles for this most important journey. As will be explained, the Puritan idea of using the state to enforce and otherwise support a tax-based public education for all youths set an early pattern of organization and governance for American public education that was sustained long after state and church went their separate ways (Cubberley, 1947).

As in most colonial settlements, the Puritan home or family unit was considered to be the wellspring for moralistic and religious education. A family, in fact, was not considered very civilized if it did not attend properly to the religious education of its children (Rippa, 1984). Given the hardships of life in the New World, however, many parents proved to be neglectful of their duty, so much so that the Puritans enacted legislative statutes compelling families, under the threat of fines or removal of custodial rights, to teach reading and religion to their children. The result was the Massachusetts Law of 1642, passed at the behest of the church, which made education compulsory for all youths in the Massachusetts Bay Colony. No distinction was made in the law between the education of boys and of girls. To the Puritans, the eternal souls of both boys and girls were at stake.

FIGURE 5-1

Massachusetts Law of 1647

It being one chiefe project of that ould deluder, Satan, to keepe men from the knowledge of the Scriptures, as in former times by keeping them in an unknowne tongue, so in these latter times by perswading from the used of tongues, that so at least the true sence and meaning of the originall might be clouded by false glosses of saint seeming deceivers, that learning may not be buried in the grave of our fathers in the church and commonwealth, the Lord assisting our endeavors,–

It is therefore ordered, that every towneship in this jurisdiction, after the Lord hath increased them to the number of 50 householders, shall then forthwith appoint one within their towne to teach all such children as shall resort to him to write and reade, whose wages shall be paid either by the parents or masters of such children, or by the inhabitants in generall, by way of supply, as the major part of those that order the prudentials of the towne shall appoint; provided, those that send their children be not oppressed by paying much more than they can have them taught for in other townes; and it is further ordered, that where any towne shall increase to the number of 100 families or househoulders, they shall set up a grammer schoole, the master thereof being able to instruct youth so farr as they may be fited for the university, provided, that if any towne neglect the performance hereof above one yeare, that every such towne shall pay £5 to the next schoole till they shall performe this order.

SOURCE: Shurtleff, N. B. (1853–54), *Records of the governor and company of Massachusetts Bay in New England*. In S. Cohen, *Education in the United States: A documentary history* (1974, Vol. I) (New York: Random House), p. 394.

The law empowered town officials, also known as selectmen, to ensure that each child in the community received an education that included, among other things, reading and understanding the principles of religion. The officials periodically paid visits to homes, where they expected parents or masters (hired teachers) to account for the education of the children in the household. Thus, the 1642 law made education compulsory, but it did not necessarily establish schools. Education was now a requirement, but its operation was still largely a family matter, conducted in the home.

Within five years, however, the Puritans took an even larger step toward establishing a public system of schooling by passing a law, known as the Massachusetts Law of 1647, that specifically required all townships to maintain schools and hire teachers. Figure 5-1 reproduces the law. The actual maintenance of some type of school represented a much stronger commitment to education because it required public monies and enforced public accountability. Again, the driving force behind the legislation was the church. As far as the church was concerned, children could not be expected to understand the Bible unless they possessed the basic rudiments of reading. The thinking in the church was that the "old deluder" (Satan) was always among the people, looking for opportunities to exploit them. Direct measures had to be taken to protect the community, especially its children, from Satan's clutches. The best protection, of course, was to be charged with the word of the Lord, and at least to the Puritans, the best way to secure this effect was to erect a school system that imbued all youths with the spirit of the Bible and the skills needed to read the Bible. In the words of the law, schools had to be maintained to thwart the "chief project of the old deluder Satan to keep men from the knowledge of the scriptures" (Meriwether, 1907).

Thus, the Massachusetts Law of 1647, also known as the Old Deluder Act, authorized, depending on the size of the town, the provision of schools and the employment of teachers. For towns with at least fifty households, a teacher of reading and writing had to be employed at a wage determined by the town; for towns with at least a hundred households, the same requirements applied, but a Latin grammar school (secondary school) was required as well (Colony of Massachusetts, 1853). The Massachusetts law was copied in Connecticut in 1650, although compliance became increasingly problematic as populations spread along the frontier (Noble, 1959).

The Dame School and the Latin Grammar School

The Puritans essentially had two types of schools: dame schools and Latin grammar schools. Dame schools were elementary or primary schools typically conducted out of the home of a widowed or otherwise unmarried townswoman. Early in their development, they were either private neighborhood schools that survived on small weekly fees paid by parents or semipublic schools that received marginal assistance from the town treasury (Small, 1969). Without the compulsion of law, dame schools emerged rather idiosyncratically. As a mother taught her own children the rudiments of reading, other neighborhood children might be included for a small fee of perhaps a few pence per week (Small, 1969). But as the dame schools began to receive some public support, they took on a sharper focus. With the passage of legislation compelling the establishment of schools, the dame schools eventually garnered more substantive support from town sources and evolved into town elementary schools.

The town schools, in effect, became the elementary schools of New England, providing an essential education in the ABCs and in elementary reading up to the ages of about 7 or 8, an age limit that slowly extended upward over time. Such schools were moved out of the household and into their own facilities. These town schools ultimately set the early tradition of instruction in the three R's and compelled the increasing use of local taxes to support public education.

As reported by Rippa (1984), the dame schools were characterized by a harsh, dogmatic atmosphere. The teaching revolved around the letters of the alphabet and the Scriptures in the Bible. In most cases, the formal education of children in the dame school was concluded by age 7, and for the overwhelming majority of the population, no further opportunity for public education existed. Household duties awaited the girls while various apprenticeships or work on the farm awaited the boys (French, 1964). And for both boys and girls, it was the household that continued to be the strongest source of education (Cremin, 1977).

For a small group of boys, however, formal schooling continued in an institution known as the Latin grammar school, a school design imported from England. The sole purpose of the Latin grammar school was to educate an elite group of boys for college study. Latin was at the center of instruction because it was the sacred language of religion, which presumably made it good for the mind and for the soul. Education in the Latin grammar school among the Puritans started at about age 7 and ran until approximately age 15. Upon graduation, the boys in the Latin grammar schools were expected to enroll at Harvard College.

Girls generally were excluded from the grammar schools and from higher education. Many males believed that higher education came at the cost of a female's health, revealed her innate mental inferiority, deprived her of her most effeminate qualities, and led to the neglect of children (Douglas and Grieder, 1948). As Figure 5-2 shows, among those who shared this view was John Winthrop, the first governor of the Massachusetts Bay Colony. Few male colonists saw any contradiction between their religious views and their disregard for the education of girls beyond the most rudimentary levels (Harris, 1899). French (1964) cites sources that claim very high illiteracy rates for women in the colonies, especially in relation to the rates for men. Woman would only begin to benefit from an opportunity for a higher education during the early nineteenth century.

Like the dame school, the Latin grammar school featured religious exercises and a rote/recitation style of learning. Educators placed great faith in the act of memorization, which was encouraged through skill-drill exercises and repeated recitations. Memorizing grammatical rules and a multitude of Latin equivalents for English words, and translating Latin passages to English and back again to Latin, constituted a large share of the pedagogy (Cohen, 1974). Students also read noted classical authors, such as Cicero, Horace, Tully, Ovid, and Virgil, and received rigorous religious training,

> **FIGURE 5-2**
> ## John Winthrop of Massachusetts on the Education of Women (1645)
>
> Mr. Hopkins, the governour of Hartford upon Connecticut, came to Boston, and brought his wife with him, (a godly young woman, and of special parts,) who was fallen into a sad infirmity, the loss of her understanding and reason, which had been growing upon her divers years, by occasion of her giving herself wholly to reading and writing, and had written many books. Her husband, being very loving and tender of her, was loath to grieve her; but he saw his errour, when it was too late. For if she had attended her household affairs, and such things as belong to women, and not gone out of her way and calling to meddle in such things as are proper for men, whose minds are stronger &c. she had kept her wits, and might have improved them usefully and honourably in the place God had set her. He brought her to Boston, and left her with her brother, one Mr Yale, a merchant, to try what means might be had here for her. But no help could be had.

SOURCE: Winthrop, J. (1826), *The history of New England from 1630–1649*. In S. Cohen, *Education in the United States: A documentary history* (1974, Vol. 1) (New York: Random House), p. 383.

including daily recitation of prayers and catechisms and translation of the New Testament from Latin (Cohen, 1974). Greek was also taught. Writing and the fundamentals of arithmetic were optional, but in most cases were ignored (French, 1967). Class discussions were abhorred, and a climate of control and order, with all of its attendant punishments and regulations, pervaded the school. The entrance requirements for Harvard College testified to the instructional priorities of the Latin grammar schools. In 1642, the entrance requirement read: "When any scholar is able to read Tully, or such like classical Latin author *extempore,* and make and speak true Latin in verse and prose, *suo (ut aiunt) Marte:* and decline perfectly the paradigms of nouns and verbs in the Greek tongue, then may he be admitted into the College" (Mayer, 1964, p. 55).

Graduates of the Latin grammar schools were essentially innumerate and unable to write with much fluency, but they usually were quite literate in Latin (Cubberley, 1947). No allowance was made in such schools for technical, business, or commercial education, or for what were viewed then as "polite accomplishments" such as music or dancing (Cohen, 1974). Ultimately, the failure of the Latin grammar school to be in touch with the everyday demands of colonial life led to its demise (Tanner and Tanner, 1987). Life in the New World, on a new frontier, surely called for more useful knowledge than Latin.

The teachers in colonial schools were poorly trained, and the conditions for teaching did not encourage very thoughtful experiences in the classroom. The schoolchildren followed more or less the same instructional pattern in the classroom, as they memorized and recited their way through their lessons. Except for some reading materials, there was no classroom equipment to facilitate instruction. Paper and individual desks were rare, and slates would not appear in the school until the early 1800s.

The buildings themselves were undersized and often decrepit (Cohen, 1974). For instance, the most common building design was a simple "carpenter box," usually 25 feet by 25 feet, 6 to 9 feet high, and presumably big enough for sixty pupils (Small, 1969). These schools, more often than not, were built cheaply and hastily, and were known for falling into quick and dramatic disrepair. A Roxbury citizen recorded one complaint in 1681: "The inconveniences I shall instance no other than that of the schoolhouse, the confused and shattered and nasty picture that it is in, not fitting for to reside in; the glass broken and thereupon very raw and cold; the floor very much broken and torn up to kindle fires; the hearth spoiled; the seats, some burnt and others out of kilter, so that one had as well nigh as good keep school in a hog-sty as in it" (Small, 1969, p. 258).

In most cases, the furnishings in the school buildings were threadbare, consisting of planks on barrels or stakes for desks, and benches for seats (Small, 1969). In the winters, many schools went unheated, and those that were heated relied on poorly ventilated fireplaces or stoves, such that it sometimes became difficult to breathe (Small, 1969). The heating of the school building also consumed much wood, which was the only heating fuel available, and frequently led to a wood tax levy on families with children attending school (Small, 1969).

Some of the schoolrooms were equipped with whipping posts, which were used with unruly students (Cubberley, 1947). Even the use of the whipping posts had an ecclesiastical rationale: Children were believed to be born sinful and often had to have "old Adam beaten out of them" (Knight, 1951, p. 127). Because children were believed to be better off being whipped than eternally damned, schoolmasters could easily justify such punitive measures, but the reasons they gave for punishment often were arbitrary. Small (1969) cites the example of a boy who made a bad recitation, causing his teacher to flog "another boy for not exercising a better influence over the delinquent" (p. 386). Other teachers were more creative in their punishments. One schoolmaster, after securing several offenders, ordered one to get on all fours, another to mount his back, and the third to whip the other two around the room. They then changed positions until each boy had his turn at whipping once and being whipped twice (Small, 1969). Milder forms of punishment included forcing pupils to sit on air or stand in the corner with their face to the wall, tapping them on the head with a steel-thimbled finger, and slapping them with a rawhide ruler (Small, 1969).

Curriculum Materials

Throughout colonial America, the curriculum materials used in the various schools were wedded to the notion of building knowledge in reading as a way to build knowledge in religion. To this end, the hornbook was among the earliest pedagogic devices used. Brought from England, the hornbook, which was used in virtually every colonial school, was not really a book in the sense that we know it today. Rather, it was made out of a thin piece of wood with a handle, looked much like a paddle, and was, by some accounts, periodically used for the purpose of hitting children (Meriwether, 1907). On the top of the wood laid a paper that usually contained the alphabet, various letter combinations, and the Lord's Prayer. The paper was covered with a thin sheet of cow's horn, made transparent by boiling and scraping, that protected the book and made it quite durable for use in school. The hornbook kept instruction fixed on phonemic representations of letters (B as in bear, H as in horse) and on nonsense jingles that represented the sounds that the letters made (Art we add, Ben is bad, Cat she can, Dad or dan, Ear and eye). Some hornbooks also carried the emblem of Christ's cross at the very top of their front side. Once the children finished all of their lessons on the hornbook, they were ready for catechism, which entailed the memorization and recitation of various religious texts. At the level of catechism, the children were subjected to texts like the *Westminster Catechism* and the Reverend John Cotton's revealingly titled *Spiritual Milk for American Babes Drawn Out of the Breasts of Both Testaments for Their Souls' Nourishment* (Callahan, 1963).

The most influential text used in the education of young colonists, which eventually replaced the hornbook as introductory reading material, was *The New England Primer,* a document that embodied much of the Puritan view of moral depravity in humankind (Ford, 1899). The primer, which first appeared in 1690, was saturated with religiosity—moral maxims, hymns, and prayers. It dutifully represented the language of the Bible (the Ten

Commandments, the Lord's Prayer, various passages from the Old Testament, and unique verses that taught literacy within the story of Christianity). The primer used rhymes and poems to help children learn the phonetic sounds symbolized in the letters and letter combinations of the alphabet. These rhymes were also used to teach children something about their own innate proclivity toward sin. The book, for instance, covered the alphabet in the following manner: A—"In Adam's Fall, we sinned all"; B— "Thy life to mend, this book attend" (a pictured Bible); and so on (Rippa, 1984). One particularly popular poem, reproduced in Alexander Rippa's (1984, p. 39) history of the schools, captures the rather miserable moralistic tone to which children were subjected. The poem reminded children of their sinful nature and of their destiny in the fires of hell. Children often memorized and performed this poem in school:

> *You sinners are, and such a share*
> *as sinners may expect*
> *Such you shall have, for I do save*
> *none but mine own elect.*
> *Yet to compare your sin with theirs*
> *who liv'd a longer time,*
> *I do confess yours is much less,*
> *though ev'ry sin's a crime:*
> *A crime it is; therefore in bliss*
> *you may not hope to dwell;*
> *But unto you I shall allow*
> *the easiest room in hell.*

The merging of reading instruction with the moralistic preachments of the Puritan faith was the rule of thumb in *The New England Primer*. Proper child-rearing practices promoted the need to instill in children the values of fear, obedience, and discipline (Karier, 1967). However, with changing social conditions, later editions of *The New England Primer* deemphasized stories about sin and eternal punishment, and instead stressed patriotic themes and the practical values of learning to read (Butts, 1955). *The New England Primer* was used in schools for well over a century, with an estimated 3 million copies sold during that time. It was said to have "taught millions to read, and not one to sin" (Callahan, 1963, p. 116).

The education of black and Native American children in New England was an outgrowth of missionary work. Some early missionaries even managed to translate the Bible into Algonquin, which resulted in small numbers of Algonquin converts settling in Puritan towns (Cohen, 1974). Depending on the town, separate schools could be found for Native American children at virtually all age levels. Even Harvard College opened a college for Native Americans, housed in a separate building, in the 1650s. Because of the nature of life in New England, chattel slavery never took hold in the region. As a result, there were few blacks in New England during the seventeenth and eighteenth centuries. Cohen (1974) estimates that blacks made up slightly more than 2 percent of the total population in the region in the late eighteenth century. There were no laws against educating blacks, but there was discrimination. Thus, although compulsory school laws covered black children, most were educated in separate sectarian schools, with no real opportunity for an education beyond the town elementary school. To get another perspective on the overall life conditions in colonial America, see Feature 5-1.

VIRGINIA AND THE MIDDLE COLONIES

Not all of the colonists were as strongly committed to establishing a public school system as were the Puritans in New England. In the southern colonies, for instance, religion was simply not as strong a factor in daily life or in schooling. The character of life in Virginia, with its dispersed plantations, as opposed to towns, and its general lack of good transportation, made public schooling more problematic (Cubberley, 1947). Moreover, the South was much slower to establish local colleges and to set up printing presses that might have provided printed matter to the populace (Cremin, 1977). Wealthy parents relied on tutors and private schools for the education of their children, while the children of the poor were left to the largess of charity, which often meant church-sponsored pauper schools.

In most cases, the children of the poor, whose parents were under no legal compulsion to educate their children, were left to labor in the fields without any literate education. In 1642, the Virginia legislature passed a law providing apprenticeship education for the children from the indentured servant classes and children who were orphaned or otherwise indigent. But there were no guarantees that any apprenticeship program offered anything other than vocational training; no stipulation was made for reading or religious education (Cohen, 1974).

The societal fabric of the South was also quite different from the more homogeneous North. Black slaves and white indentured servants working on the plantations were considered too lowly to deserve publicly supported

5-1 WEB POINTS
A Colonial Family and Community

The Henry Ford Museum, together with the Greenfield Village, has put together an interactive website (www.hfmgv.org/smartfun/colonial/intro) that takes you through various dimensions of colonial life, as it existed in the context of a family living in Connecticut in the 1700s. The focus is on all aspects of life, not just education or schooling.

A Colonial Family and Community

Be a history detective. Go back in time and investigate the daily lives of the Daggetts, a colonial family from northeastern Connecticut. Collect clues to uncover answers to 7 questions about colonial life in the 1700s. Then prove your skills as a history detective by discovering "What's wrong with this picture?"

Begin!

From the Collections of Henry Ford Museum and Greenfield Village.

education. Such a population was not likely to win legislative support for the public schooling of its children. Thus, there was little motivation, from the standpoint of public policy, for free and common public schools in the South. The idea that one school could be fashioned to serve these antagonistic social classes was simply unthinkable. As a result, literate education in the colonial South resided neither with the state nor with the church, but with private tutors and private schools for the wealthy, and charity schools for the poor.

The education of girls was probably even more restricted in the South than in the North because the Anglicans did not share the Puritan zeal for bringing the Christian creed to both sexes (Cohen, 1974). As in the North, however, the southern attitude toward women and education rarely went beyond expectations of knowledge of the values of modesty, gentleness, and piety; the domestic skills of cooking, sewing, and so on; and the rudiments of reading, writing, and arithmetic. Depending on the region, girls were able to gain an education through charity schools, dame schools, private schools, and, for the wealthiest, boarding or finishing schools, but these were all relatively rare. Most girls were taught at home to do those things that contributed most directly to their roles as wives, mothers, and housekeepers (Cohen, 1974).

The education of slave children had, by and large, no legislative support in the South during the seventeenth century. And by the early nineteenth century, the southern states were actively drafting laws prohibiting the education of slaves. As the slave markets grew in size and as the margins of profits increased, due, in part, to new farming technologies, the institution of slavery became especially vicious. Where slaves in the seventeenth century could find support for their education as a matter of Christian salvation and even, in some cases, economic benefit to the slaveholder, the nineteenth century brought nothing but educational deprivation to blacks. During the early 1800s, slaveholders were keen to create a submissive and obedient labor force. They understood that education could prove to be a liberating force, and thus a menace to their slavery-based economy. The ability to read might give slaves "dangerous" ideas about their own abilities, and ultimately, reveal to them new life possibilities (Beale, 1975). Many southerners also held to the idea that black slaves were uneducable and acted on this conviction by forbidding the teaching of blacks throughout most of the region.

However, prior to the development of the chattel slavery markets that marked the nineteenth century, blacks in the South had found some educational opportunities in the evangelical activities of the Society for the Propagation of the Gospel in Foreign Parts (SPG), in the work of the Quakers, and in the activities of northern abolitionist societies. SPG, which was chartered in England, was dedicated to conducting missionary work in English colonies. The missionaries targeted the southern colonies of America, seeking converts, distributing Bibles, and founding churches with the intention of bringing blacks, Indians, and poor whites into the Episcopalian faith (Cohen, 1974). Like the Puritans, the SPG believed in the importance of education in bringing the word of God to the people. Thus, the SPG established a network of charity schools. Taught by missionaries, the schools emphasized Episcopalian religious tenets and basic instruction in literacy and numeracy. Ultimately, the SPG succeeded in providing some semblance of a centrally administered system of schooling for black children in the South (Cohen, 1974).

The education of Native American children also had an early history in the South, starting with the efforts of Virginia settlers in 1622 to establish a school, called Henrico, to educate these children in reading and in knowl-edge of Christian principles. This effort was only intermittently successful and was often undermined by hostile relations between the English settlers and the Native American population. Attempts to enslave Native Americans proved to be problematic because of their vulnerability to European dis-eases and the local assistance they could get from fellow tribesmen to escape (Webster, 1974). In any event, education of Native Americans in the South was wholly evangelistic, a matter of saving souls.

In the middle colonies, which comprised different groups of Protestants, Catholics, and Jews, there was also no strong push for public education. As in the southern colonies, no ethnic or religious monopoly existed to fuel such a movement. Thus, in the middle colonies, where no one church dom-inated the political landscape, the state played a rather marginal role in the education of youths (Cubberley,1947). Although the belief in educating youths for personal salvation existed among the middle colonists, these educative obligations were handed to the church and to private schools. As a result, families had to depend on the church or their own resources for even a rudimentary education. The state was, for all intents and purposes, out of the picture. This laissez-faire attitude toward public education in the middle colonies continued into the nineteenth century and was not sur-mounted until the migration of New Englanders created a critical mass that helped to agitate for increased public education (French, 1964).

But various church-affiliated groups did provide an important educa-tional service to children in the colonies. Quakers, for instance, provided literacy education to both sexes and admitted poor and black children to their schools free of charge. They also sponsored a network of charity schools throughout the colonies for the education of black and Native Amer-ican children. Quakers, most of whom did not own slaves, dedicated them-selves to the abolitionist cause, as well as to the education of black children. As Button and Provenzo (1983) put it, "the Church of England had hoped to save souls . . . abolitionist Quakers aimed to save men and women" (p. 38).

All in all, the colonial educational scene was marked by three rather dif-ferent movements (Cubberley, 1947). In New England, particularly in Massachusetts, efforts were directed at establishing state-sponsored com-mon schools that carried a clear religious mandate. The preponderance of towns and the lack of religious diversity made it easy for the citizens of Massachusetts to conduct such schools. As a nation, the United States inherited its present system of governance, with some obvious changes, from the Puritan New England model; Feature 5-2 traces that evolution. In the middle colonies, which were populated mostly by Protestants and Catholics, the church stood as the main player in the education of youths. Education proceeded along denominational lines, and the people viewed

The Puritans' attraction to public education was moved by a desire to use the school as an agency for the advancement of the church doctrine.

any participation by the state in such affairs as repugnant. Southerners, for their part, favored private tutoring or private schooling, with church-sponsored pauper schools for the poor.

Of course, the New England tradition eventually prevailed nationwide. Had the middle colonists had their way, the structure of schooling in America might have evolved into a partnership between private and public schools; had the southern colonists' views become popular, the nation's schools might have developed into an openly private and parochial system (French, 1964). Clearly, then, the schooling traditions of the colonial period were central to the development of modern public schooling.

THE EARLY EDUCATION OF BLACKS

As indicated, the education of black slaves in America can be viewed in terms of two historical periods (Woodson, 1968). In the first, dating from the introduction of slaves to the New World at the beginning of the seventeenth century until the dawning of the Industrial Revolution in the 1830s, southerners were at least not hostile to the idea of education for slaves. In the second, representing a period in the growth and exploitation of slave

5-2 THINKING ABOUT THE DATA
The Evolution of Local School Governance

Examine the following schematic, paying particular attention to the historical evolution
from the Puritan ideal of local, town-supported control. Notice how the idea of local
control started as an interplay between town and church interests and evolved into a
locally elected school board that grants a lot of room for professional control.

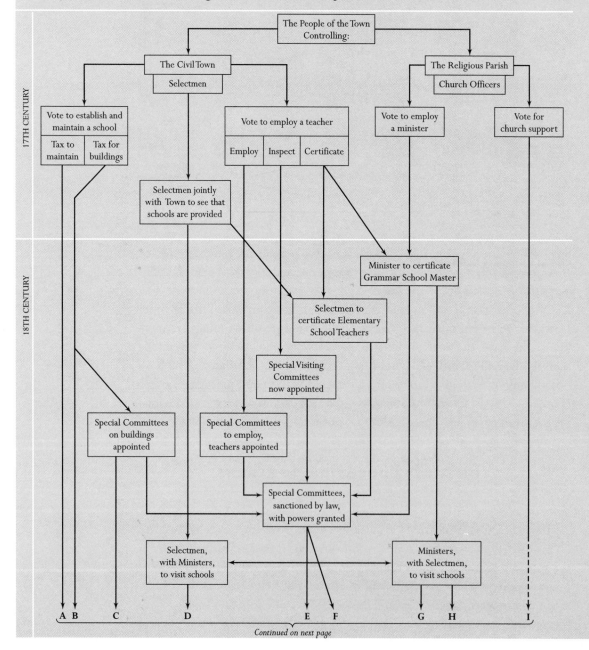

Continued on next page

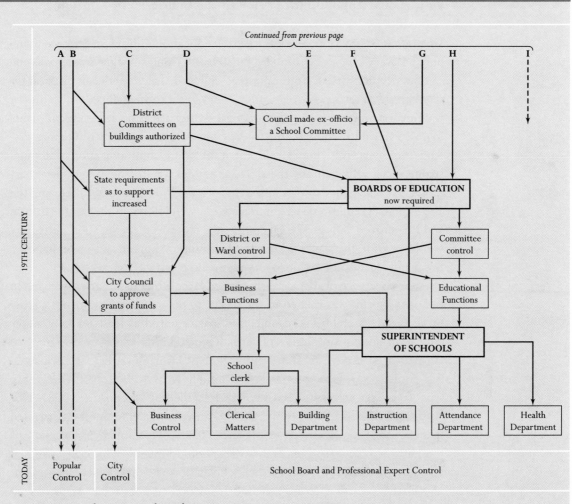

Continued from previous page

A B   C   D   E   F   G   H   I

District Committees on buildings authorized

Council made ex-officio a School Committee

State requirements as to support increased

BOARDS OF EDUCATION
now required

City Council to approve grants of funds

District or Ward control

Committee control

Business Functions

Educational Functions

SUPERINTENDENT OF SCHOOLS

School clerk

Business Control   Clerical Matters   Building Department   Instruction Department   Attendance Department   Health Department

19TH CENTURY

TODAY

Popular Control   City Control   School Board and Professional Expert Control

SOURCE: www.alumni.cc.gettysburg.edu

labor that culminated in the Civil War, virtually all of the doors that were once open for the education of slaves were slammed shut.

Educational Opportunities Prior to the Industrial Revolution

During the first period, advocacy for the education of black Americans living under slavery emerged from several sources. Ironically, one source was the slaveholder class itself. Some masters believed that the education of slaves would result only in positive economic and social consequences. Educating or training a slave force in specific practical skills, such as bookkeeping or printing, was viewed as contributing to the economic productivity of the masters. And they perceived the development of good communication skills and strong social values among the slaves as a good way to encourage social harmony and acceptance of one's place in society (Woodson, 1968). During the 1700s, in fact, educated slave artisans were well known in the South (Button and Provenzo, 1983, p. 37). Of course, the risk was that education ultimately would provide the slaves with a level of empowerment and understanding that would lead to a longing for freedom and eventual insurrection.

Another source of advocacy, motivated largely by missionaries working in the New World, was related to the desire to disseminate Christian doctrine to all of God's children, an objective that required at least a rudimentary education among potential converts. The desire to bring black slaves to Christ was even used by some as a argument favoring slavery, as slaves who had come to the faith were believed somehow to be better off than those who were free but without Christian benediction (Woodson, 1968). This argument, however, was problematic because several church officials argued that manumission (freedom from slavery) had to accompany conversion to the faith. No Christian, in other words, could be held in bondage. Thus, if the education of slaves led to their conversion to Christianity, they might legitimately demand to be released from bondage. For the Anglicans, at least, the bishop of London forestalled this possibility by ruling that the conversion of blacks to the faith should not result in manumission. With this ruling in place, missionaries were able to spread the Word in the New World without much resistance from slaveholders. As a result, as early as 1701, the Society for the Propagation of the Gospel in Foreign Parts was formed in England with the charge of moving to the New World to instruct blacks and Native Americans, and their children, in the tools needed to bring them all to an understanding of Christ. With the support of the society, various schools opened throughout the colonies. The campaign to educate blacks proceeded so rapidly that it caused some anxiety among some slaveholders and resulted in legislation prohibiting the practice. This was evident in South

FIGURE **5-3**
An Act Prohibiting Teaching Slaves to Write in South Carolina (1740)

And *whereas,* the having of slaves taught to write, or suffering them to be employed in writing, may be attended with great inconveniences; *Be it therefore enacted* by the authority aforesaid, That all and every person or persons whatsoever, who shall hereafter teach, or cause any slave or slaves to be taught, to write, or shall use or employ any slave as a scribe in any manner of writing whatsoever, hereafter taught to write, every such person and persons, shall, for every such offence, forfeit the sum of one hundred pounds current money.

SOURCE: Cooper, T., & McCord, D. (1836–41), *The statutes at large of South Carolina.* In S. Cohen, *Education in the United States: A documentary history* (Vol. 1) (New York: Random House), p. 574.

Carolina as early as 1740, as Figure 5-3 shows, but it was not a widespread prohibition, at least not yet. Many clergymen also actively opposed slavery. Even the Puritans, who did not criticize the institution of slavery as a disgrace to their faith, nevertheless insisted that all slaves be educated under the same rationale given for the education of their own children. And although church-supported education for slaves was largely motivated by a patriarchal belief in the need to enlighten the heathens, it nevertheless delivered real opportunities for education to blacks.

Another source of support for black slaves, one that was less attached to the idea of saving souls of blacks than to that of preserving their humanity, emerged from the Quakers. As early as 1693, the Quakers were on record as protesting the slave trade and openly advocating the education of blacks on the grounds that such an education would lead to their emancipation. Known as the Society of Friends, the Quakers were the first religious group to move actively against slavery, taking on abolitionist causes, organizing free schools throughout the colonies, and threatening reprisals against any Quaker who held slaves. In 1775, the Quakers established the Society for the Relief of Free Negroes Unlawfully Held in Bondage to extend an ameliorative hand into the lives of black slaves; Benjamin Franklin was its first president. The society trumpeted the issues of freedom for and education of slaves in state legislatures and religious meetings. It also worked to establish programs for black education throughout the colonies. In 1785, the Quakers also established the Manumission Society, which was designed to protect slaves from slave bounty hunters and to increase educational opportunities for black children. The Quaker-supported African free schools produced many distinguished graduates, including Benjamin Banneker (Morgan, 1995).

Led by the Quakers, antislavery abolitionists throughout the eighteenth century led campaigns to educate black slaves. Their educational plans for blacks were driven by a belief that emancipation was inevitable and that, in preparation for that event, black slaves had to begin the process of education, and in a manner that would serve them well in the future. Thus, at the turn of the eighteenth century, one could find Sunday schools, church-affiliated schools, various schools supported by individuals and nongovernment organizations, such as various abolitionist societies; in the North, legislators actively supported the education of blacks.

The effects of all this activism were manifest. Even the debasing advertisements used to sell slaves often touted their educational achievements in reading, speaking, and writing (Woodson, 1968). Educated black preachers traveled far and wide preaching the Gospels, and, against all odds, black intellectuals such as James Durham, Phyllis Wheatley, and Benjamin Banneker made their professional marks during the late eighteenth century. Feature 5-3 discusses the education of distinguished black Americans in more detail. In 1794, the American Convention of Abolition Societies recommended that the education of blacks move beyond the rudiments of achieving literacy and understanding Christian text, and into the useful arts of mechanics and agriculture. Emancipated blacks, the argument went, would eventually need to know how to till the soil, live off the land, and work as machinists and artisans.

Finally, support for the education of blacks was linked to the nascent social doctrine of democracy that fueled the American Revolution in the late 1700s. Virtually all of the leaders of the Revolution were poised, in one way or another, to put the new nation on a course to suppress the slave trade, to educate slaves for freedom, and eventually to emancipate them. The argument here was less about Christianity and more about what might be viewed as the natural rights of humanity in a democratic society. At the same time, however, these leaders were hardly militant in protesting the mistreatment of blacks and Native Americans. Blacks especially did not calculate into the rhetoric of bringing life, liberty, and happiness to all people (Woodson, 1968). For example, John Adams might have detested slavery and never owned slaves, but he had little to say about how slavery represented a contradiction to the guiding principles of the new nation. George Washington, who owned many slaves, was also generally quiet about slavery, although he did free his slaves upon his death and that of his wife. Alexander Hamilton openly opposed slavery, supported schooling for black children, and served as a trustee of the Manumission Society, but he did not actively promote antislavery prohibitions. Benjamin Franklin was probably the exception to the rule; he wrote impassioned antislavery essays and was committed to the education of black children. Feature 5-4 highlights one of Franklin's addresses on slavery.

5-3 RESEARCH INQUIRY
The Education of Distinguished Black Americans

The education of blacks in colonial America found support from a number of different sources. Nevertheless, the extension of schooling into the lives of black children was severely limited. Despite the lack of educational opportunities, several blacks during the eighteenth century and early nineteenth century achieved distinction in various areas of endeavor. Benjamin Banneker (1731–1804) was a well-known writer, astronomer, and scientist; Ira Aldridge (1807–1867) was a widely known actor; Martin DeLaney (1812–1885) was a graduate of Harvard Medical School whose career moved into journalism and political activism; Isabella Baumfree (1797–1883), also known as Sojourner Truth, was a black abolitionist and an acclaimed orator, as was Harriet Ross Tubman (1820–1913).

Research two or more of these distinguished African Americans, focusing on their early education. Where were they schooled? Who provided the schooling? What did their early education have in common?

Benjamin Banneker

© Stock Montage, Inc.

Sojourner Truth

Archive Photos

5-4 THE HISTORICAL CONTEXT
Benjamin Franklin Urging the Abolition of Slavery

As president of the Quaker's Society for Promoting the Abolition of Slavery and the Relief of Free Negroes Unlawfully Held in Bondage, Benjamin Franklin petitioned for an antislavery amendment to the Constitution. In this 1789 address, which was sent to Congress, he makes his case to the public.

It is with peculiar satisfaction we assure the friends of humanity that, in prosecuting the design of our association, our endeavors have proved successful, far beyond our most sanguine expectations.

Encouraged by this success, and by the daily progress of that luminous and benign spirit of liberty which is diffusing itself throughout the world, and humbly hoping for the continuance of the divine blessing on our labors, we have ventured to make an important addition to our original plan; and do therefore earnestly solicit the support and assistance of all who can feel the tender emotions of sympathy and compassion, or relish the exalted pleasure of beneficence.

Slavery is such an atrocious debasement of human nature, that its very extirpation, if not performed with solicitous care, may sometimes open a source of serious evils.

The unhappy man, who has long been treated as a brute animal, too frequently sinks beneath the common standard of the human species. The galling chains that bind his body do also fetter his intellectual faculties, and impair the social affections of his heart. Accustomed to move like a mere machine, by the will of a master, reflection is suspended; he has not the power of choice; and reason and conscience have but little influence over his conduct, because he is chiefly governed by the passion of fear. He is poor and friendless; perhaps worn out by extreme labor, age, and disease.

Under such circumstances, freedom may often prove a misfortune to himself, and prejudicial to society.

Attention to emancipated black people, it is therefore to be hoped, will become a branch of our national policy; but, as far as we contribute to promote this emancipation, so far that attention is evidently a serious duty incumbent on us, and which we mean to discharge to the best of our judgment and abilities.

To instruct, to advise, to qualify those who have been restored to freedom, for the exercise and enjoyment of civil liberty; to promote in them habits of industry; to furnish them with employments suited to their age, sex, talents, and other circumstances; and to procure their children an education calculated for their future situation in life, these are the great outlines of the annexed plan, which we have adopted, and which we conceive will essentially promote the public good, and the happiness of these our hitherto too much neglected fellow-creatures.

A plan so extensive cannot be carried into execution without considerable pecuniary resources, beyond the present ordinary funds of the Society. We hope much from the generosity of enlightened and benevolent freemen, and will gratefully receive any donations of subscriptions for this purpose which may be made to our Treasurer, James Starr, or to James Pemberon, Chairman of our Committee of Correspondence.

5-5 DEBATING THE ISSUES
School Namings and Slave Owners

In 1997, the Orleans (Louisiana) Parish School Board banned the use of the names of slave owners in any school namings. Thus, in the New Orleans public schools, you will not find a George Washington High School or a Thomas Jefferson Middle School. Because Washington and Jefferson owned slaves, no school in the New Orleans public school system can be named after them. The board argued that it is demeaning for the children in this overwhelmingly black school system to attend schools named after slave owners. Others counter that such a policy fails to account for the broader contributions these historical figures, some of whom owned slaves, made to the development of our democracy. The drafting of such a policy is, of course, a local prerogative, and no one questions the right of the board to make such a decision. But do you agree with it? Why or why not?

Thomas Jefferson was especially vulnerable on the issue of slavery and education. Jefferson did draft some early legislation to abolish slavery, and he supported the antislavery provisions of the Northwest Land Ordinance. But he never freed his own slaves, and he did not play much of an activist role in fighting for the causes of the slaves during his lifetime (Butts, 1978). Even Jefferson's rather modest proposals for free schooling were overwhelmingly rejected by Virginia legislators, suggesting that any hope for radical changes in the educational opportunities of slaves was slight indeed. Still, Jefferson's lack of activism was telling: Even perhaps the greatest American voice of the eighteenth century for liberty and equity did little to rally the forces needed to include blacks as free people who could be peacefully and fruitfully integrated into what was clearly developing into a pluralist constitutional democracy. This was a battle, quite literally, for another time. Today, in fact, there is lingering resentment toward Jefferson and other Founding Fathers who were slaveholders; Feature 5-5 discusses one expression of this resentment.

Increased Oppression Following the Industrial Revolution

Everything changed, however, around 1830, when the Industrial Revolution transformed the South into a plantation economy reliant on a huge slave force that was beaten down, deprived of any enlightenment, and often literally worked to death. With new mechanical appliances readily available for the processing of cotton into cheap cloth, the plantation system expanded in size and economic efficiency. In 1790, there were approximately 700,000 slaves in the nation; by 1860, by the time of the Civil War, the number had swelled to 4 million (Webster, 1974). In the South, slaves became an expendable tool for economic productivity and personal enrichment (Woodson, 1968). Not surprisingly, insurrections increased in number and in passion, which led to tightened restrictions and even more vile mistreatment of blacks. Slave owners quickly associated the education of slaves with the ability to mount insurrections. Those who in earlier times saw a rationale favoring the education of blacks now felt only anxiety over it. The consequence was the enactment of a series of state laws restricting the education, assembly, and travel of blacks. In 1814, for instance, Louisiana passed a law prohibiting the travel of free persons of color. In 1831, Georgia and Virginia passed laws prohibiting the education of blacks, and Alabama did so in 1832. In 1831, Mississippi passed a law prohibiting the congregation of more than twelve free blacks without the supervision of whites. In 1835, North Carolina passed an act prohibiting the instruction of blacks, and Missouri adopted a similar measure in 1847. As black historian Carter Woodson (1968) put it, with the passage of these prohibitions, slavery in the South now extended not only to the body but also to the mind. Nor was the North completely blameless; some northern states passed laws prohibiting the immigration of blacks to the North. In Feature 5-6, Woodson describes the prevailing antieducation mentality in the South.

Freedom of assembly, association with other slaves, and even self-initiated education (i.e., parents trying to teach something to their children)—all essentially were forbidden in the slave states. The churches now had to reconcile these prohibitions with the need to bring religious instruction to slaves. This eventually led to the employment of memory training—that is, education without letters and written words—in Christian principles for slaves. Some slave owners and local preachers continued to allow educators to operate discreetly in opposition to the law, but one manifest effect of the laws was to chase away the northern teachers, abolitionists, and other "outsiders" who had sought to enlighten the slaves. The Quakers found themselves the targets of criticism, as laws were enacted that made it difficult for them to interact with blacks, much less to help teach them. Now the southern blacks had but one place to turn for their education—themselves. Slaves, especially on the larger plantations, had to rely on their own wits and will to educate "their own." This was done through family or community

5-6 SCHOLARLY VOICES

Carter Woodson on the Education of Enslaved Blacks

Carter Woodson was a well-known black historian whose 1919 work on the history of black education still stands as a notable scholarly achievement. In this excerpt, Woodson outlines the mentality that eventually prevailed among slaveholders toward the education of enslaved blacks.

Brought from the African wilds to constitute the laboring class of a pioneering society in the new world, the . . . slaves had to be trained to meet the needs of their environment. It required little argument to convince intelligent masters that slaves who had some conception of modern civilization and understood the language of their owners would be more valuable than rude men with whom one could not communicate. The questions, however, as to exactly what kind of training these Negroes should have, and how far it should go, were to the white race . . . a matter of perplexity. . . . Yet, believing that slaves could not be enlightened without developing in them a longing for liberty, not a few masters maintained that the more brutish the bondsmen the more pliant they become for purposes of exploitation. It was this class of slaveholders that finally won the majority of southerners to their way of thinking and determined that Negroes should not be educated.

Carter Woodson

storytelling and through various clandestine meetings, which tended to focus on black folklore, on agricultural and artisan skills, and on Christian precepts (Cremin, 1977). Secret schools, clandestine meetings, field instruction, and various individualistic efforts helped to secure some enlightenment.

SUMMARY

Education in colonial America reflected regional differences in attitudes toward the idea of publicly funded schools. In homogeneous New

England, the public school was conceived as an extension of the church, as an institution that could broaden and secure the agenda of the church in the community. Uniformly committed to the cause of building a church-based society, the Puritans passed legislation that resulted in public funding for a compulsory school system. In the middle and southern colonies, geographic and demographic conditions did not allow for a uniformly supported system of public schooling. Different church affiliations and the influence of social classes resulted in a system of private schools for the well-to-do and church-sponsored charity schools for the poor. The latter also applied to the education of blacks and Native Americans, which was offered through the efforts of the Society for the Propagation of the Gospel (SPG) and other church groups, most notably the Quakers. The work of the Quakers was noticeable in other areas of concern to blacks and their children as well. Active in abolitionist causes, the Quakers provided a network of free schools for black children in both the North and the South. But even these limited opportunities for education were eventually wiped out in the wake of the nineteenth-century growth of the slave markets in the South and the concomitant treatment of slaves as commodities in a high-profit economy. Fearful that education might result in a yearning for freedom, the slaveholders sought prohibitions against any education for slaves.

QUESTIONS AND ACTIVITIES

1. Why did regional differences exist in the colonies in the provision of public education?

2. How do you account for the slight attention given to the education of women and girls in the colonies?

3. Characterize the overall nature of teaching in a New England dame school or Latin grammar school.

4. Why was the Massachusetts Law of 1647 also known as the Old Deluder Act?

5. How did the Puritans equate a literacy education with a religious education?

6. Describe the methods of and justifications for discipline in the schools of the Puritans.

7. In what way was the American public school born out of a religious mandate?

8. Why did the Puritans want to hand over the control of education to the government?

9. In what way was the (Massachusetts) Law of 1647 a greater stride toward the development of the public school than the Law of 1642?

10. What was meant by the observation that the *New England Primer* "taught millions to read and not one to sin"?

11. Why was the instructional orientation in the Latin grammar school so sharply focused on learning Latin?

12. Describe the development in the school in the three regions discussed in the chapter. What might the governance structure be like today if the school traditions of middle or southern colonies had prevailed?

13. Why was there less interest in publicly funded schools in the South than in New England?

14. Why were few slaveholders in the 1800s interested in educating their slaves?

15. What church ruling opened up opportunities for missionaries to provide education to slave children?

16. Why were most of the antieducation prohibitions against slave education passed in the 1800s?

17. What role did the SPG play in the education of black children in the South?

18. The Quakers were unique in their active protestations against slavery during the colonial period. What were some of the initiatives they undertook for this cause?

19. What was the fundamental difference between the way the Quakers approached the education of slave children and the way the missionaries approached it?

20. Assess the following according to their positions on slavery and on democracy: John Adams, Thomas Jefferson, Benjamin Franklin, and George Washington.

REFERENCES

Beale, H. K. (1975). The education of Negroes before the Civil War. In J. Barnard and D. Burner (eds.), *The American experience in education.* (New York: New Viewpoints).

Button, H. W., and Provenzo, E. P. (1983). *History of education and culture in America.* (Englewood Cliffs, NJ: Prentice-Hall).

Butts, R. F. (1978). *Public education in the United States.* (New York: Holt, Rinehart & Winston).

Butts, R. F. (1955). *A cultural history of western education: Its social and intellectual foundations.* (New York: McGraw-Hill).

Callahan, R. (1963). *An introduction to education in American society.* (New York: Knopf).

Cohen, S. S. (1974). *A history of colonial education, 1607–1776.* (New York: Wiley).

Colony of Massachusetts. (1853). *Records of the governor and company of the Massachusetts Bay in New England.* (Boston: White).

Cooper, T., and McCord, D. (eds.). (1836–41). The statutes at large in South Carolina. In S. Cohen, *Education in the United States.* (1974, Vol. 1). (New York: Random House).

Cremin, L. A. (1977). *Traditions of American education.* (New York: Basic Books).

Cubberley, E. B. (1947). *Public education in the United States.* (Boston: Houghton Mifflin).

Douglas, H. R., and Greider, C. (1948). *American public education.* (New York: Ronald Press).

Ford, P. L. (1899). *The New England Primer.* (New York: Dodd, Mead).

French, W. M. (1967). *American secondary education.* (New York: Odyssey Press).

French, W. M. (1964). *America's educational tradition.* (Boston: Heath).

Harris, W. T. (1899). *Education in the United States.* (New York: Appleton).

Karier, C. J. (1967). *Man, society and education.* (New York: Scott, Foresman).

Knight, E. W. (1951). *Education in the United States.* (Boston: Ginn).

Mayer, F. (1964). *American ideas and education.* (Columbus, OH: Merrill).

Meriwether, C. (1907). *Colonial curriculum 1607–1776.* (Washington, DC: Capital).

Morgan, H. (1995). *Historical perspectives on the education of black children.* (Westport, CT: Praeger).

Noble, S. G. (1959). *A history of American education.* (New York: Rinehart).

Rippa, S. A. (1984). *Education in a free society: An American history.* (New York: McKay).

Shurteff, N. B. (1853–54). Records of the governor and company of Massachusetts Bay in New England. In S. Cohen, *Education in the United States* (1974, Vol. 1). (New York: Random House).

Small, W. H. (1969). *Early New England schools.* (New York: Arno Press and the New York Times).

Tanner, D., and Tanner, L. N. (1987). *History of the school curriculum.* (New York: Macmillan).

Webster, S. W. (1974). *Education of black Americans.* (New York: Intext Educational).

Winthrop, J. (1826). The history of New England from 1630 to 1649. In S. Cohen, *Education in the United States* (1974, Vol. 1). (New York: Random House).

Woodson, C. G. (1968). *The education of the Negro prior to 1861.* (New York: Arno Press and the New York Times). Originally published in 1919 by Associated Publishers, Washington, DC.

CHAPTER 6

Public Schooling and the Secular Mandate

Changes in School Orientation
THE AMERICAN-STYLE ACADEMY
SCHOOL GOVERNANCE

Education in the New Nation

The Struggle for the American Public School
INSTRUCTIONAL METHODS
INDUSTRIAL DEVELOPMENT AND THE NEW NATIONAL
   CONSCIOUSNESS
EARLY FUNDING AND GOVERNANCE

Horace Mann and the Rise of State Authority

The Upward and Outward Extension of Schooling

The Birth of Teacher Education

**The Evolution of Teacher Associations
and Teacher Unions**
THE NATIONAL EDUCATION ASSOCIATION
THE AMERICAN FEDERATION OF TEACHERS

Summary

Questions and Activities

References

T HE POST-REVOLUTIONARY PERIOD IN AMERICA was a turning point for the development of the public school because it cleared the way for a new social agenda. The traditional use of the schools to perpetuate religious doctrine could no longer hold, although it would take some time to loosen the grip of religion. The birth of a new democratic nation, populated by people who represented a mosaic of religious, ethnic, linguistic, and racial identities, demanded a new kind of school experience. Secular purposes, not sacred ones, took center stage in the schools. National unity had to be strengthened, and a new generation of youths had to be socialized into the skills and behaviors needed to participate in the new constitutional democracy. The new nation, in effect, had to use the schools to find itself. During the late 1700s, in practical terms, this did little to advance the education of women and blacks, but it did set the conditions for the growth of a school system that would, over time, extend itself upward and outward.

CHANGES IN SCHOOL ORIENTATION

As an American-born generation of colonists began to expand their settlements inland during the mid-1700s, new attitudes toward schooling and religion began to prevail. Never having borne the yoke of religious oppression in Europe, this new generation of colonists were less absorbed with religious zeal and more civic-minded in their approach toward government and business. The increase in the number of denominations in the colonies made the relation between church and state much more complicated. And the hard work of frontier settlement life pointed to a more practical outlook toward life in general and toward schooling in particular.

The colonies were also beginning to develop a sense of national identification. One major consequence of the American Revolution was that schooling had to play a larger role in relation to civic affairs and economic needs. Knowledge of Latin and Greek was simply not going to take the new generation of youths far enough in dealing with the nation's economic, political, and social issues. A new method of schooling was on the horizon.

The American-Style Academy

By 1750, an entirely new vision for secondary schooling was beginning to take shape. First advanced by Benjamin Franklin, the American-style academy was designed to make the curriculum more utilitarian than the Latin grammar school and more responsive to emergent economic and social needs. These academies did not abandon the traditional courses in Latin and Greek, but they gave such courses a less exalted status in the curriculum. Franklin believed that the course work had to be broadened to include scientific inquiry and practical instruction in writing, agriculture and gardening, and navigation and surveying. Even physical education had some currency in the curriculum. Of course, the curriculum retained all of the traditional academic disciplines. Franklin also wanted to avoid religious or sectarian instruction in the academies, except as it might relate to other academic studies. In essence, his idea for schooling in the academies marked an early stage in the development of a new and comprehensive form of education.

Not only was the curriculum different, but those admitted into the school were different as well. For the first time, girls were being freely admitted into postelementary education. The Latin grammar schools, we should remember, excluded girls, largely because they were designed as a preparatory education for the ministry, which girls could not pursue. The academies, by contrast, were often coeducational, as well as openly utilitarian in their curriculum orientation. Household skills, along with the academic traditions of grammar, mathematics, languages, and English, had a place in the curriculum. The curriculum offerings, in other words, were relevant for both boys and girls.

However, the academies were still not truly public institutions. They were open to the public, but they were not free. Nor did they operate as Franklin had hoped or expected. The classical traditions provided too strong an undertow for the utilitarian brand of education that Franklin promoted, and some academies actually became breeding grounds for the college-bound elites, much to Franklin's dismay (Butts, 1955).

Still, the academies were a significant step in the development of a new philosophy of schooling according to which education should be more useful and more attentive to real-life issues and experiences (Butts and Cremin, 1953). The actual range of subjects taught in various New York academies from 1787 to 1881 is shown in Figure 6-1. Collectively, the offerings represent a much more freewheeling and practically minded approach to learning than what was typically provided in the Latin grammar schools. By the end of the eighteenth century, the Latin grammar schools had more or less expired or transformed themselves into institutions resembling the academies. A new curriculum prototype was born in the academy design, one that underscored the significance of comprehensive schooling.

FIGURE 6-1
Subjects Taught in the New York Academies, 1787–1881

Subject	Year	Subject	Year	Subject	Year
Acoustics	1850	French	1787	Music	1827
Algebra	1825	Geography	1787	Music, vocal	1832
Archaeology	1844	Geography, ancient and biblical	1826	Mythology	1829
Architecture	1830	Geography, physical	1828	Natural history	1830
Anatomy	1837	Geography, political	1830	Natural and moral chemistry	1829
Arithmetic	1787	Geology	1830	Natural theology	1828
Arts and sciences	1797	Geometry, analytical	1828	Nautical astronomy	1831
Athletic exercise	1828	Geometry, descriptive	1828	Navigation	1826
Astronomy	1797	Geometry, plane	1825	Needle-work	1828
Belles lettres	1817	Geometry, solid	1885	Optics	1831
Biblical antiquities	1832	German	1825	Orthography (spelling)	1796
Biography	1831	Globes	1827	Ornamental needle-work	1828
Blair's lectures	1827	Grecian antiquities	1828	Ornithology	1847
Bookkeeping (accountantship)	1787	Greek	1787	Painting	1826
Botany	1827	Gymnastics	1849	Penmanship (writing)	1787
Calculus	1830	Hebrew	1829	Perspective	1828
Calisthenics	1841	Higher mathematics	1825	Philosophy	1825
Carpentry	1844	History of England	1841	Philosophy, intellectual (mental)	1826
Chaldee	1838	History of France	1841	Philosophy of language	1827
Chemistry	1825	History, general	1787	Philosophy, moral	1804
Chemistry, agricultural	1841	History of Greece	1881	Philosophy, natural	1787
Chronology	1826	History of literature	1867	Philosophy, natural and chemical	1828
Classical biography	1832	History of N.Y.	1831	Philosophy, vegetable	1831
Commerce	1873	History of Rome	1881	Phonography	1846
Composition	1804	History, Tytler's	1829	Phreno-mnemotechny	1844
Conchology	1840	History of U.S.	1827	Physics	1879
Conic sections	1827	Hydraulics	1850	Physiology	1835
Constitution, New York	1841	Hydrostatics	1832	Political economy	1832
Constitution, U.S.	1841	Hydrostatics and pneumatics	1844	Pronunciation	1834
Criticism, elements of	1826	Hygiene	1849	Psychology	1847
Dancing	1837	Intellectual arithmetic	1831	Reading	1787
Declamation (elocution)	1787	Isoperimetry	1841	Rhetoric	1799
Dialing	1830	Italian	1828	Roman antiquities	1827
Domestic economy	1850	Jewish antiquities	1828	Spanish	1825
Drawing	1826	Latin	1787	Statics and dynamics	1852
Draughting	1851	Law (civics)	1826	Stenography	1831
Ecclesiastical history	1830	Laws of interpretation	1833	Stewart on the mind	1825
Electricity	1843	Lectures on English language	1833	Statistics	1831
Elements of taste	1832	Leveling	1834	Surveying	1801
Embroidery	1836	Logarithms	1825	Teaching, principles of	1831
Engineering	1828	Logic	1787	Technology	1830
Engineering, civil	1835	Mapping	1839	Technology, mathematical	1831
English, elements of grammar	1787	Mathematics	1787	Theology	1830
English literature	1804	Mechanics	1830	Topography	1830
Ethics	1827	Mensuration	1827	Trigonometry	1825
Evidences of Christianity	1827	Mental arithmetic	1826	Trigonometry, plane	1831
Evidences, Parley's	1827	Metaphysics	1827	Trigonometry, spherical	1831
Evidences of religion	1832	Meteorology	1838	Warts on the mind	1827
Extemporaneous speaking	1834	Military education	1827	Waxwork	1841
Fencing and military tactics	1828	Military tactics	1826	Zoology	1828
Fine needle-work	1827	Mineralogy	1828		
Fluxions	1825	Mnemonics	1832		

SOURCE: French, W. M. (1967), *American secondary education* (New York: Odyssey Press), pp. 74–75.

During the early phases of colonial settlement in New England, town schools were built and supported with local tax money for the education of all local youth.

School Governance

Changes were also occurring at the level of school governance. During the early phases of colonial settlement, the typical New England town was organized around facilities for public meetings and public schooling. The requirements for universal church attendance and the fear of Indian attacks had kept most settlements within a half mile of most towns (Cremin, 1951). In time, more inland settlements arose at the extreme peripheries of the central town. For those living in the more distant areas, the centrally located church and school became difficult to reach and were less widely used. Because they supported the town school with their taxes, those living in the outlying sections asked town officials to provide school facilities for them. The original solution was something known as a moving school. The town sent an itinerant schoolmaster to each of the more remote communities for a designated period of time to teach the children.

This practice, however, eventually gave way to the proportional sharing of property taxes so that each area could independently govern its own schools. Soon, these new districts opened their own dame schools and private schools, and the education of children began to be framed as a district, as opposed to a town, concern. The districts, in essence, rediscovered the dimension of local school governance that was once fundamental to the central town. For the purposes of schooling, these districts typically were restricted to the distance one could reasonably expect children to walk to school (Button and Provenzo, 1983, p. 93). The districts, however, did not have legal sanction until the passage of the Massachusetts Law of 1789. This law established the district as the basic unit of organization for the public school and reconfirmed the essential logic of the Massachusetts Law of 1647, which assigned the function of the school to local governance (Cremin, 1951). Each district was now more or less free to proceed along its own individual lines. Like the 1647 law, the new legislation also encouraged the local inspection of schools by town or district officials, stressing the responsibility that ministers had in supervising the curriculum and in encouraging attendance (Cremin, 1951).

Note, however, that the functional governance of the school was entrusted to civil authorities, not religious ones. Town funds, not church funds, were used to finance the schools. The Puritans actually had few objections to the idea of moving the school into the province of the civil government, and so it was accomplished without much friction (Cubberley, 1947). But the objectives of the church were still superordinate to the objectives of the school district. In assigning the governance of the school to the civil government, the Puritans were confident that religious instruction had a sound advocate. In this sense, the American concept of local initiative was born out of a religious agenda.

New England and some of the middle colonies made great strides in providing a basic and religious education to youths. However, with the possible exception of Massachusetts, the colonies made little progress toward universalizing even a primary education for children. Laws were permissive, and the local districts were not equally committed to the provision of common schools. Those that had the means could establish schools for their children, but for the majority of the population, life was still marked by illiteracy. However, whatever strides might have been taken in the seventeenth century toward the provision of a public education in the colonies were essentially reversed with the start of the Revolutionary War. Many colony schools closed under British occupancy, and many others fell into disarray and disrepair. Educational options decreased, and illiteracy increased.

EDUCATION IN THE NEW NATION

After achieving independence, the new nation was impoverished and was faced with the daunting task of establishing an independent government amid a society growing in cultural and religious diversity. The U.S. Constitution seemed to provide no indication of how the public school might evolve in the new nation. In England, the tradition had been to leave the state out of the affairs of education. The framers of the Constitution, virtually all privileged members of the colonial aristocracy, made no mention of education in the document. This has led to speculation about what role they envisioned for the school in society (Butts, 1978), with some scholars arguing that the framers wanted to leave education to the private sector. The fact that no direct reference to education can be found in the nation's most important legal document is not exactly an endorsement of the centrality of public education to the workings of the new democracy (Power, 1991).

But the framers' views on education were couched in other positions, the most prominent being the position taken on the separation of church and state. When the attendees of the Constitutional Convention contemplated some of the growing pains of the new nation, they were quickly drawn to the issue of how the state and church might reconcile their agendas. Among the problems facing the new nation was a growing religious diversity. The framers of the Constitution posed a solution by supporting the free exercise of religious faith for all and by banning any state-sponsored religion. The state and the church could no longer be intimates, as they had been in some of the more homogeneous colonies. Moreover, when the Tenth Amendment to the Constitution, which declared that any powers not specifically delegated to the federal government become the property of the states, was ratified in 1791, public education secured a place as a state function as opposed to a federal one. To this day, the public schools are marked by a state-specific strategy of governance that allows for the exercise of local district views—the first decentralized system of schooling in the world.

Taking religion out of the governance of the state set the course for a common, nonsectarian, state-funded public school. The use of public funds to support a religious education became more problematic. With the apparatus for publicly funded schooling already in place in Massachusetts, the common public school had just begun its transformation from an institution dominated by religiosity to one charged with enlightening a diverse citizenry for civic participation. The development of a new democracy was now dependent on a public school system that could help build functioning political communities (Butts, 1978). The very system that had its beginnings in religion was now conceived as a form of protection against it. The new mandate for the public school was civic in character and was generally associated with the need to socialize good citizens.

Many of the early advocates of a public system of schooling referred to the need for education to become a source of general enlightenment for citizens in a democracy. These were essentially the sentiments expressed by early statesmen like Thomas Jefferson, Thomas Paine, John Adams, John Jay,

James Madison, and George Washington. The dominant themes of religious fervor were replaced with more secular discussions of issues of equity, liberty, individualism, and reason. Jefferson, more than anyone in his time, directly appealed to the logic of allying a democratic society with public education. In a famous statement, he declared that "if a nation expects to be ignorant and free in a state of civilization it expects what never was and never will be . . ." (quoted in Callahan, 1963, p. 125). As early as 1779, Jefferson proposed a plan for public education in the state of Virginia that mandated free public schooling for all free white children, at public expense, for three years. At that point, the best and brightest would be chosen for secondary education at state expense, with the aim of eventually entering the College of William and Mary, again at state expense (Callahan, 1963).

But many southerners resented state-supported education, and even a statesman with the credentials of Jefferson could not convince the legislature to accept his proposal. Jefferson's dream of a state-funded system of schooling in Virginia that provided a primary education for all free children and a more advanced education for the meritorious, including what he hoped would be the first state university, was not realized until after his death.

Universal basic elementary schooling was still many decades into the future, but Jefferson and others planted the idea for it. By the end of the eighteenth century, state governments throughout the nation, with some regional variations, were beginning to confront the reality of funding public education. In 1776, for instance, Pennsylvania and North Carolina expressed a commitment to a publicly funded education in their state constitutions, and several other states followed suit (Drake, 1955, p. 141). By the late 1780s, Vermont, Massachusetts, and New Hampshire instituted general state school laws, mandating compulsory public education (Cubberley, 1947). Not only were elementary and Latin grammar schools supported in New England, but new colleges were also being founded, including Yale and Dartmouth. Thus, in New England and, eventually, New York and Ohio, the belief in state-sponsored schooling continued, even after the religious justification for it had eroded (Cubberley, 1947).

The middle Atlantic states, however, were much less attuned to the objectives of general education in the population. Some legislative support was garnered for the public financing of pauper schools, but the tradition of privately funded education continued to prevail. Similarly, the southern states (as well as Rhode Island, which was the first state to legislatively support the freedom to exercise any religion) essentially maintained that the state had no business in the affairs of educating children.

Even as various states incorporated a commitment to public schooling in their constitutions and laws, the federal government was underscoring the importance of public education through its regulation of the westward migration (Cubberley, 1947). As settlers purchased land in Ohio and other territories north and west of Ohio, Congress decreed that land surveys be conducted and that one section of the land surveyed (640 acres) in every township be reserved as a place for the maintenance of schools (Butts, 1978). Land grants provided by the Northwest (or Land) Ordinance of 1785 enticed settlers from New England to the region and helped to create a conducive climate for publicly funded schooling. Because so many New Englanders migrated West, the development of schools in the Northwest Territories (northern Ohio, northern Indiana, northern Illinois, and Michigan) often followed that same pattern set by the early Puritans. Wherever former New Englanders formed a majority in the population, particularly in Ohio, Wisconsin, and Michigan, state-funded public schooling was on firm ground. Wherever the population was dominated by settlers whose origins were in the middle Atlantic or southern states, such as Kentucky, Tennessee, and the southern portions of Ohio, Illinois, and Indiana, no such sentiments prevailed (Cubberley, 1947). Still, by 1876, nearly 20 million acres—a territory the size of Great Britain—had been allocated by the federal government for educational purposes (Harris, 1899).

THE STRUGGLE FOR THE AMERICAN PUBLIC SCHOOL

As the nation entered the nineteenth century, a philanthropic movement to offer free education to children of the poor was thriving in the cities of the North. This movement had its roots in Europe, where public education was considered to be an act of alms for the poor (Power, 1991). To wealthy Europeans, who could afford to educate their own children, the idea of public schools were unacceptable because of the associated stigma of pauperism. Despite the considerable legislative support given to the public school in America, the tradition of education as alms appealed to many wealthy citizens. At the turn of the nineteenth century, for instance, one could find public schools funded by various agencies and philanthropists, including some free schools for black children, which existed in New York City as early as 1787. Many of these charity schools were later absorbed by the public school system itself and got their charter from the state (Cubberley, 1947). Ironically, philanthropically funded public schools, as will be explained, would ultimately give a boost to the idea of publicly funded schools.

Instructional Methods

During the early 1800s, among the more significant events emanating from the philanthropic school movement was a pedagogical innovation known as the Lancaster method (sometimes also known as monitorial instruction). Named after the philanthropist Joseph Lancaster, the method originated in England and was popular in many of its pauper schools. The major appeal to the method was that it was a cheap and efficient way to educate large numbers of children in a similar manner. The idea was rather simple: The school grouped 200 to 1,000 students in one large room and seated them in rows. One student, usually a boy, was chosen as monitor of each row or a portion of it, and with the other chosen monitors was instructed by the teacher in the lessons for the day. The monitor's responsibility was to return to his row and instruct it in the very lesson that he had just completed with the teacher—hence, the phrase "monitorial instruction." This system was used for the teaching of reading, catechism, simple computations, writing, and spelling. It usually took on a competitive edge, as different groups of children, led by their monitor, competed for various rewards (Button and Provenzo, 1983, p. 69).

The beauty of the practice was that hundreds of youths presumably could be educated in one room by one teacher, with results that were no worse than those achieved in the Latin grammar schools or dame schools. With the Lancaster method, students no longer had to wait their turn at their teacher's desk to read or recite lessons. Moreover, the method protected against student idleness and promoted an orderly environment. Used on a wholesale basis, the Lancaster method greatly reduced the costs of providing a public education (Cubberley, 1947). With classroom sizes literally in the hundreds, per-pupil expenditures could be kept low. In the words of one admirer of the method, "When I behold the wonderful celerity in instruction and economy of expense and when I perceive one great assembly of a thousand children, under the eye of a single teacher, marching, with unexampled rapidity and with perfect discipline to the goal of knowledge, I confess that I recognize in Lancaster the benefactor of the human race" (Clinton, 1809, p. 121).

Another idea inspired by a philanthropist and brought to the colonies from England began to take hold at the level of primary education. In nineteenth-century England, it was not uncommon for children as young as 5 to work up to 14 hours a day in factories. One manufacturer, Robert Owen, sought to remedy this situation by offering an education to children between ages 3 and 5, partly to give them some enjoyment before entering factory life and partly to offer them moral and intellectual training. These schools were known as infant schools. In cities in the northeastern United States where similar conditions existed for poor children, various philanthropists supported infant schools for the same purposes as in England. The infant schools were especially popular in Boston, New York, and Philadelphia.

The infant schools signified an early organizational distinction between primary and elementary education. Unlike the Lancaster schools, the infant schools actually tried to advance a new theory of teaching that was driven by a psychological view of children (Cubberley, 1947). With the introduction of the infant school to America came the introduction of the learner, and his or her needs and interests, into the teaching/learning equation. This was fundamentally different from the Lancaster method, which was influenced largely by business values and efficiency concerns.

Industrial Development and the New National Consciousness

As the country grew and stabilized during the early nineteenth century, and as it moved into the early stages of industrial development and the building of its infrastructure, the ideals of equality gained popularity among settlers. The country now had to conceive of itself as a national entity, with national needs and goals, as opposed to the distinct local or regional identities that had existed among the settlers of the colonial period. During this period, the school came to be conceived, particularly among various social reformers interested in bringing equity to the social landscape of America, as a great leveler, as an agency that could provide social and economic opportunities to all.

One of the first steps toward developing a national consciousness was tied to the goal of using the schools to build a common language and a common history. Lexicographer Noah Webster (1739) took this task on as a matter of national urgency:

> It will be readily admitted that the pleasures of reading and conversing, the advantage of accuracy in business, the necessity of clearness and precision in communicating ideas, require us to be able to speak and write our own tongue with ease and correctness. . . . [We] must gradually destroy the differences of dialect which our ancestors brought from their native countries. (p. 89)

FIGURE 6-2

Sample Lesson from Webster's *American Spelling Book* (1789)

Of the Boy *that stole* Apples.

An old Man found a rude Boy upon one of his trees stealing Apples, and desired him to come down; but the young Sauce-box told him plainly he would not. Won't you? said the old Man, then I will fetch you down; so he pulled up some tufts of Grass and threw at him; but this only made the Youngster laugh, to think the old Man should pretend to beat him down from the tree with grass only.

FABLE I.—*Of the* Boy *that ſtole* Apples.
From a Webster's speller dated 1789.

Well, well, said the old Man, if neither words nor grass will do, I must try what virtue there is in Stones: so the old Man pelted him heartily with stones, which soon made the young Chap hasten down from the tree and beg the old Man's pardon.

MORAL

If good words and gentle means will not reclaim the wicked, they must be dealt with in a more severe manner.

SOURCE: Johnson, C. (1917), *Old-time schools and school books* (New York: Macmillan), p. 179.

Webster helped the schools serve the objective of fashioning a national culture by publishing his *Grammatical Institute of the English Language,* a three-part book with sections on spelling, grammar, and readings. The spelling section, which was published separately as the *American Spelling Book,* eventually superseded the *New England Primer* as the most widely used text in the schools in the late 1700s and into the 1800s. Figure 6-2 shows a sample lesson from the book. It was said to have gone West with the settlers, often being the first book printed by the local presses in the small frontier towns (Pangle and Pangle, 1993). Webster, of course, later wrote and published the *Dictionary of the English Language,* but it was his speller that provided the impetus for a common language without accents and that contributed to the ideal of a classless society. Throughout, Webster's work stressed the Puritan values of thrift, diligence, and hard work. But Webster disdained the rather stern style used in the *New England Primer* and used images of animals and other childhood pleasantries to convey his messages to children, although moralistic proclamations were in constant use (Pangle and Pangle, 1993). The influence of Webster's work in shaping a national culture earned him the title of "Schoolmaster to America" from his biographer (Drake, 1955, p. 153).

The rise of the industrial age also influenced the renewed call for public education. Industrial development brought factory work into the life of the new American, and many of these factories led to the rapid growth of cities, particularly in the northeastern and north-central regions. In the North, as manufacturing facilities developed in the cities, a concentration of capital and labor followed. Where the colonial village was once homogeneous and tied to work on the land, the new cities brought together a wide mix of people who earned a living in the factory (Cubberley, 1947).

As the United States continued to attract diverse populations to its shores, it became clear that some type of amalgamating institution was going to be needed to build political communities in the nation. The public school was one method of promoting a common national experience. By the 1850s, the annual immigration rate exceeded 500,000, with immigrants representing a wider range of national origins. Between 1840 and 1870, the population of the country doubled, and it doubled again between 1870 and 1900. At the dawn of the twentieth century, one out of every seven Americans was foreign born (Butts, 1955). No other nation had faced the challenge of socializing a largely uneducated, pluralist population into a unified entity. The argument that children needed basic reading skills to do basic manufacturing work and to become enlightened enough to stay away from crime and other socially undesirable behaviors also gained credence. Thus, the school increasingly was taking on the roles of leveler of economic differences, assimilator of ethnic differences, and communicator of what it meant to be an American.

Simultaneous with the growth of the industrial base and the increasingly overt signs of class differences was the desire to secure universal suffrage for white men. Until the early 1800s, the right to vote was restricted to men with property qualifications, those who were able to pay for the education of their own children. Therefore, Jefferson's argument about the need for an educated citizenry did not apply because most people simply did not have the full rights of citizenship. Women did not, blacks did not, and white men without means did not. But with the extension of voting rights to all white men, irrespective of class, occurring on a state-by-state basis during the early 1800s, the arguments for a free general education for all youths, especially all boys, became more compelling. In terms of suffrage, the basic hurdle of class as it related to white men was cleared. The hurdles of gender and race were still insurmountable.

Early Funding and Governance

The idea of a publicly funded school system for all youths had its share of detractors. Many argued that state-supported education was a luxury the nation could not afford and that such a system would cause industrious citizens to support the education of the stupid and the lazy. Critics also cited the old English argument that the state has no business in education, that such an institution was best left to the church and the family. There was even an aristocratic view that the poor did not need an education because they had no time to use it (Callahan, 1963).

Given this opposition, there were some battles yet to fight in gaining widespread public support for a school tax in the early 1800s. The argument for such taxation rested on a principle that equated taxation with the price that society must pay to maintain the social order (for courts, jails, roads, police, and so on). According to this rationale, free public schooling was an investment in the stability and progress of society, in making people more civilized and enlightened. In any case, many states experimented with a wide range of tools to raise monies for schools, including lotteries, occupational taxes, bank taxes, and licensing fees. Some states also used rate bills, another practice inherited from England, which were charges levied on parents whose children were in school.

But, as the population continued to grow, these sources proved inadequate, and other avenues were explored and exploited. Eventually, this led to the idea of school funding through local property taxes. In Massachusetts, the legislature passed the Law of 1789, which gave local districts full and complete power to raise taxes and to control their own schools. Such a system was well aligned with the structure of school organization established in colonial New England and was popular in several northern states. "For the purpose of public instruction," declared Daniel Webster, "we have held, and do hold, every man subject to taxation in proportion to his property; and we look not to the question whether he himself have or have not children, to be benefited by the education for which he pays" (quoted in Harris, 1899, p. 44). The idea of the local tax was grudgingly accepted (Power, 1991). But permissive laws gave local schools all kinds of leeway, and rate bills continued to be used. Still, by rejecting the European school tradition of pauperism, public education in America turned an important corner.

Under the new scheme of tax funding used in some states in the early 1800s, it became incumbent on communities to control and regulate the quality of schooling offered to its youths. But there were dangers. Public apathy, local infighting, rampant poverty, and the rise of individualism led to a decline in community interest in schooling (Cremin, 1951). Moreover, districts not disposed to funding public schools were really under no compulsion to do so. The early state laws were lenient, and there was little in the way of organized authority at the state level in the area of public education. Under these conditions, local decision making thrived, although not always in ways that were in the interests of the public school. Clearly, the universalization of the public school could not be accomplished under circumstances that allowed local initiatives to prevail without regard for state needs. Local concerns were important, but the state clearly needed to take an active hand in developing, facilitating, and supervising public education.

Eventually, the state moved in on the public schools by establishing forms of state aid, which led to the establishment of criteria to secure these funds and then to supervisory roles in accounting for the use of the funds. States often forced local taxes on schools by making state monetary commitments to local districts contingent on in-kind or matching monetary commitments at the local level. In other words, no state monies were forwarded unless the local district made an equal investment in the school. To accomplish all of its new functions, the state had to create an administrative structure, led by a state school officer, which would be responsible for supervision of the public schools. In the 1830s, James Carter, an educator and an activist for proschool legislation, argued long and hard for a more direct state role in public schooling in Massachusetts. He wanted to establish a state board so that efforts to create public high schools and normal schools (training institutes for teachers) could be linked to some central authority. In 1837, Carter won approval for a state board and helped select Horace Mann as the first state secretary of education in Massachusetts in 1837. This appointment would eventually take on historic proportions.

HORACE MANN AND THE RISE OF STATE AUTHORITY

Probably more than anyone who lived in the nineteenth century, Horace Mann was able to reawaken the Jeffersonian concept of mass education for socio-civic gain. In his leadership role in Massachusetts, Mann worked to broaden schooling opportunities for all children in the state, to elevate the base of tax support for schools, to upgrade the hygienic standards of schoolhouses, to support the training of teachers, to bring more women into the profession, to increase the number of school libraries, and to generally improve the pedagogical practices of teachers. During his tenure, teachers' salaries increased substantially in the state, the school year was lengthened, and general appropriations for schools were increased (Rippa, 1984).

Mann studied the emerging educational theories of his time, and attempted to apply the best of these ideas to the Massachusetts schools. For instance, he was among the first to try to improve reading instruction by considering what was then known as the whole-word method of teaching reading, which essentially rejected the phonetic breakdown of words in favor of whole-word recognitions (Tanner and Tanner, 1987). In his Second Annual Report, in 1838, Mann displayed remarkable sensitivity, for his time, toward the needs of learners and the need for learning to have some attachment to the life experience. His regard for learners was logically connected to his desire to develop a statewide teacher training system that would produce teachers who ventured beyond subject matter and addressed issues related to learners' best interests.

Although he understood that there was a clear limit to what he could accomplish politically, Mann was quite an activist in his own right. He was very unhappy with the district system in Massachusetts, which allowed local schools to regulate themselves and did not hold them accountable for concerns that transcended local matters. To Mann, the district schools needed to share a common civic mission under an overseeing agency devoted to maintaining certain standards in the education of all children. Mann saw little more than anarchy in the idea of local school control (Power, 1991). In his Fourth Annual Report, in 1840, he asked for a consolidation of small districts into larger ones, with the ultimate goal of bringing them under state authority.

To the chagrin of many citizens, Mann also sought to keep the functions of state-funded schools separate from sectarian religious instruction. He wanted to use the school to promote a civic community that would give children a political education and a common discourse for mutual understanding and tolerance. Although Mann was highly critical of the way schooling was conducted in Massachusetts, he understood its potential and was ever optimistic about the powers of free common schools, thinking that they would help eliminate poverty and class distinction and become "the great equalizer of the conditions of men."

Mann also had a keen political sense and generally avoided curriculum issues that might divide the populace (Butts, 1978). Religion generally was avoided in the schools, although Mann advised that the Bible be read without commentary; potentially fractious political issues were also avoided. Mann viewed the public school as a fragile institution, and he did not want to imperil its future by generating controversies in the curriculum that might spill into the community. Thus, he focused on literacy instruction, moral training, and knowledge of government (Butts, 1978). As Karier (1967) explains, Mann also viewed the American public school as a form of protection against social revolution and as an important contrast to the European model of schooling that accepted the inevitability of class differences.

Because of his many progressive ideas, Mann was not the most popular man in Massachusetts. We should remember that, historically, Massachusetts had upheld the right of the church to dictate school practices, and Mann was breaking with tradition by trying to erect a wall between the two. Thus, critics accused Mann (and the State Board of Education he led) of trying to take God out of the public schools, to make them Godless, which, in the eyes of many citizens, also made them worthless. Mann was subjected to vicious attacks from the pulpit and through the press. In his third year in office, he even faced the indignity of two legislative attempts, fueled by religious groups, to abolish the State Board of Education (Rippa, 1984). But the attempts failed, and Mann kept his position as Secretary of Education for 12 years.

Mann also made quite a few enemies among schoolmasters, mostly because he was so critical of their work. A skilled writer, Mann used the annual reports on education in Massachusetts to comment on many of the perceived educational problems of the day. In his Seventh Annual Report, in 1843, he took direct aim at the poor teaching in the schools and spoke admiringly about how education in Prussia, which he had visited, might provide some thoughtful lessons for educators in Massachusetts. In the Prussian schools, Mann (1844) observed, "I never saw a blow struck, I never heard a sharp rebuke given, I never saw a child in tears. . . . I heard no child ridiculed, sneered at, or scolded, for making a mistake" (p. 187). Could a visitor, Mann added rhetorically, spend six weeks in our schools and walk away with the same impressions? Feature 6-1 addresses early school discipline issues.

Mann also admired the style of instruction in Prussia, noting the scholarly insights of the teachers, whose books (to paraphrase Mann) were in their heads, not in their hands. He recounted classroom interactions that allowed for student questions, group discussions, and more humane and empathic treatments of youths. Not surprisingly, his report drew a harsh response from the Principals' Association in Boston and sparked a year-long written debate between Mann and the principals. In any case, each of the

6-1 RESEARCH INQUIRY
Early School Discipline

Investigate the nature of school discipline in various early schools. How was discipline handled in the academies, in the free African schools, in common district schools, by private tutors, in charity church schools, in schools run by the Quakers, and/or for boys versus girls? What were the differences and similarities?

twelve annual reports written by Mann is full of commentary on school-related issues, many of which are still relevant today (Rippa, 1984).

The genius of Horace Mann had to do with his perception of the changing social landscape of Massachusetts and America. Although he was a deeply religious man, he knew that battles over which religious creeds to read and study in the school would eventually undermine any chance of establishing a universally accessible common public school. So he worked out of a socio-civic tradition that stressed democratizing themes in the schools and the professionalization of teaching. It was largely through his work that a strong model for free common schooling developed during the 1840s in Massachusetts, a model that influenced not only other states but other countries as well. Mann and his ideas traveled widely. He advised other state authorities on matters of school administration and aided the development of public schools in such distant places as Chile and Argentina (Noble, 1959).

THE UPWARD AND OUTWARD EXTENSION
OF SCHOOLING

Like many other aspects of public education, the American high school has its roots in Massachusetts. As indicated previously, by the mid-1700s, the Latin grammar school was waning as an institution for secondary education, and the academy was on the rise. And by the mid-1800s, the Latin grammar school had essentially disappeared, supplanted by the tuition-based academy. In Massachusetts, where free public schooling at the elementary school level was becoming a reality, public schooling was also being extended into the secondary school years. The academies were still tuition-based, but Massachusetts was ahead of its time by enacting legislation in 1827 that required the establishment of tax-supported high schools in towns with 500 or more households. Over the next two decades, at least 100 public high schools were established in Massachusetts. By 1860, a free public school system existed at the elementary level in Massachusetts, while free public high schools were becoming more popular, even in more rural areas.

The idea for public high schools spread to other states, especially in the North. But the development of the public high school in other states was hindered by the district system that allowed local districts to decide whether they would erect such schools. Lenient state laws did not always compel compliance to the state's wishes. Districts sometimes abused their power, which led to uneven tax support for the schools and uneven access to schooling.

It was only a matter of time before the constitutionality of tax-supported high school education was tested. The most prominent court case was in Kalamazoo, Michigan, where a citizen challenged the school board's right to levy taxes in support of high schools (Tanner, 1972). The complainant argued that high schools were not institutions designed to educate all children and so should not be supported by tax dollars. But the state supreme court ruled that tax monies could be used to support public high schools because they aimed to provide an advanced education to rich and poor alike (Butts, 1955). Although these schools were not widely attended, they were presumably accessible to all. This was a significant ruling because it gave the high school a secure place in the common, publicly supported school system. Feature 6-2 traces enrollment trends in the American high school, showing how far the institution has come in terms of graduating students.

As the concept of the public school began to take hold in cities and towns across the nation, fundamental changes occurred in school organization. The evolving common elementary school, which had long practiced nongraded instruction, separated primary education from intermediate education (Douglas and Greider, 1948). Soon, actual grade divisions followed. This change was facilitated by the construction of new school buildings that accommodated smaller groups, with classes reduced to 50 to 75 students (Cubberley, 1947).

Thus, with the high school in place and the elementary school divided into three parts (primary, intermediate, grammar), the American ladder system of education was born. The virtue of the ladder (grade 1 through college) was that it represented a unified pathway for schooling that all students theoretically could access, as opposed to the dual ladders that existed in Europe (one for the college-bound and one for the vocational-bound). Even higher education received a boost with the passage of the Morrill Act

6-2 THINKING ABOUT THE DATA
The Outward Extension of the High School

The figure below shows the graduation rates over time in terms of the percentage of the total 17-year-old population. What are the trends? What conclusions can you draw from the data?

High School Graduates as a Percentage of All 17-Year-Olds, 1869–70 to 1989–90

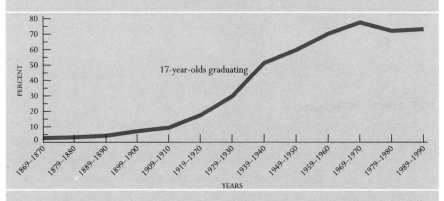

SOURCE: U.S. Department of Education (1997), *Digest of education statistics* (Washington, DC: U.S. Department of Education).

of 1862, which authorized federal subsidies and land grants for the endowment of state universities to provide members of all classes with a practical education. Many of these early land grant universities, which offered an education in agriculture and mechanics, have since become some of the largest and most comprehensive universities in the world. The land grant act also represented a new pedagogical priority in the education of young adults because practical studies, as opposed to classical studies, now had a justifiable place in the postsecondary curriculum.

THE BIRTH OF TEACHER EDUCATION

The history of teacher education, not surprisingly, also begins in New England. Teacher education was part of the general effort to elevate the common public school experience during Horace Mann's tenure as secretary of education. In the 1840s, under Mann's leadership, the State

6-3 SCHOLARLY VOICES
Horace Mann on the Importance of Teacher Education

Horace Mann was intent on developing a network of teacher training schools, explicitly and exclusively dedicated to teaching prospective teachers how to educate youngsters. He makes his case for the importance of normal schools as fundamental to the development of a common and publicly supported school system, and by implication, a mature and stable democracy

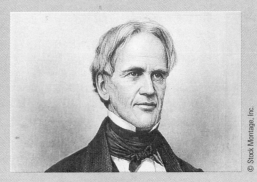

Horace Mann

I believe normal schools to be a new instrumentality in the advancement of the race. I believe that, without them, Free schools themselves would be shorn of their strength and their healing power, and would at length become mere charity schools, and thus die out in fact and in form. Neither the art of printing, nor the trial by jury, nor a free press, not free suffrage, can long exist, to any beneficial and salutary purpose, without schools for the training of teachers, for, if the character and qualifications of teachers be allowed to degenerate, the Free schools will become pauper schools, and the free press will become a false and licentious press, and ignorant voters will become venal voters, and through the medium and guise of republican form, an oligarchy of profligate and flagitious will govern the land; nay, the universal diffusion and ultimate triumph of all-glorious Christianity itself must await the time when knowledge shall be diffused among men through the instrumentality of good schools. Coiled up in this institute, as in a spring, there is a vigor, whose uncoiling may wheel the spheres. (quoted in Williams, 1937, p. 225)

Board of Education in Massachusetts had managed to fund and operate three teacher education schools, each located in a different region of the state. Because there was no legislative support for teacher education schools (known as normal schools at the time), Mann had to solicit private donations in addition to state money to get the schools opened and operating.

Horace Mann was militantly committed to the idea of teacher education. As Feature 6-3 emphasizes, it was, to him, the single most important variable in sustaining the common public school experience. The argument supporting normal schools was not complicated. As Mann put it in his Twelfth Annual Report, "Common schools will never prosper without normal schools. As well might we expect to have coats without a tailor, and hats without a hatter, and watches without a watchmaker, and houses without a carpenter or mason, as to have an adequate supply of teachers without normal schools" (quoted in Mangun, 1928, p. 412). Mann knew from firsthand experience how bad, and even abusive, some of the teachers were. He also understood how deficient many teachers were in their own academic knowledge and skills. As indicated previously, he was not hesitant about criticizing public education officials in the Massachusetts schools. Mann wanted to help cure the problem by giving teachers preparatory experiences with children, by strengthening their academic educations, and by encouraging the participation of women in the education of young people. Because the number of students attending the common schools in Massachusetts was growing precipitously (jumping 50 percent between 1840 and 1860), teacher training was especially critical.

Mann borrowed the phrase "normal school" from the Prussian system of schooling, which he visited and which featured teacher training. Apparently, the Prussian system, in the words of one admirer, could be described in eight words: "As Is the Teacher, So Is the School" (Williams, 1937, p. 193). Mann favored the phrase "normal school" because it was "short, descriptive of its etymology and in no danger of being misunderstood or misapplied" (Williams, 1937, p. 192). The idea of teacher education, however, existed in the colonies before Mann's efforts to popularize it. James Carter presented the idea of teacher seminaries in his *Essays of Popular Education,* as did Thomas Gallaudet in his essay *Plan for a Seminary for the Education of Instructors of Youth* (1825). In 1827, Carter went one step further and attempted to win legislative support in Massachusetts for the idea, but to no avail. Moreover, some private academies had included teacher training in their curricula. This was especially the case in New York, where an 1827 law provided state subsidies to academies establishing teacher training courses (Drake, 1955, p. 374).

What Mann had in mind, however, was a state-sponsored network of normal schools. He did not want teacher training to be folded into the curriculum of the academy. He wanted it to stand on its own, as an experience requiring the wholesale time and energy of its student population. "In Massachusetts," Mann stated, "the business of the normal school is to possess the entire and exclusive occupancy of all the instructors and all the pupils; to have no rival of any kind, no incidental or collateral purposes" (Williams, 1937, p. 202).

The town of Lexington, Massachusetts, agreed to the conditions for the operation of the state's first normal school in July 1839; Figure 6-3 shows the notice announcing the opening of the school. Another normal school opened in Barre, Massachusetts, in September 1839, and a third in Bridgewater, one year later. The Lexington school restricted attendance to women

> ### FIGURE 6-3
> ### Public Notice of a Normal School at Lexington
>
> #### Normal School at Lexington
>
> The Board of Education hereby give notice, that a Normal School for the qualification of *Female Teachers* for Common Schools, is to be established at Lexington, in the County of Middlesex.
>
> Applicants for admission to said School must have attained the age of *sixteen* years complete; they must be in the enjoyment of good health, and must declare it to be their intention to become school teachers after having finished a course of study at the *Normal School;* they must undergo a preparatory examination and prove themselves to be well versed in orthography, reading, writing, English, grammar, geography and arithmetic, and they must furnish satisfactory evidence of good intellectual capacity and of high moral character and principles.
>
> No pupil will be admitted to the school for a less term than one year. Provision will be made for a longer course of study. A complete course will probably occupy three years.
>
> Tuition will be free; but the pupils must supply their own board, provide themselves with all class books, and defray the incidental expenses of the school.
>
> It is expected that the school will be opened in the course of the ensuing Spring. Due notice of the time will be previously given.
>
> Applicants for admission may leave their names with the Rev. O. A. Dodge, of Lexington.
>
> JARED SPARKS,
> ROBERT RANTOUL, JR.
> GEORGE PUTNAME,
> HORACE MANN,
>
> *Visitors of the Normal School at Lexington.*
>
> Boston, February 27, 1839.

SOURCE: Mangun, V. L. (1928), *The American normal school: Its rise and development in Massachusetts* (Baltimore: Warwick & York), p. 124.

and focused on elementary education teaching. Several factors weighed into this decision. First, men typically were not interested in teaching young children because of the other means of advancement available to them. But second, and probably more important, much of the leadership on the State Board of Education, Horace Mann included, believed that women were, by their very nature, better suited to teach young children than were men. Mann saw women as freer from political ambitions and from vulgar habits, "more mild and gentle" with "stronger parental impulses" and "purer morals" than men (Williams, 1937, p. 203). And because of the need for qualified elementary school teachers, the education of female teachers was a critical mission for Mann. At the other two normal schools, in Barre and

6-4 THE HISTORICAL CONTEXT
1872 Rules for Teachers

Here is a notice of the rules and regulations that the employed teachers of one school were expected to follow in 1872.

1872 Rules for Teachers

1. Teachers each day will fill lamps, clean chimneys.

2. Each teacher will bring a bucket of water and a scuttle of coal for the day's session.

3. Make your pens carefully. You may whittle nibs to the individual taste of the pupils.

4. Men teachers may take one evening each week for courting purposes, or two evenings a week if they go to church regularly.

5. After ten hours in school, the teachers may spend the remaining time reading the Bible or other good books.

6. Women teachers who marry or engage in unseemly conduct will be dismissed.

7. Every teacher should lay aside from each day pay a goodly sum of his earnings for his benefit during his declining years so that he will not become a burden on society.

8. Any teacher who smokes, uses liquor in any form, frequents pool or public halls, or gets shaved in a barber shop will give good reason to suspect his worth, intention, integrity and honesty.

9. The teacher who performs his labor faithfully and without fault for five years will be given an increase of twenty-five cents per week in his pay, providing the Board of Education approves.

Oldest Wooden Schoolhouse
St. Augustine, Florida

SOURCE: Salvatori, M. R. (1996), *Pedagogy: Disturbing history, 1819–1929* (Pittsburgh: University of Pittsburgh Press), p. 142.

Bridgewater, enrollment was open to both sexes because the teacher training extended to the high school level. Feature 6-4 shows a reproduction of the rules of employment for a public school in the nineteenth century. Note the gender-specific nature of some of the rules.

The curriculum of the normal school required prospective teachers to learn the course of study for the common school in its entirety and to practice the art of instructing to youths, usually by means of a model school experience. Normal school attendees were graduates of the common district schools but were unevenly schooled. Thus, some attention had to be paid in the normal school to the actual knowledge and skills that the teacher would be responsible for teaching. Mann also felt that it was especially important for the normal school to offer experiences in practice teaching, under the eyes of an experienced teacher critic. Mann was said to be fond of telling the story of a skillful eye surgeon who, when asked how he learned such amazing skills of surgery replied, "by practice, but I spoiled a bushel basketful of eyes in learning how" (Williams, 1937, p. 191). To Mann, this trial-and-error method was comparable to what schoolteachers were doing to children. The normal school was designed to prevent such abuse.

In time, state-sponsored normal schools were also established in New York and in many western and southern states. In the western-most states, the "normal school studies" began to find a place in the university curriculum, leading to the development of teachers' colleges and teacher education or normal school studies departments. Normal school studies were established in many of the leading western public universities, including the Universities of Indiana (1852), Wisconsin (1856), Missouri (1856), Kansas (1876), and Iowa (1855). This was partly a function of a dissatisfaction with the work of normal schools and a desire to elevate the status of teaching. The first university department of education was founded at the University of Iowa in 1855 (Drake, 1955). In time, official state normal schools would evolve into regional, multipurpose colleges. In the South, normal schools first appeared in the 1870s; many of these were black normal schools established during Reconstruction.

THE EVOLUTION OF TEACHER ASSOCIATIONS AND TEACHER UNIONS

Professional teacher organizations historically have maintained a dual commitment to improving the welfare of the profession and the welfare of the public school. These are, after all, complementary aims. Thus, the development of teacher groups often runs parallel with historical improvements in the schools. The development of teacher groups is also entangled with political advocacy efforts, legislative initiatives, and electoral politics. The National Education Association (NEA) and the American Federation of Teachers (AFT), the nation's leading teacher groups, both have broad-ranging and often well-funded agendas. Their work influences virtually all aspects of a teacher's professional life, from local labor negotiations to state and national school policies.

The National Education Association

The National Education Association (originally known as the National Teachers' Association) was founded to bring national attention to the cause of public education, especially as it related to the professionalization of teachers. In 1857, the president of the New York State Teachers' Association invited all teachers nationwide to attend a meeting in Philadelphia dedicated to organizing a new national teachers association. The invitation was also extended to other presidents of state teachers associations. When the meeting concluded that same year, a new national group of educators, known as the National Teachers' Association (NTA), was born (Wesley, 1957). But the name of the group was largely a misnomer, because school administrators, eager to use the influence of the new organization to improve the profession of teaching, originally dominated its membership and power base.

As described in the preamble to the NEA's constitution, the mission of the NEA (or the NTA, as it was originally known) was to "elevate the character and advance the interests of the profession of teaching, and to promote the cause of popular education in the United States" (National Education Association, 1997, p. 170). Early support for the NEA and its mandate emerged from many quarters. Educational luminaries such as Horace Mann and Henry Bernard were impressed by the group's desire to make teaching a profession, as opposed to a vocation, and were happy to see efforts made to bring public education under the influence of professional leadership, instead of lay leadership. Groups such as the American Normal School Association, which concerned itself with teacher preparation, and the National Association of School Superintendents saw benefits to joining ranks with the NTA. Independent groups with varied agendas, but all connected to schooling in some way, also arrived at the NTA's door. The result was a broad coalition of educational personnel representing a wide range of professional interests. It included school administrators, teacher educators, university personnel, and, of course, public school teachers. In 1870, the NTA changed its name to the National Educational Association, and then again to the National Education Association of the United States in 1905, but its mission remained unchanged.

Originally, membership in the NTA was limited to "gentlemen." Women could be elected to honorary memberships, but they were not allowed, under any circumstances, to address the floor at the annual conventions or to hold office in the organization. But in 1866, a constitutional amendment changed the defining term for membership from "gentleman" to "person." Naturally, this change would have a positive influence on the membership rolls of the NTA and would set the stage for the election of Ella Flagg Young as its first female president in 1910. Young, a career educator with experience as a principal, teacher, and professor of education (at the University of Chicago), was the superintendent of the Chicago Public Schools when she was elected NEA president. Her election was controversial because she was originally denied the support of the nominating committee of the NEA, which was dominated by men, for the presidency. But at the annual conference, some women managed to substitute the majority report of the nominating committee, containing the nomination of a man, with the minority report, containing the nomination of Young. The convention then voted 617 to 376 in favor of the minority report, thus making Young the first female president (Wesley, 1957).

Originally, there were no racial restrictions on membership in the NEA, but because of the custom of "separate but equal," many state affiliates with white members barred blacks from membership. This, however, did not stop the NEA from seeking affiliates with both black and white state teacher associations.

As a national association, at least up until about 1892, the NTA was essentially a convention organization. In fact, the annual national convention of the NTA became an important forum for the discussion of school programs and educational practices and principles. With publications scarce and TV and radio not yet available, it was an event of some significance to the educational community (West, 1980). In 1892, the NEA increased its work in the schools by forming a series of visible and highly prestigious committees charged with making recommendations for the resolution of specific school problems. The most notable committee was probably the Committee of Ten, which published a report in 1893 that, in effect, designed the course work for high school education in America. The Committee of Fifteen, which followed the Committee of Ten, was dedicated to the same task but at the elementary school level. The well-known Cardinal Principle report, published in 1918, also came out of the NEA. We will study these reports and their influence on education in a later chapter.

Later, the NEA would shift into a legislative gear, working actively to pass federal legislation supporting the public school—a task it has maintained, with a full complement of lobbyists and political allies, into the

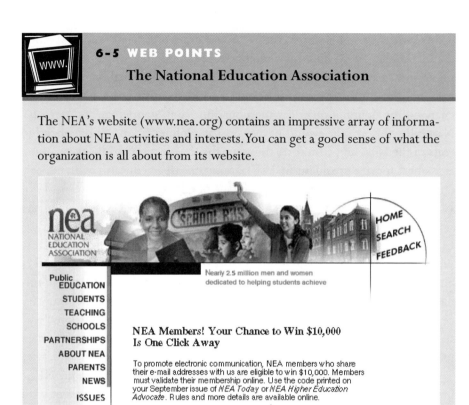

6-5 WEB POINTS

The National Education Association

The NEA's website (www.nea.org) contains an impressive array of information about NEA activities and interests. You can get a good sense of what the organization is all about from its website.

twenty-first century. The legislative accomplishments of the NEA are, historically speaking, impressive. They include the founding of a federal school agency, originally known as the Office of Education. Through NEA efforts, this agency eventually evolved into the Department of Education, now headed by a secretary with a cabinet-level appointment. The NEA traditionally has been at the forefront in lobbying for federal funds for education, a practice that has many detractors who believe that federal support translates into federal control. Despite its achievements in the federal arena, the NEA continues to target much of its legislative initiatives at the state level, largely through its affiliates. This is where most of the activity related to the actual operation of the school, and to the improvement of teacher salaries and teacher work conditions, remains.

Today, the NEA is the country's largest organization of educators, claiming a membership of 2.3 million and an annual budget approaching $200 million; Feature 6-5 show a portion of the NEA's website. Headquartered in Washington, DC, the NEA is the base for a vast network of activity that is realized through state and local affiliates. These affiliates are active in labor negotiations and work to influence school policies and school practices in their respective states. Funded by the NEA, they take complementary, if not identical, positions on the issues.

The NEA is heavily involved at the local and state level in labor and collective bargaining negotiations with school districts. It is constantly on the lookout for attempts to restrict teacher tenure, teacher autonomy, and teacher professionalism, and it supports initiatives that lead to better funded schools and more professional teachers. At the national level, it has a large publication mill that produces a considerable body of literature dealing with a vast assortment of professional issues. And it lobbies intensively in the halls of Congress to sway federal legislation in the direction of school improvements and to ally itself with various politicians and special interest groups sympathetic to NEA objectives.

Involvement in legislative affairs requires simultaneous involvement in the political and electoral process. The NEA has, over time, earned a reputation as a heavyweight in the political process. Although the NEA claims to have a bipartisan outlook, it does not shy away from endorsing political candidates whom it believes support its objectives. In the early 1970s, the organization plunged into the political process by establishing a political action group (NEA-PAC) to funnel funds to favored political candidates and political issues. The NEA-PAC money trail reveals that the NEA is tightly connected to the Democratic Party. In the 1992 elections, for instance, 92 percent of its PAC money went to Democrats, amounting to a $40-million distribution (Lieberman, 1997). The basic explanation for this has to do with the NEA's historical attachment to the objective of garnering federal funds for public school causes, a position that is fundamentally at odds with the Republican Party's philosophy of less government and less federal intervention in schools. Feature 6-6 examines some of many problems that political conservatives have with the NEA.

The NEA has endured quite a bit of criticism over the years. One criticism has to do with the perceived view that its actions are, first and foremost, unionist in orientation and are guided only secondarily by a desire to improve public schools. Critics maintain that the NEA cannot accept any idea, even if it promises to benefit schools and schoolchildren, until it first passes through a screen that determines its suitability from the standpoint of teacher welfare. Thus, for example, if performance pay for teachers was found to be something that might reward better teachers and create a more professional climate for teaching and learning, the NEA, it critics assert, could never support it because it would be counter to the "union" objective of increasing pay for all teachers. Lieberman (1997) cites the reorganization of the NEA in 1972 as evidence of the shift by the organization toward a

6-6 DEBATING THE ISSUES
Conservative Criticism of the NEA

Each year, delegates to the NEA Representative Assembly meet, discuss issues, and set association policy for the coming year. These policies take on the form of annual written resolutions, which often become the target of critics (often self-described profamily, conservative critics), who see the NEA as little more than a special interest group deeply committed to advancing a radical/liberal social agenda for America. Phyllis Schlafly, the founder of the Eagle Forum, is an especially harsh critic of the NEA. In 1999, she published a faultfinding essay on the NEA resolutions entitled, "Decoding the NEA Resolutions." Here you can read a small sample of the criticisms offered by Schlafly against some of many resolutions passed at the 1999 NEA meeting, followed by the actual resolution in question. To appreciate the friction, you are encouraged to read the full text of Schlafly's essay (August 4, 1999), which can be found on her website (www.eagleforum.org), and the full text of the NEA resolutions, which can be found on its website (www.nea.org) or its annual handbook. Consider the criticisms, and ask yourself whether you agree with them.

Phyllis Schlafly

The NEA supports bilingual education, i.e. keeping immigrant children speaking their native language instead of learning English.

NEA Resolution, Educational Programs for Limited English Proficiency Students

The National Education Association believes that limited English proficiency (LEP) students must have available to them programs that address their unique needs and that provide equal opportunity to all students, regardless of their primary language. Programs for LEP students should emphasize English proficiency while concurrently providing meaningful instruction in all other curriculum areas.

The Association also believes that LEP students should be placed in bilingual education programs to receive instruction in their native language from qualified teachers until such time as English proficiency is achieved. If no bilingual programs are available, these students should be taught in English-as-a-second-language (ESL) programs designed to meet their specific needs. Students should not be enrolled in special education classes solely because of linguistic differences.

The Association values bilingual and multilingual competence and supports programs that assist individuals in attaining and maintaining proficiency in their native language before and after they acquire proficiency in English.

Phyllis Schlafly

The NEA is so vindictively against private schools that one resolution even opposes ever renting or selling a closed public school building to a private school.

NEA Resolution, Public School Buildings

The National Education Association believes that closed public school buildings that have been deemed safe can be used effectively for public preschool, day care, job training, and adult education centers. The Association also believes that closed public school buildings should be sold or leased only to those organizations that do not provide direct educational services to students and/or are not in direct competition with public schools.

Phyllis Schlafly

Global education is the favorite of the NEA. This means teaching that patriotism and sovereignty are bad while global governance is good, that Americans should subordinate their customs and country to foreign control, and that we should distribute U.S. wealth and resources to the rest of the world.

NEA Resolution, Global Education

The National Education Association believes that global education increases respect for and awareness of the earth and its people. Global education imparts information about cultures and an appreciation of our interdependency in sharing the world's resources to meet mutual human needs.

The Association also believes that curriculum and instruction about regional and international conflicts must present a balanced view, include historical context, and demonstrate relevancy and sensitivity to all people. The achievement of this goal requires the mastery of global communication and development of an appreciation of the common humanity shared by all peoples.

The Association further believes that the goal of appreciation of and harmony with our global neighbors depends on a national commitment to strengthening the capability of the educational system to teach American children about the world.

union structure. Previously, the NEA had been organized along departmental lines that reflected interests in curriculum and instruction concerns. These included departments dedicated to, among many other things, business education, nursery education, rural education, supervision, and curriculum. But they were all wiped out in 1972, replaced by a more legalistic and bureaucratic organizational structure reflecting, according to Lieberman, employee salary and benefits issues. This change is further supported by the fact that approximately one-third of the NEA's $200-million budget in 1997 was dedicated to a program known as Uniserve. This program, operated through the state affiliates, puts the NEA in the middle of labor negotiations with local school districts. Depending on the desires of the local district members, Uniserve directors serve as negotiators, grievance representatives, and/or general labor consultants to local teachers (Lieberman, 1997).

The NEA historically has devoted considerable resources to the advancement and defense of the public school and public school children. Although some might see its actions as self-serving, few organizations have been more vocal in and more committed to lobbying for resources that directly benefit school children. And at a time when arguments for the privatization of schools have taken on a bipartisan political cast, the NEA has held firm in actively opposing any initiative that even hints at the idea of using public funds for private schooling purposes. It critics might see this action as unionist, while it advocates might see it as part of its historical dedication to promoting the cause of public education.

The American Federation of Teachers

Unlike the NEA, a spirit of unionism motivated the founding of the American Federation of Teachers (AFT). At the turn of the twentieth century, some local teachers' organizations, disenchanted with work conditions and their general lack of influence in negotiations with school boards, reached out to the American Federation of Labor (AFL) for union affiliation. Many of these local chapters did not survive for long, becoming victims of pressures by administrators and school boards (Campbell, Cunningham, McPhee, and Nystrand, 1970). As a result, there was a growing interest in a national teachers' union, a new federation of teachers that would retain its ties to organized labor and bring considerable resources to local labor struggles. The cradle for this new teacher unionism was in the Chicago area, where, in 1915, four separate local unions were engaged in embittered negotiations with their school boards. The problem came to a head when the Chicago School Board attempted to prohibit membership by teachers in any labor union. It was in this context that a handful of educators from the Chicago area, all representatives of their local union chapters, got together in 1916 to organize what one might very well view as the nation's first national teachers' union, the AFT.

Although the NEA was in existence at the time, its operations could not be characterized as unionlike yet. Recall that, although the NEA was concerned about teachers, it was very much dominated in its early years by male administrators, who saw the professional service base of the organization to be largely a matter of male experts offering female teachers their wisdom. Women, as indicated, were not even allowed to address the floor at the NEA annual convention until 1866. Through the 1890s, only 11 percent of the NEA membership was teachers, and it was not until 1912 that teachers were even recognized with their own department in the NEA (Murphy, 1990). So, the AFT, with its grass-roots contacts in the workplace and its more visible female leadership, appealed to teachers, especially female teachers, in a way that the NEA did not. Today, the remnants of this early difference are still evident. The NEA, for instance, has kept its membership open to school administrators, seeing them as part of the same professional body. By contrast, the AFT has denied membership for top-level administrators, believing that they cannot be trusted to operate in the best collective bargaining interests of teachers.

But the early difference between the two groups is perhaps best expressed historically, in the clashes between union representatives and NEA officials at the annual conventions of the NEA. Under the leadership of Margaret Haley, teachers from the Chicago Teacher Federation, a teachers' union folded into the AFT (and later removed from it), had tried to petition NEA officials to discuss their objections to some NEA policies and resolutions. Among the more aggravating issues to the union was the NEA's support for the idea of centralizing administrative control in the financing of the school and the supervision of teachers. While the NEA was busy trying to solidify administrative control over teachers, the union argued, real problems related to corruption in state and local politics, inadequate school revenues, and deplorable working conditions simply weren't getting the attention they deserved. Haley and her union forwarded a hard-knuckled agenda to the NEA, portraying the problems facing teachers in terms of ongoing combat against antidemocratic forces, as a workers' struggle to obtain justice and equity for teachers and schoolchildren. The more gentile NEA could only interpret this position as heresy. Haley, to the NEA, was an insurrectionist tainted by Socialist leanings, who wanted teacher interest to march with class interest. Class struggle was not on the agenda of the NEA, and annual dalliances at a conference, where one listened to elitist experts in education, did not register on the more unionist agenda of the AFT.

Although there was early agreement on issues related to securing higher teacher salaries and other teacher benefits, the differences in perspective between a professional organization led by administrators and a union manifested in many ways. For instance, when the NEA worked to help a establish a federal department of education, believing that such a department, with a cabinet-level secretary, would bring increased investment in the problems of public education, the AFT hedged. It wanted to know what the payoff of a federal department of education would be for teachers: better salaries, benefits, and working conditions, or more centralized administrative authority and power, and less room for negotiations (Urban, 1982)? Although the NEA might have had its own designs on power in the Department of Education, it did successfully lobby for a stronger federal presence in education. The AFT, for its part, focused more exclusively on the issue of what was best for the teacher as worker.

Given the differences between the NEA and the AFT, it is not surprising that the AFT began to win the membership contest among teachers. In the 1910s, its membership actually exceeded that of the NEA (Lieberman, 1997). But antiunion activities after World War I, coupled with an active teacher recruitment campaign led by school administrators in the NEA, brought membership numbers back up for the NEA. As teachers moved into the NEA, its more unionlike stance began to take form.

Today, the two groups fundamentally have the same agenda, so much so that some commentators believe a merger is imminent (Lieberman, 1997). Interesting, the NEA has moved boldly into more unionlike activism, while the AFT has moved, with equal conviction, into more professionally based activities. The AFT is still proudly and securely committed to union activity, working directly to improve salaries, work conditions, and job security for teachers. But it now also has a social agenda reflecting a commitment to public schooling, democracy, and social justice—an agenda very similar to the NEA's. The AFT, like its counterpart, is legislatively conscious, politically active, and pro-Democratic. Its membership approaches 1 million, including nurses and health care workers, as well as noneducation personnel, a vestige of its early identification with workers.

SUMMARY

As the twentieth century loomed, the nature of instruction in the common schools of New England and elsewhere was no longer dominated by religious concerns. Rather, the development of national consciousness resulted in a comprehensive vision of schooling that included teaching not only the rules of arithmetic and grammar, and the conventions of spelling and reading, but also the occupational matters and even some holdover academic studies from the Latin grammar school. The American public school turned a corner in the mid-1800s, emerging as a public agency supported by public law and a public mandate, a clear rejection of the pauper school tradition practiced in England. At the same time, the American school looked to Europe for new ideas, focusing largely on the advances made in the Prussian system, which included the development of teacher training institutes, known as normal schools, and new theoretical outlooks on the classroom and the curriculum. Horace Mann's tenure as state superintendent of education in Massachusetts set many of the early precedents for the relation between state and community-based school interests. He led the way for the development of a state-regulated system of schooling, showing others how to balance state and district concerns in ways that ensured properly funded and properly managed schools, stressing the role of the educated teacher. Teacher education, in this sense, was an especially important development because it helped plant the roots for the professionalization of teaching and the founding of teacher associations dedicated to the livelihood of the public school.

The development of the public school in New England had indeed pointed the way for public education in America. On principle, the foundation for tax-supported public education was secure at the turn of the century. Opportunities for an education were no longer dependent on the philanthropy of industrialists and other elites or on the church. In the decades to come, the public school would emerge at the very forefront of a civil rights struggle, continuing to try to find its way as an agency of and for the people.

A new democratic vista was now before the nation—public schools, free and open to all, supported by tax dollars, regulated by the state, free from sectarian control, and still responsive to local conditions and priorities. Figure 6-4 highlights the main events in the establishment of public education in America between the colonial period and the mid-1800s.

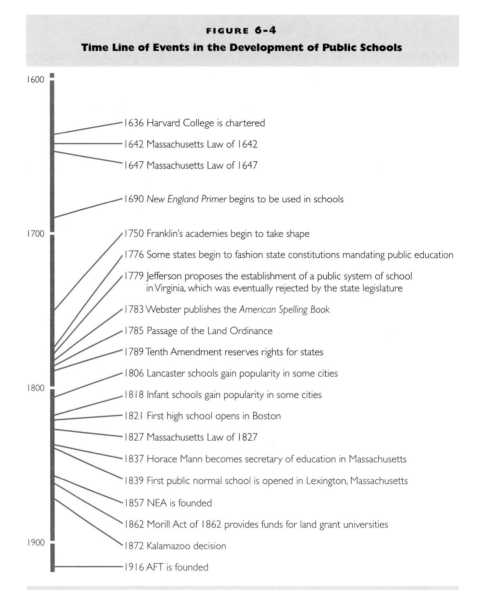

FIGURE 6-4
Time Line of Events in the Development of Public Schools

1600

1636 Harvard College is chartered

1642 Massachusetts Law of 1642

1647 Massachusetts Law of 1647

1690 *New England Primer* begins to be used in schools

1700

1750 Franklin's academies begin to take shape

1776 Some states begin to fashion state constitutions mandating public education

1779 Jefferson proposes the establishment of a public system of school in Virginia, which was eventually rejected by the state legislature

1783 Webster publishes the *American Spelling Book*

1785 Passage of the Land Ordinance

1789 Tenth Amendment reserves rights for states

1806 Lancaster schools gain popularity in some cities

1800

1818 Infant schools gain popularity in some cities

1821 First high school opens in Boston

1827 Massachusetts Law of 1827

1837 Horace Mann becomes secretary of education in Massachusetts

1839 First public normal school is opened in Lexington, Massachusetts

1857 NEA is founded

1862 Morill Act of 1862 provides funds for land grant universities

1900

1872 Kalamazoo decision

1916 AFT is founded

QUESTIONS AND ACTIVITIES

1. How was the academy more responsive to the prevailing postrevolutionary societal changes than the Latin grammar school?

2. How did the Lancaster method of teaching contribute to the argument for publicly funded education?

3. Explain the decline of religious bodies in the control of education.

4. Explain the shift from religious instruction to socio-civic objectives in the historical development of the public school.

5. How did the constitutional recognition of religious freedom contribute to the growth of the public school?

6. Explain the logic behind the district system of schooling.

7. How did the national government support the development of the public school through its regulation of westward settlements?

8. What were some of the early arguments against publicly funded education?

9. In what way was the virtue of the district system also its fundamental weakness?

10. How could Noah Webster be viewed as "Schoolmaster of America"?

11. What was Horace Mann's main argument for more active state control over public schools?

12. Why did Horace Mann not support the introduction of controversial topics in the school curriculum?

13. Why was Horace Mann not always the most popular public official in Massachusetts?

14. Why did many consider Horace Mann to be extending Jefferson's ideas on public education?

15. What is the general difference between a pauper system of public education, popular in England during the nineteenth century, and a publicly funded system of education?

16. What made the American school ladder unique for its time?

17. Why did Horace Mann favor women as prospective teachers of young children?

18. Explain the connection of the normal school movement to the common school movement in Massachusetts.

19. Explain the fundamental historical difference in outlook or orientation between the NEA and the AFT.

20. Explore the affiliation of the NEA and the AFT to the Democratic Party.

21. Explore the biographical background of Margaret Haley and Emma Flagg Young. Explain their connection to the development of both the NEA and the AFT.

REFERENCES

Button, H. W., and Provenzo, E. P. (1983). *History of education and culture in America.* (Englewood Cliffs, NJ: Prentice-Hall).

Butts, R. F. (1978). *Public education in the United States.* (New York: Holt, Rinehart & Winston).

Butts, R. F. (1955). *A cultural history of western education: Its social and intellectual foundations.* (New York: McGraw-Hill).

Butts, R. F., and Cremin, L. A. (1953). *A history of education in American culture.* (New York: Rinehart & Winston).

Callahan, R. (1963). *An introduction to education in American society.* (New York: Knopf).

Campbell, R. F., Cunningham, L. L., McPhee, R. F., and Nystrand, R. O. (1970). *The organization and control of American schools.* (Columbus, OH: Merrill).

Clinton, D. W. (1809). Address on the opening of a new school building. In D. Calhoun (1969), *Educating of Americans: A documentary history.* (Boston: Houghton Mifflin).

Cremin, L. A. (1951). *The American common school: A historic conception.* (New York: Teachers College Press).

Cubberley, E. B. (1947). *Public education in the United States.* (Boston: Houghton Mifflin).

Douglas, H. R., and Greider, C. (1948). *American public education.* (New York: Ronald Press).

Drake, W. E. (1955). *The American school in transition.* (New York: Prentice-Hall).

French, W. M. (1967). *American secondary education.* (New York: Odyssey Press).

Harris, W. T. (1899). *Education in the United States.* (New York: Appleton).

Karier, C. J. (1967). *Man, society and education.* (New York: Scott, Foresman).

Lieberman, M. (1997). *The teachers unions: How the NEA and AFT sabotage reform and hold students, parents, teachers and taxpayers hostage to bureaucracy.* (New York: Free Press).

Mangun, V. L. (1928). *The American normal school: Its rise and development in Massachusetts.* (Baltimore: Warwick & York).

Mann, H. (1844). Seventh annual report of the Board of Education. In D. Calhoun (1969), *Educating of Americans: A documentary history* (Boston: Houghton-Mifflin).

Murphy, M. (1990). *Blackboard unions: The AFT and the NEA, 1900–1980.* (Ithaca, NY: Cornell University Press).

National Education Association. (1997). *Handbook, 1997–98.* (Washington, DC: National Education Association).

Noble, S. G. (1959). *A history of American education.* (New York: Rinehart).

Pangle, L. S., and Pangle, T. L. (1993). *The learning of liberty.* (Lawrence: University Press of Kansas).

Power, E. J. (1991). *A legacy of learning.* (Albany: SUNY Press).

Rippa, S. A. (1984). *Education in a free society: An American history.* (New York: David McKay).

Tanner, D. (1972). *Secondary education.* (New York: Macmillan).

Tanner, D., and Tanner, L. N. (1987). *History of the school curriculum.* (New York: Macmillan).

Urban, W. J. (1982). *Why teachers organized.* (Detroit: Wayne State University Press).

Webster, N. (1739). The call for a national culture. In D. Calhoun (1969), *Educating of Americans: A documentary history.* (Boston: Houghton Mifflin).

Wesley, E. B. (1957). *NEA: The first hundred years.* (New York: Harper).

West, A. M. (1980). *The National Education Association: The power base for education.* (New York: Free Press).

Williams, E. I. F. (1937). *Horace Mann: Educational statesman.* (New York: Macmillan).

CHAPTER 7

The School Experience at the Turn of the Twentieth Century

The Ascendancy of the Traditional Liberal Arts
THE DOCTRINE OF MENTAL DISCIPLINE
THE COMMITTEE REPORTS AND THE IDENTIFICATION OF THE
CURRICULUM

The Child-Centered Counterreaction
THE DOCTRINE OF ORIGINAL GOODNESS
EUROPEAN PIONEERS IN PEDAGOGIC PRACTICES

American Child-Centeredness
THE AMERICANIZATION OF JOHANN PESTALOZZI
G. STANLEY HALL AND THE CHILD STUDY MOVEMENT
THE AMERICAN KINDERGARTEN AND THE RISE—AND FALL—
OF FROEBEL
THE PROGRESSIVE CRITICISM OF CHILD-CENTEREDNESS

Summary

Questions and Activities

References

A NEW ERA WAS DAWNING for the American public school at the turn of the twentieth century. The school gates were just beginning to swing open, and the very idea of pedagogy was taking on new scientific and philosophical slants. A progressive force was gathering strength in American education, counterbalancing traditionalist thinking and raising new questions about curriculum content and instructional practices. The American public school was about to get an injection of ideas that would set the course for an entirely new way of looking at teaching and learning. At the same time, traditional methods of teaching were themselves getting a boost from advocates in the liberal arts, who were pushing for a highly academic, subject-centered curriculum. The conditions were set for a debate over the practices of the American school, a clash of ideas that featured a child-centered form of progressivism and the traditional subject-centered approach (Bode, 1938; Dewey, 1902).

THE ASCENDANCY
OF THE TRADITIONAL LIBERAL ARTS

The progressive backlash in the schools at the turn of the century was due in part to the ascendancy of traditionalism in the schools during the late nineteenth century. In most schools at this time, traditional approaches to teaching youths, which stressed the Old World methods of rote and recitation, were still popular. In fact, new advocates for such instruction were emerging from the ranks of the liberal arts, equipped with a new psychology and an associated doctrine of learning that justified the old pedagogy. Many of these thinkers were what we might classify as traditional humanists (Kliebard, 1986)—scholars who believed that a good education entailed an immersion in the liberal arts and the Great Books. In Chapter 3, this broad conservative group was described as representing essentialist and perennialist philosophical perspectives on the school. During the early stages of development of the American high school, from the late nineteenth century into the twentieth century, such thinkers dominated the educational scene.

The Doctrine of Mental Discipline

The type of education supported by the traditional humanists is probably best understood, first, in terms of the learning doctrine that underscored their thinking about the curriculum. The traditionalists rationalized virtually everything that was done in school through a learning doctrine known as mental discipline. The central principle of the doctrine was derived from a theory of learning, known as faculty psychology, holding that several separate faculties collectively made up the human mind. According to faculty psychology, responses related to emotions, affections, the will, and the intellect all had their "place" in the mind. More progressive thinkers, such as Johann Pestalozzi, used faculty psychology to argue for a more holistic approach to education that encompassed all of the so-called faculties—mental, physical, moral, emotional. By contrast, advocates of the doctrine of mental discipline used it to justify a preoccupation with the task of finding a way to train the intellectual faculties. In instructional terms, according to the doctrine of mental discipline, the intellectual faculties could be developed and improved only through certain mental exercises. Proponents believed that such exercises could so strengthen the mind that the benefits to learners would be transferable to virtually all life situations, making them better able to live intelligently.

The key to the teaching/learning process, given these assumptions, was ensuring that students were exposed to subject areas believed to be intrinsically empowered to cultivate the mind's intellectual faculties. This meant that students needed to be trained in the study of certain subjects. Skills of memory, judgment, imagination, and other mental processes could only be sharpened if students were regularly immersed in the proper academic subjects. The "mind as muscle" metaphor came to be associated with the doctrine of mental discipline because it captured the idea that the mind, like a muscle, had to be rigorously exercised. Such a workout, however, could only be accomplished with the "heavy mental equipment" that the traditional academic disciplines provided. Thus, Latin, Greek, mathematics, rhetoric, grammar, and the Great Books were at the core of a good mental routine. However, anything that dealt with vocational, interdisciplinary, or more experiential studies was not up to the task of building up the mind's muscle. The idea was to absorb the intellectual force of the subject matter through intensive drill and practice, as well as student memorization (Rippa, 1971).

Mental discipline was clearly an expression of a classical dualism in education that placed the power of the mind over the power of the body. It fostered a bias toward "mindful" intellectual activity, as it might be construed in its purist academic sense, over vocational and experiential activity. This would seemingly have made it an untenable idea for the prevailing institution of public schooling, which was increasingly committed to broadening its scope of learning opportunities. But the doctrine of mental discipline also represented a pulling back from the ideal of comprehensiveness and a movement away from the academy tradition. In fact, as mentioned previously, the academies themselves were drawn to the doctrine of mental discipline, so much so that many became purely scholastic centers for highly discipline-centered learning.

Mental disciplinarians could argue effectively for their place in the school curriculum because they had answers to two essential curriculum questions: (1) what should be taught, and (2) how should it be taught. What one taught in school from the standpoint of mental discipline was a traditional body of academic knowledge built largely on the liberal arts. But because the subject matter did the "teaching," through its inherent intellective capacities, mental disciplinarians did not believe that any particular instructional methodology was needed to actualize the connection between the subject matter and the mind. Teachers, of course, had to be well schooled in the subject matter, but their prime role in the classroom was as purveyors and guardians of the liberal arts tradition. Thus, the teacher, who frequently came to the classroom with little professional training, was not expected to do much more than maintain order in the classroom, fulfill the primary need for basic skills instruction (which was typically approached through skill-drill strategies), provide an example of moral rectitude to the school community, and ensure an exposure to the proper academic traditions. The high regard placed on basics skills, especially in the elementary school, had to do with the fact that such skills were seen as preparatory for later academic study. In other words, mental disciplinarians held few worries about instructional methods. They opted to put their faith in the power of the subject matter.

Because of its fixation on mental manipulations, the school (especially the high school) was characterized by a uniformity of instructional routines that did little to attract the learners' interests or attend to their needs. And as long as mental discipline prevailed as a learning doctrine, things were unlikely to change. Any studies that could not find a rationale for the doctrine of mental discipline were dismissed as potential distractions from the central function of cultivating the mind.

The adherents of mental discipline were convinced that they had identified the central core of studies needed to develop the human mind. But they also had an even more important revelation. They maintained that this core of studies was appropriate for the education of all youths, not simply for those aiming to go to college. The mental training afforded to the individual by academic studies represented the best preparation not only for the college-bound but also for ordinary citizens. This egalitarian principle in the traditional humanist position turned out to be crucial for the school curriculum. It gave the traditional humanists a platform upon which the education of all youths could be maintained. At the level of the high school, this position was made quite clear in a curriculum document sponsored by the National Education Association (NEA) and published in 1894 by a committee of traditional humanists known as the Committee of Ten.

The Committee Reports and the Identification of the Curriculum

The Committee of Ten report (1893) was written under the leadership of Charles Eliot, who was, at the time of the writing of the report, president of Harvard University. Funded by the NEA for the purpose of providing some curriculum direction to the American high school, the Committee of Ten fashioned a clear statement of what should be taught. Many secondary schools, which served less than 5 percent of the student population in the 1890s, were facing a dizzying set of requirements from different universities and colleges, and were quite confused over how to best prepare their students to succeed. Moreover, participation in public secondary education was on the rise, forcing educators to think about high school as preparation not only for college but also for life itself. The committee (1893) took note of this trend, stating that "a secondary school programme tended for national use must be made for those children whose education is not to be pursued beyond the secondary school. The preparation of a few pupils for college . . . should in the ordinary secondary school be the incidental, and not the principal object" (p. 481).

The Committee of Ten was dominated by strong believers in the doctrine of mental discipline. The membership included five college presidents, one professor, two private school masters, a public school principal, and the sitting U.S. commissioner of education (Rippa, 1971). The actual report provided a single curriculum prescription for the high school, advancing what was, in effect, a highly traditional set of studies, rooted in the liberal arts, believed to be valuable to the goal of disciplining the mind. The Committee supported nine broad subjects: Latin, Greek, English, modern languages, physics, astronomy and chemistry, natural history, history, and geography. The inclusion of science courses was unusual for the time and was likely the result of the influence of Eliot, who, as a former professor of chemistry, believed that there were mind-training possibilities in studies not traditionally conceived in the liberal arts. But the report made no provision for physical education, the fine arts, or any vocational subjects, which were thought to have no relevance to the strengthening of the mind.

Thus, by virtue of what it included and excluded, the Committee of Ten created a high school curriculum based on nine subjects conceived as equally able to train the mind. As indicated, these nine subjects were upheld as appropriate for the education of all youths, including those who did not plan to attend college. Although the committee asked for four different curriculum tracks (classical, Latin-scientific, modern languages, and English), there was little difference between them, as Figure 7-1 shows. Each track or program represented a slight variation on the nine core subjects.

Interestingly, Charles Eliot did not fully support the committee's work. Eliot had already been on record for his support of free electives in the curriculum, a cause he championed at Harvard during his tenure as president (Rippa, 1971). At Harvard, Eliot had managed to reduce the number of classical courses in the interests of expanding the curriculum offerings, providing more space for the technical and scientific (Tanner and Tanner, 1987). Eliot accepted the value of mental training, but he did not agree that only certain subject areas had a monopoly on mind development. Eliot thought, in fact, that virtually all subjects had value in this regard as long as they were taught in a manner that cultivated reason and morality. This was a radical alteration on the orthodoxy of mental discipline. But, when the Committee of Ten limited its recommendations to nine essential subjects, Eliot had to compromise. But the committee had to compromise as well, because without Eliot's influence it probably would not have supported even as many as nine core areas of study. Eliot's lobbying helped to secure a place for courses in the modern sciences in the curriculum, which was a breakthrough for the time.

Still, the frictions with the committee underscored a fundamental issue in the development of the school. Eliot had raised an important question: Should the school stand by a uniform academic curriculum that treated every student more or less the same, or should it broaden its offerings beyond the core academic subjects? That is, should the school experience be tethered to the acquisition of a formalized body of knowledge, or should it look more comprehensively at student and societal needs? At the secondary school level, the Committee of Ten had opted for uniformity and for focused instruction in nine academic areas.

Before the dust had settled from the Committee of Ten report, another NEA-sponsored committee, known as the Committee of Fifteen, reconsidered elementary education in America. Charles Eliot was in the thick of the debate related to this report as well. Although not a member of the Committee of Fifteen, Eliot used various forums to argue that the elementary school curriculum had to be broadened and enriched with more diverse offerings. This was a matter of considerable significance to Eliot. He believed that too much time and energy were being spent on a narrow range of subjects, including holdover subjects from the Latin grammar school, such as Latin and grammar. He also thought that it was wrong to conceive of elementary education as a single program of studies for all students and that it was important to recognize the value of some individualization in the curriculum. Eliot wanted to integrate a new science course in the elementary school and to reduce the time devoted to traditional courses.

When the Committee of Fifteen submitted its recommendations in 1895, however, it was clear that Eliot's views had only been partially accepted. The report of the committee (1895) advocated the inclusion of some new courses, including one dedicated to "Natural Science and Hygiene." Overall, however, the report sanctioned the status quo and helped to solidify the traditionalists' grasp on the curriculum (Tanner and Tanner, 1987). Even where new courses were added, the time devoted to them, relative to the traditional subject-centered courses, was slight. The central subjects that the committee recommended for the elementary school were those that the traditionalists viewed as most worthy—grammar, literature, arithmetic, geography, and history.

The central figure in the Committee of Fifteen's work was its chair and main author, William Torrey Harris, then U.S. commissioner of education. Harris had a background in philosophy and once held the job of superintendent of schools in St. Louis. At the turn of the century, he was emerging as one of the more outspoken and articulate proponents for a conservative liberal arts education. Harris, in fact, had cultivated a new rationale for the subject-centered thinking that dominated the curriculum for years to come. He believed that public education had everything to do with transmitting the "race experience" (as in the human race experience) of the nation. Further, he was convinced that this could best be accomplished by elevating the importance in the curriculum of five central academic areas —grammar, literature and art, mathematics, geography, and history— which he likened to the five windows of the soul. To Harris's (1888) thinking, the schools could best serve the nation by actively transmitting the high accomplishments of humanity, or the culture of Western civilization, which was embodied in the five windows. These windows, the argument went, gave the learner a view of all that was worthy in our culture (Cremin, 1988). Hence, it was through the windows that society became civilized and enlightened; life was in the subject matter.

Due, in part, to his high standing as commissioner, Harris strongly influenced the deliberations of both the Committee of Ten and the Committee of Fifteen. Because of his high regard for subject-centered study, Harris became an active critic of anyone who argued for the inclusion of student course work (at the post–primary school level) in the natural sciences, the

FIGURE 7-1

Committee of Ten Program for Secondary Schools, 1893

Year	Classical. Three foreign languages (one modern).		Latin-Scientific. Two foreign languages (one modern).	
I.	Latin	5p.	Latin	5p.
	English	4p.	English	4p.
	Algebra	4p.	Algebra	4p.
	History	4p.	History	4p.
	Physical Geography	3p.	Physical Geography	3p.
		20p.		20p.
II.	Latin	5p.	Latin	5p.
	English	2p.	English	2p.
	German (or French) begun	4p.	German (or French) begun	4p.
	Geometry	3p.	Geometry	3p.
	Physics	3p.	Physics	3p.
	History	3p.	Botany or Zoology	3p.
		20p.		20p.
III.	Latin	4p.	Latin	4p.
	Greek	5p.	English	3p.
	English	3p.	German (or French)	4p.
	German (or French)	4p.	Mathematics $\left\{\begin{array}{l}\text{Algebra 2}\\\text{Geometry 2}\end{array}\right\}$	4p.
	Mathematics $\left\{\begin{array}{l}\text{Algebra 2}\\\text{Geometry 2}\end{array}\right\}$	4p.	Astronomy ½ yr. & Meteorology ½ yr.	3p.
		20p.	History	2p.
				20p.
IV.	Latin	4p.	Latin	4p.
	Greek	5p.	English $\left\{\begin{array}{l}\text{as in Classical 2}\\\text{additional 2}\end{array}\right\}$	4p.
	English	2p.	German (or French)	3p.
	German (or French)	3p.	Chemistry	3p.
	Chemistry	3p.	Trigonometry & Higher Algebra or History $\left.\right\}$	3p.
	Trigonometry & Higher Algebra or History $\left.\right\}$	3p.	Geology or Physiography ½ yr. and Anatomy, Physiology, & Hygiene ½ yr.	3p.
		20p.		20p.

SOURCE: Committee of Ten (1893), *Report of the Committee of Ten on secondary school studies* (Washington, DC: National Education Association).

Year	Modern Languages. Two foreign languages (both modern).		English. One foreign language (ancient or modern).	
	French (*or* German) begun	5p.	Latin, or German, or French	5p.
	English	4p.	English	4p.
I.	Algebra	4p.	Algebra	4p.
	History	4p.	History	4p.
	Physical Geography	3p.	Physical Geography	3p.
		20p.		20p.
	French (*or* German)	4p.	Latin, or German, or French	5 or 4p.
	English	2p.	English	3 or 4p.
II.	German (*or* French) begun	5p.	Geometry	3p.
	Geometry	3p.	Physics	3p.
	Physics	3p.	History	3p.
	Botany or Zoology	3p.	Botany or Zoology	3p.
		20p.		20p.

Year III.

	Modern Languages		English	
	French (*or* German)	4p.	Latin, or German, or French	4p.
	English	3p.	English { as in others 3 / additional 2 }	5p.
	German (*or* French)	4p.	Mathematics { Algebra 2 / Geometry 2 }	4p.
III.	Mathematics { Algebra 2 / Geometry 2 }	4p.	Astronomy ½ yr. & Meteorology ½ yr.	3p.
	Astronomy ½ yr. & Meteorology ½ yr.	3p.	History { as in the Latin-Scientific 2 / additional 2 }	4p.
	History	2p.		
		20p.		20p.

Year IV.

	Modern Languages		English	
	French (*or* German)	3p.	Latin, or German, or French	4p.
	English { as in Classical 2 / additional 2 }	4p.	English { as in Classical 2 / additional 2 }	4p.
	German (*or* French)	4p.	Chemistry	3p.
	Chemistry	3p.	Trigonometry & Higher Algebra	3p.
IV.	Trigonometry & Higher Algebra *or* History	3p.	History	3p.
	Geology or Physiography ½ yr. and Anatomy, Physiology, & Hygiene ½ yr.	3p.	Geology or Physiography ½ yr. and Anatomy, Physiology, & Hygiene ½ yr.	3p.
		20p.		20p.

vocational arts, interdisciplinary studies, and any other "nonacademic" pursuits.

THE CHILD-CENTERED COUNTERREACTION

As mentioned, part of the reaction against traditionalist thinking in the schools had to do with a desire to locate children at the center of teaching and learning formulations. Many of the early impulses on this front came from Europe. The philosophical discourses of Jean-Jacques Rousseau, the practical work supported by Robert Owens in the infant schools, the new pedagogical theorizing offered by Johann Pestalozzi and others—all delivered messages about the importance of recognizing the life of children in schools. Educators in America tapped into these influences and launched a movement dedicated to giving learners their due in the school. This commitment, however, also had the overarching effect of glorifying learners and their innate capacities to decide what was best for their own education.

The Doctrine of Original Goodness

The major philosophical voice helping to clear the way for more expressly child-centered views in education was Rousseau. His thinking was rooted in a desire to undermine the doctrine of original sin promulgated by the Calvinists and other religious groups. Children were not born sinful, proclaimed Rousseau. Quite the contrary: They were born good and innocent, and were made sinful and depraved by adults and the social institutions to which adults subjected them. Rousseau was, in effect, proclaiming a doctrine of original goodness. Rousseau's thinking on these matters likely was influenced by the manner in which children were exploited in eighteenth-century France and by his own brutal upbringing (Rippa, 1971). It is not so much that Rousseau had trouble envisioning healthy and active interactions between children and adults. Rather, he thought that nature was right in its original construction of children and that adults had to follow its lead and not interrupt its work with too frequent or too specific interventions (Thayer, 1960). Thus, spontaneity and natural interests were very important to any education justified by Rousseau.

Throughout his works, Rousseau glorified the early or primitive savagery of humanity as a natural and good period, a time when humankind was in a state of equilibrium with nature. "Civilized" humanity, according to

Rousseau, severed this connection and corrupted itself through its social inventions of greed and power. Because children were born as one with nature, without the contamination provided by society, Rousseau celebrated their innocence and their beauty. His message was that children, as a raw product of nature, were born good, but that society corrupted children and eventually made them evil. For example, in *Emil,* originally published in 1762, he stated, "Everything is good as it leaves the hands of the Author of things; everything degenerates in the hands of man. . . . He turns everything upside down; he disfigures everything; he loves deformity, monsters. He wants nothing as nature made it, not even man" (Rousseau, 1979, p. 37).

According to Rousseau, the pedagogical antidote to the depravity of "civilized" humanity was for adults to take a more limited and distant role in the education of children. That is, they could regulate, if the need arose, the education of children from afar, but they must always allow children to unfold and develop under their own initiative and will, and according to their own interests. It was the child, not the church and not the state, that was at the center of Rousseau's universe.

Rousseau's theories had a dramatic influence on the thinking and actions of a small group of school reformers in Europe, whose ideas would eventually reach America during the mid-1800s. This group, especially Johann Pestalozzi, Johann Herbart, Friedrich Froebel, and Maria Montessori, helped to set an early condition for the rise of an important branch of the American progressive education movement.

European Pioneers in Pedagogic Practices

Pestalozzi's Focus on Experiential Learning. In elementary education, the colonial rote-and-recitation style was challenged directly by a view of teaching developed in the late eighteenth century by a European reformer named Johann Pestalozzi. Inspired by the child-centered thinking of Rousseau, Pestalozzi experimented with new forms of teaching focused on what he believed to be the natural inclinations of children. Pestalozzi viewed learning from the standpoint of faculty psychology. Unlike the traditional humanists, however, he argued for a school experience that nurtured all of the mind's discrete faculties (emotional, intellectual, physical, moral), which he believed could only be accomplished through experiential, or sensory, learning. He vested discipline in the activities of learning, rather than in external prodding and compulsion, and he saw motivation as emerging out of the inner instincts and desires of children. Pestalozzi could not abide the Calvinist view of child depravity, arguing that all children

© Stock Montage, Inc.

Johann Pestalozzi.

should be disciplined gently. It was these Pestalozzian principles that so impressed Horace Mann during his visit to the Prussian schools in the 1840s.

According to Pestalozzi, teaching/learning had to move away from the acts of memorizing and reciting, which he likened to "empty chattering," and toward the acts of sensing, interpreting, observing, and questioning. Teaching had to engage students in language and thinking; it had to proceed along the lines of children's organic development and be planned and organized ahead of time. In this manner, Pestalozzi emancipated teachers, not only by liberating them from the rather dreary recitation style of instruction that bound them and their students to the text but also by giving them a reason to consider their own ideas in the light of learners' needs. As Power (1991) observed, an implication of Pestalozzi's work was that "teachers could no longer be regarded as mere hearers of lessons" (p. 203). This amounted to a virtual sea change in the school curriculum. Observations, investigations, discussions, and individual expressions and activities, all largely ignored in the early American schools, now had legitimate place in the classroom.

Pestalozzi also stressed the role of objects in teaching. He wanted children to study real objects found in nature to cultivate their sense of observation and their overall understanding of objects in the world. Relying on his own observations of children, Pestalozzi argued that sense perception was the most important path to good learning for children. This, of course, was the opposite of the memorization exercises of the colonial schools and the instructional reliance that such schools put on reciting from books. Pestalozzi wanted to connect the senses of sight, sound, and touch to the development of language and thought.

This perspective on learning had specific implications for the school curriculum. In the teaching of science, for instance, it led to a higher regard for nature study, observational insight, and outdoor learning, and a reduced emphasis on "bookish" or abstract attempts to understand the world (Cubberley, 1947). It also led to the inclusion of drawing, modeling, music, and general sense or physical activities in the school. With Pestalozzi, the schools now had a way to justify a break with the instructional tradition of memorization exercises and to offer activities that encouraged expression and sense perception. Ironically, over time, the object lesson became a kind of tradition in early childhood education that often lost its sensory and observational slant and became yet another way to teach facts (Cubberley, 1934; Meyer, 1975). As Thayer (1960) noted, Pestalozzi's object teaching did indeed "open the door of the classroom to the outside world of objects and events, but, in the course of time, it also degenerated into a barren verbalism" (p. 230). Today, we can still see the legacy of object teaching in classroom demonstrations and in the custom "show and tell" in early education.

Although Pestalozzi's work clearly advanced teacher professionalism and brought the interests of the learner into pedagogical consideration, Pestalozzi did not promote a social theory to accompany his thinking about schooling. This gave his work some currency among economic elites, who saw no real social threat in the kind of education that Pestalozzi was proposing (Karier, 1967). The Prussians apparently were attracted to Pestalozzi's methods and to the broader implications that his work had for the training of teachers precisely because his ideas were so socially neutral. As reported by Karier (1967), the rise of the normal school (teacher training institute) in Prussia was partly a function of the fact that such schools taught teachers how to teach, not what to teach. Thus, the graduates of these schools lacked the kinds of content skills or knowledge that might sow the seeds of revolution or otherwise threaten the stability of the society. In America, the normal schools developed along the same lines, and today many teacher training programs continue to stress the value of methods over content.

Herbart's Emphasis on Interdisciplinary Knowledge. Another European thinker whose ideas gained some ascendancy in the American schools in the nineteenth century was German professor of philosophy Johann Herbart. Herbart was highly sympathetic to the work of Pestalozzi, fundamentally agreeing with his open rejection of the rote-and-recitation

© Stock Montage, Inc.

Johann Herbart.

approach to instruction, with his regard for the use of real objects in teaching, and with his belief that education was a process of social and moral development. Herbart, however, asked new and different questions, approaching the problem of developing an educational theory and method with novel insights.

First, Herbart shed the Pestalozzian concern for the faculties of the mind. It was not individuals' minds that needed to be developed, but their social character and morality, of which the mind was but a part. Thus, the purpose of schooling was not to cultivate the different faculties of the mind, but to cultivate the social powers of the individual. This meant that schooling had to be more expressly social and less tied to the content of the academic traditions. Herbart maintained that school experiences had to be framed around the problems and concerns of the social environment. He contended further that the study of history and literature, which were not popular in school curricula at the time, were absolutely vital to the fulfillment of such a purpose.

As a result, Herbart (1901) sought to use history and literature to synthesize the subject matter in school so that it could be better linked to the social environment. He viewed the convention of organizing knowledge along strict disciplines as illogical and not attendant to the living conditions of individuals. No one subject area had a monopoly on the interests and needs of a child, and thus no one subject could be promulgated as most appropriate for all children. The solution was to find focal points of concentration or convergence among different disciplines that took on a historical focus and that conveyed a literary tradition.

These units of subject matter came to be known as correlations or concentrations. A concentration was simply a general topic on which the work of a whole school or grade or class could be focused for an extended period of time. Herbart often referred to the "unbroken circle of thought. Close-knit in all its parts," an idea that his protégés were convinced they had secured in the curriculum notion of concentrations. American supporters of Herbart, for instance, frequently used *Robinson Crusoe* or *The Song of Hiawatha* as a way to unify all inquiry in the third-grade classroom, which traditionalists derided as bad pedagogy. But to a Herbartian, such an activity had all the essential ingredients of a good curriculum. *Robinson Crusoe,* after all, was a literary work that represented a simple level of culture, highlighting the problem of survival; it correlated with history and with literature; and it symbolically told one part of the human story.

Charles McMurry, an American proponent of Herbart, reported on how an elementary school might use basic historical topics as correlations in the curriculum. In the fifth grade, for instance, the synthesizing theme for the curriculum was the story of John Smith, who helped found Jamestown, Virginia, in 1607. For planning purposes, the correlation could be seen as carrying a geography component that might highlight the study of the Chesapeake Bay area (its climate, its main crops, its natural resources); a science component that might focus on the flora and fauna of Virginia; a mathematics component that might offer mathematical queries into the production, marketing, and consumption of vital crops in Virginia; and a language component that might focus on the adventure of Smith's life (McMurry, 1946). Butts (1955) believed that the Herbartian effort to bring a sense of convergence to literature, history, and the social environment helped to develop the role of social studies in the school curriculum.

In a way, then, Herbart was the first to argue for a more integrated and interdisciplinary curriculum. Such a belief was anathema at the time, given the high regard in which the separate disciplines were held. In fact, when Herbart's ideas began to attract a following in the United States, they were attacked vigorously by William Torrey Harris. As the defender of the liberal arts tradition in the schools, Harris felt that the more integrated schemes proposed by the Herbartians could not effectively transmit American culture. The correlations advanced by the Herbartians eviscerated Harris's five windows of the soul. Obviously, this was no small problem to Harris, who thought that Herbart's views threatened the school's capacity to bestow children with the cultural treasures of the past, with the very tools Harris believed children needed to understand themselves and their society.

The most visible battle between Harris and the American Herbartians occurred over the release of the Committee of Fifteen report. The report raised the ire of the Herbartians because they had hoped that it would sanction the use of correlations in the curriculum. Although the committee addressed the idea of correlations, its curriculum recommendations indicated, at least to the Herbartians, a complete repudiation of the idea of correlation (McMurry, 1946). Harris was not shy about expressing his disdain for Herbartian thinking, referring at one point to the integrated use of *Robinson Crusoe* in the curriculum as "shallow and uninteresting" (Krug, 1964, p. 103).

Out of Herbart's work also arose an unusual theory of teaching that equated the maturational development of the individual with the evolutionary stages of the human culture. Known as the cultural epoch theory, this idea implied that the proper instruction of children had to be connected with the period of development in the human race that corresponded with their age. Thus, the youngest schoolchildren might be given activities dealing with primitive life and with the hunting-and-gathering period of human history. Slightly older children (grades 2 and 3) might engage in activities related to early agricultural life and early civilization. And children in the later elementary grades might engage in activities rooted in the médieval period, the early explorers and settlers, and so on, until the industrial age was reached. Thayer (1960) described these stages of human evolution as (1) prehistoric, (2) patriarchal, (3) tribal, (4) feudal, with absolute monarchy, (5) revolutionary, with constitutional monarchy, and (6) republican or self-governing. The corresponding stages in the development of the learner were (1) infancy, (2) childhood, (3) preadolescence, (4) early adolescence, (5) middle adolescence, and (6) late adolescence (pp. 234–235).

Followers of Herbart saw a wonderful sense of unity between the individual and the race experience in cultural epochs theory. Such a theory contained the vast character-building potential of historical study, and the actual cultural epochs provided focal points for a more unified arrangement of the subject matter in the curriculum. For instance, at John Dewey's laboratory school, where cultural epochs ideas were tested, children studied the race experience by focusing on people's occupations in the preindustrial period. In the course of their studies, the children made cloth from fleece (weaving, spinning, and dying), lead castings, Indian baskets, candles, and soap (McMurry, 1946).

Herbart also spoke directly to the issue of teaching methodology. Like Pestalozzi, he did not want to resort to external devices to inspire motivation; he wanted it to emerge out of the conditions of learning. Using principles taken from Pestalozzi, Herbart developed a method of instruction based on the notion that all learning is a process of assimilating knowledge based on what one already knows, of connecting new knowledge to existing conditions and understandings. According to Herbart, if such a connection was properly made, the learner would be in an ideal learning situation; his or her interests would be aroused, and his or her mind would be prepared to absorb the new material.

Herbart's followers tried to formalize this process into five steps: (1) Formally prepare by recalling or otherwise stimulating prior ideas and experiences in the child, to which the new material can be related, (2) present the new material to the child, (3) build associations, through comparisons and contrasts between the old and the new, (4) draw generalizations from the individual cases discussed in class, and (5) find examples and practical situations highlighting the generalizations (Butts, 1955). This method, which lent some sense of standardization to instruction, dominated the training given in the normal schools in the 1890s.

In fact, American Herbartianism made its greatest inroads in American education via the normal school. During the late nineteenth century, several Americans traveled to Prussia, where they studied with the disciples of Herbart at the University of Jena. This group included Charles DeGarmo, Charles McMurry, and his younger brother Frank—all graduates of the normal school. DeGarmo and the McMurrys went on to popularize Herbart on their own writings, which focused on teaching methods that could be used in the normal schools. The steps of instruction in the Herbartian method and the idea of curriculum concentration gave teachers a ready handle on what to do in the classroom. Teachers were encouraged to use a problem-focused approach that, in the tradition of Herbart, concerned itself with understanding a movement of history, a masterpiece of literature, or the operation of a social institution in one unified vision of learning (Thayer, 1960, p. 242).

Froebel's Romantic Idealism. Whereas Pestalozzi influenced instruction at the elementary school level and Herbart at the secondary school level, two more important European figures emerged to influence instruction at the primary school level: Friedrich Froebel and Maria Montessori. Froebel's interest in education was also piqued by the work of Pestalozzi. He visited Pestalozzi's schools in Switzerland and was impressed with the value Pestalozzi placed on play and on "nonacademic" pursuits, such as art and music. Froebel, however, formulated his own views on education by merging the sense perceptions that were fundamental to Pestalozzi with a philosophy of romantic idealism.

Through idealism, Froebel (1887) saw his work, in kinship with the absolute spirit of God, as drawing out the innate gifts given to children by God—gifts that allowed each child to more closely identify with the divine spirit. Froebel felt that his instructional efforts awakened the inner strengths of children, which, in turn, allowed them to find an essence of unity in the divine. Liberating children's "gifts" and encouraging their spontaneous and natural curiosity was the way that one started them down the path toward perfect unity (Butts, 1955). This was Froebel's way of facilitating the work of God. "Education," he observed, "consists in leading man, as a thinking, intelligent being, growing into self-consciousness, to a pure and unsullied, conscious and free representation of the inner law of Divine Unity and in teaching him ways and means thereto" (1897, p. 2).

Froebel opened his own school for very young children in 1840, in which singing, drawing, painting, coloring, dancing, dramatics, and self-selected activity were all encouraged. He called the school Kindergarten, which means "a garden where children grew." Froebel advanced beyond Pestalozzi in several ways. To Pestalozzi, learning still tended, despite his efforts to bring sense perceptions to bear, to be passive and mental. Froebel, however, awakened the spirit of "learning by doing," the physical/motor side of learning and the ideal of directing children in socially desirable ways. He was not preoccupied with the faculties of the mind or with the Herbartian idea of finding unity between the child and cultural history. What he wanted most was for children to find themselves through play, and he envisaged growth as a social concept, as part of the quest to find the whole self.

To this end, Froebel provided children with balls, blocks, and paper, and encouraged them to use them at their will. In this way, Froebel granted new respect and authority to children, to their individuality, and to the dynamic qualities of their personalities. After all, to Froebel, the child was anointed with the inner spirit of God, and play, liberated from the exigencies of survival, represented a high spiritual form. And this, in the end, was the moving idea that Froebel brought to educational thought—the notion that the actions of play brought one closer to finding a unity with the highest orders of life. Education, then, could not resort to prescriptive or coercive measures; it had to engage students in facilitative roles that enlivened the inner spirits of play and self-activity. Moreover, children themselves, as a kind of replica of God, were to be revered and their inner spirit cherished as the main pathway toward growth and understanding.

Over time, the metaphysical justifications that Froebel gave for his kindergarten had to give way to different criteria. Curriculum planning could not revolve around a mystical explanation about how the child's con-

Maria Montessori.

Associated Press, AP

sciousness was part and parcel of the divine spirit; in this sense, Froebel could only advance the curriculum so far. The legacy of Froebel, however, can be appreciated in the design and function of the kindergarten today. Here, children, by and large, are still allowed to play, social activities are viewed as educative, and the atmosphere, especially relative to the upper grades, is warm and protective.

Montessori's Individualized Early Education Environment. Maria Montessori worked along the same lines as Froebel, but she brought a different level of analysis to the problem of teaching children. Trained in the fields of engineering, medicine, anthropology, and experimental psychology, Montessori had a comprehensive lens with which to view the problem of educating children. She started her work in education in 1898 by focusing on the education of "idiot children" housed in the insane asylums of Italy. After spending two years preparing methods of instruction for these children, she discovered that many of their problems were educational, not biological, in nature. The children, in other words, were in many cases victimized by poor environmental experiences; they were deprived of the early stimuli needed to develop into intellectually and emotionally healthy individuals. Montessori validated her thesis by teaching these "deficient" children to read and write and to compete successfully with so-called normal children. Montessori's success with these children, which to outside observers bordered on the miraculous, inspired her to move forward with formulations on early education for all children (Rippa, 1984).

After years of advanced study in experimental psychology, Montessori opened a preschool in 1907 for the education of children living in the slum tenements of San Lorenzo, a poverty-stricken section of Rome. She noted how these poor children, like the feeble-minded children in the asylums, were at a considerable disadvantage because they were not benefiting from any of the basic early-childhood experiences that point the way to later success and health.

In her school, which was called "Casa dei Bambini" (the Children's House), Montessori set out to help correct the early education problems of the poor. She formulated a pedagogical model that used Pestalozzi's ideas about fostering the growth of intelligence through the senses as a springboard. She developed quite a few original games and tasks that highlighted the sense experience. These activities came with certain "didactic apparatus"—blocks, cylinders, and other manipulatives—that children could select at their discretion. To Montessori, the didactic materials represented a form of sensory gymnastics. Children could engage in their use freely, which meant that individual youngsters could occupy themselves by moving into and out of various tasks associated with the materials. Thus, the Montessorian classroom recognized a new level of individualization. Montessori also designed and developed classroom furniture to encourage real social interactions among the children, which included social events such as preparing lunch and cleaning up afterward. She asked teachers to be cognizant of the peculiarities of each child and to encourage free choice among the children. The success of her school took on international proportions; the children had learned the fundamental elements of cleanliness and manners and were equipped with the basic skills of reading and writing (Rippa, 1984).

Montessori clearly viewed early education as fundamental to the sound development of humans. She countered the argument for biological determinism by showing what a good early educational environment can do. Historically, her work has been criticized for being too programmatic and for relying too much on the didactic apparatus, which tended to reduce learning to the completion of predesigned tasks as opposed to creative and open-ended ones. She was also criticized for not recognizing the importance of reflecting social needs and collective group actions in her teaching (Kilpatrick, 1971). The individual was always the central variable to Montessori, and the importance of the group project and social intercourse were secondary. To this day, Montessori's ideas are implemented in early education programs throughout the nation. The idea of providing youths with early sensory experiences as an investment in later development has stayed vital long after Montessori's death.

AMERICAN CHILD-CENTEREDNESS

As indicated, Americans showed widespread interest in some of the more progressive educational ideas being tested in Europe. As applications of these new ideas were attempted on American soil, European thinkers like Pestalozzi and Herbart began to enjoy professional recognition among American educators. The embrace of the new European perspective stemmed from its clever recalculation of the learner in the teaching equation and its insistence that no good teaching could proceed without some working connection to the learner. This gave learners a new priority in the school and set the conditions for classroom innovations based on learners' interests.

The Americanization of Johann Pestalozzi

The Americanization of Pestalozzi was largely realized in the operation of the early normal schools. As indicated, the proliferation of elementary schools put a great deal of emphasis on the education of elementary school teachers during the mid-1800s; Feature 7-1 traces the growth of the normal school movement. Education in the subject matter was an uncomplicated affair in the normal schools, but education in pedagogics was something that could proceed down any number of philosophical paths. The ideas of Pestalozzi, and later of Herbart, found a warm welcome in the American normal schools because they were framed with the teacher in mind. Finding new ways to teach, grounded in a new way of running the school, was the central effect of the ideas. For Pestalozzi, other signal events in the dissemination of his ideas in America included the endorsements he received from Horace Mann in his efforts to reform the Massachusetts common schools and from various disciples in their establishment of private schools in America.

The earliest incursion of Pestalozzian thinking in American education occurred in 1809. With the support of Scottish businessman-turned-philanthropist William Maclure, the first Pestalozzian school was opened outside of Philadelphia, under the direction of Joseph Neef, a former student of Pestalozzi's whose trip to America was financed by Maclure.

7-1 RESEARCH INQUIRY
Normal Schools Across the States, 1885

The following table gives the distribution of normal schools across the United States in 1885. Notice the heavy representation of public normal schools in selected states. Research the reasons behind the distribution. Compare the numbers in the normal schools to the state populations. Explain the role of state laws in the process, as well as the virtual absence of normal schools in the South. Find out as much you can about one of the normal schools, and offer a case study analysis of its curriculum and general operating procedure.

Normal Schools—State, Private, and City— in the United States, 1885–86

	State	Pupils	Private	Pupils	City	Pupils	Total Enrollment
Alabama	5	525	4	198	—	—	723
Arkansas	1	46	—	—	—	—	46
California	2	750	—	—	1	76	826
Colorado	—	—	—	—	—	—	—
Connecticut	1	266	—	—	2	—	266
Delaware	—	—	—	—	—	—	—
Florida	—	—	1	8	—	—	8
Georgia	—	—	—	—	—	—	—
Illinois	2	658	3	833	1*	425	1,916
Indiana	1	909	6	2,910	2	22	3,841
Iowa	1	432	2	680	2	20	1,082
Kansas	1	431	1	580	—	—	1,011
Kentucky	—	—	—	—	—	—	—
Louisiana	1	75	2	200	1	100	375
Maine	4	581	2	191	1	223	995
Maryland	1	272	1	170	1	32	474

Maclure had adopted America as his country and saw a new form of democratic education in the work of Pestalozzi. He, in fact, tried to recruit the Swiss educator himself to come to America. Instead, Pestalozzi recommended Neef, whom he had known since 1800 when he arrived in Switzerland to work with Pestalozzi.

Neef arrived in America in 1807. While being supported by Maclure, Neef spend two years learning English before finally opening the school in Philadelphia. But his career as a headmaster in America would prove to be

	State	Pupils	Private	Pupils	City	Pupils	Total Enrollment
Massachusetts	5	1,128	—	—	5	233	1,361
Michigan	1	628	—	—	1	—	628
Minnesota	3	891	—	—	—	—	891
Mississippi	2	—	4	453	—	—	453
Missouri	4	1,091	1	46	1	138	1,275
Nebraska	1	248	2	80	—	—	328
Nevada	—	—	—	—	—	—	—
New Hampshire	1	50	—	—	1	12	62
New Jersey	2	128	1	270	1	60	458
New York	9	2,693	—	—	5	1,684	4,377
North Carolina	4	559	1	3	—	—	562
Ohio	—	—	3	385	3	289	674
Oregon	2	100	—	—	1	—	100
Pennsylvania	11	3,537	2	373	1	1,218	5,128
Rhode Island	1	153	—	—	—	—	153
South Carolina	—	—	3	276	1	105	381
Tennessee	1	154	4	250	—	—	404
Texas	2	215	2	41	—	—	256
Vermont	3	191	—	—	—	—	191
Virginia	3	493	—	—	1	350	843
West Virginia	6	702	—	—	—	—	702
Wisconsin	5	1,185	2	118	—	—	1,303
Arizona	1	50	—	—	—	—	50
Dakota	2	241	—	—	—	—	241
District of Columbia	—	—	2	50	—	—	50
Total	87	19,382	49	8,065	32	4,987	32,384

* Cook County Normal School.

SOURCE: Butler, N. (1899), *Education in the United States* (New York: Appleton), p. 135.

problematic, partly because of his publicly proclaimed atheism and partly because of the demographics associated with his school. After failing to sustain two different schools, Neef retired to a life of farming outside of Louisville, Kentucky.

But Maclure would call again in 1825, this time with the added voice and support of Robert Owens, the philanthropist who helped to establish the infant school movement in America. The two businessmen sought to establish a utopian commune in New Harmony, Indiana, where they could engage in an experiment in cooperative socialism. The plan was to create a community that would contain about 2,000 people, who would share land, homes, and labor for the overall benefit of all community residents (Monroe, 1907). Alarmed by the perceived evils of industrialization and large, crowded cities, Owens and Maclure envisioned a rural community of selfless cooperation, untainted by private ownership, unequal classes, ranks, and egoism. It was a kind of promised land, seeded by intellectuals whom Maclure attracted from far and wide, but propagated by ordinary people.

One key to the plan was, of course, the system of schooling used in the commune. Maclure felt that Neef was the best choice to lead the schools. Neef came to the Indiana countryside and oversaw a schooling program that included an infant school, a higher school for children between the ages of 5 and 12, and an adult school (Gutek, 1968). The education the children received represented a rejection of traditional humanism and its emphasis on disciplinary knowledge, and an embrace of a utilitarian education, including occupational learning, which was seen as vital to the sustainability of the commune. Young children collected objects for school, studied natural history, spent time outdoors, and took advantage of the stock of books provided by Owens and Maclure. Older children received a comprehensive education that included learning a trade.

However, New Harmony only lasted two years, collapsing under the weight of internal strife and financial problems. It did little to spread the word about Pestalozzi, although it did represent one of the first efforts to apply his ideas in America, a fact made all the more interesting due to its association with communitarian social reform (Gutek, 1968). It offered the first infant school in America, and given its emphasis on experience, activity, and student interest, it anticipated important elements of the progressive education movement in America by several decades (Gutek, 1968). Feature 7-2 shows a portion of the New Harmony website.

Pestalozzi's ideas, however, would penetrate the consciousness of American educators through the American normal school movement. In 1861, a teacher training school opened in upstate New York that openly claimed to apply to the teachings of Pestalozzi. Led by E. A. Sheldon, the Oswego (New York) Normal School quickly became the main American preparation center for teachers interested in Pestalozzian methods. Sheldon had established a local reputation in Oswego as a distinguished educator, founding a school there in 1848 for poor and neglected children and rising to the position of superintendent of the Syracuse schools in 1851. In 1853, he returned to Oswego as its superintendent of schools. He first encountered Pestalozzi's ideas, not in Europe, but in Canada, where he was visiting some schools in 1859. There, he purchased a set of materials produced by the

7-2 WEB POINTS
New Harmony

New Harmony was a social experiment, funded by Robert Owens and William Maclure, in social commutarianism. Its schools, directed by Joseph Neef, were among the first to feature Pestalozzian principles. This website (www.cedar.evansville.edu/~ck6/bstud/nh.html) is dedicated to the history of New Harmony. It has quite a few good links to the extended works of Owens, Maclure, Neef, and Pestalozzi.

New Harmony

Scientists, Educators, Writers & Artists

This page introduces biographical studies associated with New Harmony, Indiana - a collection of studies that celebrate the lives and works of individual scientists, educators, writers, and artists.

Just click on the underscored names, or scroll down aways and click on related subjects.

The image seen here, from *United States Illustrated*, c. 1855, is from a drawing by Karl Bodmer during his visit to New Harmony in 1832-1833.

From New Harmony. Reprinted with permission.

Home and Colonial Training Institution in London, a group that had as its principal aim the promotion of Pestalozzian principles in the education of children in England and in the colonies (Barlow, 1977, p. 94). Sheldon contacted the institution and arranged to have an instructor, Margaret E. M. Jones, travel to Oswego to begin training teachers. This eventually led to the opening of the Oswego Normal School.

The teaching at the school proceeded along classic Pestalozzian lines, with students taught the following principles:

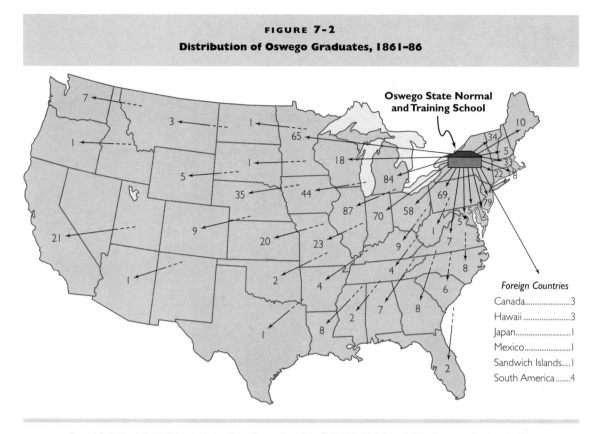

FIGURE 7-2

Distribution of Oswego Graduates, 1861–86

Oswego State Normal and Training School

Foreign Countries
Canada...................3
Hawaii 3
Japan.....................1
Mexico...................1
Sandwich Islands.....1
South America 4

SOURCE: Elwood P. Cubberly, *Public Education in the United States*. Copyright © 1947 by Houghton Mifflin Company. Reprinted with permission.

1) Begin with the senses; 2) Never tell a child what he can discover for himself; 3) Activity is a law of childhood. Train a child not merely to listen, but to do. Educate the hand; 4) Love of variety is a law of childhood—change is rest; 5) Cultivate the faculties in their natural order. First form the mind, then furnish it; 6) Reduce every subject to its elements, and present one difficulty at a time; 7) Proceed step by step. Be thorough. The measure of information is not what you give, but what the child can receive; 8) Let every lesson have a definite point; 9) Proceed from the simple to the difficult, i.e., from the known to the unknown, from the particular to the general, from the concrete to the abstract; 11) Synthesis before analysis—not the order of the subject, but the order of nature. (Barlow, 1977, p. 96)

As Figure 7-2 shows, Oswego's graduates went far and wide; so did Oswego's reputation. The Oswego school brought teachers to the classrooms of America who were committed to using object lessons, a practice that represented a clear departure from the widespread memorization and mentalistic learning in the schools; Feature 7-3 shows one such lesson. The

7-3 THE HISTORICAL CONTEXT
An Object Lesson

Here is an example of an object lesson, developed in 1835, by a teacher who worked for the Home and Colonial School Society (Gutek, 1968, p. 160). What are the essential Pestalozzian principles at work in the lesson?

Teacher: What is this which I hold in my hand?

Children: A piece of glass.

Teacher: Can you spell the word glass? (*The teacher then writes the word "glass" upon the slate, which is thus presented to the whole class as the subject of the lesson.*) You have all examined this glass; what do you observe? What can you say it is?

Children: This is bright.

Teacher: (*Teacher having written the word "qualities" writes under it—"It is bright."*) Take it in your hand and feel it.

Children: It is cold (*written on the board under the former quality*).

effect in the classroom was very real. As Cubberley (1934) observed, "What Pestalozzi tried most of all to do was to get children to use their senses and their minds, to look carefully, to count, to observe forms, to get, by means of their five senses, clear impressions and ideas as to objects and life in the world about them and then to think over what they had seen and be able to answer his questions because they had observed carefully and reasoned clearly" (p. 390). This was a long way from the mental school tradition of colonial America.

G. Stanley Hall and the Child Study Movement

The emerging recognition of the child in school deliberations was also furthered by a burgeoning child study movement in America. This movement had begun to gain momentum during the 1890s and early 1900s, particularly as it was steered by the able hand of G. Stanley Hall, an American psychologist who brought credibility to the field of child study by applying modern scientific methods. The child study movement sought to investigate children in ways that might inform the practical judgments of schoolteachers. Hall, for instance, conducted studies on children's muscle use in school

7-4 DEBATING THE ISSUES
Criticism of the Committee of Ten Report

G. Stanley Hall (1904) emerged as one the main critics of the report of the Committee of Ten. Presumably siding with learners, Hall felt that the recommendations of the report were misguided in asserting that all students should be taught the same way, that the subject areas chosen in the curriculum had standing as mind training constructs, and that no distinction should be made between those who might attend college and those who might not. Examine the report yourself in the light of Hall's criticisms. Would a more differentiated approach to the curriculum serve schoolchildren better? Would the American high school be less inclined to reflect the viewpoint of the college in its curriculum if Hall had influenced the committee?

and concluded that very young children needed opportunities for large muscle development, a finding that had clear, practical implications for the school (Tanner and Tanner, 1987). He even went so far as to develop a systematic survey of what primary school children knew about common animals, insects, plants, and other phenomena, which he wrote in an essay entitled "The Contents of Children's Minds" (Hall, 1883). This was the goal of the child study movement—to gain insights into children that might lead to better teaching. Even teachers got into the act by beginning to study children by questioning them, keeping observational notes on them, and checking their vision and hearing, so as to improve their own classroom methods.

Hall's influence in education, however, transcended his work in the child study movement. As Harvard's first doctoral graduate in psychology and as a German-schooled scientist, Hall had the credentials and the intellectual prowess to speak directly to a newly developing pedagogy, one that accounted for the natural development of children. At the turn of the twentieth century, he was indeed emerging as one of the new titans in education, as someone who spoke for the causes of children in education from a scientific perspective (Cremin, 1961). In this way, Hall represented a position that was diametrically opposed to that of William Torrey Harris, the great defender of the centrality of the liberal arts in the curriculum.

Hall, in fact, made quite a spirited criticism of the Committee of Ten report, as Feature 7-4 suggests, through which he helped to frame an important counterposition to the traditional liberal arts agenda (Kliebard, 1986). The Committee of Ten report, he stated, was faulty in fundamental ways. First, it failed to acknowledge the importance of individual differences among students by trying to force them to adjust uniformly to preexisting subject categories and learning tracks. Second, he simply did not see or appreciate the so-called transferable life-skills that were supposedly being effected in the kind of studies supported in the report. Hall was no mental disciplinarian, and he did not accept the view that certain subjects had mind training powers that were transferable as life-skills.

Clearly, Hall wanted to scuttle the traditionalist version of learning, which treated children as passive receptacles in need of having their heads filled with disciplinary knowledge. In its place, he wanted a curriculum that showed some responsiveness to individuals, a desire that inevitably led to the idea of curriculum differentiation or individualization in the school experience. Hall (1901) argued that the curriculum had to be differentiated so that each individual would have a chance to develop according to his or her own potential.

Interestingly, given Hall's concern for child study, we might expect that he was a strong believer in the formative powers of the environment. But Hall's commitment to individualizing the curriculum was justified, paradoxically, by a social Darwinian view of the world, whereby heredity, and not the environment, was the ruling law. To Hall, the school curriculum had to be determined according to student needs, but because these needs were innate to each student, the school had to encourage, through curriculum differentiation, the development of the most gifted students ("the best blood"). This also meant that all "nongifted" students could be treated in a simpler manner, all in the name of the learner. To know children, then, was to appreciate their natural endowments, something that Hall believed would become obvious to teachers as they allowed their students to develop freely. In this way, Hall helped to tow the Rousseauian line about the virtues of a laissez-faire education. That is, he encouraged teachers and parents to stay out of nature's way and to act only as guardians of the child's health and natural endowments (Cremin, 1988). Ironically, such an attitude could be seen as contradicting the very role and purpose of child development, which presumably would encourage teachers not to leave students alone but to take an interventionist role attuned to the developmental nature of the learner. But not from Hall's standpoint. Because child study pointed to certain developmental patterns in all learners, Hall argued that such patterns might help teachers foster certain learnings for children but that ultimately it was each child's unique endowments that would determine his or her progress. Teachers could facilitate the growth of the child, but without natural endowments, certain potentials could not be realized. Growth was largely preordained.

In examining the process of development among children, Hall also became a proponent of the cultural epochs theory that was gaining popularity with the American Herbartians. The theory, to recall, was tied to the notion that the development of the individual recapitulates the course of human history (from presavagery to civilization). The more sophisticated way of putting this is to say that ontogeny (the development of the individual) recapitulates phylogeny (the evolution of the race). To Hall, children developed naturally along the lines of the various stages of race experience. Making the connection between the two was essential to good pedagogy. Such ties helped students along an already predetermined path. With young children, applying the cultural epochs theory also helped to justify the indulgent treatment that these children received at the hands of teachers applying Hall's ideas. Given that young children were recapitulating the experiences of the species, they could not be expected to meet adult standards of conduct and face adult standards of discipline; they had to be treated at their level of race development (Cremin, 1988).

Although cultural epochs theory had its share of problems, it still represented a breakthrough in the curriculum that favored the child. The content of the curriculum was now arguably with and in children (part of their natural development), not in the liberal arts. Furthermore, education itself, which was long seen as a luxury or privilege, was now naturally endowed in the children (Cremin, 1961).

The American Kindergarten and the Rise—and Fall—of Froebel

Early Advocates and Rationales. Securing a publicly supported kindergarten in the ladder system of American education was an important achievement. The kindergarten, invented by Friedrich Froebel, found its first American expressions in several midwestern German American homes and schools. Most scholars acknowledge that Mary Schurz was the first American practitioner of the kindergarten. In 1856, she opened a private, German-speaking school for friends and family in Watertown, Wisconsin (Ross, 1976). However, the first signs of a national consciousness related to the kindergarten in America emerged from the work of Elizabeth Peabody. A seasoned teacher, Peabody was attracted to the idea of kindergarten after meeting Mary Schurz and being exposed to the writings of Froebel. Peabody eventually went on to study Froebelian methods in Germany during the late 1860s. When she returned to America, Peabody dedicated her life to the promotion of Froebelian causes in the schools and forcefully advocated the importance of the kindergarten and kindergarten teaching schools in the American school structure. With Peabody's advocacy, which included lecturing and writing on the subject of kindergarten, both public and private endeavors in kindergarten education became increasingly popular.

Another source of visible advocacy for the public kindergarten came from William Torrey Harris, who used his authority as superintendent of the St. Louis public schools to support the introduction of the kindergarten in his district. Harris, in fact, had received some early correspondence from Elizabeth Peabody outlining the importance of the kindergarten. His initial plan was to frame the kindergarten as a curriculum experiment. After all, Harris shared with Froebel a commitment to the philosophy of romantic idealism, which stressed the importance of bringing individuals into conformity with the absolute perfection or wholeness embodied in the divine spirit. Harris and Froebel had different ideas about the pathway toward the achievement of that perfection, but they shared the philosophic ideal. In 1873, Harris asked Susan Blow, a trainee in Froebelian methods, to oversee the kindergarten experiment in a school within the St. Louis district, the Des Peres School. Her job was to teach the kindergarten and to prepare a report on her experiences.

The arguments against including the kindergarten in the school structure were fairly well entrenched at the time. The major complaint was that the "nonacademic" mission of the kindergarten would not generate much public interest and would only waste money. Critics maintained that, if the kindergarten was going to emphasize the importance of play, as Froebel demanded, then few parents would regard it as necessary. And the resulting limited enrollment probably could not justify the expense. Other critics pointed to the actual types of experiences that the kindergarten supported. Because Froebelian notions were child-centered, many believed that the kindergarten would spoil young children and ruin their chances for later success in school. Some critics, for instance, cited the importance of silent study in the primary school experience and pointed to the kindergarten's philosophical opposition to silence. They maintained that socializing young children one way during the kindergarten years, only to reverse direction during the postkindergarten years, was educationally unsound.

As director of the experimental kindergarten in St. Louis, Susan Blow had a response to these assertions. After her first year, in 1878, she reported data showing very high attendance rates, relatively low financial expenditures, and evidence that the children outperformed primary school children on primary school tasks (Ross, 1976). St. Louis would soon become known as the center of the kindergarten universe, employing 131 paid kindergarten teachers by 1879. Blow would make a name for herself as an expert teacher and practitioner of the kindergarten. Before long, the St. Louis schools became the prime training grounds for young teachers in the kindergarten method.

Blow's work clearly convinced Harris that the kindergarten was a wise investment. Harris, in fact, began to see possibilities for the development of skills in the kindergarten that would later make it easier for primary school teachers to attend to the essential academic tasks he so valued. If kindergarten teachers could focus their efforts on the development of good manners, cleanliness, handicrafts, and manual dexterity, then primary grade teachers would be freer to direct their attention and energy to an education in the academic disciplines.

As it turned out, Froebel's romantic idealism would have its way in the kindergarten, while Harris's conception of idealism would apply in the postkindergarten years. Harris observed, for instance, that

> the kindergarten should be a sort of sub-primary education. . . . The disciplines of reading and writing, geography and arithmetic, as taught in the ordinary, primary school, are beyond the power of the average child not yet entered upon his seventh year. And beyond the seventh year the time of the child is too valuable to use it for other than general disciplines. . . . He must not take up his school time with learning a handicraft. (quoted in Blow, 1900, p. 9)

Harris also believed that the kindergarten represented an early school intervention that would eventually pay a positive social dividend. With children enrolled in school at the ages of 4 and 5, Harris was convinced that kindergarten classes could become early weapons against the poor habits and low-mindedness that many children inherited from their families (Blow, 1900). In fact, this was the same basic rationale offered by many advocates of private charity kindergartens. With so many young children living in slum conditions, the kindergarten was viewed as a kind of child-saving agency (Vandewalker, 1971). Harris, however, saw public kindergartens not only benefiting the children of the poor, who would be spared from the experiences of vice, crime, and neglect at an earlier age, but also the children of the rich, who would be saved "from the ruin of self-indulgence and the corruption ensuing on weak management in the family" (Blow, 1900, p. 9).

Classroom Methods. The early American kindergarten was deliberately Froebelian in its purpose and procedures. As mentioned, Froebel placed a high premium on play, but in forms that would develop the physical, intellectual, and moral nature of the child. He worked out a system for educating very young children by requiring that their play include the

7-5 SCHOLARLY VOICES
Froebel on the Educative Power of the Ball

Froebel (1904) developed a way of educating young children designed to bring them into some conception of unity with nature and God. Here, he states how one of the gifts, the ball, brings the child into this metaphysical state.

The ball [is] not only a great charm for the children but likewise [has] deep signifi-cance as a plaything . . . that the child, feeling himself a whole, early seeks and must seek in conformity with his human nature and his destiny, even at the stage of uncon-sciousness, always to contemplate, to grasp, and to possess a whole, but never merely a part as such. He seeks to contemplate, to grasp, and to possess a whole in all things, and in each thing, or at least, by means of and with them. . . . This whole for which the child seeks is supplied to him by the ball. (p. 33)

manipulation of a set of playthings, which he called gifts, and the adminis-tration of various handiwork activities, which he called occupations. He also stressed the importance of telling certain stories and singing certain songs. The kindergarten, in this sense, was not only a philosophy for early schooling but also a procedure for early schooling.

The playthings, or gifts, chosen and devised by Froebel, included different-colored balls, a wooden sphere, different-sized cubes and trian-gles, a cylinder, a square, small sticks, and wire rings. These materials, when manipulated by the child, allowed him or her to develop important observational capacities and to begin to understand ideas associated with the handling of the gifts, such as presence, absence, clasping, rolling, and falling (Ross, 1976). The gifts also enabled teachers to introduce concepts such as gravity and space to children (Kilpatrick, 1916).

The balls had the added power of representing a perfect form of unity, a geometric form that reminded children of the sense of unity that they needed to foster in themselves. In the words of Froebel, "The child . . . perceives in the ball the general expression of each object. . . . Even the word ball, in our significant language, is full of expression and meaning, pointing out that the ball is, as it were, an image of All" (quoted in Kilpatrick, 1916, pp. 111–12). In Feature 7-5, Froebel discusses the educative powers of the ball in more detail. The cubes, in sharp contrast to the balls, gave the child the chance to develop an understanding of contrast and variety. By playing with the cubes, cylinder, and balls, the child could develop the verbal skills needed to describe the distinguishing characteristics of the unified world (Ross, 1976).

Understanding the contrasting and opposing conditions of the universe was important to Froebel because such understandings helped the child to conceive of the endpoints of the whole. All of the gifts, or some combination, could also be used to build different geometric forms. Children, in fact, were encouraged to use different geometric parts to form different geometric wholes. Throughout the learning/playing process, the idea was to show the child the constituent parts comprised in the whole, a symbolic message that recurs in Froebel's kindergarten.

The handicraft activities, or occupations, were also vital to Froebel's kindergarten procedure. The occupations entailed a variety of activities with different materials, including sewing, drawing, paper twisting, weaving, paper folding, paper cutting, and clay modeling (Ross, 1976). These activities gave children the chance to ponder their world, to engage in a creative and productive as opposed to a receptive process of learning, and to see geometric forms as the building blocks of the world. The goal here was to give children the opportunity to synthesize and integrate the general geometric elements of the world, to find the whole (the Allness) in the synthesis of the parts. As a devotee of Froebel, Blow (1908) characterized the idea behind these kinds of activities: "As we learn the phonetic alphabet in order to get at the sense of what is written in books, so we learn the alphabet of form, in order to get at the sense of what is written in the great book of nature" (p. 41).

Where reading and writing were prominent in the early dame schools and Latin grammar schools, Froebel sought to replace these activities with experiences in song, storytelling, games, conversation, and outdoor events such as gardening. The goal, again, was to show children their place in the whole of the social group. The teacher, for instance, might sing the following rhyme as she engaged children in the manipulation of eight small cubes: "Look here and see! One whole, two halves; One half, two fourths; Two halves, four fourths; One whole, four fourths; Four fourths, eight eights; Eight eights, one whole. Here are many, here are few; It's a magic way to do" (Kilpatrick, 1916, p. 141). Froebel also developed a series of games that often stressed the significance of the circle.

Criticisms of the Early Kindergarten Method. Not surprisingly, criticism of the kindergarten method soon followed. The most basic criticism emerged from John Dewey (1916), who, despite admiring Froebel's contribution to education, felt that the kindergarten method had become too prescribed and too dependent on a particular set of materials and activities. Educator William Kilpatrick (1916) questioned the foundation of symbolism in Froebel's theories, asking how a ball or any other object could have any special claim on an organic or social construction of unity. Kilpatrick also asserted the need for the kindergarten to move beyond Froebel's preoccupation with symbolism in favor of dealing with real-world issues and problems.

G. Stanley Hall, whose own work underscored the importance of making adjustments in the learning environment based on the emerging knowledge of the learner, made a similar point. Thus, he directly attacked some kindergarten training schools for their uniform and programmatic approaches toward teaching. For instance, he argued that, because some gifts were too small for young children, they would only frustrate the children and undermine the learning experience (Ross, 1976). As founder of the child study movement, Hall argued that kindergarten teachers had to be receptive to the new knowledge available on the nature of the child and to be prepared to make appropriate changes in classroom materials, curricula, and methods. Thus, kindergarten teachers had to be less concerned with using the particular gifts and materials developed by Froebel, and more concerned with making intelligent adjustments to the learning environment in the light of the latest available knowledge on learners.

Hall's message reached a receptive audience, as kindergarten training sites began to acknowledge the importance of the child study movement in creating new insights for kindergarten teachers. However, it also galvanized a group, led by Susan Blow, committed to the orthodox interpretation of the Froebelian system. Blow claimed that the kindergarten represented a uniform plan of action based on the materials developed by Froebel. Meanwhile, other emerging scholars in the field, particularly Patty Smith Hill, argued that the kindergarten classroom had to retain some flexibility to best serve the interests of children.

Because she challenged Blow directly, Hill would emerge as an important thinker in the kindergarten movement. Her early appointment to the Teachers College in Columbia University as a lecturer on kindergarten and preschool education would give her views a visible platform. Having studied at some level with Dewey and Hall, Hill was less ideologically attached to the work of Froebel than was Blow. Hill acknowledged the significance of Froebel by crediting him with helping to bring the child into the center of curriculum formulations and with advancing the idea of making the school a happy place marked by play, games, music, and well-educated, well-intentioned teachers. But Hill believed that the school environment had to be open to change based on the best available knowledge. New songs, games, materials, and methods had to be continuously considered as new demands on and insights into learners and the society emerged.

Emerging Methods of Teaching Kindergarten. By the 1890s, kindergarten teachers were being trained nationwide. Naturally, Froebelian gifts and the principles governing their application in the classroom were an important part of the training (Ross, 1976). Prospective teachers spent much time in observation and practice teaching. But the debate that loomed between Blow and Hill pointed to two very different kindergarten training programs. Blow wanted attention to be directed at the true Froebelian procedures; Hill wanted these procedures to be reevaluated and amended not only in the light of new knowledge about learning but also in relation to the unique social context of America. Hill, for instance, moved away from teaching teachers how to use the stories and songs that Froebel chose for the kindergarten and toward encouraging teachers to create their own stories, using the issues and demands of the day to make them more suitable for American children. Because Froebel's stories and songs were originally conceived for and used with German children, Hill wanted the stories and songs used in the American kindergarten to be composed specifically for American children. Because of Hill's influence, early kindergarten teachers would, in fact, become leading authors of children's stories and original composers of simple children's tunes. For instance, with her sister, Hill composed the traditional birthday song "Happy Birthday to You" (Rudnitski, 1994). Hill also preached the selective and adapted use of the gifts, arguing that they should be bigger, as dictated by child study findings, and that many other types of objects should be brought into the school, including dolls and bean bags. She believed that the symbolic commitment to teaching children their place in a unified world took precious time away from other important objectives in the curriculum, including the development of social skills. She turned the gifts into means serving broader ends as opposed to ends in themselves.

Blow saw these developments as little more than contaminants to the true Froebelian method. To her, modifications in the Froebelian approach testified to the weakening of the kindergarten ideal. Blow was appalled by the selective use of Froebel's methods. She disdained, for instance, the manner in which some kindergarten teachers were building their curricula around Herbartian themes, or concentrations, and using the gifts and occupations to advance the knowledge and ideas inherent in the study of the concentrations (Blow, 1908). Such an approach, in Blow's view, destroyed the special value of the gifts and the occupations. Froebelian instruments, she asserted, should not be used for non-Froebelian aims. Blow was also insulted by the increasingly popular concept of a free-play kindergarten. She, of course, did not deny the importance of play, but to secure attainment with the absolute spirit of God, play had to be mediated by Froebel's gifts and occupations, and not left to the caprice of children (Blow, 1908).

In the end, the progressive views of Patty Smith Hill won the day. The American kindergarten would have to acknowledge the special vision of

Froebel and the dedication that he inspired among its early practitioners. But the growing strength of the child study movement and the awakening of the progressive commitment to the social aims of schooling led the school away from Froebelian procedures and their mystical rationales. The American kindergarten would support a form of practice better attuned to the nature of the learner and to the values and aims of democracy. As Feature 7-6 shows, the kindergarten today still struggles with some of the same types of problems that originally led to its founding.

The Progressive Criticism of Child-Centeredness

All in all, proponents of the child-centered approach were fairly successful in securing the place of the child in the curriculum equation. The problem was that, too often, the thinking started and stopped with the child. Later, a large portion of the school community embraced romantic/naturalist reasoning, so much so that many of the private schools of the 1900s featured a curriculum that encouraged children to follow their momentary interests and wishes. Many of these progressive private schools concentrated on the education of young children. But elements of the progressive community also were distressed to see the level of individualism being advanced in many of these so-called progressive schools. In 1928, Rugg and Schumaker published a book that appraised the first quarter-century of child-centered education in these mostly private schools, showing how teacher initiatives were frequently supplanted by a desire simply to reflect and cater to children's interests.

In time, the notion of child-centeredness, as expressed in its most Rousseauian form, was sullied in both traditional and progressive quarters. John Dewey, for instance, could not fathom how any form of education can deny children the wisdom and maturity of experience offered to them by adults, especially ones professionally trained to deal with children. He was usually a gentle critic, but in this case, Dewey (1929) strongly condemned child-centeredness:

> There is a present tendency in so called advanced schools of educational thought to say, in effect, let us surround pupils with certain materials, tools, appliances, etc. and let pupils respond to these things according to their own desires. Above all let us not suggest any end or plan to students; let us not suggest to them what they shall do, for that is an unwarranted trespass upon their sacred individuality since the essence of such individuality is to set up ends and aims. Now such a method is really stupid. For it attempts the impossible, which is always stupid; and it misconceived the conditions of independent thinking. (p. 153)

283

7-6 THINKING ABOUT THE DATA

Kindergartners and Mother's Education Level

The National Center for Education Statistics released a study on American kindergartners in February 2000. The data show interesting variations among the children. The following is a selective sample of differences expressed in relation to the education level of the child's mother. What does this say about the role of school education? How might Montessori and Hall have responded to these data?

	MOTHER'S EDUCATION LEVEL			
	Less Than High School	High School Diploma	Some College	Bachelor's Degree or Higher
Mean Kindergarten Reading Score (beginning sounds, ending sounds, letter recognition)	43	48	51	56
Percentage of Kindergartners, As Reported by Parents, Who Often/Very Often				
Make Friends	80%	88%	91%	91%
Comfort Others	71	82	85	85
Fight with Others	21	17	13	10
Get Angry	29	18	14	12
Percentage of Kindergartners at Risk for Being Overweight	15	13	12	9
Percentage of Kindergartners, as Assessed by Parents, as Having "Excellent" General Health	35	47	54	62
Percentage of Kindergartners, as Assessed by Parents, as Having Difficulty with				
Attention	17	14	14	10
Articulation	14	12	10	8
Percentage of Kindergartners, as Assessed by Parents, Who Are Often/Very Often				
Persistent at Tasks	65	70	74	81
Eager to Learn	85	91	94	95
Creative	73	83	88	89
Percentage of Kindergartners				
With Less Than 26 Books at Home	62	31	17	7
With No CDs, Records, or Audiotapes at Home	35	15	8	3
Who Are Read to Every Day at Home	36	39	45	59

SOURCE: National Center for Education Statistics (2000), *America's Kindergartners* (Washington, DC: U.S. Department of Education).

Dewey believed in the need to reflect the nature of the learner in school decisions. But he also believed that the learner, as an immature organism, could not be effectively socialized into the canons and learnings of the social group (the culture) without the active intervention of adults. Boyd Bode (1938), who was among the most penetrating progressive critics of his time, sided with Dewey in assailing the thinking of those who opted for child-centeredness and in worrying about the negative effects that such a view might have on the progressive education movement:

> The failure to emancipate ourselves completely from Rousseauism . . . is responsible for most, if not all, of the weaknesses of the progressive move-ment in education. . . . The insistence that we must stick uncompromisingly at all times to the "needs" of childhood has bred a spirit of anti-intellectual-ism, which is reflected in the reliance on improvising instead of long-range organization, in the overemphasis of the here and now, in the indiscriminate tirades against "subjects" [and] in the absurdities of pupil planning. (p. 70)

Dewey and Bode were at the forefront of a very different version of pro-gressivism, one that honored the child but that also incorporated other fun-damental variables in the act of teaching and learning. In the eyes of Dewey and other like-minded progressives, child development could not be con-templated without thinking about the child in the context of the society. That is, it was ridiculous to think about the child independent of the society or of the skills, attitudes, and knowledge needed to succeed in society. This new attitude pervaded the progressivism, as discussed in the next chapter.

SUMMARY

The early struggle to influence the course of the American school experi-ence was won by the traditional humanists, whose views represented an extension of the old colonial idea of mental learning in the context of selected subject areas. The Committee of Ten and Committee of Fifteen reports made it clear that the first pattern of course work to be established in a more universalized version of public schooling would be subject-centered. But there were changes in the air, blowing mostly from the conti-nent of Europe.

The European notion of child-centeredness began to take hold in Amer-ica in the 1860s and left an indelible impression on the American school scene. Because of it, normal schools found real opportunities to teach teachers about children, rather than simply subject matter. And the recalcu-lation of the curriculum with the child in mind gave way to new visions of subject matter organization, such as the Herbartian notion of concentration, and also set the conditions for the study of the learner as an important component in the teaching/learning process. Some of these elements helped to form the pillars of the progressive education movement.

At the same time, child-centeredness ran the risk of reaching too far in the direction of the child, creating schools openly dedicated to the romantic/naturalist view of learning by permitting anything that the child was interested in pursuing. In this sense, child-centered thinking represented a classic counterreaction to the traditionalism that had dominated the schools at the end of the nineteenth century. The traditional school, long a bastion of order and control, had deliberately squelched student expression and initiative, and showed little regard for the interests and welfare of learners. Child-centeredness found its way as a palliating force against traditional extremes. But by casting its floodlights on the child, the child-centered school created its own counterextreme. Thus, much of the early twentieth-century debate over the school curriculum was waged between subject-centered (traditionalist) views and child-centered views. This was an inadequate framing of the curriculum problem because it posed the curriculum in dual terms—as either subjected-centered or child-centered. As we will see in the next chapter, another progressive group demanded that both factors (the learner and the subject matter) be integrated with yet another important factor (the society).

QUESTIONS AND ACTIVITIES

1. What was the doctrine of mental discipline, and how did it help give rise to a subject-centered view of learning?

2. What was the central recommendation of the Committee of Ten report, and how did such a recommendation influence the character of high school education?

3. In what ways did Charles Eliot, the chair of the Committee of Ten, disagree with the committee's recommendations?

4. Describe the fundamental differences between William Torrey Harris's and Charles Eliot's conceptions of the school curriculum.

5. Both Pestalozzi and the mental disciplinarians used faculty psychology to justify their school actions. Explain how this could be so.

6. What was the central message that Johann Pestalozzi wanted to send to the school?

7. Why were supporters of Johann Herbart turning toward thematic treatments in the curriculum, using, as described, the novel *Robinson Crusoe* as a way to unify all studies in the third-grade classroom?

8. Describe how the Herbartian idea of correlations might be used in a elementary school today.

9. Why was William Torrey Harris utterly distressed by what the Herbartians were advocating in the curriculum?

10. Describe cultural epochs theory, and explain why many Herbartians were attracted to the idea.

11. Explain how Friedrich Froebel believed that he was facilitating the work of God through his method of educating small children.

12. How did Maria Montessori's work with "feeble-minded" children lead her toward early childhood instruction?

13. In what ways was Maria Montessori's work in early childhood education criticized?

14. How did the philosophical work of Jean-Jacques Rousseau contribute to the child-centered movement in education?

15. What was the significance of the New Harmony commune in the late 1820s?

16. Explain the attraction of Johann Pestalozzi and Johann Herbart to the American normal school curriculum.

17. What was the significance of the founding and operation of the Oswego Normal School?

18. Explain the significance of G. Stanley Hall in the development of the child-centered movement in education.

19. In what ways did Hall's social Darwinism arguably contradict his work in the area of child development?

20. What was behind William Torrey Harris's attraction to the kindergarten?

21. What were the main principles distinguishing Susan Blow from Patty Smith Hill?

22. How and why was the Froebelian version of kindergarten in America eventually supplanted by a different view?

23. What was the essential argument that John Dewey and other progressives made against child-centered thinking?

24. In what ways was the child-centered movement a counterreaction to the traditionalist curriculum?

REFERENCES

Barlow, T. A. (1977). *Pestalozzi and American education.* (Boulder, CO: Este Press).

Blow, S. (1908). *Educational issues in the kindergarten.* (New York: Appleton).

Blow, S. (1900). Kindergarten education. In N. M. Butler (ed.), *Education in the United States.* (Albany: Lyons).

Bode, B. H. (1938). *Progressive education at the crossroads.* (New York: Newson).

Bode, B. H. (1927). *Modern educational theories.* (New York: Macmillan).

Butts, R. F. (1955). *A cultural history of western education: Its social and intellectual foundations.* (New York: McGraw-Hill).

Childs, J. (1956). *American pragmatism and education.* (New York: Holt).

Committee of Fifteen. (1895). *Report of the Committee of Fifteen.* (New York: Arno Press [1969]).

Committee of Ten. (1893). *Report of the Committee of Ten on secondary school studies.* In D. H. Calhoun (1969), *Education of Americans: A documentary history.* (New York: Houghton Mifflin).

Cremin, L. A. (1988). *American education: The metropolitan experience.* (New York: Harper & Row).

Cremin, L. A. (1961). *The transformation of the school.* (New York: Knopf).

Cubberley, E. (1947). *Public education in the United States.* (New York: Houghton Mifflin).

Dewey, J. (1929). Individuality and experience. In J. Dewey, *Art and education.* (Merion, PA: Barnes Foundation Press).

Dewey, J. (1916). *Democracy and education.* (New York: Free Press).

Dewey, J. (1902). *The child and the curriculum.* (Chicago: University of Chicago Press).

Eliot, C. (1893). Can school programs be shortened and enriched? In *National Education Association proceedings.* (Washington, DC: NEA).

Froebel, F. (1887). *The education of man.* (New York: Appleton [1826]).

Gutek, G. L. (1968). *Pestalozzi and education.* (New York: Random House).

Hall, G. S. (1901). The ideal school as based on child study. In D. H. Calhoun, *Educating of Americans: A documentary history.* (New York: Houghton Mifflin).

Hall, G. S. (1883). The contents of children's minds. In D. H. Calhoun, *Educating of Americans: A documentary history.* (New York: Houghton Mifflin).

Harris, W. T. (1888). What shall the public schools teach? *The Forum,* 4:573–81.

Herbart, J. F. (1901). *Outlines of educational doctrine.* (New York: Macmillan).

Karier, C. J. (1967). *Man, society and education.* (New York: Scott Foresman).

Kilpatrick, W. H. (1971). *The Montessori system examined.* (New York: Arno Press and the New York Times [1914]).

Kilpatrick, W. (1918). The project method. *Teachers College Record,* 19(4):319–35.

Kilpatrick, W. (1916). *Froebel's kindergarten principles.* (New York: Macmillan).

Kliebard, H. (1986). *The struggle for the American curriculum.* (New York: Routledge & Kegan Paul).

Krug, E. A. (1964). *The shaping of the American high school.* (New York: Harper & Row).

McMurry, F. (1946). *Herbartian contributions to history instruction in American elementary schools.* (New York: Bureau of Publications, Teachers College, Columbia University).

Meyer, A. E. (1975). *Grandmasters of educational thought.* (New York: McGraw-Hill).

Monroe, W. S. (1907). *History of the Pestalozzian movement in the United States.* Syracuse, NY: Bardeen).

Pestalozzi, J. H. (1894). *How Gertrude teaches her children.* (Syracuse, NY: Bardeen).

Power, E. J. (1991). *A legacy of learning.* (Albany: SUNY Press).

Rippa, A. (1984). *Education in a free society: An American history.* (New York: McKay).

Ross, E. D. (1976). *The kindergarten crusade.* (Athens: Ohio University Press).

Rousseau, J. J. (1979). *Emile.* Trans. A. Bloom. (New York: Basic Books [1762]).

Rudnitski, R. A. (1994). Patty Smith Hill and the progressive kindergarten. *Current Issues in Education.* 11(1):25–34.

Rugg, H., and Schumaker, A. (1969). *The child-centered school.* (New York: Arno Press and the New York Times [1928]).

Tanner, D., and Tanner, L. N. (1987). *The history of the school curriculum.* (New York: Macmillan).

Thayer, V. T. (1960). *The role of the school in American society.* (New York: Dodd, Mead).

Vandewalker, N. C. (1971). *The kindergarten in American education.* (New York: Arno Press and the New York Times [1908]).

CHAPTER 8

The School Experience into the Twentieth Century

Progressivism and the Cause of Social Reform
JOHN DEWEY AND THE DEMOCRATIC COMMUNITY
LESTER WARD AND THE PROGRESSIVE PRINCIPLE OF
ENVIRONMENTALISM

Progressive Ideas in Action
BOOKER T. WASHINGTON, W. E. B. DU BOIS,
AND THE BLACK STRUGGLE FOR SCHOOLING
FRANCIS PARKER AND THE QUINCY METHODS
JANE ADDAMS AND THE SETTLEMENT HOUSE MOVEMENT
THE CARDINAL PRINCIPLES REPORT OF 1918 AND
A TIDAL CHANGE FOR SECONDARY EDUCATION
GEORGE COUNTS AND A MORE RADICAL PROGRESSIVISM

Education and the Rise of Social Efficiency
FREDERICK TAYLOR AND THE IDEAL OF EFFICIENCY
FRANKLIN BOBBITT, CURRICULUM DESIGN,
AND SOCIAL EFFICIENCY
SPECIFICITY IN THE CURRICULUM AND IQ TESTING

Summary

Questions and Activities

References

W HILE MUCH OF THE EARLY DEBATE between progressives and traditionalists revolved around child-centered versus subject-centered views, other progressive thinkers began to think about the design of the school in terms of its democratizing function in society. As a result, the dominant issue was no longer whether the child or the omnipotent subject matter was being served in the school. Instead, the focus shifted toward the question of how to use the school to build a good society. This was always the implicit concern, as both child-centered and subject-centered advocates felt that their own brand of education would yield well-educated individuals who would contribute to a better society. But the new progressive focus was explicitly attached to a social democratic theory and to the use of the school as a tool for social reform. Thus, the struggle over the school curriculum became part of a broader struggle over how the school would contribute to social progress. Educational concerns, such as those affecting blacks (especially in the South), women, the poor, and immigrants, were fundamentally public policy matters, tied to social improvements and social corrections. But different progressives had different ideas about how to develop the school along these lines.

PROGRESSIVISM AND THE CAUSE OF SOCIAL REFORM

Led by John Dewey, one progressive rank emerged in the early twentieth century that sought to reawaken the social democratic ideal of public schooling. For Dewey and others, the conception of the child in relation to curriculum development had to be tempered with a vision of the school as an agency for the improvement of social conditions, the advancement of democratic principles, and the formation of common democratic communities. The child-centered movement focused on the individual and promoted a pedagogic agenda that valued individualistic pursuits of self-expression, self-meaning, and self-development. By contrast, the progressivism of Dewey emphasized the importance of developing social insights and a sense of community consciousness. Dewey conceived of the school as a miniature unit of democracy, consciously conceived to produce a comprehensive and enlarging social experience, where children learn about their differences and their commonalties, where vocational pursuits coexist with academic ones, and where the ideals of tolerance and social mutuality coexist with critical mindedness.

THE SCHOOL EXPERIENCE INTO THE TWENTIETH CENTURY   CHAPTER 8

John Dewey and the Democratic Community

Background and Philosophical Development. Born in 1859 in prein-dustrial Vermont, John Dewey entered the University of Vermont at age 16 (Wirth, 1989). Graduating in 1879, Dewey became a high school teacher. Within three years, however, he entered into a doctoral program at Johns Hopkins University, where he was tutored by some of the academic stars of his time, including G. Stanley Hall. Dewey took only two years to complete his doctoral studies, at which time he was hired by the University of Michigan as an instructor of psychology and philosophy. In 1884, he moved to the University of Chicago, where he quickly developed a laboratory school that allowed him to test his school-related ideas against the actual experience of teaching children (see Dewey (1902b) *School and the Society*). But in 1905, in a squabble over leadership of the laboratory school, Dewey left Chicago for Columbia University. He remained at Columbia until his retirement; he died in New York City at the age of 92.

During his long life, Dewey engaged in a philosophy that not only addressed traditional pursuits in logic, ethics, political science, religion, psychology, and aesthetics but also spoke to issues in the public arena. Dewey, for instance, had substantive things to say about issues related to the suffragette movement, labor unions, birth control, world peace, social class tensions, and societal transformations in Mexico, China, and Russia (Dworkin, 1954). A complete collection of Dewey's works is contained in a thirty-seven-volume work edited by Jo Ann Boydston (1979). Feature 8-1 suggests some ways to learn more about Dewey from the Center for Dewey Studies.

Although Dewey started his career in the field of psychology, he soon came to know and appreciate the philosophical work of the American pragmatists. The philosophy of pragmatism appealed to Dewey largely because it stressed a social psychology that examined human behaviors and that resonated with democratic values and traditions. In the context of American pragmatism, thought and knowledge were relevant only as action, as practical power in the conduct of the individual and the society. Truth itself was a tentative condition, always under inspection and always being tested by the consequences that it produced under real-life conditions (Childs, 1956).

Similarly, society was an ever-changing arrangement that required close examination and reasoned treatment of its problems. The very sustenance and health of the society, according to pragmatism, depended on a commitment to understanding the problems of present living conditions. This, in turn, meant that some method of intelligence or inquiry, qualified by democratic values, had to be found as a way to regulate, understand, and,

8-1 WEB POINTS
Center for Dewey Studies

The Center for Dewey Studies (www.siu.edu/~deweyctr) is one of several groups interested in better understanding and promoting Dewey's ideas. Other groups include the John Dewey Society (www.cuip.uchicago.edu/jds) and the John Dewey Project on Progressive Education (www.uvm.edu/~dewey).

What Is the Center for Dewey Studies?

The Center for Dewey Studies at Southern Illinois University at Carbondale was established in 1961 as the "Dewey Project." In the course of collecting and editing Dewey's works, the Center amassed a wealth of source materials for the study of America's quintessential philosopher-educator, John Dewey. By virtue of its publications and research, the Center has become the international focal point for research on Dewey's life and work. Its location at the University makes it possible for visitors to take advantage of the resources and professional expertise of the faculty and staff of the Department of Philosophy, the College of Education, Special Collections in Morris Library, and the Southern Illinois University Press.

From Special Collections, Morris Library, Southern Illinois University.

ultimately, ameliorate current conditions. The present, to the early pragmatists, was "holy ground," to borrow Whitehead's (1929) metaphor, that gave the past relevance and that provided the working conditions for a better future.

Dewey eventually made his own contributions to American pragmatism by stressing the role that the scientific method could play in improving the human condition and by openly linking his philosophy to the values and aims of democracy. To Dewey, democracy was less a political concept than a moral one. Dewey, in this sense, became the chief voice for the values and morals of American pragmatism, a role that likely led George Herbert Mead to observe that "in the profoundest sense John Dewey is the philosopher of America" (quoted in Morris, 1970, p. 8).

Learning as Real-Life Inquiry and Reconstruction. In 1902, based on his work in his laboratory school, Dewey put forth what he believed to be the three crucial factors in the learning process: (1) the nature of the learner, (2) the values and aims of the society, and (3) the wider world of knowledge represented in the subject matter. This was his way of saying that all good teaching must be attuned to (1) the character of learners (interests, problems, developmental nature), (2) the highest values of the society (democratic principles of cooperation, tolerance, critical mindedness, and political awareness), and (3) the reflective representation of the subject matter (the knowledge in the various disciplines that helps the teacher present material that resonates with both learner and society). These factors are not discrete, but work together as interrelated and complementary elements. Thus, the learner had to be seen in the context of the society, forcing a consideration of the needs and interests not just of the learner but also of the learner living in a democracy. Similarly, the choice of subject matter in the curriculum had to be made based on what was most worth knowing for a learner living in a democracy.

Dewey's ideas about the school curriculum can be cautiously classified, as noted in Chapter 3, as experimentalist-progressive (Tanner and Tanner, 1987a). The reference to experimentalism has to do with Dewey's advocation of the scientific method in teaching and learning. According to Dewey, science had given humans a method of intelligent inquiry by which they could transform problems into progress. Convinced of the need to develop autonomously thinking, socially responsible citizens through the school, Dewey embraced the scientific method as an educational mainstay. However, he merged his embrace of science with the ethics of democracy. In this way, he hoped to instill in schoolchildren a scientific attitude toward truth and understanding informed by and associated with democratic ideals and principles.

Dewey (1916), who wrote extensively about the act of thinking, structured the act of learning along lines that resembled the scientific method. Good learning, he believed, is based on a method of inquiry. It originates in real-life experiences, framed and intellectualized in terms of a problem to be investigated. This leads invariably to the careful consideration of the condition of the problem and to the positing of tentative resolutions. Such resolutions are then further refined into hypotheses and developed in a way that anticipates their overall effect in experience. Finally, the hypotheses are brought to bear on the real-life problem and are tested for the purpose of yielding new insights on the original problem. Dewey wanted the spirit of such inquiry to be marked by social problems rooted in the soil of democratic communities. He wanted schooling to ingrain youths with an experimental habit of mind and with an ethical disposition toward the aims of democracy. Under the conditions just described, learning is anchored in the real problems of experience, is problem focused and democratic in purpose and intent, and is based on the principle that truth is never absolute.

This latter point was particularly relevant to Dewey. In fact, he often discussed the need for education to proceed as an act of reconstruction. By this, he meant that the school had to continuously look at society's problems as opportunities for improvement and growth. When one subjected social problems to a method of intelligent inquiry, found in the admixture of science and democracy, one allowed for experience to be reconstructed with new insight and value. More than anything, Dewey's commitment to the reconstruction of experience made him a progressive in the true sense of the word—one who looks for progress and change.

Dewey, however, balanced this regard for reconstruction through inquiry with an argument that spoke to the value of common communities, particularly as unifying and conserving forces. One could not have a community, he argued, unless the people shared elements of commonality—common problems, common ideals, a common language, and a common history. Given the pluralistic character of the U.S. population, Dewey thought that it was imperative to use the school to build common bases of understanding. The school, in other words, had to transmit a heritage of ideals to schoolchildren and to provide a common ground for discourse that would bond the nation in some basis of commonality (Dewey, 1916). He did not want the school simply to transmit culture through the liberal arts, as William Torrey Harris and others did. He wanted this foundation of commonality to be built on conversation and to be devoted to problems and principles rather than preexisting subject matter.

The Laboratory School. Dewey's entrance into the school reform fray at the turn of the century was to become legendary. After spending ten years as a professor of psychology and philosophy at the University of Michigan, he moved more directly into educational circles by accepting a position at the University of Chicago, which entailed, among other duties, directing a university laboratory school.

Like many progressives of his time, Dewey started to test his ideas in an actual school. In developing his school, he was naturally drawn to questions of what knowledge was most worthwhile and what instructional procedures could be employed to promote an experiential and democratic education. Dewey, of course, wanted to integrate the problems of actual experience in the education of the children, but he also wanted to be sure that this process did not collapse into child-centeredness. Dewey's curriculum, it should be remembered, had to be attuned not only to the learner but to the society and to a sense of subject matter as well. Dewey understood that, if children were going to learn to control their own destinies, they obviously had to learn basic literacy skills and acquire basic knowledge embodied in organized subject matter.

As a result, he decided to build the lab school curriculum around what he called social occupations—cooking, carpentry, and sewing (Dewey, 1902b; Wirth, 1989). Out of these occupations, children could learn arithmetic, reading and writing, and the sciences. The subject matter came to the occupations, as it were, which meant that it was interdisciplinary in its organization. The occupations themselves were worthwhile only to the extent to which they informed problems and needs in experience.

For instance, the 12-year-olds in the laboratory school had at one time made it clear to their teachers that they needed their own meeting place in school. They were apparently unhappy about not having a place of their own where they could hold meetings without interruption and could store materials for ongoing projects. Out of this need, the children developed a plan to build a clubhouse. In consultation with adults,

> committees on architecture, building, sanitation, ways and means, and interior decoration were formed. . . . The site for the building was chosen under the guidance of the teachers in the different departments; plans were made and the cost estimated. A scheme for decoration was worked out, designs for furniture made. The choice of a location was prefaced by a study of the formation of soil, the conditions of drainage, climate, exposure to light or wind, which must be taken into account in building a house. (Mayhew and Edwards, 1936, p. 229)

All of this activity led to the actual building of the clubhouse and to the more extended study of the physical geography of Chicago (where the school was located) in relation to its building sites. It was out of such problem-driven projects that Dewey taught children to think, act, and express themselves in intelligent ways while simultaneously developing basic skills and knowledge.

Dewey's desire to integrate skills and knowledge into real-life experiences also led to a very different attitude toward interest and motivation (Tanner and Tanner, 1987a). Whereas the idea of motivating children had long been seen as dependent on threats or coercion, Dewey argued that interest and motivation had to be vested in the actual conduct of the learning experience. If one had to resort to pleadings, threats, punishments, or trickery to get children to do their schoolwork, it probably meant that the work was not very worthwhile and not likely connected to ideas and experiences. The development of student interest and motivation was always an act of curriculum development. It had everything to do with the construction of attractive and engaging learning experiences.

8-2 SCHOLARLY VOICES
Lester Ward and the Idea of Environmentalism

Lester Ward combatted the social Darwinism of his time by strongly supporting the idea that the environment controls human destiny. He resisted prevailing efforts to see education as biologically determined and the more extended eugenic efforts to make such an argument in reference to categories of ethnicity and race. In this way, he was an early voice for the expansion of educational opportunity, a centerpiece to the progressive education project.

The brain power of the world is the same at every level, even the lowest slaves and serfs that have ever existed on the globe have the same faculties as those who have had them under control, who have owned them . . . there is no difference. (quoted in Tanner and Tanner, 1987b, p. 541)

Lester Ward and the Progressive Principle of Environmentalism

Dewey was not alone in trying to create a new form of education openly devoted to the idea of using the school for social democratic purposes. Other scholars were advocating the very same idea, the most notable being Lester Ward. In 1883, Ward produced a two-volume work entitled *Dynamic Sociology,* which helped earn him the title among some as the "father of American sociology."

Ward was trained as a geologist, but he used his analytical talents to test the prevailing social doctrines of the day. His two-volume book took direct aim at social Darwinism, which presumed that a "survival of the fittest" attitude was the best policy in the schools and in society. Recall that even G. Stanley Hall, the champion of the child study movement, had bowed to social Darwinism, believing that children were genetically wired for success. Ward, however, came to quite a different conclusion. He believed that environmental factors were at the forefront of an individual's chance to succeed in life and that the uneven distribution of wealth and all of its concomitant inequalities (access to knowledge, nutrition, the fulfillment of material needs, and so on) ensured the continued poverty of underclass citizens. Intelligence, to Ward, was evenly distributed across social, economic, and gender lines, as Feature 8-2 indicates. The trick was to develop a system of education that distributed equal qualities of experience. There was no lack of intelligence among poor people or among women; there was only lack of opportunity (Tanner and Tanner, 1987b).

To Ward, securing the quality of the learning environment was the pre-condition for securing the opportunity to learn and, ultimately, to improve oneself. There could be no learning without a systematic opportunity to learn. And this could not occur by happenstance. Dewey (1916), whose work followed in the intellectual tradition of Ward, agreed, referring to the school environment as a "purified medium of action," a place that deliberately eliminated, as much as possible, the miseducative features of the environment, that simplified the environment in the interest of securing various important effects, and that broadened the living context of schoolchildren with a world beyond their community or home. According to Dewey, this required, in part, that the schoolchildren of America learn together, in one unified setting and in a common universe of knowledge and problems, where equal opportunities could be assured and where common bonds of understanding could be formed.

Ward, not surprisingly, also put his faith in the public school, believing that it was the most important function of government—the main engine for social correction and social improvement. Through the school, he wanted to lay to rest the idea of biological inheritance in intelligence and to operationalize the idea that healthy environmental interventions were the key to improving the lives of people. He was also not shy about encouraging government intervention to help close the chasm of inequity in people's lives, a view that has led some to describe him as "the prophet of the welfare state" (Kliebard, 1986). While Ward underscored the sociological need for schools to contribute to social progress and social change, Dewey put the flesh on the bones of this idea, as it were, by specifying how schools should conduct themselves based on these priorities. Ward helped to cripple the inherent laissez-faire attitude of social Darwinism and provided the main rationale and conceptual foundation for a method of schooling that looked to prepare a new generation for social insight and social gain.

PROGRESSIVE IDEAS IN ACTION

The progressive education movement in America was partly a protest movement. The movement, after all, was partly an effort to reconcile the untenable dualism that had prevailed between subject-centered and child-centered views. But the progressive education movement had a full supply of practical ideas as well as criticisms. The school world would become a very different place because of the hands-on work of the progressives. Among the earliest and most important progressive issues was captured in the debate between Booker T. Washington and W. E. B. Du Bois, as they struggled to influence the public school experience for black Americans.

Booker T. Washington, W. E. B. Du Bois, and the Black Struggle for Schooling

Although 4 million blacks gained their constitutional freedom following the Civil War, they did not gain freedom from private discrimination nor obtain much in the way of social or economic stability, especially in the South. Largely destitute, they had to find their way to a new life with limited assistance. One important legislative mechanism that existed, however, was the Bureau of Refugees, Freedmen, and Abandoned Lands, or simply the Freedmen Bureau. The agency operated from 1865 until 1872, carrying out a comprehensive mandate to help resettle blacks, among other concerns. One of its more successful endeavors was the construction and operation of schools for black children. Under the leadership of General O. O. Howard, the Freedmen Bureau collected money from various private aid agencies and benevolent societies and applied the money to the development of a schooling infrastructure for all black children. This included the purchase of buildings and curriculum materials and the hiring of teachers for the schools. The bureau had no appropriations from Congress during its first several years of existence. Instead, the benevolence of northern aid societies and Howard's creative collection of rent money on abandoned lands gave the bureau its early working budget (Harlan, 1988).

But it wasn't money that would stand in the way of the movement to educate the children of former slaves. Aggressive white racism in several southern states resulted in threats and actual violence directed at Freedmen and school personnel and facilities. The "problem of the color line" was just beginning to take form. Jim Crow laws prevailed, and overt racism in the management of restaurants, hotels, trains, and theaters, which was not illegal under the provisions of the Fourteenth Amendment, helped to oppress blacks. In the South, "separate but equal" became the dominant social doctrine of the time, eventually receiving the sanction of law under the *Plessy v. Ferguson* ruling in 1896. Reflecting the tensions of the time, hate groups like the Ku Klux Klan became popular in the South.

Booker T. Washington's Accommodationist Approach. Booker T. Washington was a product of this period of untamed agitation and racism. Because of his inclination to peacefully accommodate paternalistic racism, he has become a controversial figure in the history of the African American

© Stock Montage, Inc.

Booker T. Washington.

struggle for freedom and equal opportunity. There is little question, however, that Washington was among the most influential voices in the turn-of-the-century movement to improve the life condition for blacks.

Born in 1856, Washington was the child of a white father and a black mother. His mother's duties as a slave cook placed her and her child in relatively close proximity with the master class. As a result, Washington's early socialization was marked by frequent and immediate interactions with the family of the slave master. Historians speculate that this gave Washington an early orientation in the skills of accommodation and compromise. His mother subsequently married Washington Ferguson, a black slave on a neighboring farm; in 1865, the newly freed family found wage-earning work in a mining town in West Virginia. Here, due to the efforts of the local black Baptist church, Washington experienced his first lessons in reading and writing. However, he did not stay with his family for long. At the age of 10 or 11, he took a job as servant in the home of a well-to-do general in town. Again, Washington found himself in the close company of paternalistic racists. The general's wife, who was from New England, was a strict disciplinarian, scrupulous about cleanliness and order. Living with this family, Washington personalized some of these same values, but access to the books in the home also gave him the opportunity to further his own self-education (Harlan, 1988).

Washington eventually made his way to the Hampton Normal and Industrial Institute, where he came under the influence of benevolent white racists. No one was more influential in this respect than General Samuel Armstrong, who founded the Hampton Institute in 1869. Armstrong, who had a missionary background and who commanded black troops in the Civil War, was committed to providing an industrial education for blacks and Native Americans. His focus on industrial education was moved by a mixture of racism and well-intentioned concern for the livelihood of southern blacks. At one level, the belief that blacks (and Native Americans) could best advance themselves by obtaining industrial skills could be viewed as bowing to the idea that such groups were incapable of performing in higher education (in the true collegiate tradition) and in the professional-class jobs that awaited college graduates. Armstrong, however, portrayed the idea of industrial education for blacks as a dignified pursuit and as a reasonable first step in assisting them in the turbulent postslavery transition period. Thus, he sought to convince business interests that trained blacks could become an important force in the economy, which, in the end, could only contribute to their assimilation. Moreover, to Armstrong, industrial education carried a collateral effect of teaching blacks the attitudes and morals of industriousness (thrift, abstinence, order, cleanliness). Washington adopted Armstrong's philosophy and promoted the idea of industrial education for blacks throughout his life. Armstrong's views were criticized by no less a figure than William Torrey Harris, who saw little promise in any educational idea that strayed from the intellectual traditions he held so dear (Morgan, 1995, p. 84). But the real debate on this issue would take shape in a long-running feud between Washington and his most dogged critic, W. E. B. Du Bois.

Washington is probably best known for his association with the Tuskegee Institute, which he was appointed to lead in 1881. The Tuskegee Institute was a school dedicated to the improvement of the life condition for blacks in America. Supported by both public and private funds, the Tuskegee Institute was established as a normal and industrial school that trained teachers, farmers, and tradesmen. Washington encouraged graduates to return to their communities, where they could become beacons for the next generation (Harlan, 1988). Bringing educated teachers back to the communities from which they came, just as Washington had returned from Hampton, was Washington's way of multiplying the effects of a Tuskegee education. As he put it, "We wanted to give [the students at Tuskegee] such an education as would fit a large proportion of them to be teachers and at the same time cause them to return to the plantation districts and show the people there how to put new energy and new ideas into farming, as well as into the intellectual and moral and religious life of the people" (Washington, 1901, pp. 347–48). But education at Tuskegee, to paraphrase Washington, was not only of the hand; it was also of the heart. Washington aimed to shape the character of Tuskegee graduates according to certain attitudes toward thrift, honesty, hard work, cleanliness, and racial conciliation, all of which, Washington believed, were needed to facilitate the social assimilation of blacks and the establishment of a firm economic foundation for their futures:

> We wanted to teach the student how to bathe; how to care for their teeth and clothing. We wanted to teach them what to eat, and how to eat it properly, and how to care for their rooms. Aside from this, we wanted to give them such a practical knowledge of some one industry, together with the spirit of industry, thrift and economy, that they would be sure of knowing how to make a living after they had left us. (Washington, 1901, p. 347)

The school started with 30 students in 1881; but by 1916, over 1,000 were enrolled.

Washington abided by what many view as a pragmatic vision for the improvement of blacks. The problem, however, as many of his critics saw it, was that his vision for a good life in America did not aim as high for blacks as it did for whites. Washington tended to see the improved future for blacks in America as a long-term battle that had to be won in small increments. The main methods for improvement included a qualified version of educational opportunity, full economic participation, and the embrace of Puritan values regarding God and work. He did not see full participation in the political life of the country as especially important, and he discouraged blacks from recognizing the act of voting or the holding of political office as a working solution to their problems, a view he likely inherited from his mentor, General Armstrong (Anderson, 1978). Rather, Washington wanted blacks to obtain a practical education that would give them a decent and dignified living and that would help show the world how capable blacks were of achieving their own high standard of independence and livelihood. With this in mind, he set his sights on only certain educational opportunities and promoted the hope that a practical, industrially based education would light the way for black Americans as they climbed out of the depths of generational experiences in slavery. "Tuskegee," he declared,

> emphasizes industrial education training for the Negro, not with the thought that the Negro should be confined to industrialism, the plow or the hoe, but because the undeveloped material resources of the South offer at this time a field peculiarly advantageous to the worker skilled in agriculture

and the industries, and here are found the Negro's most inviting opportunities for taking on the rudimentary elements that ultimately make for a permanently progressive civilization. (Washington, 1905, p. 356)

Washington's own experience of rising up from slavery to become a national political figure reflected what he thought could happen to all blacks if they were given an education and an opportunity to show the world their talents and values. In his mature years, Washington became an advisor to several U.S. presidents and to philanthropists seeking to donate money to advance causes benefiting blacks in America. If there was a black political broker at the turn of the twentieth century, it was Booker T. Washington. He personally dispensed a large share of the endowments that came from philanthropists like Andrew Carnegie, and he emerged as the favored choice by white patrons in virtually all matters of philanthropy involving blacks (Harlan, 1988).

Washington might have been weighted down by an accommodationist perspective that encouraged a kind of peaceful apartheid between blacks and whites, but he worked tirelessly to develop educational and economic opportunities for blacks. "In all things that are truly social, we [blacks and whites] are as separate as the fingers," he declared, "yet one as the hand in all things essential to mutual progress" (Washington, 1895, p. 350). This kind of language, with its clear separatist implications, satisfied many whites, but it also rankled some black intellectuals looking for a very different solution to the problems associated with skin color in America.

W. E. B. Du Bois' Demand for Full Integration.   To this end, black social thought was also very much affected by the work of W. E. B. Du Bois, who articulated a much more pervasive social agenda for black Americans. Specifically, Du Bois demanded full political and civil gains (including voting rights), access to liberal education (not industrial education), and equal economic opportunities for all blacks. Du Bois' familial background was quite different from Washington's. Born and raised in the North in a family of means, he traveled to Germany for his graduate studies and ultimately earned a Ph.D. from Harvard University. Du Bois' broader, more radical perspective on social reform in America was embodied in an intellectual movement known as the Niagara movement. Comprised of a small group of black intellectuals educated largely in elite northern universities, the Niagara movement emerged as the countervoice to Washington's, as the foil that represented "the talented tenth" of the black population (the very subpopulation that would be stifled by Washington's insistence on an industrial education for blacks). Du Bois' idea was that, at a minimum, 10 per-

UPI/Corbis-Bettmann

W. E. B. Du Bois.

cent of the black population had to receive a classical education at the leading universities of the country, much like the education he received. Du
Bois (1903) pulled no punches in condemning Washington: "Mr. Washington came, with a definite single programme. . . . His programme of industrial education, conciliation of the South, and submission and silence as to
civil rights and political rights, was not wholly original. . . . But Mr. Washington . . . put enthusiasm, unlimited energy and perfect faith into this programme and changed it from a by-path into a veritable Way of Life" (p.
352).

The main battleground for the debate between Washington and Du Bois
emerged in the constitution of the National Negro Business League, which
Washington founded in 1899. Under Washington's leadership, the league
pressed for a segregated black economy, which, from Washington's viewpoint, would eventually achieve its own high status and make it clear to
whites that broader social changes had to follow (Harlan, 1988). The league
stressed the power of the purse in improving the lives of blacks. Black
money had to be directed toward black merchants, who through a first-rate
practical education could provide quality goods and services to consumers.
Earning, saving, and ultimately spending the dollar was to become a political activity for black Americans. Washington believed that, to the extent
that blacks were able to demonstrate the virtues of conducting a good business, of working hard, and of obtaining private property, even within separatist lines, the demand for more extended gains in civil rights would grow.

In a way, the natural segregation that manifested after the emancipation of blacks was to Washington a natural business opportunity for them. This was the opportunity that whites had given to blacks: the chance to work within the cracks of a system designed to keep them down and to transcend it by proving to the world that there was no way to keep down a people who worked hard, lived thriftily, and embodied Godly virtues.

Du Bois, however, continued to push for full equal rights for all blacks, and in 1909, he founded the National Association for the Advancement of Colored People (NAACP). The original members of the group included the leading black intellectuals of the day, as well as other intellectual activists like John Dewey and Jane Addams (Morgan, 1995). The NAACP has, of course, achieved legendary status as an agency in the historical fight for civil rights.

Some critics have looked upon Washington's leadership as one that was too willing to compromise and too unwilling to agitate for radical change. Despite the fact that Washington was born into slavery, he is nevertheless viewed by some as a bourgeois conservative who accommodated white supremacist views. Further, the argument goes, he sent racists exactly the wrong message—that blacks could settle for a humble, segregated niche in society and tolerate the hostility toward their social mobility and improvement. Others argue that his methods were appropriate for the time and that his single-minded focus on self-improvement through education has a lasting legacy. In either case, we could consider both Washington and Du Bois as working in the progressive tradition of social change, making different arguments but still both seeing the school and educational opportunity as the basis for the improvement of social conditions for blacks. Feature 8-3 summarizes the ideological clash between Du Bois and Washington.

Francis Parker and the Quincy Methods

Other notable progressives tested their ideas in the schools as well. In fact, Francis Parker, whom Dewey called the "father of progressive education," was advancing progressive ideas in the school several years before Dewey even got started in education. Unlike Dewey, who operated out of a private laboratory school, Parker's ideas found expression in the public schools that he led as superintendent of schools in Quincy, Massachusetts, from 1875 to 1880.

Influenced by progressive Europeans like Pestalozzi and Froebel, Parker approached his superintendency with a rather comprehensive reform mandate. Prior to hiring Parker, the Quincy schools tested their students to dis-

8-3 DEBATING THE ISSUES
Booker T. Washington Versus W. E. B. Du Bois

In *The Souls of Black Folks,* W. E. B. Du Bois attacked the views of Booker T. Washington, accusing him of asking blacks to give up their political power, their civil rights, and access to the kind of higher education Du Bois had experienced. He believed that Washington not only was not helping the causes of blacks but actually was hindering them with his obvious deference to white racism and his willingness to compromise. Washington, for his part, offered a rejoinder to Du Bois in *Tuskegee and Its People,* arguing that blacks could best achieve advancement in increments, starting with access to normal and industrial education. This would, he claimed, have the effect of equipping the black population with wage-earning skills and would establish the foundations for self-sustaining segregated communities that, in time, could demand and expect expanded opportunities. Read both of these accounts and secondary source material on both thinkers (see Hawkins' *Booker T. Washington and His Critics*) for a juxtaposition of the views of each. Who do you prefer to stand with, Washington or Du Bois?

cern their levels of skill and knowledge. The findings were discouraging, to say the least. Children knew the rules of grammar but not how to write; they could read from their texts but not from any other materials (Cremin, 1961). They had essentially been trained for specific examinations but had no generalizable skills. As one school committee member put it, the school "had turned our scholars into parrots and made a meaningless farce of education" (Adams, 1881, p. 318). Change was definitely in the air in Quincy, making Parker the right man for the job.

Among Parker's first actions was to try to integrate more natural methods of learning in the classroom, methods built around child play and activity. Here, his bias for Pestalozzi was most evident. More natural methods included the whole-word reading strategy, the use of field trips, the embrace of conversations in the classroom, and the willingness to bring motor activities into teaching (Cremin, 1961). Object lessons were used in the teaching of geography, and teachers were encouraged to look at ways to individualize instruction. His interest in field trips, which was unique for its time, was his way of expanding the classroom, of bringing children not only to nature and the outdoors but also to the hard realities of society, factory life, and poverty. Parker did not tolerate the whipping or flogging of children because he openly rejected the doctrine of depravity. Likewise, he abhorred uniformity in school practice, believing it to be neglectful of individual (natural) differences. "Any teacher who pretends to have a perfect method of teaching any subject," he observed, "is a quack" (quoted in Mayer, 1964, p. 314). Later, Parker brought his ideas on teaching to the Cook County Normal School, where he served as principal from 1883 until 1899.

In reading education, Parker is considered to be among the first to connect reading with children's interests. He preferred to use the children's own compositions as reading material. At the Cook County Normal School, he had hundreds of children's stories professionally printed for the purposes of enhancing reading instruction (Kline, Moore, and Moore, 1987). He also managed to connect reading education to virtually all facets of the curriculum, tying it to the study of other subjects and to expressive skills in drawing, speaking, and writing. Most radically, Parker experimented with what is known today as whole-language instruction, an instructional method that teaches children to construct associations between spoken and written words.

Parker was on the side of the child in the curriculum, but he was also energized by the social reform spirit of education, referring to the school as an upbuilder of democracy and as an embryonic democracy, descriptors that Dewey himself would later use in his work. Parker understood the socio-civic purposes of education and thoroughly supported the idea of using the school to build communities and to teach tolerance and understanding. He was an early advocate of legislation to benefit the working class and feared the potential effects of industrialization on working-class children. The means that he used in combating such effects, however, were child-centered; they were primarily Pestalozzian and Froebelian, in that, through individualization, he sought to promote social unity and cohesion.

Thus, while Parker's rhetoric supported the expression of schooling as a democratizing institution, his heart was always with the child. The child was the focal point on which all else depended, including the growth of a democratic society. As a result, Parker put forward a child-centered strategy as a means for obtaining socio-civic objectives. The school would have to wait for Dewey and others to supply social democratic means for achieving social democratic objectives. Feature 8-4 provides a historical overview of Parker's Quincy methods.

Although Parker was one of the first progressives to apply his ideas in the public schools, his school, as indicated, was more Froebelian than Deweyan. However, over time, other school reform efforts were more closely aligned with the emerging experimentalist thinking of the early decades. Many of these are described in the *Twenty-Sixth Yearbook of the*

National Society for the Study of Education, edited by Harold Rugg (1927), and in a small book that John Dewey co-authored with his daughter, Evelyn Dewey, called *Schools of Tomorrow* (1915).

Jane Addams and the Settlement House Movement

Lester Ward's concept of environmentalism got an early test at the hands of educational progressives, but some other social reformers were working from a broader agenda. Driven by the need to take direct action against the poverty and squalor of city life, social activists like Jane Addams and Lillian Wald opened settlement houses for the indigent. Located in the poorest urban neighborhoods, settlement houses were community centers that provided local residents, including children, with educational experiences that helped them to deal with the emergent needs of their difficult and often painful lives. Cremin (1961) describes the kinds of questions that inspired the settlement houses:

> Were the streets dirty and the tenements infested with vermin? Settlements founded antifilth societies to induce people to rid their rooms of bedbugs, lice, cockroaches, and rats. Were gangs of street urchins a menace to life and property? Settlements established boys' and girls' clubs to channel the ebullient energy of adolescence into athletics, arts and crafts, and constructive recreation. Were death and disease rates in the slum pitifully high? Settlements became first-aid centers, clinics, headquarters for visiting nurses, and schools of preventive medicine. Were young men unable to obtain jobs? Settlements experimented not only with trade education but with devices for fitting individuals to the trades for which they were best suited. Were mothers required to work? Settlements introduced kindergartens and day nurseries. Were workingmen illiterate? Settlements taught them to read. Was summer oppressive in the city? Settlements established playgrounds and vacation centers. (pp. 60–61)

The most prominent director of a settlement house in America, Jane Addams, established her house in 1893 in a Chicago neighborhood populated by poor immigrants living under the most horrific conditions. At her settlement, called Hull House, Addams placed education at the center of all of the action. There was a kindergarten for toddlers and clubs for boys and girls. For adults, there were classes in English, cooking, nutrition, dressmaking, childcare, the trades, and the like (Cremin, 1961). There were also music and drama clubs; the Working People Social Science Club, which looked into issues of social relevance; a club for young working women called the Jane Club; the Electrical Club, which taught about electricity; a Men and

8-4 THE HISTORICAL CONTEXT
The Quincy Methods

Here, a disciple of Francis Parker's Quincy methods outlines what she believes to be some of the main principles of Parker's pedagogy. What makes these methods unusual for their time? What ideas listed, if any, are still relevant today?

I found that there were multitudes of teachers who were disappointed with the results of their hard but unsatisfactory labors, and were anxious to know of better ways.
   To them I presented the distinguishing features of the Quincy work:

1. The joyous life of the schools and the comradeship of teacher and pupils.

2. By grouping their pupils (in the lower grades) they obtained many of the benefits of individual teaching.

3. The skillful use of a great amount and variety of "Busy-Work."

4. Lessons in subjects not usually taught—Drawing, Modeling, Form, Color, Natural History, etc.

5. The constant use of Drawing as a means of expression.

6. Use of text-books as repositories of knowledge.

7. Amount and variety of Supplementary Reading.

8. Substitution of the expression of original thought on the part of the pupils for the old-fashioned memoriter recitation.

9. Carefully varied programme, *whose order was known only to the teacher.*

10. The atmosphere of happy work which encompassed teachers and pupils.

11. Disorder not worrying the teacher and wasting her time.

12. The confidence, courtesy, and respect characterizing the attitude not only of pupils to teacher, but teacher to pupils.

Women's Club; and clubs devoted to the works of Shakespeare and Plato. In addition, there were public forums, an art gallery, college extension courses, free concerts, a reading room, a coffee shop, a nursery, a labor museum, and a branch of the Chicago Public Library on the grounds (Colky, 1987). For children, Addams tried to provide a comprehensive education that went beyond the three R's offered in the schools, stressing art, literature, and his-

13. The absence of scolding, snubbing, or spying.

14. The dignity, self-possession, and lack of self-consciousness of pupils.

15. The making of the child the objective point, and not Courses of Study, examinations, or promotions.

16. The great economy, naturalness, and practicability of the devices employed.

17. The marked attention paid to the so-called dull pupils.

18. The evident growth of moral power.

19. The remarkable skill of the teachers evidencing their comprehension of underlying principles.

20. The wonderful originality and individuality of the teachers—none being imitators; the devices used varying from day to day.

21. The high ideal set before the teachers by the Superintendent, and their hearty co-operation with him in striving to attain it.

22. The absence of machinery, and the absolute freedom from any fixed or prescribed mode of work, each teacher being encouraged to invent and try any device not violating fundamental laws.

23. Examinations aimed to test the teacher's power to teach.

24. Examinations such as to test the children's power to do, not their power to memorize.

SOURCE: Partridge, L. A. (1885), *The Quincy methods illustrated* (New York), pp. xii–xiii.

tory in ways that related to industrial life. Moreover, Addams agitated for legislation to improve factory conditions and city services for the poor. In the tradition of Lester Ward, she committed herself to providing environmental stimuli for those who had little means and often even less hope. Addams wanted to reduce the suffering of the poor, but she also wanted to help them develop the life skills, power, and initiative needed to combat poverty.

Here was an example of progressive ideas in their full bloom of practice. Addams worked directly with people needing help, using the very problems of their lives as targets for instruction and improvement. She was driven by the ideal of developing and liberating communities to work in the interest of political reform and social reconstruction. Whereas Dewey turned to the school to fulfill his hopes for broad social reform, Addams remained anchored in the community, living amid the very problems and perturbations that plagued poor people. Dewey was a frequent visitor to Hull House even before he opened the doors to his own school. He became a great admirer of Hull House and of Addams herself. He and Addams, in fact, became the closest of friends, so much so that Addams became the namesake for John and Alice Dewey's daughter, Jane Dewey. Dewey himself acknowledged a deeper faith in the guiding forces of democracy after witnessing Addam's work at Hull House (Cremin, 1988). Addams eventually achieved worldwide recognition for her work, winning the Nobel Peace Prize in 1931 for the humanitarian causes she championed in Hull House (Lagemann, 1985).

Addams' philosophy clearly was rooted in progressivism and very much committed to the provision of comprehensive educational services well into adulthood, predating the idea of adult education as it is known today. Addams once declared that the settlement house was a protest against a restricted view of education (Cremin, 1988, p. 176). To Addams, schooling was a matter of socialization for participation in democracy, which required an encompassing form of education. Teaching immigrants English and knowledge of American government were priorities, to be sure. But teaching about community-based issues, including problems related to corruption and workers' rights, and widening immigrants' knowledge of and insight into virtually all aspects of life also were important. This was education as an Americanization process, something that Addams accomplished while still sympathizing with and showing respect for elements of the immigrants' ancestral culture, a point we will return to in a later chapter.

The Cardinal Principles Report of 1918
and a Tidal Change for Secondary Education

Serious changes in the composition of the secondary school curriculum were effected in yet another famous committee report sponsored by the National Education Association (NEA). Like its 1898 counterpart (the Committee of Ten report), the Cardinal Principles Report of 1918, more than any document of its time, led to a national call to change the high school curriculum. Unlike the earlier report, however, it asked for sweeping changes that resulted in a broadening of the fundamental scope of the schools' curricular offerings. As mentioned, the Committee of Ten and Committee of Fifteen reports had kept the schools focused largely on academics, within the limits of a very few subject areas. The Cardinal Principles report changed this radically.

In 1913, the NEA appointed a committee, aptly named the Commission on the Reorganization of Secondary Education, to reconsider course work in the high schools. After five years of deliberation, the commission offered its recommendations in its Cardinal Principles report. Whereas the Committee of Ten report itemized subject areas to be taught, the Cardinal Principles report detailed practical objectives to be met. These objectives included command of the fundamental processes (basic skills), worthy home membership, health, vocation, citizenship, worthy use of leisure time, and ethical character. These were, in fact, the seven cardinal principles of the report.

The listing of seven principles or objectives for the school foretold a whole new conception of education. If the report was to be taken seriously, the character of secondary education now had to shift from its academic emphasis on the traditional liberal arts to a more comprehensive emphasis that placed equal value on vocational development, citizenship education, and personal needs. It was precisely in the context of these recommendations that the blueprint for the comprehensive high school was fashioned.

The American comprehensive high school now had two main functions: (1) the provision of specialized studies dealing with issues related to individual interests and talents in areas of college and vocational preparation and personal development; and (2) the provision of unifying studies dealing with the vital problems of social life in a democracy as they related to citizenship, ethical character, and worthy home membership. Where individual needs had to be met—including needs for tailored programs, needs for specific career or vocational preparation, and needs related to student interests and aptitudes—the specialized facet of the curriculum delivered the experiences. Where a common experience was needed—to forge common identities, a common core of knowledge and understanding for civic participation, and a common basis of values—common learnings were provided. The point is that the school now looked to the development of the whole student.

The notion of providing new breadth in the curriculum had direct effects in the way the school was organized. Differentiation in the curriculum was needed to allow students to pursue their own plans and interests and to meet their needs. The curriculum could no longer be seen as one monolithic block of courses, a problem that hounded the Committee of Ten report from its inception. As a result, specialized courses designed to meet vocational, college preparatory, and special interest needs were all supported in the Cardinal Principles report. At the same time, course work in general education was needed. Such courses had to be expressly designed to provide a common social discourse for students. They represented a place where schools could broach socio-civic issues and teach common ideals and common understandings. In the Cardinal Principles report, the unifying studies of general education represented the curriculum base for democracy. Through common experiences, a pluralistic population could find a common ground—diversity could be turned into unity. See Feature 8-5 for the nature of high school course offerings in one city district in 1930.

The Cardinal Principles report has often been cited as a turning point in American education, primarily because it offered a comprehensive school model as an alternative to the strictly academic traditional curriculum. Partly as a result of the report, the idea of mental discipline was rejected, and the search for life activities responsive to individual and social needs was enacted. As Butts (1955) put it, "What the seven cardinal principles did was shift the emphasis in schooling away from the preoccupation with the academic and intellectual disciplines and to broaden the social role of education almost beyond recognition" (p. 194). The report can be viewed as a uniquely American effort to educate youths in a unified setting in ways that allowed for both socio-civic (general) education and specialized education. Such a system diverged markedly from the separatist, dual system that existed in Europe. Instead of going to separate trade schools, American students interested in vocational education found a hospitable climate in the unified cosmopolitan school. Vocational education was, after all, one of the cardinal principles. But no matter what their specialization might be, students were always required to participate in heterogeneously grouped, common learning environments, where they could develop a sense of community based on common knowledge and common values.

Not surprisingly, the comprehensive school would run into some problems. Although the specializing function of the curriculum was designed to meet key individual differences, it sometimes resulted in a system of curriculum tracking that came at the expense of lower-achieving students. And although the idea of common leaning was designed as a school experience in common democratic living, it sometimes resulted simply in the drafting of core academic courses required for graduation. Still, the commitment to educating all high school students under one roof, irrespective of their background and their career expectations, has remained vital in American

8-5 THINKING ABOUT THE DATA

High School Course Offerings in Five Schools, 1930

The following table shows the percentage distribution of subjects completed in grades 9–12 by the graduates of five Denver high schools in 1930. The ranks are used to sort the student population into achievement quartiles, with rank 4 indicating the lowest 25 percent and rank 1 the highest 25 percent. What might the members of the Commission on the Reorganization of Secondary Education have had to say about the distribution? What questions might they have asked to learn more about the curriculum offerings in these schools?

PERCENTAGE DISTRIBUTION OF SEMESTER
HOURS BY SUBJECT GROUP IN FIVE DENVER SCHOOLS, 1930

	Rank 4	Rank 3	Rank 2	Rank 1	Total
English	22.2%	21.7%	21.9%	21.5%	21.8%
Social Studies	19.1	18.5	18.0	17.5	18.3
French	1.1	1.8	2.5	3.2	2.2
Spanish	6.0	6.3	6.6	5.6	6.1
German	0.1	0.2	0.2	0.3	0.2
Latin	4.0	5.2	6.4	9.2	6.3
Mathematics	12.8	13.4	13.6	15.3	13.8
General Science	0.6	0.4	0.5	0.5	0.5
Biology	3.2	3.0	2.8	2.9	3.0
Chemistry	2.5	3.1	3.1	3.4	3.0
Physics	2.3	2.1	2.1	2.7	2.3
Other Science	2.6	1.9	1.9	1.3	1.9
Stenography	1.6	2.2	2.8	2.9	2.4
Bookkeeping	1.3	1.5	1.4	1.3	1.4
Typing	2.3	2.4	2.5	2.4	2.4
Other Commerce	4.4	3.9	2.9	1.8	3.2
Home Economics	3.2	3.4	3.0	2.3	2.9
Industrial Arts	4.3	3.1	2.4	1.2	2.7
Art	2.3	1.9	1.8	1.6	2.0
Music	2.4	2.4	2.2	1.9	2.2
Psychology	1.6	1.6	1.4	1.2	1.4

SOURCE: U.S. Department of the Interior (1932), *The program of studies* (Washington, DC: U.S. Government Printing Office), p. 230.

education and continues to point the way toward new progressive possibilities in the curriculum.

George Counts and a More Radical Progressivism

Also arising out of the movement to promote the school's role in achieving social progress and social consciousness was a more radical group of thinkers who wanted the school to intervene directly in making America into a classless workers' society built largely on Socialist principles. Much of this thinking started with the social class analysis of George Counts, who in the 1920s attempted to show empirically how the goals of democracy and equal opportunity were unfulfilled in the public school. Counts had a keen eye for demonstrating how schools not only failed to ameliorate economic disparities but also how they actually had a hand in their perpetuation. "In a very large measure," wrote Counts in 1922, "participation in the privilege of secondary education is contingent on social economic status" (p. 149). Counts showed how socioeconomic factors affected various levels of school operation. He observed, for instance, that the members of school boards were drawn predominantly from favored socioeconomic classes, which had little interest in drafting educational policy that altered the status quo (Counts, 1927). Elsewhere, he bemoaned the disproportionately large numbers of dropouts who came from poor backgrounds, noting that a high school education "was a privilege being extended at public expense to those very classes that already occupy the privileged positions in modern societies" (Counts, 1922, p. 152).

To Counts, the problems with schooling had less to do with the institution itself than with the socioeconomic conditions in which the institution found itself operating. According to Counts, in America, the masses barely got by while a small culture of elites flourished. The implication was that, unless the economic order was changed, the school would always be a handmaiden to economic interests. On this point, Counts forthrightly stated that the maintenance of existing patterns of economic inequities would always lead to differential forms of education constructed along class lines. To avoid this condition, Counts reasoned, the schools needed to deliberately resist the dominance of the economic aristocracy by championing collectivist democratic causes and principles. Economic oppression infused the school with the philosophy of economic individualism, which fostered egoistic and competitive values in education. Thus, the schools themselves, particularly the teachers, needed to defuse this power by committing themselves to a restructuring of the economic order in the direction of a collectivist or workers' society. This attitude removed Counts from the progressive-experimentalism of Dewey and placed him more directly in what could be called the social reconstructionist realm.

Counts articulated his Socialist themes most powerfully in a speech delivered at a meeting of the NEA in 1932. Counts' voice reflected the temperament of the Great Depression and his overwhelming concerns with social and economic inequalities:

> Here is a society that manifests the most extraordinary of contradictions: a mastery over the forces of nature, surpassing the wildest dreams of antiquity, is accompanied by extreme material insecurity; dire poverty walks hand in hand with the most extravagant living the world has ever seen; an abundance of goods of all kinds is coupled with privation, misery, and even starvation; . . . breakfastless children march to school past bankrupt shops laden with rich foods gathered from the ends of the world; strong men by the million walk the streets in a futile search for employment and with the exhaustion of hope enter the ranks of the damned; great captains of industry close factories without warning and dismiss the workmen by whose labor they have amassed huge fortunes over the years; . . . racketeers and gangsters with the connivance of public officials fasten themselves on the channels of trade and exact toll at the end of the machine gun; . . . the wages paid to the workers are too meager to enable them to buy back the goods they produce; . . . the science of psychology is employed to fan the flames of desire so that men may be enslaved by their wants and bound to the wheel of production; . . . federal aid to the unemployed is opposed on the ground that it would pauperize the masses when the favored members of the society have already lived on a dole; an ideal of rugged individualism, evolved in a simple pioneering and agrarian order at a time when free land existed in abundance, is used to justify a system which exploits pitilessly and without thought of the morrow the natural and human resources of the nation and of the world. (1932, pp. 33–35)

Here, Counts used attention-commanding language to make a case for the primacy of economic factors in the rehabilitation of our democracy. He wanted the schools to be open about indoctrinating youth according to certain "democratic" tenets, which to Counts meant the embrace of a more Socialist societal arrangement.

Bode and Dewey criticized Counts and other social reconstructionists for misconceiving the functioning of a democracy. Using a strategy that resonates with current discussions about politically correct thinking, Bode (1938) observed that what the social reconstructionists were proposing was not education at all, but training toward a particular programmatic position

8-6 RESEARCH INQUIRY
George Counts and the Social Frontier

In 1934, George Counts helped to publish the inaugural issue of *The Social Frontier,* a journal dedicated to social-reformist ideas in education. The journal lasted for only five years, but during its run it contained commentary of some of the leading progressive voices in education, including John Dewey, often in a format that highlighted a debate. Go to the first few editions of *The Social Frontier,* and research some of the educational problems that were on the minds of some of the leading educational thinkers of the day.

Contents of October 1934 Edition of *The Social Frontier*

Launching THE SOCIAL FRONTIER . . . . .WILLIAM H. KILPATRICK   2
Editorials
       Orientation   3
       "Educating for Tomorrow"   5
       The Ives Law   7
       Professional Security   9
       On the Eve of a New School Year   10
Can Education Share in Social Reconstruction . . . . .JOHN DEWEY   11
Property and Democracy . . . . .CHARLES A. BEARD   13
A Sociologist Views the New Deal . . . . .HENRY P. FAIRCHILD   15
The Importance of a Point of View . . . . .SIDNEY HOOK   19
Education *Is* the Social Frontier .GOODWIN WATSON   22
Who Are the Friends of Human Rights?   23
The Teacher's Bookshelf
       Verdicts of Experts . . . . .NATHAN REICH   24
       Revolutionary Gradualism   25
       Sweet Freedom   27
       Brief Reviews   27
       Books Received   28
Notes for the Future Historian   29
Voices from Olympus   30

that equated democracy with a specific scheme of ownership and distribution. The problems that concerned Counts also concerned Dewey, but Dewey believed that the judgments of a democracy had to be rendered democratically. Such problems were opportunities for reconstruction—a process, as discussed, that was scientific and moral in its orientation, and that harbored no prior commitment to a Socialist collectivism. Counts wanted revolutionary change; Dewey wanted evolutionary change. This difference in scholarly outlook can be found in the pages of *The Social Frontier,* a journal edited by Counts and highlighted in Feature 8-6.

Thus, where Dewey and like-minded progressives were interested in dealing with socioeconomic issues in the school for the purpose of developing a critical consciousness about the society, the social reconstructionists framed the same issues in terms of creating a workers' society. And this difference is crucial. To Dewey, ideas proceeded from inquiry and could not be predetermined to democratic and scientific procedures. To Counts, the primacy of economic problems in the society made him unapologetic about predetermining the kind of social and economic arrangements that were best for America. To experimentalists, learning could not be democratic and intelligent if it was encumbered with a mission of imposing and inculcating particular ideological viewpoints. This did not mean that schooling had to be neutral. But it did mean that the methods used in dealing with socioeconomic factors in the school had to be those of investigation and cooperative discussion.

The work of Counts and other social reconstructionists helped to inform and develop a neo-radical group of educators in educational studies that became vital in later decades and that focused most of its attention on issues of race, class, and gender. Just as importantly, however, together with the more moderate branch of the progressive movement, Counts and the social reconstructionists made it clear that the child-centered perspective was fundamentally inadequate. As Counts stated in 1932, "The weakness of Progressive Education lies in the fact that it has elaborated no theory of social welfare, unless it be that of anarchy or extreme individualism" (pp. 6–7).

EDUCATION AND THE RISE OF SOCIAL EFFICIENCY

There was yet another group of thinkers intent on bringing life activities to the curriculum. But these thinkers differed substantively from most progressive groups in that they supported the application of business values and principles to the public school education. Advocates of this view wanted to use the curriculum to promote order, control, and social harmony; they saw the curriculum as a mechanism to sort and slot students to their proper place in society. Thus, this group of thinkers proposed a new conception of curriculum that was management oriented, efficiency driven, and highly prescriptive. It was out of this early tradition, which is known in the literature as the tradition of social efficiency, that later formulations revolving around competency-based instruction arose. It was also out of this tradition that the concept of measurement began to take primacy in the school.

Several forces shaped the movement toward social efficiency concerns in the curriculum. First, educators recognized that they might use modern methods of science to standardize methods and curricula. Given the general disillusionment with the traditional school, some scholars saw standardization as the only way to ensure high-quality outcomes. Rather than seeking to tap the intelligence of teachers, they argued that teachers should be programmed or scripted. Second, the rise of industrialization and the embrace of business values in the American ethic gave way to a new set of principles in education that stressed waste elimination, procedural compulsion, cost savings, and efficiency.

Frederick Taylor and the Ideal of Efficiency

The commitment to social efficiency in the curriculum was naturally preceded by a commitment to social efficiency in society. In the early 1900s, the business community led the way with a new efficiency strategy known as scientific management. Developed by an engineer named Frederick Taylor (1911), scientific management promised to provide a method for businesses, particularly factories, to increase production and lower costs.

The basic premise of scientific management was that there was one best way to do any job and that such a way could be discerned through careful study. To Taylor, if the most productive worker had an output of x, then there was no reason all workers could not meet the same output level. Using various methods, Taylor identified the very best workers, meaning those who produced the most in the least amount of time. He then analyzed their actions and tried to note, in behavioral terms, what made them so productive. After having secured a sense of what factors were central to the most productive workers, Taylor itemized and then standardized the practice so that other workers could be taught to produce at the same level.

It is instructive to explain how Taylor's management system worked in an actual case study taken from Taylor's own writing (Callahan, 1962). The setting was the Bethlehem Steel Company at the turn of the century. After building up a huge surplus of pig iron during an economic downturn in the 1890s, Bethlehem Steel entered healthier economic times, and the vigorous sales promised to reduce the accumulated surplus. The company hired Taylor to examine how the pig iron could be moved out for sale as quickly and efficiently as possible. Each bar of pig iron weighed 92 pounds and had to be carried approximately 40 feet to a railway car for shipment.

When Taylor arrived on the scene, each workman was moving about 300 bars over the course of his 10-hour shift. Armed with the tools of scientific management, Taylor set out to improve this figure. First, he conducted time and motion studies that itemized exactly what was involved in moving the pig iron. Specifically, he recorded the time per foot of travel and the time taken to pick up, throw down, and stack the bars. Taking various fatigue factors into account, Taylor's time and motion studies indicated that each man was capable of carrying 1,100 bars per day, a more than threefold increase that translated into a daily rate of over 47 tons per man. Thus, according to Taylor, the men were not accomplishing what science indicated a healthy man could accomplish. Perhaps they were dawdling or simply were lazy, but the bottom line was that they were not working efficiently or producing optimally.

Having determined his target efficiency levels, Taylor tried to find the men whom he thought would be best able to meet his productivity objectives. He finally settled on one, a man whom he witnessed trotting a mile to and from work each day and who was building a house for himself in the morning before work and in the hours remaining after work. Taylor provided this worker with a monetary incentive to increase his productivity to the target level. The man received a 60 percent increase in pay (from $1.10 to $1.85 per hour) and was followed during the ensuing workdays by an efficiency expert who told him exactly when to pick up the pig iron and when to rest. The results spoke for themselves: The man received a 60 percent increase in pay, but he met Taylor's objective by more than tripling his productivity. And the company, to its delight, was getting more for less: a threefold increase in output with only a 60 percent increase in input (wages). Stories of Taylor's successes spread through the business community, and in time, the road to success in business was paved with the insights of scientific management.

The lesson that Taylor provided to businesses soon reached the schools. Applied to the curriculum, scientific management was deceptively simple: Find the best practices, standardize them, and make them part of the school routine. The "best" practices under Taylor's conditions, however, were always those that managed to secure the highest productivity with the least amount of effort. Applied to education, there were going to be complications. It was one thing to note the productivity of an assembly line worker or a laborer lifting pig iron, but it was quite another to make similar judgments about something as complex and dynamic as the education of children. For scientific management to work in the schools, substantive changes had to be made in the way the curriculum was conceived. The idea of productivity in the school meant that actual learning outcomes had to be identified and that measurements had to be taken to determine whether they had been reached. The Taylorian regard for efficiency had, in fact, set the wheels in motion for a whole new science of school measurement, a numerical way of demonstrating achievement and mastery.

Franklin Bobbitt, Curriculum Design, and Social Efficiency

The effects of Taylor's work were evident in the early curriculum construction designs being promoted by like-minded thinkers in the burgeoning field of curriculum studies, the most prominent being a University of Chicago professor named John Franklin Bobbitt. For the curriculum to be manageable and operative, Bobbitt believed that it had to achieve an unprecedented specificity. Many social progressives, including those who supported the Cardinal Principles report, had framed the school experience in terms of generalizability, pointing to the need for broadly framed objectives that were more statements of principle than specific actions to be undertaken. But Bobbitt (1924a) thought that such thinking was unrealistic and irresponsible, and he wanted to change it:

> Objectives that are only vague, high-sounding hopes and aspirations are to be avoided. Examples are: "character building," "the harmonious development of the individual," "social efficiency," "general discipline," "self-realization," "culture," and the like. All of these are valid enough; but too cloud-like for guiding practical procedure. They belong to the visionary adolescence of our profession—not to its sober and somewhat disillusioned maturity. (p. 32)

Out of this demand for a new level of specificity arose a method of curriculum development known as activity analysis. An admitted admirer of Taylor's work, Bobbitt believed that the school curriculum was best served by preparing learners for specific activities in adult life. He wanted the school to survey all of the relevant activities in the lives of adults (as they related to occupations, family, society, and so on) and then, similar to Taylor's standardized production model, to teach directly to each activity. Bobbitt (1918) expressed his theory in clear terms:

> The central theory is simple. Human life, however varied, consists in the performance of specific objectives. However numerous and diverse they may be for any social class, they can be discovered. This requires only that one go out into the world of affairs and discover the particulars of which these affairs consist. These will show the abilities, attitudes, habits, appreciations and forms of knowledge that men need. These will be the objectives of the curriculum. They will be numerous, definite and particularized. The

curriculum will then be that series of experiences which children and youth must have by way of attaining those objectives. (p. 42)

The intent was to be as specific as possible in the framing of activities because the job of the curriculum was to prepare learners for specific tasks through a process of habit formation. "The most significant feature of the work of practical curriculum making today," stated Bobbitt (1921), "is the tendency first to particularize with definiteness and in detail the objectives" (p. 607). As a result, Bobbitt filled the curriculum with thousands of skills and behaviors that were, by virtue of their specificity, often fixed at rather low, mechanistic levels. This made the method of activity analysis amenable to the behavioristic psychology emerging at the time. The following list of objectives, taken from a reading program designed for the Los Angeles schools, reflects this detailed, mechanistic approach:

You will be ready to undertake A-1 reading when you can do the following things:
1. When you are spending at least sixty minutes a day on reading and phonetics
2. When you know at sight one hundred words from the list of one hundred and twenty-five on flash cards chosen from the main list
3. When you can use any of the one hundred words in sentences with the following word phrases: This is, I see, I have, We have, I can, We can, Can you, Have you, I like, We like; a, the, an
4. When you can read the first, second, fourth and fifth stories in the Free and Treadwell Primer
5. When you are able to read no less than ten pages of your Supplementary Unit Primer
6. When you can speak the English language well enough to understand the work of the next grade intelligently
7. When you read a sentence as a whole and not word by word. If a sentence is long, you will phrase it properly
8. When you can read print from the flash cards or from your books, also standard script as written on the blackboard by your teacher
9. When you can read silently and interpret sentence units with our required vocabulary as "Was the cat black?" or "Can a dog fly?"
10. When you have read the Jack Straw Stories (optional) (Bobbitt, 1921, p. 609)

This style of fragmenting the curriculum and instruction methods applied to virtually every facet of the school experience, including reading, arithmetic, spelling, language, and penmanship. As Bobbitt (1924b) claimed, activity analysis is intent on discovering the specific forms of behaviors for humans to follow: "It would discover the five or ten thousand words they spell, the several score mathematical operations they perform, the several hundred specific practical home activities in which they engage, the main things they do in the care of their health, the specific things involved in managing a checking account at the bank, and the like" (p. 50). It is important to note that Bobbitt worked out of a functionalist perspective, trying to train students to perform real-life functions or activities. He was not concerned with the nature of the learner or with the ideals of society. He simply observed the environment and chose objectives that emerged from the common judgments of teachers and other curriculum participants. His advice to curriculum makers was, as Jackson (1975) phrased it, "Keep your eye on behavior and particularize it" (p. 125).

Bobbitt believed that education could be reduced to a conveyor belt–like process that yielded a completed product. Bobbitt (1913) was not subtle about such matters. "Education," he declared, "is a shaping process as much as the manufacturing of steel rails" (p. 11). This factory metaphor captured the essence of education that Bobbitt promoted. Students were the raw products, the school was the assembly line, and society was the consumer. Philosophical concerns related to social reform and socio-civic growth were simply not important considerations. The mission of the school was to fit individuals into life slots to ensure order and stability.

To its advocates, the method of activity analysis promised to yield certain positive results. By virtue of the method, for instance, the school curriculum was undoubtedly more closely connected to life. It was based, after all, on activity. This was not an insignificant claim, because Bobbitt believed that activity analysis reflected the progressive regard for "learning as doing." To Bobbitt, activity analysis was a good practical alternative to the tradition of mental discipline, which placed misdirected attention, to use Bobbitt's phrase, on the "memory reservoir" of students, on the idea of "subject storage," and on the image of student "as knower." Armed with activity analysis, Bobbitt could claim that he was interested in conduct, action, behavior, and the construction of the learner "as doer." Activity analysis also presumed to be better suited for teachers because it offered prefashioned, ready-made activities that did not require teachers to think independently. "The burden of finding the best methods," stated Bobbitt (1913), "is too large and too complicated to be laid on the shoulders of the teachers" (pp. 51–52).

Clearly, this idea differed from those being proposed by the experimentalists, who wanted to liberate teacher intelligence and teacher judgment in the interests of shaping school experiences based on the nature of learners and the values of society. Activity analysis also pointed the way to the elimination of waste and the maintenance of institutional order by making it clear that scales of measurement were needed for assessment purposes. Finally, the method, by aiming to teach children according to their needs and abilities, represented a victory for proponents of differential experiences in the school, ones that led to different social and vocational outcomes. In fact, the ultimate implication of Bobbitt's work was that each child deserved a school experience based on his or her own unique individuality. This willingness to differentiate in the school curriculum helped to secure a world in which everyone could find his or her place.

Bobbitt certainly had his share of critics, but none was more penetrating and thoughtful than Boyd Bode. Bode attacked Bobbitt for the manner in which he discerned his objectives, noting how Bobbitt drew largely from adult activities. Bode (1927) contended that Bobbitt had set into motion a condition for education that simply served the status quo. To Bode, activity analysis represented little more than training for adjustment to existing social conditions. In a democracy, Bode continued, society would be better served if education proceeded from the level of general training, in areas such as problem solving and communication skills. Individuals and society could grow and develop only if they had the skills needed to deal with emergent problems and issues, as opposed to being adjusted to and knowledgeable about preexisting conditions. Specific activities change over time; for example, the activities involved in being a citizen or a farmer are different now from what they were decades ago. Thus, to view specificity as the answer to the curriculum was to promote outdated training that would not likely have much currency beyond the present. Bobbitt was no progressive in Bode's estimation.

Specificity in the Curriculum and IQ Testing

Despite the criticisms, activity analysis received a boost from the landmark experimental work of Edward Thorndike in the area of mental training. Thorndike had conducted experiments to test the validity of the doctrine of mental discipline, which was, to recall, the belief that certain subjects had greater disciplinary value in developing intelligence than others. Thorndike's (1924) experiment was elegantly simple. After correcting for initial ability and special training, Thorndike tested the disciplinary value of Latin by comparing the gains in intelligence scores of students who studied a series of subjects plus Latin to those of students who studied an identical series of subjects plus shop work. This same experimental procedure was used to test each of the subject areas. The results were clear: No one subject had a higher claim to developing intelligence; there was no hierarchy of studies. In Thorndike's (1924) words, "We found notable differences in gain in ability to think as measured by these tests, but they do not seem to be due to what one studies" (p. 94).

This finding was a boon for Bobbitt and others smitten with the notion of activity analysis. If Thorndike was right, then the academic subjects clearly were not instruments of intelligence, as was originally believed. Bobbitt and others could say with more confidence that education had to follow a direct route, teaching each activity and condition in life.

Bobbitt's advocacy of specificity drew support from other sources as well, including the prominent journalist and educational critic Joseph Rice. During the late nineteenth and early twentieth centuries, Rice wrote several important pieces about the state of education on America. Rice, who wrote in the style of the muckraking journalism that was popular at the turn of the century, was a tough critic with a searing style. Having surveyed American elementary school education over a thirty-six-city tour, Rice began to inform the American public about what was actually happening in its schools. In city after city, he outlined the pervasive incompetence, corruption, and apathy that was, in his view, ruining the hearts and minds of schoolchildren. Although he did report on some positive developments in the schools, particularly in the Indianapolis schools, where the Herbartians influenced the curriculum, Rice clearly believed that schools in general were in a calamitous state. In his writing, he frequently targeted the mindlessness of the pedagogical exercises used in schools and the pettiness and triviality that characterized much of the teaching. In an elementary school in St. Louis, for instance, Rice (1969) observed the following scene:

> During several daily recitation periods, each of which is from twenty to twenty-five minutes in duration, the children are obliged to stand on the line, perfectly motionless, their bodies erect, their knees and feet together, the tips of their shoes touching the edge of the board in the floor. The slightest movement on the part of a child attracts the attention of the teacher. The recitation is repeatedly interrupted with cries of "Stand straight," "Don't bend the knees," "Don't lean against the wall," and so on. I heard one teacher ask a little boy: "How can you learn anything with your knees and toes out of order?" . . . The teacher never forgets the toes; every few moments she casts her eyes "toeward." (p. 98)

Discouraged by what he saw in the schools, Rice could conceive of only one solution. Believing that teachers were the main perpetrators of stupidity in the school, Rice recommended that the curriculum be built around specific objectives and skills, so that teachers would know exactly what they were to do. Rather than attempt to cultivate teachers' intelligence and creativity, Rice wanted to find a way to protect children from teachers' incompetence. In this manner, he opted for a Bobbitt-like design that featured specificity.

This inclination to teach by direct route and to provide a differentiated curriculum that led to different social and vocational outcomes was also bolstered by a new faith in the measurement of intelligence. To have confidence in measures of the intelligence quotient (IQ) of students was also to be confident of their place in the differentiated curriculum. Given quantifiable numbers, curriculum developers could be sure that they had identified the proper intellectual ranks of individuals. In turn, this paved the way for the creation of curriculum tracks that provided an appropriate education for each rank of intelligence. Ross Finney, a professor of sociology, expressed this attitude with stunning openness. Armed with IQ data, Finney envisaged a curriculum for "dullards" and a curriculum for "leaders," both of whom would make their contribution to the order and maintenance of society. "Instead of trying to teach the dullards to think for themselves," Finney (1928) observed, "the intellectual leaders must think for them, and drill the results, memoriter, into their synapses" (p. 395). Along the same lines, other sociologists argued that separate schools, divided along vocational and academic lines, were needed to teach to the different intelligence levels (Snedden, 1914).

The IQ test was developed in 1905 by Alfred Binet and Theodore Simon, two French psychologists (Cremin, 1961). Over the course of a decade or so, discussions related to IQ testing were confined to professional circles. But during the early stages of World War I, the IQ test attracted the attention of the U.S. Army, which was looking for a way to "quantify" the intelligence of its recruits, particularly those soldiers at either extreme of the scale. Although the developers of the IQ test admitted that the test was irrelevant to character concerns, they asserted that the test had the capacity to assign mental ages to all test takers. Using norms taken from children, which turned out to be quite a mistake, the Army found that the average "mental age" of the American soldier was 14. This was a dangerous turn for American education because various commentators now could claim that schooling beyond a certain age was essentially worthless. Students with an IQ that corresponded with a mental age of 13 presumably did not need to go to school beyond age 13—their inherent skills could take them only so far. Clearly, Lester Ward's hope to enliven the social environment and to expand educational opportunities for all youths was imperiled by the prospect of educational retrenchment based on IQ scores.

In time, progressives and traditionalists alike challenged the worth of IQ scores. They tried to demonstrate how hazardous the IQ was as a measurement, and they also argued that even accurate IQs were not fixed and changeless, but were very much influenced by educational opportunity. Bagley (1925), for instance, conducted studies showing a high correlation between IQ scores and educational opportunity (Cremin, 1961). He made it clear that the results of the IQ tests spoke not for educational restriction, but for educational opportunity. Dewey offered similar objections to IQ tests, fearing that teachers might see IQ measures as complete and final statements of a student's ability to learn. He saw children as always in the state of becoming, of growing and developing. This was his faith as an educator, to be more concerned about what might be than what is. "At all events," observed Dewey (1928), "quality of activity and of consequence is more important for the teacher than any quantitative element" (p. 174). Dewey could see some value in the IQ score if it assisted teachers in designing individually responsive learning experiences, but he was wary about using it to classify students and about its role in supporting the idea that education was largely a biologically predetermined affair.

In the end, those who supported efficiency strategies in the curriculum helped to give life to various new curriculum trends in the school. New trends toward specificity, toward differentiation, toward life adjustment, toward instructional scripting, toward measurement, and toward the power of activity over mentalism—all were fruits of the social efficiency movement.

SUMMARY

Many child-centered thinkers in American education viewed themselves as on the side of progressivism, largely because they opposed the subject-centered and mentalistic views of the traditional humanists. But other progressives saw as much danger in the child-centered perspective as in the subject-centered view it was designed to counter. Chief among these was John Dewey, who succeeded in galvanizing a new progressivism that deliberately shaped the school as an agency of and for democracy. The school, as a result, was moved, as never before, by a social democratic theory. The effects were palpable. A new generation of freed slaves and their children could begin to look to the school for uplift. Booker T. Washington and W. E. B. Du Bois offered opposing views on how the school could act as a corrective agency in the lives of blacks, but they both had high expectations for the school.

Other progressive initiatives rested on the same foundation of high expectations. The settlement house movement, popularized by Jane Addams, gave hope to poor and immigrant populations. A new reconfiguration for the secondary school curriculum, as set forth in the Cardinal Principles report, created the early model for the American comprehensive high school. A heady protest literature, mostly from the hand of George Counts, used a social class analysis to voice concerns with disparities in educational opportunity. Finally, a social efficiency movement placed a new emphasis on activity in the school experience while also setting the conditions for the role of specific objectives and intelligence measurement in the curriculum.

QUESTIONS AND ACTIVITIES

1. Describe in general terms what John Dewey supported as the main factors in the educative process.

2. How did the scientific method relate to John Dewey's ideas about learning?

3. John Dewey balanced his regard for change with an equal regard for conservation through a sense of commonality. Explain this position.

4. Explain John Dewey's curriculum experiment with social occupations. Why was he attracted to using social occupations as focal points in the curriculum?

5. What were some of the main principles of American pragmatism, and how did they inform John Dewey's thinking?

6. What was Lester Ward's main contribution to the progressive education movement?

7. What were settlement houses, and how did they fit into Lester Ward's thinking about school and society?

8. What was the general nature of the debate between Booker T. Washington and W. E. B. Du Bois?

9. What was Booker T. Washington's rationale for supporting industrial and normal school education for blacks?

10. Why did John Dewey call Francis Parker the "father of progressive education"?

11. How did Francis Parker differ in his thinking from John Dewey?

12. Why did the Cardinal Principles report of 1918 represent a proverbial tidal change in the way that high school education was conceived?

13. What are the two main curricular functions of the school according to the Cardinal Principles report?

14. Explain the social reconstructionism of George Counts, and describe how John Dewey and others criticized Counts.

15. What was scientific management, and how did it relate to the development of the school curriculum?

16. What was the main rationale behind the use of activity analysis in the curriculum?

17. How did Edward Thorndike help to overcome the dominance of mental discipline as a learning doctrine, and in what way was such a development helpful to Franklin Bobbitt and activity analysis?

18. Who was Joseph Rice, and how did his work contribute to the rise of scientific management procedures in the school?

19. Explain how the development of IQ testing led to curriculum differentiation and educational restrictionism.

REFERENCES

Adams, C. F. (1881). The development of the superintendency. In D. Calhoun (1969), *Educating for Americans: A documentary history.* (New York: Houghton Mifflin).

Anderson, J. D. (1978). The Hampton model of normal school industrial education, 1868–1900. In V. P. Franklin and J. D. Anderson, *New perspectives on black educational history.* (Boston: Hall).

Bagley, W. (1925). *Determinism in education.* (Baltimore: Warwick & York).

Bobbitt, J. F. (1924a). *How to make a curriculum.* (Boston: Houghton Mifflin).

Bobbitt, J. F. (1924b). The new technique of curriculum-making. *Elementary School Journal,* 25:45–54.

Bobbitt, J. F. (1921). A significant trend in curriculum-making. *Elementary School Journal,* 21:607–15.

Bobbitt, J. F. (1918). *The curriculum.* (Boston: Houghton Mifflin).

Bobbitt, J. F. (1913). The supervision of city schools: Some general principles of management applied to the problems of city-school systems. In *Twelfth yearbook of the National Society for the Study of Education,* Part I. (Bloomington, IL: Public School).

Bode, B. H. (1938). *Progressive education at the crossroads.* (New York: Newson).

Bode, B. H. (1927). *Modern educational theories.* (New York: Macmillan).

Boydston, J. A. (ed.). (1979). *The complete works of John Dewey.* (Carbondale: Southern Illinois University Press).

Butts, R. F. (1955). *A cultural history of Western education.* (New York: McGraw-Hill).

Callahan, R. E. (1962). *Education and the cult of efficiency.* (Chicago: Phoenix Books, University of Chicago Press).

Childs, J. (1956). *American pragmatism and education.* (New York: Holt).

Colky, M. (1987). Janes Addams' Hull House: Early contributions to adult education. *Journal of Midwest History of Education Society,* 15:32–43.

Commission on the Reorganization of Secondary Education. (1918). *The cardinal principles of secondary education.* (Washington, DC: U.S. Government Printing Office).

Counts, G. S. (1932). *Dare the schools build a new social order?* (New York: John Day).

Counts, G. S. (1927). *The social composition of boards of education.* (Chicago: University of Chicago Press).

Counts, G. S. (1922). *The selective character of American secondary education.* (Chicago: University of Chicago Press).

Cremin, L. A. (1988). *American education: The metropolitan experience, 1876–1980.* (New York: Harper & Row).

Cremin, L. A. (1961). *The transformation of the school.* (New York: Knopf).

Du Bois, W. E. B. (1903). The souls of black folk. In D. Calhoun (1969), *Educating for Americans: A documentary history.* (New York: Houghton Mifflin).

Dewey, J. (1928). Progressive education and the science of education. In R. D. Archambault (ed.), *John Dewey on education.* (New York: Modern Library).

Dewey, J. (1916). *Democracy and education.* (New York: Free Press).

Dewey, J. (1902a). *The child and the curriculum.* (Chicago: University of Chicago Press).

Dewey, J. (1902b). *The school and society.* (Chicago: University of Chicago Press).

Dewey, J., and Dewey, E. (1915). *Schools of tomorrow.* (New York: Dutton).

Dworkin, M. (1954). *Dewey on education.* (New York: Teachers College Press).

Finney, R. L. (1928). *A sociological philosophy of education.* (New York: Macmillan).

Harlan, L. R. (1988). *Booker T. Washington in perspective.* (Jackson: University of Mississippi Press).

Jackson, P. W. (1975). Notes on the aging of Franklin Bobbitt. *Elementary School Journal,* 75:118–33.

Kliebard, H. M. (1986). *The struggle for the American curriculum.* (New York: Routledge & Kegan Paul).

Kline, E., Moore, D., and Moore, S. A. (1987). Colonel Francis Parker and beginning reading instruction. *Reading Research and Instruction,* 26(3):141–50.

Lagemann, E. (1985). *Jane Addams on education.* (New York: Teachers College Press).

Mayer, F. (1964). *American ideas and education.* (Columbus, OH: Merrill).

Mayhew, K. C. and Edwards, A. C. (1936). *The Dewey school.* (New York: Atherton Press).

Morgan, H. (1995). *Historical perspectives on the education of black children.* (Westport, CT: Praeger).

Morris, C. (1970). *The pragmatic movement in American philosophy.* (New York: George Braziller).

Rice, J. M. (1969). *The public school system of the United States.* (New York: Arno Press [1893]).

Rugg, H. O. (1927). *Twenty-sixth yearbook of the National Society for the Study of Education,* Part I: Curriculum making: Past and present. (Bloomington, IL: Public School).

Snedden, D. (1914). Vocational education. *The New Republic,* 3 (May):40–42.

Tanner, D., and Tanner, L. N. (1987a). *The history of the school curriculum.* (New York: Macmillan).

Tanner, L. N., and Tanner, D. (1987b). Environmentalism in American pedagogy: The legacy of Lester Ward. *Teacher College Record,* 88(4):537–48.

Taylor, F. W. (1911). *The principles of scientific management.* (New York: Harper).

Thorndike, E. L. (1924). Mental discipline in high school studies. *Journal of Educational Psychology,* 15:1–22, 82–98.

Ward, L. F. (1883). *Dynamic sociology.* (New York: Appleton).

Washington, B. T. (1905). Tuskegee and its people. In D. Calhoun (1969). *Educating for Americans: A documentary history.* (New York: Houghton Mifflin).

Washington, B. T. (1901). Up from slavery. In D. Calhoun (1969), *Educating for Americans: A documentary history.* (New York: Houghton Mifflin).

Washington, B. T. (1895). The Atlanta compromise. In D. Calhoun (1969), *Educating for Americans: A documentary history.* (New York: Houghton Mifflin).

Whitehead, A. N. (1929). *Aims of education and other essays.* (New York: Macmillan).

Wirth, A. (1989). *John Dewey as educator.* (Lanham, MD: University Press of America).

PART III

The School and Society

*The conception of education as a social
process and function has no definite meaning until
we define the kind of society we have in mind.*

—JOHN DEWEY

CHAPTER 9

The Structure
of American Education

Grade- and School-Level Orientations

School Governance

THE ROLE OF THE STATE

THE ROLE OF LOCAL SCHOOL DISTRICTS

THE ROLE OF THE FEDERAL GOVERNMENT

Funding Public Education

Church, State, and Public Education

THE ESTABLISHMENT AND FREE EXERCISE CLAUSES

SCHOOL PRAYER

RELIGIOUS HOLIDAYS AND RELIGIOUS SYMBOLS

THE TEACHING OF CREATIONISM

STATE AID TO RELIGIOUS SCHOOLS

Summary

Questions and Activities

References

T HE ORGANIZATION OF THE AMERICAN SCHOOL historically
has been built on a relation between state and local jurisdictions.
Some early state laws gave local school districts considerable liberties. But as the nation developed and as the teaching profession began to
acquire a theoretical foundation, the state became increasingly adamant
about the establishment of public schools in local districts and more
focused on how such schools should go about educating youths. As discussed, the historical model for the state supervision of local schools was
set by Horace Mann during his tenure as the first state superintendent of
schools in Massachusetts. But the very notion of allowing the state to guide
the schools is rooted in the Massachusetts laws of 1642 and 1647. The legislators of the Massachusetts Bay Colony were the first to mandate public
education, the first to require the maintenance of town schools, and the
first to use tax dollars to fund public schools.

The role of the federal government in the governance of the schools was
decided with the 1791 ratification of the Tenth Amendment to the Constitution, which essentially gave the states full powers in the operation of the
public schools. Although the Constitution itself delegated no specific powers to the federal government in the arena of public education, the federal
government still had a legislative role to play. In fact, the precedent for federal intervention in schooling was set early on, when Congress drafted the
Northwest (or Land) Ordinance of 1785, which required that federal land
grants be contingent on the parceling of land for local public schools. Here,
the federal government was promoting the general welfare of the nation by
encouraging public schools without stipulating how such schools should be
structured (Cremin, 1951).

GRADE- AND SCHOOL-LEVEL ORIENTATIONS

The American system of education, which is structurally organized as one
path, or ladder, from kindergarten to college, came into existence through
an interplay of various influences. In the eighteenth century, the public
schools in America were organized without a grade-level structure. Dame
schools and common elementary town schools were largely ungraded and
made no effort to form a systematic whole with more advanced schools,
such as the Latin Grammar schools or the academies (Douglas and Grieder,
1948). In order words, the elementary school did not flow curricularly into
the secondary school; they were not component parts of one larger unit.
But as the nation took on a national identity, so did the school, and the

Middle schools are designed to be attuned to the nature of the preadolescent.

establishment of the graded educational ladder gave the whole system a unified focus. Figure 9-1 shows the rungs in this ladder.

Almost all American public schools use grade levels to organize instruction, but the grade configuration in individual schools varies (Jones, Salisbury, and Spencer, 1969). Many school districts use a 6-3-3 configuration, which includes seven years of elementary school (counting kindergarten), three years of junior high school, and three years of high school. Increasingly, however, school districts are recognizing the value of a middle school, as opposed to a junior high school, for the education of preadolescents. School districts so inclined lean toward the adoption of a 4-4-4 or 5-3-4 pattern, which places the ninth grade in high school and the sixth grade in middle school.

Middle schools were developed in response to the accusation that traditional junior high schools were little more than imitations of senior high schools (Tanner, 1972). Focused on the needs of preadolescents in the curriculum, the middle schools promised to provide learning experiences that were less concerned with a college track and more directly committed to exploratory, enrichment, and general education opportunities. The junior high school originally was conceived as a transitional or intermediate institution between the self-contained classroom setting of elementary school and the departmentalized setting of the senior high school. But it had failed

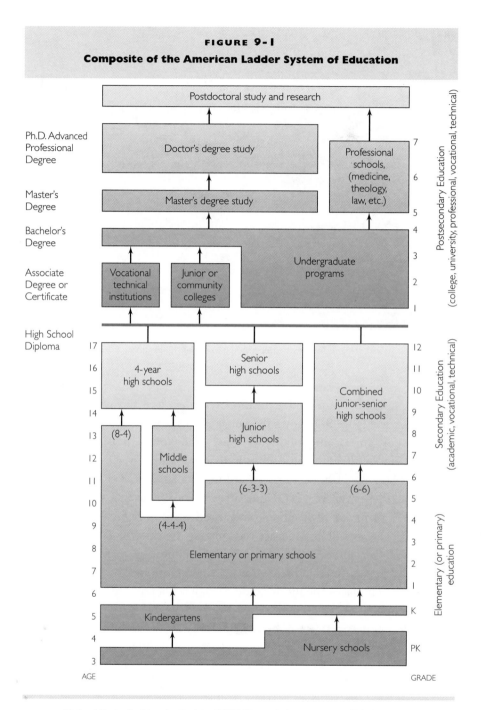

FIGURE 9-1

Composite of the American Ladder System of Education

SOURCE: National Center for Education Statistics (1995), *Digest of education statistics* (Washington, DC: U.S. Department of Education), p. 7.

to become a distinctive institution for preadolescents. Moving the course work for the ninth grade out of the middle school or junior high setting was significant because ninth-grade course work is recorded on the high school transcript used for admission to college. Similarly, moving the sixth grade into the middle school setting better served the developmental level of preadolescents. Thus, under the new grade configuration, the middle school could explore curriculum options that were more attuned to the early adolescent, stressing interdisciplinary themes, exploratory learning, and more multi-age grouping strategies (Wiles and Bondi, 1993).

For every rule in American education, there are always notable exceptions. Because the educational system is decentralized, with states and local school districts holding authority, it is difficult to make generalizations about American schooling. Thus, the structural configurations discussed previously are by no means universally adopted. Small rural districts might organize their schools with a 6-6 configuration, and where the population is especially small, the district might adopt one unified K-12 arrangement. Moreover, the manner in which a school district structures its grade levels may have nothing to do with pedagogical principles and everything to do with the size of its facilities and its enrollment distributions across age levels.

However, there are some common threads. For instance, most school districts recognize the divisions of elementary, middle or intermediate, and secondary schools. In doing so, they also recognize the accompanying pedagogical orientations of each division. Thus, while secondary schools and junior high schools traditionally have been openly departmentalized in how they structure teaching, elementary schools and the new middle schools have been less inclined toward departmentalization.

Much teaching at the elementary school level continues to occur along rather traditional subject lines (math, science, language arts, and so on). However, the actual elementary school classroom is often self-contained, with one educator responsible for teaching all the standard academic subjects to one heterogeneously grouped classroom. The rationale behind this is that elementary education should be more attendant to interdisciplinary lines because it does not need to be as concerned about college preparation (which tends to support disciplinary studies). Moreover, the elementary classroom is often supported by a child development strategy that sees the classroom as a miniature society, where young people can learn basic principles of cooperation and other facets of group living. Elementary schools are designed to be responsive to the developmental tasks of early, middle, and late childhood. They center on social adjustment, physical development, self-awareness, academic readiness, and sensory development

(Wiles and Bondi, 1993). Subject-centered learning should not be a major consideration.

The self-contained classroom design used in elementary schools is ideal for group-centered learning that promotes interdisciplinary visions, but it has been criticized for its failure to deal properly with individual variations. Critics have argued that, in self-contained classrooms containing heterogeneous groups of youths, teachers have no good way of dealing with individual talents and skills. Further, the classroom is said to follow the pace of the slowest learner, thereby compromising the education of the more academically inclined students. As a result of these problems, grouping procedures have become quite popular in self-contained settings, especially in the elementary subjects of reading and mathematics. Note that intraclass grouping within the self-contained classroom differs from ability-based interclass grouping, or curriculum tracking, which is discussed in the next chapter.

In some school districts, the self-contained system in the elementary schools has been abandoned in favor of departmentalization. Today, some elementary schools are teaching children within an organizational scheme not unlike what might be found at a high school level. Specialized teachers are teaching specialized subjects, sometimes in ability-grouped settings. Some elementary schools employing specialized teachers have tried to temper the arrangement by using heterogeneous groups sometimes known as a house or unit, taught by a team of teachers. This team teaching arrangement allows for collaborative curriculum planning, some connection across subjects and grades, and combined group meetings. This arrangement is also used in some larger middle schools and high schools to preserve the intimacy of the school experience.

Middle schools have, by and large, featured curriculum designs that resemble those found in self-contained elementary schools rather than those found in the high schools. That is, they seek connections between subject areas for the purpose of providing integrated and socio-centered learning opportunities. Like the elementary school, the middle school is not under direct college preparatory pressures. Under ideal circumstances, the middle school curriculum should focus on the psychosocial development of early adolescents and deal with issues related to health, social responsibility, basic communication, and human relations. The development of more complex thinking skills should be at center stage because, developmentally speaking, many preadolescents are just entering into the Piagetian stage of formal operations, which stresses hypothetical thinking. The academic subject areas of the curriculum should not be disciplinary, but should aim at socio-personal issues that speak to life interests, peer relations, questions of social identity, and the like. And exploratory learning should be valued as a way to open the world up to the preadolescent and to develop early interests in various new ideas and subjects.

At the secondary school level, public education follows two different styles. Many high schools are comprehensive institutions that provide educational programs for all students—college- and non-college-bound—in a unified setting. Thus, college preparatory programs are offered to youths on a college track, and vocational programs are offered to students destined for blue-collar work. All youths, however, have opportunities to participate in exploratory, enrichment, and general education programs, with the latter representing socio-civic learnings in common heterogeneous settings (see Chapter 1). The other secondary school style is the specialized high school, which, depending on the school, offers specialized training in a particular academic or vocational area. Specialized vocational schools, in fact, are popular in some states. Specialized magnet schools, which can offer unique academic or vocational programs for students, are growing in stature and popularity in school districts across the nation, especially in large urban districts.

SCHOOL GOVERNANCE

The Role of the State

Today, the ladder system of American education is governed by three interrelated sources: the federal government, state governments, and local school boards. But the legal governance of the school rests entirely in the hands of the state. Each state conducts its schools as it sees fit, as long as it abides by the laws of the nation. Thus, in effect, fifty states translates into fifty systems of education. Although each state is, of course, influenced by the federal government and the national media, there is no centralized national control of education. In fact, the public school system in the United States is one of the few worldwide to be governed by a decentralized system. Other advanced nations, such as Japan, Russia, and most European nations, have central ministries of education that dictate national policy and practices for schooling.

Ultimately, state legislatures are responsible for the public schools. They authorize funding and pass legislation for the schools. But the state board of education and its main administrative unit, the state department of education, is responsible for the actual day-to-day supervision of the state system. All the states in America except one (Wisconsin) have state boards of education. Their services extend into the areas of policy development, school personnel, budget appropriations, curriculum, and the law. Among other duties, state boards of education appoint and supervise the chief state officer or state superintendent of education and oversee budgetary appropriations for school spending, licensure regulations for the preparation of teachers, standards for accrediting schools, compliance with state school laws, and the distribution of state and federal funds to various local districts. Some state boards of education are more interventionist than others. In Texas, for instance, the state board appoints a committee to screen textbooks for the purpose of creating an adoption list from which schools can make their selections. It also tries to supervise the instruction offered by teachers in each local school district by providing a statewide model of pedagogy; and, at one time, it required all professional educators to take a basic literacy examination. Differences between school governance in the states are explored in Feature 9-1.

In most states, the members of the state board are appointed by the governor. But in fifteen states, membership is by popular vote, and in five states, the state legislature appoints school board members. Still other states use some combination of these methods. In most cases, the board is composed of laypeople. Membership rarely requires professional educator status, although in Indiana, four of the eleven members must be educators. Different states attach different conditions to the composition of the board. In Georgia, board members must have been a resident of the state for at least five years; in Kentucky, board members must be at least 30 years old and hold at least an associate's degree; in Delaware, at least two board members must have local school board experience; and in New Jersey, at least three of the thirteen board members must be women. The number of voting members on a state board ranges from seven, which is the case in ten states, to sixteen for the New York State Board of Education. Term lengths range from three years in Rhode Island to nine years in West Virginia and Mississippi.

The chief officer of the state typically answers to the state board of education, especially if he or she is an appointed official. Frequently, the chief officer of education is also the executive chair of the state board. This official makes appointments to the state education department, offers budgetary and legislative recommendations to the state board, and determines the status and the needs of public education, particularly as they relate to improving the conditions of schooling. The state superintendent is also responsible for the function of the state department of education, which often operationalizes the work of the state board with regard to teacher certification, school accreditation, attendance, financial, and other pertinent issues. The state department of education is often active in compiling statistical data on the schools and in filing the annual state report on educational progress. It is the main administrative agency for education in the state.

The chief school officer is an elected position in eighteen states and an appointed position in the remaining states. The appointment can come from the state board of education or from the governor; in thirty-two states, this represents two sides of the same coin because state boards of education in such states are also appointed by the governor. Only a handful of states require the superintendent to have had experience as a professional educator.

Often overlooked is the power that governors have in this arrangement of authority. In most cases, the governor appoints the executive state officer of education and members of the state board of education. And it is the governor who gives final approval to the state school budget. The governor can propose bills to the legislature, veto bills brought forward by the legislature, and use the office as a platform for the promotion of reform. During the 1980s, state governors became quite active in the school reform movement. Because the Reagan administration abhorred the idea of federal intervention in schooling and tried to reduce the federal presence in education, the torch for reform was taken up by the governors, whose consolidated efforts led to widespread institutional changes in school practices (U.S. Department of Education, 1984). With federal programs being slashed, the status assumed more financial and program responsibilities. The governors targeted everything from the length of the school day to the requirements for teacher certification.

The Role of Local School Districts

Except for Hawaii, which has one statewide school district, every public school is part of a local school district, and in this sense, local communities still have a voice in their schools. In fact, the local district is the basic administrative unit for the implementation of state policy. But the local district is an agent of the state, essentially sanctioned by the state to carry out its functions. The state can intervene virtually as it wishes in local school matters. For example, it can change district boundaries, authorize an evaluation of its curriculum, or, if warranted, entirely usurp its governing powers.

Each local district also has its own local school board, whose members, again depending on the district, might be appointed or elected, although the overwhelming majority are elected. Although local districts, in most

9-1 RESEARCH INQUIRY
State-by-State School Governance Profile

Research the public school governance structure in one state, and use it as a basis for comparison with another state. You can start with the National Association of State Boards of Education, which has a website (www.nasbe.org) that allows you to access a public school profile for each state (see the example below), as well as to examine state department of education links and the actual education governance structure of each state. Delving into education department websites gives you insight into the regulatory structure of each state with regard to public schooling and into the general issues confronting the public schools in each state. Pick two different states, perhaps your own state and a state with a similar demographic, and write an analysis of the similarities and differences.

Public School Profile, New York

Governance Structure
Number of State Board Members: 16
Length of Term: 5 years
Selection Process: Appointed by the Legislature
Selection of Chief State School Officer: Appointed by the State Board of Education
Official Role of Chief on State Board: Chief Executive Officer

1. Number of students enrolled in grades K–12	2,825,000
2. Number of teachers	185,063
3. Number of schools	4,149

cases, have wide latitude in decision making, they have to comply with state requirements, especially in areas of institutional regulation. State laws and regulations might specify the length of the school year, the standards of preparation required of teachers, minimal teacher salaries, required subject areas to be taught, and other essential aspects of the school's operation. But within this framework of regulations, the local school district usually has ample opportunity to follow its own prerogatives. Local school boards, after all, authorize the funds to be raised through local taxes. They hire the district superintendent of schools, and they make all the decisions related to personnel and property. Within certain limitations, local school boards

4. Number of school districts	719
5. Student/teacher ratio	16:1
6. Average teacher salary	$49,560
7. High School graduation rate	90.9%
8. Average daily attendance	2,388,973
9. Percentage of teachers with advanced degrees	74.90%
10. Average SAT score (verbal/math)—Percentage of graduates tested	419/473—74%
Average composite ACT score—Percentage of graduates tested	22—16%
11. Student-multimedia computer ratio	25:1
12. Percentage of students living in poverty	23.6%
13. Federal contribution to school revenue	$1,196,994,000
—Share of total revenue	4.8%
14. State contribution to school revenue	$10,127,462,000
—Share of total revenue	40.7%
15. Local contribution to school revenue	$13,330,601,000
—Share of total revenue	53.6%
16. Per-pupil expenditure, excluding state administration	$9,623

plan school policy and appraise the work of the personnel they hire, especially the superintendent. They also approve budgets, determine school and attendance boundaries within the district, enter into labor negotiations, and make many curriculum decisions. Their work, however, is bound to the formation of policy, not to its implementation. The local boards are composed of lay citizens, most of whom serve without pay and who are under a state directive to operate as a public body in deliberate discussions with the public, a principle that gave birth to the public school board meeting.

The actual implementation of the local board's policies typically is delegated to the superintendent of schools. Thus, the superintendent is the

Local school boards are typically comprised of lay people. They have an obligation to operate as a public body in deliberate discussion with the public.

main representative of the board when it is not in session, as well as its official executive agent, making decisions in accordance with board policy and in close contact with board personnel. But, the school superintendent also acts in an advisory capacity. As the chief officer of the school district, he or she makes recommendations to the local board on various fronts, including the appointment of personnel, the drafting of labor policies, curriculum reforms, physical plant issues, and public relations concerns. The local school superintendent is also responsible for submitting a budget to the board for its analysis and eventual approval.

The idea of the local school district is distinctively American; it is a function of our unique history. Advocates of localism have long promoted the idea of keeping the schools close to the people. But local school control also has its share of problems. As we will see, the district system tends to lead to funding inequities between schools, a problem that many states have been unable to solve. And, too often, local school boards overstep their responsibilities and attempt to micromanage their schools, which sometimes results in the promotion of narrow political or even religious agendas. The state, of course, oversees these actions and can apply remedies. Unfortunately, such controversial practices can lead to bitter court battles and often prove costly to schoolchildren.

The Role of the Federal Government

The federal government also plays a role in the governance of schools. Historically, its role has been to implement any federal legislation related to the functioning of the school, which has frequently meant providing funds to schools through federal programs approved by Congress. The federal government also is responsible for evaluating the status of American education at the national level. However, it has little jurisdiction in the area of policy or practices.

Most of the educational actions of the federal government has been operationalized through the Department of Education, which is led by a cabinet-level secretary of education. The secretary has no power to dictate educational changes or prescriptions to the states. There is no centralizing national power for school policy and school practice. The secretary, however, can be enormously persuasive and influential in state-level school policy, largely because of the national visibility of the position, the federal grant money underpinning Department of Education causes, and the easy access that the secretary has to national media sources.

The Department of Education and the secretary also oversee the Office of Educational Research and Improvement, which is responsible for analyzing the reported achievements of American children. This office conducts the National Assessment of Educational Progress (NAEP), which provides insight into the level of comprehension and competence achieved by American students in various subject areas, including math, science, reading, and writing, using the variables of gender, race, and age.

The federal government traditionally has played a prominent role in the promotion of public education. Among its more significant initiatives was the Morrill Act of 1862, which was largely responsible for the development of the nation's state universities, and the Smith-Hughes Act of 1917, which provided massive funding for the support of vocational education in secondary schools. More recently, the federal government has sponsored a variety of initiatives and programs. For example, the GI Bill supported the cost of postsecondary education for military veterans. The National Science Foundation has maintained a presence in the area of math and science education. The National Defense Education Act of 1958 funneled federal funds for the improvement of instruction in math, science, and foreign language, and for the development of early instructional technologies, while the Elementary and Secondary Act of 1965 targeted the education of children in low-income brackets. The National Merit Scholarship program recognizes and supports the most academically talented students in the country, and a host of initiatives have addressed special education, bilingual education,

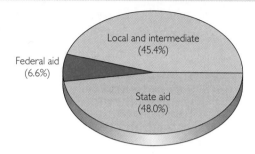

FIGURE 9-2

Distribution of School Revenues for Public Elementary and Secondary Education by Source, 1996–97

NOTE: Percentages may not sum to 100 due to rounding. Intermediate revenues were combined with local revenues.

SOURCE: National Center for Education Statistics (1997), Common core data, National Public Education Financial Survey, school year 1996–97. (Washington, DC: U.S. Department of Education).

vocational education, and compensatory education. Various branches of the federal government, including the Department of Defense, the Department of Justice, the Department of the Interior, and the Department of Labor, have also, at one time or another, provided federal education programs for youths at some level of the educational ladder.

FUNDING PUBLIC EDUCATION

The education of American schoolchildren is supported by taxes collected at the local, state, and federal levels. In general, school funding is more or less evenly split between local districts and the state, with each taking on between 40 and 50 percent of the burden. But in some states, such as Hawaii, there is full state funding, and in others, such as New Hampshire, there is heavy reliance on locally raised revenues. Nationwide, the federal government accounts for less than 10 percent of the school funding. Figure 9-2 shows the national breakdown of school revenues; Table 9-1 gives a state-by-state profile of the sources of school revenues.

The typical pattern for financial support in the American schools follows the governance structure discussed previously. Thus, the state creates local school districts and authorizes taxes to raise funds for the support of the schools. The local districts raise most of these funds through property taxes. Obviously, the value of real estate properties will affect how successful a district is in providing a proper level of financial support. The basic capacity of a local school district to raise funds for schools is always a function of the property wealth of the district combined with the tax burden that the community is willing to accept. This can lead to remarkable disparities in spending between different local districts—disparities that the state is responsible for closing.

Differences in funding at the local level usually result from differences in the amount and value of local commercial and residential property. A district with high property values can raise more revenue for its students, and often at a lower tax rate, than can a property-poor district. When local districts have no state restrictions over their school budgets, the differences in outlays between high- and low-spending districts can reach astounding proportions. For example, in some states, the highest-spending district has a per-pupil expenditure rate eight times greater than that of the lowest-spending district. Table 9-2 shows the differences, adjusted for cost and need, in school spending among the states; cost adjustments account for differences in cost of living, while need adjustments account for the money required for the education of special needs students.

Although local districts rely almost exclusively on property taxes, states can turn to a number of sources for revenue. Each state is different, but states typically generate revenue through a combination of general sales taxes, personal income taxes, and corporate taxes. Recently, state lotteries have also become popular fund-raising mechanisms. Once the state collects its money for public education, it has to decide how much each district will receive.

Because one of the functions of the state is to help equalize differences in per-pupil expenditures across school districts, local districts that are less wealthy and less able to invest large sums of money in the education of their children are supposed to find relief from the state. Many states tackle this problem by applying a minimal provision philosophy toward finance whereby, essentially, each school district in the state must meet a minimal baseline investment. The baseline represents a commitment of funds that will supposedly ensure an adequate education for all youths in the state (Guthrie, Garms, and Pierce, 1988).

In recent decades, several lawsuits have been filed against states alleging a failure to provide equality of educational opportunity. As of 1998, eighteen states have had their method of financing public schools declared unconstitutional by their state supreme courts (Linn, 1998). This litigation is in the state courts because the U.S. Supreme Court does not view public education as a right protected by the Constitution. The Court took this position in 1973 in *Rodriguez v. the San Antonio Independent School District,* in which the plaintiffs charged that inequities in the funding for local

TABLE 9-1

Percentage Distribution of Revenues for Public Schools by State, 1996–97

	SOURCE		
	Local	State	Federal
National	45.4%	48.0%	6.6%
Alabama	27.1	63.2	9.6
Alaska	24.8	63.4	11.8
Arizona	41.8	45.0	9.3
Arkansas	31.9	60.1	7.8
California	31.8	60.0	8.2
Colorado	50.6	44.1	5.2
Connecticut	59.4	37.1	3.6
Delaware	27.6	64.8	7.6
District of Columbia	89.5	0.0	10.5
Florida	43.8	48.8	7.4
Georgia	39.4	53.7	6.8
Hawaii	2.4	89.5	8.1
Idaho	29.8	63.5	6.7
Illinois	66.7	27.0	6.3
Indiana	44.7	50.5	4.2
Iowa	42.7	52.0	5.1
Kansas	34.0	56.2	5.6
Kentucky	27.8	62.9	9.3
Louisiana	38.1	50.3	11.7
Maine	47.4	47.2	5.4
Maryland	56.0	38.8	5.2
Massachusetts	55.3	39.9	4.8
Michigan	27.8	65.5	6.6
Minnesota	37.1	55.0	4.3
Mississippi	30.5	55.5	14.0
Missouri	53.3	40.3	5.9

schools violated their children's equal protection guarantees under the Fourteenth Amendment to the Constitution. The equal protection clause of the Fourteenth Amendment states that "no state shall . . . deny to any person within its jurisdiction the equal protection of the laws." The Supreme Court, however, did not see a constitutional violation in

	SOURCE		
	Local	State	Federal
Montana	34.1	47.4	9.4
Nebraska	61.2	32.1	6.0
Nevada	64.0	31.9	4.2
New Hampshire	89.2	7.4	3.5
New Jersey	57.8	38.7	3.5
New Mexico	14.3	73.1	12.7
New York	54.8	39.4	5.4
North Carolina	27.4	65.4	7.2
North Dakota	45.3	41.4	12.0
Ohio	53.1	40.7	6.1
Oklahoma	27.7	62.3	8.3
Oregon	39.8	52.6	6.2
Pennsylvania	55.2	39.1	5.5
Rhode Island	54.0	40.6	5.4
South Carolina	39.1	52.5	8.4
South Dakota	53.6	35.5	9.7
Tennessee	42.9	48.5	8.5
Texas	51.6	40.3	7.7
Utah	30.9	62.8	6.3
Vermont	66.7	28.6	4.6
Virginia	62.6	32.5	5.0
Washington	27.1	67.1	5.9
West Virginia	28.6	63.0	8.3
Wisconsin	42.6	53.1	4.3
Wyoming	37.3	48.5	6.6

SOURCE: National Center for Education Statistics (1999), *Statistics in brief: Revenues and expenditures in public elementary and secondary education* (Washington, DC: U.S. Department of Education).

Rodriguez, holding that no particular group was damaged by the system of funding (the property-poor district was not wholly composed of a single homogeneous group) and that interdistrict differences in funding did not undermine the adequacy of education provided to children in different school districts and were, in fact, a reasonable byproduct of the state's

TABLE 9-2
Adjusted Revenues per Student in Terms of District Spending by State, 1991–92

	REVENUE		
	Low-Spending Districts	Intermediate-Spending Districts	High-Spending Districts
National	$3,178	$4,476	$6,851
Alabama	2,902	3,334	4,335
Alaska	5,234	5,515	9,845
Arizona	3,484	4,187	6,424
Arkansas	3,482	3,930	5,669
California	3,099	3,788	4,882
Colorado	3,921	4,395	5,312
Connecticut	5,309	6,111	8,046
Delaware	4,537	4,956	5,753
District of Columbia	7,863	7,863	7,863
Florida	4,717	5,099	6,007
Georgia	3,645	4,238	5,559
Hawaii	5,476	5,476	5,476
Idaho	2,924	3,298	4,355
Illinois	3,062	3,926	6,660
Indiana	3,662	4,371	5,355
Iowa	4,093	4,606	5,763
Kansas	4,090	4,950	7,096
Kentucky	3,355	3,820	4,248
Louisiana	3,395	4,311	4,876
Maine	4,006	4,738	5,955
Maryland	3,960	5,057	6,661
Massachusetts	3,681	4,442	6,419
Michigan	3,891	4,695	6,665
Minnesota	4,149	5,008	6,116
Mississippi	2,752	3,191	4,180
Missouri	2,970	3,814	6,144

interest in maintaining local control. Children in poorer districts were likely getting an education inferior to that of children in wealthy districts, but they were still getting an adequate education. The effect of this ruling was to shift school finance litigation to the state courts. In fact, Justice

	REVENUE		
	Low-Spending Districts	Intermediate-Spending Districts	High-Spending Districtsl
Montana	3,193	4,102	8,153
Nebraska	4,039	4,905	7,323
Nevada	4,512	4,622	5,419
New Hampshire	3,598	4,500	6,625
New Jersey	5,336	6,721	9,112
New Mexico	3,540	3,695	5,536
New York	4,531	6,096	9,099
North Carolina	3,699	4,223	4,939
North Dakota	3,348	4,028	6,035
Ohio	3,210	3,992	6,498
Oklahoma	3,099	3,649	5,106
Oregon	3,563	4,506	5,817
Pennsylvania	4,441	5,132	6,965
Rhode Island	3,810	4,554	5,430
South Carolina	3,624	4,100	4,849
South Dakota	3,345	4,028	5,664
Tennessee	2,627	3,349	4,307
Texas	3,836	4,520	5,717
Utah	2,619	2,862	3,560
Vermont	4,546	6,223	9,735
Virginia	3,861	4,774	6,129
Washington	3,807	4,519	5,299
West Virginia	4,639	4,934	5,592
Wisconsin	4,559	5,153	6,287
Wyoming	4,625	5,755	8,375

SOURCE: National Center for Education Statistics (1998), *Inequities in public school district revenues* (Washington, DC: U.S. Department of Education).

Thurgood Marshall almost encouraged challenges at the state level when he asserted in the *Rodriguez* ruling that "nothing in this court's decision today should inhibit further reviews of state educational funding schemes under state constitutional provisions."

But litigation challenging the state constitutionality of state funding schemes was already underway in California in the late 1960s, as documented in the well-known *Serrano v. Priest* case. John Serrano, a parent of a child in a Los Angeles–area school, noticed the poor quality of school services made available to his child. When he protested to the school, he was told that the school simply could not afford any improvements. The principal of the school actually advised the father to move to a wealthier school district if he wanted better instruction for his child (Guthrie, Garms, and Pierce, 1988). At the time of the trial, the disparities between the per-pupil expenditures in the Los Angeles area schools were striking. Serrano, who could not afford to move, eventually brought suit against state officials, arguing that the method of school funding, which was heavily dependent on a district's local wealth, violated provisions of the state constitution.

The California Supreme Court agreed and eventually pronounced the entire system of financing schools in California to be in violation of the state's constitution. The problem was that educational opportunities were too closely tied to the taxable wealth of a given school district. This was not an argument, as in the *Rodriguez* case, over the adequacy of the educational provisions offered in an inequitable system, but one over the actual fiscal inequalities in the funding structure of the state system. The court simply would not tolerate a system of school funding that allowed district spending to be related to district wealth. The new catchword became fiscal neutrality, which meant that no relation should exist between educational spending per pupil and local district property wealth. In other words, the quality of education had to be a function of the entire state's wealth, not of the local district's. California, like many other states, relied on property taxes as a major source of local revenue for the schools. Because of the *Serrano* ruling, this had to change. Either local school revenue had to be equalized through state aid or a state system of funding had to be explored.

Historically, when states began to give money to schools, their thinking was that each district, irrespective of its local investment, should be given a flat-rate grant that would be sufficient for a minimal education (Swanson and King, 1991). These were known as flat-grant programs. Schools spending more than the amount of the flat grant were believed to be indulging in a luxury that was their right. The minimal guarantees of an adequate education were thought to be supported under this scheme; basic equalization, in this sense, was upheld. The problem, of course, was that the amount needed for a "minimal education" was an arbitrary figure, especially because the conditions for learning across urban and rural settings varied so widely. Some schools, moreover, were already vested with local monies at a rate well above the flat-grant line drawn by the state. Because the flat grant provided an equal amount of money for each district, it had absolutely no impact on the variance in spending across districts. Flat-grant programs were eventually abandoned by most states in favor of what is known as the foundation program.

The foundation program is also driven by a minimal provision philosophy, but it is a wiser way of setting an adequate minimal level of funding for each school district. As with the flat-grant program, the foundational program sets a minimal funding level that represents what each district must provide to ensure an adequate education. At the same time, in most cases, it requires that each district levy a property tax at a fixed rate. If a property-rich local district meets the baseline or foundational figure with its local tax dollars, it receives nothing from the state in general aid; but if a less wealthy district falls short of this figure, the state makes up the difference. The architects of this program also designed a recapture clause that requires any district that spent above the foundational level to return funds in the amount of the surplus spending to the state for redistribution (Guthrie, Garms, and Pierce, 1988). Few states, however, have been willing to add this clause, arguing that a property-rich district cannot be so compelled. Under the foundation program, the state does not provide money to districts spending above the minimal line, and it can set considerably higher minimal investment levels than was possible with flat grants. Today, some form of foundation program is in operation in about forty states.

The problem with foundation funding, however, is that local funding disparities are often so wide that many states simply cannot afford to bring the lower-spending districts up to a competitive level. Further, the typical state action in closing the funding gap is to ensure that students in lower-spending districts receive a fair and basic education, which means that these states provide a minimal compensation figure rather than a full and comprehensive one. In Montana, litigation was filed against the state for operating a foundation program that set its minimal provision at a level below the average spending of districts. But even if average levels are met, the poorest districts will still be at a disadvantage because in most cases their needs and problems are not average. In many cases, the problems resulting from poverty make education in such places more costly, and thus require an above-average investment.

Researchers concerned about the equity of school finance systems have tried to address this problem by developing the idea of vertical equity. According to this concept, some students, such as those who are disabled or are limited in their English proficiency, need additional educational services that are going to be more costly to the district than would normally be the case. Thus, when school funding is calculated with vertical equity in mind, adjustments have to be made to give added weight to those districts with pupils who need extra or special educational services. With vertical equity, funding levels must be calculated as a per-weighted, pupil figure.

Vertical equity provisions usually are made through categorical aid programs. Thus, each school district, irrespective of its wealth, receives some funds from the federal government, often as a result of categorical aid programs that designate monies for special purposes such as the education of the handicapped or students from low-income backgrounds. States also provide categorical aid to school districts, as well as supplemental funding for special education programs. And some states provide categorical monies for limited-English-proficiency programs and for compensatory education programs. It is fair to say that high-poverty schools receive more categorical aid than low-poverty schools, but this does not always eliminate inequities. Sometimes, weighing schemes are built into foundation programs by recalibrating the way special needs students are counted. Thus, an educable mentally retarded student might be counted at 1.5, meaning that the associated costs with educating such a student would be 1.5 times the cost of educating a "normal" or nonclassified student; the weight factor for the education of a deaf student could be as high as 4, and for a home- or hospital-bound student perhaps 10 (Guthrie, Garms, and Pierce, 1988).

The state usually handles somewhere between 40 to 50 percent of the total financial commitment to public schooling. These state funds typically are drawn from sales and income taxes, but many states also engage in special programs, such as state lotteries, to raise funds for education. In Georgia, for instance, lottery income is used to fund a scholarship program that pays for the tuition, fees, and books of any Georgia high school graduate who has maintained a B or better average and attends a state university or college within the state. Although there is quite a bit of variance, on average, 33 percent of state tax revenue for public schools comes from sales or gross receipt taxes, 30 percent from personal income taxes, 8 percent from corporate taxes, and the remainder from excise and business taxes. Most states are, as indicated, under increasing pressure to find ways to distribute revenues to school districts to equalize the conditions of schooling. Many states have long looked at equalization as simply a matter of meeting a base or minimal level of funding. But these minimal or foundational provisions are usually not sufficient to compete with the dramatic per-pupil expenditures occurring in property-rich districts. As a result, many states are exploring funding structures that allocate revenues to school districts according to their rank on a scale of wealth, on weighted formula scales that account for the special needs of children in the district, and on formulas that provide state aid inversely proportional to the local property wealth (Munley, 1993).

The Percentage Equalization Program (PEP) is a case in point. It abandons the minimal provision ideal and allows districts to offer any budget that they are prepared to carry out. This is done by using a formula to calculate the percentage contribution that the state will make to the local district budget. The purpose of PEP is not to equalize aid but to equalize the opportunity of local districts to support public schooling at any chosen level of involvement. PEP allows the local district to decide the size of its budget, knowing that the state guarantees a certain percentage of funding and that the local district itself provides the remainder. The state percentage is calculated by dividing the average per-pupil wealth of the district by the average per-pupil wealth of the state, which is then factored by an aid ratio, sometimes representative of the average state funding contribution to the public schools. Thus, a school district with an average per-pupil wealth of $10,000 in a state where the average per-pupil wealth is $20,000 and where the state contributes, on average, 50 percent of the overall financial investment in public schooling, will be calculated as follows:

$$1 - \frac{\text{assessed local district average}}{\text{assessed state average}} \times \text{state aid ratio}$$

$$or$$

$$1 - \left(\frac{10{,}000}{20{,}000} \times .50\right) = 1 - \left(\frac{1}{2} \times \frac{1}{2}\right) = 1 - .25 = .75$$

Under the conditions just described, the state would contribute 75 percent of the overall local district budget. The important thing to remember is that the size of the budget is up to the local district, understanding that in this case it will be responsible for about 25 percent of it. We can see from this formula that, if the locally assessed value of the district is equal to the state's assessed value, then the state contribution will be 50 percent. If the local school district's assessed value is double the state's assessed value, the district will get nothing, notwithstanding categorical aid. And if it is more than double, the state might invoke a recapture clause.

PEP represents a departure from the minimal provision philosophy and reflects increasing faith in financing local/community budgetary requests. PEP is not popular with many states because they fear the possibility of having to provide funding for local districts with large budgets. In fact, some states that have used PEP have placed limits on the per-pupil expenditures, making PEP much like a foundation program (Guthrie, Garms, and Pierce, 1988).

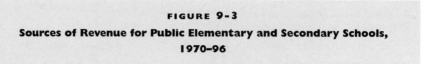

FIGURE 9-3

Sources of Revenue for Public Elementary and Secondary Schools, 1970–96

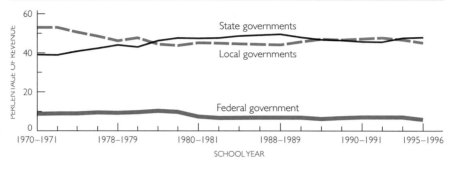

SOURCE: National Center for Education Statistics (1997), *Statistics of state school systems, revenues and expenditures for public elementary and secondary education,* and Common Core of Data, school year 1996–97 (Washington, DC: U.S. Department of Education).

Increasingly, there is also talk of full state funding, which means that each state would assume the costs of running each of its school districts. Local revenues in this case would likely become state property and be redistributed to achieve equity across local districts. Of course, such a system might also result in the forfeiture of local decision making and the overlooking of local preferences and priorities. Currently, Hawaii is funded as one statewide system, and Washington State uses a modified form of full state funding by collecting from local districts, pooling the revenues with state funds, and then redistributing the money to schools on a equal per-pupil basis (Linn, 1998).

Over the past decade, the states have taken a more active hand in the financing of schools, as Figure 9-3 shows. And this trend likely will continue because a reliance on state taxes will probably be the only way to equalize the resources of the schools. This fact was made quite clear in the recent voters' decision in Michigan to opt for a revamped tax structure that puts much of the financial burden for public schooling on the state. In 1993, voters supported a school finance reform plan that diminished the state's reliance on local property taxes as a source of funding. In 1993–94, the statewide average millage rate for the operation of local schools was just under 34 mills on all property, which is another way of saying $3.40 for every $100 of assessed property value or $34 for every $1,000. The mill is a denomination used in school finance, associated with an old English coin long out of use, which represents a tenth of a cent (.001). The millage rate for operating local schools is now 6 mills on all property in Michigan and

18 mills on nonhomestead property (mostly business and industry). This money remains within the school district and serves as part of the district's foundation allowance. The schools in Michigan were able to shift away from a reliance on local property taxes by increasing the state sales tax from 4 to 6 percent and tripling the tax on cigarettes. Under this new scheme, all of the schools in the state now draw most of their funds from the state coffers and are guaranteed a minimum or foundation level of $5,000 per student, giving most poor districts in the state about $1,000 more per student than they have been used to spending. Wealthier school districts in the state can spend above the foundation level, but their capacity to generate the kinds of local revenue that previously led to large disparities has been curtailed.

The Michigan plan has been criticized by the state teachers union, which believes that a reliance on sales taxes for school funding is dangerous. Because sales revenues fluctuate, there will be years, the union claims, when the state's sales tax revenues will not be sufficient to properly fund the schools. The union petitioned for an increase in the state income tax, instead of the sales tax, arguing that it was a more dependable source of revenue. Others have argued that, because the sales tax is a regressive tax, it forces citizens with lesser means to assume a disproportionately large share of the burden in funding the schools. In any case, the shift toward state-level funding and away from local funding by property taxes that occurred in Michigan may be a sign of things to come in other states.

Funding inequities also occur across the states, but these rarely get as much attention. The issue of disparities is no less an issue simply because it is happening among states rather than within them. But because public schooling is controlled at the state level, most of the research interest is focused on variations within states. From an interstate perspective, however, we can see that school funding revenues differ considerably. The adjusted per-pupil expenditures for schoolchildren in intermediate-spending districts in New Jersey, for instance, is $6,721, while it is $2,862 for schoolchildren of Utah (National Center for Education Statistics, 1998; also see Table 9-2). The funding disparities between states are so large in some cases that, if we compare the per-pupil expenditures in the highest-spending districts of a low-revenue state to per-pupil expenditures in the lowest-spending districts of a high-revenue state, we will find that the schoolchildren in the latter situation are probably better off. In Mississippi, for instance, students in the highest revenue districts ($4,180 per pupil) still receive less than the children in the lowest revenue districts in twenty-nine states. And students in the lowest revenue district in New York benefited from a higher per-pupil expenditure than in the majority of other states, where the school funding system was found to be more equitable. Thus, children in low-equity, high-revenue states still might be better off than children in high-equity, low-revenue states. Feature 9-2 on page 362 examines per-pupil expenditures across the nation, disaggregated by household income and minority enrollment.

Despite the changes occurring at the state level in school funding, the role of the federal government likely will remain stable. The federal role in school financing is essentially limited to aid enacted by congressional legislation. This includes direct grant programs and compensatory aid for children of poor families, as well as indirect categorical aid given to states or geographical regions, which trickles down to school districts. As indicated, the overall financial investment in public schools by the federal government amounts to less than 10 percent of the system's total budget. With such a limited role, the federal government's effort to assist districts with large concentrations of poor students has not had a significant impact on the funding disparities between schools. Historically, the federal government has invested in the expansion of educational opportunities, playing a prominent role in the education of handicapped children and in bilingual instruction and compensatory education. It has also been active where a compelling national defense interest has been involved and where the economic livelihood of the country has been in question. Feature 9-3 on page 364 offers multiple resources for continued inquiry into school finance issues.

CHURCH, STATE, AND PUBLIC EDUCATION

The Establishment and Free Exercise Clauses

One of the fundamental legal principles regulating the relation between the church and the state derives from the First Amendment to the Constitution: "Congress shall make no law respecting an establishment of religion, or prohibiting the free exercise thereof." This principle ensures religious freedom for all by prohibiting any governmental establishment of a religion (the Establishment Clause of the First Amendment) and by protecting against government restrictions of any individual religious expression (the Free Exercise Clause of the First Amendment). The Fourteenth Amendment to the Constitution extended these restrictions to state and local governments, including public school districts.

"A Wall of Separation." In 1947, the Supreme Court, in *Everson v. Board of Education,* offered its first major ruling on the relation between church and state. It spoke to the meaning of both the Establishment and Free Exercise clauses of the First Amendment. *Everson* concerned a New Jersey law that allowed for the public payment of transportation for students attending parochial schools. Although the Court upheld the law, in doing so it also outlined broad separationist lines between church and state, harkening back to the words of Thomas Jefferson, reprinted in Feature 9-4, urging that there must be a "wall of separation between church and state." The Court stated outright that the government cannot set up a church, that it cannot pass laws aiding one religion or even aiding the religious over the nonreligious, and that no tax can be levied to support religious activities. These were all Establishment Clause issues. At the same time, the Court offered safeguards for the rights of people to practice religion without state interference, stating that no persons can be forced to remain away from church or to profess a belief against their will, that no persons can be punished for professing a religious thought or engaging in a religious action, and that the government cannot participate in the affairs of religious organizations. These were all Free Exercise Clause issues. Embodied in these ideas was the brick and mortar for the wall of separation. According to the notion of separation, the state would not only be prohibited from favoring any religious belief system but would also actively protect the rights of people to practice religion without government interference.

The metaphor of a wall of separation has endured over the years. It has helped the courts to offer important prohibitions against certain religious activities in the school. But the image of a wall of separation between church and state does not capture the actual relation between schooling and religion very precisely. The school, in fact, cooperates with the church in the interests of students' free expression rights (Power, 1991). Jefferson's famous metaphor notwithstanding, the relation between church and state, in the words of Justice Warren Burger, is represented by a "blurred, indistinct and variable barrier, depending on the circumstances of a particular relationship" (quoted in Patrick and Long, 1999).

Contrary to popular belief, schools are not designed to be religion-free. Although there have been episodes in public schools, especially in the development of curriculum materials, when religion has been systematically and unreasonably culled from the learning experience (Nord, 1995; Vitz, 1986), many, if not most, public schools have been accommodating to religion. Students, for instance, have the right to pray individually or in groups when attending public school, as long as they do so in private and do not disrupt the school environment. Student prayer groups, in fact, enjoy some popularity in the public schools. According to some estimates, 12,000 Bible clubs are operating in American public schools (Prayer in Public Schools, 1994). Students may also carry and read religious materials

9-2 THINKING ABOUT THE DATA

Spending in Rich and Poor School Districts and in High- and Low-Minority Districts

School spending differences occur across and within different states, and sometimes, the disparities are astonishing. Here are four graphical representations of school spending analyzed at a national level in terms of both household income levels and minority enrollment levels. The first two figures show school expenditure levels in relation to the variables of income and minority enrollment. The second two figures show the same expenditure levels adjusted for cost of living and educational need, categorized as "buying power." The idea is that an expenditure of, say, $5,000 has be adjusted as it might be used in New York as opposed to, say, North Dakota, and as it might be used in school districts with higher numbers of special needs students as opposed to districts with few special needs students. What conclusions can you draw from these data?

Public Education Expenditures in the United States by the Median Income of Households Located Within District Boundaries, 1989–90

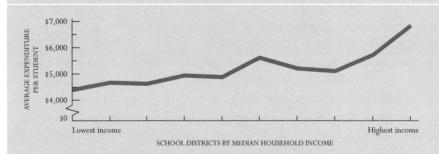

Education Expenditures in the United States in Relation to the Percentage of Minority Enrollments, 1989–90

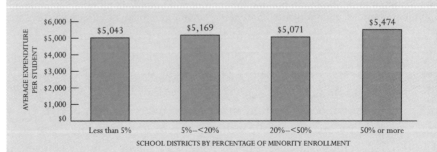

Public Education "Buying Power" in the United States by the Median Income of Households Located Within District Boundaries, 1989–90

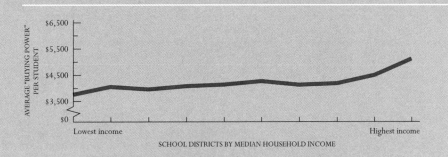

Education "Buying Power" in the United States in Relation to the Percentage of Minority Enrollments, 1989–90

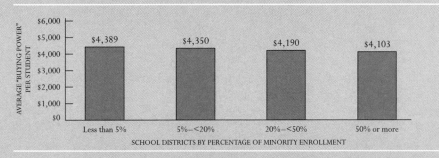

SOURCE: National Center for Education Statistics (1996), *Do rich and poor districts spend alike?* and National Center for Education Statistics (1996), *Do districts enrolling high percentages of minority students spend less?* These Issues Brief were authored by Thomas Parrish and can be accessed online (www.nces.ed.gov).

9-3 WEB POINTS

Education Finance Statistics Center

The National Center for Education Statistics has a website that features issues related to education finance (nces.ed.gov). The site offers access to the latest publications of the NCES on school finance, various graphical representations of school finance data, and survey information. It also provides links to other websites dealing with school finance.

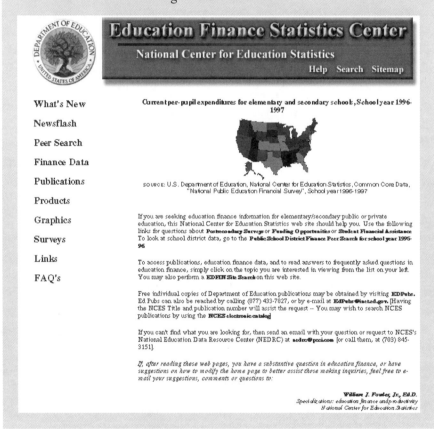

in school and, within certain boundaries, even distribute such materials in school. Further, they have every right to be excused from school to attend to religious obligations or desires and, with certain qualifications, to be excused from classroom activity if it is offensive to their religious beliefs. Many high schools offer comparative religion courses, and many of the new content standards developed for the teaching of history, social studies, and civics include references to teaching about religious beliefs and practices.

9-4 SCHOLARLY VOICES
Thomas Jefferson on the Separation of Church and State

Thomas Jefferson, a staunch supporter of religious freedom, made a clear separation between religious and government affairs. In a letter to the Danbury Baptist Association of Connecticut, Jefferson made his legendary reference to the "wall of separation between church and state," noting that the separation was the basis for the two clauses of the First Amendment:

Believing with you that religion is a matter which lies solely between man and his God, that he owes account to none other for his faith of his worship, that the legislative powers of government reach actions only, and not opinions, I contemplate with sovereign reverence that act of the whole American people which declared that their legislature should "make no law respecting an establishment of religion, or prohibiting the free exercise thereof," thus building a wall of separation between church and state. (quoted in Fraser, 1999, p. 19)

Thomas Jefferson.

The inclusion of religion in the curriculum cannot be denied if it reflects established secular purposes. One, for instance, cannot effectively study the history of early America without understanding how religious faith drove much of the actions and thinking of the colonists. Similarly, one cannot understand the civil rights movement in America without learning that much of the prominent leadership came out of the Southern Christian Leadership Conference or that the concept of nonviolent civil disobedience was partly justified by Christian doctrine. In such cases, religion is justly integrated within a secular instructional purpose.

In 2000, state education officials in Florida revamped the curriculum for "Bible history" high school courses after the State Supreme Court found them to be unconstitutional. The schools, which had taught the courses from a Christian perspective, were accused of promoting Christian faith, which is unconstitutional. But, the court ruled that the schools could continue to teach such courses if they modified them in a way that placed the Bible in the context of other religious traditions, thereby enabling the schools to claim the secular purpose implied in the comparative study of religion. According to the First Amendment, if the Bible, or any other sacred text, is used in a way that attaches itself to secular school purposes, it cannot be excluded from the curriculum.

FIGURE 9-4
Sample of Department of Education Report,
"A Teacher's Guide to Religion in the Public Schools"

Teaching about Religion in Public Schools

Is it constitutional to teach about religion?

Yes. In the 1960s school prayer cases (that prompted rulings against state-sponsored school prayer and Bible reading), the U.S. Supreme Court indicated that public school education may include teaching about religion. In *Abington v. Schempp,* Associate Justice Tom Clark wrote for the Court:

[It] might well be said that one's education is not complete without a study of comparative religion or the history of religion and its relationship to the advancement of civilization. It certainly may be said that the Bible is worthy of study for its literary and historic qualities. Nothing we have said here indicates that such study of the Bible or of religion, when presented objectively as part of a secular program of education, may not be effected consistently with the First Amendment.

Why should study about religion be included in the curriculum?

Growing numbers of educators throughout the United States recognize that study about religion in social studies, literature, art, and music is an important part of a well-rounded education. "Religion in the Public School Curriculum: Questions and Answers," issued by a coalition of 17 major religious and educational organizations— including the Christian Legal Society, the American Jewish Congress, the National Education Association, the American Federation of Teachers, the American Association of School Administrators, the Islamic Society of North America, the National Council for the Social Studies, the Association for Supervision and Curriculum Development, the Baptist Joint Committee on Public Affairs, the National Association of Evangelicals, and the National School Boards Association—describes the importance of religion in the curriculum thus:

Nevertheless, quite a bit of confusion regarding the relation between religion and the school still prevails. In 1995, President Clinton asked the Department of Education to draw up guidelines to help public school teachers understand what is generally permissible school behavior in relation to religion. The guidelines, of course, do not carry the force of law, but they do make it clear that the school need not be dismissive of religion. Figure 9-4 offers a small sample of what is contained in the guidelines.

In adjudicating cases on potential government intrusion in the religious lives of citizens, the courts target two main questions. One is whether there has been excessive government support for a particular religion, which, as indicated, involves the Establishment Clause. The other, which is less well known but equally important, is whether an individual's religious faith has

Because religion plays a significant role in history and society, study about religion is essential to understanding both the nation and the world. Omission of facts about religion can give students the false impression that the religious life of humankind is insignificant or unimportant. Failure to understand even the basic symbols, practices, and concepts of the various religions makes much of history, literature, art, and contemporary life unintelligible.

Study about religion is also important if students are to value religious liberty, the first freedom guaranteed in the Bill of Rights. Moreover, knowledge of the roles of religion in the past and present promotes cross-cultural understanding essential to democracy and world peace.

A number of leading educational groups have issued their own statements decrying the lack of discussion about religion in the curriculum and calling for inclusion of such information in curriculum materials and in teacher education.

Three major principles form the foundation of this consensus on teaching about religion in public schools:

1. As the Supreme Court has made clear, study *about* religion in public schools is constitutional.

2. Inclusion of study about religion is important in order for students to be properly educated about history and cultures.

3. Religion must be taught objectively and neutrally. The purpose of public schools is to educate students about a variety of religious traditions, not to indoctrinate them into any tradition.

been handicapped or burdened by the government, which involves the Free Exercise Clause.

The Courts and the Establishment Clause. To deal with the Establishment Clause, the Supreme Court has, since the 1970s, advanced a three-part framework, sometimes known as the Lemon test, based on the 1971 *Lemon v. Kurtzman* ruling. In the *Lemon* case, the Supreme Court prohibited public money from being used to support instruction in secular subjects at parochial schools. The law that the Court struck down aimed to assist religious schools with the education of low-income children by offering a partial reimbursement to the schools for the costs of educating such children in secular subjects. But the Court viewed the subsidies as fostering an excessive entanglement between church and state. In the words of the Court, "A dedicated religious person, teaching at a school affiliated with his or her faith and operated to inculcate its tenets, will inevitably experience great difficulty in remaining religiously neutral" (Witte, 1999, p. 158).

The Lemon test asks the following: (1) Does the government's (in this case, the public school's) action fulfill a clear secular purpose? If it does not, a constitutional violation may result. (2) Does the government's action advance religion as a primary effect? If it does, again, a constitutional violation may be the consequence. And (3) Does the effect of the government's action foster an "entanglement" with a religion? Entanglement, in the context of schooling, can mean any number of things. For instance, if important school personnel, such as a teacher or principal, display behaviors that can be interpreted as being strongly associated with a religious point of view, one could argue that the effect is entanglement. The courts are especially concerned about the actions of teachers because of their influence on pupils and because of the role model expectation placed on teacher behavior. For instance, a teacher who offers a sectarian prayer in class clearly becomes entangled with a sectarian view and, by implication, privileges or advances a sectarian view in the presence of students. This would be tantamount to the establishment of a religion in the school. The idea of entanglement, as a criterion for judging establishment issues, emphasizes the importance that the Court placed on government neutrality. As Chief Justice Burger stated, "The general principle is that we will not tolerate either government established religion or government interference with religion. Short of those expressly proscribed government acts, there is ample room for play in the joints productive of a benevolent neutrality which will permit religious exercise without sponsorship and without interference" (Witte, 1999, pp. 157–58).

In recent years, the Supreme Court has criticized and even departed from the Lemon test. Historically, the Lemon test was the best example of the Supreme Court treating church and state concerns from the standpoint of strict neutrality and strict separation. Although today's Supreme Court has not entirely rebuffed the Lemon test, and its commitment to neutrality and separation, it has explored other criteria for legal interpretation. One is the coercion test, which is simply a way of saying that there must be clear evidence of government coercion in moving individuals to profess or accept a religion for a violation of the Establishment Clause to exist. Such a test, which is largely supported by political conservatives and others favoring an increased role for religion in schooling, would open up new channels between the school and church, making "lack of coercion" the defining element for the expression of religious views in the school. The question, of course, revolves around legal nuances in operational definitions of "coercion"—whether, for instance, audible school prayer could represent a form of indirect or subtle coercion, as it might arise from social pressures and the desire to yield to school-sponsored norms. Still, coercion, as a term, has a connotation of exercise by force or by penalty of law, a standard that would probably increase the options for religion in the school experience. Anything less than coercion could be allowed. Justice William Kennedy has argued that permitting the noncoercive endorsement of religion in school is fundamentally constitutional, because it is the only way to prevent the unconstitutional practice of state hostility to religion (Finkelman, 2000, p. 96). This is another way of saying that, if the school has to maintain neutrality and separation with regard to religious concerns, which is the case under the Lemon test, the result will be the secularization of religion—which violates the Free Exercise Clause.

Another way of judging Establishment Clause concerns is through something known as the endorsement test, which essentially means that government action must be struck down if it has the purpose or effect of endorsing a religion (McCarthy, Cambron-McCabe, and Thomas, 1998). The endorsement standard is similar to the Lemon framework. In fact, it is a kind of reinterpretation of the Lemon test stating that, even if the school causes, as a primary effect, the advancement of a religion (one prong of the Lemon test), its action ultimately must be judged according to whether evidence exists that the effect is government endorsement of a religion. The endorsement test could be viewed as the weaker sister of the Lemon test, because it leaves open the possibility that schools could be entangled with religious points of views without necessarily endorsing them. The endorsement test was conceived by Justice Sandra Day O'Connor in her effort to distinguish between government actions that advance religion and government actions that advance and endorse a religious point of view. "What is crucial," O'Connor stated, "is that government practice not have the effect of communicating a message of government endorsement or disapproval of religion" (Finkelman, 2000, p. 287). Thus, if a school celebrates, say, the Easter season, such a celebration would be unconstitutional only if it could be shown to endorse that particular religious point of view.

Yet another way to judge Establishment Clause concerns involves what is known as nonpreferentialism, or equal treatment. This position, favored by Chief Justice William Rehnquist, recasts the relation between church and state by saying, in effect, that the government can actively support religion as long as it does so equally and nonpreferentially for all denominations

(Patrick and Long, 1999). Thus, financial aid to religious schools, under nonpreferentialism, is no problem as long as funds are equally and nonpreferentially distributed. Just how nonpreferentialism would apply to issues like school prayer is not clear. Under such a doctrine, the school might have to offer any number of denominational prayers on an equal opportunity basis.

The Courts and the Free Exercise Clause. Establishment issues represent only half of the problems in the realm of church/school relations. Schools also need to be conscious about not showing hostility toward or interfering with the personal religious convictions of students. This is the central concern of the Free Exercise Clause. In dealing with the Free Exercise Clause, the courts have to weigh the interests of the school to conduct its mandate against the religious expression rights of the individual. In this balancing test, the courts must try to determine the sincerity and legitimacy of individual religious views, the extent to which such views might be impeded by government action, and the extent to which an important state interest is served in imposing some limit or burden on the exercise of particular religious views. These are the factors that are "balanced." Everyone, of course, is free to think and believe according to his or her own will, but there are qualified restrictions on the freedom to engage in public religious activities in school (Sendor, 1988). For example, the Free Exercise Clause will not protect disruptive religious observances or religious views that pose an unreasonable hardship on the school.

In cases in which classroom activities are viewed by parents as impeding the free exercise of their childrens' religious beliefs, an excusal policy or alternative assignment might be used. If a certain book or school assignment, for instance, offends an individual's religious view, the teacher typically will find another book or assignment. But the school might not always be able to offer alternative experiences, for any number of reasons, or it might believe that an excusal from a particular assignment or book is inappropriate and educationally unsound. For instance, in 1972, in *Wright v. Houston Independent School District,* a Texas court refused to allow students to be excused from classes on evolution because of religious objections to the theory. The court was not convinced that the teaching of evolution was a burden on the free exercise rights of the students. At the same time, in *West Virginia Board of Education v. Burnett,* in 1943, the Supreme Court found mandatory school exercises, such as the flag salute and Pledge of Allegiance, to be unconstitutional because of free exercise issues.

The Supreme Court, in *Wisconsin v. Yoder* (1972), even found free exercise violations in mandatory school attendance requirements. In Wisconsin, all children between the ages of 7 and 16 are required to attend school. When Jonas Yoder refused to send his children to school after they completed the eighth grade, the state prosecuted him. Yoder, who was a member of an Amish community, claimed a violation of his First Amendment free exercise rights. His refusal to send his children to school was dictated by a desire to keep them away from competing views that might undermine the religious communitarianism that marked the Amish way of life. The key word here is "religious." The Supreme Court, using a balancing test, sided with Yoder, holding that, because Amish culture was rooted in centuries of religious thought, it was valid grounds for an exemption from the attendance requirement. In other words, the very act of going to school was seen as a burden on the religious views of the community. The Court, however, also noted that this was a unique situation and that, if the exemption for the Amish resulted in any disruption to the state system of schooling, it would be withdrawn.

In more recent years, the well-known *Mozert v. Hawkins County* (1988) case illustrates the tension between the exercise of school policies and practices and the Free Exercise Clause. The case raised questions about how far schools must go to protect individual religious expression when someone accuses their own policies and practices of offending individual religious views.

It all started when a group of fundamentalist Christians objected to the required reading materials used in the Hawkins County elementary school, materials that the group claimed violated the Free Exercise Clause of the Constitution. Their children, they asserted, were being forced to read materials objectionable to their religious faith. They further claimed that the reading series used in the school promoted a secular religion that supported world government, nontraditional gender roles, moral relativism, nonreligious views of death, critical views of the founders of the country, socialism, universal communication, magic, environmentalism, disarmament, gun control, kindness to animals, vegetarianism, negative views of hunting and war, and several other unacceptable perspectives (Delfattore, 1992).

The parents offered many examples. They objected, for instance, to the reading and teaching of the Jack London story, "To Build a Fire." The main character in this short story is a Yukon traveler who accidentally gets his feet and legs wet, which in the Yukon can be a life-threatening condition. The man has to build a fire to survive, but when he fails because of a series of bad decisions, his death is inevitable. The parents complained that the man failed to recognize that God was responsible for the physical survival of individuals and failed to pray for wisdom and salvation. The children who read the story would not learn that it was the will and wisdom of God, not the shortcomings of the man, that dictated his destiny. The complainants also objected to the fact that the man's death made no reference to an after-life. This lack of reference presumably taught children to accept the human-istic view that there is no God and no hereafter, a view that was highly offensive to the parents (Delfattore, 1992). The parents had similar objec-tions to the *Wizard of Oz* and *Cinderella,* in which, it was alleged, the satanic practice of witchcraft is condoned. Clearly, the plaintiffs simply did not want their children to be exposed to any ideas that went against their par-ticular religious views. The issue was whether the school had to accommo-date such views because they were based on religion.

The school's response to these complaints was that it was simply con-ducting reading instruction, well within its secular mandate, and that it could not, given the importance of reading instruction to all academic achievement, excuse the children from such instruction. The school further maintained that critical reading was one of the key components to the read-ing program, a skill that would allow all children to read all material with a critical, if not nonaccepting, eye. Finally, the school claimed that it could not provide an alternative reading program because of the number of stu-dents involved and the integrative nature of reading instruction in the sub-ject matter of the curriculum. The school consequently asserted that any accommodation would be disruptive to the whole school and would result in considerable financial duress for the school.

A circuit court eventually agreed that there was indeed a free exercise violation and that the stories did indeed pose a threat to the religious sensibilities of the children. Observing that a uniform series of books and stories was not a necessary condition for teaching children to read, the court looked for a solution in some accommodation strategy. It under-stood, however, that asking the school to provide an alternative assignment in alignment with the religious views of the children might constitute an establishment violation. So, instead, it ordered the school to provide a read-ing program outside of the school and suggested that the children be taught privately. This meant that the complainants' children would now do their reading at home or in some other private setting, apparently in accordance with their religious faith.

This ruling, however, was eventually overturned by an appeals court panel. The judges on the panel argued that the mere exposure to beliefs in books did not constitute an active advocacy for or against a particular reli-gion. All areas of learning, after all, have the potential to communicate val-ues that might offend a student's or parent's religious beliefs. The court also stated that, because reading was integrated into other aspects of the curriculum, the removal of students from the reading class would have a ripple effect throughout the curriculum and seriously undermine the whole educational process. The court further observed that, even if the school offended the religious views of the plaintiffs, it did so with a compelling state interest in mind.

In the end, the plaintiffs lost the case, but there were lessons learned for public school authorities. The *Mozert* case made it clear that school districts should honor excusal requests from parents as long as such requests do not result in unreasonable financial, pedagogical, or administrative hardships for the school and as long as the overall educational environment of the school is not disrupted.

School Prayer

Historically, the schools used biblical texts and invoked Christian prayers with some frequency. Over the years, however, school prayer has been litigated as a First Amendment violation, and the courts have, by and large, judged that the conditions of the Establishment Clause ("to make no law respecting the establishment of a religion") could not be met when one considered the place of prayer in the school (Sendor, 1988). Generally, the courts found that, by allowing audible prayer and Bible reading, the school district (the government) was no longer acting toward a clear secular purpose and was advancing religion as a primary effect (see, for example, *Engel v. Vitale* [1962] and *Abington v. Schempp* [1963]).

In *Engel v. Vitale,* the landmark case on school prayer, the Supreme Court ruled that the state of New York could not require the daily recitation of a state-composed prayer in its public schools. The schoolchildren in the state started each school day with the following prayer: "Almighty God, we acknowledge our dependence upon Thee, and we beg Thy blessing upon us, our parents, our teachers and our country." Even though the prayer was voluntary and nondenominational, it was nevertheless publicly practiced and was ultimately viewed by the Court as promoting religious practice. The Court, in effect, declared that any state-sponsored prayer—voluntary or not, denominational or not—was a violation of the Establishment Clause. In writing the majority opinion, Justice Hugo Black observed that "it is no part of the government to compose official prayers" (Patrick and Long, 1999, p. 162). The *Engel* ruling unleashed widespread public fury, causing the Court to engage in the unprecedented event of explaining its decision to the press (Finkelman, 2000, p. 442). In *Abington v. Schempp,* the Court extended the logic of *Engel* by not allowing Abington High School to dedicate any time to prayer or to Bible readings. The school had selected various biblical verses to read over the school's public address system, but the Court found these to be purely religious exercises. These early rulings revealed the Court's inclination to demand neutrality from the school on issues related to religion.

In his dissent to this ruling, Justice Potter Stewart asserted that prohibitions against prayer were less a manifestation of state neutrality and more a representation of state hostility toward and discrimination against religious exercises. Stewart outlined the basic elements of the coercion test, arguing that voluntary noncoercive prayer, free from embarrassment and pressures, should be allowable (Finkelman, 2000, p. 442). Feature 9-5 excerpts Black's majority opinion and Stewart's dissent. And Stewart went further and maintained that the refusal to permit noncoercive religious experiences in school resulted in the establishment of the religion of secularism. The majority opinion in *Schempp* took this accusation seriously and stressed the fact that prohibitions against sectarian prayer and the reading of sacred texts could not be interpreted as an endorsement of a secular religion. There was nothing in the two cases that precluded the study of the Bible or religion in the school experience. Such study was allowable if it fulfilled a manifestly secular school purpose.

Because there is constitutional protection for the freedom to hold religious beliefs, the school cannot prevent individuals or groups from engaging in private prayers, as long as such prayers are voluntary, nonofficial, and nondisruptive. The school cannot tell students that they may not pray, and students can pray to themselves at any time. In fact, private prayer is a protected right in the public schools. What the school cannot do is condone any form of public prayer.

However, the courts have treated so-called moments of silence more leniently because they are less vulnerable to being interpreted as violating the conditions of the Establishment Clause. If the school designates a "moment of silence" or "silent meditation" without formally sanctioning prayer or any other denominational method of reflection, it will likely be on more solid constitutional ground than if it refers to a period of "voluntary prayer." This was the issue in *Wallace v. Jaffree* (1985), which involved a father's effort to stop his daughters' school from practicing voluntary devotional exercises. In 1978, the Alabama legislature had passed a law mandating that each school day begin with a moment of silence for meditation purposes. In 1981, the legislature added the option of voluntary prayer to the law, and in 1982, it added further that willing students could be led in prayer by teachers. Jaffree, a resident of Mobile County and an avowed agnostic, had complained to the school about the ridicule his daughters

9-5 THE HISTORICAL CONTEXT
Engel v. Vitale (1962)

The 1962 ruling in *Engel v. Vitale* was historic because it explicitly struck down public prayer in the school. It was not a popular decision with the majority of Americans, but the Supreme Court was almost unanimous, voting 8 to 1, in ruling against state-mandated public prayer in school. The following are excerpts taken from the statements of the justices who offered both the majority and dissenting views (quoted in Patrick and Long, 1999, pp. 162–63).

Justice Hugo Black offered the majority opinion:

We think that by using the public school system to encourage recitation of the Regents' prayer, the State of New York has adopted a practice wholly inconsistent with the Establishment Clause. There can, of course, be no doubt that New York's program of daily classroom invocation of God's blessings, as prescribed in the Regents' prayer, is a religious activity. It is a solemn avowal of divine faith and supplication for the blessings of the Almighty. . . .

Justice Hugo L. Black.

Neither the fact that the prayer may be denominationally neutral nor the fact that its observance on the part of the students is voluntary can serve to free it from the limitations of the Establishment Clause. . . . The Establishment Clause . . . does not depend upon showing of direct government compulsion and is violated by the enactment of laws which establish an official religion whether those laws operate directly to coerce nonobserving individuals or not.

Justice Potter Stewart delivered the dissent:

With all respect, I think the court has misapplied a great constitutional principle. I cannot see how an "official religion" is established by letting those who want to say a prayer say it. On the contrary, I think that to deny the wish of these school children to join in reciting this prayer is to deny them the opportunity of sharing in the spiritual heritage of our Nation. . . .

Justice Potter Stewart.

endured as a result of their nonparticipation in any of the exercises. Eventually, he took his concerns to court. The Court struck down all provisions except the 1978 statute, largely because it was the only one that was free and clear from any reference to or entanglement with official prayer.

A period of meditation seems to be more closely attached to a secular purpose. It has no real connection with advancing a religion, because youths who are asked to participate in moments of silence (or meditation) can presumably think about anything they choose to. All this assumes, however, that there is no compulsion in the school to embrace a particular form of reflection or meditation. This means that teachers have to be scrupulous about their own behaviors during official moments of silence. Some school districts have instructed their teachers not to bow their heads, fold their hands, close their eyes, or otherwise hint that they may actually be praying (When quiet is pervasive in schools, 1994). The concern here is with the issue of perceived teacher entanglement with a religious or prayerful view. Laws mandating a moment of silence at the beginning of the school day exist in Alabama, Georgia, South Carolina, and Tennessee; several other states allow for a moment of silence but do not require it. In any event, some legal scholars believe that the Supreme Court will hear a case on silent meditation in the near future (Finkelman, 2000, p. 445).

A variation of this problem is the issue of prayer held at special school ceremonies. The Supreme Court, in *Lee v. Weisman* (1992), held that prayers at graduation ceremonies advance religion, noting the importance of the event in the lives of the students and the coercive elements at work in attending and participating (or passively listening) to an explicit state religious exercise. But the Supreme Court is divided on this issue, and it is likely that another case will be needed to bring it all into better focus. Some legal arguments favor school prayer at graduation ceremonies. The claim is that there should be little concern over Establishment Clause issues because the exercise is not an official part of the school curriculum program and can be viewed as ceremonial rather than educational in purpose. Moreover, because attendance at such events typically is voluntary and because many adults usually are present, there is less concern over potential proselytizing. This is a fundamentally different scenario from, say, prayer at a mandatory public school meeting (pep rallies, assemblies, homeroom activities, and other special school events) without the buffeting presence of parents. The use of devotional or prayerful student speech at graduation ceremonies likely will turn out to be easier to protect because it is harder to argue that such speech is government speech endorsing religion, which the Establishment Clause forbids, as opposed to private speech endorsing religion, which the Free Exercise Clause protects (McCarthy, Cambron-McCabe,

---

FIGURE 9-5
Principles and Guidelines on School Prayer

---

1. School-sponsored prayer is unconstitutional. Prayers cannot be offered in classrooms or in opening morning exercises.

2. Moments of silence, as long as they are voluntary and not part of any devotional activity, are less likely to violate the Establishment Clause.

3. Individual or group prayer is protected as long as it is done in private and does not disrupt the school.

4. Prayers offered at school-sponsored events outside regular school hours are judged by the context of the event. Prayers offered at graduation ceremonies are typically viewed as less problematic because these are ceremonial events that attract many adults. Prayers are easier to protect if they are student-led than if they are part of the school's program.

---

and Thomas, 1998). However, this legal argument has yet to be recognized as valid by the Supreme Court. In fact, in 2000, the Supreme Court held that student-led public prayer at high school football games was an Establishment Clause violation. In a 6-3 decision, the Court ruled that school-sanctioned prayer at Santa Fe (Texas) High School was unconstitutional. The school had implemented a policy that allowed the student population to choose two students to recite a prayer before each football game. But the Court interpreted the student-led prayers as representing school support (and by extension, government support) for a religious point of view. It did not view the prayers as solely private speech. As Justice John Paul Stevens put it, "An objective Santa Fe High School student will unquestionably perceive the inevitable pregame prayer as stamped with her school's seal of approval" (Walsh, 2000). Figure 9-5 summarizes the current principles and guidelines for school prayer.

Religious Holidays and Religious Symbols

The observation of holidays that have clear religious overtones is also an issue that has been debated in the courts. Holidays such as Christmas, Easter, St. Patrick's Day, and others are all religious occasions with some basis in secularity. One could argue that Christmas, through the actions of some people, has actually become a kind of commercial holiday without any religious affiliation. According to the three conditions of the Lemon test, a school cannot observe holidays like these if such observations advance a religious belief or fail to reflect a clear secular purpose. Thus, holidays such as Christmas can be observed in the school as long as the instruction is clearly secular in orientation. Teachers can discuss the commercial aspects of the holiday, the folklore surrounding it, and its festival traditions, but if they raise ideas related to the celebration of the birth of Jesus, who is seen by Christians as the savior of the world, they will likely be on shaky Establishment Clause grounds.

Classroom and school displays fall under the same principle. During the winter holiday season, displays of snowflakes, wreaths, and even Santa Clauses usually reflect a secular intention to enjoy the gaiety of the season and can be offered without much problem. Displays that come closer to sanctioning the actual sacred character of Christmas, such as Christmas trees—which, despite being a paganistic symbol historically, could still be symbolically viewed as a place where gifts are offered in celebration of the birth of Jesus—are more problematic. Actual portraits of Jesus and his birthplace in the manger are probably out of the question unless, again, they are offered with a clear secular purpose in mind.

In a recent case in Kentucky, the public schools of Harlan County displayed a copy of the Ten Commandments on their walls. Knowing that it had to secure a secular purpose to mount such a display, the school showcased the Ten Commandments along with other important historical documents, claiming that the exhibit was little more than a history of the American government. But a district court judge disagreed, ruling that the inclusion of the Ten Commandments served no secular purposes and was patently religious in nature. The judge issued an order to have the display removed (Federal judge orders, 2000).

Music teachers who direct school choir and band performances during various holiday seasons have sometimes run into trouble in this area. Can "Silent Night," for instance, be sung without violating the Establishment Clause? Unambiguous references to a "holy night" and to "Christ, the savior" seem to suggest a religious intent. But a song like "Silent Night" can, in fact, be offered with secular intent. The teacher simply has to demonstrate that the choice of songs to be performed by the students advances a secular learning purpose. The teacher might justify the singing of "Silent Night" on the grounds that the song has secular artistic value; after all, many of the world's greatest musical compositions are religious in orientation. But the more likely rationale for the singing of "Silent Night" would be to appreciate and recognize festival songs typically sung during the winter holiday season. To make such an argument, however, the teacher must teach the

The religious apparel of students generally cannot be regulated unless it is found to be disruptive to the learning environment of the school.

students to perform other festival songs, including perhaps Hanukkah and Kwanza songs. Thus, the performance of "Silent Night" might not be viewed as an Establishment Clause issue if the teacher can show that it was one of several important festival songs sung by the choir in the interests of fostering appreciation for and recognition of a variety of winter holiday songs. If, however, the song was sung for devotional purposes or without any palpable secular purpose in mind, it could be viewed as an Establishment Clause violation.

Similar controversies are raised when a teacher openly wears religious apparel to school. Some courts have reasoned that attire itself is not objectionable because it represents an affiliation with a faith but not the open promotion of a faith. As long as the attire is not part of an overt attempt by the teacher to impose personal religious views on others, it is not a problem. Other courts have maintained that the wearing of religious attire on a daily basis represents a subtle signal about religious faith and leads to clear associations between the supervisory authority (the teacher) and a particular religious faith, which itself would be indicative of an excessive entanglement of school personnel with a religion (Sendor, 1988).

Students, of course, generally have no restrictions on their religious apparel unless it disrupts the learning environment. This was precisely the problem that surfaced in an interesting case in California. Three elementary school students of the Sikh faith were banned by their principal from carrying their sacred knives, 4-inch blades known as kirpans, to school. The students, whose faith required them to carry their kirpans as a sign of their devotion to God, were in violation of the schools' weapons policy, and in the mind of the principal, they created an unsafe condition for learning. The question was whether the safety and security of the student population was compromised by the presence of kirpans and whether the Sikh students were subjected to an unreasonable burden on their freedom of religious expression. A circuit court ruled in the favor of the Sikhs, stating that every reasonable accommodation had to be made to allow the Sikh youngsters to wear their knives. In this case, the court, using a balancing test, was convinced that the Free Exercise Clause could be secured without harming the educative environment of the school. The court, in fact, suggested that certain safeguards be taken, such as blunting the knives and sewing them into their cloth sheaths (Sikh students return, 1994).

In a more recent case, a pair of students in an Indiana school fought for their right to wear pentagrams as symbols of their Wiccan religion. The girls were working in a junior teaching program that brought them in contact with third-grade students when they were dismissed from the program over fears that the five-pointed pentagrams were satanic and therefore disruptive to the school. The court, however, failed to find any evidence of disruption caused by the wearing of the pentagrams and so ruled in favor of the students, allowing them to return to the program wearing their pentagrams (Federal judge upholds, 2000). Figure 9-6 summarizes the principles and guidelines for religious holidays and symbols in the schools.

The Teaching of Creationism

In recent years, objections have been raised over the manner in which science educators have privileged the theory of evolution over biblical accounts of the origins of human life. The controversy, of course, dates back to the Scopes monkey trial of 1925, when it was argued that even in science class teaching should not conflict with the Bible. As late as the 1960s, several states had laws on the books prohibiting the teaching of evolution. In 1968, a schoolteacher in Arkansas challenged the antievolution law in her state on the grounds that it existed for the sole purpose of privileging a sectarian view of human origin. In *Epperson v. Arkansas* (1968), the Supreme Court agreed with this position and ruled the Arkansas law unconstitutional.

FIGURE 9-6
Principles and Guidelines on Religious Holidays and Religious Symbols

1. Religious holidays that have some basis in secularity may be treated in the school experience as long as a secular school purpose is being fulfilled.

2. Religious songs, symbols, and displays are allowable if used for a legitimate secular school purpose.

3. Teachers may not wear religious garb or religious jewelry if it is found to have the effect of promoting a religious faith. Teacher dress may not be stridently and obviously religious in its visual effect.

4. Schools must make reasonable accommodations to students' religious views, including accommodations related to religious dress and the wearing of religious symbols. Only if the school can demonstrate or anticipate that the student dress will have (or has had) some disruptive impact on the school can it be limited.

But the issue was still not resolved. Believing that the courts would uphold a balanced treatment of creationism and evolution, some states sought to gain equal standing for the two competing views in the science curriculum. The belief was that, if the secular purpose was to teach the origins of humankind, creationism had a legitimate place in the school curriculum. Creationism, after all, certainly had no less to say about the secular topic of human origins than did evolutionary theory.

As a consequence, Tennessee introduced a law in 1971 requiring an "equal amount of emphasis" on alternative theories, including, of course, the Genesis account, and in 1981, Arkansas and Louisiana followed suit (Fraser, 1999). It was not long, however, before the courts were involved. In 1982, in *McLean v. Arkansas Board of Education,* a federal court found that Arkansas' balanced treatment statute violated the Establishment Clause. Specifically, the court flatly asserted that creationism was not a science. The teaching of a scientific theory such as evolution had to be sanctioned by a method of science, not by a preexisting religious faith. The fact that the National Academy of Science, a distinguished association of scientists, did not recognize creationism as a science added weight to the argument. The court also noted the emphasis given in the statute to creationist literature as an alternative to the theory of evolution, which it took as evidence that the law was less interested in posing alternative views than in promoting a particular alternative view, one with clear linkages to the Bible.

A similar situation prevailed in Louisiana. In the Louisiana law, known as the Creationism Act, the schools were obligated, as a matter of fairness and neutrality, to teach evolution on an equal basis with creation science, or not to teach it at all. In *Edwards v. Aguillard* (1987), the state portrayed its mandate for equal time as reasonable because evidence could be brought into the science classroom to support and to refute both evolutionary and creationist views of the world. But the legal challenge offered against the Louisiana law also claimed that the state's effort was moved by the singular purpose of promoting a sectarian view in the science curriculum. Few could deny the fact that creationism was an unambiguously Christian version of truth that the school was being asked to legitimate as science. The teaching of the origins of humankind was indeed a secular purpose, but the place of creationism in such a context could not be justified on secular (scientific) grounds. Using the Lemon test, the Supreme Court struck down the Louisiana law, arguing that it was designed primarily to benefit or advance one particular religious belief (one prong of the Lemon test).

In 1995, the issue was again tested, but this time in the context of the classroom. In Capistrano, California, a schoolteacher refused to follow the district's requirement to teach evolution in science class. The teacher claimed that evolution was a religion and that the requirement to teach it was a patent infringement on the Establishment Clause. Yet again, the courts disagreed, ruling that in biology class evolution has a legitimate secular claim while creationism does not (Fischer, Schimmel, and Kelly, 1999).

Despite these rulings, creationism continues to find its way into the news. One recent controversy revolved around the decision of the Kansas State of Board of Education to keep any reference to evolution out of the state-approved standards for science education. Because local control prevails in Kansas, local schools are free to set their own standards, which means they can comfortably ignore evolution in the science curriculum (Kansas evolution controversy, 1999). Critics assert that this turns out to be little more than an effort to impose a de facto prohibition on the teaching of evolution.

Interestingly, creationism can be taught in the schools, but under a different secular objective. If one wanted to teach it in a comparative religion class or in a class dedicated to religious views on the origin of humanity, no violation would occur. As a science, however, it poses an Establishment Clause violation because it offers a religious message for a nonreligious purpose. Figure 9-7 summarizes the principles and guidelines in the teaching of creationism.

FIGURE 9-7

Principles and Guidelines on the Teaching of Creationism

1. Creationism may be taught in the school when justified by a reasonable secular purpose, as in a comparative religion class or a class that explores different views of human origin.

2. State laws prohibiting the teaching of evolution have been struck down as Establishment Clause violations because their intent was to erect an alternative sectarian view on the origins of humankind.

3. State laws mandating equal treatment of evolution and creationism have been struck down as Establishment Clause violations because their intent was to support an alternative sectarian view on the origins of humankind.

4. Evolution has been declared to be a legitimate scientific theory in the context of science education, and not a secular religion posing an Establishment Clause threat.

State Aid to Religious Schools

Public funds have long been used to aid children attending private schools, including religious or parochial schools. The design of the aid structure has been based on something known as the child benefit doctrine. That is, public monies may be directed to the education of children attending private school if the children are the primary beneficiaries of the money, but not if the aid is viewed as primarily benefiting the religious institution (see *Board of Education v. Allen* [1968]). Thus, public transportation aid and aid in the form of loaned textbooks and other instructional materials generally are permissible under the child benefit doctrine. But aid in the form of physical space and certain instructional services is viewed as benefiting the religious enterprise per se.

But even under the child benefit doctrine, states can offer aid to religious schools only under certain conditions. In the 1985 *Aguilar v. Felton* ruling, the Supreme Court barred public school teachers from going into parochial schools to provide federally sponsored remedial education to disadvantaged students (a program justified under Title 1 of the Elementary and Secondary School Act). The prohibition against public school teachers working on parochial school grounds did not mean that parochial school children would be denied Title 1 services. Such services were their right according to the child benefit doctrine. But it did affect where such services would be provided. Because of the *Aguilar* ruling, the federal government spent $100 million building and operating off-site mobile classrooms for the purpose of providing Title 1 services to children attending parochial schools (Fraser, 1999).

In *Aguilar,* the Court found that, because the Title 1 remedial instruction put public school employees on parochial school grounds, it created a symbolic link between religion and schooling (an entanglement) that had the effect of advancing religion. Even though teachers participating in the program had been instructed to avoid involvement in religious activity and were monitored in an attempt to guard against the dissemination of religious views, the Court believed that their presence in the religious setting of the school (and the accompanying mechanism of state supervision) constituted state sanctioning of a religious point of view. Under the conditions of the partnership between public and private school personnel, educators would have worked together to resolve issues related to scheduling, classroom assignments, and instructional implementation. And this amounted to excessive entanglement.

In the same year, in *School District of the City of Grand Rapids v. Ball,* the Supreme Court struck down a Michigan law aiming to publicly fund special education (remedial and enrichment) programs in nonpublic parochial schools, ruling that direct aid to an instructional program had the primary effect of advancing religion. In this case, public subsidies were used to fund a shared-time program in which public school teachers came into private schools and to make payments to parochial school teachers working in after-school programs. The Court was convinced that neither program could prove that it was neither advancing not inhibiting a religious point of view in educating these children.

But the Supreme Court fundamentally changed it outlook on both cases in 1997. The decisions in both *Aguilar* and *Ball* were overruled in the 1997 case of *Agostini v. Felton,* which revisited the earlier rulings. In the new ruling, the Court moved away from the Lemon test, with Justice O'Connor arguing that not all entanglements (one prong of the Lemon test) have the effect of advancing a religion. Because Title 1 services had to be offered to parochial school children, either on or off parochial school grounds, there would have to be some entanglement (Patrick and Long, 1999). The question was whether the entanglement was excessive. O'Connor felt that the safeguards in place related to the monitoring of teachers in the parochial settings and to the teachers' obligation to remain neutral on matters of religion protected against excessive entanglement. Justice David Souter, in dissent, observed that any state-sponsored instruction on parochial school grounds was excessive entanglement, and certainly more of an entanglement than would otherwise be the case. The setting, he argued, tempted the teacher to reflect the religious mission of the school.

State aid to parochial schools was also adjudicated from another angle. In 1972, New York State proposed a tuition reimbursement program for parents of children attending private schools (of which 90 percent were parochial schools), along with a program designed to funnel money to private schools for the maintenance and repair of their facilities. The law was challenged in the 1973 case of *Committee for Public Education and Religious Liberty v. Nyquist*. The Supreme Court's response to the law was to determine whether the two programs constituted an Establishment Clause violation. In examining the tuition reimbursement program, the Court could not find assurances that the money given to the parents would be used exclusively for secular purposes. To the Court, granting money to parents for the religious education of their children was tantamount to state sponsorship of religion. Similarly, the facilities maintenance fund was struck down because it, too, resulted in aid that had the primary benefit of subsidizing and advancing the religious mission of sectarian schools.

The issue of school vouchers is the latest wrinkle in the controversy over state aid to religious schools. On the one hand, the *Agostini* ruling makes it clear that the Court is willing to entertain the prospect of church/state entanglements that do not result in the endorsement of a particular religious point of view or that are noncoercive in nature. This might be a short step away from allowing public funds to be used to empower parental choice in a school voucher program that includes religious schools. On the other hand, the *Nyquist* ruling explicitly denies public revenue to parents for the religious education of their children. It seems, however, that the conceptual tide is moving more in the direction of the *Agostini* judgment.

In Wisconsin, in *Jackson v. Benson* (1998), for instance, the State Supreme Court allowed public monies to be used for the education of a limited group of low-income children in private schools, including private religious schools. The court ruled that the Milwaukee-based program, known as Milwaukee Parental Choice Program (MPCP), was upholding the principle of neutral and indirect aid to religious schools, the defining idea in *Agostini*. The court decided that giving public vouchers, worth over $4,000 per child, to a limited group of low-income parents simply allowed parents to decide which school best benefited their own children. The parents could use their vouchers to send their children to a private nonsectarian school or

9-6 DEBATING THE ISSUES
Publicly Supported Vouchers for Religious Education

Are school vouchers constitutional? The Supreme Court has yet to give a definitive answer to this controversial question. On one side of the argument is the traditional position of strict separation and neutrality. That is, any public money given to parents for the purpose of choosing a religious education for their children, no matter how the money is distributed, is a direct benefit to the religious enterprise itself and is therefore little more than public funding of religious instruction, which is unconstitutional. This is the position usually supported by the Lemon test, as it seeks to determine if the primary effect of a publicly supported program is secular. But according to the counterposition, using public money to empower parents to choose a school for their children's education actually passes the Lemon test, because it is driven by the fundamentally secular purpose of expanding choices for parents, which include private parochial and nonparochial schools as well as public schools. The latter argument was the essential basis for the 1998 State Supreme Court decision in Wisconsin in *Jackson v. Benson*.

What is your view on this matter? To get access to more information, read the excerpts from the *Jackson v. Benson* decision (Excerpts from the ruling, 1998), and read the legal analysis, researched and written by Susan Batte, questioning the constitutionality of vouchers, on the Separation of Church and State Home Page (www.au.org).

a private parochial school. They also, of course, had the nonvoucher option of the neighborhood school. And if their child attended a religious school with public money, the child could not be compelled to participate in school-based religious activities. Given the range of choices available, the court believed that the program in no way skewed the decision toward religion. To the court, the primary effect of the program was secular— to expand educational opportunities for low-income children in a low-performing school district. It is noteworthy that the court made no reference to entanglements; rather, it cited the maintenance of neutrality, a slight shift away from one prong of the Lemon test.

In 1998, the Supreme Court declined to review the constitutionality of MPCP. Although the decision by the Supreme Court not to review the case

---

FIGURE 9-8
Principles and Guidelines on State Aid to Religious Schools

1. Under the doctrine of child benefit, state aid may be offered to the direct benefit of a child schooled in a parochial setting. This would include transportation costs, certain instructional services, and any federally sponsored program designed to serve legislatively targeted student populations.

2. Title I services to parochial school children, as taught by public school teachers and supported with public money, may be offered in parochial schools. Certain monitoring safeguards are used to ensure that religion is not being advanced in such programs.

3. Limited voucher programs, which give low-income parents an opportunity to choose a school for their child from a menu of sectarian and nonsectarian schools, have been upheld in some states. The Supreme Court has not yet offered an opinion on these programs.

---

has no legal standing, it does send a positive political message to other states attempting limited voucher programs. In fact, a similar program has been launched in Cleveland, Ohio, although it encountered some legal turmoil when a judge found that the participating schools were overwhelmingly religious, which resulted in options being skewed in the direction of religion. Feature 9-6 gives more information on the voucher controversy; Figure 9-8 summarizes the principles and guidelines for state aid to religious schools.

SUMMARY

The governance structure of the American public schools resides within the states, as guaranteed by the Tenth Amendment to the Constitution. Despite the decentralized nature of the educational system, the nation's schools have some semblance of commonality. They are organized broadly along elementary, intermediate, and secondary school lines, and within a unified system of education that, in most cases, represents one progression from the elementary school to postsecondary options. The main administrative base for almost all public schools is the state board of education (and its partner, the state department of education), which regulates the extent and the nature of local participation and involvement in public schooling. School are funded mostly from state and local coffers, with the state monitoring financial disparities among districts and implementing monetary distribution plans designed to keep the gaps in spending among districts within a reasonable range. The federal government's financial role in schooling is limited largely to categorical aid for special needs students.

The relation between church and state priorities in the schools is defined by two clauses in the First Amendment to the Constitution: "Congress shall make no law respecting an establishment of religion, or prohibiting the free exercise thereof." The Supreme Court has adjudicated many cases that posed a threat to the First Amendment, as summarized in Figure 9-9. Since the 1970s, a guiding legal mechanism known as the Lemon test has been used to determine violations. The Lemon test, which underscores the importance of government neutrality in and separation from religious concerns, has in recent years fallen out of favor with the Court. But it still remains, with some modifications, the main test for determining First Amendment violations.

QUESTIONS AND ACTIVITIES

1. Why is the ninth grade typically excluded from the middle school arrangement?

2. Why is the self-contained classroom more popular in elementary schools than in secondary schools?

3. What is the fundamental difference between a comprehensive high school and a specialized secondary school?

4. What makes a state governor especially influential in public education?

5. Explain the relation between local and state school authorities.

6. What were some of the more significant educational initiatives sponsored by the federal government over the years?

7. What was at issue in the case of *Rodriguez v. the San Antonio Independent School District?*

8. What is the main difference between flat-grant and foundation financial programs?

9. Why do foundation programs often fail to have much impact on local funding disparities?

10. How does a reliance on property taxes help create funding inequities in public education?

11. What basic change occurred in California in school funding in the wake of the *Serrano v. Priest* ruling?

12. What is a minimal provision philosophy in the area of school finance?

13. Explain the Establishment and Free Exercise clauses as they relate to the relation between church and state.

14. Describe the main features of the Lemon test.

15. What other tests has the Supreme Court used to determine constitutional violations of the First Amendment?

16. Why is a moment of silent meditation probably more defensible in terms of Establishment Clause violation than public prayer?

17. What is a balancing test, and what are the main factors used in it?

18. Defend the position of the plaintiffs in the *Mozert v. Hawkins* case. Make the case for a free exercise violation.

19. How have the courts dealt with the place of creationism in science education?

20. Can religion be properly and honestly integrated in the school curriculum? If so, how?

21. What are the essential rules governing "religious dress" among teachers and among students?

22. How can a music teacher get away with teaching a song such as "Silent Night" during the winter holiday season?

23. What is the child benefit doctrine?

24. Explain the fundamental shift in thinking that occurred on the Supreme Court between the first ruling on *Aguilar v. Felton* and the later ruling on *Agostini v. Felton*.

25. Investigate one of the cases listed in Figure 9-9. Focus on whether the violation was an establishment or free exercise issue. Explain the rationale behind the thinking of both the majority and the dissenting opinions.

REFERENCES

Cremin, L. A. (1951). *The American common school: A historic conception.* (New York: Teachers College, Columbia University).

Delfattore, J. (1992). *What Johnny shouldn't read.* (New Haven, CT: Yale University Press).

Douglas, H. R., and Greider, C. (1948). *American public education.* (New York: Ronald Press).

Excerpts from the ruling in *Jackson v. Benson.* (1998). *Education Week* (17 June).

Everson v. Board of Education (1947)

Can the cost of public transportation for children attending parochial schools be supported with public money? The Court approved the public payment for transportation under the child benefit doctrine, but in doing so, it described broad separationist lines between church and state.

Engel v. Vitale (1962)

Can audible and public nondenominational prayer be offered in school by school officials? The Court found any official public prayer, denominational or not, to be unconstitutional.

Abington v. Schempp (1963)

Can Bible verses or the Lord's Prayer be publicly read or recited in school under official school sanction? The Court found such Bible readings unconstitutional.

Epperson v. Arkansas (1968)

Can the state of Arkansas uphold a law prohibiting the teaching of evolution? The Court found such a law to be an Establishment Clause violation and thus unconstitutional.

Board of Education v. Allen (1968)

Can school textbooks be loaned to private parochial schools? The Court found such loans to be clear of Establishment Clause violations and thus constitutional.

Lemon v. Kurtzman (1971)

Can public subsidies be used to support the teaching of secular subjects in parochial schools? The Court found such support to be unconstitutional because of the entanglement of religious personnel in the teaching of secular subjects.

Wisconsin v. Yoder (1972)

Can certain groups be exempted from mandatory school attendance on religious grounds? The Court ruled affirmatively but made it clear that the case for religious exemption was unique and would be withdrawn if it disrupted the state school system.

Committee v. Nyquist (1973)

Can parents with children attending parochial school be reimbursed by the state? The Court ruled that a New York law attempting to do this was unconstitutional.

Aguilar v. Felton (1985)

Can public school teachers, supported by Title I funds, teach parochial school students on the grounds of the parochial schools? The Court ruled that such an arrangement was unconstitutional. The remedial education of children attending religious schools must occur off grounds if it is supported by Title I funds.

Grand Rapids v. Ball (1985)

Can public monies be used to support the special education of parochial school children (remedial and enrichment) in a shared-time program with public school teachers? The Court ruled the program unconstitutional because its primary effect was to advance religion.

Wallace v. Jaffree (1985)

Can a state pass a law requiring a moment of silent meditation or voluntary prayer at the beginning of the school day? The court struck down such a law in Alabama as unconstitutional.

Edwards v. Aguillard (1987)

Can a state pass a law requiring the equal or balanced treatment of creationism and evolution in the science curriculum? The Court struck down such a law in Louisiana as unconstitutional.

Lee v. Weisman (1992)

Can school prayers be offered at graduation ceremonies? The Court ruled school sponsored prayer at graduation ceremonies to be unconstitutional.

Agostini v. Felton (1997)

Is the original *Aguilar v. Felton* ruling still valid? The Court overturned the original ruling, clearing the way for public school teachers to offer federally sponsored remedial education to children attending religious schools.

Federal judge orders religious codes out of Kentucky schools, courthouses. (2000). By the Associated Press *Freedom forum online* (8 May). (www.freedomforum.org).

Federal judge upholds Indiana students' right to wear Wiccan symbols. (2000). By the Associated Press *Freedom forum online* (1 May). (www.freedomforum.org).

Finkelman, P. (2000). *Religion and American law.* (New York: Garland).

Fischer, L., Schimmel, D., and Kelly, C. (1999). *Teachers and the law,* 5th ed. (White Plains, NY: Longman).

Fraser, J. W. (1999). *Between church and state.* (New York: St. Martin's Press).

Guthrie, J. W., Garms, W. I., and Pierce, L. C. (1988). *School finance and education policy.* (Englewood Cliffs, NJ: Prentice-Hall).

Jones, J. J., Salisbury, G. J., and Spencer, R. L. (1969). *Secondary school administration.* (New York: McGraw-Hill).

Kansas evolution controversy gives rise to national debate. (1999). *Education Week* (8 Sept.).

Linn, D. (1998). Financing America's public schools. *NGA online:* The National Governor's Association and NGA Center for Best Practices (1 Sept.).

McCarthy, M. M., Cambron-McCabe, N. H., and Thomas, S. B. (1998). *Public school law.* (Boston: Allyn & Bacon).

Munley, V. (1993). The structure of K-12 school finance in the United States. In R. J. Thornton and A. P. O'Brien (eds.), *The economic consequences of American education.* (Greenwich, CT: JAI Press).

National Center for Education Statistics. (1998). *Inequalities in public school district revenues.* (Washington, DC: U.S. Department of Education).

Nord, W. (1995). *Religion and American education.* (Chapel Hill: University of North Carolina Press).

Patrick, J. J., and Long, G. P. (1999). *Constitutional debates on freedom of religion: A documentary history.* (Westport, CT: Greenwood Press).

Power. E. J. (1991). *A legacy of learning.* (Albany: SUNY Press).

Prayer in public schools? It's nothing new for many. (1994). *New York Times* (22 Nov.).

Sendor, B. B. (1988). *A legal guide to religion and public education.* (Topeka, KS: National Organization on Legal Problems of Education).

Sikh students return. (1994). *Education Week* (21 Sept.).

Swanson, A. D., and King, R. A. (1991). *School finance.* (New York: Longman).

Tanner, D. (1972). *Secondary education.* (New York: Macmillan).

U.S. Department of Education. (1984). *A nation responds.* (Washington, DC: U.S. Department of Education).

Vitz, P. (1986). *Censorship: Evidence of bias in our children's textbooks.* (Ann Arbor, MI: Servant Books).

Walsh, M. (2000). Supreme Court strikes down student-led prayer. *Education Week* (21 June).

When quiet is pervasive in school. (1994). *New York Times* (4 Sept.).

Wiles, J., and Bondi, J. (1993). *The essential middle school.* (New York: Macmillan).

Witte, J. (1999). *Religion and the American constitutional experiment: Essential rights and liberties.* (Boulder, CO: Westview Press).

CHAPTER 10

School Equity Issues

Curriculum Tracking
DEFINING TRACKING
REASONS FOR USING TRACKING
INEQUITIES IN TRACKING
RESPONSES TO CRITICISMS OF TRACKING
ALTERNATIVES TO TRACKING

School Desegregation
LEGAL AND LEGISLATIVE INFLUENCES
THE EFFECTS OF DESEGREGATION

Gender and School Education
GENDER BIAS
SEXUAL HARASSMENT

Summary

Questions and Activities

References

THE ROLE OF THE PUBLIC SCHOOL can only be understood in the context of the values and aims of society. As social institution, the public school is obligated to reflect the highest ideals of society and to provide an experience that is rich in what it means to be, "a good person leading a good life in a good society." As Plato explained, to understand the good life, one is inevitably drawn to the ideal of the good society, which itself leads us to contemplate how such a society is created and sustained. For Plato, this had everything to do with the development of educational policy and practice (Cremin, 1966).

A simpler way of thinking about this is to realize that the aims of a public school should always be contiguous with the aims of society—that a democratic society demands a democratic school system, one that molds intelligent, socially responsible, and autonomously thinking individuals. In the context of the United States, this means that the public schools should embody, among others, the ideals of tolerance, equity, justice, dissent, and liberty. It should also teach youths how to make intelligent, ethical decisions. In the United States, the public school system has been described as being central to the functioning of virtually every aspect of life—from building a good economy to building good character, a common group identity, and individual identities. Public schools have long been perceived as the great equalizers in society and as the key element in economic and social mobility.

Not surprisingly, the very notion of universalizing secondary education and opening higher education to the masses has its roots in America. To this day, many other advanced countries offer secondary and postsecondary education to a comparatively small percentage of the student-age population. The United States, however, has high school retention rates that are among the highest in the world (despite our dropout problem), and high school graduates can choose from a large group of colleges and universities, public and private. The United States also leads the world in the percentage of 22-year-olds obtaining bachelor's degrees and in the percentage of degrees obtained by women and minorities, in both technical and nontechnical fields. And the U.S. schools, relative to the schools of other advanced nations, historically have had a low socioeconomic bias (Husen, 1983; Tanner and Tanner, 1995; Tyler, 1981).

There is, however, a dark side to American education that runs counter to its egalitarian and democratic ideals. American schools continue to suffer from clear inequities both across and within public schools. Many of these inequities affect children from poor families, the very children for whom the schools typically claim to provide an equal opportunity for personal success and growth. Many schools are inequitably funded, racially stratified, and curricularly sorted in a way that works against those who already have the least. And many schools reinforce gender stereotypes in a way that is damaging to the education of both boys and girls. This chapter will explore issues of school inequity from the standpoint of curriculum tracking, segregation, and gender bias.

CURRICULUM TRACKING

Curriculum tracking involves providing differential instruction for students with different ability levels. This is usually accomplished by grouping students based on various measures of intelligence and skill, often for the purpose of providing more homogeneous instructional targets for teachers. In essence, tracking structures entire classes according to students' ability levels.

Defining Tracking

There is a difference between tracking and ability grouping. Almost all tracking is a form of ability grouping, but not all ability grouping results in tracking. The use of reading groups based on ability in a self-contained heterogeneous classroom, for instance, technically is not tracking because such a classroom presumably will offer inclusive classroom experiences as well. That is, a student might participate in an ability-based reading group but still experience mixed-group instruction in every other phase of the curriculum. In elementary school, the idea is to target instruction according to ability in a limited area (usually reading, and occasionally math) while also maintaining the inclusive nature of the self-contained classroom. On the whole, it would be difficult to see this practice as a tracked experience when the majority of the instruction is conducted without ability grouping.

Because of the predominance of the mixed-ability self-contained classroom in elementary education, curriculum tracking is rarely viewed as much of a problem in the early grades. But it can and does occur in elementary education, especially if the school does not embrace the self-contained classroom. If young readers, for instance, are sorted by ability and taught in separate classrooms, and if a similar sorting system is used to teach science, math, and language arts, then it would be fair to say that the elementary school is tracked.

For our purposes, we can consider tracking to be the wholesale grouping of students into curriculum programs that result in some identification of

In elementary school, the self-contained classroom encourages mixed-ability groupings.

high-, middle-, and low-ability (and -status) groups. Tracking is marked by the absence of heterogeneously grouped experiences and by clear ability designations between entire classrooms.

Tracking usually starts in middle school. Although middle schools are ideally designed to keep learners away from tracked experiences, in the interests of keeping them involved in exploratory and general education, national survey data suggest the persistent presence of tracking in schools serving preadolescents. According to Braddock (1990a), close to one-fourth of middle-level schools (grades 5–8) engage in a rigid form of tracking by using between-class ability grouping in all subject areas. Approximately one-third of the middle schools (depending on the grade level) report no ability grouping between classes, while the remaining report between-class ability grouping in some subjects. Rates of ability grouping in English, math, science, and social studies increase substantially from the fifth to the eighth grade, and the percentage of schools using no ability grouping decreases substantially between these grades. These data do not apply to ability groups formed within classrooms, but only to the designation of whole classes by ability. See Table 10-1 for a complete breakdown of the national survey.

TABLE 10-1
Grouping Practices in Middle-Level Schools

	GRADE			
	5	6	7	8
All Subjects	23%	22%	22%	23%
Some Subjects	40	44	47	50
Reading	96	86	63	54
English	24	44	54	54
Math	57	77	84	88
Science	4	5	14	16
Social Studies	4	4	10	10
No Subjects	37	34	31	27

SOURCE: Braddock, J. H. (1990). *Tracking in the middle grades: National patterns of grouping for instruction, Phi Delta Kappan,* 71(6):445–49. Reprinted with permission.

At the high school level, tracking continues to grow in scope, but not necessarily in intensity. According to another study by Braddock (1990b), only about 8 percent of the nation's comprehensive high schools use between-class ability grouping (curriculum tracking) in all subject areas, but the remaining 92 percent use between-class ability grouping in some subjects. Curriculum tracking is most popular in English, with 59 percent of the comprehensive schools using between-class ability grouping. Approximately 42 percent of the schools engage in tracking in math/science, and 38 percent in social studies (Braddock, 1990b). In most high schools, only one or two academic tracks can be found (usually math and English), with the remainder of the school curriculum undifferentiated.

Two basic forms of tracking exist in the schools. One type attempts to identify ability groups irrespective of the subject matter taught, with entire classes marked by a high, middle, or low designation. Thus, students in each group will be tracked together for instruction in English, math, social studies, science, and so on. For example, a high track might represent some honors or advanced placement group (or groups) bound for college; a middle track might contain a smattering of college-bound and vocational education students with middle-range academic aptitudes; and a low track likely will represent low-functioning students (low aptitude and/or low motivation) who typically are not college bound.

The other form of tracking reconstitutes the ability levels according to the subject matter, making it possible for a student to be placed in a high-level math course but a low-level English course, and so on. Even this form of tracking, however, typically results in the same students being placed in the same levels across the board. A national survey, for instance, indicated that 60 to 70 percent of tenth graders enrolled in honors math also were enrolled in honors English; a similar pattern held for remedial math and remedial English (Oakes, Gamoran, and Page, 1992). Carey and colleagues (1994) found considerable overlap between ability levels enrollment patterns in math and English courses offered in the tenth grade.

Curriculum tracking in the high school also has to be understood in relation to the school's obligation to provide enrichment and remediation experiences. The availability of honors or advanced placement courses at the secondary level for a small percentage of high-ability students does not necessarily manifest in tracking, especially if placement in these courses is based on prior performance in heterogeneously grouped courses. Tracking is not the prevailing condition if students experience mixed-ability instruction in a series of academic subjects from, say, grades 9 to 10 and are then moved, based on their performance, into advanced placement courses during their last two years of high school. Moreover, if there is open access to enrollment in differentiated courses, the conditions for tracking (wholesale ability-based experiences) are less likely to occur. In many high schools, however, tracking identifies honors or advanced placement groups as early as the ninth grade—and sometimes even earlier. The group then moves en masse through the curriculum, experiencing course work preparatory for admission into top colleges and universities, and clearly distinguished from the course work offered to lower-track groups.

Reasons for Using Tracking

Tracking is used in the schools for several reasons. First, as mentioned, tracking is expressly designed to respond to the varying abilities of students. Thus, students who may not be as skilled as others in, say, mathematics, are said to be served by a slower pace and a more deliberate and detailed approach, while those who are more skilled are free to go forward without restraint. Second, it is commonly believed that when students of mixed abilities are all taught in one common classroom, the achievement of the high-ability student is hindered. The thinking is that teachers pace their classrooms according to the slowest "runner," so that the faster ones never hit their full stride. Some evidence exists to support this conclusion, at least in the area of mathematics instruction. According to Loveless (1998), low-achieving students seem to learn more in heterogeneous math classes, while high- and average-achieving student sustain achievement losses in these settings. Third, many believe that it is simply too much to expect teachers to be responsive to a wide range of student skills in one classroom, that such an expectation is counter to good pedagogy, and that teachers can benefit from having a less wide-ranging ability target at which to aim their instruction.

Some data point to tracking as a rather negative function in the curriculum, and even as an instrument of inequity. Some critics claim that tracking serves as a kind of sorting mechanism that provides high-quality instructional experiences for students who already have the greatest social and economic advantages, and low-quality experiences for those who have the least. The problem, critics say, is that tracking has consequences that extend well beyond the stated goal of providing appropriate instructional opportunities for youths of varying ability levels. Tracking has, in effect, become a way of providing differential qualities of experience. That is, compared to their peers in low-level groups, students in high-level groups benefit from higher teacher expectations, more idea-oriented learning engagements, more meaningful curriculum materials, a better classroom climate, and more challenging teaching methodologies. The fact that this phenomenon cuts across racial and economic lines, meaning that the low-level groups have a disproportionately large representation of minority and economically poor children, places tracking at the center of our discussion on equity.

Inequities in Tracking

Much of the best work done on the inequitable nature of tracking was drawn from a national sample of schools (Oakes, 1985). Taking her data from Goodlad's landmark study of schooling, Jeannie Oakes documented the qualitative differences in the various tracks of a school curriculum. Oakes, for instance, reported on how the content of the curriculum varied at different track levels. Higher track levels were marked by a focus on college preparatory topics and were not likely to emphasize basic skills instruction. Generally, higher-track students engaged in higher cognitive work than their counterparts in the lower tracks—making judgments, drawing inferences, and engaging in idea-oriented forms of instruction. Low track levels were dedicated primarily to rote learning and to basic skills instruction such as filling out a job application. Table 10-2 lists some representative statements from students in the different tracks.

TABLE 10-2
Selected Student Responses to Curriculum Tracking

Students' written responses to the question: "What is the most important thing you have learned or done so far in this class?"

Mathematics

HIGH-TRACK STUDENTS

1. There is no one important thing I have learned. Since each new concept is built on the old ones, everything I learn is important. —Senior High
2. Learning to change my thought processes in dealing with higher mathematics and computers. —Senior High
3. Inductive reasoning. —Senior High
4. Learned many new mathematical principles and concepts that can be used in a future job. —Senior High
5. I have proved to myself that I have the discipline to take a difficult class just for the knowledge, even though it has nothing to do with my career plans. —Senior High

LOW-TRACK STUDENTS

1. Really I have learned nothing. Only my roman numerals. I knew them, but not very good. I could do better in another class. —Junior High
2. I have learned just a small amount in this class. I feel that if I was in another class, that I would have a challenge to look forward to each and every time I entered the class. I feel that if I had another teacher I would work better. —Junior High
3. How to do income tax. —Senior High

Science

HIGH-TRACK STUDENTS

1. Basic concepts and theories have been most prevalent. We have learned things that are practical without taking away some in-depth studies of the subject. —Senior High
2. Things in nature are not always what they appear to be or what seems to be happening is not what really is happening. —Senior High
3. Probably the most important thing I've learned is the understanding of the balance between man and his environment. —Senior High
4. I have learned to do what scientists do. —Junior High

LOW-TRACK STUDENTS

1. I can distinguish one type of rock from another. —Senior High
2. How to ride motorcycles and shoot trap. —Senior High
3. To be honest, nothing. —Senior High
4. Nothing outstanding. —Senior High
5. Nothing I'd use in my later life; it will take a better man than I to comprehend our world. —Senior High

English

HIGH-TRACK STUDENTS

1. I have learned things that will get me ready for college entrance examinations. Also, many things on how to write compositions that will help me in college. —Junior High
2. To me, there is not a most important thing I learned in this class. Everything or mostly everything I learn in here is IMPORTANT. —Junior High
3. It teaches you how to do research in a college library. —Senior High
4. The thing we did in class that I enjoyed the most was writing poetry, expressing my ideas. We also had a poet come and read to us. —Senior High

LOW-TRACK STUDENTS

1. I learned that English is boring. —Senior High
2. Job applications. Job interviews. Preparation for the above. —Junior High
3. To spell words you don't know, to fill out things where you get a job. —Junior High
4. Job training. —Junior High

Social Science Studies

HIGH-TRACK STUDENTS

1. The most important thing is the way other countries and places govern themselves economically, socially, and politically. Also different philosophers and their theories on government and man and how their theories relate to us and now. —Junior High
2. I have learned quite a deal about peoples of other nations, plus the ideas of creation and evolution, ideas that philosophers have puzzled over for years. —Senior High
3. Learning political and cultural trends in relation to international and domestic events. —Senior High

LOW-TRACK STUDENTS

1. I don't remember. —Junior High
2. A few lessons which have not very much to do with history. (I enjoyed it). —Junior High
3. To learn how to listen and follow the directions of the teacher. —Senior High
4. I learned about being quiet when the teacher is talking. —Junior High
5. Learned to work myself. —Junior High
6. How to go through a cart and find a folder by myself. —Junior High

SOURCE: Oakes, J. (1985), *Keeping track: How schools structure inequality.* (New Haven, CT: Yale University Press). Reprinted with permission.

Although one would naturally expect ability tracks to vary in cognitive intensity and perhaps in content, the existing situation can be more properly framed in terms of two separate cultures. One culture provides high-level cognitive experiences for children believed to have "higher" skills, and the other provides low-level cognitive experiences for those believed to have "lower" skills. This is verified in what teachers reported to be the desired behavioral outcomes for students in the different tracks. Teachers were more likely to describe behaviors like self-direction, critical thinking, creativity, and active involvement in learning as appropriate outcomes for the high track, and behaviors like working quietly, being punctual, conforming to rules, and getting along with others as appropriate for the low track (Oakes, 1985). Such disparities reflect base inequities in the way we educate youths; they cannot be justified as outcomes appropriate for varied levels of ability.

Not surprisingly, teacher expectations for the children in the different tracks also vary. This results in considerable instructional advantage for the high-level tracks, not only because of the obvious benefits of being marked as having ability but also in terms of the actual classroom instruction. High-ability tracks, for instance, were reported to be less punitive in nature, less inclined to be preoccupied with discipline and control, and more environmentally friendly than the low tracks. Students in high-ability tracks saw their teachers as more concerned with their personal needs and interests, and their own peers to be more friendly, than those in the low tracks. The high track also outscored the low track on scales of teacher clarity, organization, and enthusiasm (Oakes, 1985).

Oakes (1990) also examined how race and class affect students' opportunities to learn in a tracked math and science program, asking particularly whether such factors affect access to programs, qualified teachers, and resources. Again, she uncovered several disturbing trends. Using a national sample of schools, she found, for instance, that the basic qualification patterns of teachers was noticeable not only across schools, varying according to race and social class, but within schools as well. Regarding the qualifications of the teachers assigned to teach math and science in the various ability tracks of secondary schools, a clear trend emerged. Compared to the higher tracks, the lower tracks attracted significantly more uncertified teachers, significantly fewer teachers with a B.A or B.S., significantly fewer teachers with master's degrees, and significantly fewer teachers carrying the endorsement or qualification of the National Science Teachers Association; Table 10-3 breaks these findings down. In general, teachers working in lower tracks seem less well prepared academically and professionally than

TABLE 10-3
**Teacher Qualification Differences Across Ability Tracks
and Socioeconomic Status (SES) Levels**

	LOW ABILITY CLASSES		HIGH-ABILITY CLASSES	
	Low-SES, Minority, Urban	High-SES, White, Suburban	Low-SES, Minority, Urban	High-SES White, Suburban
Certified in Science/Math	39%	82%	73%	84%
Bachelor's in Science/Math	38	68	46	78
Master's in Science/Math	8	32	10	48
NSTA* Qualified	11	36	5	47
NCTM† Qualified	23	26	4	16
Computer Course Work	41	61	69	62

*National Science Teachers Association
†National Council of Teachers of Mathematics
SOURCE: Oakes, J. (1990), *Multiplying inequalities,* (Santa Monica, CA: Rand Corporation), p. 67. Reprinted with permission.

their colleagues in higher-track settings, at least in secondary math and science instruction. And the picture is not any better with regard to social class and race. In other words, the differences between the qualifications of teachers working in the tracks of a low-income, largely minority and urban school and those of teachers working in the tracks of a high-income, largely white and suburban school are notable.

Critics have responded to these findings by observing that it makes no sense to have more qualified teachers—especially those with more advanced knowledge in subject areas, such as math—teach basic remediation courses, and less qualified teachers teach advanced courses (Loveless, 1998). If the teaching staff is varied in its base of qualifications, the staffing distribution that brings more qualified teachers to high-level groups might make some sense (Loveless, 1998).

Oakes' work has been widely read and cited and has had considerable sway in turning school leaders and school commentators against the practice of curriculum tracking. Even mainstream critics have damned the practice. Harold Howe, secretary of education during the Johnson administration in the 1960s, has called tracking "one of the most destructive aspects of factory-model schooling," arguing that it perpetuates disadvantage, fosters racial and cultural isolation, and encourages low expectations for black and Hispanic students (Howe, 1993, p. 144). Similarly, as documented by Loveless (1999), popular journals such as *Better Homes and Gardens* and *U.S. News & World Report* have run articles criticizing the practice of tracking, and organizations with some national visibility, including the National Governor's Association, the Children's Defense Fund, the Carnegie Corporation, the College Board, and the National Education Association, have done the same. In response, many school districts have moved to either reduce or eliminate the practice of curriculum tracking.

Responses to Criticisms of Tracking

But the negative portrayal of tracking and ability grouping has not gone uncontested. Several researchers have been critical of Oakes' data on tracking, claiming that she lacked good controls and made selective use of the literature to bolster her antitracking arguments (Kulik, 1993). After reviewing the evidence, two groups of researchers claim that within-class ability grouping has positive achievement effects, thus validating the kind of grouping practices found in elementary schools (Kulik, 1993; Slavin, 1990). As far as between-class tracking is concerned, Kulik (1993) claims that students in lower and middle groups have achievement scores virtually indistinguishable from those of similar students in mixed groups, and that there are no discernible negative effects on the self-esteem of students. Kulik goes further, stating that students in high-level groups outperform similar students in mixed-group settings. He concludes that tracking benefits high-level students but does no harm (or at least is no worse than mixed groups) in the education of middle- and low-achieving students.

As far as the accusation of racial bias in assignments to the curriculum tracks, Loveless (1998) claims that, if we control for the achievement status of students assigned to the high-curriculum track (their achievement scores), black students actually enjoy a 10 percent advantage over whites in being assigned to the high track. In effect, it is easier for black students to get assigned to a high track even though their overall percentage is underrepresented. This fact, combined with evidence indicating that the achievement gap between white and black students is widest at grade 8, essentially before the onset of the most severe forms of ability grouping and tracking, leads Loveless to conclude that tracking has little culpability in the achievement differences that exist between white and black students. A stronger case, in fact, can be made for class discrimination. That is, some evidence indicates that students from poor families are more likely to be assigned to a low track than wealthier students with identical achievement records (Loveless, 1998).

Alternatives to Tracking

What alternatives to tracking might schools consider? All children, after all, need to be challenged at their own level, and high- and low-ability children naturally need to be free to pursue their learning in the most conducive climate. The complete elimination of ability grouping and access to advanced placement or honors courses is probably not advisable. The idea has little support from parents or teachers, who are surprisingly supportive of tracking.

In thinking about this, remember the design of the comprehensive school, in which tracking theoretically is frowned on. Even though curriculum tracking often has flourished in comprehensive schools (Nasaw, 1979; Oakes, 1985), the concept of the comprehensive curriculum balances the individualistic phase of the curriculum, which provides students with opportunities for advanced and accelerated instruction, with other curriculum features, including commonly grouped core learnings. At the high school level, individual ability needs can be dealt with through elective studies, advanced placement, and individualization within heterogeneous settings. Moreover, is the very idea of tracking flawed, or is it a matter or poor implementation? Can some of the problems related to teacher expectations, curriculum selection, classroom climate, and instructional differences in tracked classes be dealt with without necessarily eliminating ability grouping and some forms of tracking?

SCHOOL DESEGREGATION

The struggle to desegregate the American public school became most visible after the Supreme Court in 1954 ruled that "separate educational institutions are inherently unequal." This ruling, handed down in *Brown v. the Board of Education of Topeka,* reversed the "separate but equal" doctrine supported by the Court almost sixty years earlier in another famous court case, *Plessy v. Ferguson.* Over forty years have passed since the historic ruling in *Brown,* and its effects have been dramatic in making public education a more integrated experience. It is fair to say that school desegregation efforts have triumphed in America. Segregation by state enforcement has been outlawed, interactions between the races in public schools have increased enormously, and courts throughout the country continue to exercise supervision over schools that have not yet fulfilled the mandate to free themselves from past discriminatory practices. The struggle for desegregation, which has been fought through legal and legislative channels, clearly has yielded progress. But, as with many problems in a democracy, the struggle is never over, and new challenges continue to compel the attention of educators and other school leaders in their quest to secure equal opportunities for all youths.

Legal and Legislative Influences

The story of school desegregation starts at the turn of the twentieth century, in *Plessy v. Ferguson* (1896), which tested the constitutionality of state-enforced segregation justified under the doctrine of "separate but equal." In *Plessy,* the Supreme Court upheld a Louisiana statute requiring the segregation of passengers in railroad coaches. The Court put its faith in the "separate but equal" doctrine, explaining that separate facilities for the races were constitutionally allowable as long as the facilities were equal. This line of reasoning gave legal sanction to the de jure segregation (segregation by law or state enforcement) found in virtually all aspects of life in the South —public schools, restaurants, hotels, mass transportation systems, universities, and so on. The Court reasoned that there could be no presumption of deliberate discrimination toward minorities in a system that maintained separate and equal standards.

But the "separate but equal" standard was vulnerable, mostly because there was little reality to the "equal" side of the standard. As stated by Whitman (1993), "separate but equal" was producing "grotesque inequalities," which were manifested in obvious ways, including huge differences in funding for white and black schools in many parts of the South. Few could disagree that the "separate but equal" doctrine was anchored in racism and intolerance, and in accompanying beliefs in black inferiority. Justice John Harlan underscored this point in his dissenting opinion in *Plessy:*

> What can more certainly arouse hate, what more certainly create and perpetuate a feeling of distrust between the races, than state enactments which in fact proceed on the ground that colored citizens are so inferior and degraded that they cannot be allowed to sit in public coaches occupied by white citizens? That, as all will admit, is the real meaning of such legislation as was enacted in Louisiana. (quoted in Whitman, 1993, p. 16)

Justice Harlan's dissent was a precursor to what the Court would later say in the 1954 *Brown* ruling—that the idea of "separate but equal" was inherently unequal because it was moved by racist intentions and racist projections of inferiority of blacks. Feature 10-1 gives a more complete text of Harlan's dissent. Because the "equal" side of the equation had little basis in reality, the "separate" side could have no standing.

This was the central principle in the 1954 *Brown* ruling. Because Linda Brown was black, she had to attend a grade school across town, while her white peers attended a school close by. The Topeka school system, in which Brown was enrolled, was segregated by race, an arrangement that was legal and widely practiced. When the Brown family sued on the basis that the separate facilities were inherently unequal, the school district's position was that it fulfilled its obligation to maintain equal facilities. But plaintiffs in *Brown* challenged not the equality of the facilities, but the very idea of segregation, claiming that the design of a segregated system had a hurtful (and inequitable) effect on the education of black children.

The Supreme Court ultimately agreed with the Browns' position and, in a strongly-worded ruling, rejected the *Plessy* standard of "separate but equal." The *Brown* ruling ushered in a new day for race relations in America, outlawing de jure segregation in public schools on the grounds that it victimized black children. In the words of the Court,

> Segregation of white and colored children in public schools has a detrimental effect upon the colored children. The impact is greater when it has the sanction of the law; for the policy of separating the races is usually interpreted as denoting the inferiority of the Negro group. A sense of inferiority affects the motivation of a child to learn. Segregation with the sanction of law, therefore, has a tendency to retard the educational and mental development of Negro children and to deprive them of some of the benefits they would receive in a racially integrated school system. (quoted in Whitman, 1993, pp. 121–22)

Because of the *Brown* ruling, the dual system of schooling practiced in the South had to be dismantled. Besides prohibiting de jure segregation, the Supreme Court put school districts on notice that they had to design desegregation plans that pointed toward reasonable integration, or what the Court would later call unitary status. In a ruling one year after *Brown,* known as *Brown II,* the Supreme Court attempted to articulate how and when school desegregation could be achieved. Although the message that the segregated system had to be razed was clear enough, the Court unfortunately put no time constraints on the matter, merely advising school districts to

The ruling in *Plessy v. Ferguson* sanctioned the "separate but equal" doctrine and allowed de jure segregation to be widely and lawfully practiced in the South. The Supreme Court, in an 8-1 decision, ruled that as long as equal standards were upheld the separation of the races on railroad coaches, and by implication, on other facilities and in various government services (including public education) was not unconstitutional. But in a sternly worded dissent, Justice Harlan anticipated what the Court would say decades later in *Brown v. Board of Education*.

The 13th Amendment . . . not only struck down the institution of slavery as previously existing in the United States, but it prevents the imposition of any burdens or disabilities that constitute badges of slavery or servitude. It decreed universal civil freedom in this country. . . . But that amendment having been found inadequate to the protection of the rights of those who had been in slavery, it was followed by the 14th Amendment, which added greatly to the dignity and glory of American citizenship, and to the security of personal liberty. . . . It was said in argument that the statute of Louisiana does not discriminate against either race, but prescribes a rule applicable alike to white and colored citizens. But . . . everyone knows that the statute in question had its origin in the purpose, not so much to exclude white persons from railroad cars occupied by blacks, as to exclude colored people from coaches occupied by or assigned to white persons. . . . The thing to accomplish was, under the guise of giving equal accommodation for whites and blacks, to compel the latter to keep to themselves while traveling in railroad passenger coaches No one would be so wanting in candor as to assert the contrary. The fundamental objection, therefore, to the statute, is that it interferes with the personal freedom of citizens. . . . If a white man and a black man choose to occupy the same public conveyance on a public highway, it is their right to do so, and no government, proceeding alone on grounds of race, can prevent it without infringing the personal liberty of each. . . .

If a state can prescribe as a rule of civil conduct, that whites and blacks shall not travel as passengers in the same railroad coach, why may it not so regulate the use of the streets of its cities and towns as to compel white citizens to keep on one side of the street and black citizens to keep on the other? Why may it not, upon like grounds, punish whites and blacks who ride together in street cars or in open vehicles on a public road or street? Why may it not require sheriffs to assign whites to one side of a court-room and blacks to the other? And why may it not also prohibit the commingling of the two races in the galleries of legislative halls or in public assemblages convened for the political questions of the day? Further, if this statute of Louisiana is consistent with the personal liberty of citizens, why may not the state require the separation in railroad coaches of native and naturalized citizens of the United States, or of Protestants and Roman Catholics?

In my opinion, the judgment this day rendered will, in time, prove to be quite as pernicious as the decision made by this tribunal in the Dred Scott case. . . . Sixty millions of whites are in no danger from the presence here of eight millions of blacks. The destinies of the two races in this country are indissolubly linked together, and the interests of both require that the common government of all shall not permit the seeds of race hate to be planted under the sanction of law.

SOURCE: Quoted in Whitman, M. (1998), *The irony of desegregation law, 1955–1995* (Princeton, NJ: Markus Wiener), pp. 15–16.

Linda Brown stands in front of the school where she was refused admission because of a segregationist school policy.

proceed "with all deliberate speed" and giving no advice on how desegregation might be implemented or how progress toward it might be evaluated. This gave school districts little incentive to move quickly and little sense of what the Court might be looking for in a desegregated school system.

Among the more popular schemes used in schools during the early stages of desegregation was the open enrollment system, or freedom-of-choice plan, which allowed families to choose the school they believed to be most appropriate for the education of their children. The thinking was that the goal of integration could be served by allowing minority (and majority) families the option of enrolling their children in a public school within their district lines. But the open enrollment system was problematic on several fronts. First, many black children had developed a sense of identification and intimacy with their segregated schools, and black school administrators, perhaps fearing a loss of work, often did little to encourage black families to opt for a "white" school (Whitman, 1998). Second, there were clear psychological and social factors influencing black parents' decision not to opt for a white school. Given the history of segregation, many black families felt that it was neither safe nor wise to send their children to a school where they were likely not wanted. And harassment from racist groups, including the Ku Klux Klan, gave these fears a terrifying basis in reality. Third, freedom of choice allowed families to opt out of schools that were beginning to show signs of integration. In this way, freedom of choice was a mechanism that could not only serve integration but also work against it.

In 1968, the Supreme Court heard *Green v. County School Board of New Kent, Virginia,* which centered around a freedom-of-choice plan a school district had conceived as a device for desegregation. Parents in the district could send their children to either of two schools, both of which historically had been segregated. After three years, however, the plan had yielded no significant enrollment crossover between the races: No white children were enrolled in the historically black school, and only a small percentage of black children were enrolled in the historically white school. The district maintained that it had done its best and was not practicing de facto segregation. The segregation that prevailed in the district, it claimed, was a function of parental choice, not district action. The Court disagreed, stating that the only desegregation plan it would accept was one that worked. It demanded that the district rethink its strategy so as to achieve the "root and branch" elimination of segregation. At the same time, the Court established criteria to help districts to determine whether they had succeeded in achieving what the Court labeled unitary (or integrated/desegregated) status. To achieve unitary status, they would have to show that racial identification had been eliminated in several key areas, including the composition of the student body, faculty, and staff; transportation systems; extracurricular activities; and facilities. These became known as the Green criteria or Green factors. They are still used by the courts today to determine if a school has officially eliminated race-based segregation.

In 1969, almost fifteen years after the Court offered its infamous "with all deliberate speed" decree to schools, the Court declared in *Alexander v. Holmes County* that all desegregation plans had to be implemented immediately and that only unitary schools could prevail. Its patience worn thin, the Court changed the rules of the desegregation game.

Several events influenced the more aggressive stance taken by the Court. In 1966, the well-known Coleman report revealed that "the great majority of American children attend schools that are largely segregated . . . where almost all of their fellow students are from the same racial background as they are" (p. 4). The congressionally mandated Coleman report also revealed a nationwide achievement gap between white and black youngsters, one that widened as the students proceeded through the grades. It also argued, somewhat surprisingly, that the physical facilities of the schools in America were more or less equal but that such resources were marginal to the achievement of the children. The expectation had been that the study would show clear differences in the resources used to educate the average black child and the average white child. But the report instead pointed to the family background of children as the more significant factor in school achievement. It also claimed that school achievement among black youngsters would improve if they attended schools with white youngsters who were from homes supporting education. This finding had strong parallels to the central themes of the *Brown* ruling, which maintained that segregation itself had a negative effect on the achievement and the general academic outlook of black children. Integration, it seemed, was the key to equal opportunity and shared school success.

These findings, one should keep in mind, came in the wake of a broader civil rights movement, which itself pointed out inequities in employment practices, social and economic mobility, and access to higher education. Approximately two years before the release of the Coleman report, the federal government undertook a series of initiatives to combat poverty and racial discrimination. The federal action commenced in 1964 with the signing of the Economic Opportunity Act, which led to the establishment of the Office of Economic Opportunity and the creation of intervention programs like Upward Bound, the Job Corps, and the widely publicized Head Start. In general, this act provided financial aid to low-income and mostly minority students hoping to achieve a higher education and sponsored instructional programs in adult education and early learning. Its ambitions were far-reaching. In the summer of 1965, for instance, Head Start enrolled close to half a million poor, mostly nonwhite, children so that they could be exposed to early academic experiences that would translate into later academic success. The program was designed to bring disadvantaged children up to speed so that they could compete in elementary school.

In 1964, President Johnson signed into law the Civil Rights Act, which provided funds and resources for various desegregation efforts. Title IV of the act gave federal financial support to school districts preparing school desegregation plans and empowered the attorney general to file suit against schools still practicing discrimination; Title VI threatened the loss of federal moneys to school districts found to be using federally sponsored programs in a racially discriminating manner. One year later, Johnson signed the Elementary and Secondary Act of 1965 into law. The provisions of this legislation also were centered around educational programs for the underprivileged. Title I of this act provided funds to schools for the general purpose of advancing the education of low-income children, while Title II authorized the purchase of curriculum materials. The act also funded efforts to bring the resources of the community and various agencies together to improve the school lives of disadvantaged children. Each of these legislative mandates gave the federal government a visible role in dealing with issues of educational opportunity, racial isolation, and underachievement.

During this period, a new voice had emerged in the South, preaching a social gospel of civil disobedience, which helped lay the groundwork for black resistance to segregation and for federal involvement in the enforcement of desegregation edicts. Martin Luther King's charismatic leadership would move the issue of segregation into the more expansive realm of civil rights. He was committed to blurring the color line and to bringing a sense of humanity and common decency to race relations. King did not accept any position advancing some form of peaceful or harmonious segregation. He expected nothing less than full and complete integration in the fabric of American society and assurances of equal rights and equal opportunities for all Americans. Feature 10-2 gives a sample of the website devoted to King.

Given the national consciousness over race relations and the emergence of a more aggressive Supreme Court, the prospects for desegregation were improved going into the 1970s. School districts, feeling legal and political pressure, explored various desegregation strategies. Some school districts used a tactic known as majority-to-minority transfer, a practice that allowed children to move or transfer from any district school in which their race was in the majority to a school in which their race was in the minority. This tactic limited transfers to ones having a desegregating effect, but such programs did not produce the desired effect. To encourage more enrollment crossover, school districts designed magnet schools that offered a special curriculum or some instructional feature that would pull students to its doors. By placing well-funded, highly regarded magnet schools that served some special academic end (science education, fine arts education, and so forth) in a segregated neighborhood, school districts were convinced that they could attract nonminority participation in these schools. As it turns out, they were more right than wrong. Magnets schools undoubtedly served the purpose of desegregation by helping to put a halt to the "white flight" that many urban school districts were experiencing. They thus represent an important component in a multifaceted desegregation strategy.

But where such desegregation methods were not successful, the schools sometimes were placed under a court-ordered prescription. In this case, involuntary methods were used—like the gerrymandering of school zones, which sometimes involved transporting children to schools outside their neighborhoods, or the forced pairing of existing segregated schools for the purpose of swapping half of the students in one school with those in the other for either a partial or full schoolday experience. Both of these compulsory strategies usually involved at least some forced busing.

10-2 WEB POINTS
Martin Luther King, Jr.

The struggle for desegregation and the broader civil rights movement of which it was a part were influenced by various people and events. The results were most manifest in the passage of important legislation and in the legal construction of segregation as unconstitutional. But none of this likely would have happened when it did, or happened without violent upheaval, without the presence and influence of Martin Luther King, Jr. Reverend King was a firm integrationist and a believer in the power of the American Constitution and American democracy. This website (www.stanford.edu/group/King) contains most of Dr. King's papers, including his speeches and sermons.

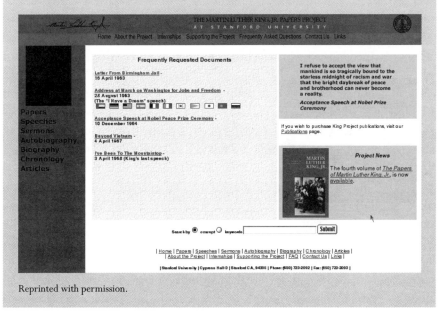

Reprinted with permission.

Transportation remedies, in fact, were typical in cases in which school segregation existed because of deeply entrenched segregated housing patterns. In 1971, in *Swann v. Charlotte-Mecklenburg Board of Education,* the Supreme Court cleared the way for more expansive desegregation plans that included the pairing of noncontiguous school districts and the busing of students across fairly large distances. Using the Green factors as its formula for integration, the Supreme Court upheld the plan of a lower court to reduce racial imbalances in the district's schools. After having experienced no success with its majority-to-minority plan, the Charlotte-Mecklenburg district, a consolidated district that included both urban and suburban schools, designed a multifaceted desegregation plan that made use of school pairings (two-way busing), satellite assignments (one-way busing), school consolidation, and redrawn attendance zones (Orfield and Eaton, 1997). Each of these strategies entailed, at some level, the transportation of some children to a school not always in closest proximity to their home. The Court had sent the strongest signal yet that desegregation meant implementing measures beyond freedom-of-choice plans, various transfer policies, and thematic magnet schools.

By 1974, however, the Court had begun to ease its aggressive posture toward desegregation. In *Milliken v. Bradley,* a circuit court had ordered the desegregation of Detroit's schools by prescribing a transportation remedy that involved fifty-three suburban school districts outside of Detroit. Unlike the Charlotte-Mecklenburg district, which was a consolidated school district that included the schools of an entire metropolitan area, Detroit's outlying areas were comprised of independent school districts. Thus, the *Milliken* case represented an important test for interdistrict remedies. The Supreme Court, however, in a close decision, shot down the plan. The Court stated that, because segregation was occurring in the Detroit schools, the problem belonged to Detroit, and not to any of its contiguous school districts. Unless the city could prove that the suburban schools (or the state) had engaged in discriminatory actions that contributed to school enrollment patterns in Detroit, the overwhelmingly white suburban schools could not be placed under any legal compulsion to participate in the desegregation remedy. Detroit would have to go at it alone in finding a way to integrate a small and dwindling white student population with a large and ever-increasing black one (Orfield and Eaton, 1998).

To the advocates of desegregation, this was a solid defeat for the mandate authorized in *Brown* and a virtual guarantee that segregation would continue to prevail in largely minority city school districts. Justice Thurgood Marshall, whose history with the landmark *Brown* ruling is well documented, referred to *Milliken* as "a giant step backwards" (Orfield and Eaton, 1997, p. 29). The Court, recognizing that long-term integration was not likely to occur in Detroit, returned to the *Milliken* ruling in *Milliken II* and ordered the state of Michigan to pay for educational programs that might help repair the harm created by segregation. Separate schools, the Court seemed to say, could now become equal through intradistrict compensatory programs. Interdistrict desegregation, however, could be authorized in districts where there was evidence of constitutional violations either by the districts or by the state overseeing them. Moreover, unitary districts could always choose to enter into voluntary interdistrict remedies (McCarthy, Cambron-McCabe, and Thomas, 1998).

In 1991, the backslide on desegregation continued when the Supreme Court ruled in *Board of Education of Oklahoma City Public Schools v. Dowell*. The Court stated that, once a school district was declared unitary, it could be released from any obligations to further maintain desegregation. The Oklahoma City public schools had operated for about five years under a court-ordered desegregation plan that relied heavily on transportation remedies. A federal court eventually declared the district to be in compliance (and unitary) and freed it from any further monitoring. The district, citing the unpopularity of the busing, adopted a neighborhood school policy that resulted in about half of its schools becoming intensely segregated. The Supreme Court upheld the action of the district, stating that even segregated housing patterns could not compel court-ordered desegregation if such patterns existed by private choice and were not a legacy of an official segregation policy. The schools, once declared unitary, could go about their business without court supervision unless faced with accusations of discriminatory practice. Justice Marshall again offered the dissent; Feature 10-3 gives a key portion.

Along these same lines, the Supreme Court ruled in *Missouri v. Jenkins,* (1995) that compensatory efforts supported by the state to assist a school district with desegregation could not be constitutionally supported unless there was evidence of discrimination on the part of the state. Over an eighteen-year period, various courts had required the state of Missouri to pay over $1 billion for improvements in the Kansas City, Missouri, School District (KCMSD), all for the express purpose of making the district attractive to nonminority students living outside the district and to district students attending private schools. The money went to the construction of state-of-the-art magnet schools, various capital improvements, salary assistance, expanded summer school programs, and so forth. Because there were not enough white children living in the district, the lower courts had allowed a remedy that aimed to bring and retain white children to the city schools voluntarily. The Supreme Court, however, had another view, noting again, as it did in *Milliken v. Bradley,* that the intradistrict problems had to be solved with intradistrict remedies. The Court was not convinced that the state had anything to do with the high black enrollments in some of the schools. Racial imbalance was not unconstitutional; only racial imbalance caused by discrimination was unconstitutional. As Justice Clarence Thomas phrased it, "Racial isolation itself is not a harm; only state-enforced segregation is" (quoted in Whitman, 1998, p. 328). The Court released the state

10-3 SCHOLARLY VOICES
Justice Thurgood Marshall's Dissent in *Dowell*

In *Dowell v. Oklahoma City,* the Supreme Court left behind the spirit of *Brown,* in the sense that once a district is declared unitary it can return to segregation as long as it is not done with discriminatory intent. Justice Marshall, in looking at the work of the Court in the area of segregation, which started for him as a young lawyer petitioning to the Court in the *Brown* case, had a different view on the idea of desegregation. Here is part of his dissent in the *Dowell* ruling:

Consistent with the mandate of Brown, our cases have imposed on school districts an unconditional duty to eliminate any condition that perpetuates the message of racial inferiority inherent in the policy of state-sponsored segregation. The racial indentifiability of a district's school is such a condition. Whether this vestige of state sponsored segregation will persist cannot simply be ignored at the point where a district court is contemplating the dissolution of a desegregation decree. In a district with a history of state-sponsored segregation, racial separation, in my view, remains inherently unequal.

Justice Thurgood Marshall.

© Stock Montage, Inc.

SOURCE: Quoted in Whitman, M. (1998), *The irony of desegregation law 1955–1995.* (Princeton, NJ: Markus Wiener), p. 317.

of Missouri from its court-imposed obligation, leaving the matter of desegregation to the KCMSD.

The series of cases since *Milliken* represent a clear movement away from the *Brown* mandate. As matters stand now, once a school district has eliminated any signs of prior discriminatory practices and has been declared unitary, using the six factors identified in *Green,* and as long as no resegregation occurs as a result of discriminatory practices, it is free to go its own way even if segregation again prevails.

Thus, the historic series of Court decisions on school segregation represent a shifting line of thinking. The *Brown* decision represented a rousing defeat of *Plessy*'s "separate but equal" mandate. It evolved into an insistence that segregation, even if de facto in nature, was inimical to the education of black children. Schools districts faced the prospect of being put under court supervision if they failed to offer a successful desegregation plan. The "root and branch" eradication of segregation, the term used in the *Green* ruling, was the defining principle. But now the Court seems more willing to give districts more leeway in conducting their own desegregation plans and to release districts from any further obligations if they have demonstrated unitary status. After four decades of struggle over school segregation, this is perhaps as it should be. Time will tell if the Court's willingness to loosen its supervisory grip in the area of segregation was premature. But over 1,000 districts are still under court supervision, and many still have trouble demonstrating unitary status (the Topeka schools, of *Brown* fame, were denied in 1992). And if it can be proven that any public schools are engaged in discriminatory practices, they will find themselves back in court. The stage now appears set for the reduction of judicial control in the area of desegregation and the return of school operations to local control (McCarthy, Cambron-McCabe, and Thomas, 1998, p. 486). Figure 10-1 summarizes the major Supreme Court cases on school segregation.

The Effects of Desegregation

Did all the efforts to desegregate the schools have a positive effect on minority children? Have the schools made significant inroads in the area of desegregation? The national data, collected and collated by Gary Orfield, director of the Harvard Project on School Desegregation, show some gains in the area of desegregation. Table 10-4 shows the percentage of minority students (blacks and Hispanics) attending predominantly minority schools (defined as schools with 50 to 100 percent minority student enrollments) and attending intensely minority schools (defined as schools with 90 to 100 percent minority student enrollments). For blacks, the effects of desegregation are clear. In 1968, about 76 percent of black children attended predominantly minority schools; by 1996, the number had been reduced to about 68 percent. But the data on black children attending intensely minority schools are even more telling—with a precipitous drop from 64 percent in 1968 to 35 percent in 1996. Thus, where segregation had been most intense, the desegregating gains have been most impressive. Among Hispanic children, however, the opposite has occurred, with more Hispanic children attending predominantly minority schools in 1996 than in 1968. Part of the problem here is increased immigration, which has contributed to the number of low-income Hispanics living in concentrated areas. Segregation, in fact, has some association with poverty in general, as Feature 10-4 on page 422 shows.

The problem of desegregation still exists mainly in the cities and suburbs. As shown in Table 10-5 on page 423, the percentage of minority

---

FIGURE 10-1

Important Supreme Court Cases Related to School Segregation

Plessy v. Ferguson (1896)

The Court upheld the principle of "separate but equal." It supported the legality of a Louisiana statute that required whites and blacks to use separate railroad coaches. This meant that the government had declared that separate facilities for the races were lawful as long as they were equal.

Brown v. Board of Education (1954)

The Court renounced the doctrine of "separate but equal' as inherently unequal and mandated the abolishment of de jure segregation. The Court was persuaded that government-approved segregation was laden with racist intentions and was injurious to black schoolchildren.

Brown II (1955)

Faced with the prospect of razing de jure segregation in the public schools of the South, the Court advised schools to proceed "with all deliberate speed" in designing and implementing their own desegregation plans. But the Court was not clear in setting a timeline or even a standard against which desegregation could be assessed.

Green v. County School Board of New Kent County (1968)

The Court ruled that school segregation must be eliminated "root and branch," and developed six factors, known as the Green factors, to be used in assessing a school district's progress in the area of desegregation. The factors have since been used as guideposts for determining whether a school has achieved integrated (unitary) status.

Alexander v. Holmes County Board of Education (1969)

The Court aimed to accelerate desegregation efforts in the South by declaring that schools had to achieve desegregation at once and operate only as unitary schools.

---

children enrolled in predominantly minority schools is considerably higher in large metro areas than in small metro areas and towns. The urban communities are not only more segregated but much larger than the nation's large metropolitan areas. Given the fact that interdistrict remedies cannot be mandated unless there is evidence of discrimination in the action of the state or the outlying communities, the desegregation efforts in these areas typically involve magnet schools, choice plans, and, in districts not yet declared unitary, some transportation remedies.

Not surprisingly, in states with large urban populations, segregated schools continue to be the rule of thumb for blacks and Hispanics. For instance, in Michigan, over 61 percent of black students attend intensely minority schools, and only 14 percent attend majority white schools. Simi-

Swann v. Charlotte-Mecklenberg Board of Education (1971)

In an attack on de facto segregation, the Court ruled that transportation remedies could be employed to encourage desegregation in schools within a school district.

Milliken v. Bradley (1974)

The Court disallowed an interdistrict busing remedy to help desegregate the isolated inner-city schools of Detroit. Suburban schools could not be legally compelled to participate in a desegregation plan unless it could be proved that they took discriminatory actions that contributed to the segregation in the city schools. Because the ruling made it difficult to use interdistrict options for desegregation purposes, it was seen as a major setback for largely segregated urban school districts.

Milliken II (1977)

Recognizing that desegregation was difficult to achieve in racially isolated school districts, the Court ordered the state of Michigan to pay the Detroit school district to help offset the harm caused by segregation. This ruling cleared the way for courts to order states to pay for programs tailored to remedy the harm caused by segregation.

Board of Education of Oklahoma City v. Dowell (1991)

The Court held that, once a district was ruled unitary, it could be released from court supervision, even if the district reverted to resegregation, unless the resegregation resulted from discriminatory practices.

Missouri v. Jenkins (1995)

The Court ruled that the use of state funds to remedy the effects of segregation, via *Milliken II*, had time limitations, and these funds did not have to be reauthorized unless there was evidence of discriminatory practices.

---

lar percentages prevail in the states of California, New York, and Illinois, each of which possesses extremely large urban areas (New York City, Los Angeles, and Chicago are the three largest school districts in the country). Table 10-6 ranks the most segregated states for black students in America. Integration is most easily served in states where the minority population is small. For instance, in Iowa, Montana, Nebraska, New Hampshire, Vermont, and a few other states, no intensely minority schools even exist. The New York City public schools, which enroll over a million students (only 16 percent of whom are white), will easily serve more minority students than the entire public school system in the state of Iowa.

Interestingly, southern schools, which historically have been among the most segregated schools in the nation, are now more integrated than

TABLE 10-4

**Percentage of Black and Hispanic Students
in Predominantly Minority and Intensely Minority Schools**

	PREDOMINATELY (50–100%) MINORITY		INTENSELY (90–100%) MINORITY	
	Blacks	Hispanics	Blacks	Hispanics
1968–69	76.6%	54.8%	64.3%	23.1%
1972–73	63.6	56.6	38.7	23.3
1980–81	62.9	68.1	33.2	28.8
1986–87	63.3	71.5	32.5	32.2
1991–92	66.0	73.4	33.9	34.0
1996–97	68.8	74.8	35.0	35.4

SOURCE: U.S. Department of Education, Office for Civil Rights, data in Orfield, *Public school desegregation in the United States, 1968–80*, Tables 1 and 10; 1991–92 and 1996–97, NCES Common Core of Data.

10-4 THINKING ABOUT THE DATA
Segregation and Poverty

The following table shows the relation between segregation and poverty. Many of the most highly segregated high-minority schools in the nation enroll the poorest children in the nation. Why is this association significant? Is segregation by income a problem that threatens the public school mandate? Why has it not received anywhere near the attention accorded to race-based segregation?

PERCENT BLACK AND HISPANIC STUDENTS

Percent Poor in Schools	0–10%	10–20%	20–30%	30–40%	40–50%	50–60%	60–70%	70–80%	80–90%	90–100%
0–10%	31.0%	21.2%	10.2%	6.1%	5.9%	4.7%	5.6%	4.7%	4.5%	3.2%
20–25%	35.1	37.1	31.1	20.7	11.7	7.1	5.2	3.7	3.2	1.8
25–50%	26.2	32.5	43.8	49.0	45.4	38.2	26.3	15.7	11.4	8.3
50–100%	7.7	9.1	14.9	24.2	37.0	50.0	62.9	75.8	80.8	86.6
Total	100.0	100.0	100.0	100.0	100.0	100.0	100.0	100.0	100.0	100.0
% of U.S. Schools	47.1	10.8	7.7	6.4	5.6	4.5	3.7	3.2	3.2	7.7

SOURCE: 1996–97 NCES Common Core of Data, Public School Universe; Harvard Project on Desegregation.

	LARGE METRO (400,000+)		SMALL METRO (200,000+)		TOWN	
	City	Suburb	City	Suburb	25,000+	Small
Blacks	92%	57%	62%	43%	45%	44%
Hispanics	93	63	70	51	44	60

TABLE 10-5
Percentage of Minority Children Enrolled in Predominantly Minority Schools in City, Suburban, and Town Settings

SOURCE: Orfield, G., et al. (1993), *The growth of segregation in American schools: A report to the National School Boards Association* (Cambridge, MA: Harvard Graduate School of Education).

schools in the Northeast and Midwest (Orfield et al., 1993). Progress in the South, in fact, has been nothing short of spectacular. As shown in Table 10-7, the percentage of black children attending white majority schools has climbed enormously in the South. Prior to 1954, no black children attended white majority schools; state-enforced segregation made it unlawful. By 1988, the number had reached 43 percent, although it slipped to 34 percent in 1996. The Court's willingness to release districts from court supervision after being declared unitary has probably contributed to some of the reversal in percentages. Still, these numbers show that public schooling in the South is a different experience today than it was prior to the *Brown* ruling. Feature 10-5 provides the results of a Gallup poll that asked Americans about the perceived effects of desegregation efforts.

GENDER AND SCHOOL EDUCATION

In recent years, the issue of gender discrimination has found its way into the public discourse on education. In the past, the term *sex* was more typically used in discussing differences between males and females, but such a term points to biological factors rather than important social, educational, and cultural factors. Today, discussions of gender in schools relate directly to school environment concerns—and specifically, to the school curriculum. To what extent, for instance, can gender discrimination be found in what is studied in the curriculum, in how things are studied in the curriculum, and in achievement differences between boys and girls?

TABLE 10-6
Most Segregated States for Black Students
on Two Measures of Segregation

RANK	PERCENTAGE IN MAJORITY WHITE SCHOOLS		RANK	PERCENTAGE IN INTENSELY MINORITY (90–100%) SCHOOLS	
1	New York	14.0%	1	Michigan	61.6%
2	California	15.8	2	Illinois	60.4
3	Michigan	17.5	3	New York	58.2
4	Illinois	19.5	4	New Jersey	55.2
5	Hawaii	22.7	5	Maryland	47.5
6	Mississippi	24.1	6	Pennsylvania	45.9
7	Maryland	24.8	7	Alabama	40.5
8	Louisiana	25.8	8	Mississippi	39.2
9	New Jersey	25.9	9	Louisiana	38.9
10	Wisconsin	26.9	10	Tennessee	38.9
11	Texas	29.0	11	California	34.9
12	Pennsylvania	30.4	12	Texas	33.7
13	Georgia	30.5	13	Connecticut	33.7
14	Ohio	31.3	14	Georgia	31.0
15	Connecticut	32.4	15	Wisconsin	30.6
16	Alabama	33.0	16	Florida	27.2
17	Missouri	34.2	17	Missouri	26.8
18	Tennessee	34.3	18	Ohio	26.7
19	Arkansas	35.7	19	Indiana	21.9
20	Massachusetts	36.6	20	Massachusetts	19.7

SOURCE: 1996–97 NCES Common Core of Data Public School Universe; Harvard Project on Desegregation.

Gender Bias

Several feminist commentators have argued that schools are designed to promote the success of males. Logic might suggest otherwise. Because most schoolteachers are women, one might think that schools would be places where girls might find some advantage over boys. But critics, many of whom are self-identified as feminists, have suggested that schools do not operate this way. The problem, they claim, is that teachers are largely subordinate in the structure of school power. And because the superordinates in the schools (principals and superintendents) are still mostly males,

TABLE 10-7
Percentage of Black Students in Majority White Schools in the South

YEAR	PERCENTAGE
1954	0.001%
1960	0.1
1964	2.3
1967	13.9
1968	23.4
1970	33.1
1972	36.4
1976	37.6
1980	37.1
1986	42.9
1988	43.5
1991	39.2
1994	36.6
1996	34.7

SOURCE: DBS Corp., 1982; 1987; 1991–92 NCES Common Core of Data Public Education Agency Universe; 1994–95 NCES Common Core of Data School Universe; 1996–97 NCES Common Core of Data Public School Universe.

schools tend to promote so-called male values—typically described as marked by the importance of competition, individuality, and rationality. The schools simply reflect what it means to be competent and successful in a society ruled by male values. In the meantime, so-called female values—typically described as marked by the importance of subjectivity, empathy, and caring—are said to be given short shrift. Ultimately, the emphasis on male values comes at the educational and psychological cost of girls.

This line of thinking helped spark the investigation of gender bias in public schooling during the early 1990s. Observational research conducted by Myra and David Sadker (1994) pointed to the conclusion that boys dominated classroom processes in a way that compromised the education of girls. A report published by the American Association of University Women (AAUW), entitled *How Schools Shortchange Girls,* added fuel to the fire by noting the low self-esteem girls suffer in school and the low interest levels exhibited by girls in math and science. The AAUW (1992) report brought national attention to the issue of gender bias and touched off a national debate over the viability of single-sex classrooms. Attention to the problem

10-5 RESEARCH INQUIRY
Public Opinion on School Desegregation

In 1994, on the fortieth anniversary of the *Brown* ruling, Gallup released the results of a national survey on the topic of school desegregation (McAneny and Saad, 1994). Eighty-four percent of the respondents agreed with the decision and with the view that children should be allowed to go to the same school, irrespective of their race. Here are some similar questions asked in 1999. What might be the responses to these questions if you directed them to particular populations (schoolteachers, parents, lawyers, school administrators) and if you cross-analyzed the responses against variables such as race, age, or gender?

How do you feel about school integration? Do you feel it has improved the quality of education received by Black students?

	1999 (Whites)	1999 (Blacks)
Yes	68%	66%
No	26	31
No Opinion	6	3

How do you feel about school integration? Do you feel it has improved the quality of education received by White students?

	1999 (Whites)	1999 (Blacks)
Yes	48%	64%
No	46	19
No Opinion	6	17

SOURCE: Moore, D. & Saad, L. (1999, July). CNN/USA Today/Gallup Poll. Reprinted with permission.

continued with the release of a second AAUW (1993) report that examined the issue of sexual harassment in schools. Critics challenged some of the research findings of the Sadkers and the AAUW, but whether one agreed with the work or not, there was clearly a new awareness of the role of gender in the education of both boys and girls.

Even old antisexist legislation was given new life. During the early 1970s, Congress had passed Title IX legislation that made it illegal for any educational programs receiving federal funds to discriminate on the basis of sex or gender. According to the law, "No person in the United States shall, on the basis of sex, be excluded from participation in, be denied the benefit of, or be subjected to discrimination under any education program or activity receiving Federal financial assistance." This meant that school systems had to appoint Title IX officers to coordinate compliance and handle emerging complaints regarding sex discrimination. Title IX does recognize gender differences in relation to safety issues, privacy concerns, and ability levels. Thus, separate classes for contact sports, separate classes dealing with specific issues of human sexuality, and musical choruses based on a particular voice range are all permitted (Salomone, 1999). Exceptions, however, generally are not permitted in any core academic areas. Compliance with Title IX was slow in coming, and federal sanctions against offending schools generally were not substantial (Hansot, 1993). During the 1990s, however, Title IX had new life. Its impact was first felt in athletic programs, in which girls sports had long been treated as a stepchild. For instance, in 1971, 294,000 girls participated in high school athletics, as compared to 3.6 million boys; in 1994, 2.2 million girls participated in high school athletics, as compared to 3.5 million boys. Title IX provisions also began to alter the pattern of sex-segregated courses in health, vocational, and physical education, and in some higher levels of mathematics and science.

Research on gender and school education has targeted school textbooks, classroom interactions, testing mechanisms, and subject-specific curricula, among other areas. As early as the 1970s, for instance, the inadequate depiction of girls in the curriculum materials used in schools was widely documented. Girls appeared relatively infrequently, and the portrayals tended to reinforce stereotypic traits of passivity and dependence (Stacey, Bereaud, and Daniels, 1974). Similar problems have been found in the area of testing, a concern that is particularly problematic because of the linkage of test achievement to high-stakes educational opportunities, such as scholarships based on test results, admission to various school-based programs, and admission to college. And observational research has revealed that the nature of student-teacher interactions in the classroom, at both elementary and secondary school levels, can be interpreted as favorable to boys. Teachers, for instance, tend to give boys more attention (including listening and counseling), to offer them more thought-provoking questions, and to reward them more often, though they also criticize and punish them more often (Sadker, Sadker, and Klien, 1991).

Yet girls, as a group, earn higher grades than boys throughout their school careers in all subject areas and are less likely to be placed in special education programs. The lack of female representation in special education categories can be viewed as a sign of gender bias against girls, indicating a failure to be responsive to their special learning needs or as a way to marginalize boys. Girls outperform boys on writing skills assessments and historically have outscored boys in all age groups on verbal abilities. They drop out of school less often than boys, although when they do drop out it seems to have a more lasting negative effect.

Many of these findings also point to the possibility that boys can be short-changed and marginalized in school as well, and that gender stereotypes are at the core of the problem. The historical underperformance of boys in verbal areas, for instance, might also have something to do with stereotypic views that equate reading, especially the reading of certain kinds of materials, with feminine behavior. The issue of why boys are disproportionately classified into special education categories might have something to do with their more aggressive and attention-commanding behavior. When such behavioral problems tax the teacher's ability to keep children educationally engaged, his or her inclination might be to construe it as a learning problem (Greenberg, 1985). The paradox is that the stereotype of quiet passivity that we expect from girls might save them from unfair special education classifications. The gender factor, in this sense, can work both ways, and not always to the benefit of boys.

This is not to say that girls are not victimized by these stereotypes. According to Belenky and colleagues (1986), there is a "silence" expected from girls that does wide-ranging damage. In their interviews with women and girls, Belenky and colleagues (1986) found that many women viewed their schooling experiences in terms of sitting in classes silently, watching and listening to other students, mostly boys, talk. Because our culture traditionally has valued girls who are polite and submissive, these women and girls felt that their voices were not valued and that any effort to exercise an opinion might be construed as rude behavior. Belenky and colleagues (1986) cited the importance of verbalizing one's thoughts in the development of crucial reasoning skills to reinforce their indictment against the schools for silencing girls' voices. Given the role of silence in the school lives of girls, Belenky and colleagues (1986) argued that girls also tend to see themselves as receivers rather than mediators of knowledge in the classroom, as receptacles into which other people make "deposits" of knowledge. Receivers of knowledge tend to believe that other people have important things to say but that their own thoughts are unimportant. Thus, women and girls who think of themselves as receivers of knowledge are apt to rely on authorities to tell them what is right and wrong. They do not

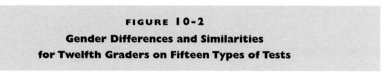

FIGURE 10-2

Gender Differences and Similarities for Twelfth Graders on Fifteen Types of Tests

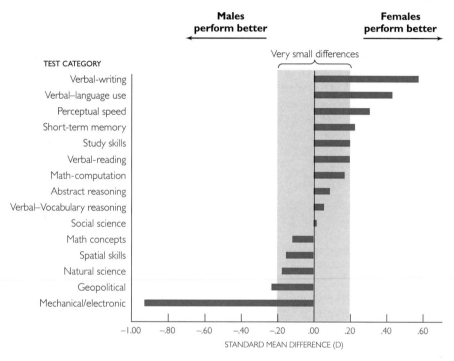

NOTE: Based on seventy-four tests for twelfth graders nationally

SOURCE: Cole, N. (1997), *The ETS gender study: How females and males perform in educational settings* (Princeton, NJ: Educational Testing Service), p. 12. Reprinted by permission of Educational Testing Service, the copyright owner.

believe that they can develop their own ideas. Again, received knowledge is an attribute that is basic to the stereotypic passivity expected from women.

Despite these criticisms, the achievement data in most cases show little evidence of a gender gap, with a few very important exceptions. In 1997, the Educational Testing Service (ETS) reviewed the findings from all of the best studies on the relation between gender and school achievement to find out what they might have to say in the aggregate (Cole, 1997). The results point to some interesting differences. Figure 10-2 shows these differences at the twelfth-grade level, at the conclusion of the whole public school experience. The data show that most achievement categories fall within margins of difference considered to be very small, attesting to the fact that in most areas there is not much of a gender gap.

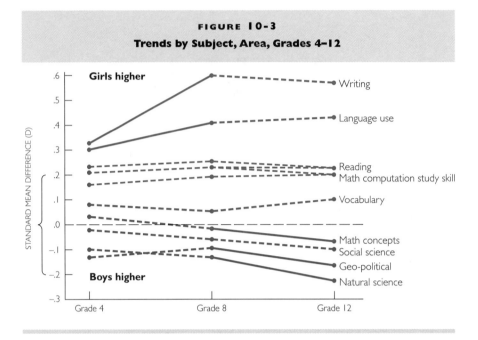

FIGURE 10-3
Trends by Subject, Area, Grades 4–12

NOTE: Solid lines indicate a significant grade-to-grade change in degree of gender difference.
SOURCE: Cole, N. (1997), *The ETS gender study: How females and males perform in educational settings* (Princeton, NJ: Educational Testing Service), p. 5. Reprinted by permission of Educational Testing Service, the copyright owner.

However, more notable differences manifest in a few categories. For example, females in the twelfth grade clearly outperform twelfth-grade boys in writing and language use, while the boys clearly outperform the girls in mechanical/electronic know-how. One could interpret the news in Figure 10-2 as worse for boys than girls if only because verbal, writing, and language use skills all have high utility and relevance in life—arguably more so, at least, than knowledge of mechanics and electronics. At the same time, however, mechanical know-how might offer access to higher-paying jobs. Interestingly, differences between girls and boys in math and science performance were small; boys showed slightly better skills with math concepts and girls slightly better computational skills.

In most cases, the differences among twelfth graders were evident as early as elementary school and grew bigger as students progressed through the school system. As Figure 10-3 shows, the superiority that girls show in writing and language use was evident, on a smaller scale, in the fourth grade. It magnified by the eighth grade and even more so by the twelfth grade. A similar, though less dramatic, pattern can be seen in the areas in which males score higher than females. This could mean that the schools have a hand in

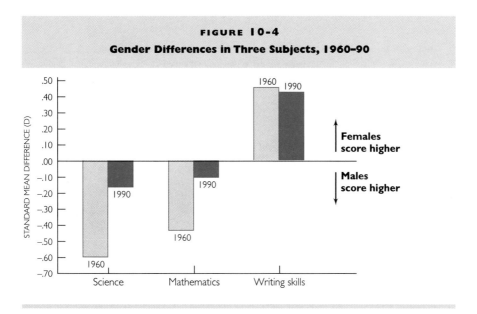

FIGURE 10-4
Gender Differences in Three Subjects, 1960–90

SOURCE: Cole, N. (1997), *The ETS gender study: How females and males perform in educational settings* (Princeton, NJ: Educational Testing Service), p. 14. Reprinted by permission of Educational Testing Service, the copyright owner.

exacerbating achievement differences between boys and girls, or at least in failing to do much to prevent the differences from worsening.

Figure 10-4 shows the differences in achievement between boys and girls in certain subject areas over a thirty-year period. The small differences between boys and girls in math and science achievement are part of a historical trend that attests to a closing or narrowing of the gap between boys and girls (Cole, 1997). What were once wide differences in math and science achievement between boys and girls had been reduced considerably by 1990. This is likely the effect of acknowledging and reducing the gender bias that worked against girls in the past. Although families, legislative initiatives, and even the courts have all likely helped with the cause, the schools probably deserve some credit for closing the achievement gap, given their involvement in direct math and science instruction. No such positive trend or movement, however, can be found between boys and girls in the area of writing. Boys have been outperformed by girls in writing for decades and have made no significant gains to close the gap. And, in this case, the school probably deserves some of the blame.

Girls, as indicated, achieve higher grades than boys in all major subjects. They exceed the grade performance of boys most in English, and less so in social studies, science, and math. The grade performance of girls in science is especially interesting because they demonstrate no commensurate superiority in the tested achievement levels of math and science. In other

TABLE 10-8
**Percentage of Postsecondary Degrees and Certificates
Awarded to Women, 1993–94**

DEGREE LEVEL	PERCENTAGE OF DEGREES AWARDED TO WOMEN
Certificate of less than one-year programs	51.6%
Certificate of one-, but less than two-year programs	58.2
Associate's degree	59.2
Bachelor's degree	54.5
Master's degree	54.5
Doctorate	38.5
First professional	40.7
Total	55.4

SOURCE: U.S. Department of Education (1996), *Digest of education statistics, 1996* (Washington, DC: National Center for Education Statistics).

words, girls get better grades in math and science, but slightly worse test scores. Some critics have interpreted this phenomenon as a function of the school reward structure for compliant behavior—that grades offer little in the way of reliable assessments of academic performance. Girls, in other words, get better grades because they behave better and act nicer to teachers than boys do. There might be something to this criticism, but school grades are still one of the best predictors of academic performance after high school and are associated with productive skills, such as doing homework and participating in class (Cole, 1997). Good grades seem to reflect productiveness. Yet, despite achieving better grades in math and science, girls typically stay clear of mathematics and science as a career. They are also less inclined to enroll in advanced placement courses in math and science. Many factors may be at play here, including a testing bias and a potential stereotypic socialization pattern in schools (and in society in general) that upholds mathematics and science as suitable career paths for men. According to some surveys, girls learn to think that they are not mathematically capable as early as the elementary grades (AAUW, 1992).

Still, there are encouraging trends in higher education for women. Recent annual growth rates for women enrolled in higher education have outstripped the rate for men. In the 1993–94 academic year, 55 percent of all degrees awarded were to women (National Center for Educational Statistics, 1998). In 1978, males earned more bachelor's, master's, and doctoral degrees than females, but as Table 10-8 shows, females have now

TABLE 10-9
Average Earnings of Year-Round, Full-Time Workers
Age 25 and Older by Gender, 1995

LEVEL OF EDUCATION	MALES	FEMALES
Less than 9th grade	$20,461	$13,349
9th to 12th grade, no diploma	24,377	16,188
High school graduate, includes equivalency	31,081	21,383
Some college, no degree	35,639	24,787
Associate's degree	38,944	26,903
Bachelor's degree or higher	61,008	39,271
Total	41,118	27,162

SOURCE: U.S. Department of Commerce (1996), *Statistical abstract of the United States: 1996* (Washington, DC: Bureau of the Census), p. 471.

overtaken males. And statistical projections indicate that women will maintain a strong presence in higher education.

However, there is less cause for optimism with regard to earnings. The average earnings of women and men by levels of educational attainment are given in Table 10-9. In 1995, women earned two-thirds of what men earned. Part of the difference is due to the fact that women still are more likely than men to prepare for jobs that historically have low income potential. Six out of 10 minimum wage earners are women, and women head 8 out of 10 single-parent households and 7 out of 10 families living below the poverty line (Scollay, 1994). Ninety-eight percent of all secretaries (the leading occupation overall for women), 84 percent of all elementary school teachers, and 90 percent of nurses are women; 76 percent of all physicians and 89 percent of all engineers are men (U.S. Department of Labor, 1999). But differences between the sexes in starting salaries also exist within the same field (National Center for Education Statistics, 1998).

Schools clearly have to get serious about remedying any role they might play in gender discrimination, especially because there are so many gender-based stereotypes perpetuated by the family and by society in general. Olivares and Rosenthal (1992) cite several studies that point to the role parents play in gender stereotyping. Parents, for example, still encourage sex-typed activities for their children (Lytton and Romney, 1991), continue to choose stereotyped toys and colors for infants and toddlers (Pomerleau, Boldice, et al., 1990), and frequently evaluate children negatively, especially boys, when they engage in cross-sex play or exhibit cross-sex personality traits

(Martin, 1990). Some scholars believe that sex-linked toys also have a place in the gender construction puzzle. Toys, for instance, that might help children develop an attitude of caring, such as baby dolls, have too often been seen as appropriate only for girls. Young boys, in fact, could learn important values related to fatherhood and child care in general by playing with dolls. Interestingly, boy dolls are typically superheroes who engage in fantastic physical feats. Similarly, toys that might serve as an introduction to science and mechanics, such as building blocks, have too often been reserved for boys (Noddings, 1992). Gender discrimination is clearly a problem that transcends the school.

Gender inequities have led some schools to consider gender-segregated classes. The presumption here is that boys undermine the education of girls through their attention-getting and competitive behaviors and the preferential treatment they receive from teachers. Others believe that girls simply learn differently from boys and are best taught away from boys. Proponents of single-sex classes cite the low self-esteem of girls, their low levels of interest in math and science, the sexual harassment they suffer at the hands of boys, and the omnipresent "boys curriculum."

Gender-segregated classes, however, are problematic for several reasons. First, they may violate a basic principle of the public school mandate, which is to provide integrated experiences for all youths irrespective of race, ethnicity, social class, and gender. In fact, some legal analysts argue that gender-segregated classes are violations of Title IX. Citing the Title IX provision, some states have made gender-segregated classes illegal. The federal Office of Civil Rights, however, has yet to get aggressive in its treatment of single-sex classes as Title IX violations. School districts, it should be remembered, do have some justification for single-sex classes. Title IX provisions allow exceptions that try to "overcome the effects of conditions which resulted in limited participation therein by persons of a particular sex." In other words, a school district could document a case for single-sex classes as a matter of "affirmative action," as a way to overcome past impediments to female school achievement. This makes math and science education more of a candidate for single-sex schooling than, say, reading education. Title IX also allows for something known as the comparability clause, whereby comparable courses or services can be offered to formerly excluded groups (Salomone, 1999).

The research findings on the topic of all-girl classes are equivocal. Some of it suggests that girls experience more comfort, improved self-confidence, and higher achievement in single-sex settings, with these effects being more pronounced with low-income black and Hispanic girls (Salomone, 1999). Critics of gender segregation, however, argue that all-girl classes are a peculiar response to accusations of school-based gender

Students in an experimental all-girls classroom.

Associated Press, Courier-Post

bias, because they are themselves based on a benevolent sexism implying that girls cannot perform in the same classrooms as boys. This sets the stage for the legitimization of stereotypic views of girls and creates the possibility for further misunderstandings between the sexes.

Other critics observe that making gender the salient factor in classroom enrollments ignores other important factors, especially race- and class-based ones, that have at least as much of an impact on inequity concerns as does gender. They also question why gender-based problems need to be remedied through class segregation when so many other solutions are available. If boys, for instance, are ridiculing girls, can a method be found to prevent such episodes without resorting to class segregation? If teachers are unwittingly providing advantages to boys, can the school seek a remedy, built on in-service training or even extra classroom programs that keep the classroom integrated? And if gender segregation finds a compelling argument in terms of enhancing the school performance of girls, can similar arguments be made for ethnic-, class-, or race-based education? Feature 10-6 offers an opportunity to further pursue the debate.

Sexual Harassment

Today, increasing attention is being given to the issue of sexual harassment in school, especially against female students. The problem can start in the

10-6 DEBATING THE ISSUES
Single-Sex Schools

The lines have been drawn in the debate over single-sex schools. Believing that coeducation shortchanges girls, advocates of single-sex schools are convinced that the self-esteem of girls, their confidence in the classroom, their interest in math and science, and the overall quality of their educational experience can best be served in gender-segregated classrooms. Opponents claim that such views themselves are sexist, because they imply the inability of girls to perform in the same classroom as boys and set the conditions for true gender-based differences. They also claim that segregation by class, race, or gender is antithetical to the public school mandate and the heterogeneous experience. Finally, they raise issues about the legality of single-sex classrooms in the light of Title IX legislation. What do you think?

To become fully informed on the issue, examine the views of the American Civil Liberties Union (ACLU) and the National Organization for Women (NOW); both of which see single-sex schools as unconstitutional. For a middle-ground view, examine the 1998 report of the American Association of University Women Education Foundation, *Separated by Sex: A Critical Look at Single Sex Education for Girls.* Views supporting single-sex schools can be found in the work of Riordan (1990), Sadker and Sadker (1994), and the National Coalition of Girl Schools.

early grades, when boys use sexually loaded terms to describe and taunt their female peers, often without knowing what they are saying. In high school, it can be deliberate sexual harassment that places unhealthy pressure and anxieties on teenage girls. The 1993 AAUW report *Hostile Hallways* reported on the problems. Eight-one percent of girls claimed to have been subjected to some form of unwanted sexual advance, and 65 percent said they had been touched or grabbed in a sexual manner. Although boys also reported high levels of harassment, girls were more seriously affected by the harassment, with 33 percent stating that they did not want to talk in class or attend school because of it. The emotional and behavioral impact of harassment also took more of a toll on girls than boys, with 43 percent of girls who had some experience of sexual harassment reporting that they felt scared (as opposed to 14 percent of boys) and 69 percent stating that they avoided the person who bothered them (as opposed to 27 percent of boys). Table 10-10 lists some key findings from the study.

TABLE 10-10
The Educational Impact of Sexual Harassment

RESPONSE	BOYS	GIRLS
Not wanting to go to school	12%	33%
Not wanting to talk as much in class	13	32
Finding it hard to pay attention in school	13	28
Staying home from school or cutting a class	7	24
Making a lower grade on a test or paper	9	23
Finding it hard to study	9	22
Making a lower grade in class	6	20
Thinking about changing schools	6	18
Doubting whether you have what it takes to graduate from high school	4	5

Base: the 81% of students who report some experience of sexual harassment in school

SOURCE: Reprinted with permission from AAUW, *Hostile Hallways,* 1993, p. 15.

Student-to-student harassment is what is typically known as hostile environment harassment. It includes any number of harassing behaviors, including verbal, nonverbal, and physical contact of a sexual nature, that creates an environment hostile to learning and to the well-being of the student. In *Hostile Hallways,* a variety of sexual harassment experiences were documented, and as Table 10-11 shows, harassment is a serious matter.

What has not been clear until recently is the extent of liability that a school carries for student-to-student harassment. In *Davis v. Monroe County Board of Education,* a circuit court ruled that the school district was not liable for a fifth grader's acts of harassment against another student. But the Supreme Court, in a close decision, overturned the ruling in 1999, observing that schools are indeed responsible and liable for student-to-student harassment, as long as it can be documented that they knew about the harassment and failed to act against it (Stein, 1999). The ruling confirmed the decision in another case, *Gebser v. Lago Vista Independent School District* (1998), which involved teacher-to-student sexual misconduct. A ninth-grade student had a year-long sexual relationship with her teacher, but the school was not aware of the problem, and the girl never reported it to

TABLE 10-11 Types of Sexual Harassment Experienced in School		
ACT	BOYS	GIRLS
Sexual comments, jokes, gestures, or looks	56%	76%
Touched, grabbed, or pinched in a sexual way	42	65
Intentionally brushed up against in a sexual way	36	57
Flashed or mooned	41	49
Had sexual rumors spread about them	34	42
Had clothing pulled at in a sexual way	28	38
Shown, given, or left sexual pictures, photographs, illustrations, messages, or notes	34	31
Had their way blocked in a sexual way	17	38
Had sexual messages/graffiti written about them on bathroom walls, in locker rooms, etc.	18	20
Forced to kiss someone	14	23
Called gay or lesbian	23	10
Had clothing pulled off or down	17	16
Forced to do something sexual other than kissing	9	13
Spied on while dressing or showering	8	7

SOURCE: Reprinted with permission from AAUW, *Hostile Hallways,* 1993, p. 9

anyone. The Supreme Court did not find the school liable because it had no knowledge of the problem and therefore could not respond to it. The defining principles in the eyes of the Court were knowledge of the problem and the adequacy of the response. If sexual harassment is occurring in the schools at the hands of fellow students or teachers, the school has clear liability if it has knowledge of the harassment and if it fails to adequately respond to it.

SUMMARY

The school equity issues raised in this chapter range from the sorting of students in academic programs by ability (and de facto by race and income), to manifest race-based segregation, to the differential, if not inequitable, treatment of the sexes in school. In the case of curriculum tracking, the need to manage differential abilities and talents clashes with the need to provide equitable experiences. Schools have to provide differential experiences responsive to individual aptitudes, interests, and remedial needs in a way that does not marginalize any students or ghettoize their experience. The controversy is whether some reformed version of tracking will be able to secure this balance.

In the area of segregation, the *Brown* ruling made it clear that segregation sanctioned by the law was inherently unequal and was in fact state-sponsored racism. The historical trend has been to integrate the schools in districts that traditionally practiced discrimination against blacks. The effects have been impressive. But the Supreme Court's inclination now is to see segregation as a problem only if it is a function of discriminatory practices. As a result, some resegregation has occurred. The public schools nevertheless are integrated today at a level that would have been unimaginable half a century ago.

With regard to gender bias, the question is whether the schools have conducted themselves in a manner that has come at the expense of the education of girls. Although there is clearly a persuasive argument that schools have indeed committed some gender-based offenses against girls, the school achievements of girls are impressive. They get better grades than boys, drop out of school less often, and are better readers and writers. For their part, boys show some slight superiority in math and science and considerable superiority in mechanical know-how, and select into math and science careers at a disproportionally high rate. Scholars concerned about the education of girls cite self-esteem and self-confidence factors, as well as observational data speaking to the neglect of girls in mixed classrooms, in making a case for single-sex schools. Opponents see gender-segregated classrooms as laden with benevolent sexist attitudes and as potential violations of Title IX provisions.

QUESTIONS AND ACTIVITIES

1. What are the typical justifications for the use of curriculum tracks in schools?

2. How have critics argued that curriculum tracking practices are inequitable and unfair to poor and minority students?

3. What is the difference between curriculum tracking and ability grouping?

4. Why is curriculum tracking rarely considered to be a problem in elementary schools?

5. Explain the different forms of tracking that can exist in high schools.

6. How have school districts responded to the mandate to desegregate?

7. In what way was the ruling *Brown v. Board of Education* a repudiation of *Plessy*?

8. What are the Green factors, and what role have they played in the historical struggle to desegregate the schools?

9. What were some of the educational strategies embraced by the federal government in the 1960s as it dealt with issues of segregation and poverty?

10. What was the essential implication behind the *Swann* ruling?

11. Why did Justice Thurgood Marshall believe that the *Milliken* ruling was a "giant step backward" for desegregation efforts?

12. Explain the significance of the *Oklahoma City v. Dowell* ruling.

13. What are the national trends in the area of school segregation? Where has segregation been most intractable, and where has the most progress been made?

14. Make a case demonstrating how schools might shortchange girls.

15. Make a case demonstrating how schools might shortchange boys.

16. Do you believe that schools embrace male values in their conduct and in a way that compromises the education of girls?

17. What are the essential points of difference in the achievement of boys and girls once they reach the twelfth grade? Speculate on how these differences arose.

18. Explain the strong classroom performance of girls in math and science against their slight underperformance on standardized tests in math and science and against their lack of interest in pursuing math and science careers.

19. What are the general arguments for and against single-sex classrooms? What are your personal views on the matter?

20. What is Title IX, and what role has it played in regulating gender bias issues in the schools?

21. Explain and interpret the significance of the sexual harassment survey data presented in the chapter.

REFERENCES

American Association of University Women. (1993). *Hostile hallways: The AAUW survey on sexual harassment in America's schools.* (Washington, DC: National Education Association).

American Association of University Women. (1992). *How schools shortchange girls.* (Washington, DC: National Education Association).

Belenky, M., Clinchy, B., Goldberger, N., and Tarule, J. (1986). *Women's way of knowing.* (New York: Basic Books).

Braddock, J. H. (1990a). Tracking in the middle grades: National patterns of grouping for instruction. *Phi Delta Kappan,* 71(6):445–49.

Braddock, J. H. (1990b). *Tracking implications for student race ethnic groups* (Report no.1). (Baltimore Center for Research on Effective Schooling for Disadvantaged Students).

Carey, N., et al. (1994). *Curricular differentiation in public high schools* (ED379-338). (Washington, DC: National Center for Education Statistics).

Cole, N. (1997). *The ETS gender study: How females and males perform in educational settings.* (Princeton, NJ: Educational Testing Service).

Coleman, J., et al. (1966). *Equality of educational opportunity.* (Washington, DC: Office of Education).

Cremin, L. A. (1966). *The genius of American education.* (New York: Random House, Vintage Books).

Greenberg, S. (1985). Educational equity in early education environments. In S. Klien (ed.), *Handbook in achieving sex equity through education.* (Baltimore: Johns Hopkins University Press).

Hansot, E. (1993). Historical and contemporary views of gender and education. In S. K. Biklen and D. Pollard (eds.), *Gender and Education. Part 1, Ninety-Second Yearbook of the National Society for the Study of Education.* (Chicago: NSSE).

Howe, H. (1993). *Thinking about our kids.* (New York: Free Press).

Husen, T. (1983). Are standards in the U.S. schools really lagging behind those in other countries? *Phi Delta Kappan,* 64(7):455–61.

Kulik, J. (1993). An analysis of the research on ability grouping. *National Research Center on the Gifted and Talented Newsletter,* 8/9 (ED367-095).

Loveless, T. (1999). *The tracking wars: State reform meets school policy.* (Washington, DC: Brookings Institution Press).

Loveless, T. (1998). *The tracking and ability grouping debate.* Fordham Report. (www.eduexcellence.net/library).

Lytton, H., and Romney, D. (1991). Parents' differential socialization of boys and girls. *Psychological Bulletin,* 109:267–96.

Martin, C. L (1990). Attitudes and expectations about children with nontraditional and traditional gender roles. *Sex Roles,* 229(3/4):131–65.

McCarthy, M. M., Cambron-McCabe, N. H., and Thomas, S. B. (1998). *Public school law: Teachers' and students' rights.* (Boston: Allyn & Bacon).

Nasaw, D. (1979). *Schooled to order.* (New York: Oxford University Press).

National Center for Education Statistics. (1998). *Gender differences in earning among young adults entering the labor market.* (Washington, DC: NCES).

Noddings, N. (1992). Gender and the curriculum. In P. Jackson (ed.), *Handbook of research on curriculum.* (New York: Macmillan).

Oakes, J. (1990). *Multiplying inequalities.* (Santa Monica, CA: Rand Corporation).

Oakes, J. (1985). *Keeping track: How schools structure inequality.* (New Haven, CT: Yale University Press).

Oakes, J., Gamoran, A., and Page, R. (1992). Curriculum differentiation: Opportunities, outcomes and meanings. In P. Jackson (ed.), *Handbook of research on curriculum.* (New York: Macmillan).

Olivares, R. A., and Rosenthal, N. (1992). *Gender equity and classroom experiences: A review of research.* (ED366-701).

Orfield, G., and Eaton, S. (1997). *Dismantling desegregation: The quiet reversal of Brown v. Board of Education.* (New York: New Press).

Orfield, G., et al. (1993). *The growth of segregation in American schools: A report to the National School Boards Association.* (Cambridge, MA: Harvard Graduate School of Education).

Pomerleau, A., Boldice, D., et al. (1990). Pink or blue: Environmental stereotyping in the first two years of life. *Sex Roles,* 22(5/6):359–67.

Riordan, C. (1990). *Girls and boys in school: Together or separate?* (New York: Teachers College Press).

Sadker, M., and Sadker, D. (1994). *Failing at fairness.* (New York: Touchstone).

Sadker, M., Sadker, D., and Klien, S. (1991). The issue of gender in elementary and secondary education. In G. Grant (ed.), *Review of research in education.* (Washington, DC: American Educational Research Association).

Salomone, R. (1999). Single sex schooling: Law, policy and research. In D. Ravitch (ed.), *Brookings papers on education policy.* (Washington, DC: Brookings Institution Press).

Scollay, S. J. (1994). The forgotten half. *The American School Board Journal,* 181(4):46–48.

Slavin, R. (1990). Achievement effects in ability grouping in secondary schools. *Review of Educational Research,* 60(3):471–99.

Stacey, M., Bereaud, S., and Daniels, J. (eds.). (1974). *And Jill came tumbling down.* (New York: Dell Books).

Stein, N. (1999). *Classrooms and courtrooms: Facing sexual harassment in K-12 schools.* (New York: Teachers College Press).

Tanner, D., and Tanner, L. N. (1995). *Curriculum development: Theory into practice.* (New York: Macmillan).

Tyler, R. W. (1981). The United States and the world: A comparison of educational performance. *Phi Delta Kappan,* 62(5):307–18.

U.S. Department of Labor. (1999). *Labor statistics in the Women's Bureau.* (www.dol.gov).

Whitman, M. (1998). *The irony of desegregation law 1955–1995: Essays and documents.* (Princeton, NJ: Markus Wiener).

Whitman, M. (1993). *Removing a badge of slavery: The record of Brown v. Board of Education.* (Princeton, NJ: Markus Wiener).

CHAPTER 11

The Condition of American Education

The Issue of School Achievement

The National Assessment of Educational Progress
THE READING REPORT CARD
THE MATHEMATICS REPORT CARD

School Dropouts

Poverty, Home Environments, and School Achievement

School Safety

Summary

Questions and Activities

References

NE DOES NOT HAVE TO GO VERY FAR or dig very deep to encounter less than complimentary commentary on the public schools. The national media have been especially quick to remind the public of any deficiencies in the public schools. In recent years, for example, we have been told that SAT scores are declining, that comparative cross-national achievement scores are less than encouraging for U.S. students, that dropout rates are embarrassingly high, and that most academic achievement measures point to serious flaws in the public education system. The media portrayal typically has been phrased in attention commanding language about educational crisis and calamity, which has lent itself well to the preferred rhetoric of politicians, who themselves have rarely been friendly to the public school.

The schools have had to endure this type of criticism at least since the mid-twentieth century. It is no exaggeration to say that public schools, from the period of the Cold War onward, have been blamed for virtually every perceived failure or decline in the nation's industrial, commercial, military, and technological status. During the late 1950s, for example, when the Soviet Union was believed to hold a military and technological advantage over the United States, the public school was blamed for not producing enough quality scientists, mathematicians, and engineers to meet the Soviet challenge.

During the early 1980s, a similar connection was made when the Japanese economy was thriving and taking the lead in the development of technological advancements. Again, the presumed lack of American ability to compete with the Japanese was publicly attributed to failings in the American public school. A spate of books followed advising Americans to imitate the Japanese educational system. In 1983, a national commission appointed by President Reagan to study the condition of public education in America was so appalled by the alleged low state of achievement in the public schools that it declared the nation to be "at risk" (National Center for Education Statistics, 1983).

What has been so striking about such criticisms is that the public school always seems to be central to any perceived failure in society but somehow insignificant or incidental to any signs of societal progress and success. Where there have been economic, technological, and military successes (and there have been many), the schools have received no credit. In truth, if one were to judge the schools according to the nation's success on various nationalistic and techno-industrial scales, one would necessarily have to make a positive judgment, as the United States currently is the world's only superpower. The association between the sociopolitical temper of different decades and public school reform is detailed in Chapter 13.

Indignant about the barrage of criticisms of the schools, some commentators have tried to correct "the big lie" that they believe has been told to the American people about public education (Berliner and Biddle, 1997; Bracey, 1993). For instance, SAT scores have indeed been on the decline, but the drop is mostly attributable to a rise in the number of students taking the exam (and going on to college) from low-income and minority backgrounds. This is an effect that should be viewed, in its broadest democratic context, with some satisfaction. Similarly, international test data might not always point to a superior performance by American students, even though they sometimes do. But few people understand that the basis of comparison between the United States and other advanced nations is not always fair, and that the extension of public schooling in American results in secondary and postsecondary enrollments not imaginable in many other advanced nations. Complaints about the dropout rate in public schools persist, often associated with nostalgic views about earlier times. However, the American public school's holding power has never been better, and the number of minority and low-income children staying in school has never been higher. And, although it is fashionable to talk about the low state of achievement in the public schools, the data show not only no appreciable decline in national achievement in recent decades but considerable progress and gain in selected areas.

The school, of course, has its share of problems. It is no more perfect than any other societal institution. Clearly, much still needs to be done to make it a more enlightened and thoughtful place. But the condition of education in America is marked by both failures and achievement, and can be fully understood only after taking account of the various sociological factors that influence school achievement.

THE ISSUE OF SCHOOL ACHIEVEMENT

School achievement is typically framed in reference to some form of standardized test, such as the Iowa Test of Basic Skills, or for graduating seniors the SAT or ACT. Each of these tests attempts to gauge what a student has learned in the classroom. Determining what children have been taught, or what they were supposed to have been taught, is the first step in the design of a valid and reliable measurement of achievement. An achievement test is only valid to the extent that it actually tests what has been taught. Thus, school achievement is a gauge not only of what students have learned but also of how effectively they have been taught.

© Joel Gordon 1990

An achievement test is not only a gauge of what students have learned, but also a gauge of how effectively they have been taught.

Achievement is sometimes confused with aptitude. They are related but fundamentally different ideas. An aptitude test is directed at determining a student's intrinsic ability in a particular area of knowledge or set of skills. A musical aptitude exam, for instance, might attempt, among other things, to determine an individual's ability to discern different pitches or tones, while a musical achievement exam might attempt to target an individual's knowledge of music theory or music history. Aptitude is more of an intrinsic ability, while achievement can be externally influenced because one cannot know the terms and principles of music theory or history without their being taught at some level. IQ tests are aptitude exams; basic skill tests and teacher-made subject area tests are achievement exams. School achievement in its most traditional construction is largely concerned with reading and mathematical skills at the elementary level and subject knowledge at the secondary level. Obviously, aptitude influences achievement, because having an innate skill in a particular area makes it easier to achieve in that area.

Almost all classroom teachers have given exams that "covered" the material taught in the classroom. When thinking about achievement, the idea of coverage is important. Achievement is directly related to a student's instructional exposure to the various items on the achievement exam. This instructional exposure is something others have referred to as opportunity to learn (OTL). OTL helps us to understand some of the achievement gaps witnessed between various groups. One could argue, for instance, that at least some of the achievement differences found between low-track and high-track ability groups, between girls and boys, between children from different income and racial backgrounds, and between various school districts (or even whole countries) are attributable to OTL differences.

OTL factors can manifest in many ways. The degree of commonality that exists between what is covered in a textbook and what is actually tested speaks to an OTL issue. Commercial publishers of texts are aware of this and often tout the linkage that their books have to various important tests. The availability of course work, especially advanced placement courses, that could extend a student's exposure to knowledge is another OTL factor. Students exposed to more advanced course work, not surprisingly, have higher achievement levels. The overall linkage between a school's curriculum and the test is another OTL factor. This, in fact, has become such a concern in many school districts that schoolwide curriculum alignment strategies have been used to bring the whole of the school curriculum into alignment with state-mandated tests. The liberties that teachers take with course materials—the extent they emphasize or deemphasize certain points—also contribute to OTL.

Berliner and Biddle (1997) have facetiously emphasized the power of OTL as it relates to achievement in the "Berliner and Biddle's student achievement law," which states that "regardless of what anyone claims about student and school characteristics, *opportunity to learn* is the single most powerful predictor of student achievement" (p. 55). This is another way of saying that one cannot expect students to know something that they have never been taught and that in some cases achievement can be improved simply by providing more equitable opportunities to learn.

When achievement data are used to compare groups, whether in classrooms, schools, school districts, or national school systems, it is important to understand the role of OTL. Because the governance structure of the public school in the United States is decentralized, the linkage between a school's curriculum and any standardized test is generally unknown and not always likely to be very tight. Different states have different graduation requirements, different subject area mandates, and different means of regulating local districts. Some states have strict curriculum requirements, while others hardly have none. In fact, the movement to embrace national (or statewide) standards is largely motivated by a desire to centralize the curricular presentation of the public school in the interests of securing clearer, more equitable OTL standards, which will, many believe, help to elevate achievement. Many other advanced nations have a centralized system of school governance, often regulated by a national ministry of education, that mandates a national curriculum and sometimes even national examinations. This results, in the most extreme cases, in every student being, in effect, on the same page in the same text, doing the same thing, at the same time. If these standardized national systems are closely coupled with an achievement test, as they often are on international tests, one can imagine the benefits for achievement. As it turns out, this is one of the key reasons achievement in the United States is sometimes lower than in other advanced nations.

THE NATIONAL ASSESSMENT OF EDUCATIONAL PROGRESS

One of the responsibilities of the U.S. Department of Education is to provide a picture of the state of achievement in the nation's public schools. As a result, the National Center for Education Statistics (NCES) collects data on criterion-based measures of achievement in reading, mathematics, science, writing, literature, geography, history, civics, art, music, and computer skills. These tests are known collectively as the National Assessment of Educational Progress (NAEP), the results of which are popularized by the NCES as "the nation's report card of educational progress." The tests are ongoing and congressionally mandated.

The NAEP is not designed to compare individual achievement or even the aggregate achievement of school districts. No individual student or school-specific results are even reported. Instead, it is designed to track longitudinal achievement on a set of skills and knowledge in various subject domains. The NAEP reports state-by-state results and, of course, national composite scores. The results of the exams are analyzed against any number of variables, including gender, race, income level, OTL factors, home environment conditions, and attitudes. The NAEP is administered to a national sample of students, usually fourth, eighth, and twelfth graders.

The NAEP is a criterion-referenced exam, which means that it assesses students across a range of increasingly complex criterion levels. The exam yields an absolute measure; that is, the assessment is made against some predefined set of criterion knowledge or skills. The criterion levels for the NAEP indicate who has achieved or mastered a basic, an intermediate (often gauged as the expected proficiency level), and an advanced level of understanding within a subject area. This makes the NAEP exams different

Reading achievement data are especially important to our society because reading is a foundation for intelligent and informed participation in society.

from the popular norm-referenced standardized exams. The Iowa Test of Basic Skills, the SAT and ACT, and most other standardized achievement exams are norm-referenced exams. They are designed to measure student performance, not against criterion levels, but against (or relative to) the performance of other students. Norm-referenced exams thus are relative measures, with results that discriminate between average, below-average, and above-average performances. These kinds of tests typically have percentile ranking associated with the raw scores.

The Reading Report Card

The NAEP reading exam, which was first offered in 1969, is a comprehensive measure of reading ability. As with all NAEP tests, it is given to a national sample of 9-, 13- and 17-year-olds, and is based on a wide range of reading assessments, from simple narrative passages to complex articles dealing with specialized topics. Reading selections in the NAEP include poems, essays, passages from selected texts, and stories, and questions are both multiple choice and open-ended.

Reading achievement data are especially important to our society because reading provides a foundation for intelligent and informed participation in society. Reading, after all, is a widely applicable skill that provides independent access to ideas, knowledge, and information. It is a skill that transcends all subject areas, in that it is required in the study of mathematics, science, social studies, and so forth.

As indicated, NAEP examinations are built on criterion measures of achievement. In reading, three criterion levels are used to delineate the sophistication of the reading ability—basic, proficient, and advanced—with each level calibrated to the three age groups tested. Figure 11-1 describes what is tested at each criterion level and shows the numerical value associated with each level.

In 1998, the NCES released its latest reading report card. The average score for the nation's fourth graders was 217; for eighth graders, 264, and for high school seniors, 291. By examining Figure 11-1, one could conclude that the average fourth grader is reading slightly above the basic level, the average eighth grader is reading somewhere between the basic and proficient level, and the average high school senior is reading close to the proficient level. One could interpret these data negatively as indicating that the average American schoolchild is not even a proficient reader, at least according to the NAEP criteria. Or one could interpret them positively as indicating that the average schoolchild is better than a basic reader. Or one might hold the schools to the highest of standards and demand that the average child should be an advanced reader, as many politicians are inclined to remark. But this is where it is important to understand the nature of a criterion-based examination. If the average examinee achieved the advanced level, our definition of "advanced" probably would need to change. After all, if the average student was advanced, the design of the "advanced" criterion level would not be very advanced. Feature 11-1 on page 456 provides a state-by-state profile of NAEP reading scores for three different years.

So, how should we begin to assess the value of these scores? Because NAEP tests are longitudinal, the scores can be examined in relation to past performances. NAEP measures of reading performance have existed since the early 1970s, so there is some basis for comparability over time. During the 1990s, the overall NAEP reading scores held steady; in fact, the national average scores for all three grade levels were higher in 1998 than in 1994, as Table 11-1 on page 458 shows. And compared to the data for 1971, the numbers are especially impressive. Students at each of the three grade levels are significantly better readers today than their counterparts were in 1971. The difference between the average scores of the students who took the exam in 1971 and those who took it in 1998 is approximately 10 scale points for 9- and 13-year-olds, and 6 scale points for 17-year-olds. These are significant differences (National Center for Education Statistics, 1999a).

What makes this improvement especially interesting, and even profound, is the fact that most of the gains have come from minority group populations, particularly black students. Thus, while the overall scores for white students have stayed more or less the same, the overall scores for black students have improved. As Figure 11-2 on page 458 shows, the result is a significant reduction in the gap between the average reading performances of white and black students. And although the narrowing of the differences was interrupted in the 1990s, it is still a notable achievement, especially in light of the fact that the dropout rate has decreased among black students. Minority students who might have dropped out in previous school years are now staying in school. This being the case, the average score might be expected to drop, but until the 1990s, the opposite had been the case.

Lest the race/ethnicity data be misinterpreted, it should be made clear that the underperformance of black and other minority children is a function of several interrelated factors. Disproportionately high numbers of minority children live below the poverty line, and the legacy of racism against minority children, and black children in particular, has sometimes resulted in the denial of equal opportunities to learn. Moreover, some evidence suggests that there are lower-quality teachers in predominately black schools. And according to proponents of cultural explanations, stereotyping and racism in society have encouraged some black children to disassociate from school and even to equate success in school with "acting white." The high incidence of single-parent homes in the black community and the relatively low involvement of black parents in the schooling enterprise might also be factors (Johnson and Viadero, 2000). The gap between black and white children in early reading- and math-related skills however, exists even before they enter kindergarten. For example, the vocabulary development scores of a typical black four-year-old fall below the twentieth percentile of the national distribution (Jencks and Phillips, 1999). This points to factors in the early life of black children, with the preschool and the home environment being likely places to look for problems and for solutions.

The reading achievement scores of male and female students also reveal some interesting trends, with females clearly superior (National Center for Education Statistics, 1999b). As Table 11-2 shows, at each age level, the gap narrowed in the 1980s only to open up again in the 1990s. The differences in reading achievement between boys and girls is significant, but it is not nearly as profound as the differences between the races. This is probably because equal numbers of boys and girls live below the poverty line. The differences in reading achievement between boys and girls may not be as dramatic as the differences between the races, but it certainly is more intractable and more resistant to improvement.

FIGURE 11-1
Reading Achievement Levels

Grade 4

Basic (208)
Fourth-grade students performing at the Basic level should demonstrate an understanding of the overall meaning of what they read. When reading text appropriate for fourth graders, they should be able to make relatively obvious connections between the text and their own experiences and extend the ideas in the text by making simple inferences.

Proficient (238)
Fourth-grade students performing at the Proficient level should be able to demonstrate an overall understanding of the text, providing inferential as well as literal information. When reading text appropriate to fourth grade, they should be able to extend the ideas in the text by making inferences, drawing conclusions, and making connections to their own experiences. The connection between the text and what the student infers should be clear.

Advanced (268)
Fourth-grade students performing at the Advanced level should be able to generalize about topics in the reading selection and demonstrate an awareness of how authors compose and use literary devices. When reading text appropriate to fourth grade, they should be able to judge text critically and, in general, give thorough answers that indicate careful thought.

Grade 8

Basic (243)
Eighth-grade students performing at the Basic level should demonstrate a literal understanding of what they read and be able to make some interpretations. When reading text appropriate to eighth grade, they should be able to identify specific aspects of the text that reflect overall meaning, extend the ideas in the text by making simple inferences, recognize and relate interpretations and connections among ideas in the text to personal experience, and draw conclusions based on the text.

Proficient (281)
Eighth-grade students performing at the Proficient level should be able to show an overall understanding of the text, including inferential as well as literal information. When reading text appropriate to eighth grade, they should be able to extend the ideas in the text by making clear inferences from it, by drawing conclusions, and by making connections to their own experiences—including other reading experiences. Proficient eighth graders should be able to identify some of the devices authors use in composing text.

Advanced (323)

Eighth-grade students performing at the Advanced level should be able to describe the more abstract themes and ideas of the overall text. When reading text appropriate to eighth grade, they should be able to analyze both meaning and form and support their analyses explicitly with examples from the text; they should be able to extend text information by relating it to their experiences and to world events. At this level, student responses should be thorough, thoughtful, and extensive.

Grade 12

Basic (265)

Twelfth-grade students performing at the Basic level should be able to demonstrate an overall understanding and make some interpretations of the text. When reading text appropriate to twelfth grade, they should be able to identify and relate aspects of the text to its overall meaning, extend the ideas in the text by making simple inferences, recognize interpretations, make connections among and relate ideas in the text to their personal experiences, and draw conclusions. They should be able to identify elements of an author's style.

Proficient (302)

Twelfth-grade students performing at the Proficient level should be able to show an overall understanding of the text which includes inferential as well as literal information. When reading text appropriate to twelfth grade, they should be able to extend the ideas of the text by making inferences, drawing conclusions, and making connections to their own personal experiences and other readings. Connections between inferences and the text should be clear, even when implicit. These students should be able to analyze the author's use of literary devices.

Advanced (346)

Twelfth-grade students performing at the Advanced level should be able to describe more abstract themes and ideas in the overall text. When reading text appropriate to twelfth grade, they should be able to analyze both the meaning and the form of the text and explicitly support their analyses with specific examples from the text. They should be able to extend the information from the text by relating it to their experiences and to the world. Their responses should be thorough, thoughtful, and extensive.

SOURCE: National Center for Education Statistics (1999b), *NAEP 1998 Reading: Report card to the nation and the states* (Washington, DC: U.S. Department of Education), p. 19.

11-1 THINKING ABOUT THE DATA

State-by-State NAEP Reading Achievement

Here are the scale scores for the NAEP fourth grade reading exam disaggregated by the thirty-nine rated states. For 1998, Connecticut earned the highest score, over 32 points higher than the lowest-performing state, Hawaii. But several states show significantly higher scores in 1998 than in 1994 and 1992, and none showed significantly lower scores in 1998 than in 1994. Look into the demographics of some of the lower- and higher-performing states, and see if a pattern emerges. What happens in Connecticut that caused it to score so much higher than many other states?

AVERAGE SCALE SCORE ON NAEP READING EXAMS
GRADE 4

	1992	1994	1998
Nation	215	212	215
Alabama	207	208	211
Arizona	209	206	207
Arkansas	211	209	209
California	202	197	202
Colorado	217	213	222
Connecticut	222	222	232
Delaware	213	206	212
Florida	208	205	207
Georgia	212	207	210
Hawaii	203	201	200
Iowa	225	223	223
Kansas	—	—	222
Kentucky	213	212	218
Louisiana	204	197	204
Maine	227	228	225

The differences between average reading scores among students eligible and ineligible for free/reduced-price lunches, which is one way the government distinguishes between children living near or in poverty and those living outside of poverty, are quite wide. One could see how this relates to differences between the races. But the data on poor children also testify to the fact that, irrespective of race or ethnicity or gender, considerable achievement differences exist between schoolchildren living near or in poverty and those living outside of it. Table 11-3 shows the differences in

	AVERAGE SCALE SCORE ON NAEP READING EXAMS GRADE 4		
	1992	1994	1998
Maryland	211	210	215
Massachusetts	226	223	225
Michigan	216	—	217
Minnesota	221	218	222
Mississippi	199	202	204
Missouri	220	217	216
Montana	—	222	226
Nevada	—	—	208
New Hampshire	228	223	226
New Mexico	211	205	206
New York	215	212	216
North Carolina	212	214	217
Oklahoma	220	—	220
Oregon	—	—	214
Rhode Island	217	220	218
South Carolina	210	203	210
Tennessee	212	213	212
Texas	213	212	217
Utah	220	217	215
Virginia	221	213	218
Washington	—	213	217
West Virginia	216	213	216
Wisconsin	224	224	224
Wyoming	223	221	219

SOURCE: National Center for Education Statistics (1999b), *NAEP 1998 reading: Report card for the nation and the states* (Washington, DC: U.S. Department of Education), p. 113.

average reading scores in 1998 by race/ethnicity, gender, and eligibility for free/reduced-price lunches.

NAEP data also reveal some of the conditions supporting reading and literacy at home, and confirm the long-standing belief that home reading conditions are associated with reading achievement (White and Dewitz, 1996). The data show, for instance, that a negative association exists between television viewing and reading achievement, with children who watch a lot of TV less likely to be good readers than children who watch less TV. Frequent

TABLE 11-1

Average Reading Performance by Age, for Selected Years

	AGE 9	AGE 13	AGE 17
1971	208	255	285
1992	217	260	292
1994	214	260	287
1998	217	264	291

SOURCE: National Center for Education Statistics (1999b), *NAEP 1998 reading: Report card for the nation and the states* (Washington, DC: U.S. Department of Education).

FIGURE 11-2

Differences in Average Reading Performance Scores Between White and Black Students by Age, 1971–96

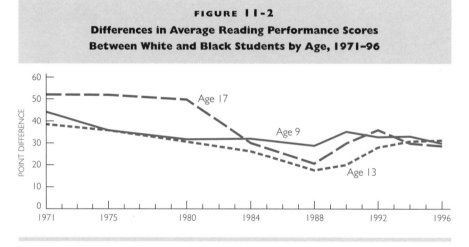

NOTE: The difference refers to the gap between the average reading score for white and black students.
SOURCE: National Center for Education Statistics (1999a), *The condition of education* (Washington, DC: U.S. Department of Education), p. 35.

TV watching likely displaces activities in the home that might make a stronger contribution to literacy, such as going to the library, subscribing to and reading a monthly magazine, reading for pleasure, telling stories, and conversing about reading materials. In addition, homes with less TV watching might be homes with higher parent education levels, which itself might explain the association.

NAEP data revealed other associations between reading achievement and home conditions. For example, children from homes with more literary materials like magazines, newspapers, encyclopedias, and books were more likely to have higher NAEP reading scores than children from homes with less literary materials. The difference, in fact, between students who

TABLE 11-2			
Differences in Average Reading Performance Scores			
Between Female and Male Students by Age, 1971–98			
	AGE 9	*AGE 13*	*AGE 17*
1971	13	11	12
1975	12	12	11
1980	10	9	7
1984	6	9	10
1988	8	9	8
1990	9	12	13
1992	8	13	6
1994	10	15	13
1998	6	13	16

SOURCE: National Center for Education Statistics (1999a), *The condition of education* (Washington, DC: U.S. Department of Education), p. 34.

TABLE 11-3			
Differences in Average Reading Achievement by Race/Ethnicity,			
Gender, and Eligibility for Free/Reduced-Price Lunches, 1998			
	RACE/ETHNICITY		*GENDER*	*ELIGIBILITY FOR FREE/REDUCED-PRICE LUNCHES*
	White-Black	*White-Hispanic*	*Female-Male*	*Not Elig.-Elig.*
Grade 4	33	31	6	29
Grade 8	28	27	13	24
Grade 12	28	23	16	22

SOURCE: National Center for Education Statistics (1999b), *NAEP 1998 reading: Report card for the nation and the states* (Washington, DC: U.S. Department of Education), pp. 48, 59.

reported four types of literary materials in the home and those who reported two or less was 30 scale points on the NAEP. Again, the association probably speaks to the importance of children having access to a wide range of reading materials. Or it might simply be that homes that are wealthier in reading materials are wealthier in general. But other associations continue to point to a strong case in support of reading at home. Students who engage in leisure-time reading (reading for fun) and who spend time discussing their readings with family members and friends are likely to

	GRADE 4	GRADE 8	GRADE 12
TABLE 11-4 Home Reading Factors and NAEP Reading Achievement Scores by Grade, 1994			
Presence of Literary Materials at Home (magazines, newspapers, encyclopedias, at least 25 books)			
4 Types	227	270	295
3 Types	216	258	286
2 or Fewer Types	197	241	269
Frequency of Reading on Students' Own Time			
Almost Every Day	223	277	302
Once or Twice a Week	213	264	294
Once or Twice a Month	208	257	285
Never or Hardly Ever	197	246	273
Frequency with Which Students Discuss Studies or Books with Family or Friend			
Almost Every Day	219	269	296
Once or Twice a Week	215	264	292
Once or Twice a Month	208	257	287
Never or Hardly Ever	199	250	274

SOURCE: White, S., and Dewitz, P. (1996), *Reading proficiency and home support* (Washington, DC: U.S. Department of Education).

be higher achievers in reading. We cannot know for sure if students who read for fun gain more reading practice and therefore have higher achievement, or if students with higher achievement are more inclined to read for fun. Probably both factors are at work. Still, it seems incumbent on the school and the family to encourage and support leisure-time reading and to be responsive to opportunities to discuss what students have read. As Table 11-4 shows, the research bears out the fact that where families or homes support reading, the achievement dividend is significant.

The Mathematics Report Card

The NAEP math assessment also covers a comprehensive set of skills according to the same criterion levels used for reading: basic, proficient, and advanced. The content areas for the three age groups are number sense, properties and operations; measurement; geometry and spatial sense; data analysis, statistics and probability; and algebra and functions. The exam includes multiple-choice items and questions requiring students to construct responses. In 1996, more than half of the overall items for the exam were constructed-response questions. Figure 11-3 provides an outline of the topics covered on the NAEP test for eighth graders; Feature 11-2 provides actual questions from the fourth-grade exam.

The NAEP math results from 1996 show continued progress in average scores across the nation. In 1996, the average score for fourth graders was 224; for eighth graders, 272; and for twelfth graders, 304. Each of these scores represents a statistical improvement from the 1990 and 1992 average scores, as Figure 11-4 on page 464 shows. The rate of progress, although modest, seems to contradict the public perception of a decline in the mathematical skills of school children.

But the NAEP results also reflect a few disturbing trends. The most prominent has to do with the differences in achievement between blacks and whites and between children living at or below the poverty line and those living above it. As Table 11-5 on page 464 shows, in the area of race/ethnicity, the differences range from 24 to 39 scale points, and in the area of income, from 24 to 28 scale points—which in both cases is equivalent to two or three grade levels (Grouws and Cebulla, 1999). This is not good news, but it represents at least in relation to race, a small improvement since 1973, when the differences in NAEP math achievement between white and black children was approximately 40 scale points for each age group (slightly lower than 40 for the 9-year-olds, and slightly higher than 40 for the 13- and 17-year-olds) (National Center for Education Statistics, 1999a).

Boys outperformed girls on the 1996 math NAEP in two of the age groups, but contrary to public perception, the difference is not very dramatic (National Center for Education Statistics, 1997a). In fact, it has never been very dramatic. In 1973, 17-year-old boys outperformed 17-year-old girls by approximately 6 scale points, but girls actually scored slightly higher than boys in the other two groups. This is an interesting phenomenon in light of the amount of attention given to the issue of gender bias in math and science, although it is understandable because of the unwillingness of girls to pursue math-/science-related careers.

Interestingly, patterns of course taking reflect equal access to all math courses, including the most advanced ones. Table 11-6 on page 465 shows the percentage of males and females who took selected mathematics courses in high school. The numbers for algebra I are slightly depressed for both sexes because they measure only credits earned in high school and do not include students who took high school–level courses prior to entering high school. The data for more advanced courses, however, represent an accurate accounting of overall enrollments (National Center for Education Statistics, 1997b).

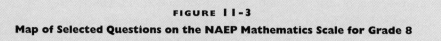

FIGURE 11-3
Map of Selected Questions on the NAEP Mathematics Scale for Grade 8

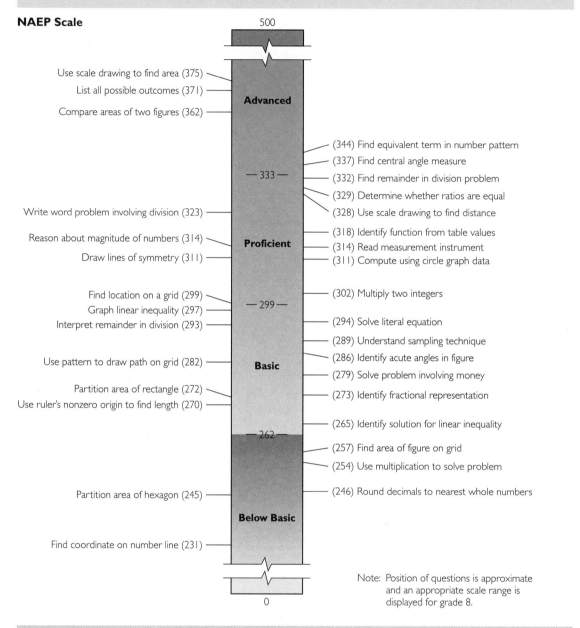

SOURCE: National Center for Education Statistics (1997a), *NAEP 1996 mathematics: Report card for the nation and the states* (Washington, DC: U.S. Department of Education), p. 11.

Obviously, access to math courses is crucial to mathematical achievement. As Berliner and Biddle's student achievement law suggests, students

11-2 RESEARCH INQUIRY
NAEP Math Exam Items

Here are three items taken from the 1996 NAEP math exam for fourth graders. The table below shows the overall percentage of students who got the correct answers and the percentage of correct answers according to overall achievement or criterion levels. If possible, give these three items to students in your preservice fourth-grade class and see how they do. Compare the results to the NAEP figures. Disaggregate the results by gender or any other variables.

1. N stands for the number of stamps John had. He gave 12 stamps to his sister. Which expression tells how many stamps John has now?
   a. $N + 12$
   b. $N - 12$
   c. $12 - N$
   d. $12 \times N$

2. Ms. Hernandez formed teams of 8 students each from the 34 students in her class. She formed as many teams as possible, and the students left over were substitutes. How many students were substitutes?

3. Sam can purchase his lunch at school. Each day he wants to have juice that costs 50¢, a sandwich that costs 90¢, and fruit that costs 35¢. His mother has only $1.00 bills. What is the least number of $1.00 bills that his mother should give him so he will have enough money to buy lunch for five days?

ITEM	OVERALL PERCENTAGE CORRECT/SATISFACTORY	BELOW BASIC (213 and below)	BASIC (214 to 248)	PROFICIENT (249 to 281)	ADVANCED (282 and above)
1	67%	44%	73%	90%	—
2	39	5	42	86	—
3	17	1	14	44	—

with greater opportunities to learn mathematics will learn more mathematics. The average NAEP math score is closely associated with the highest mathematical course taken, as Table 11-7 shows. The difference between students taking precalculus or calculus as their highest math course and students taking algebra I as their highest math course is over 50 scale points on the math NAEP (National Center for Education Statistics, 2000). There may, in fact, be wisdom in the recent calls to increase graduation requirements, to include more math courses in the curriculum, and to standardize the curriculum in a way that equalizes OTL.

FIGURE 11-4
Average Mathematics Scale Scores

SOURCE: National Center for Education Statistics (1997a), *NAEP 1996 mathematics: Report card for the nation and the states* (Washington, DC: U.S. Department of Education), p. 25.

TABLE 11-5
Differences in Average Math Achievement by Race/Ethnicity, Gender, and Eligibility for Free/Reduced-Price Lunches, 1996

	RACE/ETHNICITY		GENDER	ELIGIBILITY FOR FREE/REDUCED-PRICE LUNCHES
	White-Black	White-Hispanic	Male-Female	Not Elig.-Elig.
Grade 4	32	26	4	24
Grade 8	39	31	0	28
Grade 12	31	24	2	28

SOURCE: National Center for Education Statistics (1999a), *The condition of education* (Washington, DC: U.S. Department of Education), p. 28.

The data suggest that simply taking a course might contribute to overall achievement. But we are still left with the dilemma of associational evidence. Are students who are good in mathematics inclined to take more math courses, or are students who take more math courses better at math? In either case, the mandate should be to increase opportunities to learn mathematics. The reality of the situation is that, nationwide, only 51 percent of all high school students are required to take three years of mathematics to graduate; 46 percent are required to take only two years (National Center for Education Statistics, 1997a). Many students take more

TABLE 11-6
Percentage of High School Graduates
Taking Selected Mathematics Courses by Sex, 1994

	MALE	FEMALE
Algebra I	64%	68%
Geometry	68	72
Algebra II	55	61
Trigonometry	16	17
Pre-calculus	16	18
Calculus	9	9

SOURCE: National Center for Education Statistics (1997b), *The condition of education* (Washington, DC: U.S. Department of Education), Indicator 24.

TABLE 11-7
Average Mathematics Performance of 17-Year-Olds
by Highest Math Course Taken, 1996

	NAEP SCORE
Prealgebra	269
Algebra I	283
Geometry	298
Algebra II	316
Precalculus or Calculus	339

SOURCE: National Center for Education Statistics (2000), *Digest of education statistics, 1999* (Washington, DC: U.S. Department of Education), Table 128.

courses because of college entrance requirements, but these are generally not the students who are lower on the achievement scale. The percentage of students who actually took calculus was less than 9.2 percent in 1994. About 92 percent of all high school graduates took algebra, and about 70 percent took geometry (National Center for Education Statistics, 1997a).

NAEP data are collected on virtually every subject area in the high school curriculum. Feature 11-3 gives you the opportunity to peruse NAEP data findings in these others areas, as they are offered free of charge by the NCES.

11-3 WEB POINTS
The National Assessment of Educational Progress

The National Center for Education Statistics offers free and easy access to all of the NAEP studies conducted over the years. Recent ones include NAEP Reading, NAEP Civics, and NAEP Arts. Each of these full-scale reports can be either downloaded or ordered, free of charge, from the NCES (http://nces.ed.gov/nationsreportcard/site/home.asp). Specially designed research articles that use NAEP data are also available.

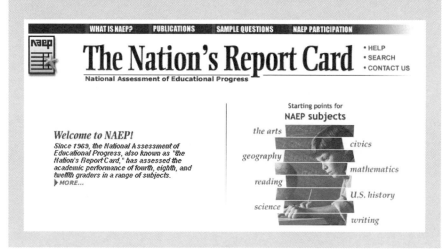

SCHOOL DROPOUTS

A high school diploma has long been a valued achievement in America—and for good reason. For young adults, documented lifetime benefits accrue from staying in school. The lifetime earning power of an individual and the general indices of quality in an individual's life are profoundly tied to education levels (National Center for Education Statistics, 1995a). It has been estimated, for instance, that the average dropout will, over a lifetime, earn about $212,000 less than the average high school graduate and $812,000 less than the average college graduate (Schwartz, 1995). Those who stay in school are less likely to be unemployed, to land in jail, or to be the victims of crime. Girls who drop out are more likely to become pregnant at a young age and to become single parents (National Center for Education Statistics, 1993).

A high school education also pays broader societal dividends. A democracy is obligated to enlighten the population. In this sense, access to and completion of a high school education is a societal requirement, not a luxury or privilege. No advanced democratic society can expect to sustain itself without extending education to the general population. The historical effort to universalize secondary education in the United States has always been driven by the belief that the greatest public good will be served. Little wonder that people often become upset over the dropout rate in America. There is a lot at stake.

In many schools, especially in the cities of America, the dropout rate is tragically high, indicative perhaps of the failure of the school to keep youths interested and engaged in meaningful learning. But the implications of the dropout rate are not as cut and dried as it might seem. Dropping out of school, for example, is not always a final condition. Students who drop out sometimes return to school or decide to pursue a high school equivalency diploma, also known as the general educational development certificate (GED). A recent study using a national sample of longitudinal data showed that 84 percent of the high school sophomore class graduated on time in 1982 and that two-thirds of the remaining 16 percent completed high school over the next ten years—and the vast majority over the first four years. Over the ten-year period, the graduation or completion rate of the class of 1982 went up to 93.7 percent (National Center for Education Statistics, 1995b). This is not to say that a GED is an effective replacement for a high school diploma. Although the evidence is conflicting, various studies have found that GED recipients do less well than high school graduates in terms of earnings, employment, wage rates, and progression into postsecondary education (National Library of Education, 1996). The compelling evidence points to the power of the school experience embodied in the attainment of a high diploma.

Different dropout procedures can also confuse matters. Some procedures count children whose school status is unknown as dropouts. In Arizona, for instance, 65 percent of the students who were labeled as "dropouts" in the ninth grade were students whose status was unknown (Shoemaker, 1994). Because some schools accept transfers without prior records, many of these students may have reenrolled in school. The classification of "status unknown" means that the school does not know whether the student simply left school or left town for another school. To complicate matters further, in the case of some immigrant populations, students who have never even enrolled in school are counted as dropouts. This is especially the case among immigrant Hispanic teenagers, whose interest in public education in America might be frustrated by language difficulties and

467

TABLE 11-8
Event Dropout Rates for Those in Grades 10–12 by Gender, Race/Ethnicity, and Family Income, 1978, 1988, 1998

	TOTAL	GENDER		RACE/ETHNICITY			FAMILY INCOME		
		Male	Female	White	Black	Hispanic	Low	Middle	High
1978	6.7%	7.5%	5.9%	5.8%	10.2%	12.3%	17.3%	7.3%	3.0%
1988	4.8	5.1	4.4	4.2	5.9	10.4	13.7	4.7	1.3
1998	4.8	4.6	4.9	3.9	5.2	9.4	12.7	3.8	2.7

SOURCE: National Center for Education Statistics (1999a), *The condition of education* (Washington, DC: U.S. Department of Education), p. 136.

poor academic preparation. These students never dropped in, let alone dropped out, but they are still counted as dropouts (Carson, Huelskamp, and Woodall, 1993).

The NCES measures the dropout rate two main ways. It tracks the proportion of youths who leave high school (between grades 10 and 12) each year. These are known as "event dropouts." This is not a comprehensive gauge of all dropouts; it is simply a picture of the proportion of students who leave school each year. A more comprehensive measure of dropouts taken by the NCES tracks the proportion of 16- to 24-year-olds who have not completed high school and are not currently enrolled in high school. These are known as "status dropouts." This statistic gives us a sense of the overall retention power of the schools.

With regard to event dropout rates, over a two-decade span, considerable progress has been made keeping students in school. The overall decline from 6.7 event dropouts in 1978 to 4.8 in 1998 represents about a 30 percent decrease. Similar progress can be seen in virtually all of the subgroups. Interestingly, income is the best predictor of whether a student will drop out. As Table 11-8 shows, children from low-income families are about three times as likely to drop out as students from middle-income families. The differences across income lines are more severe than anything related to gender or race, although the Hispanic dropout rate continues to be quite high, a point that will be raised later.

To get a good composite picture of the overall status of dropouts nationwide, the NCES also calculates high school completion rates; these graduates include not only students who obtained a high school diploma but also those who completed an alternative equivalency. Figure 11-5 shows the

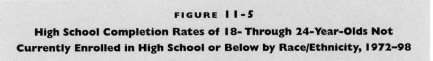

FIGURE 11-5

High School Completion Rates of 18- Through 24-Year-Olds Not Currently Enrolled in High School or Below by Race/Ethnicity, 1972–98

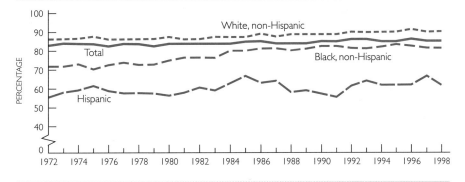

SOURCE: National Center for Education Statistics (1999c), *Dropout rates in the United States: 1998* (Washington, DC: U.S. Department of Education).

total high school completion rate since 1972 against the variable of race. The figure shows substantial gains among black children but a lack of progress among Hispanic children. In 1998, 84 percent of all 18- to 24-year-olds had completed high school or its equivalent. Eighty-seven percent of females completed high school as opposed to 82 percent of males, and 90 percent of whites as opposed 81 percent of blacks and 62 percent of Hispanics. As Table 11-9 shows, the alternative method of high school completion has gained in popularity over the past five years.

As indicated, the Hispanic dropout rate represents an anomaly in the national trends. Hispanic dropout rates have fluctuated over the years but have remained quite high and have not followed the positive trend seen among black students. These are disturbing data that have to be examined from all reasonable angles. However, researchers for NCES (1992) found that a significant number of the Hispanic dropouts are immigrant youths who are sometimes not even educated in their own native language. They found that the reported national dropout rate for Hispanic youths clearly is affected by immigration patterns and likely can be cut in half if limited to U.S.-born Hispanics. In 1997, 41 percent of all Hispanics between the ages of 16 and 24 were born outside of the United States. Of this sizable group, 38 percent were status dropouts, having not completed high school and not being currently enrolled in school. Compare this to first-generation Hispanics between the ages of 16 and 24, whose status dropout rate is only 15 percent. Hispanics born outside of the country are more than two times as likely to drop out as first-generation Hispanics. About 60 percent of all

TABLE 11-9

**High School Completion Rates and Method of Completion
of 18- Through 24-Year-Olds Not Currently Enrolled in High School
or Below, 1988–98**

	TOTAL	DIPLOMA	ALTERNATIVE
1992	86.4%	81.2%	5.2%
1993	86.2	81.2	4.9
1994	85.8	78.8	7.0
1995	85.3	77.5	7.7
1996	86.2	76.5	9.8
1997	85.9	76.7	9.1
1998	84.8	74.7	10.1

SOURCE: National Center for Education Statistics (1999c), *Dropout rates in the United States: 1998* (Washington, DC: U.S. Department of Education).

TABLE 11-10

**Percentage of Hispanic 16- to 24-Year-Olds Not Enrolled in School and
Not Having Completed High School by Recency of Immigration, 1997**

	ALL HISPANICS AGES 16–24	ALL HISPANIC DROPOUTS	NOT ENROLLED IN SCHOOL AND NOT HAVING COMPLETED HIGH SCHOOL
Born Outside of the United States	41.5%	64%	38.6%
First Generation	34.1	20	15.4
Later Generation	24.4	16	17.7

SOURCE: National Center for Education Statistics (1999a), *The condition of education* (Washington, DC: U.S. Department of Education), p. 138.

Hispanic status dropouts (between the ages of 16 and 24) were born outside of the United States; these are dramatic numbers (National Center for Education Statistics, 1999d). Accounting for the immigration factors brings the Hispanic dropout number down considerably, as evidenced by how much the numbers improve when one examines the dropout rates of students from first- and second-generation families. Table 11-10 presents data summarizing these findings.

Researchers have tried to find the variables around which dropouts might cluster and have asked why some students find the choice to leave school attractive. Interesting work has been done at the state level in this area. Many states provide comprehensive statewide data on the characteristics of dropouts. In Texas, for instance, about 50 percent of the dropouts were not identified as "at risk" the year they dropped out, showing how daunting it is to anticipate just who might be a candidate for dropping out. In Texas, 75 percent of the dropouts were also overage (older than their grade peers), and most dropouts occurred in urban areas, irrespective of school size (Texas Education Agency, 1995). In North Carolina, almost 70 percent of the dropouts were enrolled in the general education curriculum; less than 5 percent were enrolled in college preparation course work. Over 60 percent of the dropouts were in grades 9 and 10, and about 75 percent of the pool were performing below the fiftieth percentile on standardized tests. Most of the students cited "academic problems" and "choosing work over school" as their main reasons for leaving school (North Carolina State Department of Health, 1994).

The national data are similar. Based on a national database, researchers found that about one-fifth of all status dropouts (ages 18–24) were married, living with someone, or divorced, with females more likely to be married than males. Forty percent had a child or were expecting one. More than half moved during their high school years, as opposed to only 15 percent of school graduates. One-fourth, in fact, changed schools two or more times. Twelve percent, twice as many as school graduates, ran away from home. One-half was enrolled in general high school programs; very few were in college preparatory studies. One-half missed school at least ten days, one-third cut class at least ten times, and one-third was either suspended or put on probation. Students who repeated one or more grades were twice as likely to drop out as those who had never been held back (Schwartz, 1995).

Studies conducted by the NCES (1993) found that, when dropouts were asked why they left school, many simply reported that they did not like school. Other popular reasons included not being able to keep up with the academic work, not being able to get along with teachers, and not performing well in school; Table 11-11 gives data on these and many other reasons.

One could conceive of the school-related reasons for dropping out as factors that push students out of schools and the job-/family-related reasons as factors that pull students from school. Factors internal to the school, such as poor teaching, unfair disciplinary policies, and unresponsive curriculum offerings can contribute to pushing students out of school. Schools must be

TABLE 11-11
Reasons for Dropping Out of Grades 10–12

REASON	RATE
School-Related	
Did not like school	42.9%
Was failing at school	38.7
Could not keep up with schoolwork	31.3
Felt they didn't belong	24.2
Could not get along with teachers	22.8
Was suspended or expelled	15.5
Could not get along with students	14.5
Changed school and didn't like it	10.6
Did not feel safe at school	6.0
Job-Related	
Found a job	28.5
Could not work and go to school at the same time	22.8
Family-Related	
Was pregnant	26.8
Became pregnant	14.7
Got married	12.1
Had to care for family member	11.9
Had to support a family	11.2
Wanted to have a family	7.5
Other	
Wanted to travel	8.1
Friends dropped out	8.0
Drug problem	4.4

SOURCE: National Center for Education Statistics (1993), *Dropout rates in the United States* (Washington, DC: U.S. Department of Education).

aware of how they might contribute to school failure and to student resentment of schooling. This involves being aware of OTL factors, as they might be differentially distributed across curriculum tracks and ability groups, and of grade promotion policies that leave overage students in difficult, if not humiliating, classroom environments. Schools have less influence on factors outside the school environment, but they can still offer services to prevent students from being pulled away from the school. In this regard, ancillary services, such as afterschool programs, special summertime programs, counseling services, mentoring programs, homework assistance centers, and work-study programs, could be used. Given the role that pregnancy plays in dropping out, comprehensive sex education and community outreach programs that deal with issues of sexuality might help prevent dropping out. Finding ways to accommodate and support a student's situation once she or he becomes a parent might be viewed in a similar way.

POVERTY, HOME ENVIRONMENTS, AND SCHOOL ACHIEVEMENT

In a nation as prosperous as the United States, the idea of poverty is constructed in relative, not absolute terms. Much of the struggle in Third World nations involves keeping people above absolute poverty levels. Under these conditions, running water, refrigeration, a roof over one's head, and basic health care provisions cannot be taken for granted. In America, poverty is determined using an index that weighs family income against family size. In 1999, the U.S Department of Education (National Center for Education Statistics, 2000) used a poverty threshold of $13,000 in annual income for a family of three. The index increases by about $3,000 for each incremental increase in the size of the household. So, for a family of four, the threshold is about $16,000; for a family of five, about $19,000; and so on. Families living in relative poverty typically receive support from the government in the form of food stamps, free school lunches, Medicare, and housing subsidies. Despite this, in 1996, 4 percent of children under age 18 in America experienced modest to severe hunger, and 6 percent had no health care (National Center for Education Statistics, 1999d).

In 1998, over 34 million people lived in poverty in America, or about 12 percent of the total population (National Center for Education Statistics, 2000). The percentage of Americans living below the poverty level has remained between 12 and 15 percent of the population since 1970. Of the 34 million living in poverty in 1998, over 12 million were children under the age of 18, or about 18 percent of all the children in the nation.

The issue of poverty, as indicated previously, intersects with race. In 1998, about 8 million white school-age children lived in poverty in the United States, as compared to about 4 million black school-age children and 3.6 million Hispanic school-age children. Thus, the single largest impoverished group in the American schools is white children. But when one examines the distribution of the poor as a percentage of each racial and ethnic group, a

TABLE 11-12

Percentage of Children Ages 3–5 Not Yet Enrolled in Kindergarten Who Participated in Home Activities with a Family Member Three or More Times in the Past Week by Poverty Status and Family Type, 1999

	POVERTY STATUS		FAMILY TYPE	
	Below Poverty Threshold	Above Poverty Threshold	Two Parents	No Parents or One Parent
Read to	69%	85%	85%	72%
Told a Story	42	52	52	44
Taught Letter, Word, or Number	58	66	64	65
Taught a Song or Music	49	49	48	50
Did Arts and Crafts	34	41	41	34
Visited a Library	24	40	40	29

SOURCE: Nord, C. W., Lennon, J., Liu, B., and Chandler, K. (2000), "Home literacy activities and signs of children's emerging literacy," 1993 and 1999, *Education Statistics Quarterly* (Spring).

different picture emerges. About one in four black and Hispanic children live in poverty, as opposed to more than one in ten white children (National Center for Education Statistics, 2000). So, with regard to income data, two important factors need to be considered. One is that minority children are more than three times as likely as white children to be affected by poverty, but the majority of the poor in the school population are white.

Poverty factors can play an especially strong role during the preschool years. For instance, home literacy experiences, which include activities such as being read to, told a story, and taught letters and words and numbers, are less likely to occur regularly in families living in poverty. Something as seemingly simple as visiting the library with a family member, an experience obviously connected to literacy development, is significantly less likely to happen to a child living in poverty than to one who is living above the poverty threshold, as Table 11-12 shows. Not surprisingly, school readiness skills, which include recognizing letters, counting to twenty or higher, writing one's name, and reading or pretending to read a storybook, all are less developed among children living below the poverty line than among those living above it (Nord, Lennon, Liu, and Chandler, 2000). Poverty is, in many ways, associated with a way of life, as Feature 11-4 addresses.

Home-bound resources for school success, such as computer usage, are also problematic for the poor. As Table 11-13 shows, an enormous gap

II-4 SCHOLARLY VOICES
Michael Harrington on Poverty in America

Michael Harrington's best-selling book on poverty in America, *The Other America*, describes what it's like to be poor in America. It is required reading for anyone interested in the topic. Here Harrington describes the ubiquitous and permeating effects of living in poverty:

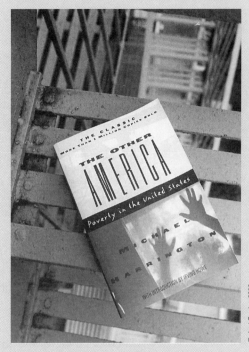

There is a famous anecdote about Ernest Hemingway and F. Scott Fitzgerald. Fitzgerald is reported to have remarked to Hemingway, "The rich are different." And Hemingway replied, "Yes, they have money." Fitzgerald had much the better of the exchange. He understood that being rich was not a simple fact, like a large bank account, but a way of looking at reality, a series of attitudes, a special type of life. If this is true of the rich, it is ten times truer of the poor. Everything about them, from the condition of their teeth to the way they love, is suffused and permeated by the fact of their poverty. And this is sometimes a hard idea for Hemingway-like middle class America to comprehend.

SOURCE: Harrington, M. (1993), *The other America: Poverty in the United States* (New York: Collier Books [1962]), p. 16.

TABLE II-13
Percentage of Students Grades 7–12 Who Used a Computer at School and/or at Home by Income, 1997

	USED A COMPUTER AT:	
	Home	*School*
Low Income	14.9%	67.9%
Middle Income	44.2	74.1
High Income	78.6	75.4

SOURCE: National Center for Education Statistics (1999a), *The condition of education* (Washington, DC: U.S. Department of Education), p. 65.

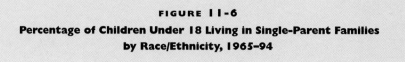

FIGURE 11-6

Percentage of Children Under 18 Living in Single-Parent Families
by Race/Ethnicity, 1965–94

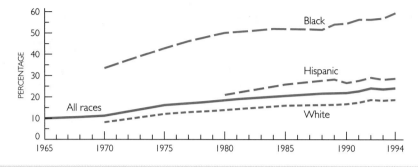

SOURCE: National Center for Education Statistics (1996a), *The condition of education* (Washington, DC: U.S. Department of Education), Indicator 11.

exists between the computer usage of children from low-income families and children from middle- and high-income families. For instance, in 1997, 78 percent of high-income children in grades 7–12 reported using a computer at home, whereas only 14 percent of low-income students reported home computer usage (National Center for Education Statistics, 1999a). Given OTL factors in this important area of proficiency, the handicap presented to the poor is obvious. Schools have responded by enhancing opportunities for computer usage by low-income children while in school; 75 percent of high-income children in grades 7–12 reported having used the computer at school, compared to 65 percent of low-income children.

The demographics of the American family also have posed new problems for the public school. In recent decades, a dramatic change has occurred in the nature of the family. Certainly, the nuclear family is not what it used to be, and today's American family is different from the American family of the 1960s and 1970s. Since 1960, the divorce rate in America has more than doubled, as have the number of births to unmarried women (National Center for Education Statistics, 1996b). As a result of these two factors, the number of single-parent families has climbed significantly over the years, as Figure 11-6 shows. Because such families are at higher risk of descending into poverty (46 percent of all female householders with children under the age of 18 live in poverty) and because they often result in the decreased involvement of the father in family life, the effects on the children in these families can be profound. The fracture of the traditional nuclear family has affected black children more than any other race or ethnic group (National

TABLE 11-14

**Percentage of Children Living in Poverty
in Female-Headed Households by Race, for Selected Years**

	TOTAL	WHITE	BLACK	HISPANIC
1960	23%	21%	29%	—
1970	45	36	60	—
1980	52	41	75	43%
1990	57	46	80	47
1994	57	46	82	45

SOURCE: National Center for Education Statistics (1996a), *The condition of education* (Washington, DC: U.S. Department of Education), Indicator 44.

Center for Education Statistics, 1996a). As Table 11-14 shows, in 1994, 82 percent of black children in female-headed households lived in poverty, compared to 46 percent of poor white and poor Hispanic children. It is yet another factor to consider when contemplating some of the achievement differences discussed earlier.

The traditional family, of course, has no monopoly on providing an enlightened, loving environment for children. Against all odds, many single-parent families provide their children with a very healthy upbringing. But the association between poverty and single-parent homes cannot be ignored. In fact, as Table 11-12 showed, similar differences of involvement in home literacy activities exist between single-parent families and two-parent families and between low- and high-income families (Nord et al., 2000).

Another factor emerging in the literature has to do with the role of fathers in the school education of children. The data show that single-parent families headed by either the father or the mother are every bit as involved in their child's school education as mothers in two-parent homes (National Center for Education Statistics, 1998a). But a nonresident father's involvement drops off considerably. Only 8 percent of all nonresident fathers displayed high involvement in their children's school education. Not surprisingly, as Table 11-15 shows, the children of fathers with high levels of involvement in their schools, at all grade levels, were more likely than children of fathers with low levels of school involvement to get better grades, to enjoy school, and to participate in extracurricular activities. They were also less likely to be expelled or suspended from school or to repeat a grade (National Center for Education Statistics, 1998a). Low-income children are

TABLE 11-15
Selected School Outcomes by Family Type
and Level of Fathers' Involvement, 1996

	FATHERS IN TWO-PARENT FAMILIES		NON-RESIDENT FATHERS	
	Low Involvement (47%)	High Involvement (26%)	Low Involvement (82%)	High Involvement (8%)
Child Gets Mostly A's	34%	50%	29%	35%
Child Enjoys School	33	49	34	44
Child Participates in Extracurricular Activities				
Grades K–5	73	79	73	86
Grades 6–12	79	94	75	92
Child Has Repeated a Grade	14	6	18	7
Child Has Been Expelled/Suspended				
Grades 6–12	17	9	27	14

SOURCE: National Center for Education Statistics (1999a), *The condition of education* (Washington, DC: U.S. Department of Education), p. 102.

disproportionately affected by the negative outcomes associated with non-resident, low-involvement fathers.

Finally, the changing role of women in the workplace needs to be considered. As Figure 11-7 shows, in 1960, only about 18 percent of married women with children under the age of 6 were in the labor force; by 1993, close to 60 percent were. Similarly, in 1960, about 40 percent of women with children ages 6–18 were participants in the labor force; by 1993, 75 percent were (National Center for Education Statistics, 1996b). Divorced or separated women have always been much more likely to be employed than married women. The percentage of divorced or separated women participating in the workforce has more or less held steady at between 80 and 85 percent over the years, but there are more of them today than ever before. The implied message here is not that women should stay home to raise children, but that familial conditions for the raising of healthy children have changed in ways that reflect on the schools. Over 20 million school-

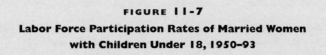

FIGURE 11-7

Labor Force Participation Rates of Married Women with Children Under 18, 1950–93

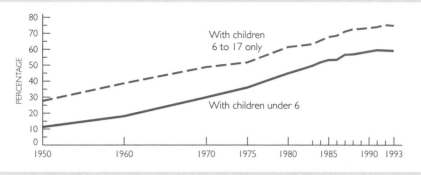

SOURCE: National Center for Education Statistics (1996b), *Youth indicators* (Washington, DC: U.S. Department of Education), p. 51.

children, for instance, are without adult supervision after school each day (Hodgkinson, 1991).

Public school teachers often see parental involvement as a key factor in a successful school education. Clearly, the home environment has a significant effect on a child's achievement in school. School readiness, opportunities to learn, home resources for learning, home literary activities, and parental involvement are all part of the picture. Given the disintegration of the nuclear family, children are more likely than ever to be living in single-parent families with low-involvement fathers. Moreover, children living in single-parent household are, in about six out of ten cases, living in poverty.

SCHOOL SAFETY

Obviously, 1999 was not a good year for the public perception of school safety. Eleven schoolchildren and one teacher were shot to death at Columbine High School, the most deadly school crime in history. School shootings also occurred in small communities in Kentucky, Arkansas, and Oregon. In each case, the perpetrators of the crimes were students in the school. This has put added pressure on schools to monitor the conduct of their student populations. Responses have included increased policing measures, the adoption of policies requiring students to wear school uniforms, the development of mechanisms for the early identification of

TABLE 11-16
Percentage of Public Schools with Zero-Tolerance Policies for Various Student Offenses, 1996–97

	FIREARMS	WEAPONS OTHER THAN FIREARMS	ALCOHOL	DRUGS	TOBACCO
All Public Schools	94%	91%	87%	88%	79%
Elementary Schools	93	91	87	88	82
Middle Schools	95	90	86	90	77
High Schools	96	92	86	89	72

SOURCE: National Center for Education Statistics (1999e), *School crime and safety* (Washington, DC: U.S. Department of Education), Table A1.

potentially violent children, and the widespread implementation of zero-tolerance policies.

Zero-tolerance policies prescribe predetermined consequences or punishments for specific offenses and typically result in automatic suspension or expulsion, depending on the violation. As Table 11-16 shows, most public schools have zero-tolerance policies for serious student offenses—mainly weapons, drug, and alcohol offenses. A majority of schools also have zero-tolerance policies for tobacco use. Zero tolerance is intended to send a strong message to youths about the seriousness of certain offenses and the lack of justification for certain violations. Clearly, the school shootings have made schools and communities more willing to adopt zero-tolerance policies. According to a 1999 Phi Delta Kappa/Gallup Poll, 92 percent of public school parents favor zero-tolerance drug and alcohol policies (Phi Delta Kappa/Gallup Poll, 1999).

The problem, of course, is that zero-tolerance policies are inflexible and often result in bureaucratic responses to personal problems. Consequently, many students are being suspended, and even expelled, for seemingly petty offenses that would probably be treated far less harshly if zero-tolerance policies were not in place. For example, a second grader who brought his grandfather's watch to show-and-tell was suspended for a weapons violation because the watch had a pocketknife attached to it. A child who brought a butter knife to school to cut up a pan of brownies she made for her friends on the occasion of her birthday was suspended for a weapons violation. A seventh grader who shared some cough drops with a friend was suspended for a drug violation. And there is, of course, the nationally known case of the six-year-old who kissed a classmate and was suspended

11-5 DEBATING THE ISSUES
Zero-Tolerance Policies

Zero-tolerance policies certainly have their share of critics. To pursue the topic further, consider reading the following:

- Ayers, W., and Dohrn, B. (1999). Have we gone overboard with zero tolerance? *Chicago Tribune* (21 Nov.).

- American Federation of Teachers. (1997). Where we stand: Zero tolerance. *USA Today* (26 Jan.).

- Cauchon, D. (1999). Zero tolerance lacks flexibility. *USA Today* (13 Apr.).

- Skiba, R., and Peterson, R. (1999). The dark side of zero tolerance: Can punishment lead to safe schools? *Phi Delta Kappan,* 80(5).

- Smartt, K. (1997). Courtside: The midol case. *Phi Delta Kappan,* 78(9).

- Steinberg, N. (1998). Fad for zero tolerance is leaving a moral void. *Chicago-Sun Times* (17 May).

The source for much of this information is Zero Tolerance = Zero Common Sense = Zero Justice (www.crossmyt.com/hc/zerotol).

based on the school's zero tolerance policy toward "unwarranted and unwelcome touching." These are some of the less-than-positive side effects of zero tolerance. Because zero tolerance fails to account for individual circumstances and motivations, some legal experts have argued that it is not a policy that can withstand a legal challenge. It denies students their right to due process, which is the right to defend oneself against charges that have serious personal consequences. Feature 11-5 lists some resources for investigating zero-tolerance policies.

The prevalence of zero-tolerance policies seems to imply that the schools are suffering from rampant crime and unruly students, but the policing measures used in public schools certainly do not testify to large-scale problems. Over 90 percent of schools require visitors to sign in, and most control access to school buildings and grounds. In addition, 19 percent of public schools conduct general drug sweeps. But 78 percent of all public schools have no law enforcement officers stationed at the school (National Center for Education Statistics, 1998b), and only 1 percent of all schools (2 percent of all high schools) require students to pass through

About 1 percent of all schools require students to pass through a metal detector each school day.

metal detectors each day. Only 2 percent of all school principals claim that student possession of weapons or the sale of drugs on school grounds is a moderate or serious concern in their school (National Center for Education Statistics, 1998c).

Interestingly, as Figures 11-8 and 11-9 show at least when it comes to violent crimes (serious violent crimes and simple assault) and serious violent crimes (rape, sexual assault, robbery, and aggravated assault), children are safer in school than away from school. This is as it should be given the high value placed on the integrity of learning in the schools. Thefts, however, are more likely to occur in school than away from school.

Despite public perceptions to the contrary, there is little evidence to support the conclusion that school-based violence has increased in recent years. School victimization rates have not changed much in recent years, and student drug and alcohol use is down considerably, as Feature 11-6 discusses. But there is some cause for concern among educators because students seem to feel more unsafe in school. As Table 11-17 shows, between 1989 and 1995, the percentages of students who felt unsafe while they were in school or coming from and going to school increased significantly. The fact the students feel less safe is a serious concern.

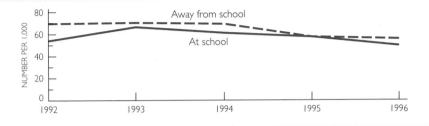

FIGURE 11-8

Number of Violent Crimes Against Students Ages 12–18, 1992–96

NOTE: Violent crimes include serious violent crimes and simple assault. Serious violent crimes include rape, sexual assault, robbery, and aggravated assault. "At school" includes on school property or on the way to or from school.

SOURCE: National Center for Education Statistics (1998b), *Indicators of school crime and safety* (Washington, DC: U.S. Department of Education).

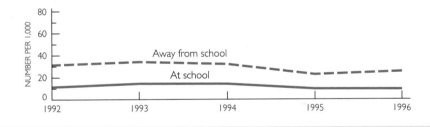

FIGURE 11-9

Number of Serious Violent Crimes Against Students Ages 12–18, 1992–96

NOTE: Serious violent crimes include rape, sexual assault, robbery, and aggravated assault. "At school" includes on school property or on the way to or from school.

SOURCE: National Center for Education Statistics (1998b), *Indicators of school crime and safety* (Washington, DC: U.S. Department of Education).

According to Abraham Maslow's (1962) learning theory, various fundamental needs must be met before any learning can occur. Maslow described these needs in a hierarchical order, arguing that the most fundamental needs were physiological ones (food, shelter, sleep), followed by a succession of needs that included safety, love, acceptance, self-esteem, and self-actualization. This was Maslow's way of saying that if children come to school tired or hungry they will likely not be able to learn much. Maslow's work, in fact, helped provide the rationale for congressional authorization

483

11-6 THE HISTORICAL CONTEXT
Student Drug Use Rates

Most people would agree that alcohol and drug use among today's high school students is a problem. But taken in historical context, it seems to be less of a problem today than it was twenty-five years ago. Examine the rate of student alcohol and drug use since 1976 depicted below. How does one explain the dramatic drop in almost all areas of drug use? Because drug and alcohol use can interfere with learning, such a drop probably has contributed to improved school performance. Find out more by examining the work of the Institute for Social Research at the University of Michigan, which monitors student drug and alcohol use in America (www.isr. umich.edu).

Reported Drug and Alcohol Use by High School Seniors During the Previous Year, 1976–98

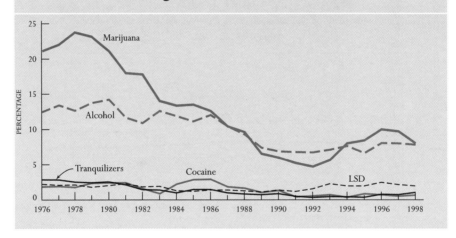

TABLE 11-17
Percentage of Students Ages 12–19
Who Reported Fears for Safety, 1989 and 1995

	FEAR BEING ATTACKED IN SCHOOL	FEAR BEING ATTACKED GOING TO AND FROM SCHOOL	AVOID ONE OR MORE PLACES IN SCHOOL
1989	6%	4%	5%
1995	9	7	9

SOURCE: National Center for Education Statistics (1998b), *Indicators of school crime and safety* (Washington, DC: U.S. Department of Education).

of the National School Lunch Program, which provides free or reduced-price lunches to low-income children, and the Child Nutrition Act, which provides free or reduced-price breakfasts to needy children.

The safety of the learning environment is also essential to Maslow's hierarchy. Anxieties about safety speak to the potential disruption of the school environment. If the safety of the school is compromised, learning is compromised. Even the perception of a lack of safety can undermine the learning environment of the school. So, the fact that more students fear for their safety in school, even though the school is no less safe, is disconcerting. Part of it might have to do with the visible media coverage given to school shootings and to the overtly drastic safety measures some schools have taken.

SUMMARY

The condition of public education in America is mixed. Most achievement measures are stable, as are the national dropout rates. The NAEP achievement indices in reading and mathematics show no appreciable decline in overall performance and significant improvements in select areas. The composite averages, however, mask the differences that exist between the performances of various subgroups. Although the achievement gap in reading and math that exists between white and nonwhite children has narrowed considerably in recent decades, it is still quite wide. Some of the differences might be explained by the disproportionately high representation of minority groups living in poverty and perhaps by differential OTL factors in the school. But some of the achievement gaps can be detected among 4-year-olds, which points to the family and to preschool environments as contributing factors. The achievement differences between males and females, although considerable in the area of reading, are significantly smaller than anything witnessed across income and race categories.

The factor of poverty seems to be closely associated with lower reading achievement. First, children living in poverty seem to have fewer home literacy experiences that contribute to reading achievement. Second, more than half of all children living in poverty live in single-parent homes, most of which have low-involvement, nonresident fathers. The presence of high-involvement fathers, in both single-parent homes and two-parent homes, is positively associated with successful school experiences.

The gap in the dropout rates between white and black children has been closing, and the graduation rates of black children have improved tremendously. The Hispanic population, however, has not experienced the same kind of improvements, and its dropout rate remains quite high. But the Hispanic population is unique because it is very much affected by immigration factors. Most Hispanic status dropouts, for instance, were born outside of the United States and are counted as dropouts even though in many cases they never attended public school. In any case, factors internal to the school tend to push students out, and factors external to the school tend to pull students out. The internal factors seem to play a more significant role than the external ones.

Although much has been written about the alarming incidences of crime and violence in school, the data show that there is no crisis of school violence. Most public schools have adopted zero-tolerance policies related to weapons, drug, and alcohol violations. But security measures in most schools are not stringent, school crime rates are stable, and very few school principals consider drugs or weapons to be modest or serious problems in their schools. Zero-tolerance policies have, of course, become controversial because they leave no discretionary room for individual circumstances and contexts. Some evidence does exist that students perceive the school to be more unsafe today than in past years. This is of obvious concern because the perception of an unsafe school can undermine the learning environment.

QUESTIONS AND ACTIVITIES

1. What is school achievement, and how does it differ from school aptitude?

2. Explain how OTL factors play into achievement and how OTL factors can explain differences in achievement between various groups.

3. What is the NAEP?

4. What is the fundamental difference between a criterion-referenced and a norm-referenced test?

5. What are the overall trends in NAEP reading results?

6. What is the general relation between reading achievement and home reading conditions?

7. Why is there a wide gap in reading achievement measures between white and black children, between boys and girls, and between children living above and below the poverty line?

8. What are the overall trends in NAEP math results?

9. Do course-taking patterns in mathematics suggest OTL differences between boys and girls?

10. What is the difference between an event dropout and a status dropout?

11. Explain why the dropout rate has remained high among Hispanic youths.

12. Outline a strategy to further improve the holding power of schools, given the data presented on dropouts.

13. Explain how dropouts can be pushed out of school as well as pulled out of school.

14. Explain the characteristics of the intersection between race and poverty.

15. What is the official poverty line index used by the Department of Education?

16. How are home literacy experiences affected by poverty levels?

17. What is the relationship between poverty, single-parent homes, divorce rates, and out-of-wedlock births?

18. How is the involvement of fathers a factor in school achievement, and how is it an especially important issue for children living in poverty?

19. How have the characteristics of the American family changed in recent decades, and how have they affected public education?

20. What are zero-tolerance policies, and what is your opinion on their implementation in schools?

21. Explain why students seem to believe that the school is more unsafe today even though the rates of violent and nonviolent crime have not increased significantly.

REFERENCES

Berliner, D. C., and Biddle, B. J. (1997). *The manufactured crisis: Myths, fraud and the attack on America's public schools.* (White Plains, NY: Longman).

Bracey, G. W. (1993). The third Bracey report. *Phi Delta Kappan,* 75(2):104–17.

Carson, C. C., Huelskamp, R. M., and Woodall, T. D. (1993). Perspectives on education in America. *Journal of Educational Research* (May/June):259–310.

Grouws, D. A., and Cebulla, K. J. (2000). Elementary and middle school mathematics at the crossroads. In T. Good (ed.), *American education: Yesterday, today and tomorrow,* The Ninety-Ninth Yearbook for the National Society for the Study of Education (Chicago: University of Chicago Press).

Hodgkinson, H. (1991). Reform versus reality. *Phi Delta Kappan,* 73(1):9–16.

Jencks, C., and Phillips, M. (1998). America's next achievement test: Closing the black-white score gap. *The American Prospect online,* 40.

Johnson, R. C., and Viadero, D. (2000). Unmet promise: Minority achievement. *Education Week* (15 March).

Maslow, A. H. (1962). *Toward a psychology of being.* (New York: Van Nostrand Reinhold).

National Center for Education Statistics. (2000). *Digest of education statistics, 1999.* (Washington, DC: U.S. Department of Education).

National Center for Education Statistics. (1999a). *The condition of education.* (Washington, DC: U.S. Department of Education).

National Center for Education Statistics. (1999b). *NAEP 1998 reading: Report card for the nation and the states.* (Washington, DC: U.S. Department of Education).

National Center for Education Statistics. (1999c). *Dropout rates in the United States: 1998.* (Washington, DC: U.S. Department of Education).

National Center for Education Statistics. (1999d). *America's children: Key national indicators of well-being: 1999.* (Washington, DC: U.S. Department of Education).

National Center for Education Statistics. (1999e). *School crime and safety.* (Washington, DC: U.S. Department of Education).

National Center for Education Statistics. (1998a). *How involved are fathers in their children's school?* (Washington, DC: U.S. Department of Education).

National Center for Education Statistics. (1998b). *Indicators of school crime and safety.* (Washington, DC: U.S. Department of Education).

National Center for Education Statistics. (1998c). *Violence and discipline problems in U.S. public schools.* (Washington, DC: U.S. Department of Education).

National Center for Education Statistics. (1997a). *NAEP 1996 mathematics: Report card for the nation and the states.* (Washington, DC: U.S. Department of Education).

National Center for Education Statistics. (1997b). *The condition of education.* (Washington, DC: U.S. Department of Education).

National Center for Education Statistics. (1996a). *The condition of education.* (Washington, DC: U.S. Department of Education).

National Center for Education Statistics. (1996b). *Youth indicators, 1996.* (Washington, DC: U.S. Department of Education).

National Center for Education Statistics. (1995a). *Digest of education statistics.* (Washington, DC: U.S Department of Education).

National Center for Education Statistics. (1995b). *Dropouts and late comers.* (Washington, DC: U.S. Department of Education).

National Center for Education Statistics. (1993). *Dropout rates in the United States.* (Washington, D.C: U.S. Department of Education).

National Center for Education Statistics. (1992). *Are Hispanic dropout rates related to immigration?* (Washington, DC: U.S. Department of Education).

National Committee on Excellence in Education. (1983). *A nation at risk.* (Washington, DC: U.S. Department of Education).

National Library of Education. (1996). *Educational and labor market performance of GED recipients.* (Washington, DC: U.S. Department of Education).

Nord, C. W., Lennon, J., Liu, B., and Chandler, K. (2000). Home literacy activities and signs of children's emerging literacy: 1993 and 1999. *Education Statistics Quarterly* (Spring).

North Carolina State Department of Mental Health. (1994). *Dropout data report and program summary.* (Raleigh: North Carolina State Department of Mental Health).

Phi Delta Kappa/Gallup Poll. (1999). The 31st annual Phi Delta Kappa/Gallup Poll. *Phi Delta Kappan,* 81(1):41–56.

Schwartz, W. (1995). *School dropouts: New information about an old problem.* ERIC/Cue Digest #109 ERIC. (New York: Clearinghouse in Urban Education). (ERIC document 38655).

Shoemaker, C. R. (1994). *Dropout rate study, 1992–93.* (Phoenix: Arizona State Department of Education).

Texas Education Agency. (1995). *Public school dropouts, 92–93* report. (Austin: Publications Distribution Division of Texas Education Agency). (ERIC #384685).

White, S., and Dewitz, P. (1996). *Reading proficiency and home support for literacy.* (Washington, DC: U.S. Department of Education).

CHAPTER 12

The Culture and Language of Schooling

Cultural Diversity and Commonality

The Culture of Schooling

SOURCES OF A COMMON CULTURE

MULTICULTURAL EDUCATION

CULTURE AND CRITICAL THEORY

The Language of Schooling

BILINGUAL EDUCATION

Summary

Questions and Activities

References

P UBLIC EDUCATION IN THE UNITED STATES has always reflected a tension between two important cultural agendas. The first has to do with building a common culture based on a common language, knowledge base, and foundation of values. This agenda is fulfilled through the assimilation process of schooling—that part of the school experience aiming to create a national identity. But in a pluralistic nation such as ours, the assimilation process is complicated by the vast diversity of the populace. Thus, the second cultural agenda has to do with the diversifying process of schooling—that part of the school experience showing sensitivity toward and tolerance of the family-based ancestral heritage of various Americans. Sometimes these two processes clash in the school, resulting in accusations of cultural imperialism on the one side and cultural divisiveness on the other.

This tension, however, is the natural consequence of living in a pluralistic constitutional democracy that claims no nationally identifiable ethnic, religious, or racial prototype. Our ancestors were either immigrants or slaves, and the nation continues to be favored by immigrants today. In 1997, the foreign-born population of the United States was almost 26 million persons, or about 10 percent of the total population (Census Bureau, 1997).

We can therefore say that in many respects the common culture in America is multicultural, and the idea of cultural diversity exists in delicate balance with the idea of cultural commonality. In this way, the forces of assimilation, which aim to make a common culture, work together with the forces of diversity. They exist in a kind of partnership.

CULTURAL DIVERSITY AND COMMONALITY

Consider for a moment the notion of diversity without a context of commonality. The effect would be cultural relativity, such that all cultural values and actions are equally moral and equally acceptable. The effect is little regard for the cultural agreements or commonalities that unify society. Moreover, where diversity stands alone, it often creates a situation in which differences become sources of antagonism or worse. We have seen how issues of ethnic diversity have wreaked havoc around the world, in places like the former Yugoslavia and parts of Africa and the Mideast. The very history of the humanity has been marked by conflicts fueled largely by ethnic, religious, and racial differences.

But the idea of a common culture, without any appreciation for diversity, is also troubling because it can result in cultural imperialism. This was

© Underwood & Underwood/Corbis

These youngsters went to school on Ellis Island while waiting for final admittance into the U.S. Today, about 10 percent of the U.S. population is foreign-born.

the case in the former Soviet Union, a nation that tolerated little diversity and imposed rigid guidelines on the thoughts and actions of its people. Similarly, Nazi Germany promoted one of the most extreme and frightening forms of cultural imperialism. Still, even the fiercest advocates of diversity in the school curriculum reach a point at which their tolerance runs thin, usually as it relates to highly racist or sexist views, or to unlawful views. The common culture helps us all to draw the line between the tolerable and the intolerable, between the type of diversity that contributes to the common good and the type that destroys it. This is essentially what it means to have a common culture.

In 1908, Jane Addams wrote a short essay titled "The Public School and the Immigrant Child," in which she argued that immigrant traditions were fundamental to the assimilation of foreign-born children into American culture. To Addams, our differences were at the heart of our commonalities; who we were individually had everything to do with whom we become collectively. She believed that at some level our differences had to be circulated, understood, and accommodated into a community of common concerns and principles. Hence, Addams had little tolerance for those who aimed to educate children in a manner that ignored the cultural dynamics of the child's life. She wanted to use these dynamics to give children a broad, multiethnic view of life in a way that related to the problems, issues, and values of American democracy. She expressed this idea clearly in her 1908 essay:

> Can we say, perhaps, that the schools ought to do more to connect these [immigrant] children with the best things of the past, to make them realize something of the beauty and charm of the language, the history, and the traditions which their parents represent. It is easy to cut them loose from their parents, it requires cultivation to tie them up in sympathy and understanding. The ignorant teacher cuts them off because he himself cannot understand the situation, the cultivated teacher fastens them because his own mind is open to the charm and beauty of that old country life. In short, it is the business of the school to give to each child the beginnings of a culture so wide and deep and universal that he can interpret his own parents and countrymen by a standard which is world-wide and not provincial. (p. 138)

Addams may have been unique for her time, but the problem of forging a common culture without disrupting the pluralistic elements of American society is one that continues to be debated by policymakers and practitioners alike. How is it possible, after all, for the public schools to acculturate children, whose identification with ethnicity, class, language, religion, and politics is overwhelmingly varied, into an American culture without destroying the very essence of diversity that makes our democracy so vital? Immigrant and first-generation American students of various ethnic and language traditions have always had to reconcile their family culture with the broader societal culture. But does this mean that these youths had to reject their own family or community culture or language in the interests of assimilating into a larger or more dominant national culture?

The truth is that the schooling process has not always resulted in a happy resolution between the forces of assimilation and diversity. For some children, the process of assimilation can sometimes lead to the severing of community- or family-based cultural connections. This could mean that students give up the use of their first language in school or even that they lose some identification with cultural traditions in the home. Students sometimes come to school with value systems not typically associated with what we might see as American culture; some of these values may even be at odds with the ideals of democracy. The school and the family may have different outlooks on gender roles, language usage, career choices, and racial tolerance, to name just a few. How should these cultural differences be treated in the curriculum? For example, should sexist views be tolerated because they have the sanction of the family or ethnic culture? Is ebonics a form of communication that should be celebrated and respected? Should the school teach children to take pride in their own ethnic or racial identity, or should it teach them about the holidays and traditions of different cultures around the world? What about the many students from multigenerational American families who do not have a strong ethnic identification? Should the school celebrate cultural differences, or should it provide a forum for the discussion, analysis, and criticism of cultural differences? These are difficult questions that do not always have definitive answers.

THE CULTURE OF SCHOOLING

The concept of culture is complicated, and acceptable definitions are hard to frame. For our purposes, we will examine culture in terms of the forces it exerts in binding people together and in establishing rules, norms, and customs for behavior. The key issue is this: How does the school contribute to the formation of American culture, to the rules, knowledge, and traditions with which we can all identify? Clearly, the "culture" of the school should reflect the wider culture, but how can the school animate this culture in its daily operations?

Sources of a Common Culture

In *The Interpretation of Cultures,* Clifford Geortz (1973) observed that "cultural patterns are programs: they provide a 'template' or 'blueprint' for the organization of social and psychological processes" (p. 216). The use of the words "template" and "blueprint" as analogies for the way a culture guides a group of people suggests that, despite individual variations, those who share a culture follow a set of underlying "directions" for living. This so-called set of directions depends on a foundation of commonality—a common language, common problems and concerns, and common values and principles. As John Dewey (1916) pointed out, humans live in communities by virtue of the things they have in common, and they communicate as a way to share and eventually possess things in common. Thus, without a sense of commonality, there can be no communication, and without communication, there can be no community. The conceptual anchor for community is the idea of commonality.

Language. Of course, language is our best way of ensuring some basis of commonality, although obviously language alone is not enough. We are endowed with the capacity to speak, but the kind of language that we speak is obviously culturally derived; that is, it includes us in one culture, but it might also exclude us from another. People consistently use language and other cultural commonalities to help define who they are and, equally important, who they are not. Thus, societies always have some semblance of a common language. In this sense, the current debate over the place of English in the school experience is really a debate about how to define a common culture.

This was exactly the situation when the Oakland Unified School District in 1997 declared its intention to include the African-derived language of ebonics in the school curriculum, asserting that it was the "primary," unique, and "genetically based" language of the descendants of slaves. The announcement of the district's new policy touched off a heated national argument over the place of English in the curriculum. Advocates of teaching English only believed that the teaching of ebonics would not only fail to properly assimilate black children into American culture but would create deeper divisions between the races. The district eventually retreated from its original position and redefined the role of ebonics in the school curriculum as a means to assist in the education of English language proficiency, a tradition of teaching well established in bilingual education programs (Schnaiberg, 1997). We will return to this topic later in the chapter.

History. A common culture is also created through a common history. The history of America testifies to a struggle to build what is now the world's oldest democracy, but many people question whether the whole story is being told. Here, again, the diversity agenda complicates our sense of commonality. For example, from the perspective of Native Americans and African Africans, the founding of America was hardly a call to freedom or to democracy. Similarly, women, minorities, laborers, gays, members of various ethnic groups, and the poor all provide different historical perspectives on living in America. Our common history thus is marked by interesting and telling subtexts.

Core Values and Knowledge. Obviously, socialization in a common set of values and a common basis of knowledge also contributes to the development of a common culture. Some evidence suggests that, despite the considerable diversifying elements in society, American youths embrace a common core of values. For example, in 1992, People for the American Way released a study that found widespread consensus among all youths on core values, including the significance of the family, the importance of personal responsibility, and the belief in social equity (Schmidt, 1992). It also showed definitively that the school is still the one place where youths have regular contact with people of other races and ethnicities—more so than at work, in the neighborhood, during sports activities, or during religious observances. The overwhelming majority of youths also approved of interracial dating, and more than 70 percent said they had a "close personal friendship" with a person of another race.

But any set of core values must also include some appreciation for cultural diversity and a willingness and ability to deliberate about relevant disagreements (Gutmann, 2000). Such discussions require an understanding of cultural differences and a shared sense of historical perspective. As indicated in Chapter 3, conservatives and progressives alike have argued that the notion of a shared base of common knowledge is essential to social discussion and the sense of community required to educate good citizens. As Feature 12-1 shows, the National Assessment of Educational Progress (NAEP) data indicate that 17-year-olds have little common knowledge of history and literature (Ravitch and Finn, 1987); NAEP civics data indicate a similar problem. According to the 1998 report, only 42 percent of fourth graders reported studying how their government works, only 55 percent studied the laws of government, and only 50 percent learned the rights and responsibilities of citizens (National Center for Education Statistics, 1999). The percentages are slightly better at the eighth- and twelfth-grade levels. Still, as Table 12.1 indicates, a core of civic topics, related mostly to citizenship, does not have an ongoing presence in the curriculum. Given what we know about opportunity-to-learn (OTL) factors, this is not a promising condition for building a common core of civic values and knowledge.

The "Melting Pot" and "Salad Bowl" Metaphors. In most cases, the thinking on the formation of a common culture in the school embraces either of two frameworks. According to one view, the school's role in the acculturation of youth is as a source of heat in the "melting pot" society, in which individual differences are dissolved. Under such conditions, exclusive immersion in the English language is required, and finding ways for children to fit into one cultural design is the very purpose of schooling. The melting pot perspective typically upholds the Western canon in the liberal arts curriculum. The main purpose here is to teach a core foundation of knowledge that can be used for common understanding and discourse. Feature 12-2 gives an idea of how the melting pot metaphor was dramatized in the early twentieth century, during a period of massive immigration to the United States.

12-1 THINKING ABOUT THE DATA

Test Items from the NAEP Test on Historical and Literary Knowledge

Here is a selective sample of test items taken from the 1988 NAEP history and literature exam given to 17-year-olds. A check mark indicates the correct response for each item, and the percentage of respondents for each of the answer options is given as well. Do you find these results to be a sign of an erosion in our common culture, or do you think that such results are not indicative of anything important?

Literature

1. *The Return of the Native, Tess of the D'Urbervilles,* and *The Mayor of Caster-bridge* were written by

___	Sir Walter Scott	34.1
✓	Thomas Hardy	24.4
___	Oscar Wilde	21.1
___	Robert Louis Stevenson	20.4

2. *Billy Budd,* "Benito Cereno," and "Bartleby the Scrivener" were written by

___	Washington Irving	22.9
✓	Herman Melville	35.9
___	Jack London	22.7
___	James Fenimore Cooper	18.6

3. Who is the Spanish knight who attacked windmills thinking they were giants?

___	Sancho Panza	21.4
✓	Don Quixote	47.9
___	El Cid	15.8
___	Zorro	14.9

4. *Julius Caesar* by Shakespeare is a play about Caesar's

___	discovery of and escape from a plot to kill him	22.1
___	ultimate triumph in the Gallic wars	11.2
✓	death and the fate of his assassins	48.0
___	love affair with Cleopatra	18.8

5. Which of the following is a play about the experiences of a black family as they made plans to move into an all-white, suburban neighborhood?

___	*The River Niger*	16.2
✓	*A Raisin in the Sun*	53.2
___	*Porgy and Bess*	14.2
___	*Blues for Mister Charlie*	16.4

6. What is the moral of Aesop's fable "The Tortoise and the Hare"?
   - ✓ Slow and steady wins the race   67.7
   - ___ Don't trust flatterers   8.9
   - ___ The race is to the swift and strong   8.0
   - ___ Look before you leap   15.4

7. Who wrote *Native Son,* a novel of black life in Chicago, and *Black Boy,* which is highly autobiographical?
   - ✓ Richard Wright   32.3
   - ___ Eldridge Cleaver   25.2
   - ___ LeRoi Jones   22.3
   - ___ Malcolm X   20.2

History

8. Who was the leader of the Soviet Union when the United States entered the Second World War?
   - ___ Yuri Gagarin   10.2
   - ___ Marshal Tito   5.9
   - ✓ Joseph Stalin   53.6
   - ___ Nikita Khrushchev   30.3

9. What is Magna Carta?
   - ___ The Great Seal of the monarchs of England   15.9
   - ✓ The foundation of the British parliamentary system   30.6
   - ___ The French Declaration of the Rights of Man   16.6
   - ___ The charter signed by the Pilgrims on the Mayflower   36.8

10. The idea that each branch of the federal government should keep the other branches from becoming too strong is called
    - ___ strict constructionism   4.4
    - ✓ the system of checks and balances   59.9
    - ___ federalism   18.9
    - ___ implied powers   16.7

11. President Abraham Lincoln wrote
    - ___ the Bill of Rights   13.6
    - ✓ the Emancipation Proclamation   68.0
    - ___ the Missouri Compromise   9.9
    - ___ *Uncle Tom's Cabin*   8.5

(continued)

12-1 THINKING ABOUT THE DATA *(continued)*

Test Items from the NAEP Test on Historical and Literary Knowledge

12. Which of the following was NOT addressed by New Deal legislation?

___	Agricultural price supports	20.6
___	Labor unions	17.7
___	Social Security	23.9
✓	Restrictions on immigration	37.8

13. The purpose of the authors of *The Federalist* papers was to

___	win foreign approval for the Revolutionary War	15.0
___	establish a strong, free press in the colonies	41.0
✓	gain ratification of the United States Constitution	40.1
___	confirm George Washington's election as the first President	3.9

14. The controversy surrounding Senator Joseph R. McCarthy focused on

✓	investigations of individuals suspected of Communist activities	42.6
___	agitation to secure civil rights for Irish immigrants	15.1
___	leadership of the movement protesting the war in Vietnam	29.4
___	leadership of the movement to improve veterans' benefits	12.9

The melting pot approach might lead to a common culture, but critics have argued that it fails the interests of democracy because it does not embrace the idea of diversity. In fact, the very idea of unity in the context of this metaphor can be construed as having imperialistic qualities. This is because all differences are melded away and recast in the image of only one privileged culture, which, historically speaking, has roots in the traditional liberal arts, with the attendant emphasis on so-called Euro-centered Western thinking and Western literature. Howe (1993) has extended this argument, claiming that the problem with the melting pot approach is that it produces exactly the opposite outcomes as originally intended. That is, the melting pot process actually creates the conditions for ethnic divisiveness, not unity, because it forces minority groups to huddle together to protect their cultural identity from dominant forces.

Another way of looking at acculturation is to frame it as a process that cultivates a dual identity—one with the larger American tradition and the other with the more community-based or familial tradition. This has been

TABLE 12-1
Levels of Civics Instruction in Grades 8 and 12, 1998

	GRADE 8		GRADE 12	
	Percentage Yes	Percentage No	Percentage Yes	Percentage No
This Year Studied				
U.S. Constitution	79%	14%	71%	27%
Congress	75	17	71	27
President and Cabinet	55	32	63	32
How Laws Are Made	67	24	64	32
The Court Systems	60	30	64	32
State and Local Government	67	22	69	28
Political Parties, Elections, Voting	69	22	70	27
Other Countries' Governments	40	45	48	44
International Organizations	33	43	45	45

SOURCE: National Center for Education Statistics (1999), *NAEP Civics: Report card for the nation* (Washington, DC: U.S. Department of Education), p. 90.

12-2 THE HISTORICAL CONTEXT
The Melting Pot

Israel Zangwill dramatized the idea of assimilation at the turn of the century in his 1909 play, appropriately titled *The Melting Pot*:

It is in the fire of god round his Crucible. There she lies, the great Melting pot——listen! Can't you hear the roaring and the bubbling? There gapes her mouth——her harbor where a thousand mammoth feeders come from the ends of the world to pour in their human freight. Ah, what a stirring and seething! Celt and Latin, Slav and Teuton, Greek and Syrian——black and yellow——Jew and Gentile.

Yet, East and West, and North and South, the palm and the pine, the people and the equator, the crescent and the cross——how the great Alchemist melts and fuses them with the purging flame! Here shall they all unite to build the republic of Man and the Kingdom of God. Ah, Vera, what is the glory of Rome and Jerusalem where all nations come to worship and look back, compared with the glory of America, where all races and nations come to labour and look forward! (pp. 184–85) expressed by some in terms of a "salad bowl" metaphor, such that differences are essential to the overall composition and quality of the whole. Thus, national identity does not come at the expense of an ethnic identity, but is vested in a multitude of ethnic identities, with an emphasis on democratic principles of tolerance and understanding. To be different, then, is to be normal, as long as these differences have some basis in common understandings. The curriculum design associated with this metaphor is less oriented toward the traditional liberal arts than the curriculum justified by the melting pot metaphor, and is more issue-centered and interdisciplinary.

Some see this latter approach as a more appropriate way of handling acculturation in the American schools, although there are potential dangers here as well. The implication is that all diverse elements are reconcilable, but they often represent deep contrasts that cannot be easily incorporated into a harmonious whole.

Multicultural Education

The call for multicultural education has been reverberating in the discussions on public education for at least three decades. The strength of the current movement to include multicultural education in the school curriculum is, in some ways, indicative of the problems that the schools have had in trying to diversify their experiences. Multicultural education seeks to prevent prejudice and stereotyping, promote a better understanding of the different ethnic groups in society, and identify some commonality among diverse groups. Multicultural education allows schools to infuse the curriculum with a strong sense of America's pluralistic society.

Various scholars have argued that the systematic bias favoring a so-called European culture in the school has helped to prevent minority students from succeeding. Not many years ago, the curriculum materials and textbooks of American schools treated nonwhite groups not only infrequently, but also often less than truthfully and even blatantly offensively. These kinds of abuses have led to a call for a reduction in the use of the Western canon in the school curriculum and for the broadening of school experiences along different cultural lines. The claim is that, if Euro-American children can experience a Euro-centered curriculum in the school, then children from other ethnic groups should enjoy the same type of benefit.

Consequently, some advocates of multicultural education have argued for ethnocentric forms of instruction, meaning that black youths should receive an Afro-centric education, Latino youths a Latino-centered education, and so on. Supporters of these views do not see any contradiction in

A group of Jewish boys with their teacher. Multicultural education has an important place in the school.

advancing a form of multicultural education that encourages ethnic separatism. The rationale is that children need to be exposed to their own ancestral culture and to be taught to respect and appreciate their own heritage. The result, they claim, is improved self-esteem and increased awareness of their ancestors' role in the experience of the human race. This view has been touted mostly by some black scholars for the education of black children (Schlesinger, 1991).

Criticism of this view has emerged from various quarters. In *The Disuniting of America,* Arthur Schlesinger (1991) shows how ethnocentric views on multiculturalism have given rise to multicultural curricula less interested in historical accuracy and good pedagogy, and more interested simply in making children feel good about their ancestry. The effect is the loss of a common experience, a common history, and a common core of knowledge needed to encourage positive communication and mutual understanding. As Schlesinger documents, black ethnic separatists often frame their ancestral cultures in the most felicitous terms while assuming the worst from the so-called white European tradition. Ultimately, they ask black children to study their ethnicity more intensely than their own common American culture, because they supposedly can learn more by studying African culture

12-3 SCHOLARLY VOICES
Arthur Schlesinger
on the Dangers of Diversity

Arthur Schlesinger (1991) has criticized the tendency of public schools to glorify diversifying ideals while neglecting unifying or assimilating ones:

Instead of a transformative nation with an identity all its own, America increasingly sees itself as preservative of old identities. Instead of a nation composed of individuals making their own free choices, America increasingly sees itself as composed of groups more or less indelible in their ethnic character. The national ideal had once been e pluribus unum. Are we now to belittle unum *and glorify* pluribus? *Will the center hold? Or will the melting pot yield to the Tower of Babel? (p.18)*

than by studying American culture. Schlesinger's main point is encapsulated in Feature 12-3.

Ravitch (1990) labeled this perspective as particularistic multiculturalism. Rather than focusing on the broadest interpretation of the common culture in America, in the interests of creating a more enriching common discourse, particularistic multiculturalists reject the very idea of an American common culture. Ravitch argues that particularistic multiculturalism can lead to a proliferation of culturalized or ethnicized versions of what gets taught in school and how it gets taught—for example, African math with African pedagogical techniques for black children, ethnic science for immigrant children, and history from the Japanese perspective for Japanese American students. And this undermines a key purpose of public schooling, which is to immerse all learners in the pluralistic values and dimensions of American culture. Progressive educators have long argued that the school curriculum should provide countervailing experiences to the more parochial, or particularistic, experiences in the home, thereby facilitating ethnic, racial, religious, and political understandings.

Multicultural education does, of course, have an important place in the school. As indicated, America's common culture actually is multicultural, and any effort to understand its differences contributes to the whole of the American experience. Thus, for example, the study of our nation's history cannot be properly managed unless it embraces its many multicultural aspects. This means recounting the considerable hardships that members of various ethnic groups had to endure over the years—stories of discrimination and xenophobia and bigotry, stories about assimilation, and stories about legal, political, and social struggles to make America the pluralistic democracy that it is.

Banks (1988) and Cornbleth and Waugh (1995) have suggested other ways to conceive of multicultural education in the schools. For example, with the additive approach, the schools append multicultural elements onto the existing curriculum. Thus, a high school might offer a series of elective studies that relate to minority cultures and groups. In the classroom, a teacher using an additive approach might add an ethnic feature onto a conventional unit or offer a unit on the food, language, and music of a particular culture. However, such "plug-in" tactics are not ideal because they tend to fragment multiculturalism. Also, teachers who use an additive approach tend to focus mostly on the heroic contributions of ethnic groups, denying students a wider multicultural perspective (Cornbleth and Waugh, 1995).

Another form of multicultural education, known as the multiperspectives approach, seeks to integrate multiple cultural perspectives into most, if not all, school studies. The goal is to infuse the curriculum with multiple perspectives, making multiculturalism the overarching theme in the design of the school experience. In mathematics, for instance, discussions of numbers, probability, geometric form, and algebra could be situated in the context of culture. In fact, some mathematics educators have recognized the place of ethnomathematics in the school curriculum, emphasizing the study of math as a tool for the study of culture (Ascher, 1991). Hence, various mathematical properties and functions can be used both to illuminate the culture and to build math skills. Similarly, in teaching about major historical events, such as the founding of the nation, various perspectives not usually presented—such as the roles of women, blacks, and indigenous peoples— would be brought into the curriculum. For example, students could examine the antislavery petition filed in the General Court of Massachusetts by free African Americans in 1777, or the letter from three Seneca leaders to President Washington in 1790 expressing concerns about the effects of the American Revolution on native populations, or the letter Benjamin Banneker sent to Thomas Jefferson in 1791 outlining the obvious discrepancies between the ideals of the Revolution and the life conditions of blacks (Patrick, 2000).

But does this mean that all perspectives—including those of, say, white supremacists or the Nazis in 1930s Germany—have a place in the curriculum? Certainly such positions can and should be examined critically, but it would be difficult to see how, in the parlance of multicultural advocates, they could be honored, celebrated, or even tolerated. Because such extremist views are not consistent with the values and aims of democracy, their inclusion in the curriculum is difficult to justify.

12-4 RESEARCH INQUIRY
Parent Survey on Multiculturalism

Here are some of the results from the 1998 Public Agenda survey on parents' views on multicultural education. Give the same survey questions to your peers or to parents whom you know. Disaggregate the results to see if any differences emerge across race, income, or even gender lines. Compare your results to the national poll.

Percentage Responding "Very/Somewhat Close" to Their Own Views to Each of the Following Statements About the Public Schools

	Parents Overall	White Parents	African American Parents	Hispanic Parents	Foreign-Born Parents
The schools should make a special effort to teach new immigrants about American values and beliefs	88%	88%	89%	91%	87%
To graduate from high school, students should be required to show they understand the common history and ideas that tie all Americans together	85	88	83	89	88
The best place for kids to learn to take pride in their ethnic or racial identity is at home—school is where they should be learning what it means to be an American	80	81	81	87	80
In the past, the schools unfairly overlooked the contributions that minorities made to U.S. history	73	70	80	76	74
The schools these days pay too much attention to the differences between different ethnic and racial groups and not enough to what they have in common	70	70	69	70	66
The schools should teach students about the holidays and traditions of different cultures from around the world	69	67	78	77	80

SOURCE: © Data copyrighted by Source. © Graphics copyrighted by Public Agenda 2000. No reproduction/distribution without permission.

In 1998, Public Agenda, a nonpartisan agency dedicated to helping Americans understand social problems and issues, published a report documenting the views of parents on the issue of multicultural education in the schools. The results are interesting because they reveal how parents expect the schools to balance diversifying and assimilating agendas. The results are given in Feature 12-4. Interestingly, the parents expressed no strong negative views toward diversity but were much more conservative and cautious about multiculturalism than we might expect. In fact, the respondents communicated strongly patriotic sentiments in their responses and were concerned that their children took their country for granted. Choices made in the school curriculum are not, of course, up for vote, and many times educators will include objectives that do not have the full support of parents or the community. But what makes the parents' guarded views toward multiculturalism in the school especially interesting is the fact that multicultural education is partly offered in the interests of being responsive to the family and the community.

Culture and Critical Theory

Over the past decade, a group of radical scholars in education has examined schools in terms of socioeconomic and minority group issues (Apple, 1990; Giroux, 1983; McLaren, 1994). These scholars have tried to reveal the supposed injustices and inequities of public schooling, focusing on practices such as "low-ability" curriculum tracks and special education labels that affect disproportionately large numbers of minority children and children living in poverty. They have also examined the nature of "culture" perpetuated in the schools. Specifically, they have accused the public schools of practicing cultural hegemony by imposing one cultural tradition on the diverse ethnic and cultural groups in the American public schools.

This outlook can be said to be informed by critical theory, which is, in essence, a neo-Marxist belief that American public schools reproduce, rather than ameliorate, socioeconomic conditions (Gibson, 1986). In this sense, schools are seen as instruments of oppression, designed to keep certain groups down while lifting a few others up. Differential access to knowledge, differential opportunities to think and use language, and the privileging of different subject matter are all part of this process.

Critical theorists would claim, for instance, that the decision to teach English in high school with a list of readings drawn from the Western canon reflects the overt privileging of one set of writings over another and the concomitant privileging of one cultural perspective over another. Table 12-2 presents the results of one reading list survey. Given these results, the critical theorists might ask why Shakespeare should have such a prominent place in the English curriculum and whose interests are being served by this practice. That is, why is the reading list in an American high school English class representative mostly of white, male, European voices? The critical theorists might also ask why certain types of students seem to find their way into low-ability curriculum tracks. Critical theorists see political conservatives as the main villains in the story of the school's oppression. Conservatives are the ones, they claim, who want to build the curriculum on

TABLE 12-2

**Percentage of Public Schools Assigning Each Book in English Class,
Grades 7–12, 1988**

1. *Romeo and Juliet*	Shakespeare	90%
2. *Macbeth*	Shakespeare	81
3. *Huckleberry Finn*	Twain	78
4. *To Kill a Mockingbird*	Lee	74
5. *Julius Caesar*	Shakespeare	71
6. *The Pearl*	Steinbeck	64
7. *The Scarlet Letter*	Hawthorne	62
8. *Of Mice and Men*	Steinbeck	60
9. *Lord of the Flies*	Golding	56
9. *The Diary of a Young Girl*	Anne Frank	56
9. *Hamlet*	Shakespeare	56
12. *The Great Gatsby*	Fitzgerald	54
13. *Animal Farm*	Orwell	51
13. *Call of the Wild*	London	51
15. *A Separate Peace*	Knowles	48
16. *The Crucible*	Miller	47
16. *The Red Badge of Courage*	Crane	47
18. *Great Expectations*	Dickens	44
18. *Our Town*	Wilder	44
20. *A Tale of Two Cities*	Dickens	41

SOURCE: A. Applebee (1989), A study of book-length works taught in high school English. Report Series 1.2 (Albany: Center for the Learning and Teaching of Literature, State University of New York).

Western texts and traditions; they are the ones who want to convey a narrow set of values and knowledge to schoolchildren. Even the notion of conservation (the ideal of conservatives) is seen as dangerous because it begs the question of what should be conserved, which always benefits those in power.

One of the ways that critical theorists seek to address the so-called cultural hegemony in the schools is to question and analyze the rationalizations used by educators to justify their various actions. Thus, for example, when a school labels students as "emotionally disturbed" or "learning disabled" or even "gifted," the critical theorist would remind us that such labels are artificial constructs, vulnerable to all kinds of problems and prejudices. Similarly, critical theorists observe that special education, although legitimated by research findings, not only is ineffective at serving special needs students but actually leads to the further deterioration of their academic competence and life skills. The problem is that, once assigned the label, the student tends to become the label, irrespective of whether it really applies. Such labels might result in access to various special instructional services but it also sends a psychological message to students about their own skills and about the school's expectations for their education.

In this way, the critical theorists treat scientific or rational explanations of social phenomena in the schools with considerable skepticism. Methods of scientific inquiry, they argue, are weapons of control that employ a technical and often dazzling numerical approach to hide the social realities of oppression and inequity. It is not the neutral, nonpolitical method that its advocates claim it to be. Rather it is a highly ideological method that imposes rational solutions on social problems, that disguises socially repressive conditions with complex explanations and that rejects imaginative and more subjective judgments as essentially unworkable. These alleged effects play into the radical theorists' belief that science itself is responsible for creating an amenable social arrangement for dominant economic groups. The role of standardized examinations in the schools is a prime example. Good performances on standardized exams often unlock the doors to scholarships, to admission to the better colleges and universities, and to various certifications. Proponents of these exams point to their statistical reliability and validity to remind everyone of their supposed fairness and to support their claim of a level playing field. But the exams themselves, and the system in which they operate, critics charge, restrict the access to knowledge of certain children and perpetuate bias against certain groups.

The critical theorists also view the schools as places that indoctrinate youths into political compliance and into acceptance of their place in the socioeconomic order. For example, children learn that their worth can be literally measured through testing devices and that their success is dependent on the merit of their work. Therefore, those who fail in school don't recognize the source or nature of their oppression and so can only blame themselves. Interestingly, teachers become the unwitting accomplices in the process of alienating and oppressing these students.

Some critical theorists also believe that the repressive force of the school is exercised in the economic arena. In fact, much has been written about the alleged correspondence between the needs of capitalism and the methods of public schooling. The school, according to this argument, exists to serve capitalism. Specifically, it acts to stratify the labor force, creating low-level and high-level workers, and to socialize youths to accept a class-based economic system as inevitable. The schools not only produce the needed variance of skills for the workforce, including nonskilled workers, but also

© Courtesy of the Archives/Paulo Freire Institute

Paulo Freire.

inculcate habits and personality traits to accompany such skills, such as docility for the low-level worker and self-direction for the high-level worker. The school, in this sense, does not create inequities but rather reproduces them. As noted by Bowles and Gintis (1976), the heart of this reproduction is found in the social encounters of the school, encounters that "correspond closely to the social relations of dominance, subordination, and motivation in the economic sphere" (p. 265). According to Bowles and Gintis, the schools teach youths their place in the capitalistic working order.

One of the more interesting and popular commentators on how schools might provide handicapping experiences to certain students is the Brazilian scholar Paulo Freire. As a social activist with Marxist leanings, Freire worked to help historically oppressed Latin Americans to rise up against the system that presumably had been holding them down. In doing so, Freire (1982) formulated a theory about how schools tend to focus their instructional methods on the transmission of facts and information that, at least in Freire's eyes, prevent young children from learning how to think and to live intelligently. Freire has argued that many schools abide by what he calls "banking education," which reflects an instructional preoccupation with conveying facts and information to students in ways that stunt their thinking capacity. A banking education involves memorizing information and uncritically receiving other people's knowledge and words. In this learning environment, the teacher has dominance over students, with the teacher as "teller" and the students as "receivers." Banking education thus keeps students passive and quiescent. It does not encourage dialogue or extensive use of language in the act of learning. It also blunts the opportunities for students to develop their own consciousness and to form the skills and dispositions needed to become socially responsible and critically minded citizens. Banking education, as Freire (1982) described it, is "an act of depositing, in which the students are depositors and the teacher the depositor. Instead of communicating, the teacher issues communiqués and makes deposits which the students patiently receive, memorize and repeat" (p. 58).

Although Freire was addressing how children are socialized in oppressive Latin American societies, his idea can also be applied in the American educational context, especially with regard to minority and economically disadvantaged children. One study found that the philosophical underpinnings for more conservative banking education agendas in the classroom were more likely to be supported by principals working in minority school settings as opposed to predominantly white settings (Hlebowitsh, 1993). Some researchers have openly stated that instruction of disadvantaged youths needs to be less supportive of dialogue, less pupil-initiated, and more concerned with low-level questions (Medley, 1979; Rosenshine, 1979). Low-track curriculum experiences, which affect disproportionately high numbers of minority children, can themselves be construed as a form of banking education.

THE LANGUAGE OF SCHOOLING

The function of language in the classroom seems, on the surface, to be a simple matter. Teachers usually teach verbally, and students typically respond verbally or in writing. The choice of language in the classroom seems simple as well. Because English is the most commonly spoken language in the United States, it is usually considered wise to conduct classes in that language. But language also has a broader function that cannot be overlooked. Cazden (1988) has studied the use of language in the classroom and has identified three very distinct features of classroom language. The first feature is obvious: Language in the classroom does what we all expect it to do—it communicates messages. The second feature of language in the classroom, however, speaks to the effects of these manifest messages and the ways in which they establish and maintain social relationships. The third feature is associated with the process by which individuals establish their self-identity. Cazden contends that this last feature of language is the least recognizable but perhaps the most important. We are all defined in large measure by the specific language we use. Our language use clearly contributes to who we are, to how others see us, and, inevitably, to how we see ourselves.

If we acknowledge that language in the classroom has at least three basic purposes, then we also have to admit that what we say, how we say it, what others say, and how we react to it all relate prominently not only to the function of communication but also to the construction of social relations and self-identities. Language use in this sense is more than merely communicating; language always communicates something that will influence the social environment.

How, then, do we respond to the clear need to teach youths standard English in the school? If students use a different style of English (for instance, ebonics), how should teachers respond? If teachers "correct" it, are they doing damage to the student's self-identity and to the social relationship with the student? If they privilege it, are they contributing to the marginalization of the youth's language skills in a society in which advancement typically depends on the use of standard English? The question should not necessarily be framed in either/or terms—it is not a question of teaching either standard English or nonstandard English, or of teaching either English or a foreign language. Rather, the question should be how we can teach children not only standard English but also all the other forms of language beneficial to the life experiences of youths.

Bilingual Education

Bilingual education is perhaps the most misunderstood feature of modern schooling. Many citizens believe that tax dollars are being spent to teach American children a foreign language instead of English. Such sentiments have been voiced as well by various politicians, and especially conservatives, who often speak of the dangers of bilingualism, of the linguistic schisms that it is likely to create in the nation, of the centrality of English to economic opportunity in our society, and of the historic decision to teach immigrant children in English.

The Legal and Political History of Bilingual Education. Obviously, such views are driven by an assimilationist position that embraces monolingual English instruction in public education. The American schools, the argument goes, historically have ignored the native languages of immigrant children in the interests of furthering the integration of such children into the society. Although some schools made accommodations toward dual language instruction, especially in the late nineteenth century among German immigrants in the Midwest, the twentieth-century assimilationist impulses eventually triumphed. The commitment to assimilation caused some states to actually draft laws prohibiting the teaching of a foreign language in private and public schools alike, laws that were eventually struck down as unconstitutional (Ravitch, 1985). Many point to the vast assimilation project of twentieth-century America and argue that today's children should be treated no differently.

Given the linguistic diversity of the nation, the debate between advocates of English immersion and advocates of dual language instruction is certain to be with us for some time; Feature 12-5 lists some resources to consult to further pursue the debate. English obviously is the national language, but many people in America do not speak it or do not speak it very well. In fact, close to 32 million Americans, or 14 percent of the population, speak a language other than English in their homes. In the 1993–94 academic year, 46 percent of all public schools had programs for limited-English-proficient (LEP) students (National Center for Education Statistics, 1997). More than 325 languages are spoken in the homes of America; in 1995, New York City alone witnessed the arrival of children from over 200 different nations (Crawford, 1997).

But the ever-increasing linguistic variety in the nation has not necessarily translated into a national call for dual language instruction; in fact, some evidence indicates quite the opposite. According to national polling data, most Americans support the immersion approach to language education in the school, believing that non-English-speaking children should learn mostly in English. As shown in Table 12-3, this includes Hispanic parents and foreign-born parents, who are the strongest supporters of English-only instruction. Such polls, however, have been criticized for placing bilingual instruction in opposition to immersion, conveying to parents the false impression that bilingual instruction will not cultivate proficiency in English (Crawford, 1997). Krashen (1999) has found strong support among parents for views inherent in bilingual instruction, such as "developing literacy in the first language facilitates literacy development in English."

Federal legislation mandating bilingual education in America was passed in 1968. Federal funds for bilingual education were first authorized through Title VII of the Elementary and Secondary School Act of 1968, which is also known as the Bilingual Education Act. The bilingual programs emerging from this legislation were compensatory in nature, serving poor students born to families in which English was not the dominant language. The goal

12-5 DEBATING THE ISSUES
Immersion Versus Dual Language Instruction

What are your views on the bilingual education debate? Here are some resources to consider as you further refine your position.

Websites

- English First, Internet Source for Information on Official English: www.englishfirst.org

- English as a Second Language: www.rong-chang.com

- ERIC Clearinghouse on Language and Linguistics: www.cal.org/ericcll

- National Association of Bilingual Education: www.nabe.org

- The English Speakers Union of the United States: www.english-speaking.org

Commentary

- King, Robert. (1997). Should English be the law? *Atlantic Monthly* (Apr.).

- Krashen, Stephen. (1997). Why bilingual education? (27 Apr.). (Posted on www.englishfirst.org).

- Pedalino-Porter, Rosalie. (1998). The case against bilingual education. *Atlantic Monthly* (May).

Research Reports

- Crawford, James. (1997). *Best available evidence: Research foundations of the Bilingual Education Act* (Washington, DC: National Clearinghouse for Bilingual Education).

- Cazden, Courtney. (1992). *Language minority education in the United States* (Posted on the National Center for Research on Cultural Diversity and Second Language Learning website: www.ncbe.gwu.edu).

was to assist low-income children who were believed to be at an instructional disadvantage due to their limited English. The program was intended not to further develop or strengthen the native cultural and linguistic abilities of these students, but to compensate for them. Another rationale for bilingual education was that non-English-speaking children were suffering

TABLE 12-3
Percentage Identifying What the Public School Should Do for Students Who Are New Immigrants

	Parents Overall	African American Parents	Hispanic Parents	Foreign-Born Parents
Teach them English as quickly as possible, *even* if this means they fall behind in other subjects	67%	68%	66%	75%
or				
Teach them other subjects in their native language, *even* if it takes them longer to learn English	27	27	30	21

SOURCE: © Data copyrighted by Source. © Graphics copyrighted by Public Agenda 2000. No reproduction/distribution without permission.

from low self-esteem brought about by the absence of their native language in the classroom.

The scope of Title VII has expanded considerably since 1968. The government now funds a variety of bilingual education programs, including programs committed to developing both English and the native language, and sponsors bilingual research and bilingual teacher training (Aleman, 1993). In 1969, the federal government funneled $7.5 million through Title VII; in 1996, the annual federal commitment for Title VII was around $120 million (Crawford, 1997).

Despite the presence of Title VII funds, the legal responsibility of school districts to offer bilingual programs was not formally resolved until 1974, in the Supreme Court ruling in *Lau v. Nichols*. This case originated in 1970 as a class action suit brought by Chinese American public school students against the San Francisco Unified School District. The essential complaint was that the school district had failed to provide bilingual education to these pupils and that such a neglect represented a violation of their right to an equal educational opportunity. How could these students have an equal opportunity to learn, asserted the complainants, when the language used in the school was completely foreign to them? The school district openly admitted that only half of its close to 3,000 limited-English-proficient (LEP) students were receiving second-language assistance. But it asserted that the right to an equal educational opportunity was not violated because all the students were receiving the same curriculum, although some in a language foreign to them. All students, the district argued, come to school with advantages and disadvantages, including linguistic ones, and the school cannot be legally bound to provide special programs to respond to all such differences.

The Supreme Court disagreed with this line of reasoning, holding that the Chinese American students who were without bilingual assistance were effectively shut off from meaningful education due to their lack of English-speaking skills. Basing part of its decision on the Civil Rights Act of 1964, which bars discrimination because of race, color, or national origin in any program sponsored by the federal government, the Supreme Court stated that merely providing students with the same facilities, textbooks, teachers, and curriculum does not constitute equality of treatment. The lesson of the ruling was clear: It makes little sense to attempt to teach non-English-speaking students to read and write in a language that they do not yet speak. In elementary education, the clear implication was that instruction in the child's first or native language for the initial years of his or her education lays a foundation for learning to read and write in a second language. This would become the rationale for a national movement in support of bilingual education. Thus, the schools had to find some educationally sound way to deal with the English language deficits of their students, including, depending on the district's desires, programs with a heavy reliance on "sheltered English" or programs more in the direction of dual language instruction (Ravitch, 1985).

Types of Bilingual Education. Bilingual instruction for LEP students can take several forms (Malakoff and Hakuta, 1990). The most popular is known as transitional bilingual education, in which students are subjected to dual language instruction and grade-appropriate materials prior to being mainstreamed in English-speaking classrooms. The intent is to begin with native-language instruction in almost all the core subject areas and to slowly add English instruction until full mainstreaming into the regular classroom has been achieved. In America, the bilingual classroom is most often populated by Spanish-speaking children, whose numbers in some school populations allow entire classrooms to be designed with bilingual materials and activities.

Contrary to popular opinion, the transitional model of bilingual education aims at assimilation; the goal is to use the student's native language to teach English and to eventually make English the dominant language. In other words, transitional bilingual education uses bilingual means to achieve a monolingual result. Although some bilingual programs also maintain or advance the native language, transitional bilingual education offers

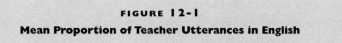

FIGURE 12-1
Mean Proportion of Teacher Utterances in English

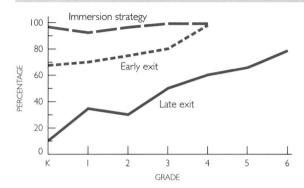

SOURCE: Cazden, C. (1992), Language minority education in the United States: Implications of the Ramirez Report (www.ncbe.gwu.edu).

what its title implies—a bilingual educational process designed to provide a transition from first-language usage to English usage. Usually, transitional programs are divided into two types: (1) early exit transitions and (2) late exit transitions. The early exit programs limit the exposure to bilingual instruction to about two years, while the late exit programs allow bilingual instruction to continue up until sixth grade (Baker, 1993).

Another popular instructional model used with LEP students is the English-as-a-second-language (ESL) approach. ESL is used mostly in settings in which LEP students come from a wide range of linguistic backgrounds. Under such conditions, there would not be enough students who spoke one particular language to justify a transitional bilingual program. With the ESL approach, LEP students are pulled out of their mainstream settings for special instruction in English for part of the school day. This "sheltered English" instruction carefully manages the vocabulary and language used. But these ESL students will actually spend a greater part of the day with their English-speaking peers in a mainstream setting. Thus, ESL typically operates in an English-only context that offers limited supplemental experiences in sheltered English and, in some cases, even sheltered math and sheltered science. Although it is officially a minority language program, ESL is clearly an approach favored by those who support English immersion. In fact, ESL is sometimes known as "structured immersion." Figure 12-1 illustrates the differences in the amount of English used in a structured immersion program, such as ESL, and in early exit and late exit bilingual education programs. The higher frequency of teacher utterances in

English found in early exit versus late exit programs is probably the result of the pressure the teachers in early exit programs might feel to move the student along more quickly in English.

We should remember that the aim of both transitional bilingual education and ESL education is to take students who are, in most cases, monolingual in a foreign language and achieve proficiency in English. In this sense, both transitional bilingual and ESL programs take a "subtractive" approach to education. That is, the native language serves as a bridge to English proficiency, and there is no concern with maintaining the native language once the student becomes an English speaker.

The Department of Education examined each of the three "subtractive" approaches and found that there were essentially no differences in the measured performances of the students on tests of English language proficiency, reading, and mathematics (Ramirez, Yuen, and Ramsey, 1991). One possible interpretation is that time spent using the native language in the classroom is wasted effort. But the authors of the report were cautious about making such a generalization, noting that school districts using late exit programs, which make extensive use of the native language, promote the higher involvement of parents. The report also stressed the fact that the distribution of teacher qualifications across the three approaches probably affected the findings. The Department of Education chose to interpret the report as an affirmation of its policy of encouraging a variety of minority language education programs. The fact that there were no differences among the programs suggested that each could be viewed as equally effective and that school districts should decide how to configure their own minority language programs.

Schools can, in fact, combine bilingual and ESL resources (Krashen, 1999). For instance a late exit program might teach all core subjects to LEP students in their first language, with a sheltered English approach as a supplemental experience and with art, music, and physical education mainstreamed. After or year or so, math and science would move into a sheltered ESL setting, and then, a year later, into a mainstreamed setting. At the same time, everything else also moves either into sheltered ESL approach or the mainstreamed classroom. Eventually full mainstreaming is achieved. Several have argued that once full mainstreaming is reached, the bilingual program should then turn its attention toward the further development of the student's first language or heritage language.

In 1998, voters in the state of California overwhelmingly passed a law known as Proposition 227 which mandated that all LEP students be instructed in a "sheltered language" ESL-style program. This has meant the

TABLE 12-4
Languages of Instruction in Two-Way Bilingual Immersion Programs, 1995–99

LANGUAGE OF INSTRUCTION	NUMBER OF SCHOOLS
Spanish/English	240
Chinese/English	6
French/English	4
Korean/English	4
Japanese/English	2
Navajo/English	2
Arabic/English	1
Portuguese/English	1
Russian/English	1
	Total: 261

SOURCE: Center for Applied Linguistics (1999), (www.cal.org). Reprinted with permission.

demise of most transitional bilingual education programs in California. Proposition 227 also mandated that LEP students should be enrolled in a sheltered English program, in most cases, for no more than a year. The law, however, allowed for some waivers. Parents can ask for a waiver if their children are 10 years old or older and if they believe that they will learn English more in an alternative program, or if their children, at any age, have special needs that could be better served in an alternative program. Charter schools (a concept explained in Chapter 14) are exempt from the law. With close to 2 million LEP students, California's decision to embrace a program dedicated to structured immersion is notable. Some legal advocates see the California law as a violation of the Supreme Court decision of *Lau v. Nichols,* but because the law mandates sheltered English, it has thus far been upheld by a circuit court as constitutional.

Other, less popular methods of bilingual education take an "additive" approach by teaching students proficiency in two languages. Such programs teach everything in two languages and are appropriate for youths who speak the minority and youths who speak the majority language. One additive approach, known as "two-way" bilingual education, teaches both the majority and minority languages to children from both linguistic groups.

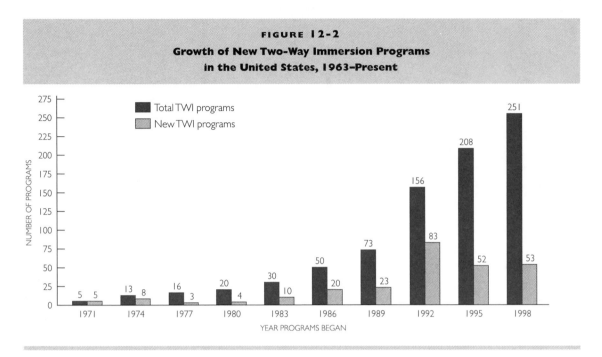

FIGURE 12-2
**Growth of New Two-Way Immersion Programs
in the United States, 1963–Present**

SOURCE: Center for Applied Linguistics (1999), (www.cal.org). Reprinted with permission.

For instance, a two-way program in Spanish and English might teach in each language on alternate days or in alternate instructional periods to all of the children in the school. Here, the objective is for all the students to add a language to their communicative repertoire. Of course, such a program requires fluent bilingual teachers. In states like Texas, California, Florida, and New York, where Spanish is spoken widely in many communities and where one can encounter the language in various contexts, including in the popular culture, two-way bilingual education makes quite a bit of sense. As shown in Figure 12-2 and Table 12-4, two-way bilingual education has grown in popularity over the years and is typically done in a Spanish/English setting.

Continued Resistance to Bilingual Education. If the reasoning behind bilingual education seems sound, why does there continue to be so much resistance to it? Part of the problem turns on an argument that returns us to our melting pot versus salad bowl metaphors. The assimilationist impulses

Here the media are presented with Proposition 227, a proposal to end bilingual education in California. Survey data indicate that Hispanic and foreign-born parents are strong supporters of English-only instruction.

of the melting pot advocates call for an immersion approach to teach youths mostly, if not exclusively, in English. Historically, this has been done with a wide range of immigrant populations, for whom the loss of the mother tongue has been the norm. Salad bowl advocates, by contrast, claim that initial instruction in a native language not only will contribute to the eventual acquisition of English but also will give the student skills in another language and another social or cultural context.

Although the research on the effects of bilingual education is conflicting, there is an overall belief, supported by the federal government and the courts, that children should be initially instructed in their native languages as a way to assist their acquisition of English. Advocates of bilingual education are convinced that it carries social and cognitive benefits for students and for society, especially in relation to international economic markets, in which multilingual competence is important. Much of the debate over the effects of bilingual education is complicated by the need to control for income, parent education, and immigration factors, and by the penchant to limit assessments of the effects of bilingual education to achievement in the

12-6 WEB POINTS

Center for Research on Education, Diversity, and Excellence (CREDE)

The CREDE website contains a vast array of information on multicultural and multilingual issues. This includes access to various papers, research documents, and reports on educational practices (www.crede.ucsc.edu).

English language, ignoring important data on self-esteem, moral development, social adjustment, and employability. Feature 12-6 gives more information about bilingual education programs.

SUMMARY

Public schooling in America has always had to find some way to build a common nation out of people from multiple ethnic, religious, linguistic, and racial backgrounds. Establishing a common culture, with a common language, knowledge base, and common value system, has not been easy for the American educational system. The assimilationist movement of the twentieth century embraced a melting pot approach whereby all Americans were melded from many forms into a uniform one. In recent decades, however, increasing attention has been directed at finding a way to better balance a common culture with the culture and ethnic heritage of students. The design of multicultural education approaches has resulted in particularistic forms of multicultural thinking, which lean in the direction of ethnocentrism, and in multiple perspective forms, which lean in the direction of fully integrated diversity.

A similar situation has prevailed in bilingual education. The Supreme Court has ruled that LEP students must be given some language assistance, but the extent of this support is widely debated. The lines are still drawn between advocates of structured immersion, also known as sheltered English, and advocates of extended dual language education.

QUESTIONS AND ACTIVITIES

1. What are the curricular consequences of a "melting pot" outlook on common learning?

2. How might you deal with the need to present a common experience in a diverse classroom environment?

3. How is it that assimilating and diversifying processes exist in a kind of partnership in the public schools?

4. According to a Public Agenda poll (see www.publicagenda.org), when parents were asked to prioritize between raising academic standards/academic achievement and achieving more diversity and integration in the school, they overwhelmingly (both black and white parents) chose academics. Is this an unexpected finding? Do you see this as an important finding?

5. Do you believe that Afro-centric or Latino-centered schools serve the causes of multicultural education?

6. Data compiled by the National Center for Education Statistics (1996) show that high school seniors have fundamentally different views from their parents on various issues of social importance. Although there is widespread consensus between parents and their children on the value of education, only 67 percent of twelfth graders agreed with their parents on racial issues, and 71 percent on roles for women. How might you begin to interpret these data?

7. In 1993, the National Center for Education Statistics surveyed parents on the topic of respect in the school environment. Parents were asked whether they strongly agreed, agreed, disagreed, or strongly disagreed with the following statement: "Most students and teachers at school respect each other." Eighty-four percent of all parents were either strongly in agreement or in agreement with the statement. Eighty-nine percent of parents of white children in mostly white schools answered the same way, as did 81 percent of parents of whites in mixed schools, 83 percent of parents of blacks in mixed schools and 88 percent of parents of blacks in nonwhite schools. What conclusions might you draw from these numbers?

8. Explain how a multiple perspective approach to multicultural education might be used in a high school history class or in an elementary school math class.

9. In *Losing Our Language,* Stotsky (1999) analyzed the "ethnic" content of popular basal reading books used in elementary schools and found that as much as 100 percent of the total foreign content in the books was non-European. What are the implications of her findings?

10. An African American scholar recently wrote that "naturally, the person of African descent should be centered in his or her historical experiences as an African" (Asante, 2000, p. 40). Do you agree with this assertion?

11. McLaren (2000) has referred to the effort to merge diversity with assimilationist goals as "conservative multiculturalism." Naming Schlesinger and Ravitch as conservative multiculturalists, McLaren states that such a position "uses the term diversity to cover up the ideology of assimilation. . . . In this view, ethnic groups are reduced to 'add-ons' to the dominant culture. Before you can be added on to the dominant U.S. culture, you must first adopt a consensual view of culture and learn to accept the essentially Euro-American patriarchal norms of the 'host' country" (p. 217). How would you respond to McLaren's analysis?

12. How can a "banking education" result in the oppression of youths?

13. What are the essential assumptions of critical theory?

14. Why might a critical theorist object to the dominance of Shakespearean readings in a high school English class?

15. What do you think of the view supported by critical theorists that equates schooling with preparation for a preordained place in the socioeconomic status quo?

16. In your view, how should schools handle the language education of LEP and ESL children?

17. What is the difference between an additive and a subtractive approach to bilingual education?

18. What are the potential advantages and disadvantages of a two-way bilingual program?

19. Explain the issues involved in the *Lau. v. Nichols* case.

20. Investigate the decision of California voters to pass Proposition 227, which, in effect, eliminated bilingual education in the state.

REFERENCES

Addams, J. (1908). Immigrants and their children. In E. C. Lagemann (ed.), *Jane Addams on education*. (New York: Teachers College Press, 1985).

Aleman, S. R. (1993). *Bilingual Education Act: Background and reauthorization issues*. (Washington, DC: Congressional Research Service).

Apple, M. (1990). *Ideology and curriculum*. (London: Routledge & Kegan Paul).

Asante, M. K. (2000). The Afrocentric idea in education. In E. Duarte and S. Smith (eds.), *Foundational perspectives in multicultural education*. (New York: Longman).

Ascher, M. (1991). *Ethnomathematics: A multicultural view of mathematical ideas*. (Pacific Grove, CA: Brooks/Cole).

Baker, C. (1993). *Foundations of bilingual education and bilingualism*. (Philadelphia: Multilingual Matters).

Banks, J. (1988). Approaches to multicultural curriculum reform. *Multicultural Leader,* 1(2):1–3.

Bowles, S., and Gintis, H. (1976). *Schooling in capitalist America*. (New York: Basic Books).

Cazden, C. (1988). *Classroom discourse*. (Portsmouth, NH: Heinemann).

Census Bureau. (1997). *Current population reports: The foreign-born population in the United States*. (Washington, DC: U.S. Department of Commerce).

Cornbleth, C., and Waugh, D. (1995). *The great speckled bird*. (New York: St. Martin's Press).

Crawford, J. (1997). *Best evidence: Research foundations of the Bilingual Education Act*. (Washington, DC: National Clearinghouse for Bilingual Education).

Dewey, J. (1916). *Democracy and education*. (New York: Free Press).

Freire, P. (1982). *The pedagogy of the oppressed*. (New York: Continuum).

Geortz, C. (1973). *The interpretation of cultures*. (New York: Basic Books).

Gibson, R. (1986). *Critical theory and education*. (London: Hodder & Stoughton).

Giroux, H. (1983). *Theory and resistance: A pedagogy for the opposition*. (New York: Bergin Garvey).

Gutmann, A. (2000). Challenges of multiculturalism in democratic education. In E. Duarte and S. Smith (eds.), *Foundational perspectives in multicultural education*. (New York: Longman).

Hlebowitsh, P. S. (1993). Philosophical orientations on the school curriculum. *NASSP Bulletin,* 77(557): 92–104.

Howe, H. (1993). *Thinking about our kids.* (New York: Free Press).

Krashen, S. (1999). *Bilingual education: Arguments for and (bogus) arguments against.* (www.ourworld.compuserve.com).

Malakoff, M., and Hakuta, K. (1990). History of language minority education in the United States. In A. Padilla, H. H. Fairchild, and C. M. Valadez (eds.), *Bilingual education.* (Newbury Park, CA: Sage).

McLaren, P. (2000). White terror and oppositional agency: Toward a critical multiculturalism. In E. Duarte and S. Smith (eds.), *Foundational perspectives in multicultural education.* (New York: Longman).

McLaren, P. (1994). *Life in schools.* (New York: Longman).

Medley, D. (1979). The effectiveness of teachers. In P. L. Peterson and H. J. Walberg (eds.), *Research on teaching.* (Berkeley, CA: McCutchan).

National Center for Education Statistics. (1999). *NAEP civics: Report card for the nation.* (Washington, DC: U.S. Department of Education).

National Center for Education Statistics. (1997). *Condition of education.* (Washington, DC: U.S. Department of Education).

National Center for Education Statistics. (1996). *Youth indicators.* (Washington, DC: U.S. Department of Education).

National Center for Education Statistics. (1993). *Parent and student perceptions of the learning environment in school.* (Washington, DC: U.S. Department of Education).

Patrick, J. (2000). *Multicultural education and the civic mission of schools.* In W. G. Wraga and P. S. Hlebowitsh (eds.), *Research review for school leaders.* (Mahwah, NJ: Lawrence Erlbaum).

Public Agenda. (1998). *A lot to be thankful for: What parents want children to learn about America.* (New York: Public Agenda).

Ramirez, J. D., Yuen, S. D., and Ramsey, D. R. (1991). *Longitudinal study of structured immersion strategy, early exit and late exit transitional bilingual education programs for language minority children.* (San Mateo, CA: Aguirre International).

Ravitch, D. (1990). Multiculturalism: E pluribus plures. In K. Ryan and J. M. Cooper (eds.), *Kaleidoscope: Readings in education.* (Boston: Houghton-Mifflin).

Ravitch, D. (1985). Politicalization and the schools: The case of bilingual education. In J. W. Noll (ed.), *Taking sides.* (Guilford, CT: Dushkin).

Ravitch, D., and Finn, C. E. (1987). *What do our 17-year-olds know? A report on the first national assessment of history and literature.* (New York: Harper & Row).

Rosenshine, B. (1979). Content, time and direct instruction. In P. L. Peterson and H. J. Walberg, (eds.), *Research on teaching.* (Berkeley, CA: McCutchan).

Schlesinger, A. (1991). *The disuniting of America.* (New York: Norton).

Schmidt, P. (1992). New survey discerns deep divisions among U.S. youths on race relations. *Education Week* (25 March).

Schnaiberg, L. (1997). Oakland Board revises "ebonics" resolution. *Education Week* (22 Jan.).

Stotsky, S. (1999). *Losing our language: How multicultural classroom instruction is undermining our children's ability to read, write and reason.* (New York: Free Press).

Zangwill, I. (1909). *The melting pot.* (New York: Macmillan).

CHAPTER 13

School Reform and the Sociopolitical Context Since the 1950s

Getting "Back to Basics" in the 1950s
THE COLD WAR AND THE SPACE RACE
THE SUBJECT-CENTERED FOCUS ON MATH AND SCIENCE

Humanizing the Schools in the 1960s
A NEW RADICAL/ROMANTIC RHETORIC
OPEN EDUCATION

Getting "Back to Basics"—Again—in the 1970s

Promoting Academic Excellence in the 1980s

Extending Academic Excellence into the 1990s
NATIONAL STANDARDS AND SCHOOL CHOICE OPTIONS
CRITICISMS OF NATIONAL STANDARDS

Summary

Questions and Activities

References

O VER THE PAST FIVE DECADES or so, American schools have been beset by changes that some scholars have characterized as swings on a reform pendulum (Goodlad, 1966; Tanner, 1986). Not surprisingly, each era in American education has been marked by a curriculum emphasis reflecting the sociopolitical temper of the time. School reform ideas believed to be most vital during the height of the Cold War in the 1950s, for instance, were fundamentally different from, if not at odds with, school reform ideas believed to be most vital in succeeding periods, especially during the turbulent 1960s.

When educational reform is moved by prevailing sociopolitical conditions, the schools run the risk of embracing a reform logic tied to narrow nationalistic causes as opposed to broad professional ones. Such a situation sets the conditions for reactionary change. Thus, when the dominant sociopolitical ideology of a given era runs its course and the changes that it wrought lose their appeal, the schools are vulnerable to new sociopolitical imperatives. In many cases, one extreme is undone by a counterextreme that itself is undone, in time, by yet another counterextreme. This principle, in fact, is reflected in the pattern of American curriculum reform since the mid-twentieth century.

In practical terms, these school reforms led to practical changes in how teachers dealt with their students in the classroom. All of the major reforms discussed in this chapter received quite a bit of support from external agencies—the government or private foundations—and were trumpeted in the media. And the reforms generally were practical movements that had a constituency in the schools and staunch advocates in the professional literature. They are described here by decade, but the movements were fluid and often overlapped between the decades.

GETTING "BACK TO BASICS" IN THE 1950s

In the early 1950s, curriculum reform was shaped by a "back to basics" retrenchment inspired mainly by conservative forces that wielded power during the early stages of the Cold War. There were many influential thinkers at the time, but Arthur Bestor (1953, 1956) and Hyman Rickover (1959) were especially instrumental in getting the schools to accept this reductionist plan. Bestor was a professor of history who lobbied for the restoration of a strict academic curriculum in the public schools; Rickover was an admiral in the U.S. Navy who wrote extensively about the shortcomings of American education relative to academic achievement in other advanced countries. Each could be characterized as an essentialist, a philosophical position explained in Chapter 3.

The Cold War and the Space Race

Buoyed by a nationalistic fervor to compete with the former Soviet Union to achieve global domination, Bestor and Rickover submitted what they viewed as a no-nonsense reform directive for the schools. The approach they advocated was practical and straightforward: (1) Center the curriculum on disciplined intellectual training; (2) reduce the course work in the high school to the core academic disciplines; (3) relegate vocational studies, art, music, and physical education to secondary status; and (4) focus the early years of schooling on the inculcation of basic skills. In many ways, this approach embraced the humanist tradition of the early twentieth century.

Bestor and Rickover embodied a strong conservative reaction to the progressivism of the 1940s. In that decade, the public schools had embraced a rather wide range of initiatives reflecting a new enthusiasm for curriculum experimentation and a new regard for real-life concerns in teaching and learning. Dismayed by these trends, Bestor and Rickover believed that the time had come for the schools to recover their subject-centered core, to fulfill their overtly academic function and to cease their attempts to build learning experiences around children's needs and interests. They were convinced that the schools were engaging in anti-intellectual programs that would eventually destroy America. It was the soft pedagogy of this earlier era, they claimed, that had already eroded America's status as a world power. Their solution was to restore rigorous intellectual training in the schools. In Rickover's (1959) words, "The educational process must be one of collecting factual knowledge to the limit of the [learner's] capacity. . . . Nothing can really make it fun" (p. 61). This was clearly a movement to revitalize the role of disciplinary knowledge in the curriculum. Feature 13-1 expands on Rickover's views in this area.

This high regard for basic academic skills and strict academic training continued to hold sway into the early 1960s. Dismayed by the Soviets' successful launching of the first space satellite, *Sputnik I,* in 1957, U.S educators inaugurated a new discipline-centered curriculum, focusing on the national security–related areas of mathematics and science. A general "get tough" attitude pervaded the classroom. The key reforms included the strengthening of graduation and curriculum standards, the provision of special services for gifted and talented students, and the elevation of subject-centered thinking.

13-1 **THE HISTORICAL CONTEXT**

The Cold War Message of Admiral Hyman Rickover

With the escalating tensions of the Cold War, educational priorities began to shift toward maintenance of an inviolate national defense. Not surprisingly, an acclaimed defense expert emerged as one of the new movers and shapers of education. Known to many as the "father of the nuclear submarine," Admiral Hyman Rickover became a driving force in imposing a narrow nationalistic framework on public schooling. Appalled by what he saw as both qualitative and quantitative deficiencies in science and engineering in the United States, Rickover sought to convince the public that the European and Soviet educational systems were superior to the system in America—so much so that the future of the nation was imperiled. This theme resurfaced in the 1983 *A Nation at Risk* report produced by the National Commission on Excellence in Education. In fact, in June 1983, just three months after the release of *A Nation at Risk,* the elderly Rickover offered a commentary in the *Washington Post,* stating, "We are told that ours is, overall, an inferior system of public education which produces mediocre high school students. But surely this is not news. I, for one, 'told you so' for more than 25 years—even before *Sputnik*" (p. B8).

© Bettmann/Corbis

Admiral Hyman Rickover.

The Subject-Centered Focus on Math and Science

Clearly, the subject- or discipline-centered changes wrought in the schools in the post-*Sputnik* era period were partly shaped by the demands of Bestor and Rickover in the early 1950s. Congress authorized massive funds for the National Science Foundation (NSF), encouraging its involvement in the development of several national curriculum programs in the areas of science and math. Responding to the Soviet achievements in space, the American schools had a new national mandate to improve mathematics and science education, and to focus on the education of the nation's most gifted children. This gave the NSF an entree into educational reform. The NSF, for instance, not only sponsored the development of curricula in high school biology, chemistry, physics, and math but also financed a nationwide network of teacher training institutes to immerse teachers in the methodology of these new curricula.

The NSF-sponsored programs and the broader effort to develop a subject-centered curriculum took their conceptual lead from psychologist Jerome Bruner's 1960 book *The Process of Education,* a report partly funded by the NSF (Tanner and Tanner, 1980). Bruner espoused a new manifesto for curriculum reform known as the "structure of a discipline" doctrine. To Bruner (1960), the term "structure" was representative of all the fundamental ideas and generalizations comprised in the subject matter. "To learn structure," he contended, "is to learn how things are related" (p. 7). But the "structure" to which Bruner referred was discipline-specific; it was all about finding the structure within disciplinary lines rather than across them. Bruner also promoted something even more provocative: that each discipline comprised a concentration of ideas that could be taught in some intellectually honest way to members of any age group. In the words of Bruner (1960), "Intellectual activity is anywhere the same, whether at the frontier of knowledge or in a third-grade classroom" (p. 14).

This kind of thinking, coming from one of America's most distinguished psychologists, helped to give scientists and other scholar-specialists an increased role in shaping the curriculum. Educators now put a great premium on discipline-specific skills and reconstructed the nature of the learner in the image of the scholar-specialist. This meant that learners could be treated as miniature scholars. When teaching math, for instance, teachers were now justified in treating learners as miniature mathematicians. This approach tended to aggrandize the abstract and the technical, and to deemphasize learning tied to life experiences. This same logic applied to all of the disciplines.

Another development central to the curriculum initiatives of the post-*Sputnik* era was the passage of the National Defense Education Act of 1958. The purpose of the legislation was to "ensure trained manpower of sufficient quality and quantity to meet the national defense needs of the United States." In the first four years following its implementation, the NDEA authorized over $1 billion worth of aid to the schools, funneling it through ten different title grants. Title III, a financial assistance program for science, mathematics, and foreign language instruction, received the bulk of the appropriations. No funds were appropriated for education in the arts or the humanities, because these areas of the curriculum simply did not fit into the war-preparedness mode that characterized the NDEA's mission.

Another significant statement on educational reform was authored by James B. Conant, who had achieved national visibility as president of Harvard University and as U.S. ambassador to Germany. Conant was commissioned by the Carnegie Corporation to oversee a study of the American high school. The fruit of his labor was the 1960 book *The American High School Today,* which outlined several basic recommendations for the reform of the public school. Essentially, Conant supported the American comprehensive high school design. Although there were considerable pressures at the time to adopt the dual model of schooling used in Europe, in which academic students were separated from vocational students during preadolescence, Conant stood by the American model of education. Specifically, he argued that a unified school should provide all youths with a general academic education, individualized elective programs, accelerated academic training for the college-bound, and first-rate vocational education programs for the noncollege-bound. In this sense, Conant "saved" the American public school system from falling prey to the dual system used in Europe, a change that was being promoted vigorously by Rickover and debated in Congress (Tanner and Tanner, 1995).

But perhaps Conant's greatest contribution had to do with the manner in which he layered his thinking about the comprehensive high school with a concern for academics and the most academically inclined. His recommendations had a strong conservative element in that they supported traditional academic studies in the core high school curriculum. There was no talk about interdisciplinary insights or socio-civic traditions in the core, although Conant did promote a senior-level course in the problems of democracy. With regard to the academically inclined, Conant advocated more advanced placement courses and more widespread use of ability groups on a subject-by-subject basis. With English courses, for example, Conant recommended at least three types of classes: one for the most able, another for the middle tier, and another for the so-called slowest learners. Besides endorsing ability groups, Conant urged that aptitude tests be used more often, that students be ranked and academic honors lists be kept, and that special counseling be provided for the most academically skilled.

Clearly, the sociopolitical climate of the Cold War and the space race affected the nature of school reform. Specifically, they highlighted the need for the schools to be attentive to the education of the academically able, to stress the importance of reform in the defense-sensitive areas of math and science, and to maintain that the most empowering forms of learning be conducted in subject-centered contexts.

The nationalistic urge to use the schools to promote military and technological domination, however, eventually gave way to a new set of prior-

The 1960s ushered in a new sociopolitical focus on domestic issues. The threat to the nation no longer came from the outside, but from the inside in the form of civil strife, urban violence, and student protest.

ities, anchored in a new sociopolitical climate. Within a decade, the emphasis shifted away from the discipline-centered curricula of the Cold War era to the "humanizing" movement of the late 1960s that called attention to society's most pervasive problems—poverty, crime, civil rights, and drug abuse. These new conditions would call for new reforms in the schools.

HUMANIZING THE SCHOOLS IN THE 1960s

As the tensions associated with the Cold War began to abate, public attention focused on the domestic front. The threat to the nation was no longer seen as external, in the form of imperialist Soviet Union, but internal, in the form of civil strife, urban violence, and abject poverty. Among the items at the top of the agenda was the issue of racial separatism in the schools and lost educational opportunities for minority groups. The federal government launched a sweeping War on Poverty designed to break the back of poverty and end racial isolation in society. The government's main tool in this war was the public school. The emphasis in the schools was no longer on the academically talented, but on the educationally disadvantaged. The watchword was a new sensitivity to learners' needs and interests, and new child-centered, rather than subject-centered, approaches gained popularity.

A New Radical/Romantic Rhetoric

This period of school reform featured a number of unconventional views. Radical critics of education, whose proposals ranged from abolishing compulsory education to framing a more humanistic pedagogy, garnered an impressive readership in the popular press. Many of these thinkers held a romantic/naturalist view of the world (see Chapter 3), taking their lead from the work of Rousseau and espousing the need for the classroom and school to be more sensitive to the needs and interests of individual children. In 1970, the flames of this fire were further fanned with the publication of Charles Silberman's *Crisis in the Classroom,* which received extensive coverage in major newspapers and journals. Silberman portrayed the American schools as mindless, joyless, and oppressive; his solution was to make education more interesting, joyful, and humane. Feature 13-2 details the type of rhetoric used to make this point.

The appearance of a new radical/romantic confederacy in American education in the 1960s was clearly a sign of the times. The rather abstract, discipline-centered initiatives that had emerged during the Cold War left a bad taste on the American educational palate. A counterreform was now in order, one characterized by humanity, openness, social purpose, and individual relevance in the schools.

The major figures emerging from the radical left in American education included John Holt, George Dennison, Herbert Kohl, Paul Goodman, Edgar Friedenberg, and Ivan Illich. These writers shared two main sentiments: (1) a deep hostility toward an allegedly profligate society and grim educational establishment, and (2) a romantic faith in the self-educating forces of a free, unhampered childhood and adolescence. Because the school, in the language of this genre, crippled the process of learning, destroyed the dignity of students, and mutilated their innate curiosity, a "do your own thing" ideology emerged.

The titles of the books and articles published by the radical/romantic element emphasized the dehumanizing and iniquitous nature of the educational establishment. Consider the following: Jonathan Kozol's *Death at an Early Age: The Destruction of the Hearts and Minds of Negro Children in the Boston*

13-2 SCHOLARLY VOICES
The Romantics

A. S. Neill (1962) admonished: "Abolish authority. Let the child be himself. Don't push him around. Don't teach him. Don't lecture him. Don't elevate him. Don't force him to do anything" (p. 58). Goodman (1964) wrote: "In the tender grades, the schools are a babysitting service during a period of collapse of the old-type family and during a time of extreme urbanization and urban mobility. In the junior and senior high school grades, they are an arm of the police, providing cops and concentration camps paid for under the heading 'Board of Education'" (p. 22). And in *Crisis in the Classroom,* Silberman (1970a) provided a concrete example of an open classroom setting: "At any one moment, some children may be hammering and sawing at a workbench, some may be playing musical instruments or painting, others may be reading aloud to the teacher or to a friend, still others may be curled up on a cot or a piece of carpet, reading in solitary absorption, oblivious to the sounds around them" (p. 224).

Do you agree with the ideas expressed by these writers? How is their rhetoric representative of the time during which they wrote?

Public Schools (1967), Paul Goodman's *Compulsory Mis-education* (1964), and Nat Hentoff's *Our Children Are Dying* (1966). Charles Silberman (1970b, 1970c) published in the *Atlantic Monthly* several essays critical of schooling under the titles "Murder in the Classroom" and "How the Public Schools Kill and Mutilate Minds." These writings were mostly about how the American school system had lost its soul.

Open Education

As far as the schools were concerned, the humanizing backlash of the 1960s manifested mainly as verbal criticism. Unlike in the 1950s, no systematic curriculum reform program emerged. In fact, it was not until 1967 that the humanizing movement began to yield practical results. These ideas were imported from England, drawn from the British Plowden Committee's report *Children and Their Primary Schools* (Central Advisory Council for Education, 1967). The report attracted attention because it advocated more child-centered schemes in British education and endorsed an undifferentiated integrated curriculum as a way to relate what was learned in school to real-life experiences. The lesson that the American schools would draw from the Plowden report, however, had less to do with an integrated, interdisciplinary curriculum and more to do with the effort to provide pleasant, meaningful experiences for children. The new goal was to promote freedom, individuality, and self-directed action in what was known as open education.

In its application, open education clearly meant different things to different people. It did not have well-articulated goals, and it never commanded the kind of foundational and government support that characterized many of the reform initiatives of the 1950s. In attempting to define the open education phenomenon, Charles Silberman (1973) maintained that it was "not a model or set of techniques to be slavishly imitated or followed," but an approach to instruction that encompassed a "set of attitudes and convictions about the nature and purposes of teaching and learning" (p. xix). Other writers tried to outline the principles central to the operation of open education: "First, the room . . . is decentralized. Second, the children are free. . . . Third, the environment is rich in learning resources. . . . Fourth, the teacher and his aides work most of the time with individual children" (Gross and Gross, 1970, p. 71).

This passage described some of the more common manifestations of open education, but like Silberman's account, it failed to point to specific curriculum goals and procedures. Not surprisingly, the open classroom came to be considered "open" according to any number of criteria. A school could promote its commitment to openness by abolishing ability groups, encouraging children to move about the classroom at will, knocking down classroom walls to foster more physical freedom, designing self-initiated learning units in a departmentalized classroom, reorganizing the curriculum into more integrated units, or any combination thereof. The open classroom, sadly, had little more to offer than the idea of openness; this made it vulnerable to some of the laissez-faire romanticism popular in that era.

The overall practical effect in the classroom during this period was a recognition of the child in the teaching/learning equation and a proliferation of child-centered views that made a virtue of any experiences the child had. At the secondary school and university levels, this same mentality led to a multiplicity of electives in the curriculum that were justified as relevant to students' interests.

Clearly, in the late 1960s, the prevailing goal was to bring the learner back into the discourse on the school curriculum. Years of neglect at the height of the Cold War, during which the subject matter was glorified and the learner was framed as the passive recipient of the knowledge inherent in the subject matter, made such a movement virtually inevitable. Similarly, the prior emphasis on math and science led to the subsequent interest in the humanities, while the prior focus on the academically inclined led to new concerns about the disadvantaged. In other words, the excesses of the 1950s reforms set the conditions for a correction in the 1960s. Unfortunately, this correction generated its own set of new excesses. It would only be a matter of time before the child-centered themes of the late 1960s would be undone by a new counterreform. On the horizon was a new wave of reform designed to bring the school "back to basics," back to the familiar ground of the subject-centered curriculum; open classrooms, open schools, and alternative education would soon become anachronisms.

GETTING "BACK TO BASICS"—AGAIN—IN THE 1970s

The problems that beset the American economy during the 1970s contributed to a conservative financial climate in which the fiscal budgets of several social institutions, including public education, were threatened. Burdened by growing inflation and unemployment rates, the U.S. economy showed few positive signs. The taxpaying public responded to these circumstances by displaying an increasing reluctance to invest in comprehensive educational programs. This climate of economic conservatism inevitably led to the promotion of cost-saving measures in public education. Efficiency values and productivity models were embraced as appropriate responses to the challenges of classroom instruction.

It was in this climate that another "bask to basics" movement was launched. The renewed effort to focus the curriculum on a strict education in the basics was accompanied by a new regard for accountability, performance assessment, and competency-based instruction. "Back to basics" also meant that the curriculum was reduced to its least common denominator, with fundamental literacy and math skills taking precedence and other aspects of the curriculum, notably the arts and writing and more interdisciplinary approaches to learning, taking a back seat. In addition, "back to basics" valued whatever was most easily measured. It set its sights on minimum standards and supported a skill-drill instructional approach to achieve these standards.

Basic skill achievement was, in effect, a cost-saving idea. The schools now could worry less about providing a comprehensive education and focus instead on the fundamentals. Competency-based strategies toward instruction seemed ideally suited for this because they enabled educators to itemize exactly what needed to be taught and to evaluate each component of the curriculum for mastery. A competency-based reading program, for instance, created a highly specific set of competencies, sequenced the competencies according to grade levels, directed the teacher to teach specifically to each competency, and regulated each student's movement through the curriculum with mastery tests for each competency. The result was a highly skill-based school experience marked by rather low-level activities. What could not be effectively measured simply was not taught. Thus, skills in oral communication, in writing, in argumentation, in problem solving, in cross-disciplinary insight, and in research, to name just a few, were not part of the instructional picture.

This period of reform also did not do much to advance the professional development of educators. Given the prevalence of competency-based systems of teaching, teachers had little room to exercise their intelligence and creativity. The most important judgments were already made for them; all they had to do was follow directions, issue the worksheets, and lead the skill-based activities already developed for them. It was in this climate, in fact, that "teacher proof" materials came into favor. These materials consisted of programmed learning workbooks, some varieties of computer-assisted instruction, and highly prescriptive learning packages that told teachers what to say and do. Their purpose was to protect the curriculum from the teacher—hence, the term "teacher proof."

Much of this retrenchment mentality was fueled by prominent studies that looked at the limitations rather than the possibilities of schooling. Christopher Jencks' *Inequality* (1972) was perhaps the most widely read. In his report, Jencks questioned whether school significantly affected economic and cognitive differences among schoolchildren. His central finding was that schools did not help to equalize the future incomes of children and that any effort to use the schools for this end would be wasted. Jencks further maintained that students' family backgrounds were far more important in the development of cognitive skills than anything the school might do. This last proposition led to the popular conclusion that schools made no difference in students' future lives, which itself turned out to be a virtual command for educational divestiture. Because people now believed that the public school was marginal to the economic and cognitive life of children, they gave more consideration and weight to alternative school options and earlier work opportunities.

Many of the alternative school ideas were discussed and promoted in a series of federally sponsored commission reports. These included reports from the National Commission on the Reform of Secondary Education (1973), the President's Science Advisory Committee (1974), and the National Panel on High School and Adolescent Education (1976). Each report sought to narrow the responsibilities of the high school by advocating the workplace and other nonschool settings as viable alternatives for education. To the panels and commissions of the 1970s, the reform emphasis was on educational reduction. An earlier compulsory school leaving age, a shortened school day and year, a narrower curriculum, and a commitment to alternative schooling arrangements were among the salient recommendations coming from the national reports.

Like the basic skills education initiative that was pushed during the early 1950s, the retrenchment trend of the 1970s eventually evolved into a pursuit of academic excellence and an effort to structure the goals of schooling according to the wishes and demands of the military-industrial complex. In 1983, influenced by the National Commission on Excellence in Education (NCEE) report *A Nation at Risk,* public education was once again subjected to a spate of charges similar to many of those made in the 1950s. As a strongly worded statement with considerable political backing, *A Nation at Risk* caught the public ear and lit the fuse for an explosion of another round of reform ideas.

PROMOTING ACADEMIC EXCELLENCE IN THE 1980s

The 1980s brought the schools full circle, back to the subject-centered traditions that were popular during the 1950s. Generally, people called for a "get tough" approach to the curriculum, which was modeled on familiar Cold War approaches. The schools, for instance, were asked to impose tougher graduation standards, to reaffirm the importance of the traditional academic curriculum, to renew their concern for the so-called gifted and talented, to examine their practices in relation to schooling in other advanced nations, to stress mathematics and science education, and, in direct contrast to what was valued only one decade earlier, to offer a longer school day and longer school year. All of these concerns were presented to the American people under the banner of "academic excellence," a Cold War–era term. Replace old fears of the military prowess of the Soviet Union with new fears of the technological and economic prowess of the Japanese, and the parallels between the two eras are virtually complete.

The NCEE report *A Nation At Risk* was undoubtedly the most influential educational document of the 1980s. Appointed by President Reagan, the

NCEE engaged in a year-long study of American schools. A significant portion of the report was dedicated to dramatizing the alleged shortcomings of the schools, often in strident language: "If an unfriendly foreign power had attempted to impose on America the mediocre educational performance that exists today, we might well have viewed it as an act of war. As it stands, we have allowed this to happen to ourselves. . . . We have, in effect, been committing an act of unthinking, unilateral educational disarmament" (p. 5).

By declaring a nationwide educational crisis and influencing various media outlets to promulgate its message, the NCEE set the stage for its own reform recommendations, which embraced the time-worn discipline-centered curriculum. Specifically, the NCEE promoted the "basics" and the subject-centered curriculum, sought to increase and strengthen graduation requirements, placed a new emphasis on math and science education, and advanced the idea of linking evaluation standards to exit and promotion decisions. The NCEE also called for new ways to educate teachers, aiming to make it easier for someone with a college degree to teach without necessarily going through teacher preparation courses. Lastly, it supported merit pay for teachers, recommended increased course loads for students, and proposed to lengthen the school day and year.

The onus for all of these so-called reforms fell squarely on the shoulders of the states. President Reagan repeatedly cited the NCEE report as evidence that reform could be accomplished without any increase in federal funding for and federal presence in education. Shortly after the release of *A Nation at Risk,* all fifty states established task forces to consider the reforms suggested by the NCEE. Within ten months, 44 states claimed to have raised their graduation requirements, 20 were considering a longer school day, and 42 were reexamining the way that they certified and prepared teachers, especially in the areas of math and science (U.S. Department of Education, 1984).

The NCEE report was hardly the only one issued during the 1980s. In that decade, a raft of education reform reports focused on the reformulation of the school curriculum. Included in the reform discussions were proposals for a conservative, one-track academic curriculum (Adler, 1982; Sizer, 1984), proposals featuring a reconceived commitment to general education (minus the placement of vocation education) in a comprehensive school program (Boyer, 1983; Goodlad, 1984), and proposals that recast the educational mission of the schools in language responsive to techno-industrial goals (National Commission on Excellence in Education, 1983; National Science Board Commission, 1983; Task Force on Education for Economic Growth, 1983).

But the effects of the academic excellence movement embodied in the *Nation at Risk* report were evident in the more stringent graduation requirements adopted at the state level and in the refocused concern for the disciplinary core of the high school academic curriculum. Most of the change was institutional in nature—longer school days, more course time for academic subjects, and so forth. But these changes had ripple effects, especially with regard to how the high school curriculum was configured, as interdisciplinary offerings lost their appeal and specialized courses in math, science, and foreign language study gained renewed popularity. This, however, served achievement concerns by allowing the states to standardize the curriculum and to better gauge what students learned in the traditional academic disciplines.

EXTENDING ACADEMIC EXCELLENCE INTO THE 1990s

As the country moved into a new decade, much of the reform rhetoric began to highlight the need for variety and choice in the school curriculum, a theme popular back in the 1960s. New opportunities for parents to choose schools for their own children opened up. The establishment of charter schools and the creation of various interdistrict and intradistrict school choice options helped to bring the issue of school choice to the forefront of school reform. Rather than working for a particular type of school reform, proponents of school choice called for new school alternatives as a way to improve public education. We will discuss the details of this still formative movement in Chapter 14.

National Standards and School Choice Options

But school reform discussions in the 1990s never quite let go of the nationalizing features that the *Nation at Risk* report highlighted. In fact, reformers in the early 1990s began to discuss seriously national education goals and standards. In a period associated with school choice, this is, at first glance, an unusual, if not paradoxical, occurrence. National goals or standards, especially if they manifest as national curricula or national tests, necessarily contradict the rationale for school choice, which is to encourage schools to proliferate in many forms as they respond to parental desires. For this reason, the national standards movement has been criticized by those who want schools to operate in a free market atmosphere and by those who

© Bettmann/Corbis

The America 2000 report grew out of
the 1989 meeting of the National
Governors' Association and included
the attendance of then Governor Bill
Clinton.

want to keep the federal government out of school policy debates. But
other commentators see a symbiotic relation between national standards
and individual choice. Believing that unregulated school choice is a practical
impossibility, advocates of national standards see a need for all schools, irrespective of their pedagogical style and curriculum emphasis, to be circum-
scribed by and accountable to a core set of standards.

The effort to simultaneously embrace school choice and national standards started with the *America 2000* report, published by the U.S. Department of Education in 1990. The report encouraged the adoption of school
choice mechanisms while also advancing national education goals, some of
which implied the need for national curriculum standards. The report grew
out of a 1989 meeting of the National Governors Association. President
Bush asked the governors of the nations (who are, in a sense, the chief operating officers of the nation's schools) to try to set some national goals for
education. They settled on six goals, which have since been adopted as
national policy; these were detailed in Chapter 1. The goals were broad
statements about improving academic achievement, assisting with school
readiness issues, increasing the holding power of the schools, and ensuring
the safety and learning integrity of the school environment.

In 1994, President Clinton, who attended the 1989 meeting of the
National Governors Association as governor of Arkansas, signed legislation,

known as Goals 2000, that not only embraced the original six goals of *America 2000,* but also introduced the idea of national standards as a way to ensure that national academic achievement goals were being met. One of the academic achievement goals, for instance, was that "American students will leave grades four, eight and twelve having demonstrated competency in challenging subject matter, including English, mathematics, science, history and geography." To realize such goals, the Goals 2000 program tried to encourage the development of some consensus among the states over generally accepted subject area standards. We should remember that in a decentralized system national standards can exist only through voluntary state compliance. Some states have resisted the notion of standards, but most others, with varying degrees of success, have embraced them. Feature 13-3 gives a state-by-state report on how the states are performing.

In any case, the emphasis on standards development clearly was an extension of the academic excellence movement of the 1980s. If the states could embrace the idea of curriculum standards, the American schools could take an important step toward improving the academic aspects of schooling. As Ravitch (1995) observed,

> Much of the movement for standards aimed to reestablish priorities by clarifying that the schools were responsible, first and foremost, for developing the intelligence of their students. This was not meant to eliminate or disparage the numerous other social functions that had been assigned to the schools, but to emphasize that instruction in skills and knowledge was the sine qua non of the school's responsibilities. (p. 5)

As a result of the influence of Goals 2000, curriculum standards have been developed for several academic subject areas. Professional educational organizations have led the way, providing states with content standards for various subject areas. The National Council of Teachers of Mathematics, the National Council of Teachers of English, the National Council for the Social Studies, the National Council for History Education, and the National Council for Geographic Education all delivered drafts on standards. Feature 13-4 gives information on major standards projects. These are typically content standards, which are usually straightforward descriptions of the actual skills and knowledge specific to a content area; Feature 13-5 gives two examples. Ideally, these standards are written in a way that allows the schools to assess student mastery.

Supporters claim that curriculum standards are empowering to students, parents, and teachers. Students benefit because standards lay the groundwork for provision of equal opportunities. They ensure that certain

13-3 THINKING ABOUT THE DATA

State Report Cards on Standards

Here is a 1998 national report card on state standards (Finn, Petrilli, and Vanourek, 1998). The table starts with the best performer, Arizona, and concludes with the three states that have refused to design any state standards, believing instead that standards development belongs at the local level. Pick a state and find out more about its standards development. Grade the states yourself, using your own criteria, or see if those states that have made progress with standards can show an achievement dividend for their efforts. Find out how one state could get an A in science standards and an F in mathematics standards. Examine the nature of the debate in the states that have refused to adopt any state-level standards.

National Report Card on State Standards Across All Subjects

	English (n = 28)	History (n = 38)	Geography (n = 39)	Math (n = 47)	Science (n = 36)	Cumulative GPA	Grade
Arizona	B	—	—	B	A	3.33	B+
California	—	B	D	A	A	3.00	B
Texas	B	B	A	B	C	3.00	B
Indiana	F	C	A	C	A	2.40	C+
Utah	C	C	C	B	B	2.40	C+
Virginia	B	A	D	B	D	2.40	C+
Massachusetts	A	B	D	F	C	2.00	C
North Carolina	—	F	C	A	—	2.00	C
Rhode Island	—	—	—	F	A	2.00	C
West Virginia	—	C	B	B	F	2.00	C
Alabama	D	C	C	B	D	1.80	C–
Louisiana	—	C	C	F	B	1.75	C–
District of Columbia	—	C	C	D	—	1.67	C–
Georgia	B	D	F	B	D	1.60	C–
Illinois	B	F	D	D	B	1.60	C–
New Hampshire	D	C	B	C	F	1.60	C–
Connecticut	—	C	F	D	B	1.50	C–
Ohio	F	D	D	A	—	1.50	C–
Colorado	F	D	A	D	D	1.40	D+

courses of study and certain learning expectations are available to all students. They also frame the school experience in a decidedly coherent, if not predictable, form. This allows educators to assess, in clear and unambiguous terms, how well their students are performing and to provide the public with information on the aggregate performance of local schools or local

	English (n = 28)	History (n = 38)	Geography (n = 39)	Math (n = 47)	Science (n = 36)	Cumulative GPA	Grade
New York	C	F	F	B	C	1.40	D+
Alaska	—	F	C	C	—	1.33	D+
Hawaii	F	—	—	F	A	1.33	D+
Vermont	—	F	F	C	B	1.25	D+
Delaware	D	F	F	C	B	1.20	D+
Florida	D	C	C	D	F	1.20	D+
New Jersey	F	F	F	C	A	1.20	D+
Wisconsin	C	F	F	C	C	1.20	D+
Mississippi	D	—	F	B	F	1.00	D
Oregon	F	—	—	D	C	1.00	D
South Carolina	—	—	—	D	D	1.00	D
Kansas	F	F	D	D	C	0.80	D–
Missouri	F	F	C	F	C	0.80	D–
Washington	D	F	F	F	B	0.80	D–
Michigan	F	F	B	F	—	0.75	D–
Oklahoma	C	D	F	F	—	0.75	D–
Idaho	F	—	C	F	—	0.67	D–
Tennessee	F	D	F	C	F	0.60	D–
Maine	—	D	F	F	D	0.50	D–
Pennsylvania	—	F	—	D	—	0.50	D–
Nebraska	—	F	—	F	D	0.33	F
North Dakota	—	—	F	D	F	0.33	F
Kentucky	—	F	F	D	F	0.25	F
Arkansas	—	F	F	F	F	0.00	F
Maryland	—	F	F	F	—	0.00	F
Minnesota	F	F	F	—	—	0.00	F
Montana	—	—	—	F	—	0.00	F
New Mexico	—	F	F	F	F	0.00	F
South Dakota	—	—	—	F	—	0.00	F
Iowa	—	—	—	—	—	—	—
Nevada	—	—	—	—	—	—	—
Wyoming	—	—	—	—	—	—	—

school districts. As Ravitch (1995) observes, "There is no such thing as Nevada science, New Jersey mathematics and Illinois English" (p. xxv). The content in these areas of study, Ravitch argues, should be coherently designed so that all students learn exactly the same mathematical, science, and English concepts. Teachers, of course, should be free to exercise their

13-4 WEB POINTS
National Standards

Almost every major professional organization concerned about teaching and learning in a particular subject area has been involved in the development of content standards. This includes, to name a short list, the National Council of Teachers of Mathematics, the National Council of Teachers of English, the National Council for the Social Studies, the National Council for Economic Education, and the American Association for the Advancement of Science. Each of the websites given here offers direct access to the content standards developed by some of these professional organizations. The Eisenhower National Clearinghouse contains the content standards developed in mathematics and science (www.enc.org). The Region 20 Education Service Center contains the national standards developed in the multiple subject areas of the social studies (www.esc20.tenet.edu).

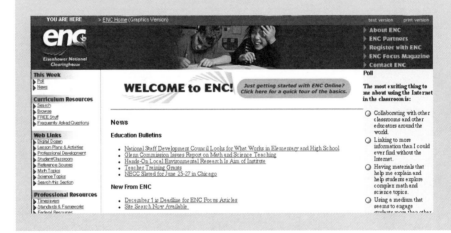

own judgment in fashioning instructional experiences, using various methods for various purposes. But all instructional choices should be grounded in some commonly defined framework of knowledge and skill.

Criticisms of National Standards

The idea of national standards does not have complete support. Many political conservatives do not like them because they represent a federal government intrusion in the school and make it less likely that local decision making will prevail. Others worry about the politicization of standards,

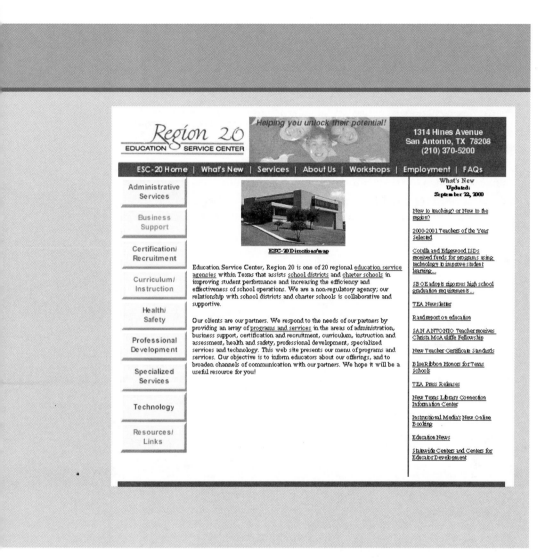

especially in cultural hotbeds such as American history or American literature. Because schools cannot teach everything, a standards-based curriculum forces choices about what gets included and excluded in the curriculum. In 1994, for example, a national controversy erupted over the release of Department of Education–sponsored history standards. Critics of the standards, mostly political conservatives, claimed that the standards were "politically correct," tainted by an overwhelmingly negative view of America, the West, and white males. The controversy led to a formal condemnation of the standards by the U.S. Senate and a subsequent revision. Some saw the battle over the history standards as emblematic of the difficulty of forging any national standards that could win broad-based support

13-5 RESEARCH INQUIRY
What Is a Good Standard?

Advocates of national curriculum standards have actively monitored standards development across the states and evaluated the quality of the standards developed or adopted within the states. Finn, Petrilli, and Vanourek (1998) have identified a number of problems with the way standards are being used. They offer examples of how good standards should be developed, arguing that they should be clear and specific statements that point to the specific knowledge or skills that children should know. Here are two examples taken from their report.

Example of a Skills-Based Standard

[The student should] (1) Locate main ideas in multiple types of sources (e.g., non-print, specialized references, periodicals, newspapers, atlases, yearbooks, government publications, etc.). (2) Take notes and develop outlines through reading, listening, or viewing. (3) Use features of books for information: table of contents, glossary, index, appendix, bibliography. (4) Distinguish between fact and opinion relating to regions/cultures. (Georgia standards, grade 7, social studies skills)

Example of a Knowledge-Based Standard

The student will identify the sources and describe the development of democratic principles in Western Europe and the United States. . . . [A]fter examining major documents (such as the Declaration of Independence, the Constitution of the United States, the English Bill of Rights, the Declaration of the Rights of Man, or the Universal Declaration of Human Rights) for specific democratic principles they contain, the student makes a comparison chart showing how certain principles appear in these documents. (California standards, standard 3, grade 10)

What is it about these examples that make them good or bad standards? Do you agree that these standards are effectively designed? Examine other standards documents, and compare and contrast them to the standards given here.

from the public (Ravitch, 1996); Feature 13-6 examines the history standards debate.

Several critics also point to the possibility that standards could result in a narrowing of the school experience, with sanction given only to content standards that are easily described and tested. Thus, aspects of the school experience not easily captured by a standard, such as the development of a

National curriculum standards have been developed in most academic areas. The National Council of Teachers of Mathematics has led the way in the development of standards for mathematics instruction.

value system marked by honesty and patience, love of learning, and ethical behavior, could be overlooked. Others argue that, far from empowering teachers, standards tend to burden them with test-driven instruction geared to the standards and with formulaic textbooks. There is also a disciplinarity implied in much curriculum standard setting, an implication that where standards exist learning must be subject-centered.

National standards have been developed in almost all subject areas of the school curriculum, and it is up to the states to decide what to do with them. They could ignore them, try to change them, or embrace them, as a national centralized system of schooling might. But whatever the trend, some reconciliation of national standards with school choice will probably follow.

SUMMARY

School reform efforts have always been influenced by sociopolitical factors, as Figure 13-1 summarizes. During the height of the Cold War, in the 1950s, concern with the Soviet "menace" shaped the curriculum in very direct ways. Congress authorized federal funds for the development of curriculum programs nationwide, mostly in the areas of math and science, designed to produce the scientists and engineers needed for the defense of

13-6 DEBATING THE ISSUES
Debating the History Standards

The release of the 1994 history standards provoked a rancorous debate over the politicization of the standards-making process. Conservative commentators such as Phyllis Schlafly referred to the history standards as an attempt to brainwash students with left-wing revisionism. The problem for Schlafly and others was that the standards represented attacks against Western civilization and offered multicultural distortions of American history. Ravitch (1994) noted, for example, that the Cold War section featured nineteen references to McCarthy and McCarthyism but not a single reference to Soviet aggression in eastern Europe or to the Communist takeover of mainland China. The history standards eventually were revised; the Department of Education would not accept them in their original form. Here is an example of a history standard dealing with immigration before and after the revision. What is the change? Is it an improvement?

The standard: *Massive immigration after 1870 and how new social patterns, conflicts, and ideas of national unity developed amid growing cultural diversity.*

Original Version

Students should be able to demonstrate understanding of the sources and experiences of the new immigrants by:

- Distinguishing between the "old" and "new" immigration in terms of its volume and the newcomers' ethnicity, religion, language, and place of origin. (Analyze multiple causation)

- Tracing the patterns of immigrant settlements in different regions of the country. (Reconstruct patterns of historical succession and duration)

the nation. In the turbulent 1960s, the civil rights and student protest movements, as well as urban decay, led to the development of humanizing initiatives in the schools, with a focus on relevant life experiences. The subject-centered tradition of the Cold War era was a distant memory. However, sociopolitical conditions would shift yet again, this time in the direction of retrenchment, efficiency, and cost-cutting measures. During the 1970s, the schools launched another back-to-basics movement, one that featured competency-based learning. The popularity of efficient and low-

- Analyzing the obstacles, opportunities, and contributions of different immigrant groups. (Evidence historical perspectives)

- Evaluating how Catholic and Jewish newcomers responded to discrimination and internal divisions in their new surroundings. (Obtain historical data)

Revised Version

The student understands the sources and experiences of the new immigrants. Therefore, the student is able to:

- Distinguish between the "old" and "new" immigration in terms of its volume and the immigrants' ethnicity, religion, language, place of origin, and motives for emigrating from their homelands. (Analyze multiple causation)

- Trace patterns of immigrant settlement in different regions of the country and how new immigrants helped produce a composite American culture that transcended group boundaries. (Reconstruct patterns of historical succession and duration)

- Assess the challenges, opportunities, and contributions of different immigrant groups. (Examine historical perspectives)

- Evaluate how Catholic and Jewish immigrants responded to religious discrimination. (Obtain historic data)

cost instructional programs kept the school experience gauged at a low conceptual mark. As the 1980s approached, the Cold War themes of academic excellence experienced a renewal, this time in the context of a global struggle for technological and economic dominance. The school curriculum, once again, became more discipline-centered. States helped to lock this shift into place by making graduation and course requirements more stringent. The academic excellence movement continued to play out during the 1990s, especially in the national call for the development of

FIGURE 13-1
Shifting Priorities in School Reform

Subject-Centered	**Learner-Centered**
Education During the Cold War in the 1950s	
1. Math and science emphasis	
2. Academic- and discipline-centered curriculum	
3. Focus on high-aptitude students	
	Humanizing of the Schools in the 1960s
	1. Emphasis on joyful and open learning experiences
	2. Student-centered curriculum, emphasizing elective study
	3. Focus on the disadvantaged
Back to Basics and Educational Retrenchment in the 1970s	
1. Back-to-basics emphasis	
2. Competency-based learning	
3. Retrenchment from the institution of public education	
Academic Excellence in the 1980s	
1. Revival of academic excellence themes, stressing discipline-centered learning	
2. Increase in graduation requirements and course work dedicated to academic subjects	
3. Math and science emphasis	
National Goals and National Standards in the 1990s	*School Choice and School Alternatives in the 1990s*
1. Development of content standards in academic subject areas	**1.** School variety and responsiveness to parental desires
2. Standardization of academic subjects	**2.** Charter schools, magnet schools, interdistrict and intradistrict choice
	3. Educational vouchers and individualistic learning agendas

national curriculum standards for all academic subject areas. The embrace of national standards, however, is tempered by a popular movement for school choice, an issue we will address in the final chapter.

QUESTIONS AND ACTIVITIES

1. Describe the pendulumlike nature of school reform since the 1950s.

2. Why are reactionary changes likely when schools respond to narrow nationalistic pressures?

3. What was the fundamental reform message offered by Arthur Bestor and Hyman Rickover during the 1950s?

4. What were some of the things that occurred in the school curriculum following the Soviet launch of *Sputnik*?

5. What was Bruner's essential contribution to the nature of school reform during the post-*Sputnik* period?

6. What was the main message emerging from the radical/romantics during the 1960s?

7. How did open education lead to a laissez-faire attitude in the curriculum?

8. Many of the schools built in the late 1960s were designed with the open education concept in mind. Can you recall an open education experience in your own school education? Find a school built during this period, and note the changes.

9. What was competency-based instruction, and why was it a popular method during the 1970s?

10. What was the essential finding of Jencks' well-known book *Inequality,* and what were the main implications for the school curriculum?

11. Explain how the idea of "teacher proof" materials fit into the context of the back-to-basics approach and educational retrenchment.

12. Compare the reforms of the 1980s to those undertaken during the post-*Sputnik* period.

13. What were the main recommendations of the *Nation at Risk* report? What is your overall assessment of the report?

14. Examine some of the major school reform documents published during the 1980s: Goodlad (1984), Boyer (1983), Sizer (1984), Adler (1982), National Science Board Commission (1983), and National Commission on Excellence in Education (1983). Analyze them from the standpoint of their responsiveness to the nature of the learner and the values and aims of democracy.

15. What are the arguments offered for and against the use of national standards in the curriculum?

16. How do you resolve the contradiction between national standards and school choice?

17. Political conservatives do not all agree about the need for national standards. What are some of the arguments that conservatives might offer for and against national standards?

18. The search for national education goals started in 1989 with a national meeting of governors. Why do you think the discussion over national goals started with state governors?

19. Look in the annual editions of the *Education Index* for the number of articles on the topic "crisis in education." Conduct a citation analysis going all the way back to the 1950s.

20. If you were asked to design a curriculum for your school, what lessons might you take from the story of school reform in America?

REFERENCES

Adler, M. J. (1982). *The paideia proposal.* (New York: Macmillan).

Bestor, A. E. (1956). *The restoration of learning.* (New York: Knopf).

Bestor, A. E. (1953). *Educational wastelands.* (Urbana: University of Illinois Press).

Boyer, E. (1983). *High school.* (New York: Harper & Row).

Bruner, J. S. (1960). *The process of education.* (Cambridge, MA: Harvard University Press).

Central Advisory Council for Education. (1967). *Children and their primary schools.* (London: Her Majesty's Stationery Office).

Conant, J. B. (1960). *The American high school today.* (New York: McGraw-Hill).

Finn, C. E., Petrilli, M. J., and Vanourek, G. (1998). The state of the state standards. *Fordham Report,* 2(5). (www.edexcellence.net).

Goodlad, J. I. (1984). *A place called school.* (New York: McGraw-Hill).

Goodlad, J. I. (1966). *The changing school curriculum.* (New York: Fund for the Advancement of Education).

Goodman, P. (1964). *Compulsory mis-education.* (New York: Horizon Press).

Gross, R., and Gross, B. (1970). A little bit of chaos. *Saturday Review* (16 May).

Hentoff, N. (1966). *Our children are dying.* (New York: Viking Press).

Jencks, C. (1972). *Inequality.* (New York: Basic Books).

Kozol, J. (1967). *Death at an early age.* (Boston: Houghton Mifflin).

National Commission on Excellence in Education. (1983). *A nation at risk.* (Washington, DC: U.S. Department of Education).

National Commission on the Reform of Secondary Education. (1973). *The reform of secondary education.* (New York: McGraw-Hill).

National Panel on High School and Adolescent Education. (1976). *The education of adolescents.* (Washington, DC: U.S. Government Printing Office).

National Science Board Commission. (1983). *Educating Americans for the twenty-first century.* (Washington, DC: National Science Foundation).

Neill, A. S. (1962). *Summerhill.* (New York: Hart).

President's Science Advisory Committee. (1974). *Youth: Transition to adulthood.* (Chicago: University of Chicago Press).

Ravitch, D. (1996). 50 states, 50 standards. *The Brookings Review,* 14(3):6–9

Ravitch, D. (1995). *National standards in American education.* (Washington, DC: Brookings Institute).

Ravitch, D. (1994). Standards in U.S. history: An assessment. *Education Week* (7 Dec.).

Rickover, H. G. (1983). We have lost that realistic sense of purpose. *The Washington Post* (19 June).

Rickover, H. G. (1959). *Education and freedom.* (New York: Dutton).

Silberman, C. E. (1973). *The open classroom reader.* (New York: Random House).

Silberman, C. E. (1970a). *Crisis in the classroom.* (New York: Random House).

Silberman, C. E. (1970b). How the public schools kill dreams and mutilate minds. *The Atlantic Monthly* (June).

Silberman, C. E. (1970c). Murder in the schoolroom. *The Atlantic Monthly* (July/August).

Sizer, T. R. (1984). *Horace's compromise.* (Boston: Houghton Mifflin).

Tanner, D. (1986). Are reforms like swinging pendulums? In H. J. Walberg, and J. W. Keefe, (eds.), *Rethinking reform: The principal's dilemma.* (Reston, VA: National Association of Secondary School Principals).

Tanner, D., and Tanner, L. (1995). *Curriculum development.* (New York: Macmillan).

Task Force on Education for Economic Growth. (1983). *Action for excellence.* (Washington, DC: Education Commission of the States).

U.S. Department of Education. (1990). *America 2000.* (Washington, DC: U.S. Department of Education).

U.S. Department of Education. (1984). *A nation responds.* (Washington, DC: U.S. Department of Education).

CHAPTER 14

The Idea of School Choice

Public School Choice Programs
   INTRADISTRICT AND INTERDISTRICT OPTIONS
   CHARTER SCHOOLS
   FOR-PROFIT EDUCATION CORPORATIONS
   MAGNET SCHOOLS

Privatization, Vouchers, and the Debate over

School Choice
   ARGUMENTS FOR AND AGAINST VOUCHERS
   THE MILWAUKEE PARENTAL CHOICE PROGRAM (MPCP)

Home Schooling

Summary

Questions and Activities

References

ODAY, MOST CHILDREN IN THE UNITED STATES are educated in a public school in their community. Neighborhood schools, as they are known, are convenient to attend and are central to the functioning of the communities they serve. Because they are charged with the responsibility of educating the neighborhood's children, these schools often become centers for community involvement and shared community undertakings. Community bonds are created this way, as families get to know each other through the school. The life of the school—its homework assignments, athletic events, and extracurricular activities—is shared by the residents of the neighborhood, and the life of the community—its common problems and concerns—is shared in the experience of the school. This is what happens when children who live together go to school together. And this was the very principle embraced by the Puritans in their efforts to provide localized schooling.

In recent years, however, the necessity of a neighborhood school arrangement has been questioned by reformers who believe in the need to broaden the menu of school choices available to parents. They argue that parents should not be content with only one option for the education of their children. Rather, parents should always have the option of sending their children to another school without being forced to resort to private schools.

Today, there is growing support for the right of parents to exercise greater choice in where their children go to school. The key issue here involves determining how far this freedom of choice should go—specifically, whether it should extend to the public funding of private schools.

PUBLIC SCHOOL CHOICE PROGRAMS

Many parents, of course, have always had the ability to choose where their children would be educated. Parents who can afford private school typically can select from among a number of schools that may abide by different philosophies or promote different religious points of view. Advocates of school choice often cite this fact, arguing that school choice exists only for the wealthy and is denied to the very group of people who need it most—poor families stuck in poor neighborhoods with poor schools.

Intradistrict and Interdistrict Options

Public school districts are increasingly aware of the need to offer more school options to parents. Many school districts have adopted open enrollment policies that give parents the option of enrolling their children in any number of schools within the district. These choices could include neighborhood schools, magnet schools, and charter schools. These limited-choice programs are known as intradistrict choice programs—schooling options made available to parents within the boundaries of a school district.

Some states also offer interdistrict choice programs in which parents can select a school for their child outside of their school district. Most of the money allocated for the student's education follows the student to the receiving school district. Interdistrict choice typically has a few restrictions attached to it. For example, in most cases, parents have to provide their own transportation, although exemptions may be made for disabled and low-income students. Also, the receiving district can deny a transfer if the school is at capacity or if racial imbalances will result. Some states have regulations that dissuade schools from using interdistrict transfers as a means of recruiting athletes.

In 1995, fewer than 2 percent of students in districts with interdistrict choice programs chose to attend schools outside of their residential districts. However, 25 percent of students in districts with intradistrict choice programs used the intradistrict option (National Center for Education Statistics, 1996). Currently, overall, about 76 percent of all schoolchildren attend neighborhood schools (also known as public assigned schools), while about 14 percent attend public chosen schools (either intradistrict or interdistrict options). The remaining 10 percent attend private schools (National Center for Education Statistics, 2000a).

Charter Schools

The public school choice option on the minds of many educators and parents today is the charter school. Charter schools are publicly supported schools created and managed by individuals or groups meeting a given state's eligibility requirements for charter school participation. In various states, charter schools are operated by parents, teachers, community leaders, public organizations, and for-profit businesses.

Charter schools typically are innovative institutions that probably would not exist in the normal policy climate of a school district. State laws permit various groups to petition the state or the local school board to authorize public funds for the design, construction, and operation of a charter school. Once approved, the charter school is free to operate without administrative control from either the state or the local district in which it is located.

Of course, a few general rules apply to all charter schools. For example, they cannot charge tuition, they must be nonsectarian, they are subject to federal and state laws prohibiting discrimination, and they must comply with all health and safety standards. Otherwise, however, charter schools are free to flex their creative muscles and to try innovations that in the regular school environment might be viewed as too risky or unusual. The idea is to allow the school to perform as it might in a free market by leaving it alone and letting teachers, parents, community members, and business leaders frame the educational experience.

Although charter schools are free to operate as they wish, they still must meet local district and/or state performance standards. Thus, the state can intervene to monitor and assess the performance of charter schools according to its expectations. In fact, if a charter school does not demonstrate adequate progress in achieving state or district outcome measures, the state can shut it down.

As of 2000, 37 states had passed charter school legislation. The nature of charter school legislation varies among the states (National Center for Education Statistics, 2000a). Thirteen of the 37 states put no limit on the number of charters granted in the state. The remaining 24 put some limit on the number, but it varies considerably, from 100 annually in California to 5 annually in New Mexico. Across the 37 states, the duration of the charter granted to a school could range from three years to fifteen. In some states, private school are not eligible for charters; in others, home schools and for-profit companies can apply for charters. Some states require the use of licensed teachers in charter schools, while others will approve schools without licensed teachers.

Because they use public funds, charter schools, as indicated, must be nonsectarian, nondiscriminatory, and tuition-free. Advocates claim that these conditions allow charter schools to maintain the common school ideal (Bierlien and Molholland, 1994). Critics, however, wonder how any common school ideal is served when the school can operate around virtually any odd gathering of ideas someone might want to try (Engel 2000). Most charter schools, for instance, are created to serve some special interest—a group of people seeking a unique school experience. If it wishes, the school could even embrace some racial or ethnic identity. For instance, in California, as reported by Wells (1998), the central focus of two such schools "included an emphasis on the ethnic culture, heritage and identity of the students. Teachers at these schools presented history and culture from the point of view of the people in their communities, not from the

As of the year 2000, 37 states have passed charter school legislation. Here, a Boston Public School bus waits outside of the Boston Renaissance Charter School.

perspective of mainstream public school textbooks and curriculum" (p. 22). Interestingly, some evidence suggests that charter schools contribute to the racial and ethnic isolation of their students. The National Center for Education Statistics (1999) found that close to one-third of all charter schools were racially distinct from the districts in which they were located. In other words, as Feature 14-1 shows, about one-third of charter schools could be considered either disproportionately white or disproportionately nonwhite in terms of districtwide enrollment. Charter schools reach out to LEP students at about the same rate as do nonchartered public schools, but are significantly less successful in reaching out to students with disabilities (National Center for Education Statistics, 2000).

As Feature 14-2 shows, charter schools have experienced enormous growth. But the enrollments in almost all charter schools represent less than 1 percent of the total school population for a given state. There are a few exceptions; for example, Arizona leads the country with 4 percent of its student population attending charter schools.

For-Profit Education Corporations

The charter school movement has also provided the impetus for a new industry of for-profit educational corporations. Private corporations have always done business with the schools, selling textbooks and school supplies, providing in-service training, and so forth. Only recently, however, have they tried to sell instruction, to actually operate a public school at a

14-1 THINKING ABOUT THE DATA
Charter Schools and Race

Here are the early results on charter enrollments in relation to race. What else might you need to know in order to determine if charter schools are perpetuating segregation?

Charter and Public School Enrollments by Race, 1999

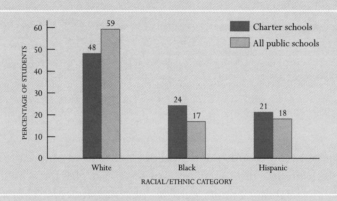

SOURCE: Charter schools and race (2000), *Education Week* (10 May).

**Charter School Enrollments
in Relation to Race/Ethnicity in the District, 1999**

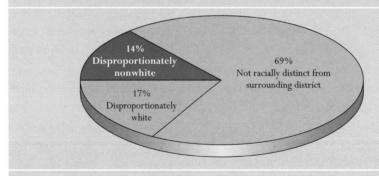

SOURCE: Charter schools and race (2000), *Education Week* (10 May).

profit. Of particular note in this regard is the Edison Schools, which is now the nation's largest private manager of public schools.

Started in 1991, the Edison Schools now operate seventy-nine schools, serving close to 40,000 students a year (Walsh, 1999). The company profits by either contracting a partnership with a public school district or by opening its own charter schools, with government funds sent directly to the corporation. The success of for-profit corporations in the charter school setting has yet to be properly evaluated. It will be another eight years, for instance, before any students move all the way through the Edison Schools program (Chubb, 1998).

The direct intrusion of a corporate culture into the affairs of the public schools, even in the limited scope of charter school involvement, has been disconcerting to critics who caution against the presence of a profit-making mindset in the schools. The classic free-market argument, of course, is that when the school is run as a business it will be sensitive to the needs and interests of its clients and strive to avoid losing paying customers. But critics wonder what happens if the parent-school relationship does not produce profits for the school. A study released by a group of Michigan researchers (Sykes, Arsen, and Plank, 2000) found that the charter schools in the state, most of which were run by for-profit companies, were targeting a low-cost market, opening elementary schools instead of secondary schools (which are more expensive) and failing to attract special-needs children. The result, as the researchers put it, was to "lower the average cost of education in charter schools, while raising the average cost in nearby public schools, which must educate all students" (p. 41). The problem, as Darling-Hammond (1992) expresses it, is that, every step of the way, for-profit schools have to decide if certain educational benefits can be skipped in order to ensure adequate profit margins, or if certain students should not be admitted because their needs are too expensive to meet. "Pursuing profits while pursuing the public's broader goals for children's education," she observes, "creates a clear and unavoidable conflict of interest." The corporate response is that most public schools operate wastefully and that, with sound planning, there is room for profit. Moreover, they might add, without a profit incentive, no good mechanism exists to motivate innovative school change.

Magnet Schools

As indicated in Chapter 10, magnet schools were originally conceived in the context of a school district's desegregation effort. The idea was to create and operate specially designed schools, often dedicated to a particular theme or area of interest, that would attract students from all the population sectors of the district. To ensure that the magnet schools were attractive enough to lure students from the various neighborhoods, school districts often invested heavily in them, making them the top schools in the district (Moore and Davenport, 1989).

14-2 THE HISTORICAL CONTEXT
Charter School Growth

As these two graphs show, charter schools have grown in number over the past decade, as more states have passed charter school laws and lifted the caps on the number of such schools that can be opened. Examine a state where charter school laws have not yet been passed, and try to determine why not.

Growth in the Number of Charter Schools, 1992–99

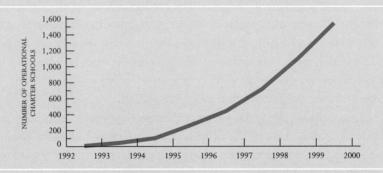

SOURCE: National Center for Education Statistics (1999), *The state of charter schools 1999: Third-year report* (Washington, DC: U.S. Department of Education).

Magnet schools continue to function along these lines, and so they are found mainly in urban and low-socioeconomic districts. But they have become more than a desegregation method. Many districts have opened magnet schools for the sole purpose of offering some school options to parents. In most cases, the magnet schools concentrate on a particular subject area, such as mathematics, science, computers and technology, music and art, or a foreign language. However, especially at the elementary school level, they also focus on particular instructional methods, such as the Montessori method. Unlike neighborhood schools, one-third of all magnet schools have a selective admissions policy.

Critics concede the role magnet schools have played in contributing to choice and variety, and to the historical effort to desegregate the schools.

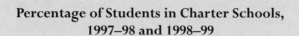

Percentage of Students in Charter Schools, 1997–98 and 1998–99

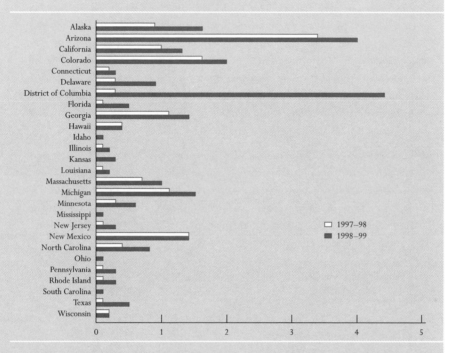

SOURCE: National Center for Education Statistics (1999), *The state of charter schools 1999: Third-year report* (Washington, DC: U.S. Department of Education).

But they claim that the magnet school has been a mixed blessing—that, despite its accomplishments, it has contributed to the deterioration of the neighborhood school, especially in urban school districts, leaving poor inner-city children worse off than ever.

The problem is that good students living in bad neighborhoods typically will opt for magnet schools, thus leaving the neighborhood schools with a disproportionately large share of the hard-to-educate. Academically motivated students from families supportive of education increasingly cannot be found in urban neighborhood schools. This problem, known as "creaming" (as in creaming off the top), has resulted in a diminished school experience for those left behind in the neighborhood schools and in the dissolution of community bonds to the neighborhood school, as Feature 14-3 describes.

14-3 DEBATING THE ISSUES
Magnet Schools and Neighborhood Schools

Here are two descriptions, taken from the *New York Times,* of some of the ways that magnet schools can affect neighborhood schools:

In the Jackson Heights section of Queens (in New York City), the parent association of a local school filed suit to have a nearby magnet school put under the local district's control, as opposed to the central board of education. The reason was that the local neighborhood school was overcrowded, operating at 139 percent capacity, while only 13 blocks away, a city-run magnet school (populated by students from all over the city) was operating at 88 percent capacity. "The city is paying for lots of yellow buses to bring children from all over Queens," a parent complained, "while denying children next door admission."

In many city school systems, zoned schools have become, in a manner of speaking, pauper schools, worthy only for those who do not care about or cannot manage a better school option. In a New York Times *article, one New York City student explained the situation. "No one wants to go to a zoned school," he observed. "It explains itself. It's like a last option. You want to try for other options. If you don't get accepted anywhere else, you just automatically go there."*

SOURCE: Hevesi, D. (1995), Neighborhood schools: Louis Armstrong to remain a magnet school, *New York Times* (26 March), Sec. 13, p. 20; Richardson, L. (1994), Being anonymous and going truant, *New York Times* (19 June), Sec. 1, p. 23.

Of course, the trade-off is that good students can find good schools, that the affluent are less likely to exit the district, and that overall more opportunities exist for integrated experiences, at least within the district.

PRIVATIZATION, VOUCHERS, AND THE DEBATE OVER SCHOOL CHOICE

The debate over school choice programs becomes most fervent when the question turns to whether private schools should be included in the menu of school choice offerings. Those who support the full inclusion of private schools in school choice programs are, in effect, endorsing the privatization of schooling.

Privatization means that the operation of public schooling is handed over to for-profit corporations and groups that would compete in the market-

© Bettmann/Corbis

Milton Friedman.

place for clients (students), offering educational services paid for through a
publicly financed voucher. The voucher is, in essence, a government certificate that represents a designated amount of money to be used for the purchase of all or some part of a child's schooling. Under privatization, the
government would likely issue redeemable vouchers or certificates to all
parents with school-age children. These parents would then be free to
enroll their children in the participating school of their choice. If they subsequently found the school to be unsuitable, they could opt for another.

Privatization obviously represents a radical departure from the current
system of financing and operating the public schools, which must follow
government guidelines and rules. No states have embraced a voucher system yet, although a few small-scale experiments have been attempted
mostly in inner-city school districts; the most well known is the Milwaukee
Parental Choice Program, which is discussed later in the section.

The first systematic effort to articulate an educational voucher plan in
the United States was by the economist Milton Friedman (1962), who
believed that offering consumer choices could only improve the schools. As
a result, Friedman advanced the now-famous argument for "schools of
choice." American public education, he claimed, could best be improved by

changing its financial and governance structure in directions that encouraged schools to compete for students and that helped parents exercise consumer options in deciding where their children should be educated. His idea was fairly simple: Provide parents with redeemable vouchers (roughly equivalent to local per-pupil expenditures) that could be spent on any school of their choice. Friedman saw no need to place any restrictions on the participating "voucher schools." Rather, each school needed only to be monitored by the government much in the way, to use his analogy, that the government inspects restaurants to ensure minimum sanitary and safety standards.

Arguments for and Against Vouchers

The idea of using vouchers to buy schooling experiences can be difficult to assess in the abstract. Marked differences of opinion exist over the size of vouchers; the eligibility requirements, if any, for the participating voucher schools; and the general nature and extent of government regulations and restrictions placed on the participating schools. For instance, will admission requirements be allowed in the schools? Will the participating schools need to follow some framework for curriculum content standards? Will some schools be allowed to ask for more money over the cost of the voucher? Will religious-affiliated schools be allowed to participate? Or should the whole system simply be left to the winds of the marketplace, as Friedman recommended? These variations might make a difference in how we react to vouchers. Still, there are general keynotes to the idea that could help clarify whether education by voucher is appropriate in the United States.

First, supporters of the general idea of vouchers claim that it will infuse the current school system with an assortment of innovative schools. They assert that vouchers will break the back of an entrenched system of schooling marked by widespread curriculum uniformity and staleness. The mechanism of market accountability is at the center of this belief, because only the "best" schools presumably will survive in the competitive climate that vouchers will generate. Second, supporters claim that the voucher system will grant new decision-making authority to members of the underclass, giving this neglected population a means of access to better schools. Supporters claim as well that vouchers will induce new openness in the area of school administration, lead to increased interaction among socioeconomic classes, and ultimately liberate teachers from the tethers of an onerous school bureaucracy. All of these claims cut across specific voucher proposals and are advanced for the general idea of vouchers.

Supporters of school choice often cite evidence from national surveys that testify to the popularity of school options among parents. Few parents, in fact, are likely to deny an interest in exercising some choice or authority over their children's public education. When parents are asked if they should have the right to choose their children's school, the response is solidly, and not surprisingly, in favor of choice (Public Agenda, 1999). The power to choose is, undeniably, not something that parents take lightly. But when the question of school choice is framed differently, in terms of a school reform strategy, parental views toward it could be interpreted quite differently. The Carnegie Foundation for the Advancement of Teaching (1992) conducted a national survey on school choice. The researchers asked parents whether American education could be best improved by giving neighborhood schools the resources they needed to achieve excellence or by letting schools compete for students with the understanding that the good schools would flourish while the weak ones would either improve or close. More than 80 percent of the respondents chose the neighborhood school option.

Nevertheless, when asked if they would send their oldest children to a private or church-affiliated school if the tuition was paid for by the government, 46 percent of public school parents answered affirmatively (Rose and Gallup, 1999). National Center for Education Statistics (2000b) data show higher levels of parental satisfaction in both public chosen and private schools than in public assigned schools, although the differences are not overwhelming. These higher ratings should be weighed against the fact that families make a financial investment in private schools, that most private schools have an affiliation with some religious group, and that private schools (and some public chosen schools) can deny certain students admission.

There is also evidence that, despite being in favor of choice and vouchers, much of the public admits to knowing very little about them. As Feature 14-4 shows, in 1999, 63 percent of the general public claimed to know "very little or nothing" about school vouchers, and 80 percent believed that they needed "to learn more about vouchers" before offering an opinion. And the lack of knowledge about charter schools was even more pronounced. But when the market rationale for school choice was explained, a large majority of parents believed that vouchers would indeed put pressure on the public school system to improve (Public Agenda, 1999).

Opponents believe that vouchers, in any form, will lead to a divided school system that fails to reaffirm the historical commitment to a common public school experience. They see the rise of an open school marketplace as a sign of abandonment of the public school ideal, as Feature 14-5

14-4 RESEARCH INQUIRY
The Public's View of School Choice

Public Agenda's survey of the general public's attitude toward school choice was revealing in that it showed that the public was admittedly uninformed. Ask the same survey questions to a group of peers or parents in your community. Are they better informed?

How much do you know about school vouchers and how they work? Percentages saying they know "very little" or "nothing."

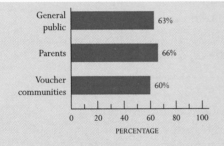

How much do you know about charter schools? Percentage saying they know "very little" or "nothing."

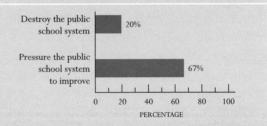

Parents should have the right to choose the school they want their child to attend. Would you say you agree or disagree?

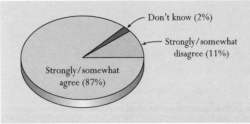

Some say school vouchers represent an effort to destroy the public school system. Others say they are an effort to pressure the public school system to improve and therefore save it. Which is closer to your view?

suggests. They argue that public money should support a public mandate, not individualistic or familial mandates.

Advocates of vouchers obviously believe that parents are the most suitable agents for determining how and where their children should be edu-

14-5 SCHOLARLY VOICES
David Tyack on the New Ideology of School Reform

Noted educational historian David Tyack (1993) observes the shift in the ideological underpinning for school reform in the direction of an economic or marketplace argument and suggests that it is a turn away from the common school ideal:

The belief systems underlying much of current educational reform seem impoverished and incomplete in comparison with earlier ideologies. . . . [They] have moved away from the tradition of a broad-based conception of democratic citizenship, revealed in action. They substitute economic competitiveness, to be certified by higher test scores. Such a narrowing of purpose omits much that is of value from the discussion of educational policy and constricts the historical vision of the common school. (pp. 25–26)

cated. In fact, a large part of the debate over vouchers revolves around the question of whether the schools should be fashioned in the best interests of the family or the best interests of society. Some advocates of choice, like Coons and Sugarman (1978), contend that the school's main objective should be the family, because maximizing the welfare of the family is the best way to maximize the welfare of the society. This view has been criticized by those who see the main objectives of the school in broader and more collective terms. Opponents of the voucher system see the idea of family choice as basically selfish and antisocial, because it focuses on the wants of the individual family rather than the needs of the larger society. Public education, the reasoning goes, must be protected from the prevailing orthodoxies of parents and must be influenced instead by the general values and aims of democratic society.

William Bennett, who supports choice programs, embodies the contradiction between the argument for choice and the argument for a common public ideal. In 1992, he wrote, "Our students should know . . . our nation's ideals and aspirations. We believe in liberty and equality, in limited government and in the betterment of the human condition. These truths underlie our society, and though they may be self-evident, they are not spontaneously apprehended by the young" (p. 62). The question, of course, is how exactly to promote these common "ideals and aspirations," these "truths," while supporting a free-market system of schooling? Wise and Darling-Hammond (1984) note the very thin line that voucher proponents walk: "If

© Candace Barbot/Miami Herald

Annette "Polly" Williams was the author of the original MPCP voucher bill in 1989.

parents' choices of schools reinforce social class stratification and socialization, [then] we must accept the outcomes as justified by choice and as being in the child's best interests" (p. 43).

The Milwaukee Parental Choice Program (MPCP)

Initiated in 1990, the Milwaukee Parental Choice Program (MPCP) is the nation's longest-running and most far-reaching publicly funded voucher program. The program was created through an unusual political alliance between Annette "Polly" Williams, a Democratic state representative who championed African American causes, and Republican governor Tommy Thompson. Both politicians supported vouchers, but Thompson embraced a more expansive free-market approach than did Williams, who believed that vouchers could best be used to address the problems of public education in predominantly poor African American neighborhoods. Williams's version of vouchers was more politically palatable, and with Thompson's support, the MPCP was born.

   The intention of the MPCP is to test whether children from poor inner-city families derive an educational benefit when their parents are given public money to purchase a private education. The original program featured several important restrictions. It offered vouchers only to low-income families living in the city of Milwaukee, excluded the participation of religious schools, capped the amount of the voucher at about $2,400, limited the number of children who could be given a voucher, and disallowed students already in private schools. In addition, the participating private schools could not discriminate on the basis of race, religion, or gender, and they had to select their students on a random basis. Finally, they were expected to meet some very modest standards for school attendance, parental involvement, and student achievement (Witte, 2000).

Since its inception, the MPCP has expanded and changed in orientation. The biggest change is that sectarian schools are now allowed to participate in the program. The maximum voucher allowance has almost doubled to $4,660, and the number of student placements has expanded dramatically, from approximately 1,000 students in 1990 to almost 8,000 students as of January 2000. According to estimates, about two-thirds of these students are now served in religious schools. In addition, students in grades K–3 who were attending private schools at their family's expense now can participate in the MPCP.

An evaluation of the first five years of the MPCP by John Witte (2000) showed no achievement differences between voucher students and comparable Milwaukee public school students. Given this fact, Witte maintains that the MPCP is no miracle cure for poor inner-city youths. But he is not willing to assert that it has been a failure either, because the program has provided new options for inner-city parents dissatisfied with their neighborhood schools. These parents report increased satisfaction with their schools and no appreciable decrease in their children's achievement. However, the MPCP parents were better educated and more highly involved than parents in the comparison group, which led Witte to speculate that had they stayed in their public schools they could have become forces for change and improvement in those schools.

This represents another variation on the creaming problem associated with magnet schools. Opponents argue that vouchers undermine a functioning school community because dissatisfied parents are encouraged to walk away from their schools rather than work to improve them. Hirschman (1970) cites this phenomenon as an example of the economist's typical preference for exit over voice. That is, rather than seek improvements in their neighborhood schools, parents are instead persuaded to shop around for other options. As Raywid (1987) put it,

> To assign parents full and unfettered responsibility for choosing their children's education in an open market is to telegraph the message that the

matter is solely their affair and not the community's concern. . . . Thus, I fear that vouchers would bring in their wake a further downplaying of education in the public agenda and a further waning of public commitment to the enterprise. (p. 763)

But advocates of choice counter that there is no stronger voice than the consumer's voice, which speaks with the power of the purse. Thus, if neighborhood schools want to serve their communities, they need to do it well enough that neighborhood families will be willing to spend their vouchers with them.

For many opponents of vouchers, the MPCP is a high-stakes enterprise that sets a bad precedent for the use of public funds for nonpublic and arguably unconstitutional purposes. According to the People for the American Way, for instance, the MPCP is a classic bait-and-switch maneuver. This group argues that the effort to win support for vouchers on the premise that vouchers will assist low-income families is simply part of a long-term plan to institute a broad-ranging voucher program with no income cap. The fact that public funds are being funneled to religious schools participating in the MPCP makes the program even more problematic for the People for the American Way, but the legality of the involvement of religious schools in the MPCP has been upheld by the state supreme court of Wisconsin. The highly critical views of the People for the American Way can be accessed on its website, as detailed in Feature 14-6.

HOME SCHOOLING

Not all children receive their schooling in a school. Some are schooled at home, usually by their parents. The kind of education received by children in the home is largely up to the family. Some families enroll their children in a school on a part-time basis, so that they can take advantage of programs the family cannot provide, such as intramural sports, advanced mathematics, or science labs. Others tap their community or even other families for activities. But with home schooling, most educational activities take place in the home, under the direct guidance of a parent.

Today, all states have compulsory education laws that validate the home as a school. In almost all states, home teachers do not need to be certified, but in many states, families must file a curriculum plan with the state and subject their children to a testing program. All states require parents to

14-6 WEB POINTS

People for the American Way

People for the American Way is a forceful critic of education vouchers and the privatization of schooling. The group monitors the education voucher movement and has taken a particular interest in the Milwaukee Parental Choice Program (www.pfaw.org/issues/education/milwaukee.shtml). Examine its critique of the MPCP against the more tempered and disinterested scholarly examination offered by Witte (2000).

PEOPLE FOR THE AMERICAN WAY   We the People

| Home Page | Issues | News | Join Us | Activist Network | About PFAW |

Milwaukee Voucher Experiment:
Rolling the Dice for Children's Future

PRESS RELEASES

Milwaukee Religious Schools Flout State Voucher Law **May 6, 1999**

24 Schools Flout Wisconsin Law, Risk Expulsion From Voucher Program, DPI Warns **March 24, 1999**

Voucher Schools Violating Wisconsin Law on Student Admissions **February 2, 1999**

Milwaukee Stands Up for Public Schools: More than 1,000 attend workshops and rallies **December 8, 1998**

Action Plan for Stronger Public Schools and Tougher Voucher School Standards Unveiled for Milwaukee **December 8, 1998**

Supreme Court Sets Stage for More Confusion Over Vouchers **November 9, 1998**

Do vouchers work and are they good for children and communities? Voucher supporters tout school "choice" as the answer to problems plaguing public schools (especially for low income families). The facts tell a different story: a story of **unprotected constitutional and civil rights for children** in private schools, **lack of accountability** to parents and public officials, and **corruption, theft**, and **fiscal irresponsibility**.

■ **Hidden Costs:** Many parents in Milwaukee opted out of the voucher program when they found their $3,600 voucher did not cover "hidden costs" for high registration fees, books, uniforms and transportation. Annual studies of the program over five years have shown high attrition rates -- as high as 46% in the first year and 28% in the fifth year. 1

■ **The Real Beneficiaries:** Only one of every six voucher students actually left Milwaukee Public Schools (MPS). Of 6,000 students participating in the Milwaukee voucher plan, 4,550 already were attending private school and paying their own way, while another 450 were just entering kindergarten. Only 1,000 students in MPS decided to take advantage of a program that allegedly was designed for their benefit. 2

notify them of their intent to home school, and some states also have education and testing requirements for parents.

Home schooling gained popularity during the child-centered period of the late 1960s, when many parents were seeking more liberating and individualized educational experiences for their children. They were convinced

A parent home schools her children. Approximately 700,000 children were home schooled in 1995.

that the emotive climate of the home and family, and the attendant flexibility to pursue individual interests and desires, made the home an ideal place for the schooling of children. Today, however, the decision to home school is more complex. Anxieties over the safety and security of the school, and disappointment with the general academic quality of the schools, play a role. Many parents are convinced that they can do a better job of educating their children than the public schools. But their idea of what constitutes a good education is sometimes tied to a particular religious ideology. Many parents believe that the best education is one that sanctions family-based values, which often are entangled with religious views. The public school system is, of course, at odds with such a position, not because it opposes the family, but because its mission is to serve the widest public good and to provide an enriching educational experience that transcends parochial or family-based prejudices.

Home schooling is a steadily growing phenomenon. According to estimates, about 700,000 American children were home schooled in 1995, a considerable increase from the 10,000 or so children who were believed to have been home schooled during the late 1970s (Lines, 1999). Home school enrollment rates are difficult to gauge because many families fail to report the practice to the state and because many students drop out of home schooling and return to the public schools (Lines, 1999). Still, it is fair to say that the number of home schoolers is roughly equal to the number of charter schoolers, who together account for around 2 percent of the national student population. In fact, several "home schools/charter schools" have opened with the purpose of giving home-schooled children opportunities for group education and for general academic assistance or remedial education.

The research on home schools, like all choice programs, is controversial. The main problem is a sampling issue, because home schoolers represent a unique demographic. According to Rudner (1999), home-schooled children live mostly in white nuclear families, with higher parent education levels and considerably more wealth than the average American family. It is difficult to say if Rudner's study accurately captured the general characteristics of the home-schooling population. But whether it did or not, unless the home-schooled children are compared with public school children representing a similar demographic, the odds are that the home-schooled children (coming from dual-parent, high-income, and well-educated families), will perform better on measures of achievement. And, in fact, they do. Rudner's study showed that the home-schooled children scored well above the national average across all grade levels and all subject areas. As Rudner stated, "I'm not saying it's the home schooling that's doing a good job. Take the same kids, similar family characteristics, and the same amount of parent involvement into the public schools and the kids would probably do just as well" (quoted in Schnaiberg, 1999, p. 5). Still, his study is a clear affirmation that home-schooled children are academically capable and prepared.

Detractors of home schooling, however, are less concerned with achievement scores and more concerned with educational outcomes not typically measured by the schools. First, they claim that there is no substitute for the group socialization that occurs in the context of the public school. Removed from students unlike themselves, home-schooled children are less likely than their public school counterparts to benefit from an interaction with others with different viewpoints, lifestyles, and political and religious orientations. They are less likely to find face-to-face engagements across racial, economic, and ethnic lines. Some home schoolers, in fact, are openly offended by the climate of diversity found in the public school. Critics also question how parents can conceivably expect to properly manage the comprehensive academic curriculum, especially when they typically have no training or experience in academic instruction or in the subject matter they are expected to teach. Finally, there is the problem of resources and the absence of the kind of equipment that might be needed to properly teach science, music, art, computer literacy, vocational education, and even physical education.

SUMMARY

Schooling is no longer a neighborhood affair. Close to one-quarter of all children go to either private schools or public chosen schools. School districts are increasingly seeking ways to attend to the new regard for choice and have opened up options to parents both within and outside of district boundaries. Charter schools, which are publicly funded schools offering variety and innovation, represent the newest arrival on the school choice scene. Because they are allowed to operate without district or state entanglements, they have created new business opportunities for profit-seeking educational corporations interested in competing with the public schools for government funds. Charter schools have been criticized for their uneven quality and their attention to narrow familial interests rather than to broad public ones.

Other by-products of the choice movement include magnet schools, especially in urban school districts. Magnet schools, which originally were created to help desegregate the schools, now also exist for the purpose of offering an educational alternative to parents. Although they have undoubtedly helped desegregate urban school districts, magnet schools also are accused of contributing to the deterioration of neighborhood schools. The presence of the magnet schools has had the effect of siphoning away good students, who come from families supportive of education, from the neighborhood schools. Many parents support the idea of school choice, but most also admit to not fully understanding the issue. The idea of choice is appealing to most parents, who cannot find themselves arguing against an opportunity to select a school that they believe is in the best interests of their children's education.

This is the basic rationale behind the drive to privatize schooling. The intention is to create a marketplace of school alternatives from which parents can select a school—public or private, religious or nonsectarian. Such choices would be empowered through a publicly funded voucher system. Supporters believe that in a free-market context schools will necessarily improve because otherwise they will be forced to close down. Detractors believe that under such a system the public school ideal will be lost and that a proliferation of alternative schools with alternative visions will lead to disastrous schisms in the society. The Milwaukee Parental Choice Program (MPCP) is the nation's most visible experiment with school vouchers. Although it is limited to low-income families and has a few other notable restrictions, it has become the main battleground for pro- and antivoucher forces. The data on achievement indicate that students participating in the MPCP do no worse—or no better, if you prefer—than their nonvoucher counterparts.

Finally, the phenomenon of home schooling has grown dramatically in recent decades. States have acknowledged the legality of home schooling but have placed various restrictions on its operation.

QUESTIONS AND ACTIVITIES

1. As one parent stated, "My experience of growing up and going to a neighborhood school was as you walked, you picked up the whole neighborhood. . . . Once you start busing and everybody is going all over the place, you don't have a community anymore. You don't have the parents going together to the PTA meetings, sports, extracurricular activities" (Smrekar and Goldring, 1999, p. 74). What is your reaction to this parent?

2. Ask your friends, classmates, and colleagues about their experiences in neighborhood schools. What seem to be the unique characteristics of neighborhood schools?

3. What is the difference between a magnet school and a charter school?

4. Interdistrict choice programs typically have a few restrictions attached to them. What are they, and why do you think they exist?

5. Explore the charter schools that have opened in your state or a state near you. Analyze them in terms of your conception of appropriate education for participation in a democracy.

6. How can someone support both school choice and the national standards? How do you reconcile these two concepts?

7. What is the main contradiction between arguing for the importance of a common curriculum and supporting school choice?

8. What do you think is the future of the charter school movement in American education?

9. What is your opinion of the involvement of for-profit corporations in the charter school movement? Do you accept the argument against a for-profit mentality in the schools?

10. Explain the problem of creaming and its association with magnet schools.

11. Explain how a school voucher system might work.

12. What are the basic arguments supporting school vouchers?

13. What are the basic arguments against school vouchers?

14. Do you agree with those who believe that free-market conditions will improve the operation of public schools? Why or why not?

15. How would you respond to someone who says, "It is a free society. If we are free to choose our own doctors and plumbers, we should also be free to choose our own child's school"?

16. Despite media reports about widespread dissatisfaction with the public schools, the majority of parents with children in public school express satisfaction with the education that their children receive. In one poll, 66 percent of public school parents gave the public school that their oldest child attended a grade of A or B (Rose and Gallup, 1999). Public confidence in the public schools, especially relative to the confidence expressed in other public institutions, could also be viewed quite positively. In the same poll, 42 percent of the respondents reported that they had either "a great deal or quite a lot" of confidence in secondary and elementary public schools. This is higher than the amount of confidence expressed in the media, health organizations, political organizations, local and state governments, and the federal government. How would you interpret these findings?

17. Raywid (1987) observed that a voucher plan "is a plan for financing schools, not improving them" (p. 764). What does she mean by this? Do you agree or disagree with her?

18. Schools in the marketplace are interested in one thing—capturing consumers. Schools for the athletically gifted, schools stressing a particular ethnic or cultural tradition, premedical elementary schools, Great Books schools, foreign language immersion schools, technology schools, back-to-basics schools, open education schools, quasi-military schools, schools run by fast-food industries, and schools stressing the virtues of capitalism—all could emerge in such an arrangement. Parents would have more choice, and the interests of educational variety would be served, but are the interests of society advanced under such an arrangement?

19. Do you think the MPCP should be continued or closed down?

20. What are your feelings about home schooling? Should parents who home school their children be closely monitored by the state? Under what circumstances, if any, might you consider home schooling your own children?

REFERENCES

Bennett, W. (1992). *The de-valuing of America.* (New York: Summit).

Bierlien, L., and Molholland, L. A. (1994). *Comparing charter school laws: The issue of autonomy.* (Tempe, AZ: Morrison Institute of Public Policy).

Carnegie Foundation for the Advancement of Teaching. (1992). *School choice: A special report.* (Princeton, NJ: Carnegie Foundation for the Advancement of Teaching).

Charter schools and race. (2000). *Education Week* (10 May).

Chubb, J. (1998). The performance of privately managed schools: An early look at the Edison Project. In P. E. Peterson and B. C. Hassel (eds.), *Learning from school choice.* (Washington, DC: Brookings Institution Press).

Coon, J. E., and Sugarman, S. D. (1978). *Education by choice.* (Berkeley: University of California Press).

Darling-Hammond, L. (1992). For-profit schooling: Where is the public good? *Education Week* (7 Oct.).

Engel, M. (2000). *The struggle for control of public education: Market ideology vs. democratic values.* (Philadelphia: Temple University Press).

Friedman, M. (1962). *Capitalism and freedom.* (Chicago: University of Chicago Press).

Hirschman, A. O. (1970). *Exit, voice and loyalty.* (Cambridge, MA: Harvard University Press).

Lines, P. M. (1999). *Homeschoolers: Estimating numbers and growth.* Office of Educational Research and Improvement Paper. (Washington, DC: U.S. Department of Education).

Moore, D., and Davenport, S. (1989). *The new improved sorting machine.* (Chicago: Designs for Change).

National Center for Education Statistics. (2000a). *The state of charter schools 2000: Fourth-year report.* (Washington, DC: U.S. Department of Education).

National Center for Education Statistics. (2000b). *The condition of education.* (Washington, DC: U.S. Department of Education).

National Center for Education Statistics. (1999). *The state of charter schools 1999: Third-year report.* (Washington, DC: U.S. Department of Education).

National Center for Education Statistics. (1996). *Public school choice programs, 1993–94: Availability and student population,* Issue Brief IB-9-96. (Washington, DC: U.S. Department of Education).

National Center for Education Statistics. (1995). *Use of school choice.* (Washington, DC: U.S. Department of Education).

Public Agenda. (1999). *On thin ice: How advocates and opponents could misread the public's views on vouchers and charter schools.* (New York: Public Agenda).

Raywid, M. A. (1987). Public choice, yes; vouchers, no! *Phi Delta Kappan,* 68(100):762–69.

Rose, L. C., and Gallup, A. M. (1999). The 31st annual PDK Gallup poll. *Phi Delta Kappan,* 81(1):41–56.

Rudner, L. M. (1999). Scholastic achievement and demographic characteristics of home school students in 1998. *Education Policy Analysis Archives,* 7(8).

Schnaiberg, L. (1999). Study finds home schoolers are top achievers on tests. *Education Week* (31 March).

Smrekar, C., and Goldring, E. (1999). *School choice in urban America: Magnet schools and the pursuit of equity.* (New York: Teachers College Press).

Sykes, G., Arsen, D., and Plank, D. (2000). School choice and school change. *Education Week* (9 Feb.).

Tyack, D. B. (1993). School governance in the United States: Historical puzzles and anomalies. In J. Hannaway and M. Carnoy (eds.), *Decentralization and school improvement.* (San Francisco: Jossey-Bass).

Walsh, M. (1999). Report card on for-profit industry still incomplete. *Education Week* (15 Dec.).

Wells, A. S. (1998). *Charter school reform in California: Does it meet expectations?* (Los Angeles: UCLA Charter School Study).

Wise, A. E., and Darling-Hammond, L. (1984). Education by voucher: Private choice and the public interest. *Educational Theory,* 24(1):29–53.

Witte, J. (2000). *The market approach to education: An analysis of America's first voucher program.* (Princeton, NJ: Princeton University Press).

INDEX

Ability grouping, 397–398
    See also Curriculum tracking
Abington v. Schempp (1963),
    373–374, 390
Abolitionist societies, 195–196,
    198
Academics
    freedom of teachers in,
        147–152
    goals related to, 16–17
    national assessment of,
        450–466
    promoting excellence in,
        541–551
    teaching for growth in,
        30–34, 35
Academies, 208–210
Accommodationist approach,
    300–304
Achievement, 447–450
Activity analysis, 322–325, 326
Adams, John, 196
Addams, Jane, 306, 309–312,
    493–494
Additive approach, 505
Adler, Mortimer, 20, 98
Adult literacy, 11
African Americans. *See* Blacks
Agostini v. Felton (1997), 384, 391
Aguilar v. Felton (1985), 383–384,
    391
Alcohol use, 484
Aldridge, Ira, 197
*Alexander v. Holmes County Board of
    Education* (1969), 412, 420
America 2000 report, 5, 544–545
American Association of Univer-
    sity Women (AAUW),
    425–426, 436
American Civil Liberties Union
    (ACLU), 436
American Federation of Labor
    (AFL), 238
American Federation of Teachers
    (AFT), 238–240
American High School Today, The
    (Conant), 534
American-style academy,
    208–210
Aptitude, 448

Armstrong, Samuel, 302
Assimilation process, 494, 513,
    520–521

Back to basics movement
    in the 1950s, 530–535
    in the 1970s, 539–541
Bagley, William, 101
Banking education, 510–511
Banneker, Benjamin, 196, 197
Batte, Susan, 386
Baumfree, Isabella, 197
Behavior Home Page, 81
Behaviorism, 82–84
Bennett, William, 100, 102, 573
Bernard, Henry, 232
Bestor, Arthur, 530–531
Bethel School District v. Fraser
    (1986), 152–153, 155,
    156
Bilingual education, 512–522
    legal and political history of,
        512–516
    public opinion on, 513, 515
    resistance to, 520–522
    resources on, 514
    types of, 516–520
Binet, Alfred, 327
Black, Hugo, 373, 375
Blacks
    achievement scores of, 453,
        458, 461, 464
    colonial education of,
        186–187, 189, 191,
        194–199
    desegregation of public
        schools and, 407–423,
        424, 425, 426
    post-Industrial Revolution
        oppression of, 199–201
    school dropout rates among,
        468–469
    struggle for schooling by,
        300–306
Bloom, Benjamin, 68
Blow, Susan, 277–278, 280, 281,
    282
*Board of Education of Oklahoma
    City v. Dowell* (1991), 417,
    418, 421

Board of Education v. Allen (1968),
    383, 390
Bobbitt, John Franklin,
    322–325, 326
Bode, Boyd, 113–114, 285, 325
Book of Virtues (Bennett), 100
Boydston, Jo Ann, 293
Brown, Linda, 409, 411
Brown v. Board of Education
    (1954), 407, 409, 410, 420
Brown II (1955), 409, 411, 420
Bruner, Jerome, 533
Bryan, William Jennings, 149
Burger, Warren, 361, 368

Cardinal Principles report
    (1918), 312–314, 316
Career-vocational education, 17
Carnegie, Andrew, 304
Carter, James, 221, 228
Censorship, 139–140, 150
Center for Dewey Studies, 294
Center for Research on Educa-
    tion, Diversity and Excel-
    lence (CREDE), 522
Charter schools, 561–563, 564,
    566–567
Child-centeredness, 111–114,
    256–285
    American educational ver-
        sions of, 267–283
    doctrine of original goodness
        and, 256–257
    European notion of, 257–267
    kindergartens and, 264,
        276–283
    progressivist criticism of,
        283–285
    school reform issues and, 554
Child study movement, 273–276
Citizenship, 15, 19
Civics, common knowledge of,
    497, 501
Civil Rights Act (1964), 413,
    516
Classrooms
    discipline and control in,
        79–87
    ethical obligation of teachers
        in, 136–142

Classrooms *(continued)*
　gender-segregated, 434–435
　kindergarten, 278–283
　self-contained, 340
　situational dynamics in,
　　60–61
　teacher effectiveness in,
　　73–76
Clinton, Bill, 366, 544
Clothing and dress codes,
　156–157, 158–161
Coercion test, 368–369
Cold War, 531, 532
Coleman report, 412–413
Colonial American schools,
　178–203
　education of blacks and,
　　186–187, 189, 191,
　　194–199
　New England colonies and,
　　178–187
　Virginia and the middle
　　colonies and, 187–191
Commission on the Reorganiza-
　tion of Secondary Educa-
　tion, 313
Committee of Fifteen report
　(1895), 252–253, 262
Committee of Ten report
　(1893), 100, 103,
　251–256, 274–275
Committee v. Nyquist (1973), 385,
　390
Commonality
　cultural diversity and,
　　492–495
　sources of, 495–502
Competency-based strategies,
　540
Comprehensive high school,
　17–22, 313–316
Computer usage, 474, 475, 476
Conant, James B., 18, 534
Concentrations, 261
Conduct of teachers, 133–142,
　143
　classroom issues and,
　　136–142
　personal issues and, 133–136
Conservative tradition of educa-
　tion, 95–105
　essentialism and, 100–105
　perennialism and, 95–100
Core Knowledge Foundation,
　105, 106
Corporal punishment, 84, 85
Correlations, 261
Cotton, John, 185
Counts, George, 18, 115–117,
　125, 316–319, 329

Court cases. *See* Legal issues;
　Supreme Court
Creationism, teaching of,
　380–383
Cremin, Lawrence, 178
Criminal offenses, 134–135
Crisis in the Classroom (Silber-
　man), 536
Critical theory, 118, 507–511
Cultural epochs theory, 262, 276
Cultural issues
　bilingual education, 512–522
　critical theory and, 507–511
　diversity and commonality,
　　492–495
　multicultural education,
　　502–507
　sources of a common culture,
　　495–502
Cultural Literacy (Hirsch),
　104–105, 123
Culture of schooling, 495–511
Curriculum
　academic growth and, 30–34,
　　35
　achievement standards and,
　　449–450
　Cardinal Principles report
　　and, 312–314
　Committee of Ten report and,
　　251–256
　correlations and concentra-
　　tions in, 261
　freedom of teachers in using,
　　147–151
　hidden, 120
　individualizing of, 275
　individual-personal growth
　　and, 22–26
　instructional judgments
　　about, 71–73
　national standards for,
　　543–551
　perennialist perspective on,
　　100, 102–103
　reading material in, 98–100,
　　120, 121, 507–508
　religious issues included in,
　　365
　school reform and, 530–555
　social efficiency and, 322–325
　socio-civic growth and, 26–30
　specificity in, 326–327
　vocational growth and,
　　34–37, 38
Curriculum tracking, 397–407
　alternatives to, 407
　defining, 397–400
　inequities in, 401–406
　reasons for using, 400–401

responses to criticisms of,
　406–407
student responses to,
　402–403

Dame schools, 181–182
Darrow, Clarence, 149
*Davis v. Monroe County Board of
　Education*, 437
Decision making
　factors in professional process
　　of, 66–73
　postmodern education and,
　　121–122
DeGarmo, Charles, 263
DeLaney, Martin, 197
Democracy
　antidemocratic attitudes and,
　　29
　essentialism and, 101–104
　learning theory and, 69
Demographics of teachers,
　46–50
Dennison, George, 536
Department of Education, U.S.,
　347, 450, 518, 544
Desegregation of public schools,
　407–423
　demographic data on, 423,
　　424, 425
　effects of, 419–423
　legal and legislative influences
　　on, 408–419
　public opinion on, 426
　Supreme Court cases on,
　　420–421
Developmental processes, 67–68
Dewey, Evelyn, 309
Dewey, Jane, 312
Dewey, John, 4, 38, 44, 60, 88,
　130, 280, 309, 495
　criticism of child-
　　centeredness, 283–285
　experimentalism and,
　　107–110, 295
　laboratory school of, 262,
　　296–297
　on motivation of students, 80,
　　82
　objections to IQ tests, 328
　progressivism and, 292–297,
　　299, 306
　social reform issues and, 306,
　　312
Discipline
　classroom control and,
　　79–87
　doctrine of mental discipline,
　　33, 69, 98, 101,
　　248–251

early American public schools
and, 224
educational goals related to,
11
structure of discipline doctrine, 533
Dismissal of teachers
classroom issues and,
136–142
common reasons for, 164–165
personal issues and, 133–136
teacher tenure and, 167
Disuniting of America, The
(Schlesinger), 503
Doctrine of mental discipline,
33, 69, 98, 101, 248–251,
325–326
Doctrine of original goodness,
256–257
Dress codes, 156–157, 158–161
Dropouts, 466–479
demographic data on,
468–470
procedures used for determining, 467–468
reasons for leaving school,
471–473
school achievement factors
and, 473–479
Drug use, 484
Du Bois, W. E. B., 302,
304–306, 307, 328
Due process rights, 163
Durham, James, 196
Duty of care, 143–145
Dynamic Sociology (Ward), 298

Eagle Forum, 236
Economic factors. *See* Socioeconomic factors
Economic Opportunity Act
(1964), 413
Edison Schools, 564–565
Education
bilingual, 512–522
child-centeredness in,
256–285
in colonial America, 178–203
conservative tradition of,
95–105
contemporary history of
reforms in, 530–555
critical theory and, 507–511
ethical issues in, 130–173
funding of, 348–360,
362–363, 364
ladder system of, 225,
336–337, 338
liberal arts curriculum in,
248–256

multicultural, 502–507
national assessment of
progress in, 450–466
professional decision making
in, 66–73
progressive tradition of, 105,
107–115
public opinion on values
related to, 96–97
radical tradition of, 115–122
separation of church and state
in, 360–361, 364–387,
390–391
social efficiency tradition and,
319–328
socioeconomic context for,
62–63
standardized testing and,
76–79
Supreme Court cases on religion and, 390–391
teacher, 226–231
See also Instructional methods;
Public schools; Teachers
Educational Testing Service
(ETS), 52, 429
Edwards v. Aguillard (1987), 382,
391
Effectiveness of teachers,
73–76
Efficiency. *See* Social efficiency
Eisenhower National Clearinghouse, 548
Elementary schools, 339–340
Elementary and Secondary Act
(1965), 347, 413–414
Eliot, Charles, 251, 252
Employment
of teachers, 157, 160–161,
163–165
of women with children,
478–479
Enculturation, 16
Engel v. Vitale (1962), 373, 375,
390
English-as-a-second language
(ESL), 517–519
Environmentalism, 298–299
Epperson v. Arkansas (1968), 380,
390
Essentialism, 100–105, 107
Establishment Clause issues,
361, 367–370, 374, 375,
376–377, 378–379,
381–382
Ethical issues, 130–142, 143
classroom conduct, 136–142
NEA code of ethics, 130,
131–132
personal conduct, 133–136

Ethnicity. *See* Race/ethnicity
European educational pioneers,
257–267
Everson v. Board of Education
(1947), 360–361, 390
Evolution, theory of, 380–383
Experimentalism, 107–110
conceptual features of, 110
pragmatism and, 109–110
scientific method and,
108–109, 295

Family issues
educational involvement of
parents, 477–479
poverty status and, 473–476,
477
reading skills and, 458–460
single-parent households,
476–477, 478
Federal government
funding of schools by, 348,
350–351, 360
governance of schools by,
347–348
Finkelman, Paul, 369, 373, 374,
376
Finney, Ross, 327
First Amendment rights,
146–157, 162
academic freedom of teachers
and, 147–151
personal views of teachers
and, 151–152
prayer in public schools and,
373
symbolic expression of students and, 156–157,
158–161
verbal expression of students
and, 152–155
written expression of students
and, 155–156
Flat-grant programs, 355–356
For-profit educational corporations, 563–565
Foundation programs, 356
Franklin, Benjamin, 196, 198,
208–209
Freedmen Bureau, 300
Freedom-of-choice plan,
411–412
Freedom of expression,
146–157, 158–161, 162
Free Exercise Clause issues, 361,
369, 370–373, 376–377,
380
Freire, Paulo, 510–511
Friedenberg, Edgar, 536
Friedman, Milton, 569–570

Froebel, Friedrich, 263–265,
    276–283
Funding
    of public education, 348–360,
        362–363, 364
    of religious schools, 383–387

Gallaudet, Thomas, 228
Gangs, 157
Gardner, Howard, 68
*Gebser v. Lago Vista Independent
    School District* (1998),
    437–438
Gender issues, 423–438
    academic bias and, 424–432
    colonial American schools
        and, 182, 183, 188–189
    early teacher education and,
        229–230
    earnings trends and, 433
    higher education trends and,
        432–433
    math achievement and, 461,
        464, 465
    postsecondary degrees and,
        432–433
    reading achievement and,
        453, 459
    school dropout rates and, 468
    segregated classrooms and,
        434–435, 436
    sex-based stereotypes and,
        433–434
    sexual harassment problems
        and, 435–438
    teacher demographics and, 46
General educational develop-
    ment (GED) certificate,
    467
Generative-creative level of pro-
    fessionalism, 65–66
Geortz, Clifford, 495
Goals for American schools,
    5–17, 544–545
Goodman, Paul, 536, 537
Governance of schools
    federal government and,
        347–348
    local school districts and,
        343–346
    states and, 341–343, 344–345
Grade-level orientation,
    336–337, 338
Grand Rapids v. Ball (1985), 384,
    391
Great Books curriculum,
    98–100, 120, 121
*Green v. County School Board of New
    Kent, Virginia* (1968), 412,
    419, 420

Haley, Margaret, 239
Hall, G. Stanley, 273–276, 281,
    293, 298
Hamilton, Alexander, 196
Hammack, Floyd, 21
Harlan, John, 408–409, 410
Harrington, Michael, 475
Harris, William Torrey, 100, 253,
    261–262, 274, 277, 278,
    296, 302
Harvard College, 179, 183, 187
Hazelwood v. Kuhlmeier (1988),
    150, 155, 156, 157
Head Start program, 413
Henry Ford Museum, 188
Hentoff, Nat, 537
Herbart, Johann, 259–263
Hidden curriculum, 120
Hierarchy of needs, 68–69, 483,
    485
High schools
    Cardinal Principles report on,
        312–314, 316
    comprehensive, 17–22,
        313–316
    curriculum tracking in,
        399–400
    dropout factors for, 466–473
    early American origins of,
        224–226
    goals for learning in, 22–37
    specialized, 341
Hill, Patty Smith, 281, 282–283
Hirsch, E. D., 104–105, 106, 123
Hispanics
    achievement scores of, 459,
        464
    desegregation of public
        schools and, 419, 422,
        423
    school dropout rates among,
        468–470
History
    common knowledge of, 496
    NAEP assessment on, 497,
        498–500
    national standards in,
        552–553
Holidays, religious, 377–380,
    381
Holt, John, 536
Home schooling, 576–579
Homosexuality, 135, 137–138
Hornbook, 185
Howe, Harold, 405–406
Hull House, 309–312
Humanizing movement,
    535–539
Hunter instructional model,
    75–76

Hutchins, Robert, 33

Illich, Ivan, 536
Imitative-maintenance level of
    professionalism, 63–64
Incompetence, 164
Individual-personal growth,
    14–15, 22–26
Induction programs, 55
Industrial Revolution
    development of public schools
        and, 219–220
    education of blacks prior to,
        194–196, 199
    national consciousness and,
        217–219
    oppression of blacks follow-
        ing, 199–201
Inequality (Jencks), 540
Infant schools, 217, 270
Injuries to students, 142–146,
    147, 148
Inquiry, method of, 295–296
In-service training programs, 56,
    75
Institute for Social Research, 484
Instructional methods
    academic growth and, 30–34,
        35
    Herbartian, 262–263
    individual-personal growth
        and, 22–26
    innovation brought to, 60
    Lancaster method, 216
    Montessorian, 265–267
    object lessons, 258–259,
        272–273, 307
    Quincy methods, 306–309,
        310–311
    socio-civic growth and, 26–30
    vocational growth and,
        34–37, 38
    See also Education
Integration of schools. *See*
    Desegregation of public
    schools
Intelligence
    influence of academic subjects
        on, 325–326
    measurement of, 327–328
Interpretation of Cultures, The
    (Geortz), 495
Intrinsic motivation, 82
IQ (intelligence quotient),
    327–328, 448

Jackson v. Benson (1998), 385,
    386
James Madison High School report
    (1987), 100, 102

Jefferson, Thomas, 4, 199, 214, 361, 365
Jencks, Christopher, 540
Job satisfaction issues, 58–59, 63
Johnson, Lyndon, 413
Jones, Margaret E. M., 271

Keefe v. Geanakos (1969), 141
Kennedy, William, 369
Kilpatrick, William, 280
Kindergarten, 276–283
    advocates and rationales for, 276–278
    criticisms of early methods in, 280–281
    early classroom methods in, 278–280
    emerging teaching methods for, 281–283
    mother's education level and, 284
    origins of, 264
King, Martin Luther, Jr., 414, 415
Knowledge-based standard, 550
Kohl, Herbert, 536
Kozol, Jonathan, 536

*Laboratory school, 296–297
Ladder system of education, 225, 336–337, 338
Lancaster method, 216
Language
    bilingual education and, 512–522
    classroom function of, 511–512
    cultural commonality and, 496
Latin grammar schools, 182–184
Lau v. Nichols (1974), 515, 519
Learner-centered reform, 554
Learning
    Dewey's three factors in, 294–295
    instructional judgments about, 66–69, 70
    theories of, 69
Lee v. Weisman (1992), 376, 391
Legal Information Institute (LII), 171
Legal issues
    bilingual education and, 513–516
    desegregation of public schools and, 408–419, 420–421
    due process rights and, 163–165

freedom of expression and, 146–157, 158–161
liability of teachers and, 142–146, 147, 148
professional ethics and, 133–142
search-and-seizure requirement and, 165, 167–170
separation of church and state, 360–361, 364–387, 390–391
website of school-related decisions, 171
Lemon test, 368–369, 384, 386
Lemon v. Kurtzman (1971), 367–368, 390
Liability of teachers, 142–146, 147, 148
Liberal arts, 248–256
Limited-English-proficiency (LEP) students, 48, 513, 515
Literacy, 11, 52, 54
    See also Reading skills
Local school districts
    desegregation of schools and, 412, 414–416
    governance of schools by, 192–193, 343–346
    public school funding and, 348–359, 362–363
Lotteries, state, 356

*Maclure, William, 267–270, 271
Madaus, George, 88
Magnet schools, 414, 565–568
Mann, Horace, 4, 221–224, 226–231, 232, 241, 258, 336
Marshall, Thurgood, 353, 416, 417, 418
Maslow, Abraham, 68, 483, 485
Massachusetts Bay Colony, 178–181
Mathematics
    achievement data for, 10, 461, 464, 465
    national assessment of, 460–465
    subject-centered focus on, 532–535
McLaren, Peter, 126
McLean v. Arkansas Board of Education (1982), 381
McMurry, Charles, 261, 263
Mead, George Herbert, 294
Mediative level of professionalism, 64–65
"Melting pot" metaphor, 497, 500, 501, 520–521

Mencken, H. L., 149
Mentoring, 55
Middle schools
    curriculum issues in, 340–341, 398–399
    origins and development of, 337, 339
Milliken v. Bradley (1974), 416, 417, 421
Milliken II (1977), 416–417, 421
Milwaukee Parental Choice Program (MPCP), 385, 574–576
Minority students
    achievement scores of, 453, 458, 459, 461, 464
    colonial education of, 186–187, 189–190, 191, 194–199
    desegregation of public schools and, 407–423, 424, 425, 426
    historical struggle for schooling by, 300–306
    poverty status of, 473–474
    public education expenditures and, 362–363
    school dropout rates among, 468–470
    See also Race/ethnicity
Missouri v. Jenkins (1995), 417, 421
Montessori, Maria, 265–267
Morality, 16, 133–142
    See also Ethical issues
Morrill Act (1862), 347
Motivation, 80, 82
Mozert v. Hawkins County (1988), 371–373
Multicultural education, 502–507
Multiperspectives approach, 505
Multiple intelligences, 68

*National Assessment of Educational Progress (NAEP), 105, 347, 450–465, 466
    civics assessment, 497, 501
    history/literary assessment, 497, 498–500
    mathematics assessment, 460–465
    reading assessment, 451–460
National Association for the Advancement of Colored People (NAACP), 306
National Association of State Boards of Education (NASBE), 344

National Center for Education Statistics (NCES), 6, 51, 53, 284, 364, 450, 466, 563, 571
National Commission on Excellence in Education (NCEE), 532, 541–542
National Defense Education Act (1958), 347, 533
National Education Association (NEA), 100, 232–238
  code of ethics, 130, 131–132
  early gender bias in, 233, 239
  relationship of AFT and, 239–240
National Education Goals Panel (NEGP), 8, 12
National Organization for Women (NOW), 436
National Science Foundation (NSF), 532–533
National standards
  criticisms of, 548–551
  development of, 543–548
  examples of, 550
  history standards debate and, 552–553
  state-by-state data on, 546–547
National Teachers Association (NTA), 232–233
Nation at Risk report (1983), 532, 541–543
Native Americans, 186–187, 189–190
Neef, Joseph, 267–270, 271
Negligence, 142–146, 147, 148
New England
  colonial education in, 178–187
  origins of public education in, 214, 221–224
New England Primer, 185–186, 219
New Harmony commune, 269–270, 271
New Jersey v. TLO (1985), 167–168
Newspapers, school-sponsored, 155–156
Normal schools, 228–231, 267, 268–269

Oakes, Jennie, 401
Object lessons, 258–259, 272–273, 307
O'Connor, Sandra Day, 369, 384
Office of Educational Research and Improvement, 347
Omission training, 85–86

Open education, 537–539
Open enrollment system, 411
Opportunity to learn (OTL), 449–450, 497
Oppositional thought, 119
Orfield, Jerry, 419
Oswego Normal School, 271–272
Other America, The (Harrington), 475
Owens, Robert, 217, 256, 269–270, 271

Parducci v. Rutland (1970), 150
Parents, school involvement by, 477–479
  See also Family issues
Parker, Francis, 306–309, 310
Parochial schools, 383–387
Pavlov, Ivan, 83
Peabody, Elizabeth, 276–277
Pedagogic strategies, 67
People for the American Way, 576, 577
Percentage Equalization Program (PEP), 357
Perennialism, 95–100, 104
Permanent studies, 96–98
Pestalozzi, Joseph, 249, 256, 257–259
  Americanization of ideas of, 267–273
Philosophies of teaching, 94–126
  conservative, 95–105
  hypothetical debate on, 124–125
  progressive, 105–115
  public opinion and, 96–97
  radical, 115–122
Piaget, Jean, 68
Pickering v. Board of Education (1968), 151–152
Plato, 4, 396
Plessy v. Ferguson (1896), 300, 407, 408, 410, 420
Political views of teachers
  classroom ethics related to, 137, 152
  demographics on, 49–50
  freedom of expression and, 151–152
Positive reinforcement, 86
Postmodernism, 118–122
Postsecondary degrees, 432–433
Poverty
  school achievement and, 456, 459, 461, 464, 473, 476–477
  segregation issues and, 422
  See also Socioeconomic factors

Pragmatism, 109–110, 293–294
Prayer in public schools, 373–377
  See also Religion
Pregnancy, of unwed teachers, 135–136
Private schools
  state aid to, 383–387
  voucher programs and, 385–386, 569–576
Process of Education, The (Bruner), 533
Profanity, 139–140, 141
Professionalism
  criteria for evaluating, 51
  decision-making process and, 66–73
  levels for teachers, 61–66
Progressive tradition of education, 105, 107–115, 292–319
  black struggle for schooling and, 300–306
  Cardinal Principles report and, 312–314, 316
  criticism of child-centeredness by, 283–285
  environmentalism and, 298–299
  experimentalism and, 107–110
  Quincy methods and, 306–309, 310–311
  romantic naturalism and, 110–115
  settlement house movement and, 309–312
  social reform and, 292–299, 316–319
Property taxes, 220, 349
Public opinion
  on bilingual education, 513, 515
  on good schooling, 96–97
  on multicultural education, 506–507
  on school choice, 572
  on school desegregation, 426
Public schools
  curriculum tracking in, 397–407
  desegregation of, 407–423, 426
  dress codes in, 156–157, 158–161
  dropout factors for, 466–473
  early American development of, 212–221, 242
  equity issues related to, 396–439

evolution of local governance for, 192–193
freedom of expression in, 146–157, 158–161
funding of, 348–360, 362–363, 364
gender issues and, 423–438
governance of, 341–348
grade-level organization of, 336–339
Industrial Revolution and, 219–220
kindergartens and, 276–283
national goals for, 5–17
nineteenth-century development of, 215–224
prayer in, 373–377
punishment in, 84–85
religion and, 223, 360–361, 364–387
safety and discipline in, 11, 62, 479–485
school choice programs for, 560–568
search-and-seizure issues in, 165, 167–170
self-contained system in, 340
separation of church and state in, 360–361, 364–387, 390–391
sexual harassment in, 435–438
socioeconomic context of, 62
taxes imposed for, 220–221
teaching of creationism in, 380–383
violence in, 59
See also Education; Schools
Punishment
classroom control and, 84–85
in colonial American schools, 184–185
Puritans, 178–187

Quakers, 190, 195–196, 202
Quantitative reasoning, 71
Quincy methods, 306–309, 310–311

Race/ethnicity
charter schools and, 564
curriculum tracking and, 404–405, 406
teacher demographics and, 46–48, 49
See also Minority students
Radical tradition of education, 115–122
postmodernism and, 118–122

school reform in the 1960s and, 536–537
social reconstructionism and, 115–118
Reading skills
achievement levels for, 454–455
economic factors in, 456, 459
gender differences in, 453, 459
home environment and, 458–460
national assessment of, 451–460
racial factors in, 453, 458, 459
state-by-state data on, 456–457
Reagan, Ronald, 541, 542
Reform movements. See School reform
Region 20 Education Service Center, 548, 549
Rehnquist, William, 369
Religion
classroom ethics related to, 136–137
colonial American schools and, 178, 179–181, 185–186
creationism debate and, 380–383
educational guidelines on, 366–367
free exercise rights and, 370–373
holidays and symbols of, 377–380, 381
public schools and, 223, 360–361, 364–387
school prayer and, 373–377
student attire reflective of, 156
Supreme Court cases on education and, 390–391
teacher demographics and, 50
Religious schools, 383–387
Rice, Joseph, 326
Rickover, Hyman, 530–531, 532
Rippa, Alexander, 186
Rodriguez v. the San Antonio Independent School District (1973), 349–353
Romantic idealism, 263–265, 278
Romantic naturalism, 110–115
conceptual features of, 115
historical context for, 113
school reform in the 1960s and, 536–537

Rousseau, Jean-Jacques, 111, 256–257
Rugg, Harold, 309

Sadker, Myra and David, 425
Safety issues, 11, 62, 479–485
zero-tolerance policies and, 480–481
"Salad bowl" metaphor, 500, 502, 521
Salaries
for teachers, 51–52, 53
for women vs. men, 433
Schlafly, Phyllis, 236–237, 552
Schlesinger, Arthur, 503–504
School choice, 560–581
charter schools and, 561–563, 564, 566–567
for-profit educational corporations and, 563–565
home schooling and, 576–579
intradistrict/interdistrict options in, 561
magnet schools and, 565–568
national standards and, 543–544
privatization and, 568–569
public opinion on, 572
voucher programs and, 569–576
School reform, 530–555
in the 1950s, 530–535
in the 1960s, 535–539
in the 1970s, 539–541
in the 1980s, 541–543
in the 1990s, 543–551
Schools
academies, 208–210
charter, 561–563, 564, 566–567
colonial American, 178–203
comprehensive, 17–22, 313–316
dame, 181–182
infant, 217
laboratory, 296–297
magnet, 414, 565–568
religious, 383–387
single-sex, 436
See also Education; Public schools
Schools of Tomorrow (Dewey and Dewey), 309
Schurz, Mary, 276
Science
achievement data for, 10
subject-centered focus on, 532–535
Science, Technology and Society (STS) movement, 32, 34

Scientific management, 320–322
Scientific method, 108–109, 295
Scopes monkey trial (1925),
    149, 380
Search-and-seizure issues, 165,
    167–170
Secondary schools. *See* High
    schools
Segregation
    gender, 434–435, 436
    poverty and, 422
    "separate but equal" doctrine
        and, 408–409, 410
    state-by-state demographics
        on, 424
    See also Desegregation of pub-
        lic schools
Self-contained classroom, 340
"Separate but equal" doctrine,
    408–409, 410
Separation of Church and State
    Home Page, 386
Serrano v. Priest, 354
Settlement house movement,
    309–312
Sexual harassment, 435–438
Sheldon, E. A., 270–271
Silberman, Charles, 536, 537,
    538
Simon, Theodore, 327
Single-parent families, 476–477,
    478
Sizer, Theodore, 20
Skills-based standard, 550
Skinner, B. F., 83
Slaves
    abolitionist societies and,
        195–196, 198
    colonial education of,
        186–187, 189, 191,
        194–199
    post-Industrial Revolution
        oppression of, 199–201
Smith-Hughes Act (1917), 347
Social Darwinism, 298
Social efficiency, 319–328
    curriculum design and,
        322–325
    intelligence testing and,
        327–328
    scientific management and,
        320–322
    specificity in the curriculum
        and, 326–327
Social Frontier, The (journal), 318
Socialism, 116–117
Social reconstructionism,
    115–118
    conceptual features of, 119

radical progressivism and,
    317–319
social class issues and,
    115–117
Social reform
    environmentalism and,
        298–299
    progressivism and, 292–299
Society
    Dewey's views on learning
        and, 293–295
    responding to values and aims
        of, 69–71
Society for the Propagation of
    the Gospel in Foreign Parts
    (SPG), 189, 194, 202
Socio-civic issues, 13, 15–16,
    26–30, 308
Socioeconomic factors
    computer usage and, 474,
        475, 476
    curriculum tracking and,
        404–407
    data on public schools and,
        62–63
    dropout rates and, 468
    school achievement and, 456,
        459, 461, 464
    social reconstructionism and,
        115–117
Souls of Black Folks, The (Du Bois),
    307
Souter, David, 384–385
Southern states
    colonial education in,
        187–191
    contemporary segregation
        data for, 425
    oppression of slaves in,
        199–201
    origins of public education in,
        214
Space race, 531
Special education
    gender bias in, 427–428
    postmodernist view of, 120
Standardized tests
    achievement standards and,
        447–450
    development of IQ tests,
        327
    ethical issues related to,
        141–142
    gender issues related to,
        429–432
    teaching influenced by,
        76–79
Standards, educational. *See*
    National standards

States
    funding of schools by,
        348–360, 362–363
    governance of schools by,
        192–193, 341–343,
        344–345
    religious school aid from,
        383–387
    rise of educational authority
        of, 221–224
    school taxes imposed by,
        220–221
Stevens, John Paul, 377
Stewart, Potter, 374, 375
Structured immersion programs,
    517
Structure of discipline doctrine,
    533
Students
    academic achievement data
        for, 9, 10, 453, 459,
        461, 464, 465
    drug and alcohol use among,
        484
    freedom of expression by,
        152–157
    liability for injury to,
        142–146, 147, 148
    per pupil expenditures and,
        352–353, 359–360,
        362–363
    punishment of, 84–85
    religious apparel worn by,
        379–380
    responses to curriculum
        tracking by, 402–403
    safety-related fears among,
        484, 485
    search-and-seizure issues and,
        165, 167–170
    sexual harassment of,
        435–438
    socioeconomic context and,
        62–63
    symbolic expression by,
        156–157, 158–161
    verbal expression by, 152–155
    violent crimes against, 482,
        483
    written expression by,
        155–156
Subject-centeredness, 112, 554
Subject matter
    conservative tradition and,
        95–105
    gender differences and,
        430–432
    instructional judgments
        about, 69–71

Supreme Court
  religion and education cases,
    390–391
  school desegregation cases,
    420–421
  website of school-related
    decisions, 171
  See also Legal issues
*Swann v. Charlotte-Mecklenburg
  Board of Education* (1971),
  415, 421
Symbolic expression, 156–157,
  158–161
  religious symbols, 377–380,
    381

Taxes for public education
  contemporary use of, 349
  historical origins of, 220–221
Taylor, Frederick, 320–322
Teachers
  academic freedom of,
    147–151
  associations and unions for,
    231–240
  certification requirements for,
    48–49
  classroom discipline and con-
    trol by, 79–87
  comprehensive schools and,
    17–22
  conduct of, 133–142, 143
  demographic characteristics
    of, 45–50
  dismissal of, 164–165
  education and training for, 10,
    55–56, 226–231, 267,
    268–269
  effectiveness of, 73–76
  employment process for, 157,
    160–161, 163–165
  ethics of, 130–142
  factors in decision making of,
    66–73
  freedom of expression by,
    147–152
  hours in workweek of, 52, 55
  job satisfaction issues for,
    58–59
  legal liability of, 142–146,
    147, 148
  levels of professionalism for,
    61–66
  professional status of, 50–58

prose literacy scores of, 52, 54
religious issues and, 50,
  136–137, 379
salaries for, 51–52, 53
tenure for, 163–165, 166, 167
See also Education
Team teaching, 340
Tenure contracts, 163–165, 166,
  167
Term contracts, 160–161, 163,
  167
Testing
  ethical issues related to,
    141–142
  gender issues related to,
    429–432
  intelligence quotient (IQ),
    327–328
  teaching oriented to, 76–79
  See also Standardized tests
Thomas, Clarence, 417
Thompson, Tommy, 574
Thorndike, Edward, 33,
  325–326
*Tinker v. Des Moines Independent
  School District* (1969), 154,
  155
Tracking. *See* Curriculum track-
  ing
Transitional bilingual education,
  516–517
Truth, Sojourner, 197
Tubman, Harriet Ross, 197
Tuition reimbursement program,
  385
Tuskegee Institute, 302–303
Tuskegee and Its People (Washing-
  ton), 307
Two-way bilingual education,
  519–520
Tyack, David, 573
Tyler, Ralph, 123

Uniforms, school, 157, 158–161
Unions, 238–240
Uniserve program, 238

Values, common, 496–497
Verbal expression, 152–155
Vernonia District v. Acton (1992),
  169–170
Vertical equity, 355–356
Violence in schools, 59, 482,
  483, 484

Virginia, colonial education in,
  187–191
Vocational education
  goals related to, 17
  specialized high schools and,
    341
  teaching for growth in,
    34–37, 38
  unified high schools and, 314
Vonnegut, Kurt, 150
Voucher programs, 569–576
  arguments for and against,
    570–574
  Milwaukee Parental Choice
    Program, 574–576
  religious school aid via,
    385–386
  See also School choice

Wald, Lillian, 309
Wallace v. Jaffree (1985), 374, 391
Ward, Lester, 4, 298–299, 309,
  311, 327
Washington, Booker T.,
  300–306, 307, 328
Washington, George, 196, 199
Watson, John, 82–83
Webster, Daniel, 220
Webster, Noah, 217–219
*West Virginia Board of Education v.
  Burnett* (1943), 370
Wheatley, Phyllis, 196
Whipping posts, 184
Whole-language instruction, 308
Williams, Annette "Polly," 574
Winthrop, John, 182, 183
Wisconsin v. Yoder (1972),
  370–371, 390
Witte, John, 368, 575
Woodson, Carter, 200, 201
*Wright v. Houston Independent
  School District* (1972), 370
Writing
  freedom of expression
    through, 155–156
  law prohibiting educating
    slaves in, 195

Young, Ella Flagg, 233

Zangwill, Israel, 501
Zero-tolerance policies,
  480–481